Game Programming Using Qt 5 Beginner's Guide *Second Edition*

Create amazing games with Qt 5, C++, and Qt Quick

Pavel Strakhov
Witold Wysota
Lorenz Haas

Packt>

BIRMINGHAM - MUMBAI

Game Programming Using Qt 5 Beginner's Guide
Second Edition

Acquisition Editor: Shweta Pant
Content Development Editor: Flavian Vaz
Technical Editor: Akhil Nair
Copy Editor: Shaila Kusanale
Project Coordinator: Devanshi Doshi
Proofreader: Safis Editing
Indexer: Rekha Nair
Graphics: Jason Monteiro
Production Coordinator: Aparna Bhagat

First published: January 2016
Second edition: April 2018

Production reference: 2230818

Published by Packt Publishing Ltd.
Livery Place
35 Livery Street
Birmingham
B3 2PB, UK.

ISBN 978-1-78839-999-9

`www.packtpub.com`

I dedicate this book to all people who are passionate about programming; live long and prosper

– Pavel Strakhov

Contributors

About the authors

Pavel Strakhov is a software architect and developer from Russia. He started working with Qt in 2011 in Moscow Institute of Physics and Technology, where it was used to build scientific image processing software. During 2012-2015, he was highly active in the Qt section of StackOverflow, helping people learn Qt and solve issues. In 2016, he started working on Qt bindings for Rust language.

> *I would like to thank all the reviewers who worked with me on this book for their invaluable feedback. I am also very grateful to all people from Packt Publishing who worked with me. Writing this book wouldn't have been possible without their support and motivation.*

Witold Wysota is a software architect and developer living in Poland. He started his adventure with Qt in 2004 and, since then, it has become his main area of expertise.

He is an active trainer and consultant in Qt, C++, and related technologies in both commercial and academic environments.

In real life, he is a passionate adept of Seven Star Praying Mantis, a traditional style of Chinese martial arts.

Lorenz Haas, a passionate programmer, started his Qt career with Qt 3. He immersed himself in this framework, became one of the first certified Qt developers and specialists, and turned his love for Qt into his profession.

Lorenz is now working as a lead software architect. He mainly develops machine controls and their user interfaces as well as general solutions for the industry sector.

Years ago, he started contributing to Qt Creator and Qt. He added a couple of refactoring options that you probably rely on regularly if you use Qt Creator. He is also the author of the Beautifier plugin.

About the reviewers

Julien Déramond is a software developer living in Paris, France. He started his career developing C++ web services until he entered the embedded world via the Orange set-top boxes in 2012. Specialized in QML, he mainly prototypes and develops user interfaces with designers. Recently, he started contributing to Qt, especially in finding bugs and proposing patches for the QML JS Reformater of Qt Creator. When he is not writing code, he enjoys traveling and drawing.

Simone Angeloni is a software engineer with over 13 years of experience in C++ and a skillset including cross-platform development, embedded systems, multi-threading, user interfaces, network communication, databases, web applications, game development, and visual design.

He is currently a senior software engineer in the R&D dept of Nikon Corporation, and he is developing software/hardware solutions to control robots used in the motion picture industry.

Packt is searching for authors like you

If you're interested in becoming an author for Packt, please visit `authors.packtpub.com` and apply today. We have worked with thousands of developers and tech professionals, just like you, to help them share their insight with the global tech community. You can make a general application, apply for a specific hot topic that we are recruiting an author for, or submit your own idea.

Table of Contents

Preface

As a leading cross-platform toolkit for all significant desktop, mobile, and embedded platforms, Qt is becoming more popular by the day. This book will help you learn the nitty-gritty of Qt and will equip you with the necessary toolsets to build apps and games. This book is designed as a beginner's guide to take programmers new to Qt from the basics, such as objects, core classes, widgets, and new features in version 5.9, to a level where they can create a custom application with the best practices of programming with Qt.

From a brief introduction of how to create an application and prepare a working environment for both desktop and mobile platforms, we will dive deeper into the basics of creating graphical interfaces and Qt's core concepts of data processing and display. As you progress through the chapters, you'll learn to enrich your games by implementing network connectivity and employing scripting. Delve into Qt Quick, OpenGL, and various other tools to add game logic, design animation, add game physics, handle gamepad input, and build astonishing UIs for games. Toward the end of this book, you'll learn to exploit mobile device features, such as sensors and geolocation services, to build engaging user experiences.

Who this book is for

This book will be interesting and helpful to programmers and application and UI developers who have basic knowledge of C++. Additionally, some parts of Qt allow you to use JavaScript, so basic knowledge of this language will also be helpful. No previous experience with Qt is required. Developers with up to a year of Qt experience will also benefit from the topics covered in this book.

What this book covers

`Chapter 1`, *Introduction to Qt*, familiarizes you with the standard behavior that is required when creating cross-platform applications and shows you a bit of history of Qt and how it evolved over time with an emphasis on the most recent architectural changes in Qt.

`Chapter 2`, *Installation*, guides you through the process of installing a Qt binary release for desktop platforms, setting up the bundled IDE, and looks at various configuration options related to cross-platform programming.

`Chapter 3`, *Qt GUI Programming*, shows you how to create classic user interfaces with the Qt Widgets module. It also familiarizes you with the process of compiling applications using Qt.

`Chapter 4`, *Custom 2D Graphics with Graphics View*, familiarizes you with 2D object-oriented graphics in Qt. You will learn how to use built-in items to compose the final results as well as create your own items supplementing what is already available.

`Chapter 5`, *Animations in Graphics View*, describes the Qt Animation framework, the property system, and shows you how to implement animations in Graphics View. It will guide you through the process of creating a game featuring 2D graphics and animations.

`Chapter 6`, *Qt Core Essentials*, covers the concepts related to data processing and display in Qt—file handling in different formats, Unicode text handling and displaying user-visible strings in different languages, and regular expression matching.

`Chapter 7`, *Networking*, demonstrates the IP networking technologies that are available in Qt. It will teach you how to connect to TCP servers, implement a TCP server, and implement fast communication via UDP.

`Chapter 8`, *Custom Widgets*, describes the whole mechanism related to 2D software rendering in Qt, and teaches you how to create your own widget classes with unique functionalities.

`Chapter 9`, *OpenGL and Vulkan in Qt applications*, discusses Qt capabilities related to accelerated 3D graphics. You will learn how to perform fast 3D drawing using OpenGL and Vulkan APIs and use the convenient wrappers Qt provides for them.

`Chapter 10`, *Scripting*, covers the benefits of scripting in applications. It will teach you how to employ a scripting engine for a game by using JavaScript or Python.

`Chapter 11`, *Introduction to Qt Quick*, teaches you how to program resolution-independent fluid user interfaces using a QML declarative engine and Qt Quick scene graph environment.

`Chapter 12`, *Customization in Qt Quick*, focuses on how to implement new graphical items in Qt Quick and implement custom event handling.

`Chapter 13`, *Animations in Qt Quick Games*, familiarizes you with the ways to perform animations in Qt Quick and give more hints for implementing games in Qt Quick.

`Chapter 14`, *Advanced Visual Effects in Qt Quick*, goes through some advanced concepts that will allow you to perform truly unique graphical effects in Qt Quick.

`Chapter 15`, *3D Graphics with Qt*, outlines using Qt's high-level API for 3D graphics and show you how to implement an animated 3D game.

`Chapter 16`, *Miscellaneous and Advanced Concepts*, demonstrates the important aspects of Qt programming that didn't make it into the other chapters but may be important for game programming. This chapter is available online at `https://www.packtpub.com/sites/default/files/downloads/MiscellaneousandAdvancedConcepts.pdf`.

To get the most out of this book

You don't need to own or install any particular software before starting to work with the book. A common Windows, Linux, or MacOS system should be sufficient. `Chapter 2`, *Installation*, contains detailed instructions on how to download and set up everything you'll need.

In this book, you will find several headings that appear frequently:

- The **Time for action** section contains clear instructions on how to complete a procedure or task.
- The **What just happened?** section explains the working of the tasks or instructions that you have just completed.
- The **Have a go hero** sections contain practical challenges that give you ideas to experiment with what you have learned.
- The **Pop quiz** sections contain short single-choice questions intended to help you test your own understanding. You will find the answers at the end of the book.

While going through the chapters, you will be presented with multiple games and other projects as well as detailed descriptions of how to create them. We advise you to try to create these projects yourself using the instructions we'll give you. If at any point of time you have trouble following the instructions or don't know how to do a certain step, you should take a pick at the example code files to see how it can be done. However, the most important and exciting part of learning is to decide what you want to implement and then find a way to do it, so pay attention to the "Have a go hero" sections or think of your own way to improve each project.

Download the example code files

You can download the example code files for this book from your account at www.packtpub.com. If you purchased this book elsewhere, you can visit www.packtpub.com/support and register to have the files emailed directly to you.

You can download the code files by following these steps:

1. Log in or register at www.packtpub.com.
2. Select the **SUPPORT** tab.
3. Click on **Code Downloads & Errata**.
4. Enter the name of the book in the **Search** box and follow the onscreen instructions.

Once the file is downloaded, please make sure that you unzip or extract the folder using the latest version of:

- WinRAR/7-Zip for Windows
- Zipeg/iZip/UnRarX for Mac
- 7-Zip/PeaZip for Linux

The code bundle for the book is also hosted on GitHub at https://github.com/PacktPublishing/Game-Programming-Using-Qt-5-Beginners-Guide-Second-Edition. We also have other code bundles from our rich catalog of books and videos available at https://github.com/PacktPublishing/. Check them out!

Conventions used

There are a number of text conventions used throughout this book.

CodeInText: Indicates code words in text, database table names, folder names, filenames, file extensions, pathnames, dummy URLs, user input, and Twitter handles. Here is an example: "This API is centered on QNetworkAccessManager,which handles the complete communication between your game and the Internet."

A block of code is set as follows:

```
QNetworkRequest request;
request.setUrl(QUrl("http://localhost/version.txt"));
request.setHeader(QNetworkRequest::UserAgentHeader, "MyGame");
m_manager->get(request);
```

When we wish to draw your attention to a particular part of a code block, the relevant lines or items are set in bold:

```
void FileDownload::downloadFinished(QNetworkReply *reply) {
    const QByteArray content = reply->readAll();
    _edit->setPlainText(content);
    reply->deleteLater();
}
```

Bold: Indicates a new term, an important word, or words that you see onscreen. For example, words in menus or dialog boxes appear in the text like this. Here is an example: "On the **Select Destination Location** screen, click on **Next** to accept the default destination."

Warnings or important notes appear like this.

Tips and tricks appear like this.

Get in touch

Feedback from our readers is always welcome.

General feedback: Email `feedback@packtpub.com` and mention the book title in the subject of your message. If you have questions about any aspect of this book, please email us at `questions@packtpub.com`.

Errata: Although we have taken every care to ensure the accuracy of our content, mistakes do happen. If you have found a mistake in this book, we would be grateful if you would report this to us. Please visit `www.packtpub.com/submit-errata`, selecting your book, clicking on the Errata Submission Form link, and entering the details.

Piracy: If you come across any illegal copies of our works in any form on the Internet, we would be grateful if you would provide us with the location address or website name. Please contact us at `copyright@packtpub.com` with a link to the material.

If you are interested in becoming an author: If there is a topic that you have expertise in and you are interested in either writing or contributing to a book, please visit `authors.packtpub.com`.

Reviews

Please leave a review. Once you have read and used this book, why not leave a review on the site that you purchased it from? Potential readers can then see and use your unbiased opinion to make purchase decisions, we at Packt can understand what you think about our products, and our authors can see your feedback on their book. Thank you!

For more information about Packt, please visit `packtpub.com`.

1
Introduction to Qt

In this chapter, you will learn what Qt is and how it evolved. We will describe the structure of the Qt framework and the differences between its versions. Finally, you will learn how to decide which Qt licensing scheme is right for your projects.

The main topics covered in this chapter are:

- Qt history
- Supported platforms
- Structure of the Qt framework
- Qt versions
- Qt licenses

A journey through time

The development of Qt started in 1991 by two Norwegians—Eirik Chambe-Eng and Haavard Nord—who were looking to create a cross-platform GUI programming toolkit. The first commercial client of Trolltech (the company that created the Qt toolkit) was the European Space Agency. The commercial use of Qt helped Trolltech sustain further development. At that time, Qt was available for two platforms—Unix/X11 and Windows—however, developing with Qt for Windows required buying a proprietary license, which was a significant drawback in porting the existing Unix/Qt applications.

A major step forward was the release of Qt Version 3.0 in 2001, which saw the initial support for Mac as well as an option to use Qt for Unix and Mac under a liberal GPL license. Still, Qt for Windows was only available under a paid license. Nevertheless, at that time, Qt had support for all the important players in the market—Windows, Mac, and Unix desktops, with Trolltech's mainstream product and Qt for embedded Linux.

In 2005, Qt 4.0 was released, which was a real breakthrough for a number of reasons. First, the Qt API was completely redesigned, which made it cleaner and more coherent. Unfortunately, at the same time, it made the existing Qt-based code incompatible with 4.0, and many applications needed to be rewritten from scratch or required much effort to be adapted to the new API. It was a difficult decision, but from the time perspective, we can see it was worth it. Difficulties caused by changes in the API were well countered by the fact that Qt for Windows was finally released under GPL. Many optimizations were introduced that made Qt significantly faster. Lastly, Qt, which was a single library until now, was divided into a number of modules. This allowed programmers to only link to the functionality that they used in their applications, reducing the memory footprint and the dependencies of their software.

In 2008, Trolltech was sold to Nokia, which at that time was looking for a software framework to help it expand and replace its Symbian platform in the future. The Qt community became divided; some people were thrilled, others were worried after seeing Qt's development get transferred to Nokia. Either way, new funds were pumped into Qt, speeding up its progress and opening it for mobile platforms—Symbian and then Maemo and MeeGo.

For Nokia, Qt was not considered a product of its own, but rather a tool. Therefore, Nokia decided to introduce Qt to more developers by adding a very liberal **Lesser General Public License** (**LGPL**) that allowed the usage of the framework for both open and closed source development.

Bringing Qt to new platforms and less powerful hardware required a new approach to create user interfaces and to make them more lightweight, fluid, and attractive. Nokia engineers working on Qt came up with a new declarative language to develop such interfaces—the **Qt Modeling Language** (**QML**) and a Qt runtime for it called **Qt Quick**.

The latter became the primary focus of the further development of Qt, practically stalling all non-mobile-related work, channeling all efforts to make Qt Quick faster, easier, and more widespread. Qt 4 was already in the market for seven years, and it became obvious that another major version of Qt had to be released. It was decided to bring more engineers to Qt by allowing anyone to contribute to the project. The Qt Project founded by Nokia in 2011 provided an infrastructure for code review and introduced an open governance model, allowing outside developers to participate in decision making.

Nokia did not manage to finish working on Qt 5.0. As a result of an unexpected turnover of Nokia toward different technology in 2011, the Qt division was sold in mid 2012 to the Finnish company Digia that managed to complete the effort and release Qt 5.0, a completely restructured framework, in December of the same year. While Qt 5.0 introduced a lot of new features, it was mostly compatible with Qt 4 and allowed developers to seamlessly migrate to the new major version.

In 2014, Digia formed the Qt Company that is now responsible for Qt development, commercialization, and licensing. All Qt-related web resources scattered across Qt Project and Digia websites were eventually unified at `https://www.qt.io/`. Qt continues to receive bug fixes, new features, and new platform support. This book is based on Qt 5.9, which was released in 2017.

The cross-platform programming

Qt is an application-programming framework that is used to develop cross-platform applications. What this means is that software written for one platform can be ported and executed on another platform with little or no effort. This is obtained by limiting the application source code to a set of calls to routines and libraries available to all the supported platforms, and by delegating all tasks that may differ between platforms (such as drawing on the screen and accessing system data or hardware) to Qt. This effectively creates a layered environment (as shown in the following diagram), where Qt hides all platform-dependent aspects from the application code:

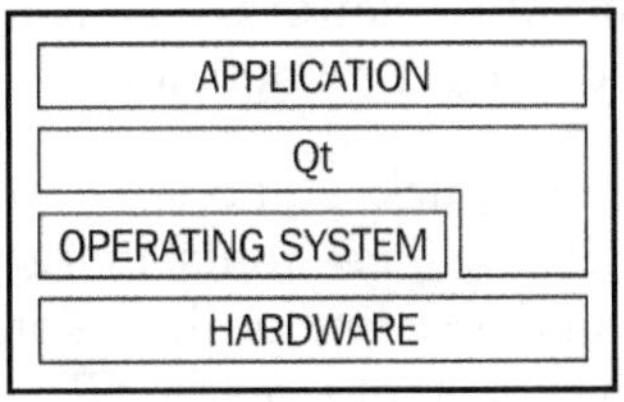

Of course, at times, we need to use some functionality that Qt doesn't provide. In such situations, it is important to use a conditional compilation for platform-specific code. Qt provides a wide set of macros specifying the current platform. We will return to this topic in `Chapter 6`, *Qt Core Essentials*.

Supported platforms

The framework is available for a number of platforms, ranging from classical desktop environments through embedded systems to mobile devices. Qt 5.9 supports the following platforms:

- Desktop platforms: Windows, Linux, and macOS
- Mobile platforms: UWP, Android, and iOS
- Embedded platforms: VxWorks, INTEGRITY, QNX, and Embedded Linux

It is likely that the list of supported platforms will change in future Qt versions. You should refer to the **Supported Platforms** documentation page for your Qt version for detailed information about supported versions of operating systems and compilers.

GUI scalability

For the most part of the history of desktop application development, specifying sizes of GUI elements in pixels was the common practice. While most operating systems had **dots per inch** (**DPI**) settings and APIs for taking it into account for a long time, the majority of existing displays had approximately the same DPI, so applications without high DPI support were common.

The situation changed when high-DPI displays became more common in the market—most notably in mobile phones and tablets, but also in laptops and desktops. Now, even if you only target desktop platforms, you should think about supporting different DPI settings. When you target mobile devices, this becomes mandatory.

If you are using Qt Widgets or Qt Quick, you often don't need to specify pixel sizes at all. Standard widgets and controls will use fonts, margins, and offsets defined by the style. If layouts are used, Qt will determine positions and sizes of all GUI items automatically. Avoid specifying constant sizes for GUI elements when possible. You may use sizes related to sizes of other GUI elements, the window, or the screen. Qt also provides an API for querying screen DPI, GUI style metrics, and font metrics, which should help to determine the optimal size for the current device.

On macOS and iOS, Qt Widgets and Qt Quick applications are scaled automatically using a virtual coordinate system. Pixel values in the application remain the same, but the GUI will scale according to the DPI of the current display. For example, if the pixel ratio is set to 2 (a common value for retina displays), creating a widget with 100 "pixels" width will produce a widget with 200 physical pixels. That means that the application doesn't have to be highly aware of DPI variations. However, this scaling does not apply to OpenGL, which always uses physical pixels.

Qt versions

Each Qt version number (for example, 5.9.2) consists of major, minor, and patch components. Qt pays special attention to forwards and backwards compatibility between different versions. Small changes which are both forwards and backwards compatible (typically bug fixes without changing any API) are indicated by changing only the patch version. New minor versions usually bring in new API and features, so they are not forwards compatible. However, all minor versions are backwards binary and source compatible. This means that if you're transitioning to a newer minor version (for example, from 5.8 to 5.9), you should always be able to rebuild your project without changes. You can even transition to a new minor version without rebuilding, by only updating shared Qt libraries (or letting the package manager of the OS do that). Major releases indicate big changes and may break backwards compatibility. However, the latest major release (5.0) was mostly source compatible with the previous version.

Qt declares **Long Term Support** (**LTS**) for certain versions. LTS versions receive patch-level releases with bug fixes and security fixes for three years. Commercial support is available for even longer periods. Current LTS releases at the time of writing are 5.6 and 5.9.

Structure of Qt framework

As Qt expanded over time, its structure evolved. At first, it was just a single library, then a set of libraries. When it became harder to maintain and update for the growing number of platforms that it supported, a decision was made to split the framework into much smaller modules contained in two module groups—Qt Essentials and Qt Add-ons. A major decision relating to the split was that each module could now have its own independent release schedule.

Qt Essentials

The Essentials group contains modules that are mandatory to implement for every supported platform. This implies that if you are implementing your system using modules from this group only, you can be sure that it can be easily ported to any other platform that Qt supports. The most important relations between Qt Essentials modules are shown in the following diagram:

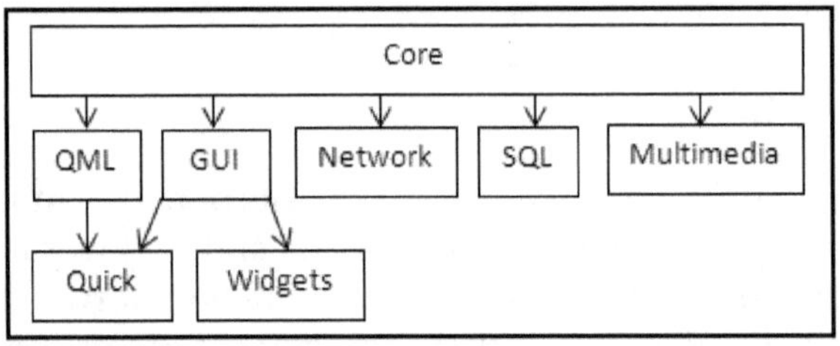

Some of the modules are explained as follows:

- The **Qt Core** module contains the most basic Qt functionality that all other modules rely on. It provides support for event processing, meta-objects, data I/O, text processing, and threading. It also brings a number of frameworks, such as the Animation framework, the State Machine framework, and the Plugin framework.
- The **Qt GUI** module provides basic cross-platform support to build user interfaces. It contains the common functionality required by more high-level GUI modules (Qt Widgets and Qt Quick). Qt GUI contains classes that are used to manipulate windows that can be rendered using either the raster engine or OpenGL. Qt supports desktop OpenGL as well as OpenGL ES 1.1 and 2.0.
- **Qt Widgets** extends the GUI module with the ability to create a user interface using widgets, such as buttons, edit boxes, labels, data views, dialog boxes, menus, and toolbars, which are arranged using a special layout engine. Qt Widgets utilizes Qt's event system to handle input events in a cross-platform way. This module also contains the implementation of an object-oriented 2D graphics canvas called Graphics View.
- **Qt Quick** is an extension of Qt GUI, which provides a means to create lightweight fluid user interfaces using QML. It is described in more detail later in this chapter, as well as in `Chapter 11`, *Introduction to Qt Quick*.

- **Qt QML** is an implementation of the QML language used in Qt Quick. It also provides API to integrate custom C++ types into QML's JavaScript engine and to integrate QML code with C++.
- **Qt Network** brings support for IPv4 and IPv6 networking using TCP and UDP. It also contains HTTP, HTTPS, FTP clients, and it extends support for DNS lookups.
- **Qt Multimedia** allows programmers to access audio and video hardware (including cameras and FM radio) to record and play multimedia content. It also features 3D positional audio support.
- **Qt SQL** brings a framework that is used to manipulate SQL databases in an abstract way.

TIP

There are also other modules in this group, but we will not focus on them in this book. If you want to learn more about them, you can look them up in the Qt reference manual.

Qt Add-ons

This group contains modules that are optional for any platform. This means that if a particular functionality is not available on some platform or there is nobody willing to spend time working on this functionality for a platform, it will not prevent Qt from supporting this platform. We'll mention some of the most important modules here:

- **Qt Concurrent**: This handles multi-threaded processing
- **Qt 3D**: This provides high-level OpenGL building blocks
- **Qt Gamepad**: This enables applications to support gamepad hardware
- **Qt D-Bus**: This allows your application to communicate with others via the D-Bus mechanism
- **Qt XML Patterns**: This helps us to access XML data

Many other modules are also available, but we will not cover them here.

qmake

Some Qt features require additional build steps during the compilation and linking of the project. For example, **Meta-Object Compiler** (**moc**), **User Interface Compiler** (**uic**), and **Resource Compiler** (**rcc**) may need to be executed to handle Qt's C++ extensions and features. For convenience, Qt provides the **qmake** executable that manages your Qt project and generates files required for building it on the current platform (such as Makefile for the make utility). qmake reads the project's configuration from a project file with the `.pro` extension. Qt Creator (the IDE that comes with Qt) automatically creates and updates that file, but it can be edited manually to alter the build process.

Alternatively, CMake can be used to organize and build the project. Qt provides CMake plugins for performing all the necessary build actions. Qt Creator also has fairly good support for CMake projects. CMake is more advanced and powerful than qmake, but it's probably not needed for projects with a simple build process.

Modern C++ standards

You can use modern C++ in your Qt projects. Qt's build tool (qmake) allows you to specify the C++ standard you want to target. Qt itself introduces an improved and extended API by using new C++ features when possible. For example, it uses ref-qualified member functions and introduces methods accepting initializer lists and rvalue references. It also introduces new macros that help you deal with compilers that may or may not support new standards.

If you use a recent C++ revision, you have to pay attention to the compiler versions you use across the target platforms because older compilers may not support the new standard. In this book, we will assume C++11 support, as it is widely available already. Thus, we'll use C++11 features in our code, such as range-based `for` loops, scoped enumerations, and lambda expressions.

Choosing the right license

Qt is available under two different licensing schemes—you can choose between a commercial license and an open source one. We will discuss both here to make it easier for you to choose. If you have any doubts regarding whether a particular licensing scheme applies to your use case, you better consult a professional lawyer.

An open source license

The advantage of open source licenses is that we don't have to pay anyone to use Qt; however, the downside is that there are some limitations imposed on how it can be used.

When choosing the open source edition, we have to choose between GPL 3.0 and LGPL 3. Since LGPL is more liberal, in this chapter we will focus on it. Choosing LGPL allows you to use Qt to implement systems that are either open source or closed source—you don't have to reveal the sources of your application to anyone if you don't want to.

However, there are a number of restrictions you need to be aware of:

- Any modifications that you make to Qt itself need to be made public, for example, by distributing source code patches alongside your application binary.
- LGPL requires that users of your application must be able to replace Qt libraries that you provide them with other libraries with the same functionality (for example, a different version of Qt). This usually means that you have to dynamically link your application against Qt so that the user can simply replace Qt libraries with his own. You should be aware that such substitutions can decrease the security of your system; thus, if you need it to be very secure, open source may not be the option for you.
- LGPL is incompatible with a number of licenses, especially proprietary ones, so it is possible that you won't be able to use Qt with some commercial components.

Some Qt modules may have different licensing restrictions. For example, Qt Charts, Qt Data Visualization, and Qt Virtual Keyboard modules are not available under LGPL and can only be used under GPL or the commercial license.

The open source edition of Qt can be downloaded directly from `https://www.qt.io`.

A commercial license

Most of the restrictions are lifted if you decide to buy a commercial license for Qt. This allows you to keep the entire source code a secret, including any changes you may want to incorporate into Qt. You can freely link your application statically against Qt, which means fewer dependencies, a smaller deployment bundle size, and a faster startup. It also increases the security of your application, as end users cannot inject their own code into the application by replacing a dynamically loaded library with their own.

Summary

In this chapter, you learned about the architecture of Qt. We saw how it evolved over time and we had a brief overview of what it looks like now. Qt is a complex framework and we will not manage to cover it all, as some parts of its functionality are more important for game programming than others that you can learn on your own in case you ever need them. Now that you know what Qt is, we can proceed with the next chapter, where you will learn how to install Qt on to your development machine.

2
Installation

In this chapter, you will learn how to install Qt on your development machine, including Qt Creator, an IDE tailored to use with Qt. You will see how to configure the IDE for your needs and learn the basic skills to use that environment. By the end of this chapter, you will be able to prepare your working environment for both desktop and embedded platforms using the tools included in the Qt release.

The main topics covered in this chapter are as follows:

- Installing Qt and its developer tools
- Main controls of Qt Creator
- Qt documentation

Installing the Qt SDK

Before you can start using Qt on your machine, it needs to be downloaded and installed. Qt can be installed using dedicated installers that come in two flavors: the online installer, which downloads all the needed components on the fly, and a much larger offline installer, which already contains all the required components. Using an online installer is easier for regular desktop installs, so we prefer this approach.

Time for action – Installing Qt using an online installer

All Qt resources, including the installers, are available at `https://qt.io`. To obtain the open source version of Qt, go to `https://www.qt.io/download-open-source/`. The page suggests the online installer for your current operating system by default, as shown in the following screenshot. Click on the **Download Now** button to download the online installer, or click on **View All Downloads** to select a different download option:

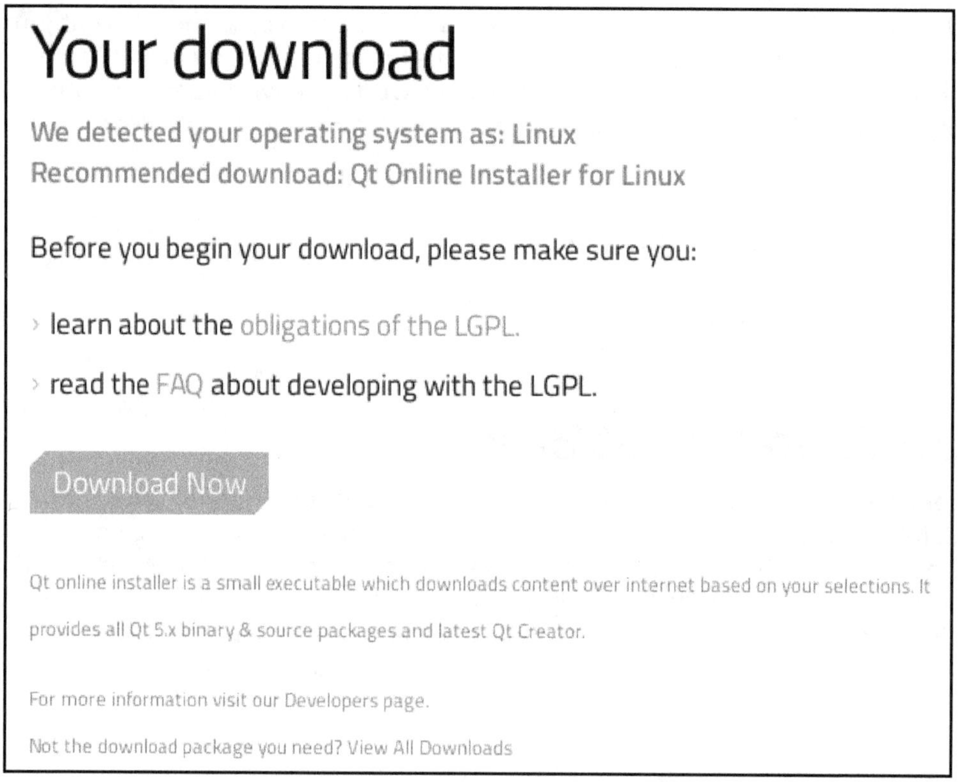

Your download
We detected your operating system as: Linux
Recommended download: Qt Online Installer for Linux
Before you begin your download, please make sure you:
learn about the obligations of the LGPL.
read the FAQ about developing with the LGPL.
Download Now
Qt online installer is a small executable which downloads content over internet based on your selections. It provides all Qt 5.x binary & source packages and latest Qt Creator.
For more information visit our Developers page.
Not the download package you need? View All Downloads

When the download is complete run the installer, as shown:

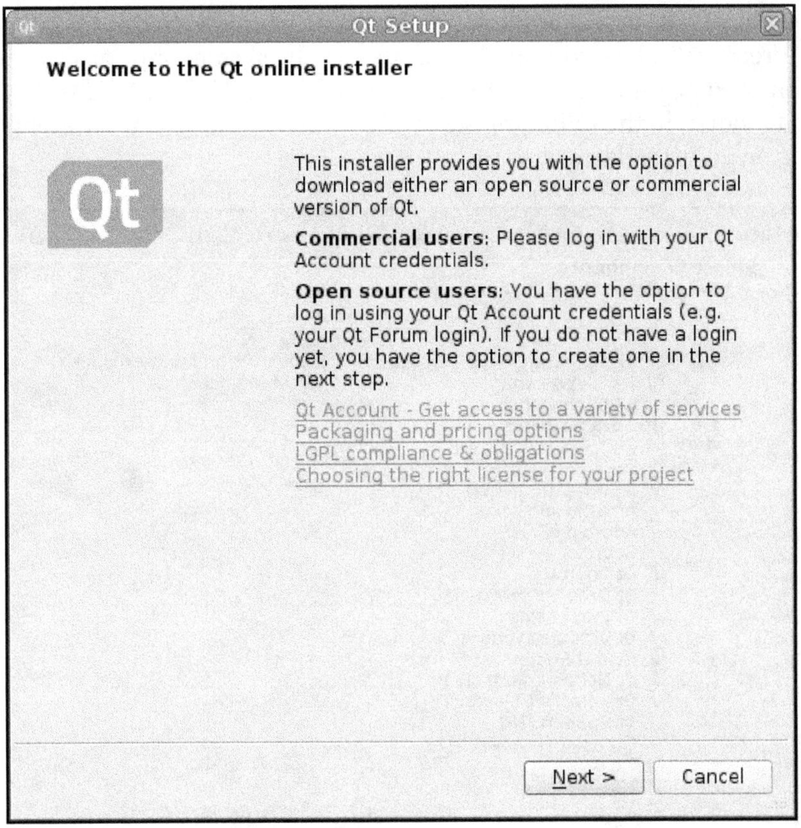

Click on **Next** to begin the installation process. If you are using a proxy server, click on **Settings** and adjust your proxy configuration. Then, either log into your Qt Account or click on **Skip**, if you don't have one.

Click on **Next** again, and after a while of waiting as the downloader checks remote repositories, you'll be asked for the installation path. Ensure that you choose a path where you have write access and enough free space. It's best to put Qt into your personal directory, unless you ran the installer as the system administrator user. Clicking on **Next** again will present you with the choice of components that you wish to install, as shown in the following screenshot. You will be given different choices depending on your platform:

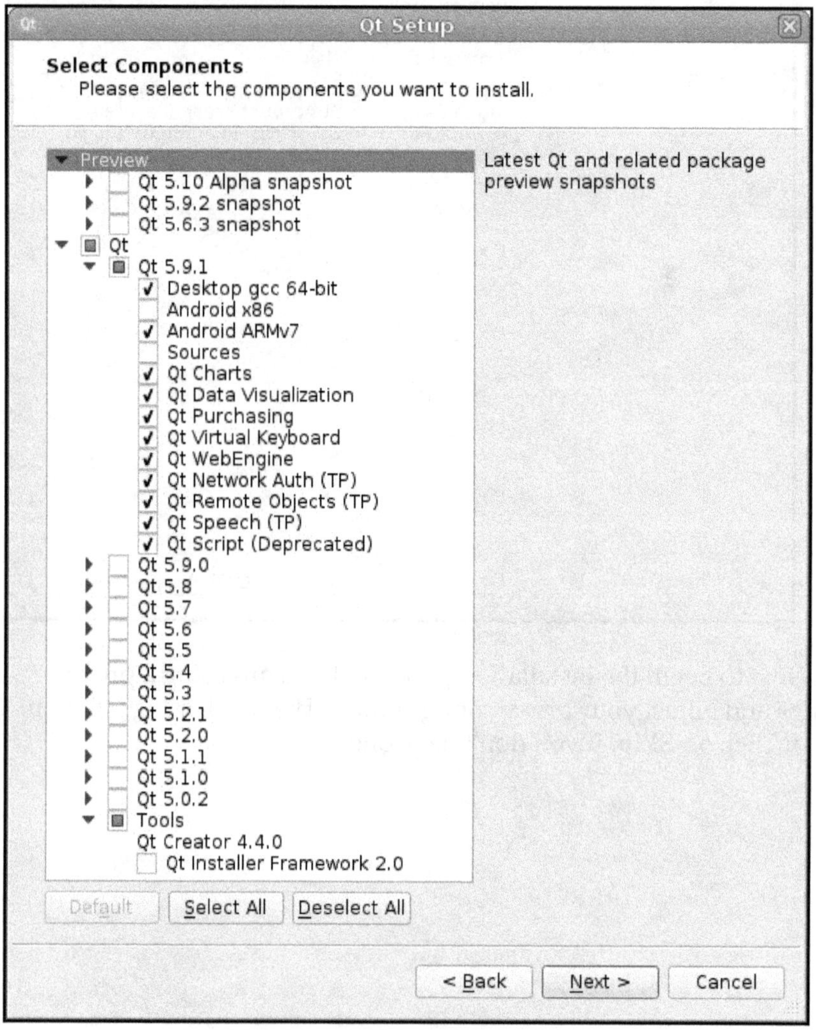

Before we continue, you need to choose which Qt version you want to install. We recommend that you use the most recent stable version, that is, the first item under the **Qt** section. Ignore the **Preview** section, as it contains prerelease packages that may be unstable. If you want to be fully consistent with the book, you can choose Qt 5.9.0, but it's not required. The installer also allows you to install multiple Qt versions at once.

Expand the section corresponding to the Qt version you want to install, and choose whichever platforms you need. Select at least one desktop platform to be able to build and run desktop applications. When in Windows, you have to make additional choices for the desktop builds. Select the 32-bit or 64-bit version and choose the compiler you want to be working with. If you have a Microsoft C++ compiler (provided with Visual Studio or Visual C++ Build Tools), you can select the build corresponding to the installed MSVC version. If you don't have a Microsoft compiler or you simply don't want to use it, choose the **MinGW** build and select the corresponding **MinGW** version in the **Tools** section of the package tree.

If you want to build Android applications, choose the option corresponding to the desired Android platform. In Windows, you can select a UWP build to create Universal Windows Platform applications.

The installer will always install Qt Creator—the IDE (integrated development environment) optimized for creating Qt applications. You may also select Qt add-ons that you want to use.

After choosing the required components and clicking on **Next** again, you will have to accept the licensing terms for Qt by marking an appropriate choice, as shown in the following screenshot:

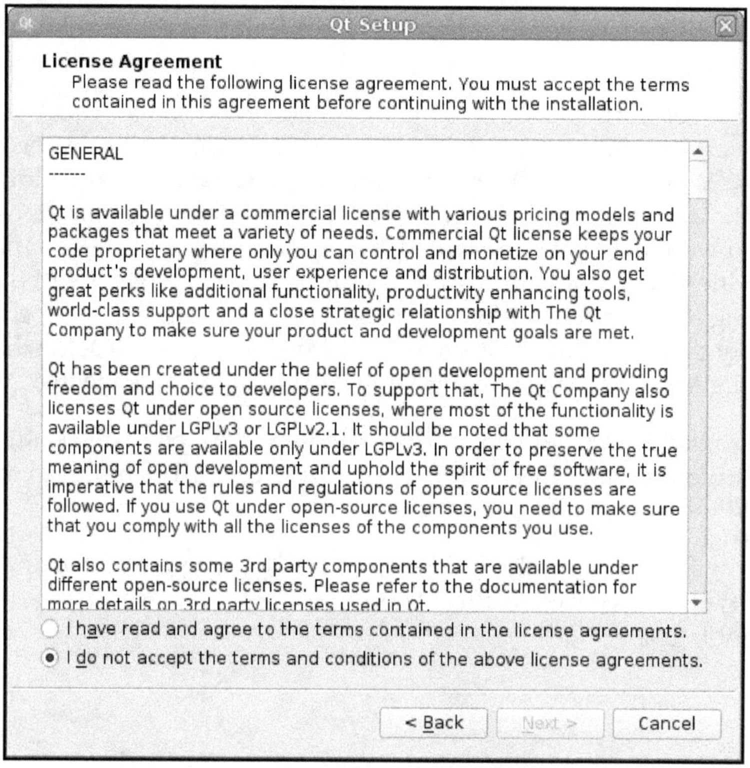

After you click on **Install**, the installer will begin downloading and installing the required packages. Once this is done, your Qt installation will be ready. At the end of the process, you will be given an option to launch Qt Creator:

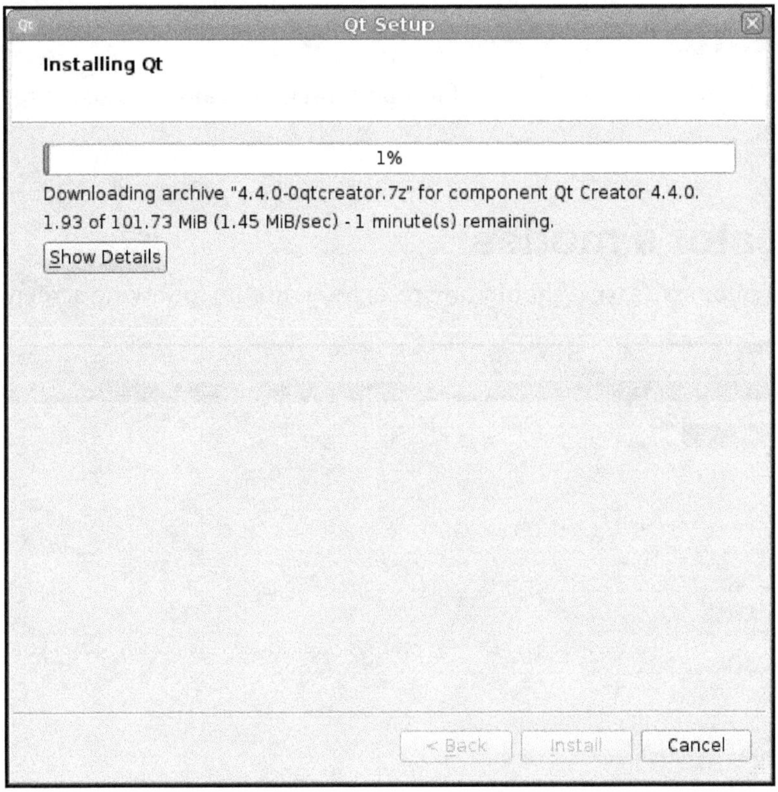

What just happened?

The process we went through results in the whole Qt infrastructure appearing on your disk. You can examine the directory you pointed to the installer to see that it created a number of subdirectories in this directory, one for each version of Qt chosen with the installer, and another one called `Tools` that contains Qt Creator. The Qt directory also contains a `MaintenanceTool` executable, which allows you to add, remove, and update the installed components. The directory structure ensures that if you ever decide to install another version of Qt, it will not conflict with your existing installation. Furthermore, for each version, you can have a number of platform subdirectories that contain the actual Qt installations for particular platforms.

Qt Creator

Now that Qt is installed, we will get familiar with Qt Creator and use it to verify the installation.

Qt Creator's modes

After Qt Creator starts, you should be presented with the following screen:

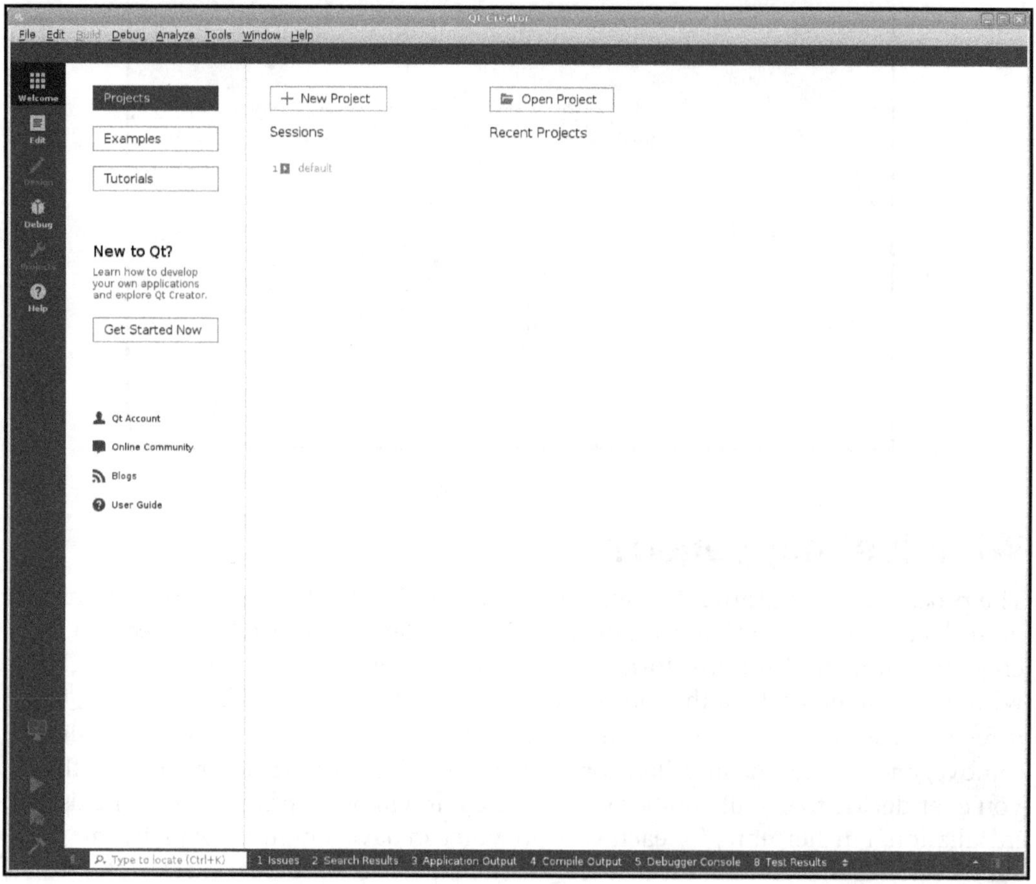

The panel on the left allows you to switch between different **modes** of the IDE:

- **Welcome** mode: Allows you to quickly open last sessions, projects, load examples, and tutorials.
- **Edit** mode: The main mode used to edit the source code of your applications.
- **Design** mode: Contains a visual form editor. Design mode is automatically activated when you create or open a Qt Widgets form file (`.ui`) or a QML form file (`.ui.qml`).
- **Debug** mode: Automatically activated when you launch the application under debugger. It contains additional views for displaying the call stack, the break point list, and values of local variables. More views (such as thread lists or values of registers) can be enabled when needed.
- **Projects** mode: Allows you to configure how Qt Creator will build and run your application. For example, you can choose which Qt version it will use or add command-line arguments here.
- **Help** mode: Provides access to the Qt documentation. We will focus on this topic later in the chapter.

Setting up compilers, Qt versions, and kits

Before Qt Creator can build and run projects, it needs to know which Qt builds, compilers, debuggers, and other tools are available. Fortunately, Qt installer will usually do it automatically, and Qt Creator is able to automatically detect tools that are available system-wide. However, let's verify that our environment is properly configured. From the **Tools** menu, choose **Options**. Once a dialog box pops up, choose **Build & Run** from the side list. This is the place where we can configure the way Qt Creator can build our projects. A complete build configuration is called a **kit**. It consists of a Qt installation and a compiler that will be executed to perform the build. You can see tabs for all the three entities in the **Build & Run** section of the **Options** dialog box.

Let's start with the **Compilers** tab. If your compiler was not autodetected properly and is not in the list, click on the **Add** button, choose your compiler type from the list, and fill the name and path to the compiler. If the settings were entered correctly, Creator will autofill all the other details. Then, you can click on **Apply** to save the changes.

Next, you can switch to the **Qt Versions** tab. Again, if your Qt installation was not detected automatically, you can click on **Add**. This will open a file dialog box where you will need to find your Qt installation's directory, where all the binary executables are stored (usually in the `bin` directory), and select a binary called `qmake`. Qt Creator will warn you if you choose a wrong file. Otherwise, your Qt installation and version should be detected properly. If you want, you can adjust the version name in the appropriate box.

The last tab to look at is the **Kits** tab. It allows you to pair a compiler with the Qt version to be used for compilation. In addition to this, for embedded and mobile platforms, you can specify a device to deploy to and a `sysroot` directory containing all the files needed to build the software for the specified embedded platform. Check that the name of each kit is descriptive enough so that you will be able to select the correct kit (or kits) for each of your applications. If needed, adjust the names of the kits.

Time for action – Loading an example project

Examples are a great way to explore the capabilities of Qt and find the code required for some typical tasks. Each Qt version contains a large set of examples that are always up to date. Qt Creator provides an easy way to load and compile any example project.

Let's try loading one to get familiar with Qt Creator's project editing interface. Then, we will build the project to check whether the installation and configuration were done correctly.

In Qt Creator, click on the **Welcome** button in the top-left corner of the window to switch to the **Welcome** mode. Click on the **Examples** button (refer to the previous screenshot) to open the list of examples with a search box. Ensure that the kit that you want to use is chosen in the drop-down list next to the search box. In the box, enter `aff` to filter the list of examples and click on **Affine Transformations** to open the project. If you are asked whether you want to copy the project to a new folder, agree.

After selecting an example, an additional window appears that contains the documentation page of the loaded example. You can close that window when you don't need it. Switch back to the main Qt Creator window.

Qt Creator will display the **Configure Project** dialog with the list of available kits:

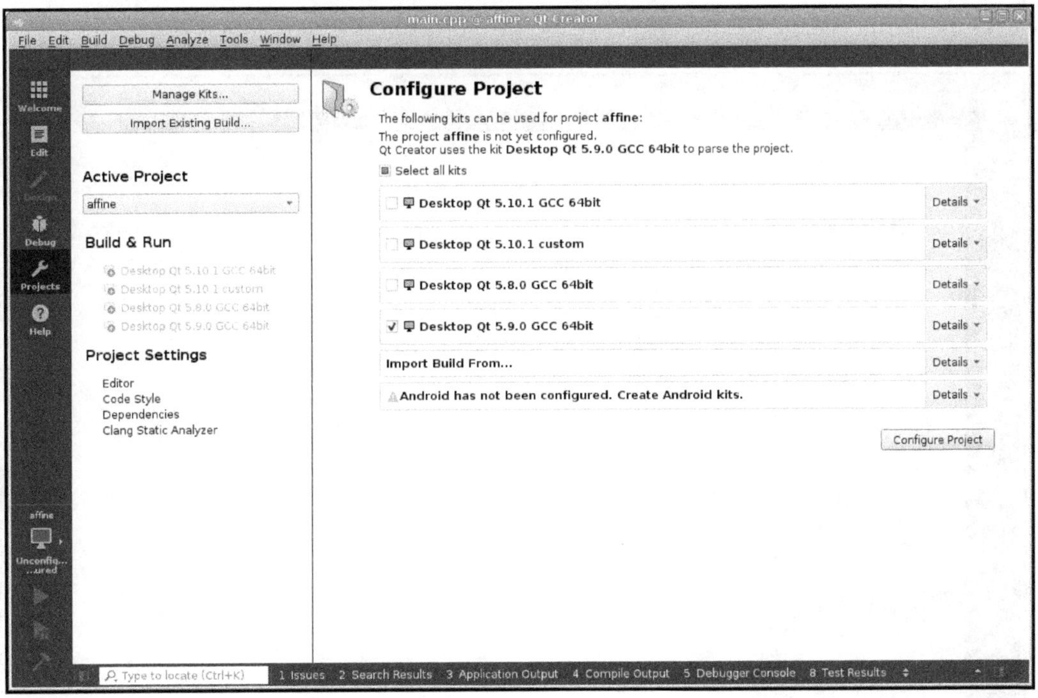

Verify that the kits you want to use are marked with check boxes, and click on the **Configure Project** button. Qt Creator will then present you with the following window:

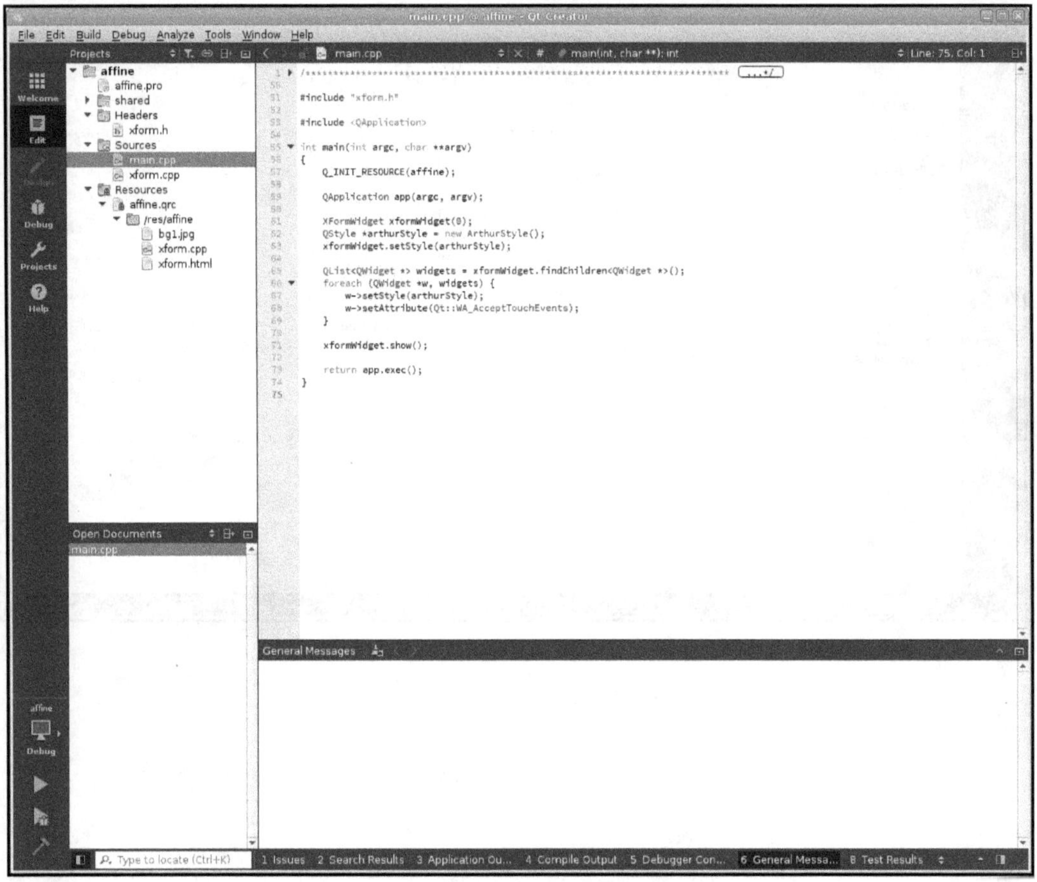

This is the **Edit** mode of Qt Creator. Let's go through the most important parts of this interface:

- **Project tree** is located at the top-left of the window. It displays all open projects and the hierarchy of files within them. You can double-click on a file to open it for editing. The context menu of projects, directories, and files in the project tree contains a lot of useful functions.

- At the bottom-left of the window, there's a list of **open documents**. The file selected in this list will appear in the code editor in the center of the window. If the selected file is a Qt Designer form, Qt Creator will automatically switch to the **Design** mode. Each file in the list has a close button.
- The **Type to locate** field is present at the left of the bottom panel. If you want to quickly navigate to another file in the project, type the beginning of its name in the field and select it in the pop-up list. Special prefixes can be used to enable other search modes. For example, the `c` prefix allows you to search for C++ classes. You can press *Ctrl* + *K* to activate this field.
- The buttons at the bottom of the left panel allow you to build and run your current project under debugger, or normally. The button above them displays names of the current project and the current build configuration (for example, **Debug** or **Release**) and allows you to change them.
- The output panes appear below the code editor when you select them in the bottom panel. The **Issues** pane contains compiler errors and other related messages. The **Search Results** pane allows you to run a text search in the entire project and view its results. The **Application Output** pane displays the text your application has printed to its standard output (`stderr` or `stdout`).

Qt Creator is highly configurable, so you can adjust the layout to your liking. For example, it's possible to change the locations of panes, add more panes, and change keyboard shortcuts for every action.

Qt documentation

Qt project has very thorough documentation. For each API item (class, method, and so on), there is a section in the documentation that describes that item and mentions things that you need to know. There are also a lot of overview pages describing modules and their parts. When you are wondering what some Qt class or module is made for or how to use it, the Qt documentation is always a good source of information.

Qt Creator has an integrated documentation viewer. The most commonly used documentation feature is context help. To try it out, open the `main.cpp` file, set the text cursor inside the `QApplication` text, and press *F1*. The help section should appear to the right of the code editor. It displays the documentation page for the `QApplication` class. The same should work for any other Qt class, method, macro, and so on. You can click on the **Open in Help Mode** button on top of the help page to switch to the **Help** mode, where you have more space to view the page.

Another important feature is the search in documentation index. To do that, go to the **Help** mode by clicking on the **Help** button on the left panel. In **Help** mode, in the top-left corner of the window, there is a drop-down list that allows you to select the mode of the left section: **Bookmarks**, **Contents**, **Index**, or **Search**. Select **Index** mode, input your request in the **Look for:** text field and see whether there are any search results in the list below the text field. For example, try typing `qt core` to search for the Qt Core module overview. If there are results, you can press *Enter* to quickly open the first result or double-click on any result in the list to open it. If multiple Qt versions are installed, a dialog may appear where you need to select the Qt version you are interested in.

> Later in this book, we will sometimes refer to Qt documentation pages by their names. You can use the method described previously to open these pages in Qt Creator.

Time for action – Running the Affine Transformations project

Let's try building and running the project to check whether the building environment is configured properly. To build the project, click on the hammer icon (**Build**) at the bottom of the left panel. At the right of the bottom panel, a grey progress bar will appear to indicate the build progress. When the build finishes, the progress bar turns green if the build was successful or red otherwise. After the application was built, click on the green triangle icon to run the project.

> Qt Creator can automatically save all files and build the project before running it, so you can just hit the **Run** (*Ctrl* + *R*) or **Start Debugging** (*F5*) button after making changes to the project. To verify that this feature is enabled, click on **Tools** and **Options** in the main menu, go to the **Build & Run** section, go to the **General** tab, and check that the **Save all files before build**, **Always build project before deploying it**, and **Always deploy project before running it** options are checked.

If everything works, after some time, the application should be launched, as shown in the next screenshot:

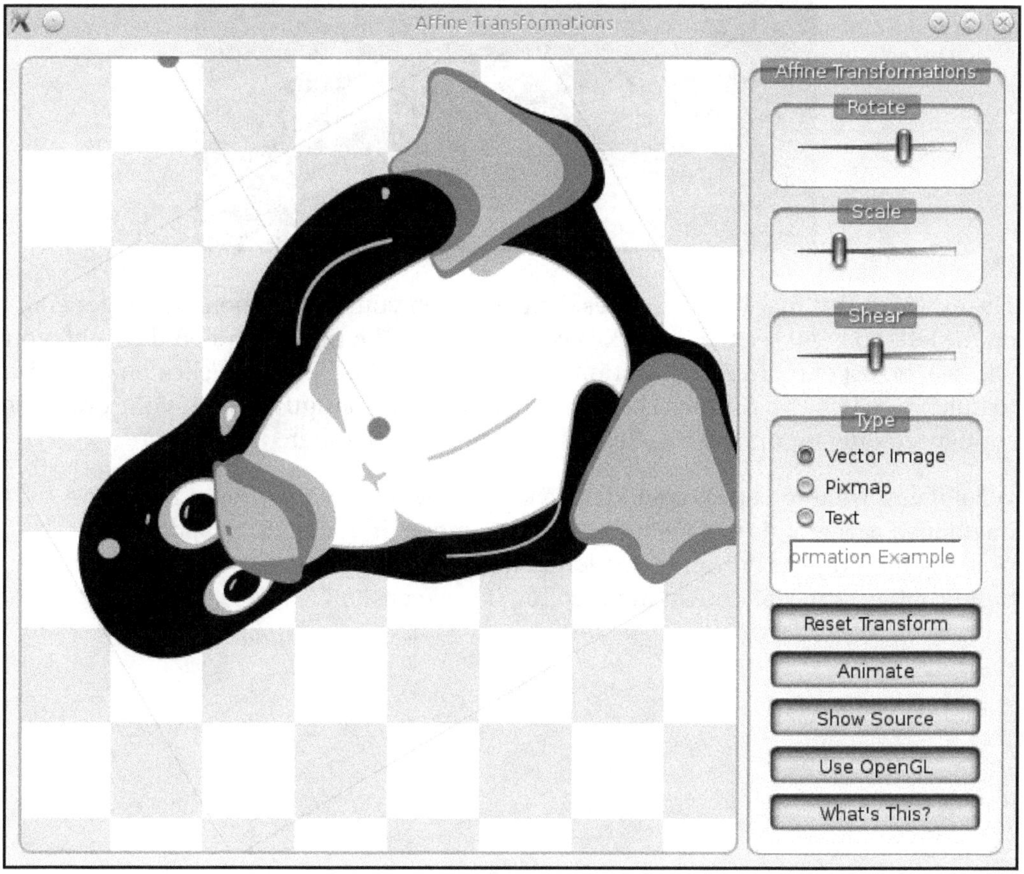

What just happened?

How exactly was the project built? To see which kit and which build configuration was used, click on the icon in the action bar directly over the green triangle icon to open the build configuration popup, as shown in the following screenshot:

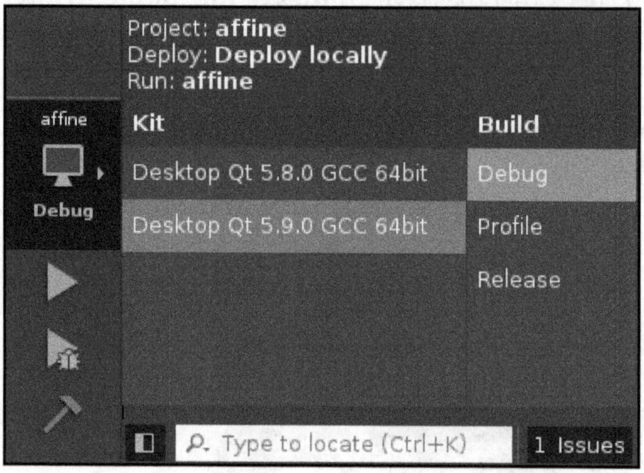

The exact content that you get varies depending on your installation, but in general, on the left, you will see the list of kits configured for the project and on the right, you will see the list of build configurations defined for that kit. You can click on these lists to quickly switch to a different kit or a different build configuration. If your project is configured only for one kit, the list of kits will not appear here.

What if you want to use another kit or change how exactly the project is built? As mentioned earlier, this is done in the **Projects** mode. If you go to this mode by pressing the **Projects** button on the left panel, Qt Creator will display the current build configuration, as shown in the following screenshot:

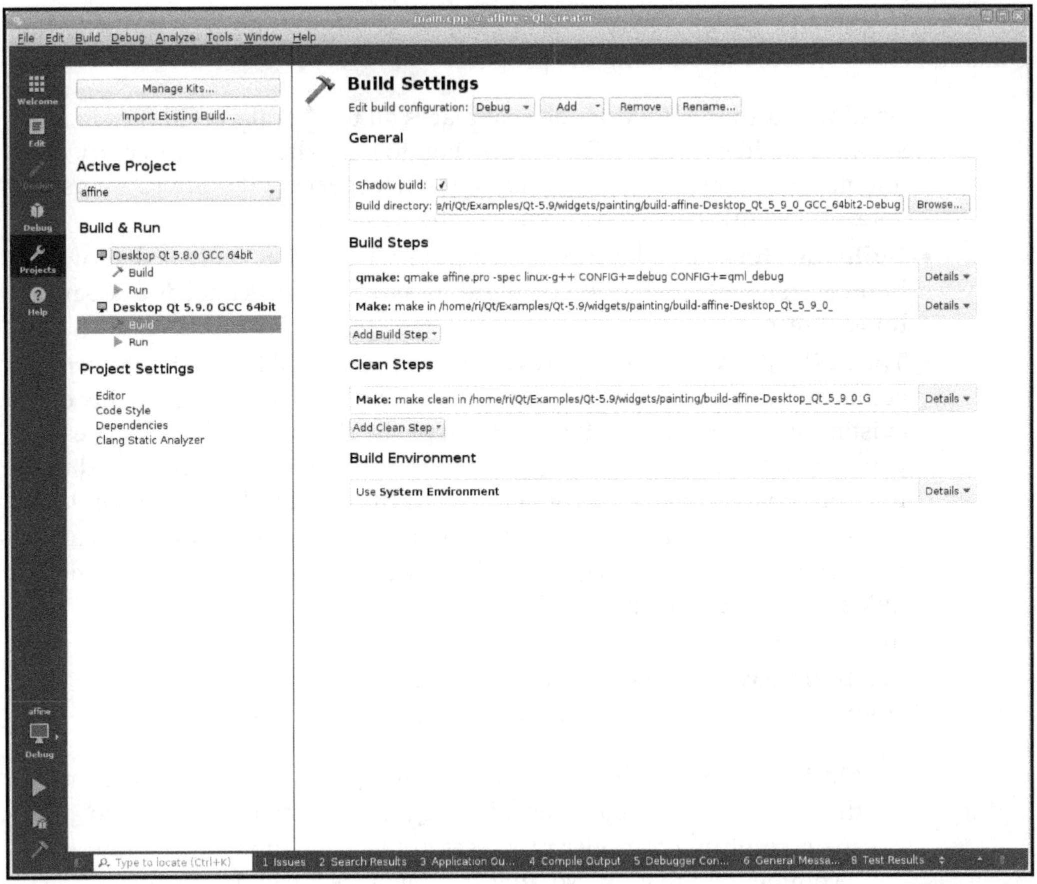

The left part of this window contains a list of all kits. Kits that are not configured to be used with this project are displayed in gray color. You can click on them to enable the kit for the current project. To disable a kit, choose the **Disable Kit** option in its context menu.

Under each enabled kit, there are two sections of the configuration. The **Build** section contains settings related to building the project:

- **Shadow build** is a build mode that places all temporary build files in a separate build directory. This allows you to keep the source directory clean and makes your source files easier to track (especially if you use a version control system). This mode is enabled by default.
- **Build directory** is the location of temporary build files (only if shadow build is enabled). Each build configuration of the project needs a separate build directory.
- The **Build steps** section displays commands that will be run to perform the actual building of the project. You can edit command-line arguments of the existing steps and add custom build steps. By default, the build process consists of two steps: `qmake` (Qt's project management tool described in the previous chapter) reads the project's `.pro` file and produces a makefile, and then some variation of `make` tool (depending on the platform) reads the makefile and executes Qt's special compilers, the C++ compiler, and the linker. For more information about `qmake`, look up the `qmake Manual` in the documentation index.
- The **Build environment** section allows you to view and change environment variables that will be available to the build tools.

> Most variations of the `make` tool (including `mingw32-make`) accept the `-j num_cores` command-line argument that allows `make` to spawn multiple compiler processes at the same time. It is highly recommended that you set this argument, as it can drastically reduce compilation time for big projects. To do this, click on **Details** at the right part of the **Make** build step and input `-j num_cores` to the **Make arguments** field (replace `num_cores` with the actual number of processor cores on your system). However, MSVC `nmake` does not support this feature. To fix this issue, Qt provides a replacement tool called `jom` that supports it.

There can be multiple build configurations for each kit. By default, three configurations are generated: **Debug** (required for the debugger to work properly), **Profile** (used for profiling), and **Release** (the build with more optimizations and no debug information).

The **Run** section determines how the executable produced by your project will be started. Here, you can change your program's command-line arguments, working directory, and environment variables. You can add multiple run configurations and switch between them using the same button that allows you to choose the current kit and build configuration.

> In most cases for desktop and mobile platforms, the binary release of Qt you download from the web page is sufficient for all your needs. However, for embedded systems, especially for ARM-based systems, there is no binary release available, or it is too heavy resource wise for such a lightweight system. Fortunately, Qt is an open source project, so you can always build it from sources. Qt allows you to choose the modules you want to use and has many more configuration options. For more information, look up **Building Qt Sources** in the documentation index.

Summary

By now, you should be able to install Qt on your development machine. You can now use Qt Creator to browse the existing examples and learn from them or to read the Qt reference manual to gain additional knowledge. You should have a basic understanding of Qt Creator's main controls. In the next chapter, we will finally start using the framework, and you will learn how to create graphical user interfaces by implementing our very first simple game.

Summary

3

Qt GUI Programming

This chapter will help you learn how to use Qt to develop applications with a graphical user interface using the Qt Creator IDE. We will get familiar with the core Qt functionality, widgets, layouts, and the signals and slots mechanism that we will later use to create complex systems such as games. We will also cover the various actions and resource systems of Qt. By the end of this chapter, you will be able to write your own programs that communicate with the user through windows and widgets.

The main topics covered in this chapter are as listed:

- Windows and widgets
- Creating a Qt Widgets project and implementing a tic-tac-toe game
- Creating widgets with or without the visual form editor
- Using layouts to automatically position widgets
- Creating and using signals and slots
- Using the Qt resource system

Creating GUI in Qt

As described in `Chapter 1`, *Introduction to Qt,* Qt consists of multiple modules. In this chapter, you will learn how to use the Qt Widgets module. It allows you to create classic desktop applications. The **user interface** (**UI**) of these applications consists of *widgets*.

A widget is a fragment of the UI with a specific look and behavior. Qt provides a lot of built-in widgets that are widely used in applications: labels, text boxes, checkboxes, buttons, and so on. Each of these widgets is represented as an instance of a C++ class derived from `QWidget` and provides methods for reading and writing the widget's content. You may also create your own widgets with custom content and behavior.

The base class of `QWidget` is `QObject`—the most important Qt class that contains multiple useful features. In particular, it implements parent–child relationships between objects, allowing you to organize a collection of objects in your program. Each object can have a parent object and an arbitrary number of children. Making a parent–child relationship between two objects has multiple consequences. When an object is deleted, all its children will be automatically deleted as well. For widgets, there is also a rule that a child occupies an area within the boundaries of its parent. For example, a typical form includes multiple labels, input fields, and buttons. Each of the form's elements is a widget, and the form is their parent widget.

Each widget has a separate coordinate system that is used for painting and event handling within the widget. By default, the origin of this coordinate system is placed in its top-left corner. The child's coordinate system is relative to its parent.

Any widget that is not included into another widget (that is, any *top-level widget*) becomes a window, and the desktop operating system will provide it with a window frame, which usually usually allows the user to drag around, resize, and close the window (although the presence and content of the window frame can be configured).

Time for action – Creating a Qt Widgets project

The first step to develop an application with Qt Creator is to create a project using one of the templates provided by the IDE.

From the **File** menu of Qt Creator, choose **New File or Project**. There are a number of project types to choose from. Follow the given steps for creating a Qt Desktop project:

1. For a widget-based application, choose the **Application** group and the **Qt Widgets Application** template, as shown in the following screenshot:

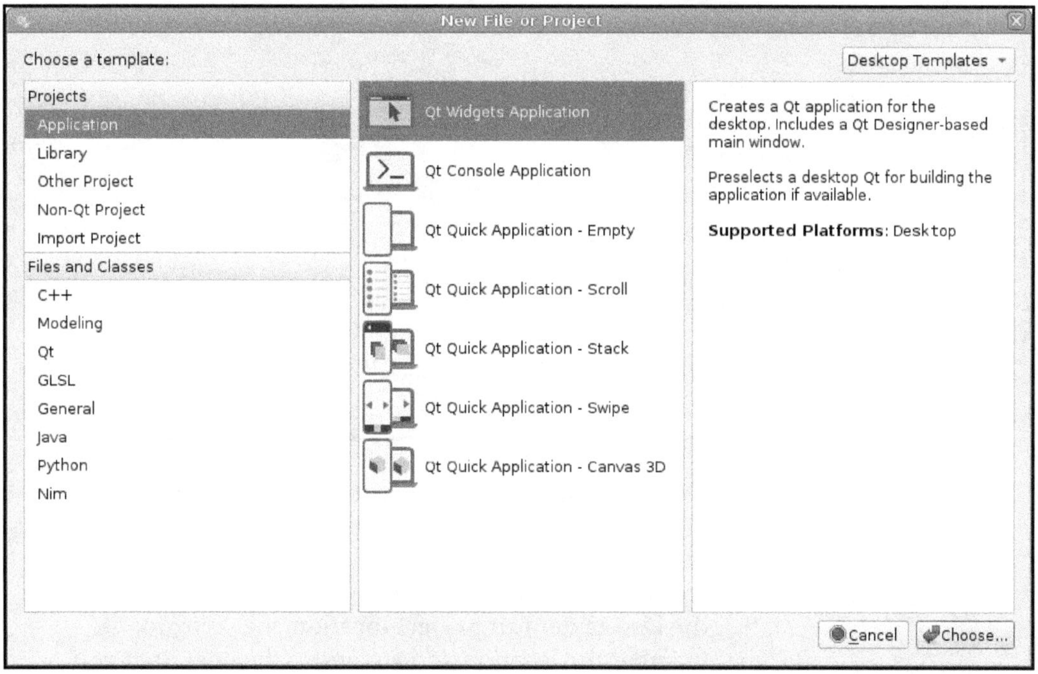

2. The next step is to choose a name and location for your new project:

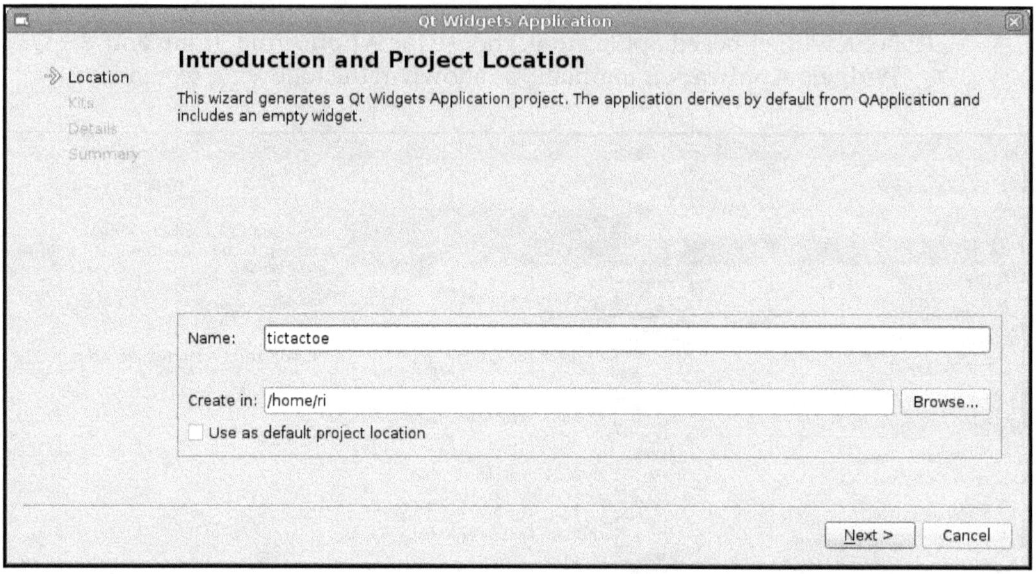

3. We will create a simple tic-tac-toe game, so we will name our project `tictactoe` and provide a nice location for it.

> **TIP:** If you have a common directory where you put all your projects, you can tick the **Use as default project location** checkbox for Qt Creator to remember the location and suggest it the next time you start a new project.

4. Next, you need to select the kit (or multiple kits) you want to use with the project. Select the Desktop Qt kit corresponding to the Qt version you want to use:

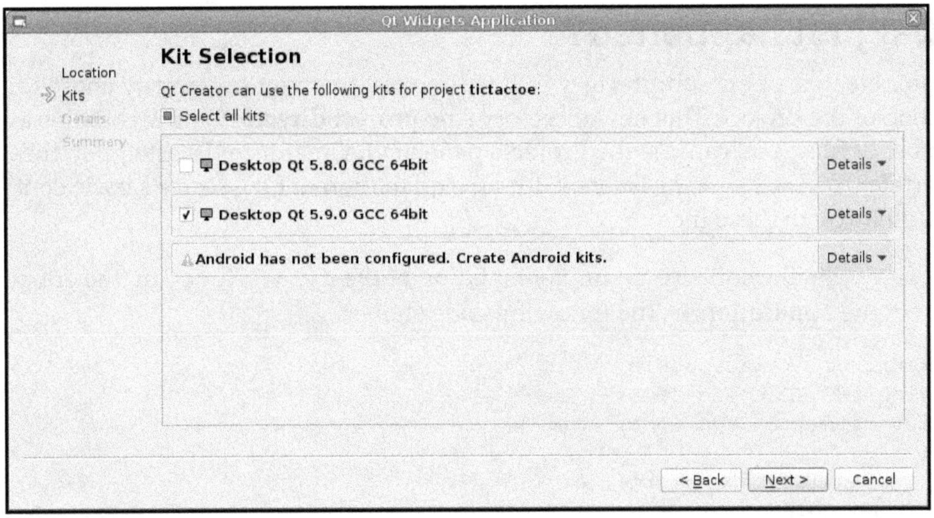

5. Now you will be presented with the option of creating the first widget for your project. We want to create a widget that will represent the main window of our application, so we can leave the **Class name** and **Base class** fields unchanged. We also want to use the visual form editor to edit the content of the main window, so **Generate form** should also be left checked:

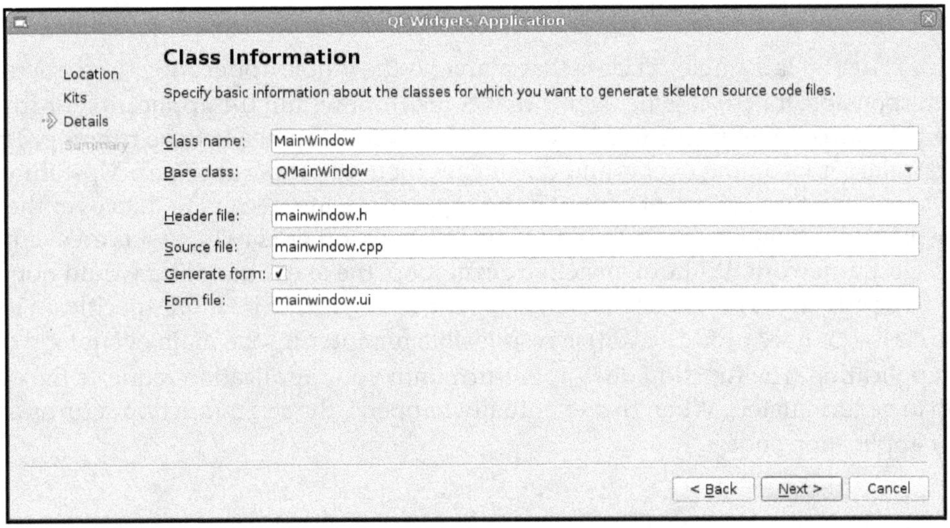

6. Then, click on **Next** and **Finish**.

What just happened?

Creator created a new subdirectory in the directory that you previously chose for the location of the project. This new directory (the **project directory**) now contains a number of files. You can use the **Projects** pane of Qt Creator to list and open these files (refer to `Chapter 2`, *Installation*, for an explanation of Qt Creator's basic controls). Let's go through these files.

The `main.cpp` file contains an implementation of the `main()` function, the entry point of the application, as the following code shows:

```
#include "mainwindow.h"
#include <QApplication>
int main(int argc, char *argv[])
{
    QApplication a(argc, argv);
    MainWindow w;
    w.show();
    return a.exec();
}
```

The `main()` function creates an instance of the `QApplication` class and feeds it with variables containing the command-line arguments. Then, it instantiates our `MainWindow` class, calls its `show` method, and finally, returns a value returned by the `exec` method of the application object.

`QApplication` is a singleton class that manages the whole application. In particular, it is responsible for processing events that come from within the application or from external sources. For events to be processed, an event loop needs to be running. The loop waits for incoming events and dispatches them to proper routines. Most things in Qt are done through events: input handling, redrawing, receiving data over the network, triggering timers, and so on. This is the reason we say that Qt is an event-oriented framework. Without an active event loop, the event handling would not function properly. The `exec()` call in `QApplication` (or, to be more specific, in its base class—`QCoreApplication`) is responsible for entering the main event loop of the application. The function does not return until your application requests the event loop to be terminated. When that eventually happens, the `main` function returns and your application ends.

The mainwindow.h and the mainwindow.cpp files implement the MainWindow class. For now, there is almost no code in it. The class is derived from QMainWindow (which, in turn, is derived from QWidget), so it inherits a lot of methods and behavior from its base class. It also contains a Ui::MainWindow *ui field, which is initialized in the constructor and deleted in the destructor. The constructor also calls the ui->setupUi(this); function.

Ui::MainWindow is an *automatically generated* class, so there is no declaration of it in the source code. It will be created in the build directory when the project is built. The purpose of this class is to set up our widget and fill it with content based on changes in the form editor. The automatically generated class is not a QWidget. In fact, it contains only two methods: setupUi, which performs the initial setup, and retranslateUi, which updates visible text when the UI language is changed. All widgets and other objects added in the form editor are available as public fields of the Ui::MainWindow class, so we can access them from within the MainWindow method as ui->objectName.

mainwindow.ui is a form file that can be edited in the visual form editor. If you open it in Qt Creator by double-clicking on it in the **Projects** pane, Qt Creator will switch to the **Design** mode. If you switch back to the **Edit** mode, you will see that this file is actually an XML file containing the hierarchy and properties of all objects edited in **Design** mode. During the building of the project, a special tool called the User Interface Compiler converts this XML file to the implementation of the Ui::MainWindow class used in the MainWindow class.

TIP

Note that you don't need to edit the XML file by hand or edit any code in the Ui::MainWindow class. Making changes in the visual editor is enough to apply them to your MainWindow class and make the form's objects available to it.

The final file that was generated is called tictactoe.pro and is the project configuration file. It contains all the information that is required to build your project using the tools that Qt provides. Let's analyze this file (less important directives are omitted):

```
QT += core gui
greaterThan(QT_MAJOR_VERSION, 4): QT += widgets
TARGET = tictactoe
TEMPLATE = app
SOURCES += main.cpp mainwindow.cpp
HEADERS += mainwindow.h
FORMS   += mainwindow.ui
```

The first two lines enable Qt's `core`, `gui`, and `widgets` modules. The `TEMPLATE` variable is used to specify that your project file describes an application (as opposed to, for example, a library). The `TARGET` variable contains the name of the produced executable (`tictactoe`). The last three lines list all files that should be used to build the project.

> In fact, `qmake` enables Qt Core and Qt GUI modules by default, even if you don't specify them explicitly in the project file. You can opt out of using a default module if you want. For example, you can disable Qt GUI by adding `QT -= gui` to the project file.

Before we proceed, let's tell the build system that we want to use C++11 features (such as lambda expressions, scoped enumerations, and range-based `for` loops) in our project by adding the following line to `tictactoe.pro`:

```
CONFIG += c++11
```

If we do this, the C++ compiler will receive a flag indicating that C++11 support should be enabled. This may not be needed if your compiler has C++11 support enabled by default. If you wish to use C++14 instead, use `CONFIG += c++14`.

What we have now is a complete Qt Widgets project. To build and run it, simply choose the **Run** entry from the **Build** drop-down menu or click on the green triangle icon on the left-hand side of the Qt Creator window. After a while, you should see a window pop up. Since we didn't add anything to the window, it is blank:

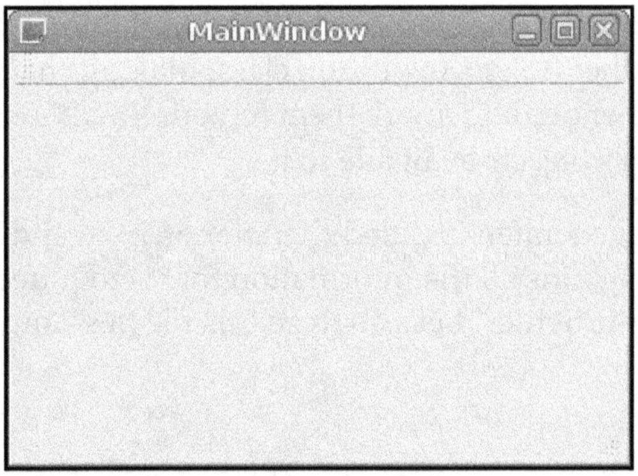

Design mode interface

Open the `mainwindow.ui` file and examine Qt Creator's Design mode:

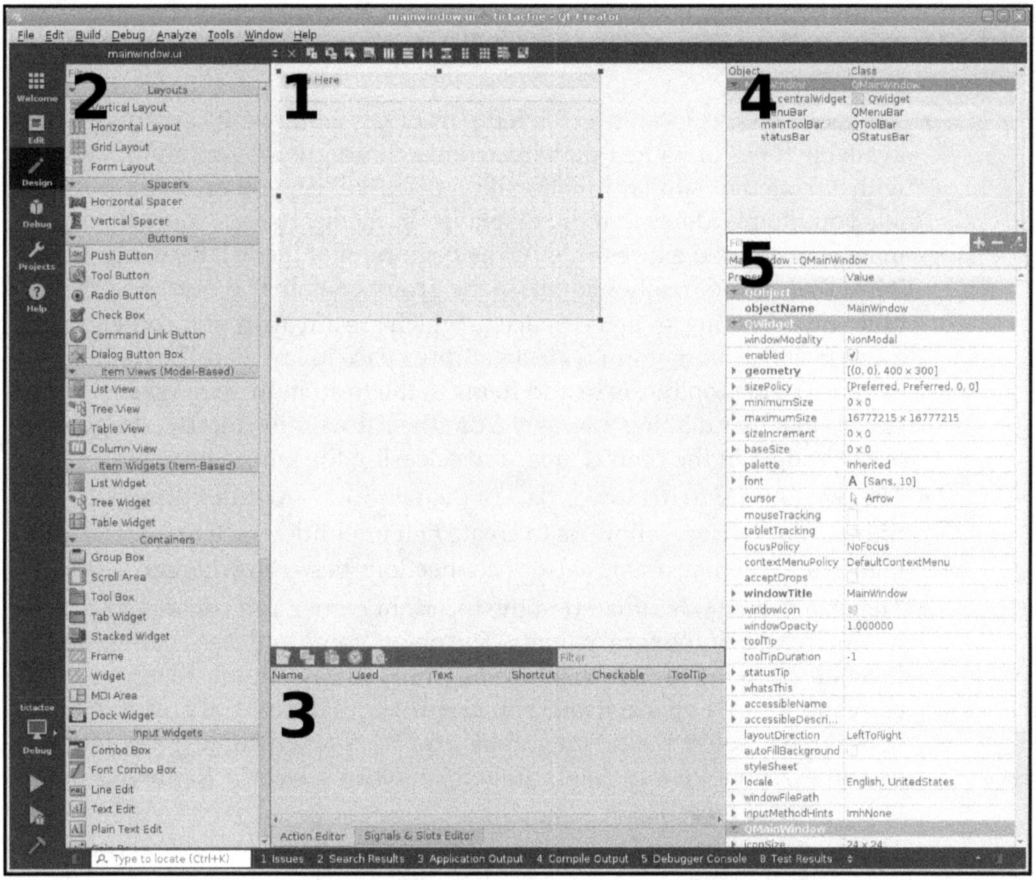

The **Design** mode consists of five major parts (they are marked on this screenshot):

- The central area **(1)** is the main worksheet. It contains a graphical representation of the form being designed where you can move widgets around, compose them into layouts, and see how they react. It also allows further manipulation of the form using the point-and-click method that we will learn later.
- The toolbox **(2)** is located in the left part of the window. It contains a list of available types of widget that are arranged into groups containing items with a related or similar functionality. Over the list, you can see a box that lets you filter widgets that are displayed in the list to show only those that match the entered expression. At the beginning of the list, there are also items that are not really widgets—one group contains layouts, and the other one contains so-called spacers, which are a way to push other items away from each other or create an empty space in layouts. The main purpose of the toolbox is to add items to the form in the worksheet. You can do that by grabbing a widget from the list with the mouse, dragging it to the widget in the central area, and releasing the mouse button.
- The two tabs **(3)** in the lower part of the window—**Action Editor** and **Signal/Slot Editor**—allow us to create helper entities such as actions for the menus and toolbars or signal-slot connections between widgets.
- The object tree **(4)** is situated in the top-right corner and contains the hierarchy tree of the form's items. The object name and class name of each item added to the form is displayed in the tree. The topmost item corresponds to the form itself. You can use both the central area and the object tree to select the existing items and access their context menu (for example, if you want to delete an item, you can select the **Remove...** option in the context menu).
- The property editor **(5)** is located in the bottom-right corner. It allows you to view and change the values of all the properties of the item currently selected in the central area and the object tree. Properties are grouped by their classes that they have been declared in, starting from `QObject` (the base class implementing properties), which declares only one, but an important, property—`objectName`. Following `QObject`, there are properties declared in `QWidget`, which is a direct descendant of `QObject`. They are mainly related to the geometry and layout policies of the widget. Further down the list, you can find properties that come from further derivations of `QWidget`, down to the concrete class of the selected widget. The **Filter** field above the properties can help you find the needed property quickly.

Taking a closer look at the property editor, you can see that some of them have ▸ arrows, which reveal new rows when clicked. These are composed properties where the complete property value is determined from more than one subproperty value; for example, if there is a property called `geometry` that defines a rectangle, it can be expanded to show four subproperties: `x`, `y`, `width`, and `height`. Another thing that you may quickly note is that some property names are displayed in bold. This means that the property value was modified and is different from the default value for this property. This lets you quickly find the properties that you have modified.

> TIP
>
> If you changed a property's value but decided to stick to the default value later, you should click on the corresponding input field and then click on the small button with an arrow to its right: . This is not the same as setting the original value by hand. For example, if you examine the `spacing` property of some layouts, it would appear as if it had some constant default value for (example, 6). However, the actual default value depends on the style the application uses and may be different on a different operating system, so the only way to set the default value is to use the dedicated button and ensure that the property is not displayed in bold anymore.

If you prefer a purely alphabetical order where properties are not grouped by their class, you can switch the view using a pop-up menu that becomes available after you click on the wrench icon positioned over the property list; however, once you get familiar with the hierarchy of Qt classes, it will be much easier to navigate the list when it is sorted by class affinity.

What was described here is the basic tool layout. If you don't like it, you can invoke the context menu from the main worksheet, uncheck the **Automatically Hide View Title Bars** entry, and use the title bars that appear to re-arrange all the panes to your liking, or even close the ones you don't currently need.

Now that you are familiar with the structure of the visual form editor, you can finally add some content to our widget. We are making a tic-tac-toe game with local multiplayer, so we need some way of displaying which of the two players currently moves. Let's put the game board in the center of the window and display the names of the players above and below the board. When a player needs to move, we will make the corresponding name's font bold. We also need a button that will start a new game.

Time for action – Adding widgets to the form

Locate the **Label** item in the toolbox (it's in the **Display Widgets** category) and drag it to our form. Use the property editor to set the `objectName` property of the label to `player1Name`. `objectName` is a unique identifier of a form item. The object name is used as the name of the public field in the `Ui::MainWindow` class, so the label will be available as `ui->player1Name` in the `MainWindow` class (and will have a `QLabel *` type). Then, locate the `text` property in the property editor (it will be in the `QLabel` group, as it is the class that introduces the property) and set it to `Player 1`. You will see that the text in the central area will be updated accordingly. Add another label, set its `objectName` to `player2Name` and its `text` to `Player 2`.

TIP: You can select a widget in the central area and press the *F2* key to edit the text in place. Another way is to double-click on the widget in the form. It works for any widget that can display text.

Drag a **Push Button** (from the **Buttons** group) to the form and use the *F2* key to rename it to `Start new game`. If the name does not fit in the button, you can resize it using the blue rectangles on its edges. Set the `objectName` of the button to `startNewGame`.

There is no built-in widget for our game board, so we will need to create a custom widget for it later. For now, we will use an empty widget. Locate **Widget** in the **Containers** group of the toolbox and drag it to the form. Set its `objectName` to `gameBoard`:

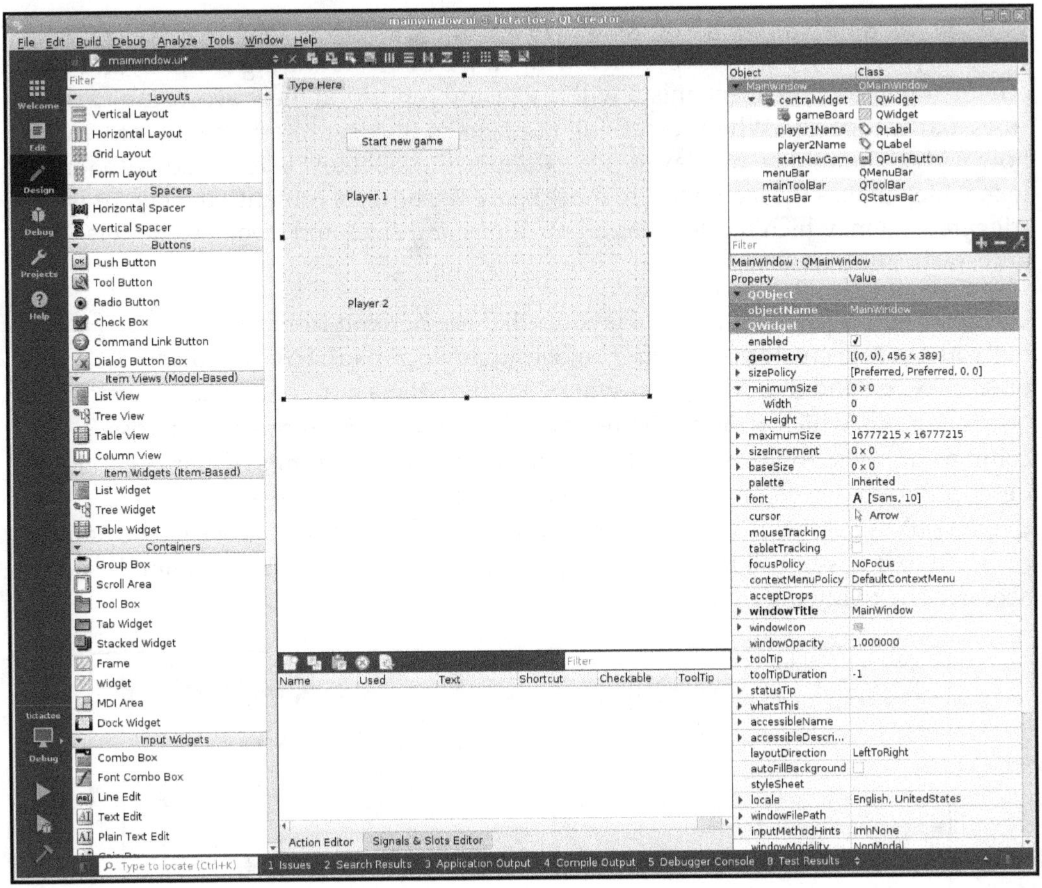

Layouts

If you build and run the project now, you will see the window with two labels and a button, but they will remain in the exact positions you left them. This is what you almost never want. Usually, it is desired that widgets are automatically resized based on their content and the size of their neighbors. They need to adjust to the changes of the window's size (or, in contrast, the window size may need to be restricted based on possible sizes of the widgets inside of it). This is a very important feature for a cross-platform application, as you cannot assume any particular screen resolution or size of controls. In Qt, all of this requires us to use a special mechanism called **layouts**.

Layouts allow us to arrange the content of a widget, ensuring that its space is used efficiently. When we set a layout on a widget, we can start adding widgets, and even other layouts, and the mechanism will resize and reposition them according to the rules that we specify. When something happens in the user interface that influences how widgets should be displayed (for example, the label text is replaced with longer text, which makes the label require more space to show its content), the layout is triggered again, which recalculates all positions and sizes and updates widgets, as necessary.

Qt comes with a predefined set of layouts that are derived from the `QLayout` class, but you can also create your own. The ones that we already have at our disposal are `QHBoxLayout` and `QVBoxLayout`, which position items horizontally and vertically; `QGridLayout`, which arranges items in a grid so that an item can span across columns or rows; and `QFormLayout`, which creates two columns of items with item descriptions in one column and item content in the other. There is also `QStackedLayout`, which is rarely used directly and which makes one of the items assigned to it possess all the available space. You can see the most common layouts in action in the following figure:

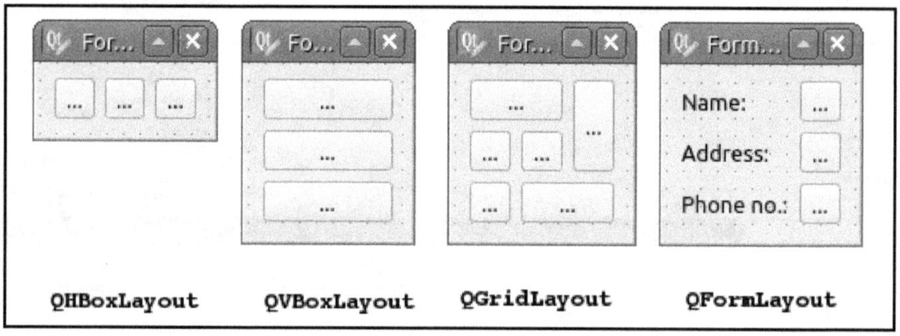

Time for action – Adding a layout to the form

Select the **MainWindow** top-level item in the object tree and click on , the **Lay Out Vertically** icon in the upper toolbar. The button, labels, and the empty widget will be automatically resized to take all the available space of the form in the central area:

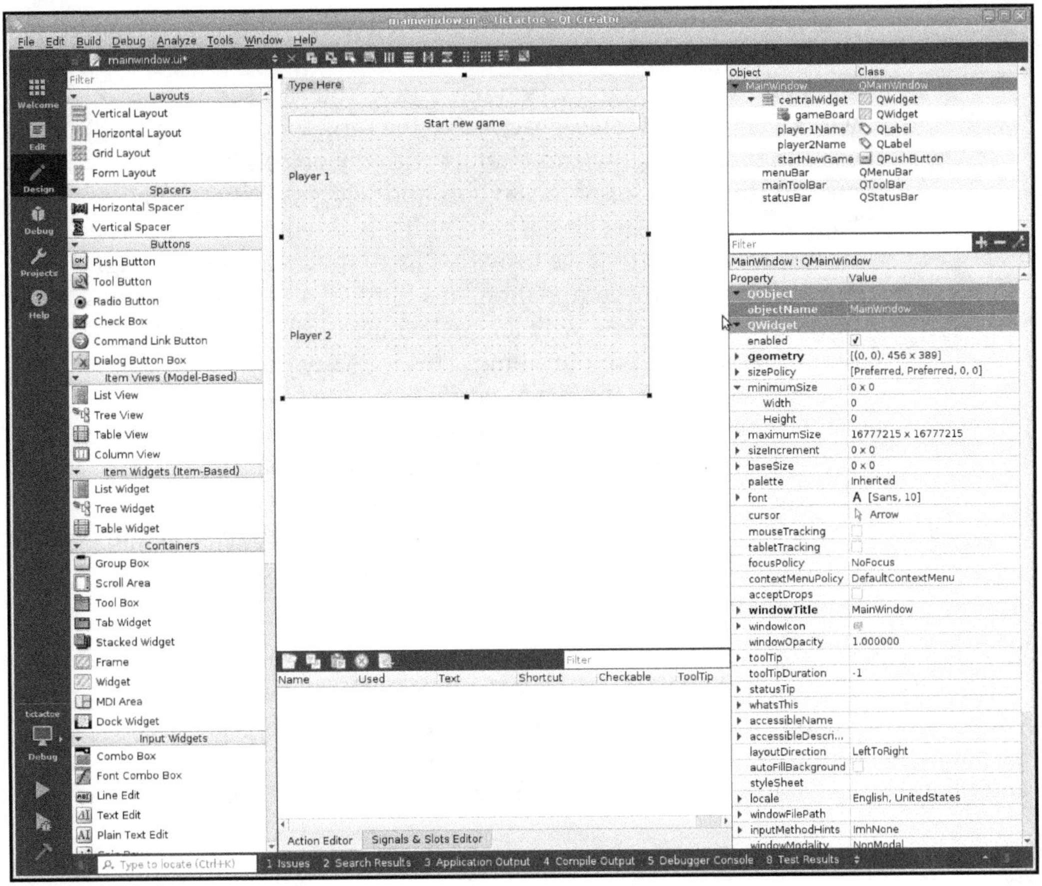

If the items were arranged in a different order, you can drag and drop them to change the order.

Run the application and check that the window's contents are automatically positioned and resized to use all the available space when the window is resized. Unfortunately, the labels take more vertical space than they really require, resulting in an empty space in the application window. We will fix this issue later in this chapter when we learn about size policies.

TIP

You can test the layouts of your form without building and running the whole application. Open the **Tools** menu, go to the **Form Editor** submenu, and choose the **Preview** entry. You will see a new window open that looks exactly like the form we just designed. You can resize the window and interact with the objects inside to monitor the behavior of the layouts and widgets. What really happened here is that Qt Creator built a real window for us based on the description that we provided in all the areas of the design mode. Without any compilation, in a blink of an eye, we received a fully working window with all the layouts working and all the properties adjusted to our liking. This is a very important tool, so ensure that you use it often to verify that your layouts are controlling all the widgets as you intended them to—it is much faster than compiling and running the whole application just to check whether the widgets stretch or squeeze properly. You can also resize the form in the central area of the form editor by dragging its bottom-right corner, and if the layouts are set up correctly, the contents should be resized and repositioned.

Now that you can create and display a form, two important operations need to be implemented. First, you need to receive notifications when the user interacts with your form (for example, presses a button) to perform some actions in the code. Second, you need to change the properties of the form's contents programmatically, and fill it with real data (for example, set player names from the code).

Signals and slots

To trigger functionality as a response to something that happens in an application, Qt uses a mechanism of signals and slots. This is another important feature of the `QObject` class. It's based on connecting a notification (which Qt calls a **signal**) about a change of state in some object with a function or method (called a **slot**) that is executed when such a notification arises. For example, if a button is pressed, it **emits** (sends) a `clicked()` signal. If some method is connected to this signal, the method will be called whenever the button is pressed.

Signals can have arguments that serve as a payload. For example, an input box widget (`QLineEdit`) has a `textEdited(const QString &text)` signal that's emitted when the user edits the text in the input box. A slot connected to this signal will receive the new text in the input box as its argument (provided it has an argument).

Signals and slots can be used with all classes that inherit `QObject` (including all widgets). A signal can be connected to a slot, member function, or functor (which includes a regular global function). When an object emits a signal, any of these entities that are connected to that signal will be called. A signal can also be connected to another signal, in which case emitting the first signal will make the other signal be emitted as well. You can connect any number of slots to a single signal and any number of signals to a single slot.

Creating signals and slots

If you create a `QObject` subclass (or a `QWidget` subclass, as QWidget inherits QObject), you can mark a method of this class as a signal or a slot. If the parent class had any signals or non-private slots, your class will also inherit them.

In order for signals and slots to work properly, the class declaration must contain the `Q_OBJECT` macro in a private section of its definition (Qt Creator has generated it for us). When the project is built, a special tool called **Meta-Object Compiler** (**moc**) will examine the class's header and generate some extra code necessary for signals and slots to work properly.

> Keep in mind that **moc** and all other Qt build tools do not edit the project files. Your C++ files are passed to the compiler without any changes. All special effects are achieved by generating separate C++ files and adding them to the compilation process.

A signal can be created by declaring a class method in the `signals` section of the class declaration:

```
signals:
    void valueChanged(int newValue);
```

However, we don't implement such a method; this will be done automatically by **moc**. We can send (`emit`) the signal by calling the method. There is a convention that a signal call should be preceded by the `emit` macro. This macro has no effect (it's actually a blank macro), but it helps us clarify our intent to emit the signal:

```
void MyClass::setValue(int newValue) {
    m_value = newValue;
    emit valueChanged(newValue);
}
```

You should only emit signals from within the class methods, as if it were a protected function.

Slots are class methods declared in the `private slots`, `protected slots`, or `public slots` section of the class declaration. Contrary to signals, slots need to be implemented. Qt will call the slot when a signal connected to it is emitted. The visibility of the slot (private, protected, or public) should be chosen using the same principles as for normal methods.

> The C++ standard only describes three types of sections of the class definition (`private`, `protected`, and `public`), so you may wonder how these special sections work. They are actually simple macros: the `signals` macro expands to `public`, and `slots` is a blank macro. So, the compiler treats them as normal methods. These keywords are, however, used by **moc** to determine how to generate the extra code.

Connecting signals and slots

Signals and slots can be connected and disconnected dynamically using the `QObject::connect()` and `QObject::disconnect()` functions. A regular, signal-slot connection is defined by the following four attributes:

- An object that changes its state (sender)
- A signal in the sender object
- An object that contains the function to be called (receiver)
- A slot in the receiver

If you want to make the connection, you need to call the `QObject::connect` function and pass these four parameters to it. For example, the following code can be used to clear the input box whenever the button is clicked on:

```
connect(button,   &QPushButton::clicked,
        lineEdit, &QLineEdit::clear);
```

Signals and slots in this code are specified using a standard C++ feature called pointers to member functions. Such a pointer contains the name of the class and the name of the method (in our case, signal or slot) in that class. Qt Creator's code autocompletion will help you write connect statements.

In particular, if you press *Ctrl* + *Space* after `connect(button, &`, it will insert the name of the class, and if you do that after `connect(button, &QPushButton::`, it will suggest one of the available signals (in another context, it would suggest all the existing methods of the class).

Note that you can't set the arguments of signals or slots when making a connection. Arguments of the source signal are always determined by the function that emits the signal. Arguments of the receiving slot (or signal) are always the same as the arguments of the source signal, with two exceptions:

- If the receiving slot or signal has fewer arguments than the source signal, the remaining arguments are ignored. For example, if you want to use the `valueChanged(int)` signal but don't care about the passed value, you can connect this signal to a slot without arguments.
- If the types of the corresponding arguments are not the same, but an implicit conversion between them exists, that conversion is performed. This means that you can, for example, connect a signal carrying a `double` value with a slot taking an `int` parameter.

If the signal and the slot do not have compatible signatures, you will get a compile-time error.

An existing connection is automatically destroyed after the sender or the receiver objects are deleted. Manual disconnection is rarely needed. The `connect()` function returns a connection handle that can be passed to `disconnect()`. Alternatively, you can call `disconnect()` with the same arguments the `connect()` was called with to undo the connection.

You don't always need to declare a slot to perform a connection. It's possible to connect a signal to a standalone function:

```
connect(button, &QPushButton::clicked, someFunction);
```

The function can also be a lambda expression, in which case it is possible to write the code directly in the `connect` statement:

```
connect(pushButton, &QPushButton::clicked, []()
{
    qDebug() << "clicked!";
});
```

It can be useful if you want to invoke a slot with a fixed argument value that can't be carried by a signal because it has less arguments. A solution is to invoke the slot from a lambda function (or a standalone function):

```
connect(pushButton, &QPushButton::clicked, [label]()
{
    label->setText("button was clicked");
});
```

A function can even be replaced with a function object (functor). To do this, we create a class, for which we overload the call operator that is compatible with the signal that we wish to connect to, as shown in the following code snippet:

```
class Functor {
public:
    Functor(const QString &name) : m_name(name) {}
    void operator()(bool toggled) const {
        qDebug() << m_name << ": button state changed to" << toggled;
    }
private:
    QString m_name;
};

int main(int argc, char *argv[])
{
    QApplication a(argc, argv);
    QPushButton *button = new QPushButton();
    button->setCheckable(true);
    QObject::connect(button, &QPushButton::toggled,
                     Functor("my functor"));
    button->show();
    return a.exec();
}
```

This is often a nice way to execute a slot with an additional parameter that is not carried by the signal, as this is much cleaner than using a lambda expression. However, keep in mind that automatic disconnection will not happen when the object referenced in the lambda expression or the functor is deleted. This can lead to a use-after-free bug.

> While it is actually possible to connect a signal to a method of a `QObject`-based class that is not a slot, doing this is not recommended. Declaring the method as a slot shows your intent better. Additionally, methods that are not slots are not available to Qt at runtime, which is required in some cases.

Old connect syntax

Before Qt 5, the old connect syntax was the only option. It looks as follows:

```
connect(spinBox, SIGNAL(valueChanged(int)),
        dial,    SLOT(setValue(int)));
```

This statement establishes a connection between the signal of the `spinBox` object called `valueChanged` that carries an `int` parameter and a `setValue` slot in the `dial` object that accepts an `int` parameter. It is forbidden to put argument names or values in a `connect` statement. Qt Creator is usually able to suggest all possible inputs in this context if you press *Ctrl* + *Space* after `SIGNAL(` or `SLOT(`.

While this syntax is still available, we discourage its wide use, because it has the following drawbacks:

- If the signal or the slot is incorrectly referenced (for example, its name or argument types are incorrect) or if argument types of the signals and the slot are not compatible, there will be no compile-time error, only a runtime warning. The new syntax approach performs all the necessary checks at compile time.
- The old syntax doesn't support casting argument values to another type (for example, connect a signal carrying a `double` value with a slot taking an `int` parameter).
- The old syntax doesn't support connecting a signal to a standalone function, a lambda expression, or a functor.

The old syntax also uses macros and may look unclear to developers not familiar with Qt. It's hard to say which syntax is easier to read (the old syntax displays argument types, while the new syntax displays the class name instead). However, the new syntax has a big disadvantage when using overloaded signals or slots. The only way to resolve the overloaded function type is to use an explicit cast:

```
connect(spinBox,
        static_cast<void (QSpinBox::*)(int)>(&QSpinBox::valueChanged),
        ...);
```

The old connect syntax includes argument types, so it doesn't have this issue. In this case, the old syntax may look more acceptable, but compile-time checks may still be considered more valuable than shorter code. In this book, we prefer the new syntax, but use the old syntax when working with overloaded methods for the sake of clarity.

Signal and slot access specifiers

As mentioned earlier, you should only emit signals from the class that owns it or from its subclasses. However, if signals were really protected or private, you would not be able to connect to them using the pointer-to-member function syntax. To make such connections possible, signals are made public functions. This means that the compiler won't stop you from calling the signal from outside. If you want to prevent such calls, you can declare `QPrivateSignal` as the last argument of the signal:

```
signals:
    void valueChanged(int value, QPrivateSignal);
```

`QPrivateSignal` is a private struct created in each `QObject` subclass by the `Q_OBJECT` macro, so you can only create `QPrivateSignal` objects in the current class.

Slots can be public, protected, or private, depending on how you want to restrict access to them. When using the pointer to a member function syntax for connection, you will only be able to create pointers to slots if you have access to them. It's also correct to call a slot directly from any other location as long as you have access to it.

That being said, Qt doesn't really support restricting access to signals and slots. Regardless of how a signal or a slot is declared, you can always access it using the old connect syntax. You can also call any signal or slot using the `QMetaObject::invokeMethod` method. While you can restrict direct C++ calls to reduce the possibility of errors, keep in mind that the users of your API still can access any signal or slot if they really want to.

> There are some aspects of signals and slots that we have not covered here. We will discuss them later when we deal with multithreading (*Online Chapter*, `https://www.packtpub.com/sites/default/files/downloads/MiscellaneousandAdvancedConcepts.pdf`).

Time for action – Receiving the button-click signal from the form

Open the `mainwindow.h` file and create a `private slots` section in the class declaration, then declare the `startNewGame()` private slot, as shown in the following code:

```
class MainWindow : public QMainWindow
```

```
{
    Q_OBJECT
public:
    explicit MainWindow(QWidget *parent = nullptr);
    ~MainWindow();
private slots:
    void startNewGame();
}
```

To quickly implement a freshly declared method, we can ask Qt Creator to create the skeleton code for us by positioning the text cursor at the method declaration, pressing *Alt* + *Enter* on the keyboard, and choosing **Add definition in tictactoewidget.cpp** from the popup.

> It also works the other way round. You can write the method body first and then position the cursor on the method signature, press *Alt* + *Enter*, and choose **Add (...) declaration** from the quick-fix menu. There are also various other context-dependent fixes that are available in Creator.

Write the highlighted code in the implementation of this method:

```
void MainWindow::startNewGame()
{
    qDebug() << "button clicked!";
}
```

Add `#include <QDebug>` to the top section of the `mainwindow.cpp` file to make the `qDebug()` macro available.

Finally, add a connect statement to the constructor after the `setupUi()` call:

```
ui->setupUi(this);
connect(ui->startNewGame, &QPushButton::clicked,
        this, &MainWindow::startNewGame);
```

Run the application and try clicking on the button. The `button clicked!` text should appear in the **Application Output** pane in the bottom part of Qt Creator's window (if the pane isn't activated, use the **Application Output** button in the bottom panel to open it):

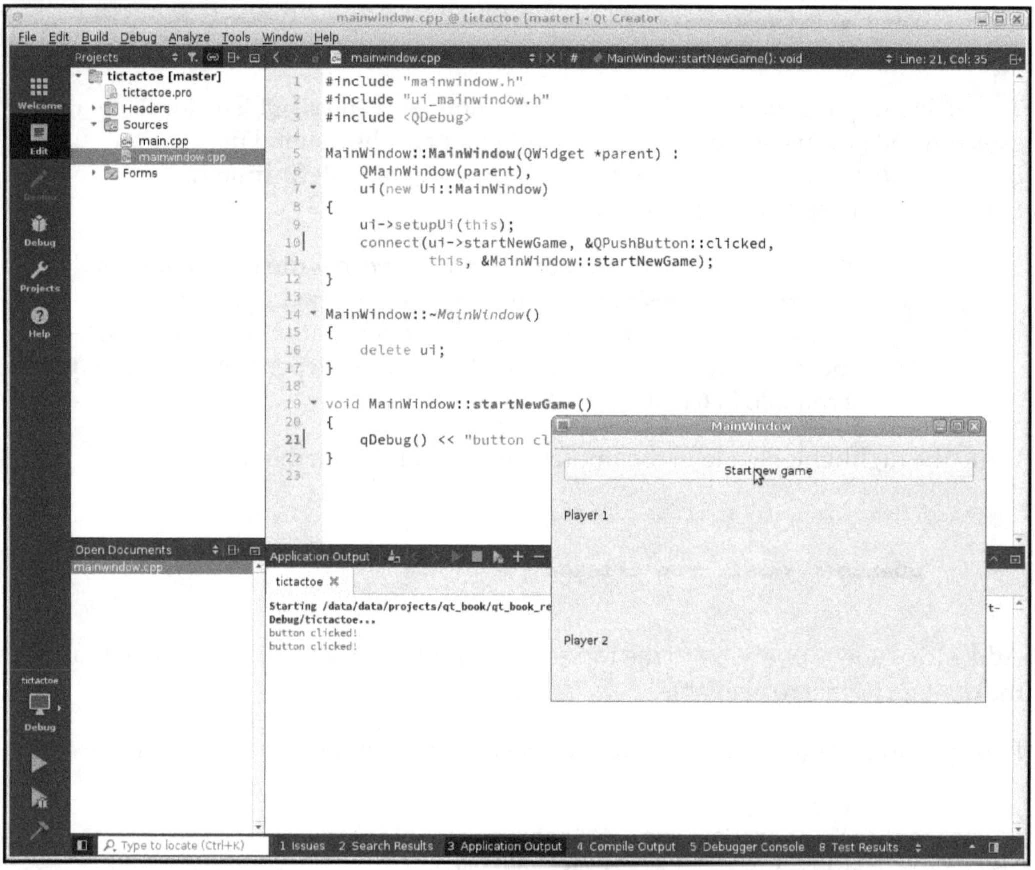

What just happened?

We created a new private slot in the `MainWindow` class and connected the `clicked()` signal of the **Start new game** button to the slot. When the user clicks on the button, Qt will call our slot, and the code we wrote inside it gets executed.

> **TIP** Ensure that you put any operations with the form elements after the `setupUi()` call. This function creates the elements, so `ui->startNewGame` will simply be uninitialized before `setupUi()` is called, and attempting to use it will result in undefined behavior.

`qDebug() << ...` is a convenient way to print debug information to the `stderr` (standard error output) of the application process. It's quite similar to the `std::cerr << ...` method available in the standard library, but it separates supplied values with spaces and appends a new line at the end.

> Putting debug outputs everywhere quickly becomes inconvenient. Luckily, Qt Creator has powerful integration with C++ debuggers, so you can use **Debug** mode to check whether some particular line is executing, see the current values of the local variables at that location, and so on. For example, try setting a break point at the line containing `qDebug()` by clicking on the space to the left of the line number (a red circle indicating the break point should appear). Click on the **Start Debugging** button (a green triangle with a bug at the bottom-left corner of Qt Creator), wait for the application to launch, and press the **Start new game** button. When the application enters the break point location, it will pause, and Qt Creator's window will be brought to the front. The yellow arrow over the break point circle will indicate the current step of the execution. You can use the buttons below the code editor to continue execution, stop, or execute the process in steps. Learning to use the debugger becomes very important when developing large applications. We will talk more about using the debugger later (*Online Chapter*, `https://www.packtpub.com/sites/default/files/downloads/MiscellaneousandAdvancedConcepts.pdf`).

Automatic slot connection and its drawbacks

Qt also offers an easier way to make a connection between signals of the form's elements and the slots of the class. You can right-click on the button in the central area of the form editor and select the **Go to slot...** option. You will be prompted to select one of the signals available in the button's class (`QPushButton`). After you select the `clicked()` signal, Qt Creator will automatically add a new `on_startNewGame_clicked` slot to our `MainWindow` class.

The tricky part is that there is no `connect()` call that enforces the connection. How is the button's signal connected to this slot, then? The answer is Qt's automatic slot connection feature. When the constructor calls the `ui->setupUi(this)` function, it creates the widgets and other objects in the form and then calls the `QMetaObject::connectSlotsByName` method. This method looks at the list of slots existing in the widget class (in our case, `MainWindow`) and searches for ones that have their name in an `on_<object name>_<signal name>` pattern, where `<object name>` is the `objectName` of an existing child widget and `<signal name>` is the name of one of this widget's signals. In our case, a button called `startNewGame` is a child widget of our widget, and it has a `clicked` signal, so this signal is automatically connected to an `on_startNewGame_clicked` slot.

While this is a really convenient feature, it has many drawbacks:

- It makes your application harder to maintain. If you rename or remove the form element, you have to update or remove the slot manually. If you forget to do that, the application will only produce a warning at runtime when the automatic connection fails. In a large application, especially when not all forms are instantiated at the start of the application, there is a significant risk that you will miss the warning and the application will not work as intended.
- You have to use a specific name for the slot (for example, `on_startNewGame_clicked()` instead of a clean-looking `startNewGame()`).
- Sometimes you want to connect signals from multiple objects to the same slot. Automatic slot connection doesn't provide a way to do this, and creating multiple slots just to call a single function will lead to unnecessary code bloat.
- Automatic slot connection has a runtime cost, because it needs to examine the available children and slots and find the matching ones, but it's usually insignificant since it only runs when the form object is created.

The basic approach shown in the previous section is much more maintainable. Making an explicit `connect()` call with pointers to member functions will ensure that both signal and slot are specified properly. If you rename or remove the button, it will immediately result in a compilation error that is impossible to miss. You are also free to choose a meaningful name for the slot, so you can make it part of your public API, if desired.

Considering all this, we advise against using the automatic slot connection feature, as the convenience does not outweigh the drawbacks.

Time for action – Changing the texts on the labels from the code

Printing text to the console is not as impressive as changing the text in our form. We don't have GUI for letting users enter their names yet, so we'll hardcode some names for now. Let's change the implementation of our slot to the following:

```
void MainWindow::startNewGame()
{
    ui->player1Name->setText(tr("Alice"));
    ui->player2Name->setText(tr("Bob"));
}
```

Now, when you run the application and click on the button, the labels in the form will change. Let's break down this code into pieces:

- As mentioned earlier, the first label's object is accessible in our class as `ui->player1Name` and has the `QLabel *` type.
- We're calling the `setText` method of the `QLabel` class. This is the setter of the `text` property of `QLabel` (the same property that we edited in the property editor of the **Design** mode). As per Qt's naming convention, getters should have the same name as the property itself, and setters should have a `set` prefix, followed by the property name. You can set the text cursor on `setText` and press *F1* to learn more about the property and its access functions.
- The `tr()` function (which is short for "translate") is used to translate the text to the current UI language of the application. We will describe the translation infrastructure of Qt in `Chapter 6`, *Qt Core Essentials*. By default, this function returns the passed string unchanged, but it's a good habit to wrap any and all string literals that are displayed to the user in this function. Any user-visible text that you enter in the form editor is also subject to translation and is passed through a similar function automatically. Only strings that should not be affected by translation (for example, object names that are used as identifiers) should be created without the `tr()` function.

Creating a widget for the tic-tac-toe board

Let's move on to implementing the board. It should contain nine buttons that can display "X" or "O" and allow the players to make their moves. We could add the button directly to the empty widget of our form. However, the behavior of the board is fairly separate from the rest of the form, and it will have quite a bit of logic inside. Following the encapsulation principle, we prefer implementing the board as a separate widget class. Then, we'll replace the empty widget in our main window with the board widget we created.

Choosing between designer forms and plain C++ classes

One way of creating a custom widget is by adding a **Designer Form Class** to the project. **Designer Form Class** is a template provided by Qt Creator. It consists of a C++ class that inherits `QWidget` (directly or indirectly) and a designer form (`.ui` file), tied together by some automatically generated code. Our `MainWindow` class also follows this template.

However, if you try to use the visual form editor to create our tic-tac-toe board, you may find it quite inconvenient for this task. One problem is that you need to add nine identical buttons to the form manually. Another issue is accessing these buttons from the code when you need to make a signal connection or change the button's text. The `ui->objectName` approach is not applicable here because you can only access a concrete widget this way, so you'd have to resort to other means, such as the `findChild()` method that allows you to search for a child object by its name.

In this case, we prefer to add the buttons in the code, where we can make a loop, set up each button, and put them into an array for easy addressing. The process is pretty similar to how the designer forms operate, but we'll do it by hand. Of course, anything that the form editor can do is accessible through the API.

> After you build the project, you can hold *Ctrl* and click on `ui_mainwindow.h` at the beginning of `mainwindow.cpp` to see the code that actually sets up our main window. You should not edit this file, because your changes will not be persistent.

Time for action – Creating a game board widget

Locate the `tictactoe` folder in the project tree (it's the top-level entry corresponding to our whole project), open its context menu, and select **Add New... Select C++** in the left list and **C++ Class** in the central list. Click on the **Choose** button, input `TicTacToeWidget` in the **Class name** field, and select **QWidget** in the **Base class** drop-down list. Click on **Next** and **Finish**. Qt Creator will create header and source files for our new class and add them to the project.

Open the `tictactoewidget.h` file in Creator and update it by adding the highlighted code:

```
#ifndef TICTACTOEWIDGET_H
#define TICTACTOEWIDGET_H
#include <QWidget>
class TicTacToeWidget : public QWidget
{
    Q_OBJECT
public:
    TicTacToeWidget(QWidget *parent = nullptr);
    ~TicTacToeWidget();
private:
    QVector<QPushButton*> m_board;
};
#endif // TICTACTOEWIDGET_H
```

Our additions create a `QVector` object (a container similar to `std::vector`) that can hold pointers to instances of the `QPushButton` class, which is the most commonly used button class in Qt. We have to include the Qt header containing the `QPushButton` declaration. Qt Creator can help us do this quickly. Set the text cursor on `QPushButton`, press *Alt* + *Enter*, and select **Add #include <QPushButton>**. The include directive will appear at the beginning of the file. As you may have noted, each Qt class is declared in the header file that is called exactly the same as the class itself.

From now on, this book will not remind you about adding the include directives to your source code—you will have to take care of this by yourself. This is really easy; just remember that to use a Qt class you need to include a file named after that class.

The next step is to create all the buttons and use a layout to manage their geometries. Switch to the `tictactoewidget.cpp` file and locate the constructor.

> TIP: You can use the *F4* key to switch between the corresponding header and the source files. You can also use the *F2* key to navigate from the definition of a method to its implementation, and back.

First, let's create a layout that will hold our buttons:

```
QGridLayout *gridLayout = new QGridLayout(this);
```

By passing the `this` pointer to the layout's constructor, we attached the layout to our widget. Then, we can start adding buttons to the layout:

```
for(int row = 0; row < 3; ++row) {
    for(int column = 0; column < 3; ++column) {
        QPushButton *button = new QPushButton(" ");
        gridLayout->addWidget(button, row, column);
        m_board.append(button);
    }
}
```

The code creates a loop over rows and columns of the board. In each iteration, it creates an instance of the `QPushButton` class. The content of each button is set to a single space so that it gets the correct initial size. Then, we add the button to the layout in `row` and `column`. At the end, we store the pointer to the button in the vector that was declared earlier. This lets us reference any of the buttons later on. They are stored in the vector in such an order that the first three buttons of the first row are stored first, then the buttons from the second row, and finally those from the last row.

This should be enough for testing the widget. Let's add it to our main window. Open the `mainwindow.ui` file. Invoke the context menu of the empty widget called `gameBoard` and choose **Promote to**. This allows us to **promote** a widget to another class, that is, substitute a widget in the form with an instance of another class.

In our case, we will want to replace the empty widget with our game board. Select **QWidget** in the **Base class name** list, because our `TicTacToeWidget` is inherited from `QWidget`. Input `TicTacToeWidget` into the **Promoted class name** field and verify that the **Header file** field contains the correct name of the class's header file, as illustrated:

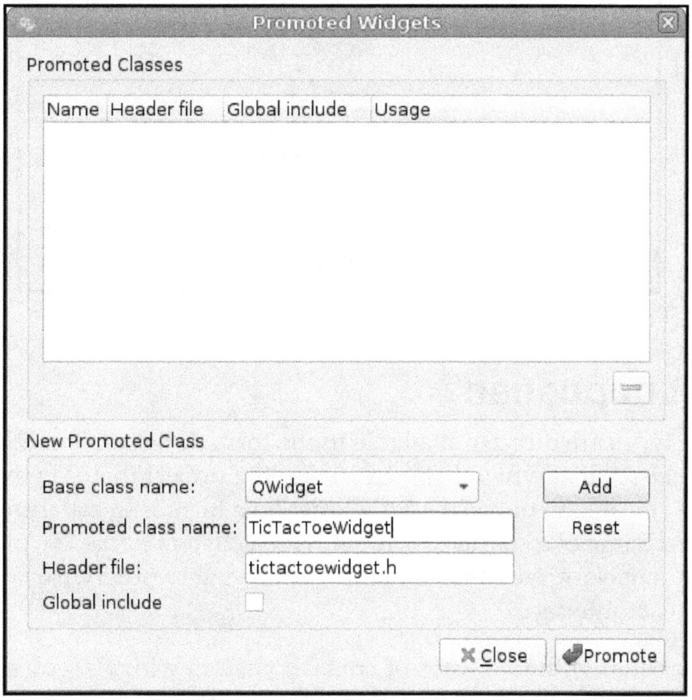

Then, click on the button labeled **Add** and then **Promote,** to close the dialog and confirm the promotion. You will not note any changes in the form, because the replacement only takes place at runtime (however, you will see the `TicTacToeWidget` class name next to `gameBoard` in the object tree).

Run the application and check whether the game board appears in the main window:

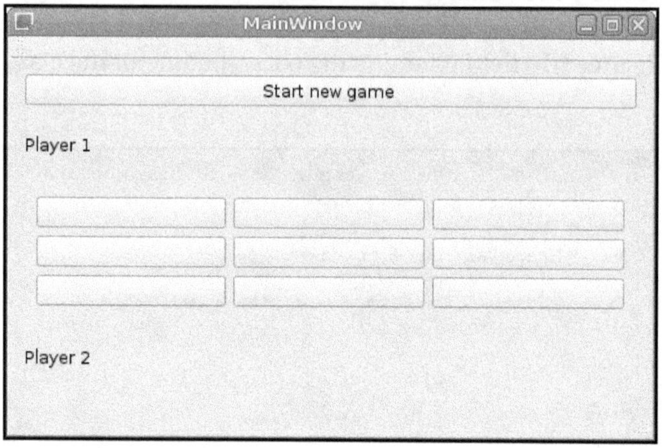

What just happened?

Not all widget types are directly available in the form designer. Sometimes, we need to use widget classes that will only be created in the project that is being built. The simplest way to be able to put a custom widget on a form is to ask the designer to replace the class name of a standard widget with a custom name. By promoting an object to a different class, we saved a lot of work trying to otherwise fit our game board into the user interface.

You are now familiar with two ways of creating custom widgets: you can use the form editor or add widgets from the code. Both approaches are valuable. When creating a new widget class in your project, choose the most convenient way depending on your current task.

Automatic deletion of objects

You might have noted that although we created a number of objects in the constructor using the `new` operator, we didn't destroy those objects anywhere (for example, in the destructor). This is because of the way the memory is managed by Qt. Qt doesn't do any garbage collecting (as C# or Java does), but it has this nice feature related to `QObject` parent–child hierarchies. The rule is that whenever a `QObject` instance is destroyed, it also deletes all of its children. This is another reason to set parents to the objects that we create—if we do this, we don't have to care about explicitly freeing any memory.

Since all layouts and widgets inside our top-level widget (an instance of `MainWindow` class) are its direct or indirect children, they will all be deleted when the main window is destroyed. The `MainWindow` object is created in the `main()` function without the `new` keyword, so it will be deleted at the end of the application after `a.exec()` returns.

When working with widgets, it's pretty easy to verify that every object has a proper parent. You can assume that anything that is displayed inside the window is a direct or indirect child of that window. However, the parent–child relationship becomes less apparent when working with invisible objects, so you should always check that each object has a proper parent and therefore will be deleted at some point. For example, in our `TicTacToeWidget` class, the `gridLayout` object receives its parent through a constructor argument (`this`). The button objects are initially created without a parent, but the `addWidget()` function assigns a parent widget to them.

Time for action – Functionality of a tic-tac-toe board

We need to implement a function that will be called upon by clicking on any of the nine buttons on the board. It has to change the text of the button that was clicked on—either "X" or "O"—based on which player made the move. It then has to check whether the move resulted in the game being won by the player (or a draw if no more moves are possible), and if the game ended, it should emit an appropriate signal, informing the environment about the event.

When the user clicks on a button, the `clicked()` signal is emitted. Connecting this signal to a custom slot lets us implement the mentioned functionality, but since the signal doesn't carry any parameters, how do we tell which button caused the slot to be triggered? We could connect each button to a separate slot, but that's an ugly solution. Fortunately, there are two ways of working around this problem. When a slot is invoked, a pointer to the object that caused the signal to be sent is accessible through a special method in `QObject`, called `sender()`. We can use that pointer to find out which of the nine buttons stored in the board list is the one that caused the signal to fire:

```
void TicTacToeWidget::someSlot() {
    QPushButton *button = static_cast<QPushButton*>(sender());
    int buttonIndex = m_board.indexOf(button);
    // ...
}
```

While `sender()` is a useful call, we should try to avoid it in our own code as it breaks some principles of object-oriented programming. Moreover, there are situations where calling this function is not safe. A better way is to use a dedicated class called `QSignalMapper`, which lets us achieve a similar result without using `sender()` directly. Modify the constructor of `TicTacToeWidget`, as follows:

```
QGridLayout *gridLayout = new QGridLayout(this);
QSignalMapper *mapper = new QSignalMapper(this);
for(int row = 0; row < 3; ++row) {
    for(int column = 0; column < 3; ++column) {
        QPushButton *button = new QPushButton(" ");
        gridLayout->addWidget(button, row, column);
        m_board.append(button);
        mapper->setMapping(button, m_board.count() - 1);
        connect(button, SIGNAL(clicked()), mapper, SLOT(map()));
    }
}
connect(mapper, SIGNAL(mapped(int)),
        this,   SLOT(handleButtonClick(int)));
```

Here, we first created an instance of `QSignalMapper` and passed a pointer to the board widget as its parent so that the mapper is deleted when the widget is deleted.

> Almost all subclasses of `QObject` can receive a pointer to the parent object in the constructor. In fact, our `MainWindow` and `TicTacToeWidget` classes can also do that, thanks to the code Qt Creator generated in their constructors. Following this rule in custom `QObject`-based classes is recommended. While the parent argument is often optional, it's a good idea to pass it when possible, because objects will be automatically deleted when the parent is deleted. However, there are a few cases where this is redundant, for example, when you add a widget to a layout, the layout will automatically set the parent widget for it.

Then, when we create buttons, we "teach" the mapper that each of the buttons has a number associated with it—the first button will have the number `0`, the second one will be bound to the number `1`, and so on. By connecting the `clicked()` signal from the button to the mapper's `map()` slot, we tell the mapper to process that signal. When the mapper receives the signal from any of the buttons, it will find the mapping of the sender of the signal and emit another signal—`mapped()`—with the mapped number as its parameter. This allows us to connect to that signal with a new slot (`handleButtonClick()`) that takes the index of the button in the board list.

Before we create and implement the slot, we need to create a useful enum type and a few helper methods. First, add the following code to the public section of the class declaration in the `tictactoewidget.h` file:

```
enum class Player {
    Invalid, Player1, Player2, Draw
};
Q_ENUM(Player)
```

This enum lets us specify information about players in the game. The `Q_ENUM` macro will make Qt recognize the enum (for example, it will allow you to pass the values of this type to `qDebug()` and also make serialization easier). Generally, it's a good idea to use `Q_ENUM` for any enum in a `QObject`-based class.

We can use the `Player` enum immediately to mark whose move it is now. To do so, add a private field to the class:

```
Player m_currentPlayer;
```

Don't forget to give the new field an initial value in the constructor:

```
m_currentPlayer = Player::Invalid;
```

Then, add the two public methods to manipulate the value of this field:

```
Player currentPlayer() const
{
    return m_currentPlayer;
}
void setCurrentPlayer(Player p)
{
    if(m_currentPlayer == p) {
        return;
    }
    m_currentPlayer = p;
    emit currentPlayerChanged(p);
}
```

The last method emits a signal, so we have to add the signal declaration to the class definition along with another signal that we will use:

```
signals:
    void currentPlayerChanged(Player);
    void gameOver(Player);
```

TIP

We only emit the `currentPlayerChanged` signal when the current player really changes. You always have to pay attention that you don't emit a "changed" signal when you set a value to a field to the same value that it had before the function was called. Users of your classes expect that if a signal is called changed, it is emitted when the value really changes. Otherwise, this can lead to an infinite loop in signal emissions if you have two objects that connect their value setters to the other object's changed signal.

Now it is time to implement the slot itself. First, declare it in the header file:

```
private slots:
    void handleButtonClick(int index);
```

Use *Alt* + *Enter* to quickly generate a definition for the new method, as we did earlier.

When any of the buttons is pressed, the `handleButtonClick()` slot will be called. The index of the button clicked on will be received as the argument. We can now implement the slot in the `.cpp` file:

```
void TicTacToeWidget::handleButtonClick(int index)
{
    if (m_currentPlayer == Player::Invalid) {
        return; // game is not started
    }
    if(index < 0 || index >= m_board.size()) {
        return; // out of bounds check
    }
    QPushButton *button = m_board[index];
    if(button->text() != " ") return; // invalid move
    button->setText(currentPlayer() == Player::Player1 ? "X" : "O");
    Player winner = checkWinCondition();
    if(winner == Player::Invalid) {
        setCurrentPlayer(currentPlayer() == Player::Player1 ?
                         Player::Player2 : Player::Player1);
        return;
    } else {
        emit gameOver(winner);
    }
}
```

Here, we first retrieve a pointer to the button based on its index. Then, we check whether the button contains an empty space—if not, then it's already occupied, so we return from the method so that the player can pick another field in the board. Next, we set the current player's mark on the button. Then, we check whether the player has won the game. If the game didn't end, we switch the current player and return; otherwise, we emit a `gameOver()` signal, telling our environment who won the game. The `checkWinCondition()` method returns `Player1`, `Player2`, or `Draw` if the game has ended, and `Invalid` otherwise. We will not show the implementation of this method here, as it is quite lengthy. Try implementing it on your own, and if you encounter problems, you can see the solution in the code bundle that accompanies this book.

The last thing we need to do in this class is to add another public method for starting a new game. It will clear the board and set the current player:

```
void TicTacToeWidget::initNewGame() {
    for(QPushButton *button: m_board) {
        button->setText(" ");
    }
    setCurrentPlayer(Player::Player1);
}
```

Now we only need to call this method in the `MainWindow::startNewGame` method:

```
void MainWindow::startNewGame()
{
    ui->player1Name->setText(tr("Alice"));
    ui->player2Name->setText(tr("Bob"));
    ui->gameBoard->initNewGame();
}
```

Note that `ui->gameBoard` actually has a `TicTacToeWidget *` type, and we can call its methods even though the form editor doesn't know anything specific about our custom class. This is the result of the *promoting* that we did earlier.

It's time to see how all this works together! Run the application, click on the **Start new game** button, and you should be able to play some tic-tac-toe.

Time for action – Reacting to the game board's signals

While writing a turn-based board game, it is a good idea to always clearly mark whose turn it is now to make a move. We will do this by marking the moving player's name in bold. There is already a signal in the board class that tells us that the current player has changed, which we can react to update the labels.

We need to connect the board's `currentPlayerChanged` signal to a new slot in the `MainWindow` class. Let's add appropriate code into the `MainWindow` constructor:

```
ui->setupUi(this);
connect(ui->gameBoard, &TicTacToeWidget::currentPlayerChanged,
        this, &MainWindow::updateNameLabels);
```

Now, for the slot itself, declare the following methods in the `MainWindow` class:

```
private:
    void setLabelBold(QLabel *label, bool isBold);
private slots:
    void updateNameLabels();
```

Now implement them using the following code:

```
void MainWindow::setLabelBold(QLabel *label, bool isBold)
{
    QFont f = label->font();
    f.setBold(isBold);
    label->setFont(f);
}

void MainWindow::updateNameLabels()
{
    setLabelBold(ui->player1Name,
        ui->gameBoard->currentPlayer() ==
            TicTacToeWidget::Player::Player1);
    setLabelBold(ui->player2Name,
        ui->gameBoard->currentPlayer() ==
            TicTacToeWidget::Player::Player2);
}
```

What just happened?

`QWidget` (and, by extension, any widget class) has a `font` property that determines the properties of the font this widget uses. This property has the `QFont` type. We can't just write `label->font()->setBold(isBold);`, because `font()` returns a const reference, so we have to make a copy of the `QFont` object. That copy has no connection to the label, so we need to call `label->setFont(f)` to apply our changes. To avoid repetition of this procedure, we created a helper function, called `setLabelBold`.

The last thing that needs to be done is to handle the situation when the game ends. Connect the `gameOver()` signal from the board to a new slot in the main window class. Implement the slot as follows:

```
void MainWindow::handleGameOver(TicTacToeWidget::Player winner) {
    QString message;
    if(winner == TicTacToeWidget::Player::Draw) {
        message = tr("Game ended with a draw.");
    } else {
        QString winnerName = winner ==
TicTacToeWidget::Player::Player1 ?
                    ui->player1Name->text() : ui->player2Name->text();
        message = tr("%1 wins").arg(winnerName);
    }
    QMessageBox::information(this, tr("Info"), message);
}
```

This code checks who won the game, assembles the message (we will learn more about `QString` in `Chapter 6`, *Qt Core Essentials*), and shows it using a static method `QMessageBox::information()` that shows a modal dialog containing the message and a button that allows us to close the dialog.

Run the game and check that it now highlights the current player and shows the message when the game ends.

Advanced form editor usage

Now it's time to give the players a way to input their names. We will do that by adding a game configuration dialog that will appear when starting a new game.

Time for action – Designing the game configuration dialog

First, select **Add New...** in the context menu of the **tictactoe** project and choose to create a new **Qt Designer Form Class,** as shown in the following screenshot:

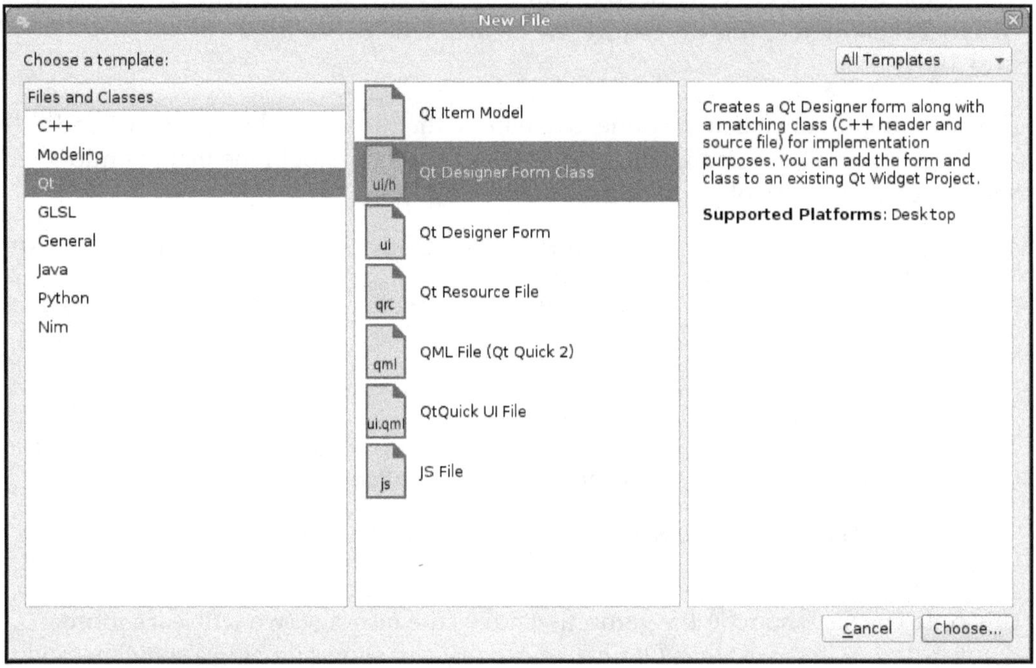

In the window that appears, choose **Dialog with Buttons Bottom**:

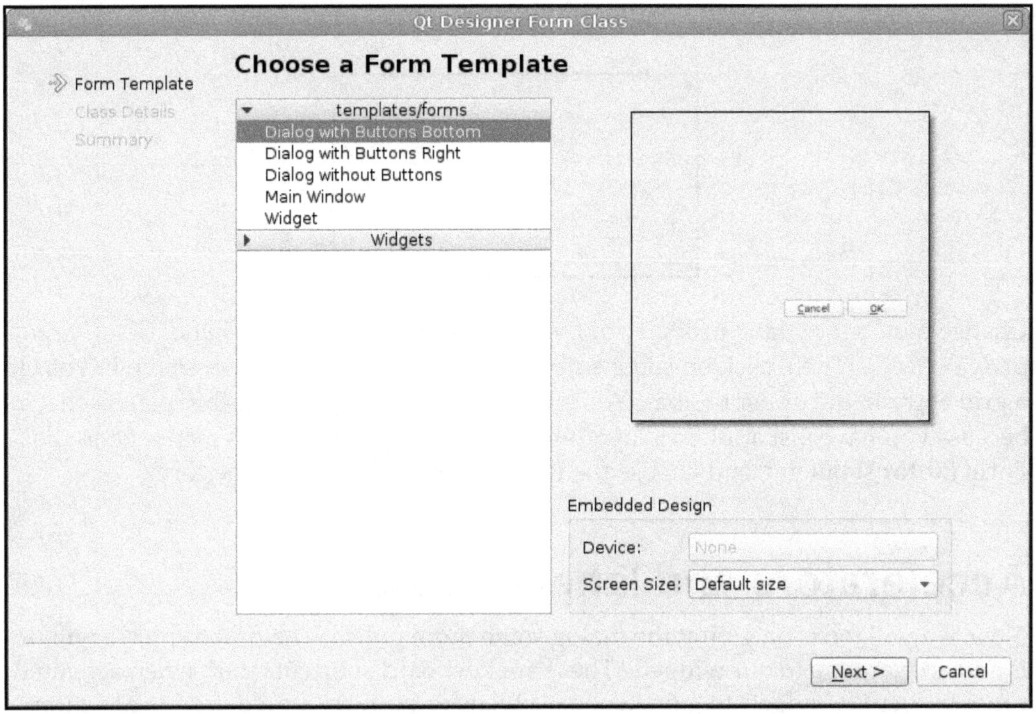

Adjust the class name to `ConfigurationDialog`, leave the rest of the settings at their default values, and complete the wizard. The files that appear in the project (`.cpp`, `.h`, and `.ui`) are very similar to the files generated for the `MainWindow` class when we created our project. The only difference is that `MainWindow` uses `QMainWindow` as its base class, and `ConfigurationDialog` uses `QDialog`. Also, a `MainWindow` instance is created in the `main` function, so it shows when the application is started, while we'll need to create a `ConfigurationDialog` instance somewhere else in the code.
`QDialog` implements behavior that is common for dialogs; in addition to the main content, it displays one or multiple buttons. When the dialog is selected, the user can interact with the dialog and then press one of the buttons. After this, the dialog is usually destroyed. `QDialog` has a convenient `exec()` method that doesn't return until the user makes a choice, and then it returns information about the pressed button. We will see that in action after we finish creating the dialog.

Drag and drop two labels and two line edits on the form, position them roughly in a grid, double-click on each of the labels, and adjust their captions to receive a result similar to the following:

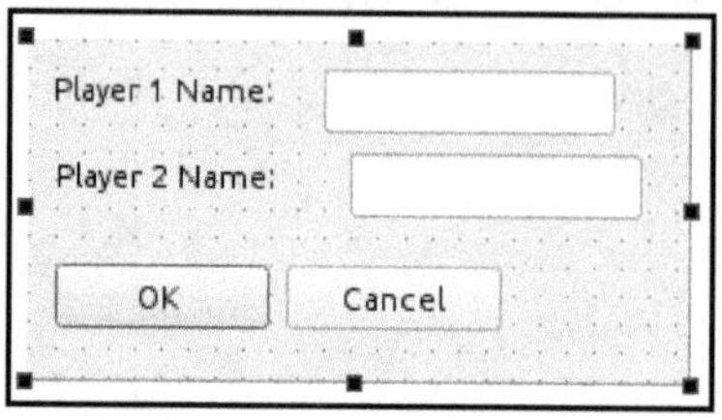

Change the `objectName` property of the line edits to `player1Name` and `player2Name`. Then, click on some empty space in the form and choose the **Layout in a grid** entry in the upper toolbar. You should see the widgets snap into place—that's because you have just applied a layout to the form. Open the **Tools** menu, go to the **Form Editor** submenu, and choose the **Preview** entry to preview the form.

Accelerators and label buddies

Now, we will focus on giving the dialog some more polish. The first thing we will do is add accelerators to our widgets. These are keyboard shortcuts that, when activated, cause particular widgets to gain keyboard focus or perform a predetermined action (for example, toggle a checkbox or push a button). Accelerators are usually marked by underlining them, as follows:

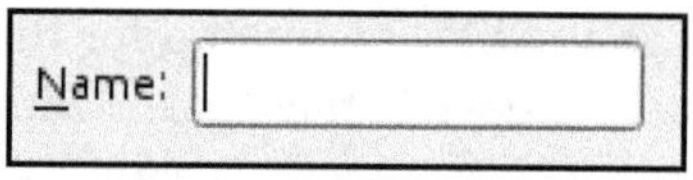

We will set accelerators to our line edits so that when the user activates an accelerator for the first field, it will gain focus. Through this, we can enter the name of the first player, and, similarly, when the accelerator for the second line edit is triggered, we can start typing in the name for the second player.

Start by selecting the first label on the left-hand side of the first line edit. Press *F2* and change the text to `Player &A Name:`. The `&` character marks the character directly after it as an accelerator for the widget. Accelerators may not work with digits on some platforms, so we decided to use a letter instead. Similarly, rename the second label to `Player &B Name:`.

For widgets that are composed of both text and the actual functionality (for example, a button), this is enough to make accelerators work. However, since `QLineEdit` does not have any text associated with it, we have to use a separate widget for that. This is why we have set the accelerator on the label. Now we need to associate the label with the line edit so that the activation of the label's accelerator will forward it to the widget of our choice. This is done by setting a so-called **buddy** for the label. You can do this in code using the `setBuddy` method of the `QLabel` class or using Creator's form designer. Since we're already in the Design mode, we'll use the latter approach. For that, we need to activate a dedicated mode in the form designer.

Look at the upper part of Creator's window; directly above the form, you will find a toolbar containing a couple of icons. Click on the one labeled **Edit buddies** . Now, move the mouse cursor over the label, press the mouse button, and drag from the label toward the line edit. When you drag the label over the line edit, you'll see a graphical visualization of a connection being set between the label and the line edit. If you release the button now, the association will be made permanent. You should note that when such an association is made, the ampersand character (`&`) vanishes from the label, and the character behind it gets an underscore. Repeat this for the other label and corresponding line edit. Click on the **Edit widgets**  button above the form to return the form editor to the default mode. Now, you can preview the form again and check whether accelerators work as expected; pressing *Alt* + *A* and *Alt* + *B* should set the text cursor to the first and second text field, respectively.

The tab order

While you're previewing the form, you can check another aspect of the UI design. Note which line edit receives the focus when the form is open. There is a chance that the second line edit will be activated first. To check and modify the order of focus, close the preview and switch to the tab order editing mode by clicking on the icon called **Edit Tab Order**  in the toolbar.

This mode associates a box with a number to each focusable widget. By clicking on the rectangle in the order you wish the widgets to gain focus, you can reorder values, thus re-ordering focus. Now make it so that the order is as shown here:

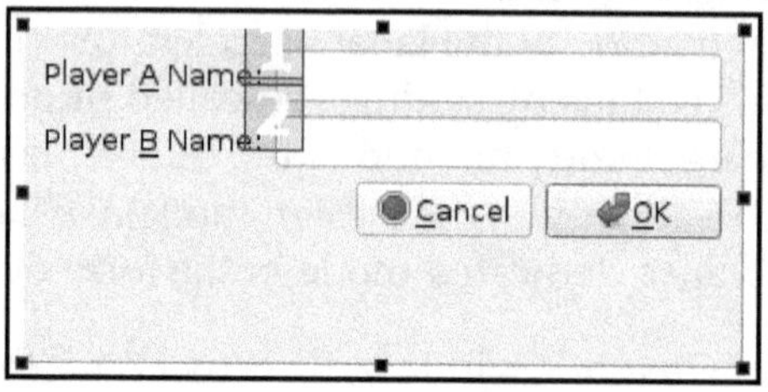

Our form only has two widgets that can receive focus (except for the dialog's buttons, but their tab order is managed automatically). If you create a form with multiple controls, there is a good chance that when you press the *Tab* key repeatedly, the focus will start jumping back and forth between buttons and line edits instead of a linear progress from top to bottom (which is an intuitive order for this particular dialog). You can use this mode to correct the tab order.

Enter the preview again and check whether the focus changes according to what you've set.

> **TIP**
>
> When deciding about the tab order, it is good to consider which fields in the dialog are mandatory and which are optional. It is a good idea to allow the user to tab through all the mandatory fields first, then to the dialog confirmation button (for example, one that says **OK** or **Accept**), and then cycle through all the optional fields. Thanks to this, the user will be able to quickly fill all the mandatory fields and accept the dialog without the need to cycle through all the optional fields that the user wants to leave as their default values.

Time for action – Public interface of the dialog

The next thing to do is to allow to store and read player names from outside the dialog—since the `ui` component is private, there is no access to it from outside the class code. This is a common situation and one that Qt is also compliant with. Each data field in almost every Qt class is private and may contain accessors (a getter and optionally a setter), which are public methods that allow us to read and store values for data fields. Our dialog has two such fields—the names for the two players.

Names of setter methods in Qt are usually started with `set`, followed by the name of the property with the first letter converted to uppercase. In our situation, the two setters will be called `setPlayer1Name` and `setPlayer2Name`, and they will both accept `QString` and return `void`. Declare them in the class header, as shown in the following code snippet:

```
void setPlayer1Name(const QString &p1name);
void setPlayer2Name(const QString &p2name);
```

Implement their bodies in the `.cpp` file:

```
void ConfigurationDialog::setPlayer1Name(const QString &p1name)
{
    ui->player1Name->setText(p1name);
}
void ConfigurationDialog::setPlayer2Name(const QString &p2name)
{
    ui->player2Name->setText(p2name);
}
```

Getter methods in Qt are usually called the same as the property that they are related to—`player1Name` and `player2Name`. Put the following code in the header file:

```
QString player1Name() const;
QString player2Name() const;
```

Put the following code in the implementation file:

```
QString ConfigurationDialog::player1Name() const
{
    return ui->player1Name->text();
}
QString ConfigurationDialog::player2Name() const
{
    return ui->player2Name->text();
}
```

Our dialog is now ready. Let's use it in the `MainWindow::startNewGame` function to request player names before starting the game:

```
ConfigurationDialog dialog(this);
if(dialog.exec() == QDialog::Rejected) {
    return; // do nothing if dialog rejected
}
ui->player1Name->setText(dialog.player1Name());
ui->player2Name->setText(dialog.player2Name());
ui->gameBoard->initNewGame();
```

In this slot, we create the settings dialog and show it to the user, forcing them to enter player names. The `exec()` function doesn't return until the dialog is accepted or cancelled. If the dialog was canceled, we abandon the creation of a new game. Otherwise, we ask the dialog for player names and set them on appropriate labels. Finally, we initialize the board so that users can play the game. The dialog object was created without the `new` keyword, so it will be deleted immediately after this.

Now you can run the application and see how the configuration dialog works.

Polishing the application

We have implemented all the important functionalities of our game, and now we will start improving it by exploring other Qt features.

Size policies

If you change the height of the main window of our game, you will note that different widgets are resized in a different way. In particular, buttons retain their original height, and labels gain empty fields to the top and bottom of the text:

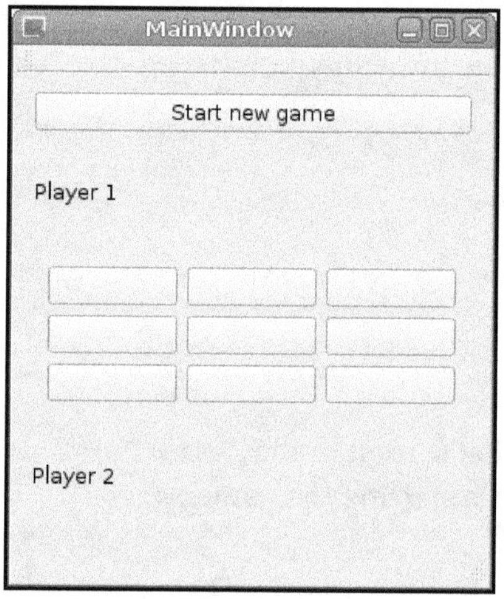

This is because each widget has a property called `sizePolicy`, which decides how a widget is to be resized by a layout. You can set separate size policies for horizontal and vertical directions. A button has a vertical size policy of `Fixed` by default, which means that the height of the widget will not change from the default height regardless of how much space there is available. A label has a `Preferred` size policy by default. The following are the available size policies:

- `Ignored`: In this, the default size of the widget is ignored and the widget can freely grow and shrink
- `Fixed`: In this, the default size is the only allowed size of the widget
- `Preferred`: In this, the default size is the desired size, but both smaller and bigger sizes are acceptable
- `Minimum`: In this, the default size is the smallest acceptable size for the widget, but the widget can be made larger without hurting its functionality
- `Maximum`: In this, the default size is the largest size of the widget, and the widget can be shrunk (even to nothing) without hurting its functionality
- `Expanding`: In this, the default size is the desired size; a smaller size (even zero) is acceptable, but the widget is able to increase its usefulness when more and more space is assigned to it
- `MinimumExpanding`: This is a combination of `Minimum` and `Expanding`—the widget is greedy in terms of space, and it cannot be made smaller than its default size

How do we determine the default size? The answer is by the size returned by the `sizeHint` virtual method. For layouts, the size is calculated based on the sizes and size policies of their child widgets and nested layouts. For basic widgets, the value returned by `sizeHint` depends on the content of the widget. In the case of a button, if it holds a line of text and an icon, `sizeHint` will return the size that is required to fully encompass the text, icon, some space between them, the button frame, and the padding between the frame and content itself.

In our form, we prefer that when the main window is resized, the labels will keep their height, and the game board buttons will grow. To do this, open `mainwindow.ui` in the form editor, select the first label, and then hold *Ctrl* and click on the second label. Now both labels are selected, so we can edit their properties at the same time. Locate `sizePolicy` in the property editor (if you're having trouble locating a property, use the **Filter** field above the property editor) and expand it by clicking on the triangle to its left. Set **Vertical Policy** to **Fixed**. You will see the changes in the form's layout immediately.

The buttons on the game board are created in the code, so navigate to the constructor of `TicTacToeWidget` class and set the size policy using the following code:

```
QPushButton *button = new QPushButton(" ");
button->setSizePolicy(QSizePolicy::Preferred,
                      QSizePolicy::Preferred);
```

This will change both the horizontal and vertical policy of buttons to `Preferred`. Run the game and observe the changes:

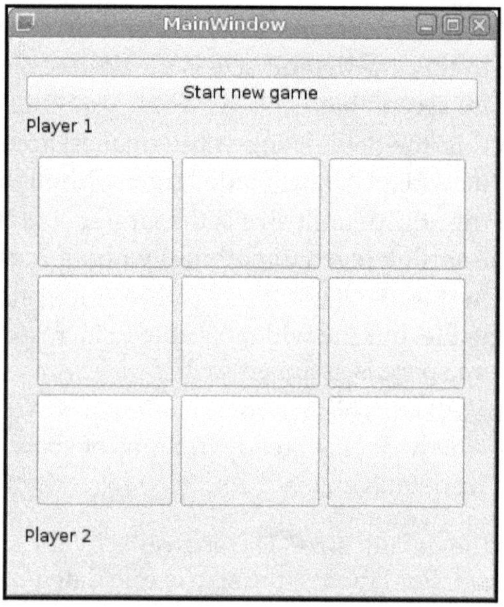

Protecting against invalid input

The configuration dialog did not have any validation until now. Let's make it such that the button to accept the dialog is only enabled when neither of the two line edits is empty (that is, when both the fields contain player names). To do this, we need to connect the `textChanged` signal of each line edit to a slot that will perform the task.

First, go to the `configurationdialog.h` file and create a private slot `void updateOKButtonState();` in the `ConfigurationDialog` class (you will need to add the `private slots` section manually). Use the following code to implement this slot:

```
void ConfigurationDialog::updateOKButtonState()
{
    QPushButton *okButton =
ui->buttonBox->button(QDialogButtonBox::Ok);
    okButton->setEnabled(!ui->player1Name->text().isEmpty() &&
                         !ui->player2Name->text().isEmpty());
}
```

This code asks the button box that currently contains the **OK** and **Cancel** buttons to give a pointer to the button that accepts the dialog (we have to do that because the buttons are not contained in the form directly, so there are no fields for them in `ui`). Then, we set the button's `enabled` property based on whether both player names contain valid values or not.

Next, edit the constructor of the dialog to connect two signals to our new slot. The button state also needs to be updated when we first create the dialog, so add an invocation of `updateOKButtonState()` to the constructor:

```
ui->setupUi(this);
connect(ui->player1Name, &QLineEdit::textChanged,
        this, &ConfigurationDialog::updateOKButtonState);
connect(ui->player2Name, &QLineEdit::textChanged,
        this, &ConfigurationDialog::updateOKButtonState);
updateOKButtonState();
```

Main menu and toolbars

As you may remember, any widget that has no parent will be displayed as a window. However, when we created our main window, we selected `QMainWindow` as the base class. If we had selected `QWidget` instead, we would still be able to do everything we did up to this point. However, the `QMainWindow` class provides some unique functionality that we will now use.

A main window represents the control center of an application. It can contain menus, toolbars, docking widgets, a status bar, and the *central widget* that contains the main content of the window, as shown in the following diagram:

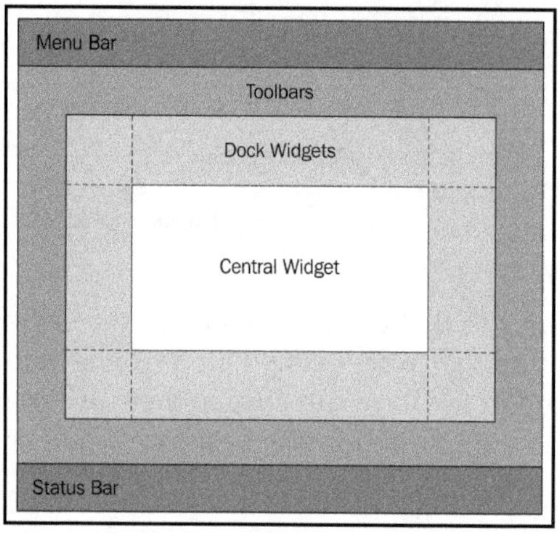

If you open the `mainwindow.ui` file and take a look at the object tree, you will see the mandatory `centralWidget` that actually contains our form. There are also optional `menuBar`, `mainToolBar`, and `statusBar` that were added automatically when Qt Creator generated the form.

The central widget part doesn't need any extra explanation; it is a regular widget like any other. We will also not focus on dock widgets or the status bar here. They are useful components, but you can learn about them yourself. Instead, we will spend some time mastering menus and toolbars. You have surely seen and used toolbars and menus in many applications, and you know how important they are for a good user experience.

The main menu has a bit of unusual behavior. It's usually positioned in the top part of the window, but in macOS and some Linux environments, the main menu is separated from the window and displayed in the top area of the screen. Toolbars, on the other hand, can be moved freely by the user and docked horizontally or vertically to the sides of the main window.

The main class shared by both these concepts is `QAction`, which represents a functionality that can be invoked by a user. A single action can be used in multiple places—it can be an entry in a menu (the `QMenu` instances) or in a toolbar (`QToolBar`), a button, or a keyboard shortcut (`QShortcut`). Manipulating the action (for example, changing its text) causes all its incarnations to update. For example, if you have a **Save** entry in the menu (with a keyboard shortcut bound to it), a **Save** icon in the toolbar, and maybe also a **Save** button somewhere else in your user interface and you want to disallow saving the document (for example, a map in your dungeons and dragons game level editor) because its contents haven't changed since the document was last loaded. In this case, if the menu entry, toolbar icon, and button are all linked to the same `QAction` instance, then, once you set the `enabled` property of the action to `false`, all the three entities will become disabled as well. This is an easy way to keep different parts of your application in sync—if you disable an action object, you can be sure that all entries that trigger the functionality represented by the action are also disabled. Actions can be instantiated in code or created graphically using **Action Editor** in Qt Creator. An action can have different pieces of data associated with it—a text, tooltip, status bar tip, icons, and others that are less often used. All these are used by incarnations of your actions.

Time for action – Creating a menu and a toolbar

Let's replace our boring **Start new game** button with a menu entry and a toolbar icon. First, select the button and press the *Delete* key to delete it. Then, locate **Action Editor** in the bottom-center part of the form editor and click on the **New** button on its toolbar. Enter the following values in the dialog (you can fill the **Shortcut** field by pressing the key combination you want to use):

Locate the toolbar in the central area (between the **Type Here** text and the first label) and drag the line containing the **New Game** action from the action editor to the toolbar, which results in a button appearing in the toolbar.

To create a menu for the window, double-click on the **Type Here** text on the top of the form and replace the text with `&File` (although our application doesn't work with files, we will follow this tradition). Then, drag the **New Game** action from the action editor over the newly created menu, but do not drop it there yet. The menu should open now, and you can drag the action so that a red bar appears in the submenu in the position where you want the menu entry to appear; now you can release the mouse button to create the entry.

Now we should restore the functionality that was broken when we deleted the button. Navigate to the constructor of the `MainWindow` class and adjust the `connect()` call:

```
connect(ui->startNewGame, &QAction::triggered,
        this, &MainWindow::startNewGame);
```

Actions, like widgets, are accessible through the `ui` object. The `ui->startNewGame` object is now a `QAction` instead of a `QPushButton`, and we use its `triggered()` signal to detect whether the action was selected in some way.

Now, if you run the application, you can select the menu entry, press a button on the toolbar, or press the *Ctrl* + *N* keys. Either of these operations will cause the action to emit the `triggered()` signal, and the game configuration dialog should appear.

TIP

Like widgets, `QAction` objects have some useful methods that are accessible in our form class. For example, executing `ui->startNewGame->setEnabled(false)` will disable all ways to trigger the **New Game** action.

Let's add another action for quitting the application (although the user can already do it just by closing the main window). Use the action editor to add a new action with text `Quit`, object name `quit`, and shortcut *Ctrl* + *Q*. Add it to the menu and the toolbar, like the first action.

We can add a new slot that stops the application, but such a slot already exists in `QApplication`, so let's just reuse it. Locate the constructor of our form in `mainwindow.cpp` and append the following code:

```
connect(ui->quit, &QAction::triggered,
        qApp,     &QApplication::quit);
```

What just happened?

The `qApp` macro is a shortcut for a function that returns a pointer to the application singleton object, so when the action is triggered, Qt will call the `quit()` slot on the `QApplication` object created in `main()`, which, in turn, will cause the application to end.

The Qt resource system

Buttons in the toolbar usually display icons instead of text. To implement this, we need to add icon files to our project and assign them to the actions we created.

One way of creating icons is by loading images from the filesystem. The problem with this is that you have to install a bunch of files along with your application, and you need to always know where they are located to be able to provide paths to access them. Fortunately, Qt provides a convenient and portable way to embed arbitrary files (such as images for icons) directly in the executable file. This is done by preparing resource files that are later compiled in the binary. Qt Creator provides a graphical tool for this as well.

Time for action – Adding icons to the project

We will add icons to our **Start new game** and **Quit** actions. First, use your file manager to create a new subdirectory called `icons` in the project directory. Place two icon files in the `icons` directory. You can use icons from the files provided with the book.

Click on **Add New...** in the context menu of the **tictactoe** project and select **Qt Resource File** (located in **Qt** category). Name it `resources`, and finish the wizard. Qt Creator will add a new `resources.qrc` file to the project (it will be displayed under the **Resources** category in the project tree).

Locate the new `resources.qrc` file in the project tree of Qt Creator and choose **Add Existing Files...** in its context menu. Select both icons, and confirm their addition to the resources.

Open the `mainwindow.ui` form, and double-click on one of the actions in the action editor. Click on the "..." button next to the **Icon** field, select **icons** in the left part of the window, and select the appropriate icon in the right part of the window. Once you confirm changes in the dialogs, the corresponding button on the toolbar will switch to displaying the icon instead of the text. The menu entry will also gain the selected icon. Repeat this operation for the second action. Our game should now look like this:

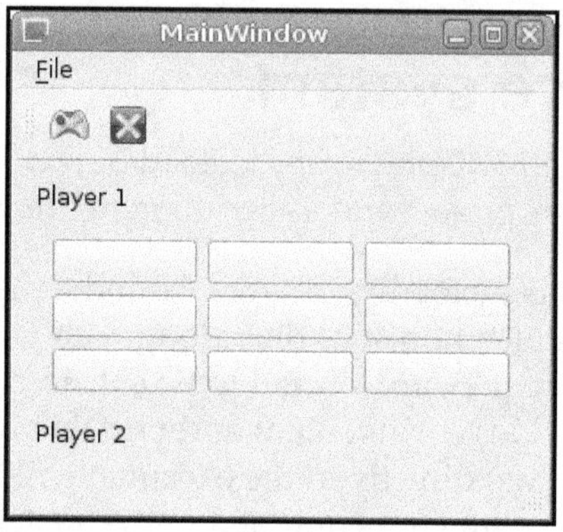

Have a go hero – Extending the game

There are a lot of subtle improvements you can make in the project. For example, you can change the title of the main window (by editing its `windowTitle` property), add accelerators to the actions, disable the board buttons that do nothing on click, remove the status bar, or use it for displaying the game status.

As an additional exercise, you can try to modify the code we wrote in this chapter to allow playing the game on boards bigger than 3 x 3. Let the user decide the size of the board (you can modify the game options dialog for that and use `QSlider` and `QSpinBox` to allow the user to choose the size of the board), and you can then instruct `TicTacToeWidget` to build the board based on the size it gets. Remember to adjust the game-winning logic! If at any point you run into a dead end and do not know which classes and functions to use, consult the reference manual.

Pop quiz

Q1. Which classes can have signals?

1. All classes derived from `QWidget`.
2. All classes derived from `QObject`.
3. All classes.

Q2. For which of the following do you have to provide your own implementation?

1. A signal.
2. A slot.
3. Both.

Q3. A method that returns the preferred size of a widget is called which of these?

1. `preferredSize`.
2. `sizeHint`.
3. `defaultSize`.

Q4. What is the purpose of the `QAction` object?

1. It represents a functionality that a user can invoke in the program.
2. It holds a key sequence to move the focus on a widget.
3. It is a base class for all forms generated using the form editor.

Summary

In this chapter, you learned how to create simple graphical user interfaces with Qt. We went through two approaches: designing the user interface with a graphical tool that generates most of the code for us, and creating user interface classes by writing all the code directly. None of them is better than the other. The form designer allows you to avoid boilerplate code and helps you handle large forms with a lot of controls. On the other hand, the code writing approach gives you more control over the process and allows you to create automatically populated and dynamic interfaces.

We also learned how to use signals and slots in Qt. You should now be able to create simple user interfaces and fill them with logic by connecting signals to slots—predefined ones as well as custom ones that you now know how to define and fill with code.

Qt contains many widget types, but we didn't introduce them to you one by one. There is a really nice explanation of many widget types in the Qt manual called **Qt Widget Gallery**, which shows most of them in action. If you have any doubts about using any of those widgets, you can check the example code and also look up the appropriate class in the Qt reference manual to learn more about them.

As you already saw, Qt allows you to create custom widget classes, but in this chapter our custom classes mostly reused the default widgets. It's also possible to modify how the widget responds to events and implement custom painting. We will get to this advanced topic in `Chapter 8`, *Custom Widgets*. However, if you want to implement a game with custom 2D graphics, there is a simpler alternative—the Graphics View Framework that we'll use in the next chapter.

4
Custom 2D Graphics with Graphics View

Widgets are great for designing graphical user interfaces, but they are not convenient if you want to use multiple objects with custom painting and behavior together, such as in a 2D game. You will also run into problems if you wish to animate multiple widgets at the same time, by constantly moving them around in the application. For these situations, or generally for frequently transforming 2D graphics, Qt offers you Graphics View. In this chapter, you will learn the basics of the Graphics View architecture and its items. You will also learn how to combine widgets with Graphics View items.

The main topics covered in this chapter are as follows:

- Graphics View architecture
- Coordinate systems
- Standard graphics items
- Pens and brushes
- Useful features of Graphics View
- Creating custom items
- Event handling
- Embedding widgets in the view
- Optimizations

Graphics View architecture

The Graphics View Framework is part of the Qt Widgets module and provides a higher level of abstraction useful for custom 2D graphics. It uses software rendering by default, but it is very optimized and extremely convenient to use. Three components form the core of Graphics View, as shown:

- An instance of `QGraphicsView`, which is referred to as **View**
- An instance of `QGraphicsScene`, which is referred to as **Scene**
- Instances of `QGraphicsItem`, which are referred to as **Items**

The usual workflow is to first create a couple of items, add them to a scene, and then show that scene on a view:

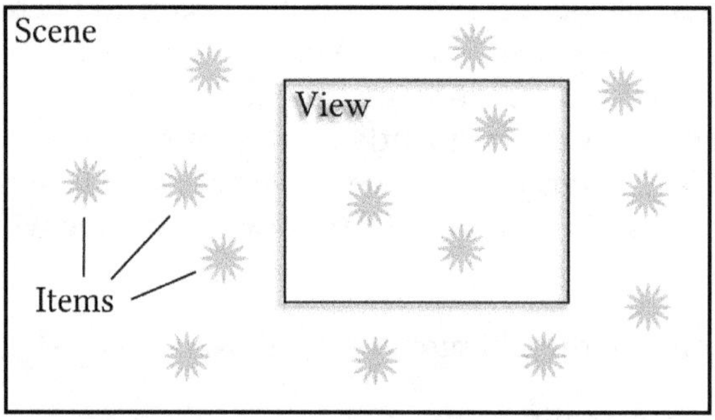

After that, you can manipulate items from the code and add new items, while the user also has the ability to interact with visible items.

Think of the **items** as Post-it notes. You take a note and write a message on it, paint an image on it, both write and paint on it, or, quite possibly, just leave it blank. Qt provides a lot of item classes, all of which inherit `QGraphicsItem`. You can also create your own item classes. Each class must provide an implementation of the `paint()` function, which performs painting of the current item, and the `boundingRect()` function, which must return the boundary of the area the `paint()` function paints on.

What is the **scene**, then? Well, think of it as a larger sheet of paper on to which you attach your smaller Post-its, that is, the notes. On the scene, you can freely move the items around while applying funny transformations to them. It is the scene's responsibility to correctly display the items' position and any transformations applied to them. The scene further informs the items about any events that affect them.

Last, but not least, let's turn our attention to the **view**. Think of the view as an inspection window or a person who holds the paper with the notes in their hands. You can see the paper as a whole, or you can only look at specific parts. Also, as a person can rotate and shear the paper with their hands, so the view can rotate and shear the scene's content and do a lot more transformations with it. `QGraphicsView` is a widget, so you can use the view like any other widget and place it into layouts for creating neat graphical user interfaces.

> You might have looked at the preceding diagram and worried about all the items being outside the view. Aren't they wasting CPU time? Don't you need to take care of them by adding a so-called *view frustum culling* mechanism (to detect which item not to draw/render because it is not visible)? Well, the short answer is "no", because Qt is already taking care of this.

Time for action – Creating a project with a Graphics View

Let's put all these components together in a minimalistic project. From the **Welcome** screen, click on the **New Project** button and select **Qt Widgets Application** again. Name the project `graphics_view_demo`, select the correct kit, uncheck the **Generate form** checkbox, and finish the wizard. We don't actually need the `MainWindow` class that was generated for us, so let's delete it from the project. In the project tree, locate `mainwindow.h` and select **Remove file** in the context menu. Enable the **Delete file permanently** checkbox and click on **OK**. This will result in deleting the `mainwindow.h` file from the disk and removing its name from the `graphics_view_demo.pro` file. If the file was open in Qt Creator, it will suggest that you close it. Repeat the process for `mainwindow.cpp`.

Open the `main.cpp` file, remove `#include "mainwindow.h"`, and write the following code:

```
int main(int argc, char *argv[])
{
    QApplication a(argc, argv);
    QGraphicsScene scene;
    QGraphicsRectItem *rectItem =
        new QGraphicsRectItem(QRectF(0, 0, 100, 50));
    scene.addItem(rectItem);
    QGraphicsEllipseItem *circleItem =
        new QGraphicsEllipseItem(QRect(0, 50, 25, 25));
```

```
        scene.addItem(circleItem);
        QGraphicsSimpleTextItem *textItem =
            new QGraphicsSimpleTextItem(QObject::tr("Demo"));
        scene.addItem(textItem);
        QGraphicsView view(&scene);
        view.show();
        return a.exec();
    }
```

When you run the project, you should get the following result:

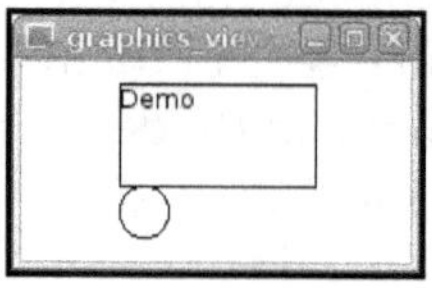

What just happened?

Our new project is so simple that all its code is located in the `main()` function. Let's examine the code. First, we create a `QApplication` object, as in any Qt Widgets project. Next, we create a scene object and three instances of different item classes. The constructor of each item class accepts an argument that defines the content of the item:

- The `QGraphicsRectItem` constructor receives a `QRectF` object that contains the coordinates of the rectangle
- The `QGraphicsEllipseItem` constructor, similarly, receives a `QRectF` object that defines the bounding rectangle of the circle
- The `QGraphicsSimpleTextItem` constructor receives the text to display

> `QRectF` is basically a helpful struct with four fields that allow us to specify four coordinates of the rectangle's boundaries (left, top, width, and height). Qt also offers `QPointF` that contains *x* and *y* coordinates of a point, `QLineF` that contains *x* and *y* coordinates of two ends of a line, and `QPolygonF` that contains a vector of points. The `F` letter stands for "floating point" and indicates that these classes hold real numbers. They are widely used in Graphics View, as it always works with floating point coordinates. The corresponding classes without `F` (`QPoint`, `QRect`, and so on) store integer coordinates and are more useful when working with widgets.

After creating each item, we use the `QGraphicsScene::addItem` function to add the item to the scene. Finally, we create a `QGraphicsView` object and pass the pointer to the scene to its constructor. The `show()` method will make the view visible, as it does for any `QWidget`. The program ends with an `a.exec()` call, necessary to start the event loop and keep the application alive.

The scene takes ownership of the items, so they will be automatically deleted along with the scene. This also means that an item can only be added to one single scene. If the item was previously added to another scene, it gets removed from there before it is added to the new scene.

> TIP: If you want to remove an item from a scene without setting it directly to another scene or without deleting it, you can call `scene.removeItem(rectItem)`. Be aware, however, that now it is your responsibility to delete `rectItem` to free the allocated memory!

Examine the resulting window and compare it to the coordinates of the rectangles in the code (the `QRectF` constructor we use accepts four arguments in the following order: left, top, width, height). You should be able to see that all three elements are positioned in a single coordinate system, where the *x* axis points to the right and the *y* axis points down. We didn't specify any coordinates for the text item, so it's displayed at the **origin** point (that is, the point with zero coordinates), next to the top-left corner of the rectangle. However, that (0, 0) point does not correspond to the top-left corner of the window. In fact, if you resize the window, you'll note that the origin has shifted relative to the window, because the view tries to display the scene's content as centered.

Coordinate systems

To use Graphics View correctly, you need to understand how the coordinate systems in this framework work. We'll go through all the levels of hierarchy and see how we can change the positioning of items and the whole scene, on each level. We will provide examples of the code that you can paste into our demo project and examine the effect.

The item's coordinate system

Each item has its own coordinate system. In our example of Post-it notes, the content of each note is defined relative to the top-left corner of the note. No matter how you move or rotate the item, these coordinates remain the same. The coordinates of a drawn object can usually be passed to the constructor of the class, like we did in our demo project, or to a special setter function (for example, `rectItem->setRect(0, 10, 20, 25)`). These are coordinates in the item's coordinate system.

Some classes, such as `QGraphicsSimpleTextItem`, do not provide the ability to change the coordinates of the content, so they're always positioned at the origin of the item's coordinate system. This is not a problem at all; as we'll see next, there are ways to change the visible position of the content.

If you try to create your own graphics item class (we'll get to it later in this chapter), you'll need to implement the `paint()` and `boundingRect()` functions, and they always operate in the item's coordinate system. That's right, when you're painting the content, you can just pretend that your item will never be moved or transformed. When that actually happens, Qt will take care of transforming paint operations for you. Additionally, coordinates in any events the item receives (for example, coordinates of a mouse button click) are expressed in the item's coordinate system.

The scene's coordinate system

Any item can be moved in the scene using the `setPos()` function. Try to call `textItem->setPos(50, 50)` and verify that the text was moved in the scene. Technically, this operation changes the **transformation** between the item's coordinate system and the scene's coordinate system. A convenience function called `moveBy()` allows you to shift the position by specified amounts.

An item can also be rotated with `setRotation()` and scaled with `setScale()`. Try calling `textItem->setRotation(20)` to see this in action. If you need a more advanced transformation, such as shearing, or you want to perform multiple translations in a particular order, you can create a `QTransform` object, apply the required transformations, and use the `setTransform()` function of the item.

> The `setRotation()` function accepts `qreal` as the argument value, which is usually a typedef for `double`. The function interprets the number as degrees for a clockwise rotation around the *z* coordinate. If you set a negative value, a counter-clockwise rotation is performed. Even if it does not make much sense, you can rotate an item by 450 degrees, which will result in a rotation of 90 degrees.

The viewport's coordinate system

The view consists of the **viewport** and two scrollbars. The viewport is a subwidget that actually contains the content of the scene. The view performs conversion from the scene coordinates to the viewport coordinates based on multiple parameters.

First, the view needs to know the bounding rectangle of everything we could want to see in the scene. It's called the **scene rect** and is measured in the scene's coordinate system. By default, the scene rect is the bounding rectangle of all items that were added at the scene since it was created. This is usually fine, but if you move or delete an item, that bounding rectangle will not shrink (because of performance reasons), so it may result in showing a lot of unwanted empty space. Luckily, in such cases, you can set the scene rect manually using the `setSceneRect` function of the scene or view.

> The difference between `QGraphicsScene::setSceneRect` and `QGraphicsView::setSceneRect` is usually marginal, since you will typically have one view per scene. However, it is possible to have multiple views for a single scene. In this case, `QGraphicsScene::setSceneRect` sets the scene rect for all views, and `QGraphicsView::setSceneRect` allows you to override the scene rect for each view.

If the area corresponding to the scene rect is small enough to fit in the viewport, the view will align the content according to the view's `alignment` property. As we saw earlier, it positions the content at the center by default. For example, calling `view.setAlignment(Qt::AlignTop | Qt::AlignLeft)` will result in the scene staying in the upper-left corner of the view.

If the scene rect area is too large to fit in the viewport, the horizontal or vertical scrollbars appear by default. They can be used to scroll the view and see any point inside the scene rect (but not beyond it). The presence of scrollbars can also be configured using the `horizontalScrollBarPolicy` and the `verticalScrollBarPolicy` properties of the view.

Try to call `scene.setSceneRect(0, 20, 100, 100)` and see how the view acts when resizing the window. If the window is too small, the top part of the scene will no longer be visible. If the window is large enough and the view has the default alignment, the top part of the scene will be visible, but only the defined scene rect will be centered, with no regard to the items outside of it.

The view provides the ability to transform the entire scene. For example, you can call `view.scale(5, 5)` to make everything five times larger, `view.rotate(20)` to rotate the scene as a whole, or `view.shear(1, 0)` to shear it. As with items, you can apply a more complex transformation using `setTransform()`.

> You may note that Graphics View (and Qt Widgets in general) uses a **left-handed** coordinate system by default, where *x* axis points right and *y* axis points down. However, OpenGL and science-related applications usually use a **right-handed** or standard coordinate system, where *y* axis points up. If you need to change the direction of the *y* axis, the simplest solution is to transform the view by calling `view.scale(1, -1)`.

Origin point of the transformation

In our next example, we will create a cross at (0, 0) point and add a rectangle to the scene:

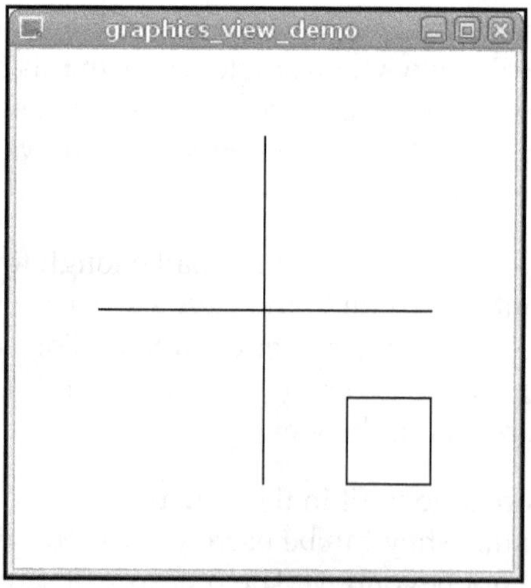

You can do it with the following code:

```
scene.addLine(-100, 0, 100, 0);
scene.addLine(0, -100, 0, 100);
QGraphicsRectItem* rectItem = scene.addRect(50, 50, 50, 50);
```

In this code, we use the `addLine()` and `addRect()` convenience functions. This is the same as creating a `QGraphicsLineItem` or `QGraphicsRectItem` and adding it to the scene manually.

Now, imagine that you want to rotate the rectangle by 45 degrees to produce the following result:

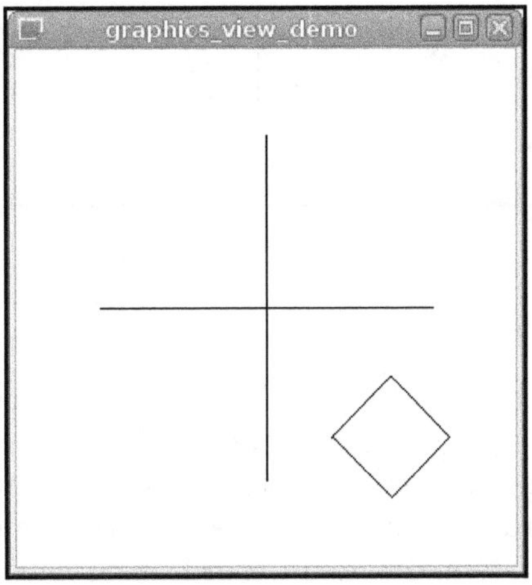

A straightforward attempt to do it will use the `setRotation()` method:

```
QGraphicsRectItem* rectItem = scene.addRect(50, 50, 50, 50);
rectItem->setRotation(45);
```

However, if you try to do that, you will get the following result:

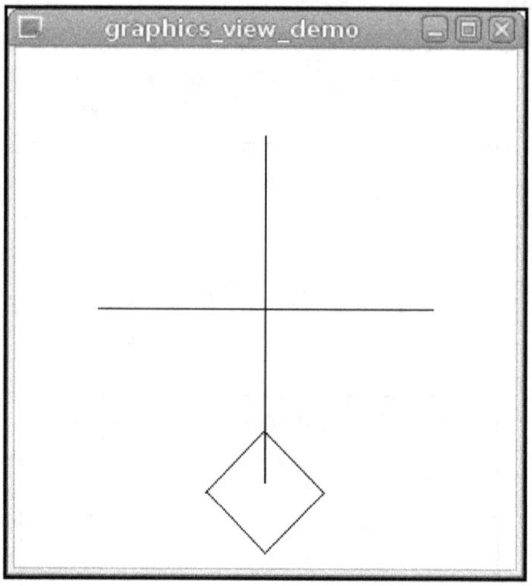

What just happened?

Most transformations depend on the **origin** point of the coordinate system. For rotation and scaling, the origin point is the only point that remains in place. In the preceding example, we used a rectangle with the top-left corner at (50, 50) and the size of (50, 50). These coordinates are in the item's coordinate system. Since we originally didn't move the item, the item's coordinate system was the same as the scene's coordinate system, and the origin point is the same as the scene's origin (it's the point marked with the cross). The applied rotation uses (0, 0) as the center of rotation, thus providing an unexpected result.

There are multiple ways to overcome this problem. The first way is to change the transform's origin point:

```
QGraphicsRectItem* rectItem = scene.addRect(50, 50, 50, 50);
rectItem->setTransformOriginPoint(75, 75);
rectItem->setRotation(45);
```

This code produces the rotation we want, because it changes the origin point used by the `setRotation()` and `setScale()` functions. Note that the item's coordinate system was not translated, and (75, 75) point continues to be the center of the rectangle in the item's coordinates.

However, this solution has its limitations. If you use `setTransform()` instead of `setRotation()`, you will get the unwanted result again:

```
QGraphicsRectItem* rectItem = scene.addRect(50, 50, 50, 50);
rectItem->setTransformOriginPoint(75, 75);
QTransform transform;
transform.rotate(45);
rectItem->setTransform(transform);
```

Another solution is to set up the rectangle in such a way that its center is in the origin of the item's coordinate system:

```
QGraphicsRectItem* rectItem = scene.addRect(-25, -25, 50, 50);
rectItem->setPos(75, 75);
```

This code uses completely different rectangle coordinates, but the result is exactly the same as in our first example. However, now, (75, 75) point in the scene's coordinates corresponds to (0, 0) point in the item's coordinates, so all transformations will use it as the origin:

```
QGraphicsRectItem* rectItem = scene.addRect(-25, -25, 50, 50);
rectItem->setPos(75, 75);
rectItem->setRotation(45);
```

This example shows that it is usually more convenient to set up the items so that their origin point corresponds to their actual location.

Have a go hero – Applying multiple transformations

To understand the concept of transformations and their origin point, try to apply `rotate()` and `scale()` to an item. Also, change the point of origin and see how the item will react. As a second step, use `QTransform` in conjunction with `setTransform()` to apply multiple transformations to an item in a specific order.

Parent–child relationship between items

Imagine that you need to create a graphics item that contains multiple geometric primitives, for example, a circle inside a rectangle. You can create both items and add them to the scene individually, but this solution is inconvenient. First, when you need to remove that combination from the scene, you would need to manually delete both items. However, more importantly, when you need to move or transform the combination, you will need to calculate positions and complex transformations for each graphics item.

Fortunately, graphics items do not have to be a flat list of items added directly into the scene. Items can be added into any other items, forming a parent–child relationship very similar to the relationship of `QObject` that we observed in the last chapter:

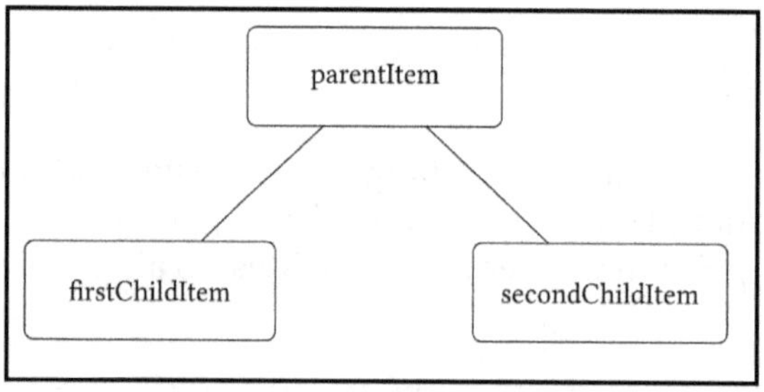

Adding an item as a child of another item has the following consequences:

- When the parent item is added to the scene, the child item automatically becomes part of that scene, so there is no need to call `QGraphicsScene::addItem()` for it.
- When the parent item is deleted, its children are also deleted.
- When the parent item is hidden using the `hide()` or `setVisible(false)` functions, the child items will also be hidden.
- Most importantly, the child's coordinate system is derived from the parent's coordinate system instead of the scene's. This means that when the parent is moved or transformed, all children are also affected. The child's position and transformations are relative to the parent's coordinate system.

You can always check whether an item has a parent using the `parentItem()` function, and check the returned `QGraphicsItem` pointer against `nullptr`, which means that the item does not have a parent. To figure out whether there are any children, call the `childItems()` function on the item. A `QList` method with the `QGraphicsItem` pointers to all child items is returned.

For a better understanding of `pos()` and the involved coordinate systems, think of post-it notes again. If you put a note on a larger sheet of paper and then had to determine its exact position, how would you do it? Probably like this: "The note's upper-left corner is positioned 3 cm to the right and 5 cm to the bottom from the paper's top-left edge". In the Graphics View world, this will correspond to a parentless item whose `pos()` function returns a position in the scene coordinates, since the item's origin is directly pinned to the scene. On the other hand, say you put a note A on top of a (larger) note B, which is already pinned on a paper, and you have to determine A's position; how would you describe it this time? Probably by saying that note A is placed on top of note B or "2 cm to the right and 1 cm to the bottom from the top-left edge of note B". You most likely wouldn't use the underlying paper as a reference since it is not the next point of reference. This is because if you move note B, A's position regarding the paper will change, whereas A's relative position to B still remains unchanged. To switch back to Graphics View, the equivalent situation is an item that has a parent item. In this case, the `pos()` function's returned value is expressed in the coordinate system of its parent. So, `setPos()` and `pos()` specify the position of the item's origin in relation to the next (higher) point of reference. This can be the scene or the item's parent item.

Keep in mind, however, that changing an item's position does not affect the item's internal coordinate system.

For widgets, the child always occupies a subarea of its direct parent. For graphics items, such a rule does not apply by default. A child item can be displayed outside the bounding rectangle or visible content of the parent. In fact, a common situation is when the parent item does not have any visual content by itself and only serves as a container for a set of primitives belonging to one object.

Time for action – Using child items

Let's try to make an item containing multiple children. We want to create a rectangle with a filled circle in each corner and be able to move and rotate it as a whole, like this:

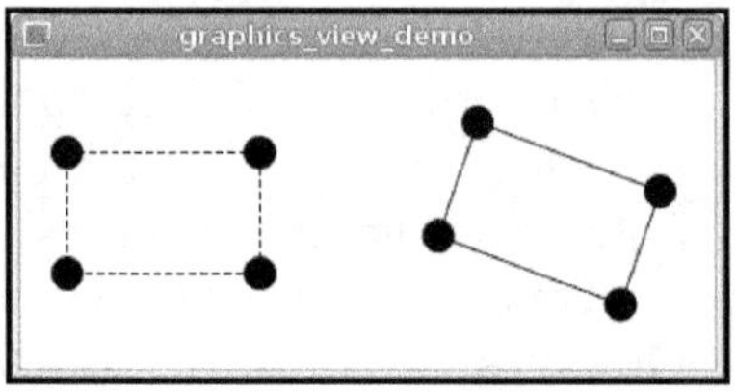

First, you need to create a function that creates a single complex rectangle, by using the following code:

```
QGraphicsRectItem *createComplexItem(
    qreal width, qreal height, qreal radius)
{
    QRectF rect(-width / 2, -height / 2, width, height);
    QGraphicsRectItem *parent = new QGraphicsRectItem(rect);
    QRectF circleBoundary(-radius, -radius, 2 * radius, 2 * radius);
    for(int i = 0; i < 4; i++) {
        QGraphicsEllipseItem *child =
            new QGraphicsEllipseItem(circleBoundary, parent);
        child->setBrush(Qt::black);
        QPointF pos;
        switch(i) {
        case 0:
            pos = rect.topLeft();
            break;
        case 1:
            pos = rect.bottomLeft();
            break;
        case 2:
            pos = rect.topRight();
            break;
        case 3:
            pos = rect.bottomRight();
            break;
        }
        child->setPos(pos);
    }
    return parent;
}
```

We start with creating a `QRectF` variable that contains the rectangle coordinates in the item's coordinate system. Following the tip we provided earlier, we create a rectangle centered at the origin point. Next, we create a rectangle graphics item called `parent`, as usual. The `circleBoundary` rectangle is set to contain the boundary rect of a single circle (again, the center is at the origin point). When we create a new `QGraphicsEllipseItem` for each corner, we pass `parent` to the constructor, so the new circle item is automatically added as a child of the rectangle item.

To set up a child circle, we first use the `setBrush()` function that enables filling of the circle. This function expects a `QBrush` object that allows you to specify an advanced filling style, but in our simple case, we use an implicit conversion from the `Qt::GlobalColor` enum to `QBrush`. You will learn more about brushes later in this chapter.

Next, we select a different corner of the rectangle for each circle and call `setPos()` to move the circle to that corner. Finally, we return the parent item to the caller.

You can use this function as follows:

```
QGraphicsRectItem *item1 = createComplexItem(100, 60, 8);
scene.addItem(item1);

QGraphicsRectItem *item2 = createComplexItem(100, 60, 8);
scene.addItem(item2);
item2->setPos(200, 0);
item2->setRotation(20);
```

Note that when you call `setPos()`, the circles are moved along with the parent item, but the `pos()` values of the circles do not change. This is the consequence of the fact that `pos()` means the position relative to the parent item (or the scene's origin, if there is no parent item). When the rectangle is rotated, circles rotate with it, as if they were fixed to the corners. If the circles weren't children of the rectangle, positioning them properly, in this case, would be a more challenging task.

Have a go hero – Implementing the custom rectangle as a class

In this example, we avoided creating a class for our custom rectangle to keep the code as simple as possible. Following the principles of object-oriented programming, subclassing `QGraphicsRectItem` and creating children items in the constructor of the new class is a good idea. Doing this doesn't require anything you don't already know. For example, when subclassing `QGraphicsRectItem`, you don't need to implement any virtual functions, because they are all properly implemented in the base classes.

Conversions between coordinate systems

If an item is simply moved using `setPos()`, conversion from the item's coordinates to the scene coordinates is as simple as `sceneCoord = itemCoord + item->pos()`. However, this conversion quickly becomes very complex when you use transformations and parent–child relationships, so you should always use dedicated functions to perform such conversions. `QGraphicsItem` provides the following functions:

Function	Description
`mapToScene( const QPointF &point)`	Maps the point `point` that is in the item's coordinate system to the corresponding point in the scene's coordinate system.
`scenePos()`	Maps the item's origin point to the scene's coordinate system. This is the same as `mapToScene(0, 0)`.
`sceneBoundingRect()`	Returns the item's bounding rectangle in the scene's coordinate system.
`mapFromScene( const QPointF &point)`	Maps the point `point` that is in the scene's coordinate system to the corresponding point in the item's coordinate system. This function is the reverse function to `mapToScene()`.
`mapToParent( const QPointF &point)`	Maps the point `point` that is in the item's coordinate system to the corresponding point in the coordinate system of the item's parent. If the item does not have a parent, this function behaves like `mapToScene()`; thus, it returns the corresponding point in the scene's coordinate system.

`mapFromParent( const QPointF &point)`	Maps the point `point` that is in the coordinate system of the item's parent to the corresponding point in the item's own coordinate system. This function is the reverse function to `mapToParent()`.
`mapToItem( const QGraphicsItem *item, const QPointF &point)`	Maps the point `point` that is in the item's own coordinate system to the corresponding point in the coordinate system of the item `item`.
`mapFromItem( const QGraphicsItem *item, const QPointF &point)`	Maps the point `point` that is in the coordinate system of the item `item` to the corresponding point in the item's own coordinate system. This function is the reverse function to `mapToItem()`.

What is great about these functions is that they are not only available for `QPointF`. The same functions are also available for `QRectF`, `QPolygonF`, and `QPainterPath`, not to mention that there are some convenience functions:

- If you call these functions with two numbers of the `qreal` type, the numbers are interpreted as the *x* and *y* coordinates of a `QPointF` pointer
- If you call the functions with four numbers, the numbers are interpreted as the *x* and *y* coordinates and the width and height of a `QRectF` parameter

The `QGraphicsView` class also contains a set of `mapToScene()` functions that map coordinates from the viewport's coordinate system to the scene coordinates and `mapFromScene()` functions that map the scene coordinates to the viewport coordinates.

Overview of functionality

You should now have some understanding of Graphics View's architecture and transformation mechanics. We will now describe some easy-to-use functionality that you'll probably need when creating a Graphics View application.

Standard items

In order to effectively use the framework, you need to know what graphics item classes it provides. It's important to identify the classes you can use to construct the desirable picture and resort to creating a custom item class, only if there is no suitable item or you need better performance. Qt comes with the following standard items that make your life as a developer much easier:

Standard item	Description
`QGraphicsLineItem`	Draws a line. You can define the line with `setLine(const QLineF&)`.
`QGraphicsRectItem`	Draws a rectangle. You can define the rectangle's geometry with `setRect(const QRectF&)`.
`QGraphicsEllipseItem`	Draws an ellipse or an ellipse segment. You can define the rectangle within which the ellipse is being drawn with `setRect(const QRectF&)`. Additionally, you can define whether only a segment of the ellipse should be drawn by calling `setStartAngle(int)` and `setSpanAngle(int)`. The arguments of both functions are in sixteenths of a degree.
`QGraphicsPolygonItem`	Draws a polygon. You can define the polygon with `setPolygon(const QPolygonF&)`.
`QGraphicsPathItem`	Draws a path, that is, a set of various geometric primitives. You can define the path with `setPath(const QPainterPath&)`.
`QGraphicsSimpleTextItem`	Draws plain text. You can define the text with `setText(const QString&)` and the font with `setFont(const QFont&)`. This item doesn't support rich formatting.
`QGraphicsTextItem`	Draws formatted text. Unlike `QGraphicsSimpleTextItem`, this item can display HTML stored in a `QTextDocument` object. You can set HTML with `setHtml(const QString&)` and the document with `setDocument(QTextDocument*)`. `QGraphicsTextItem` can even interact with the displayed text so that text editing or URL opening is possible.

`QGraphicsPixmapItem`	Draws a pixmap (a raster image). You can define the pixmap with `setPixmap(const QPixmap&)`. It's possible to load pixmaps from local files or resources, similar to icons (refer to `Chapter 3`, *Qt GUI Programming*, for more information about resources).
`QGraphicsProxyWidget`	Draws an arbitrary `QWidget` and allows you to interact with it. You can set the widget with `setWidget(QWidget*)`.

As we already saw, you can usually pass the content of the item to the constructor instead of calling a setter method such as `setRect()`. However, keep in mind that compact code may be harder to maintain than code that sets all the variables through setter methods.

For most items, you can also define which pen and which brush should be used. The pen is set with `setPen()` and the brush with `setBrush()` (we've already used it for the child circles in the previous example). These two functions, however, do not exist for `QGraphicsTextItem`. To define the appearance of a `QGraphicsTextItem` item, you have to use `setDefaultTextColor()` or HTML tags supported by Qt. `QGraphicsPixmapItem` has no similar methods, as the concepts of pen and brush cannot be applied to pixmaps.

TIP

Use `QGraphicsSimpleTextItem` wherever possible and try to avoid `QGraphicsTextItem`, if it is not absolutely necessary. The reason is that `QGraphicsTextItem` is a subclass of `QObject` and uses `QTextDocument`, which is basically an HTML engine (although quite limited). This is way heavier than an average graphics item and is definitely too much overhead for displaying simple text.

It is generally easier to use standard items than to implement them from scratch. Whenever you will use Graphics View, ask yourself these questions: Which standard items are suited for my specific needs? Am I re-inventing the wheel over and over again? However, from time to time, you need to create custom graphics items, and we'll cover this topic later in this chapter.

Anti-aliasing

If you look at the result of the previous screenshot, you can probably note that the drawing looks pixelated. This happens because each pixel in a line is completely black, and all the surrounding pixels are completely white. The physical display's resolution is limited, but a technique called **anti-aliasing** allows you to produce more smooth images with the same resolution. When drawing a line with anti-aliasing, some pixels will be more or less blacker than others, depending on how the line crosses the pixel grid.

You can easily enable anti-aliasing in Graphics View using the following code:

```
view.setRenderHint(QPainter::Antialiasing);
```

With the anti-aliasing flag turned on, the painting is done much more smoothly:

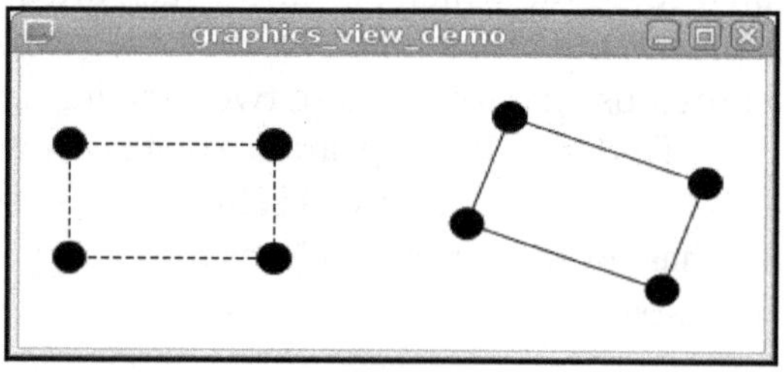

However, lines in the rectangle on the left now look thicker. This happens because we used lines with integer coordinates and 1 pixel width. Such a line is located exactly on the border between two rows of pixels, and when anti-aliased, both adjacent rows of pixels will be partially painted. This can be fixed by adding 0.5 to all coordinates:

```
QRectF rect(-width / 2, -height / 2, width, height);
rect.translate(0.5, 0.5);
QGraphicsRectItem *parent = new QGraphicsRectItem(rect);
```

Now the line is positioned right in the middle of a pixel row, so it only occupies a single row:

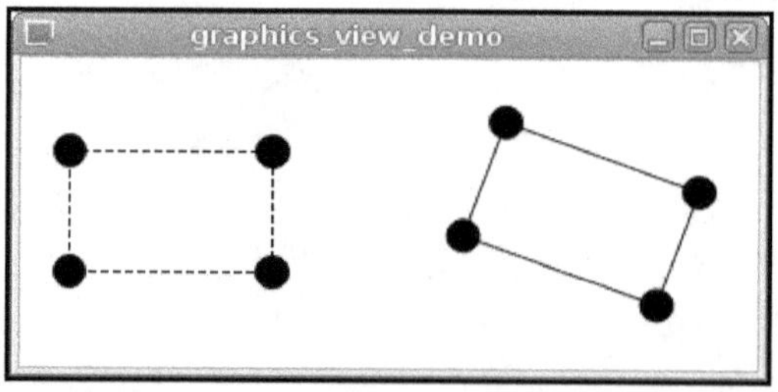

Another solution is to implement a custom item class and disable anti-aliasing when painting a horizontal or vertical line.

`QGraphicsView` also supports the `QPainter::TextAntialiasing` flag that enables anti-aliasing when drawing text, and the `QPainter::SmoothPixmapTransform` flag that enables smooth pixmap transformation. Note the anti-aliasing and smoothing impact performance of your application, so use them only when needed.

Pens and brushes

The pen and brush are two attributes that define how different drawing operations are performed. The pen (represented by the `QPen` class) defines the outline, and the brush (represented by the `QBrush` class) fills the drawn shapes. Each of them is really a set of parameters. The most simple one is the color defined, either as a predefined global color enumeration value (such as `Qt::red` or `Qt::transparent`), or an instance of the `QColor` class. The effective color is made up of four attributes: three color components (red, green, and blue) and an optional alpha channel value that determines the transparency of the color (the larger the value, the more opaque the color). By default, all components are expressed as 8-bit values (0 to 255) but can also be expressed as real values representing a percentage of the maximum saturation of the component; for example, 0.6 corresponds to 153 (0.6·255). For convenience, one of the `QColor` constructors accepts hexadecimal color codes used in HTML (with `#0000FF` being an opaque blue color) or even bare color names (for example, `blue`) from a predefined list of colors returned by a static function—`QColor::colorNames()`. Once a color object is defined using RGB components, it can be queried using different color spaces (for example, CMYK or HSV). Also, a set of static methods are available that act as constructors for colors expressed in different color spaces.

For example, to construct a clear magenta color any of the following expressions can be used:

- `QColor("magenta")`
- `QColor("#FF00FF")`
- `QColor(255, 0, 255)`
- `QColor::fromRgbF(1, 0, 1)`
- `QColor::fromHsv(300, 255, 255)`
- `QColor::fromCmyk(0, 255, 0, 0)`
- `Qt::magenta`

Apart from the color, `QBrush` has two additional ways of expressing the fill of a shape. You can use `QBrush::setTexture()` to set a pixmap that will be used as a stamp or `QBrush::setGradient()` to make the brush use a gradient to do the filling. For example, to use a gradient that goes diagonally and starts as yellow in the top-left corner of the shape, becomes red in the middle of the shape, and ends as magenta at the bottom-right corner of the shape, the following code can be used:

```
QLinearGradient gradient(0, 0, width, height);
gradient.setColorAt(0,   Qt::yellow);
gradient.setColorAt(0.5, Qt::red);
gradient.setColorAt(1.0, Qt::magenta);
QBrush brush = gradient;
```

When used with drawing a rectangle, this code will give the following output:

Qt can handle linear (`QLinearGradient`), radial (`QRadialGradient`), and conical (`QConicalGradient`) gradients. Qt provides a **Gradients** example (shown in the following screenshot) where you can see different gradients in action:

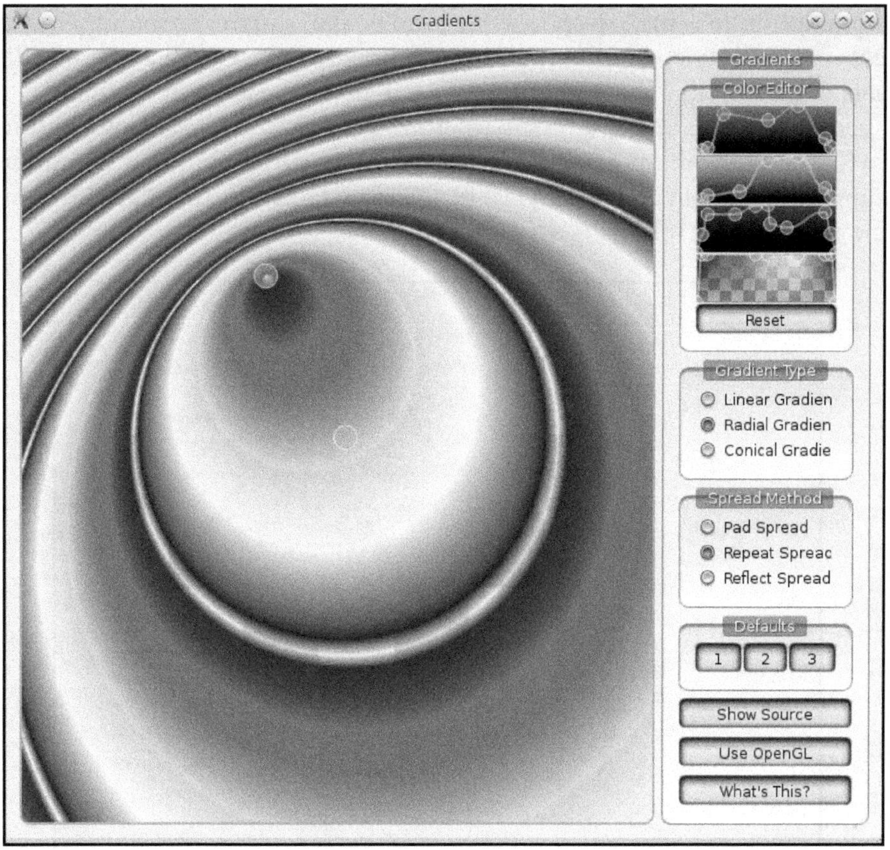

As for the pen, its main attribute is its width (expressed in pixels), which determines the thickness of the shape outline. A pen can, of course, have a color set but, in addition to that, you can use any brush as a pen. The result of such an operation is that you can draw thick outlines of shapes using gradients or textures.

There are three more important properties for a pen. The first is the pen style, set using `QPen::setStyle()`. It determines whether lines drawn by the pen are continuous or divided in some way (dashes, dots, and so on). You can see the available line styles here:

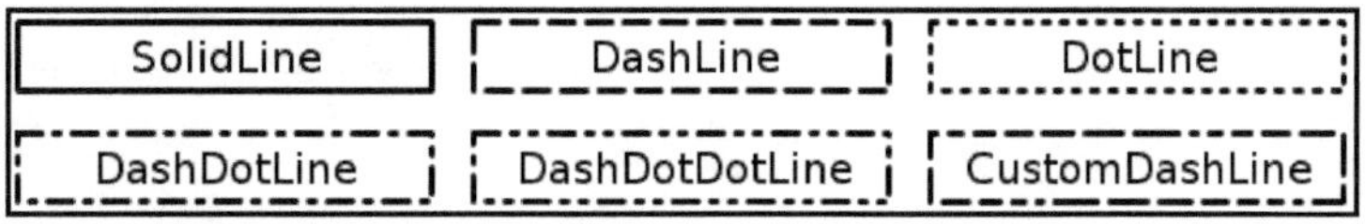

The second attribute is the cap style, which can be flat, square, or round. The third attribute—the join style—is important for polyline outlines and dictates how different segments of the polyline are connected. You can make the joins sharp (with `Qt::MiterJoin` or `Qt::SvgMiterJoin`), round (`Qt::RoundJoin`), or a hybrid of the two (`Qt::BevelJoin`). You can see the different pen attribute configurations (including different join and cap styles) in action by launching the **Path Stroking** example shown in the following screenshot:

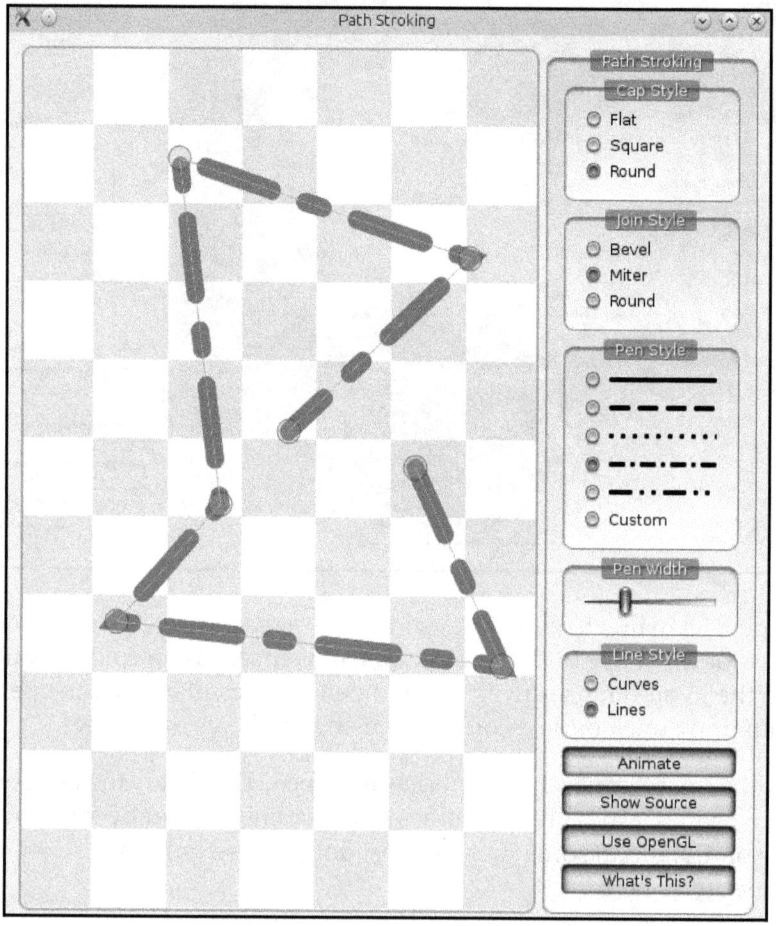

Item selection

The scene supports the ability of selecting items, similar to how you select files in a file manager. To be selectable, an item must have the `QGraphicsItem::ItemIsSelectable` flag turned on. Try to add `parent->setFlag(QGraphicsItem::ItemIsSelectable, true)` to the `createComplexItem()` function we created earlier. Now, if you run the application and click on a rectangle, it is selected, which is indicated by dashed lines:

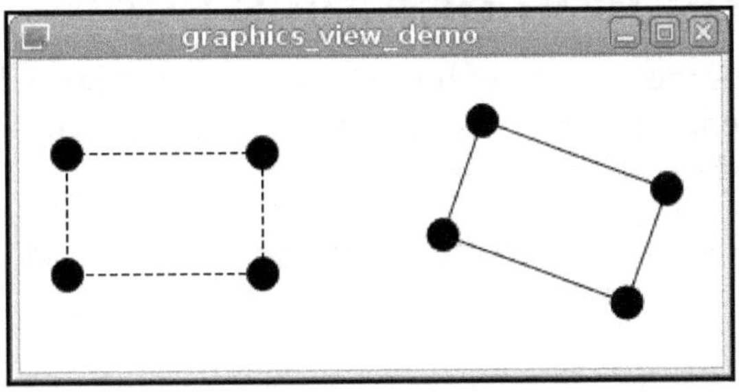

You can use the *Ctrl* button to select multiple items at once. Alternatively, you can call `view.setDragMode(QGraphicsView::RubberBandDrag)` to activate the rubber band selection for the view.

TIP

Another useful drag mode of the Graphics View is `ScrollHandDrag`. It allows you to scroll the view by dragging the scene with the left mouse button, without the need to use scrollbars.

Besides that, there are different ways to select items programmatically. There is the item's `QGraphicsItem::setSelected()` function, which takes a `bool` value to toggle the selection state on or off, or you can call `QGraphicsScene::setSelectionArea()` on the scene, which takes a `QPainterPath` parameter as an argument, in which case all items within the area are selected.

With the scene's `QGraphicsScene::selectedItems()` function, you can query the actual selected items. The function returns a `QList` holding `QGraphicsItem` pointers to the selected items. For example, calling `QList::count()` on that list will give you the number of selected items. To clear the selection, call `QGraphicsScene::clearSelection()`. To query the selection state of an item, use `QGraphicsItem::isSelected()`, which returns `true` if the item is selected and `false` otherwise.

TIP

Another interesting flag of `GraphicsItem` is `ItemIsMovable`. It enables you to drag the item within the scene by holding it with the left mouse button, effectively changing the `pos()` of the item. Try to add `parent->setFlag(QGraphicsItem::ItemIsMovable, true)` to our `createComplexItem` function and drag around the rectangles.

Keyboard focus in graphics scene

The scene implements the concept of focus that works similar to keyboard focus in widgets. Only one item can have focus at a time. When the scene receives a keyboard event, it is dispatched to the focus item.

To be focusable, an item must have the `QGraphicsItem::ItemIsFocusable` flag enabled:

```
item1->setFlag(QGraphicsItem::ItemIsFocusable, true);
item2->setFlag(QGraphicsItem::ItemIsFocusable, true);
```

Then, an item can be focused by a mouse click. You can also change the focused item from the code:

```
item1->setFocus();
```

Another way to set the focus is to use the scene's `QGraphicsScene::setFocusItem()` function, which expects a pointer to the item you like to focus as a parameter. Every time an item gains focus, the previously focused item (if any) will automatically lose focus.

To determine whether an item has focus, you again have two possibilities. One is that you can call `QGraphicsItem::hasFocus()` on an item, which returns `true` if the item has focus or `false` otherwise. Alternatively, you can get the actual focused item by calling the scene's `QGraphicsScene::focusItem()` method. On the other hand, if you call the item's `QGraphicsItem::focusItem()` function, the focused item is returned if the item itself or any descendant item has focus; otherwise, `nullptr` is returned. To remove focus, call `clearFocus()` on the focused item or click somewhere in the scene's background or on an item that cannot get focus.

TIP

If you want a click on the scene's background not to cause the focused item to lose its focus, set the scene's `stickyFocus` property to `true`.

Painter paths

If you want to create a graphics item that consists of multiple geometric primitives, creating multiple QGraphicsItem objects seems to be tedious. Fortunately, Qt provides a QGraphicsPathItem class that allows you to specify a number of primitives in a QPainterPath object. QPainterPath allows you to "record" multiple painting instructions (including filling, outlining, and clipping), and then efficiently reuse them multiple times.

Time for action – Adding path items to the scene

Let's paint a few objects consisting of a large number of lines:

```
static const int SIZE = 100;
static const int MARGIN = 10;
static const int FIGURE_COUNT = 5;
static const int LINE_COUNT = 500;
for(int figureNum = 0; figureNum < FIGURE_COUNT; ++figureNum) {
    QPainterPath path;
    path.moveTo(0, 0);
    for(int i = 0; i < LINE_COUNT; ++i) {
        path.lineTo(qrand() % SIZE, qrand() % SIZE);
    }
    QGraphicsPathItem *item = scene.addPath(path);
    item->setPos(figureNum * (SIZE + MARGIN), 0);
}
```

For each item, we first create a QPainterPath and set the current position to (0, 0). Then, we use the qrand() function to generate random numbers, apply the modulus operator (%) to produce a number from 0 to SIZE (excluding SIZE), and feed them to the lineTo() function that strokes a line from the current position to the given position and sets it as the new current position. Next, we use the addPath() convenience function that creates a QGraphicsPathItem object and adds it to the scene. Finally, we use setPos() to move each item to a different position in the scene. The result looks like this:

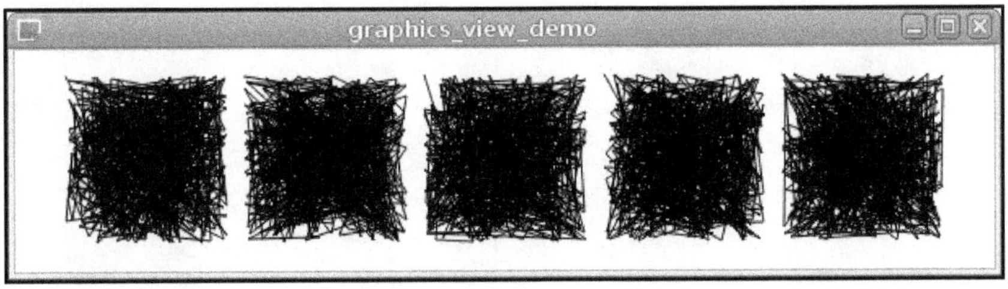

`QPainterPath` allows you to use practically every paint operation Qt supports. For example, `QGraphicsPathItem` is the only standard item able to draw Bezier curves in the scene, as `QPainterPath` supports them. Refer to the documentation of `QPainterPath` for more information.

Using painter paths in this example is very efficient, because we avoided creating thousands of individual line objects on the heap. However, putting a large part of a scene in a single item may reduce the performance. When parts of the scene are separate graphics items, Qt can efficiently determine which items are not visible and skip drawing them.

Z-order of items

Have you wondered what happens when multiple items are painted in the same area of the scene? Let's try to do this:

```
QGraphicsEllipseItem *item1 = scene.addEllipse(0, 0, 100, 50);
item1->setBrush(Qt::red);
QGraphicsEllipseItem *item2 = scene.addEllipse(50, 0, 100, 50);
item2->setBrush(Qt::green);
QGraphicsEllipseItem *item3 = scene.addEllipse(0, 25, 100, 50);
item3->setBrush(Qt::blue);
QGraphicsEllipseItem *item4 = scene.addEllipse(50, 25, 100, 50);
item4->setBrush(Qt::gray);
```

By default, items are painted in the order they were added, so the last item will be displayed in front of the others:

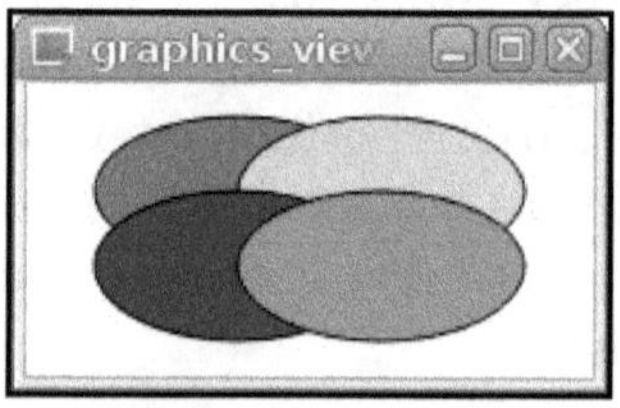

However, you can change the **z-order** by calling the `setZValue()` function:

```
item2->setZValue(1);
```

The second item is now displayed in front of the others:

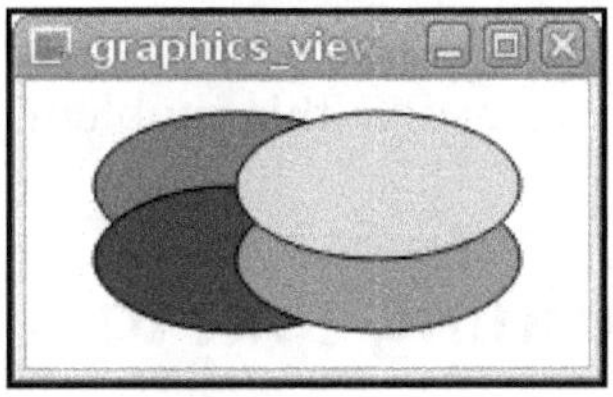

Items with a higher z value are displayed on top of the items with lower z values. The default z value is 0. Negative values are also possible. If items have the same z value, the order of insertion decides the placement, and items added later overlap those added earlier.

Ability to change the z-order of items is very important when developing 2D games. Any scene typically consists of a number of layers that must be painted in a specific order. You can set a z value for each item based on the layer this item belongs to.

> The parent–child relationship between items also has an impact on the z-order. Children are displayed on top of their parent. Additionally, if an item is displayed in front of another item, the children of the former are also displayed in front of the children of the latter.

Ignoring transformations

If you try to zoom in on our custom rectangles scene (for example, by calling `view.scale(4, 4)`), you will note that everything is scaled proportionally, as you would expect. However, there are situations where you don't want some elements to be affected by scale or other transformations. Qt provides multiple ways to deal with it.

If you want lines to always have the same width, regardless of the zoom, you need to make the pen cosmetic:

```
QPen pen = parent->pen();
pen.setCosmetic(true);
parent->setPen(pen);
```

Now, the rectangles will always have lines with one-pixel width, regardless of the view's scale (anti-aliasing can still blur them, though). It's also possible to have cosmetic pens with any width, but using them in Graphics View is not recommended.

Another common situation where you don't want transformation to apply is displaying text. Rotating and shearing text usually makes it unreadable, so you'd usually want to make it horizontal and untransformed. Let's try to add some text to our project and look at how we can solve this problem.

Time for action – Adding text to a custom rectangle

Let's add a number to each of the corner circles:

```
child->setPos(pos);
QGraphicsSimpleTextItem *text =
    new QGraphicsSimpleTextItem(QString::number(i), child);
text->setBrush(Qt::green);
text->setPos(-text->boundingRect().width() / 2,
             -text->boundingRect().height() / 2);
```

The `QString::number(i)` function returns the string representation of number `i`. The text item is a child of the circle item, so its position is relative to the circle's origin point (in our case, its center). As we saw earlier, the text is displayed to the top-left of the item's origin, so if we want to center the text within the circle, we need to shift it up and right by half of the item's size. Now the text is positioned and rotated along with its parent circle:

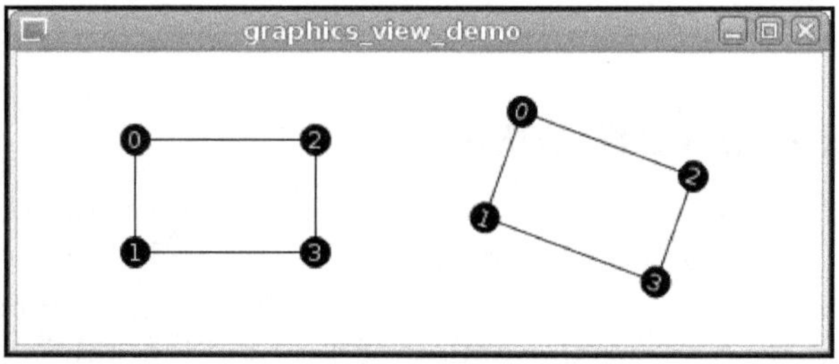

However, we don't want the text to be rotated, so we need to enable the `ItemIgnoresTransformations` flag for the text item:

```
text->setFlag(QGraphicsItem::ItemIgnoresTransformations);
```

This flag makes the item ignore any transformations of its parent items or the view. However, the origin of its coordinate system is still defined by the position of `pos()` in the parent's coordinate system. So, the text item will still follow the circle, but it will no longer be scaled or rotated:

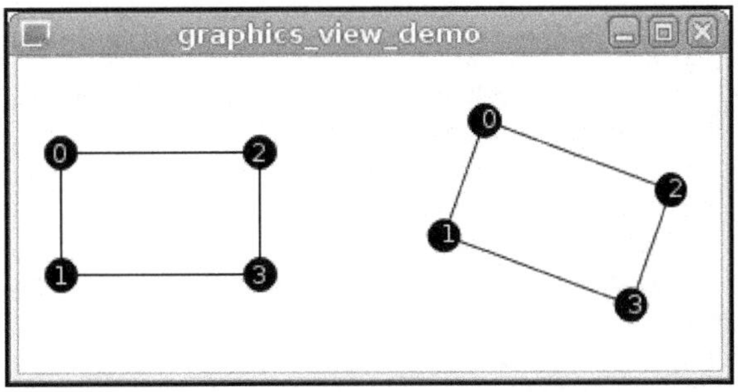

However, now we hit another problem: the text is no longer properly centered in the circle. It will become more apparent if you scale the view again. Why did that happen? With the `ItemIgnoresTransformations` flag, our `text->setPos(...)` statement is no longer correct. Indeed, `pos()` uses coordinates in the parent's coordinate system, but we used the result of `boundingRect()`, which uses the item's coordinate system. These two coordinate systems were the same before, but with the `ItemIgnoresTransformations` flag enabled, they are now different.

To elaborate on this problem, let's see what happens with the coordinates (we will consider only x coordinate, since y behaves the same). Let's say that our text item's width is eight pixels, so the `pos()` we set has `x = -4`. When no transformations are applied, this `pos()` results in shifting the text to the left by four pixels. If the `ItemIgnoresTransformations` flag is disabled and the view is scaled by 2, the text is shifted by eight pixels relative to the circle's center, but the size of the text itself is now 16 pixels, so it's still centered. If the `ItemIgnoresTransformations` flag is enabled, the text is still shifted to the left by eight pixels relative to the circle's center (because `pos()` operates in the parent item's coordinate system, and the circle is scaled), but the width of the item is now 8, because it ignores the scale and so it's no longer centered. When the view is rotated, the result is even more incorrect, because `setPos()` will shift the item in the direction that depends on the rotation. Since the text item itself is not rotated, we always want to shift it up and left.

This problem would go away if the item were already centered around its origin. Unfortunately, `QGraphicsSimpleTextItem` can't do this. Now, if it were `QGraphicsRectItem`, doing this would be easy, but nothing stops us from adding a rectangle that ignores transformations and then adding text inside that rectangle! Let's do this:

```
QGraphicsSimpleTextItem *text =
        new QGraphicsSimpleTextItem(QString::number(i));
QRectF textRect = text->boundingRect();
textRect.translate(-textRect.center());
QGraphicsRectItem *rectItem = new QGraphicsRectItem(textRect, child);
rectItem->setPen(QPen(Qt::green));
rectItem->setFlag(QGraphicsItem::ItemIgnoresTransformations);
text->setParentItem(rectItem);
text->setPos(textRect.topLeft());
text->setBrush(Qt::green);
```

In this code, we first create a text item, but don't set its parent. Next, we get the bounding rect of the item that will tell us how much space the text needs. Then, we shift the rect so that its center is at the origin point (0, 0). Now we can create a rect item for this rectangle, set the circle as its parent, and disable transformations for the rect item. Finally, we set the rect item as the parent of the text item and change the position of the text item to place it inside the rectangle.

The rectangle is now properly positioned at the center of the circle, and the text item always follows the rectangle, as children usually do:

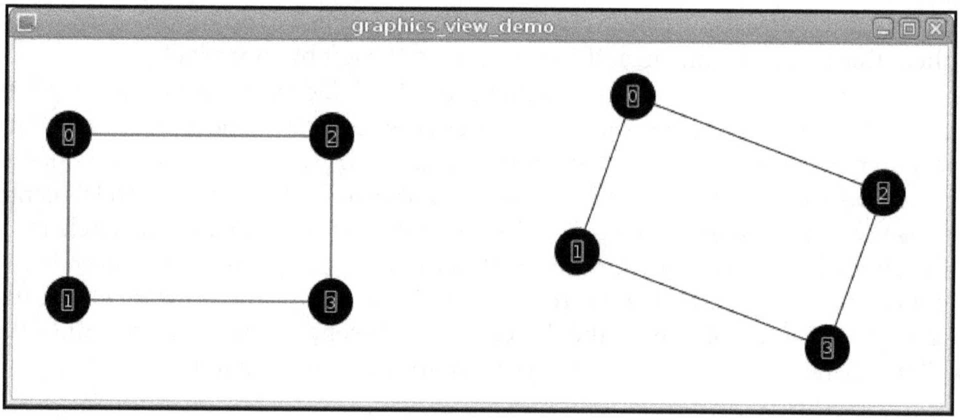

TIP

Since we didn't originally want the rectangle, we may want to hide it. We can't use `rectItem->hide()` in this case, because that would also result in hiding its child item (the text). The solution is to disable the painting of the rectangle by calling `rectItem->setPen(Qt::NoPen)`.

An alternative solution to this problem is to translate the text item's coordinate system instead of using `setPos()`. `QGraphicsItem` doesn't have a dedicated function for translation, so we will need to use `setTransform`:

```
QTransform transform;
transform.translate(-text->boundingRect().width() / 2,
                    -text->boundingRect().height() / 2);
text->setTransform(transform);
```

Contrary to what you would expect, `ItemIgnoresTransformations` doesn't cause the item to ignore its own transformations, and this code will position the text correctly without needing an additional rectangle item.

Finding items by position

If you want to know which item is shown at a certain position, you can use the `QGraphicsScene::itemAt()` function that takes the position in the scene's coordinate system (either a `QPointF` or two `qreal` numbers) and the device transformation object (`QTransform`) that can be obtained using the `QGraphicsView::transform()` function. The function returns the topmost item at the specified position or a null pointer if no item was found. The device transformation only matters if your scene contains items that ignore transformations. If you have no such items, you can use the default-constructed `QTransform` value:

```
QGraphicsItem *foundItem = scene.itemAt(scenePos, QTransform());
```

If your scene contains items that ignore transformations, it may be more convenient to use the `QGraphicsView::itemAt()` function that automatically takes the device transform into account. Note that this function expects the position to be in the viewport's coordinate system.

If you want all items that are located at some position, say in cases where multiple items are on top of each other, or if you need to search for items in some area, use the `QGraphicsScene::items()` function. It will return a list of items defined by the specified arguments. This function has a number of overloads that allow you to specify a single point, a rectangle, a polygon, or a painter path. The `deviceTransform` argument works in the same way as for the `QGraphicsScene::itemAt()` function discussed earlier. The `mode` argument allows you to alter how the items in the area will be determined. The following table shows the different modes:

Mode	Meaning
`Qt::ContainsItemBoundingRect`	The item's bounding rectangle must be completely inside the selection area.
`Qt::IntersectsItemBoundingRect`	Similar to `Qt::ContainsItemBoundingRect` but also returns items whose bounding rectangles intersect with the selection area.
`Qt::ContainsItemShape`	The item's shape must be completely inside the selection area. The shape may describe the item's boundaries more precisely than the bounding rectangle, but this operation is more computationally intensive.
`Qt::IntersectsItemShape`	Similar to `Qt::ContainsItemShape` but also returns items whose shapes intersect with the selection area.

The `items()` function sorts items according to their stacking order. The `order` argument allows you to choose the order in which the results will be returned. `Qt::DescendingOrder` (default) will place the topmost item at the beginning, and `Qt::AscendingOrder` will result in a reversed order.

The view also provides a similar `QGraphicsView::items()` function that operates in viewport coordinates.

Showing specific areas of the scene

As soon as the scene's bounding rectangle exceeds the viewport's size, the view will show scroll bars. Besides using them with the mouse to navigate to a specific item or point on the scene, you can also access them by code. Since the view inherits `QAbstractScrollArea`, you can use all its functions for accessing the scroll bars; `horizontalScrollBar()` and `verticalScrollBar()` return a pointer to `QScrollBar`, and thus you can query their range with `minimum()` and `maximum()`. By invoking `value()` and `setValue()`, you get and can set the current value, which results in scrolling the scene.

However, normally, you do not need to control free scrolling inside the view from your source code. The normal task would be to scroll to a specific item. In order to do that, you do not need to do any calculations yourself; the view offers a pretty simple way to do that for you—`centerOn()`. With `centerOn()`, the view ensures that the item, which you have passed as an argument, is centered on the view unless it is too close to the scene's border or even outside. Then, the view tries to move it as far as possible on the center. The `centerOn()` function does not only take a `QGraphicsItem` item as argument; you can also center on a `QPointF` pointer or as a convenience on an *x* and *y* coordinate.

If you do not care where an item is shown, you can simply call `ensureVisible()` with the item as an argument. Then, the view scrolls the scene as little as possible so that the item's center remains or becomes visible. As a second and third argument, you can define a horizontal and vertical margin, which are both the minimum space between the item's bounding rectangle and the view's border. Both values have 50 pixels as their default value. Besides a `QGraphicsItem` item, you can also ensure the visibility of a `QRectF` element (of course, there is also the convenience function taking four `qreal` elements).

> TIP
>
> If you need to ensure the entire visibility of an item, use `ensureVisible(item->boundingRect())` (since `ensureVisible(item)` only takes the item's center into account).

`centerOn()` and `ensureVisible()` only scroll the scene but do not change its transformation state. If you absolutely want to ensure the visibility of an item or a rectangle that exceeds the size of the view, you have to transform the scene as well. With this task, again the view will help you. By calling `fitInView()` with `QGraphicsItem` or a `QRectF` element as an argument, the view will scroll and scale the scene so that it fits in the viewport size.

As a second argument, you can control how the scaling is done. You have the following options:

Value	Description
`Qt::IgnoreAspectRatio`	The scaling is done absolutely freely regardless of the item's or rectangle's aspect ratio.
`Qt::KeepAspectRatio`	The item's or rectangle's aspect ratio is taken into account while trying to expand as far as possible while respecting the viewport's size.
`Qt::KeepAspectRatioByExpanding`	The item's or rectangle's aspect ratio is taken into account, but the view tries to fill the whole viewport's size with the smallest overlap.

The `fitInView()` function does not only scale larger items down to fit the viewport, it also enlarges items to fill the whole viewport. The following diagram illustrates the different scaling options for an item that is enlarged (the circle on the left is the original item, and the black rectangle is the viewport):

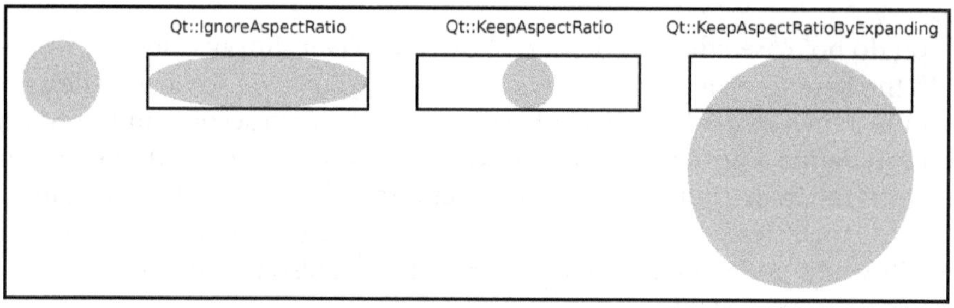

Saving a scene to an image file

We've only displayed our scene in the view so far, but it is also possible to render it to an image, a printer, or any other object Qt can use for painting. Let's save our scene to a PNG file:

```
QRect rect = scene.sceneRect().toAlignedRect();
QImage image(rect.size(), QImage::Format_ARGB32);
image.fill(Qt::transparent);
QPainter painter(&image);
scene.render(&painter);
image.save("scene.png");
```

What just happened?

First, you determined the rectangle of the scene with `sceneRect()`. Since this returns a `QRectF` parameter and `QImage` can only handle `QRect`, you transformed it on the fly by calling `toAlignedRect()`. The difference between the `toRect()` function and `toAlignedRect()` is that the former rounds to the nearest integer, which may result in a smaller rectangle, whereas the latter expands to the smallest possible rectangle containing the original `QRectF` parameter.

Then, you created a `QImage` file with the size of the aligned scene's rectangle. As the image is created with uninitialized data, you need to call `fill()` with `Qt::transparent` to receive a transparent background. You can assign any color you like as an argument both as a value of `Qt::GlobalColor` enumeration and an ordinary `QColor` object; `QColor(0, 0, 255)` will result in a blue background. Next, you create a `QPainter` object that points to the image. This painter object is then used in the scene's `render()` function to draw the scene. After that, all you have to do is use the `save()` function to save the image to a place of your choice. The format of the output file is determined by its extension. Qt supports a variety of formats, and Qt plugins can add support for new formats. Since we haven't specified a path, the image will be saved in the application's working directory (which is usually the build directory, unless you changed it using the **Projects** pane of Qt Creator). You can also specify an absolute path, such as `/path/to/image.png`.

TIP

Of course, you'll need to construct a path that's valid on the current system instead of hard-coding it in the sources. For example, you can use the `QFileDialog::getSaveFileName()` function to ask the user for a path.

Have a go hero – Rendering only specific parts of a scene

This example draws the whole scene. Of course, you can also render only specific parts of the scene using the other arguments of `render()`. We will not go into this here, but you may want to try it as an exercise.

Custom items

As we already saw, Graphics View provides a lot of useful functionality that covers most typical use cases. However, the real power of Qt is its extensibility, and Graphics View allows us to create custom subclasses of `QGraphicsItem` to implement items that are tailored for your application. You may want to implement a custom item class when you need to do the following:

- Paint something that is not possible or difficult to do with standard item classes
- Implement some logic related to the item, for example, add your own methods
- Handle events in individual items

In our next small project, we will create an item that can draw a graph of the sine function `sin(x)` and implement some event handling.

Time for action – Creating a sine graph project

Use Qt Creator to create a new Qt Widgets project and name it `sine_graph`. On the **Class Information** page of the wizard, select `QWidget` as the base class and input `View` as the class name. Uncheck the **Generate form** checkbox and finish the wizard.

We want the `View` class to be the graphics view, so you need to change the base class to `QGraphicsView` (the wizard doesn't suggest such an option). For this, edit the class declaration to look like `class View : public QGraphicsView ...` and the constructor implementation to look like `View::View(QWidget *parent) : QGraphicsView(parent) ...`.

Next, edit the `View` constructor to enable anti-aliasing and set a new graphics scene for our view:

```
setRenderHint(QPainter::Antialiasing);
setScene(new QGraphicsScene);
```

The view doesn't delete the associated scene on destruction (because you may have multiple views for the same scene), so you should delete the scene manually in the destructor:

```
delete scene();
```

You can try to run the application and check that it displays an empty view.

Time for action – Creating a graphics item class

Ask Qt Creator to add a new **C++ class** to the project. Input `SineItem` as the class name, leave **<Custom>** in the **Base class** drop-down list, and input `QGraphicsItem` in the field below it. Finish the wizard and open the created `sineitem.h` file.

Set the text cursor inside `QGraphicsItem` in the class declaration and press *Alt* + *Enter*. At first; Qt Creator will suggest that you **Add** `#include <QGraphicsItem>`. Confirm that and press *Alt* + *Enter* on `QGraphicsItem` again. Now, Qt Creator should suggest that you select **Insert Virtual Functions of Base Classes**. When you select this option, a special dialog will appear:

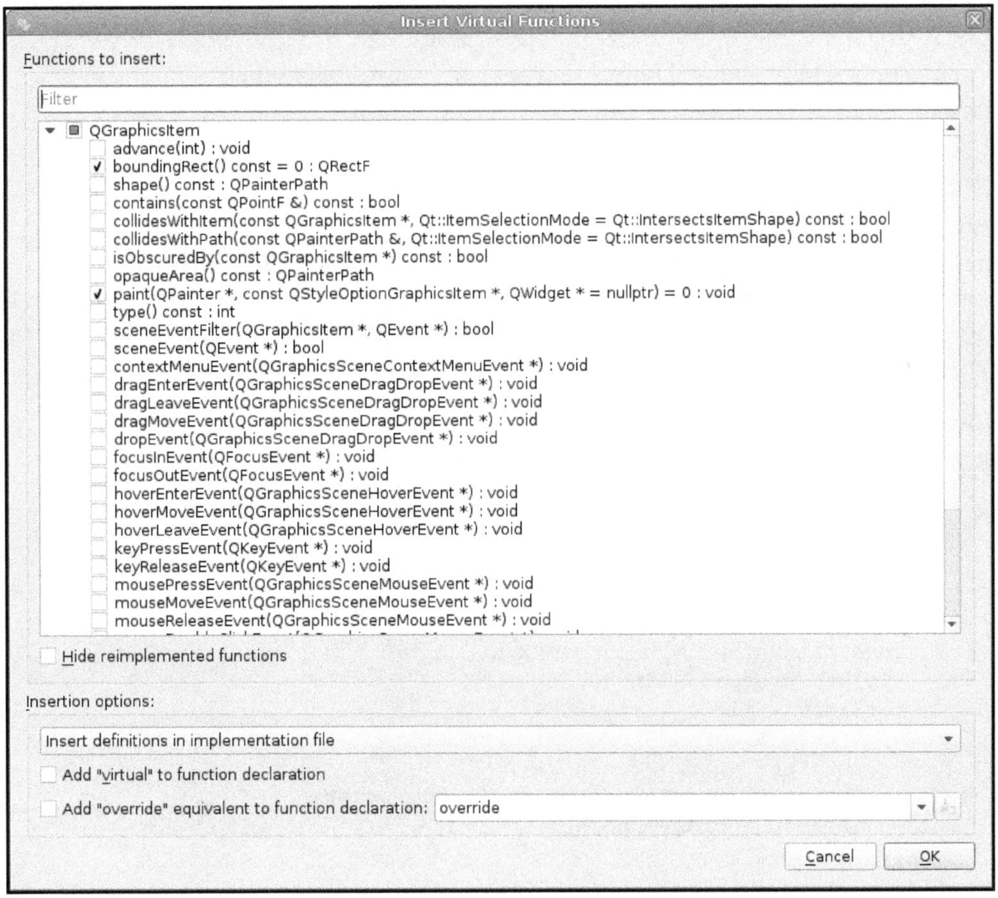

The function list contains all virtual functions of the base class. The pure virtual functions (which must be implemented if you want to create objects of the class) are enabled by default. Check that everything is set as in the preceding screenshot, and then click on **OK**. This convenient operation adds declaration and implementation of the selected virtual functions to the source files of our class. You can write them manually instead, if you want.

Let's edit `sineitem.cpp` to implement the two pure virtual functions. First of all, a couple of constants at the top of the file:

```
static const float DX = 1;
static const float MAX_X = 50;
```

In our graph, *x* will vary from 0 to `MAX_X`, and `DX` will be the difference between the two consequent points of the graph. As you may know, `sin(x)` can have values from -1 to 1. This information is enough to implement the `boundingRect()` function:

```
QRectF SineItem::boundingRect() const
{
    return QRectF(0, -1, MAX_X, 2);
}
```

This function simply returns the same rectangle every time. In this rectangle, *x* changes from 0 to `MAX_X`, and *y* changes from -1 to 1. This returned rectangle is a promise to the scene that the item will only paint in this area. The scene relies on the correctness of that information, so you should strictly obey that promise. Otherwise, the scene will become cluttered up with relics of your drawing!

Now, implement the `paint()` function, as follows:

```
void SineItem::paint(QPainter *painter,
    const QStyleOptionGraphicsItem *option, QWidget *widget)
{
    QPen pen;
    pen.setCosmetic(true);
    painter->setPen(pen);
    const int steps = qRound(MAX_X / DX);
    QPointF previousPoint(0, sin(0));
    for(int i = 1; i < steps; ++i) {
        const float x = DX * i;
        QPointF point(x, sin(x));
        painter->drawLine(previousPoint, point);
        previousPoint = point;
    }
```

```
        Q_UNUSED(option)
        Q_UNUSED(widget)
    }
```

Add `#include <QtMath>` to the top section of the file to make math functions available.

What just happened?

When the view needs to display the scene, it calls the `paint()` function of each visible item and provides three arguments: a `QPainter` pointer that should be used for painting, a `QStyleOptionGraphicsItem` pointer that contains painting-related parameters for this item, and an optional `QWidget` pointer that may point to the currently painted widget. In the implementation of the function, we start with setting a cosmetic pen in the `painter` so that the line width of our graph is always 1. Next, we calculate the number of points in the graph and save it to the `steps` variable. Then, we create a variable to store the previous point of the graph and initialize it with the position of the first point of the graph (corresponding to `x = 0`). Next, we iterate through points, calculate *x* and *y* for each point, and then use the `painter` object to draw a line from the previous point to the current point. After this, we update the value of the `previousPoint` variable. We use the `Q_UNUSED()` macro to suppress compiler warnings about unused arguments and to indicate that we, intentionally, didn't use them.

Edit the constructor of our `View` class to create an instance of our new item:

```
SineItem *item = new SineItem();
scene()->addItem(item);
```

The application should display the sine graph now, but it is very small:

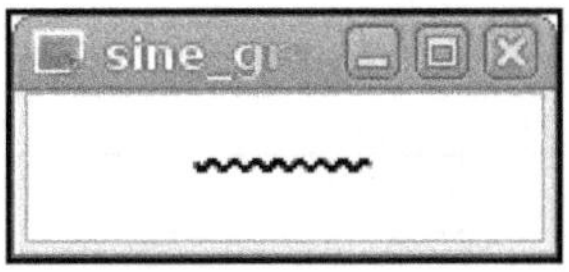

We should add a way for users to scale our view using the mouse wheel. However, before we get to this, you need to learn a little more about event handling.

Events

Any GUI application needs to react to the input events. We are already familiar with the signals and slots mechanism in `QObject`-based classes. However, `QObject` is not exactly a lightweight class. Signals and slots are powerful and convenient for connecting parts of the application, but invoking a signal for processing each keyboard press or mouse move will be too inefficient. To process such events, Qt has a special system that uses the `QEvent` class.

The dispatcher of the events is the **event loop**. Almost any Qt application uses the main event loop that is started by calling `QCoreApplication::exec` at the end of the `main()` function. While the application is running, the control flow is either in your code (that is, in the implementation of any function in the project) or in the event loop. When the operating system or a component of the application asks the event loop to process an event, it determines the receiver and calls a virtual function that corresponds to the event type. A `QEvent` object containing information about the event is passed to that function. The virtual function has a choice to **accept** or **ignore** the event. If the event was not accepted, the event is **propagated** to the parent object in the hierarchy (for example, from a widget to its parent widget, and from a graphics item to the parent item). You can subclass a Qt class and reimplement a virtual function to add custom events processing.

The following table shows the most useful events:

Event types	Description
`QEvent::KeyPress`, `QEvent::KeyRelease`	A keyboard button was pressed or released.
`QEvent::MouseButtonPress`, `QEvent::MouseButtonRelease`, `QEvent::MouseButtonDblClick`	The mouse buttons were pressed or released.
`QEvent::Wheel`	The mouse wheel was rolled.
`QEvent::Enter`	The mouse cursor entered the object's boundaries.
`QEvent::MouseMove`	The mouse cursor was moved.
`QEvent::Leave`	The mouse cursor left the object's boundaries.
`QEvent::Resize`	The widget was resized (for example, because the user resized the window or the layout changed).
`QEvent::Close`	The user attempted to close the widget's window.

`QEvent::ContextMenu`	The user requested a context menu (the exact action depends on the operating system's way to open the context menu).
`QEvent::Paint`	The widget needs to be repainted.
`QEvent::DragEnter`, `QEvent::DragLeave`, `QEvent::DragMove`, `QEvent::Drop`	The user performs a drag and drop action.
`QEvent::TouchBegin`, `QEvent::TouchUpdate`, `QEvent::TouchEnd`, `QEvent::TouchCancel`	A touchscreen or a trackpad reported an event.

Each event type has a corresponding class that inherits `QEvent` (for example, `QMouseEvent`). Many event types have the dedicated virtual function, for example, `QWidget::mousePressEvent` and `QGraphicsItem::mousePressEvent`. More exotic events must be processed by re-implementing the `QWidget::event` (or `QGraphicsItem::sceneEvent`) function that receives all events, and using `event->type()` to check the event type.

Events dispatched in the graphics scene have special types (for example, `QEvent::GraphicsSceneMousePress`) and special classes (for example, `QGraphicsSceneMouseEvent`) because they have an extended set of information about the event. In particular, mouse events contain information about the coordinates in the item's and the scene's coordinate systems.

Time for action – Implementing the ability to scale the scene

Let's allow the user to scale the scene using the mouse wheel on the view. Switch to the `view.h` file and add a declaration and an implementation of the `wheelEvent()` virtual function using the same method we just used in the `SineItem` class. Write the following code in the `view.cpp` file:

```
void View::wheelEvent(QWheelEvent *event)
{
    QGraphicsView::wheelEvent(event);
    if (event->isAccepted()) {
        return;
    }
    const qreal factor = 1.1;
    if (event->angleDelta().y() > 0) {
        scale(factor, factor);
    } else {
```

```
            scale(1 / factor, 1 / factor);
        }
        event->accept();
    }
```

If you run the application now, you can scale the sine graph using the mouse wheel.

What just happened?

When an event occurs, Qt calls the corresponding virtual function in the widget in which the event occurred. In our case, whenever the user uses the mouse wheel on our view, the `wheelEvent()` virtual function will be called, and the `event` argument will hold information about the event.

In our implementation, we start with calling the base class's implementation. It is very important to do this whenever you reimplement a virtual function, unless you want the default behavior to be completely disabled. In our case, `QGraphicsView::wheelEvent()` will pass the event to the scene, and if we forget to call this function, neither the scene nor any of its items will receive any wheel events, which can be very much unwanted in some cases.

After the default implementation is complete, we use the `isAccepted()` function to check whether an event was accepted by the scene or any items. The event will be rejected by default, but if we later add some item that can process wheel events (for example, a text document with its own scrollbar), it will receive and accept the event. In that case, we don't want to perform any other action based on this event, as it's usually desirable that any event is only processed (and accepted) in one location.

In some cases, you may want your custom implementation to take priority over the default one. In that case, move the call to the default implementation to the end of the function body. When you want to prevent a particular event from being dispatched to the scene, use an early `return` to prevent the default implementation from executing.

The `factor` parameter for the zooming can be freely defined. You can also create a getter and setter method for it. For us, 1.1 will do the work. With `event->angleDelta()`, you get the distance of the mouse's wheel rotation as a `QPoint` pointer. Since we only care about vertical scrolling, just the *y* axis is relevant for us. In our example, we also do not care about how far the wheel was turned because, normally, every step is delivered separately to `wheelEvent()`. However, if you should need it, it's in eighths of a degree, and since most mouses work in general steps of 15 degrees, the value should be 120 or -120, depending on whether you move the wheel forward or backward. On a forward wheel move, if `y()` is greater than zero, we zoom in using the already familiar `scale()` function. Otherwise, if the wheel was moved backward, we zoom out. Finally, we accept the event, indicating that the user's input was understood, and there is no need to propagate the event to parent widgets (although the view currently doesn't have a parent). That's all there is to it.

When you try this example, you will note that, while zooming, the view zooms in and out on the center of the view, which is the default behavior for the view. You can change this behavior with `setTransformationAnchor()`. `QGraphicsView::AnchorViewCenter` is, as described, the default behavior. With `QGraphicsView::NoAnchor`, the zoom center is in the top-left corner of the view, and the value you probably want to use is `QGraphicsView::AnchorUnderMouse`. With that option, the point under the mouse builds the center of the zooming and thus stays at the same position inside the view.

Time for action – Taking the zoom level into account

Our graph currently contains points with integer *x* values because we set `DX = 1`. This is exactly what we want for the default level of zoom, but once the view is zoomed in, it becomes apparent that the graph's line is not smooth. We need to change `DX` based on the current zoom level. We can do this by adding the following code to the beginning of the `paint()` function():

```
const qreal detail =
QStyleOptionGraphicsItem::levelOfDetailFromTransform(
    painter->worldTransform());
const qreal dx = 1 / detail;
```

Delete the DX constant and replace DX with dx in the rest of the code. Now, when you scale the view, the graph's line keeps being smooth because the number of points increases dynamically. The levelOfDetailFromTransform helper function examines the value of the painter's transformation (which is a combination of all transformations applied to the item) and returns the **level of detail**. If the item is zoomed in 2:1, the level of detail is 2, and if the item is zoomed out 1:2, the level of detail is 0.5.

Time for action – Reacting to an item's selection state

Standard items, when selected, change appearance (for example, the outline usually becomes dashed). When we're creating a custom item, we need to implement this feature manually. Let's make our item selectable in the View constructor:

```
SineItem *item = new SineItem();
item->setFlag(QGraphicsItem::ItemIsSelectable);
```

Now, let's make the graph line green when the item is selected:

```
if (option->state & QStyle::State_Selected) {
    pen.setColor(Qt::green);
}
painter->setPen(pen);
```

What just happened?

The state variable is a bitmask holding the possible states of the item. You can check its value against the values of the QStyle::StateFlag parameter using bitwise operators. In the preceding case, the state variable is checked against the State_Selected parameter. If this flag is set, we use green color for the pen.

TIP

The type of state is QFlags<StateFlag>. So, instead of using the bitwise operator to test whether a flag is set, you can use the convenient function testFlag().

Used with the preceding example, it would be as follows:

```
if (option->state.testFlag(QStyle::State_Selected)) {
```

The most important states you can use with items are described in the following table:

State	Description
`State_Enabled`	Indicates that the item is enabled. If the item is disabled, you may want to draw it as grayed out.
`State_HasFocus`	Indicates that the item has the input focus. To receive this state, the item needs to have the `ItemIsFocusable` flag set.
`State_MouseOver`	Indicates that the cursor is currently hovering over the item. To receive this state, the item needs to have the `acceptHoverEvents` variable set to `true`.
`State_Selected`	Indicates that the item is selected. To receive this state, the item needs to have the `ItemIsSelectable` flag set. The normal behavior would be to draw a dashed line around the item as a selection marker.

Besides the state, `QStyleOptionGraphicsItem` offers much more information about the currently used style, such as the palette and the font used, accessible through the `QStyleOptionGraphicsItem::palette` and `QStyleOptionGraphicsItem::fontMetrics` parameters, respectively. If you aim for style-aware items, take a deeper look at this class in the documentation.

Time for action – Event handling in a custom item

Items, like widgets, can receive events in virtual functions. If you click on a scene (to be precise, you click on a view that propagates the event to the scene), the scene receives the mouse press event, and it then becomes the scene's responsibility to determine which item was meant by the click.

Let's override the `SineItem::mousePressEvent` function that is called when the user presses a mouse button inside the item:

```
void SineItem::mousePressEvent(QGraphicsSceneMouseEvent *event)
{
    if (event->button() & Qt::LeftButton) {
        float x = event->pos().x();
        QPointF point(x, sin(x));
        static const float r = 0.3;
        QGraphicsEllipseItem *ellipse =
                new QGraphicsEllipseItem(-r, -r, 2 * r, 2 * r, this);
        ellipse->setPen(Qt::NoPen);
```

```
            ellipse->setBrush(QBrush(Qt::red));
            ellipse->setPos(point);
            event->accept();
        } else {
            event->ignore();
        }
    }
```

When a mouse press event occurs, this function is called and the passed `event` object contains information about the event. In our case, we check whether the left mouse button was pressed and use the `event->pos()` function that returns coordinates of the clicked point *in the item's coordinate system*. In this example, we ignored the *y* coordinate and used the *x* coordinate to find the corresponding point on our graph. Then, we simply created a child circle item that shows that point. We `accept` the event if we did understand the action performed and `ignore` it if we don't know what it means so that it can be passed to another item. You can run the application and click on the graph to see these circles. Note that when you click outside of the graph's bounding rect, the scene doesn't dispatch the event to our item, and its `mousePressEvent()` function is not called.

The `event` object also contains the `button()` function that returns the button that was pressed, and the `scenePos()` function that returns the clicked point in the scene's coordinate system. The scene's responsibility for delivering events does not only apply to mouse events, but also to key events and all other sorts of events.

Time for action – Implementing the ability to create and delete elements with mouse

Let's allow the users to create new instances of our sine item when they click on the view with the left mouse button and delete the items if they use the right mouse button. Reimplement the `View::mousePressEvent` virtual function, as follows:

```
void View::mousePressEvent(QMouseEvent *event)
{
    QGraphicsView::mousePressEvent(event);
    if (event->isAccepted()) {
        return;
    }
    switch (event->button()) {
        case Qt::LeftButton: {
            SineItem *item = new SineItem();
            item->setPos(mapToScene(event->pos()));
```

```
            scene()->addItem(item);
            event->accept();
            break;
        }
        case Qt::RightButton: {
            QGraphicsItem *item = itemAt(event->pos());
            if (item) {
                delete item;
            }
            event->accept();
            break;
        }
        default:
            break;
    }
}
```

Here, we first check whether the event was accepted by the scene or any of its items. If not, we determine which button was pressed. For the left button, we create a new item and place it in the corresponding point of the scene. For the right button, we search for an item at that position and delete it. In both cases, we accept the event. When you run the application, you will note that if the user clicks on an existing item, a new circle will be added, and if the user clicks outside of any items, a new sine item will be added. That's because we properly set and read the `accepted` property of the event.

> TIP: You may note that the scene jumps within the view when we add a new item. This is caused by changes of the scene rect. To prevent this, you can set a constant rect using `setSceneRect()` or change the alignment using `setAlignment(Qt::AlignTop | Qt::AlignLeft)` in the view's constructor.

Time for action – Changing the item's size

Our custom graphics item always displays the graph for *x* values between 0 and 50. It would be neat to make this a configurable setting. Declare a private `float m_maxX` field in the `SineItem` class, remove the `MAX_X` constant, and replace its uses with `m_maxX` in the rest of the code. As always, you must set the initial value of the field in the constructor, or bad things can happen. Finally, implement a getter and a setter for it, as shown:

```
float SineItem::maxX()
{
```

```
    return m_maxX;
}

void SineItem::setMaxX(float value)
{
    if (m_maxX == value) {
        return;
    }
    prepareGeometryChange();
    m_maxX = value;
}
```

The only non-trivial part here is the `prepareGeometryChange()` call. This method is inherited from `QGraphicsItem` and notifies the scene that our `boundingRect()` function will return a different value on the next update. The scene caches bounding rectangles of the items, so if you don't call `prepareGeometryChange()`, the change of the bounding rectangle may not take effect. This action also schedules an update for our item.

TIP

When the bounding rect does not change but the actual content of the item changes, you need to call `update()` on the item to notify the scene that it should repaint the item.

Have a go hero – Extending the item's functionality

The abilities of `SineItem` are still pretty limited. As an exercise, you can try to add an option to change the minimum *x* value of the graph or set a different pen. You can even allow the user to specify an arbitrary function pointer to replace the `sin()` function. However, keep in mind that the bounding rect of the item depends on the value range of the function, so you need to update the item's geometry accurately.

Widgets inside Graphics View

In order to show a neat feature of Graphics View, take a look at the following code snippet, which adds a widget to the scene:

```
QSpinBox *box = new QSpinBox;
QGraphicsProxyWidget *proxyItem = new QGraphicsProxyWidget;
proxyItem->setWidget(box);
```

```
scene()->addItem(proxyItem);
proxyItem->setScale(2);
proxyItem->setRotation(45);
```

First, we create a `QSpinBox` and a `QGraphicsProxyWidget` element, which act as containers for widgets and indirectly inherit `QGraphicsItem`. Then, we add the spin box to the proxy widget by calling `addWidget()`. When `QGraphicsProxyWidget` gets deleted, it calls `delete` on all assigned widgets, so we do not have to worry about that ourselves. The widget you add should be parentless and must not be shown elsewhere. After setting the widget to the proxy, you can treat the proxy widget like any other item. Next, we add it to the scene and apply a transformation for demonstration. As a result, we get this:

Be aware that, originally, Graphics View wasn't designed for holding widgets. So when you add a lot of widgets to the scene, you will quickly notice performance issues, but in most situations, it should be fast enough.

If you want to arrange some widgets in a layout, you can use `QGraphicsAnchorLayout`, `QGraphicsGridLayout`, or `QGraphicsLinearLayout`. Create all widgets, create a layout of your choice, add the widgets to that layout, and set the layout to a `QGraphicsWidget` element, which is the base class for all widgets and is, easily spoken, the `QWidget` equivalent for Graphics View by calling `setLayout()`:

```
QGraphicsProxyWidget *edit = scene()->addWidget(
  new QLineEdit(tr("Some Text")));
QGraphicsProxyWidget *button = scene()->addWidget(
  new QPushButton(tr("Click me!")));
QGraphicsLinearLayout *layout = new QGraphicsLinearLayout;
layout->addItem(edit);
layout->addItem(button);
QGraphicsWidget *graphicsWidget = new QGraphicsWidget;
graphicsWidget->setLayout(layout);
scene()->addItem(graphicsWidget);
```

The scene's `addWidget()` function is a convenience function and behaves similar to `addRect`, as shown in the following code snippet:

```
QGraphicsProxyWidget *proxy = new QGraphicsProxyWidget(0);
```

```
proxy->setWidget(new QLineEdit(QObject::tr("Some Text")));
scene()->addItem(proxy);
```

The item with the layout will look like this:

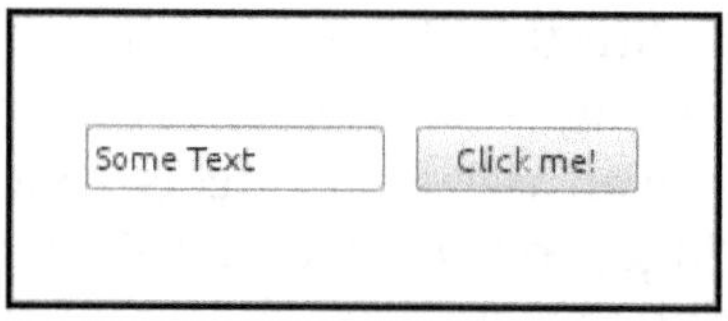

Optimization

When adding many items to a scene or using items with complex `paint()` functions, the performance of your application may decrease. While default optimizations of Graphics View are suitable for most cases, you may need to tweak them to achieve better performance. Let's now take a look at some of the optimizations we can perform to speed up the scene.

A binary space partition tree

The scene constantly keeps a record of the position of the item in its internal binary space partition tree. Thus, on every move of an item, the scene has to update the tree, an operation that can become quite time-consuming, and also memory consuming. This is especially true of scenes with a large number of animated items. On the other hand, the tree enables you to find an item (for example, with `items()` or `itemAt()`) incredibly quickly, even if you have thousands of items.

So when you do not need any positional information about the items—this also includes collision detection—you can disable the index function by calling `setItemIndexMethod(QGraphicsScene::NoIndex)`. Be aware, however, that a call to `items()` or `itemAt()` results in a loop through all items in order to do the collision detection, which can cause performance problems for scenes with many items. If you cannot relinquish the tree in total, you can still adjust the depth of the tree with `setBspTreeDepth()`, taking the depth as an argument. By default, the scene will guess a reasonable value after it takes several parameters, such as the size and the number of items, into account.

Caching the item's paint function

If you have items with a time-consuming paint function, you can change the item's cache mode. By default, no rendering is cached. With `setCacheMode()`, you can set the mode to either `ItemCoordinateCache` or `DeviceCoordinateCache`. The former renders the item in a cache of a given `QSize` element. The size of that cache can be controlled with the second argument of `setCacheMode()`, so the quality depends on how much space you assign. The cache is then used for every subsequent paint call. The cache is even used for applying transformations. If the quality deteriorates too much, just adjust the resolution by calling `setCacheMode()` again, but with a larger `QSize` element. `DeviceCoordinateCache`, on the other hand, does not cache the item on an item base but on a device level. This is, therefore, optimal for items that do not get transformed all the time because every new transformation will cause a new caching. Moving the item, however, does not invalidate the cache. If you use this cache mode, you do not have to define a resolution with the second argument. The caching is always performed at maximum quality.

Optimizing the view

Since we are talking about the item's `paint()` function, let's touch on something related. By default, the view ensures that the painter state is saved before calling the item's paint function and that the state gets restored afterward. This will end up saving and restoring the painter state, say 50 times, if you have a scene with 50 items. However, you can disable this behavior by calling `setOptimizationFlag(DontSavePainterState, true)` on the view. If you do this, it is now your responsibility to ensure that any `paint()` function that changes the state of the painter (including pen, brush, transformation, and many other properties) must restore the previous state at the end. If you prevent automatic saving and restoring, keep in mind that now the standard items will alter the painter state. So if you use both standard and custom items, either stay with the default behavior or set `DontSavePainterState`, but then set up the pen and brush with a default value in each item's paint function.

Another flag that can be used with `setOptimizationFlag()` is `DontAdjustForAntialiasing`. By default, the view adjusts the painting area of each item by two pixels in all directions. This is useful because when one paints anti-aliased, one easily draws outside the bounding rectangle. Enable that optimization if you do not paint anti-aliased or if you are sure that your painting will stay inside the bounding rectangle. If you enable this flag and spot painting artifacts on the view, you haven't respected the item's bounding rectangle!

As a further optimization, you can define how the view should update its viewport when the scene changes. You can set the different modes with `setViewportUpdateMode()`. By default (`QGraphicsView::MinimalViewportUpdate`), the view tries to determine only those areas that need an update and repaints only these. However, sometimes it is more time-consuming to find all the areas that need a redraw than to just paint the entire viewport. This applies if you have many small updates. Then, `QGraphicsView::FullViewportUpdate` is the better choice since it simply repaints the whole viewport. A kind of combination of the last two modes is `QGraphicsView::BoundingRectViewportUpdate`. In this mode, Qt detects all areas that need a redraw, and then it redraws a rectangle of the viewport that covers all areas affected by the change. If the optimal update mode changes over time, you can tell Qt to determine the best mode using `QGraphicsView::SmartViewportUpdate`. The view then tries to find the best update mode.

OpenGL in the Graphics View

As a last optimization, you can take advantage of OpenGL. Instead of using the default viewport based on `QWidget`, advise Graphics View to use an OpenGL widget:

```
QGraphicsView view;
view.setViewport(new QOpenGLWidget());
```

This usually improves the rendering performance. However, Graphics View wasn't designed for GPUs and can't use them effectively. There are ways to improve the situation, but that goes beyond the topic and scope of this chapter. You can find more information about OpenGL and Graphics View in the **Boxes** Qt example as well as in Rødal's article "Accelerate your Widgets with OpenGL", which can be found online at `https://doc.qt.io/archives/qq/qq26-openglcanvas.html`.

If you want to use a framework designed to be GPU accelerated, you should turn your attention to Qt Quick (we will start working with it in `Chapter 11`, *Introduction to Qt Quick*). However, Qt Quick has its own limitations compared to Graphics View. This topic is elaborated in Nichols's article *Should you still be using QGraphicsView?*, available at `https://blog.qt.io/blog/2017/01/19/should-you-be-using-qgraphicsview/`. Alternatively, you can access the full power of OpenGL directly using its API and helpful Qt utilities. We will describe this approach in `Chapter 9`, *OpenGL and Vulkan in Qt applications*.

Unfortunately, we can't say that you have to do this or that to optimize Graphics View as it highly depends on your system and view/scene. What we can tell you, however, is how to proceed. Once you have finished your game based on Graphics View, measure the performance of your game using a profiler. Make an optimization you think may pay or simply guess, and then profile your game again. If the results are better, keep the change, otherwise reject it. This sounds simple and is the only way optimization can be done. There are no hidden tricks or deeper knowledge. With time, however, your forecasting will get better.

Pop quiz

Q1. Which of the following classes is a widget class?

1. `QGraphicsView`
2. `QGraphicsScene`
3. `QGraphicsItem`

Q2. Which of the following actions does not change the graphics item's position on the screen?

1. Scaling the view.
2. Shearing this item's parent item.
3. Translating this item.
4. Rotating this item's child item.

Q3. Which function is not mandatory to implement in a new class derived from `QGraphicsItem`?

1. `boundingRect()`
2. `shape()`
3. `paint()`

Q4. Which item class should be used to display a raster image in the Graphics View?

1. `QGraphicsRectItem`
2. `QGraphicsWidget`
3. `QGraphicsPixmapItem`

Summary

In this chapter, you learned how the Graphics View architecture works. We went through the building blocks of the framework (items, scene, and view). Next, you learned how their coordinate systems are related and how to use them to get the picture you want. Later on, we described the most useful and frequently needed features of Graphics View. Next, we covered creating custom items and handling input events. In order to build a bridge to the world of widgets, you also learned how to incorporate items based on `QWidget` into Graphics View. Finally, we discussed ways to optimize the scene.

Now, you really know most of the functions of the Graphics View framework. With this knowledge, you can already do a lot of cool stuff. However, for a game, it is still too static. In the next chapter, we will go through the process of creating a complete game and learn to use the Animation framework.

5
Animations in Graphics View

The previous chapter gave you a lot of information about powers of Graphics View framework. With that knowledge, we can now proceed to implementing our first 2D game. Down the road, we will learn more about Qt's property system, explore multiple ways of performing animations, and add gamepad support to our application. By the end of the chapter, you will know all the most useful features of Graphics View.

Main topics covered in this chapter are as listed:

- Using timers
- Camera control
- Parallax scrolling
- Qt's property system
- The Animation framework
- Using Qt Gamepad module

The jumping elephant or how to animate the scene

By now, you should have a good understanding of the items, the scene, and the view. With your knowledge of how to create items, standard and custom ones, of how to position them on the scene, and of how to set up the view to show the scene, you can make pretty awesome things. You can even zoom and move the scene with the mouse. That's surely good, but for a game, one crucial point is still missing—you have to animate the items.

Instead of going through all possibilities of how to animate a scene, let's develop a simple jump-and-run game where we recap parts of the previous topics and learn how to animate items on a screen. So let's meet Benjamin, the elephant:

The game play

The goal of the game is for Benjamin to collect the coins that are placed all over the game field. Besides walking right and left, Benjamin can, of course, also jump. In the following screenshot, you see what this minimalistic game should look like at the end:

Time for action - Creating an item for Benjamin

Let's create a new Qt Widgets project and start making our game. Since the project will become more complex than our previous projects, we will not be giving you precise instructions for editing the code. If at any time you are unsure about the changes you make, you can look at the reference implementation provided with the book. It also contains the image files you can use to implement the game.

Let's now look at how we can mobilize Benjamin. First, we need a custom item class for him. We call the `Player` class and choose `QGraphicsPixmapItem` as the base class, because Benjamin is a PNG image. In the item's `Player` class, we further create a private field of integer type and call it `m_direction`. Its value signifies in which direction Benjamin walks—left or right—or if he stands still. Next, we implement the constructor:

```
Player::Player(QGraphicsItem *parent)
    : QGraphicsPixmapItem(parent)
    , m_direction(0)
{
    QPixmap pixmap(":/elephant");
    setPixmap(pixmap);
    setOffset(-pixmap.width() / 2, -pixmap.height() / 2);
}
```

In the constructor, we set `m_direction` to `0`, which means that Benjamin isn't moving at all. If `m_direction` is `1`, Benjamin moves right, and if the value is `-1`, he moves left. In the body of the constructor, we set the image for the item by calling `setPixmap()`. The image of Benjamin is stored in the Qt Resource system; thus, we access it through `QPixmap(":/elephant")`, with elephant as the given alias for the actual image of Benjamin. Finally, we use the `setOffset()` function to change how the pixmap is positioned in the item's coordinate system. By default, the origin point corresponds to the top-left corner of the pixmap, but we prefer to have it at the center of the pixmap so that applying transformations is easier.

TIP: When you are unsure of how to specify the path to your resource, you can ask Qt Creator about it. To do that, expand the **Resources** branch in the project tree, locate the resource, and select the **Copy Path...** entry in its context menu.

Next, we create a getter and setter function for the `m_direction` field:

```
int Player::direction() const {
    return m_direction;
}

void Player::setDirection(int direction)
{
    m_direction = direction;
    if (m_direction != 0) {
        QTransform transform;
        if (m_direction < 0) {
            transform.scale(-1, 1);
        }
```

```
            setTransform(transform);
        }
    }
```

The `direction()` function is a standard getter function for `m_direction` returning its value. The `setDirection()` setter function additionally checks in which direction Benjamin is moving. If he is moving left, we need to flip his image so that Benjamin looks to the left, the direction in which he is moving. If he is moving toward the right, we restore the normal state by assigning an empty `QTransform` object, which is an identity matrix.

> We cannot use `QGraphicsItem::setScale` here, because it only supports the same scale factors for *x* and *y* axes. Fortunately, `setTransform()` enables us to set any affine or perspective transformation.

So, we now have our item of the `Player` class for the game's character, which shows the image of Benjamin. The item also stores the current moving direction, and based on that information, the image is flipped vertically if needed.

The playing field

Since we will have to do some work on the scene, we subclass `QGraphicsScene` and name the new class `MyScene`. There, we implement one part of the game logic. This is convenient since `QGraphicsScene` inherits `QObject` and thus we can use Qt's signal and slot mechanism.

The scene creates the environment in which our elephant will be walking and jumping. Overall, we have a view fixed in size holding a scene, which is exactly as big as the view. We do not take size changes of the view into account, since they will complicate the example too much.

All animations inside the playing field are done by moving the items, not the scene. So we have to distinguish between the view's, or rather the scene's, width and the width of the elephant's virtual "world" in which he can move. In order to handle the movement properly, we need to create a few private fields in the `MyScene` class.

The width of this virtual world is defined by the `int m_fieldWidth` field and has no (direct) correlation with the scene. Within the range of `m_fieldWidth`, which is 500 pixels in the example, Benjamin or the graphics item can be moved from the minimum *x* coordinate, defined by `qreal m_minX`, to the maximum x coordinate, defined by `qreal m_maxX`. We keep track of his actual *x* position with the `qreal m_currentX` variable. Next, the minimum *y* coordinate the item is allowed to have is defined by `qreal m_groundLevel`. We have to also take into account the item's size.

Lastly, what is left is the view, which has a fixed size defined by the scene's bounding rectangle size, which is not as wide as `m_fieldWidth`. So the scene (and the view) follows the elephant while he walks through his virtual world of the `m_fieldWidth` length. Take a look at the following diagram to see the variables in their graphical representation:

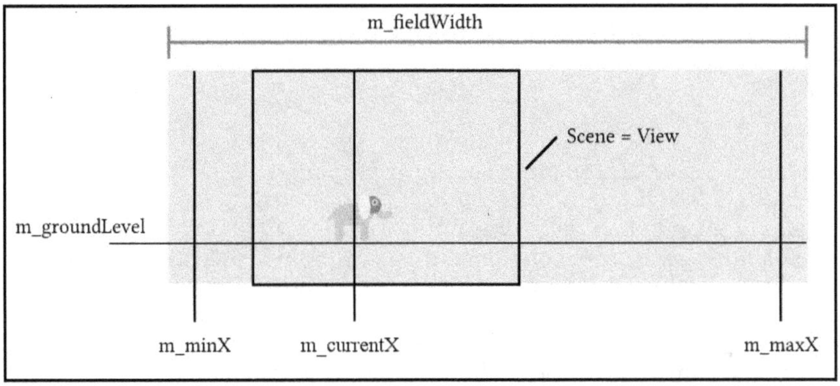

Time for action - Making Benjamin move

The next thing we want to do is make our elephant movable. In order to achieve that, we add a `QTimer m_timer` private member to `MyScene`. `QTimer` is a class that can emit the `timeout()` signal periodically with the given interval. In the `MyScene` constructor, we set up the timer with the following code:

```
m_timer.setInterval(30);
connect(&m_timer, &QTimer::timeout,
        this, &MyScene::movePlayer);
```

First, we define that the timer emits the timeout signal every 30 milliseconds. Then, we connect that signal to the scene's slot called `movePlayer()`, but we do not start the timer yet. The timer will be started when the player presses a key to move.

Next, we need to handle the input events properly and update the player's direction. We introduce the `Player * m_player` field that will contain a pointer to the player object and the `int m_horizontalInput` field that will accumulate the movement commands, as we'll see in the next piece of code. Finally, we reimplement the `keyPressEvent` virtual function:

```
void MyScene::keyPressEvent(QKeyEvent *event)
{
    if (event->isAutoRepeat()) {
        return;
    }
    switch (event->key()) {
    case Qt::Key_Right:
        addHorizontalInput(1);
        break;
    case Qt::Key_Left:
        addHorizontalInput(-1);
        break;
    //...
    }
}
void MyScene::addHorizontalInput(int input)
{
    m_horizontalInput += input;
    m_player->setDirection(qBound(-1, m_horizontalInput, 1));
    checkTimer();
}
```

As a small side note, whenever code snippets in the following code passages are irrelevant for the actual detail, we will skip the code but will indicate missing code with `//...` so that you know that it is not the entire code. We will cover the skipped parts later when it is more appropriate.

What just happened?

In the key press event handler, we first check whether the key event was triggered because of an auto-repeat. If this is the case, we exit the function, because we only want to react on the first real key press event. Also, we do not call the base class implementation of that event handler since no item on the scene needs to get a key press event. If you do have items that could and should receive events, do not forget to forward them while reimplementing event handlers at the scene.

> If you press and hold a key down, Qt will continuously deliver the key press event. To determine whether it was the first real key press or an autogenerated event, use `QKeyEvent::isAutoRepeat()`. It returns `true` if the event was automatically generated.

As soon as we know that the event was not delivered by an auto repeat, we react to the different key presses. Instead of calling the `setDirection()` method of the `Player *m_player` field directly, we use the `m_horizontalInput` class field to accumulate the input value. Whenever it's changed, we ensure the correctness of the value before passing it to `setDirection()`. For that, we use `qBound()`, which returns a value that is bound by the first and the last arguments. The argument in the middle is the actual value that we want to get bound, so the possible values in our case are restricted to -1, 0, and 1.

You might wonder, why not simply call `m_player->setDirection(1)` when the right key is pressed? Why accumulate the inputs in the `m_horizontalInput` variable? Well, Benjamin is moved by the left and right arrow keys. If the right key is pressed, 1 is added; if it gets released, -1 is added. The same applies for the left key, but only the other way around. The addition of the value rather than setting it is now necessary because of a situation where a user presses and holds the right key, and the value of `m_direction` is therefore 1. Now, without releasing the right key, they also press and hold the left key. Therefore, the value of `m_direction` is getting decreased by one; the value is now 0 and Benjamin stops. However, remember that both keys are still being pressed. What happens when the left key is released? How would you know in this situation in which direction Benjamin should move? To achieve that, you would have to find out an additional bit of information—whether the right key is still pressed down or not, which seems too much trouble and overhead. In our implementation, when the left key is released, 1 is added and the value of `m_direction` becomes 1, making Benjamin move right. Voilà! All without any concern about what the state of the other button might be.

After calling `setDirection()`, we call the `checkTimer()` function:

```
void MyScene::checkTimer()
{
    if (m_player->direction() == 0) {
        m_timer.stop();
    } else if (!m_timer.isActive()) {
        m_timer.start();
    }
}
```

This function first checks whether the player moves. If not, the timer is stopped, because nothing has to be updated when our elephant stands still. Otherwise, the timer gets started, but only if it isn't already running. We check this by calling `isActive()` on the timer.

When the user presses the right key, for example, at the beginning of the game, `checkTimer()` will start `m_timer`. Since its `timeout` signal was connected to `movePlayer()`, the slot will be called every 30 milliseconds till the key is released.

Since the `movePlayer()` function is a bit longer, let's go through it step by step:

```
const int direction = m_player->direction();
if (0 == direction) {
    return;
}
```

First, we cache the player's current direction in a local variable to avoid multiple calls of `direction()`. Then, we check whether the player is moving at all. If they aren't, we exit the function because there is nothing to animate:

```
const int dx = direction * m_velocity;
qreal newX = qBound(m_minX, m_currentX + dx, m_maxX);
if (newX == m_currentX) {
    return;
}
m_currentX = newX;
```

Next, we calculate the shift the player item should get and store it in `dx`. The distance the player should move every 30 milliseconds is defined by the `int m_velocity` member variable, expressed in pixels. You can create setter and getter functions for that variable if you like. For us, the default value of 4 pixels will do the job. Multiplied by the direction (which could only be 1 or -1 at this point), we get a shift of the player by 4 pixels to the right or to the left. Based on this shift, we calculate the new *x* position of the player. Next, we check whether that new position is inside the range of `m_minX` and `m_maxX`, two member variables that are already calculated and set up properly at this point. Then, if the new position is not equal to the actual position, which is stored in `m_currentX`, we proceed by assigning the new position as the current one. Otherwise, we exit the function since there is nothing to move.

The next question to tackle is whether the view should always move when the elephant is moving, which means that the elephant would always stay, say, in the middle of the view. No, he shouldn't stay at a specific point inside the view. Rather, the view should be fixed when the elephant is moving. Only if he reaches the borders should the view follow. Let's say that when the distance between the elephant's center and the window's border is less than 150 pixels, we will try to shift the view:

```
const int shiftBorder = 150;
const int rightShiftBorder = width() - shiftBorder;

const int visiblePlayerPos = m_currentX - m_worldShift;
const int newWorldShiftRight = visiblePlayerPos - rightShiftBorder;
if (newWorldShiftRight > 0) {
    m_worldShift += newWorldShiftRight;
}
const int newWorldShiftLeft = shiftBorder - visiblePlayerPos;
if (newWorldShiftLeft > 0) {
    m_worldShift -= newWorldShiftLeft;
}
const int maxWorldShift = m_fieldWidth - qRound(width());
m_worldShift = qBound(0, m_worldShift, maxWorldShift);
m_player->setX(m_currentX - m_worldShift);
```

The `int m_worldShift` class field shows how much we have already shifted our world to the right. First, we calculate the actual coordinate of our elephant in the view and save it to the `visiblePlayerPos` variable. Then, we calculate its position relative to the allowed area defined by the `shiftBorder` and `rightShiftBorder` variables. If `visiblePlayerPos` is beyond the right border of the allowed area, `newWorldShiftRight` will be positive, we need to shift the world by `newWorldShiftRight` to the right. Similarly, when we need to shift it to the left, `newWorldShiftLeft` will be positive, and it will contain the needed amount of shift. Finally, we update the position of `m_player` using a `setX()` helper method that is similar to `setPos()` but leaves the *y* coordinate unchanged.

Note that the value for `shiftBorder` is randomly chosen. You can alter it as you like. Of course, you can create a setter and getter for this parameter too.

The last important part to do here is to apply the new value of `m_worldShift` by setting positions of the other world items. While we're at it, we will implement parallax scrolling.

Parallax scrolling

Parallax scrolling is a trick to add an illusion of depth to the background of the game. This illusion occurs when the background has different layers that move at different speeds. The nearest background must move faster than the ones farther away. In our case, we have these four backgrounds ordered from the most distant to the nearest:

The sky:

The trees:

The grass:

The ground:

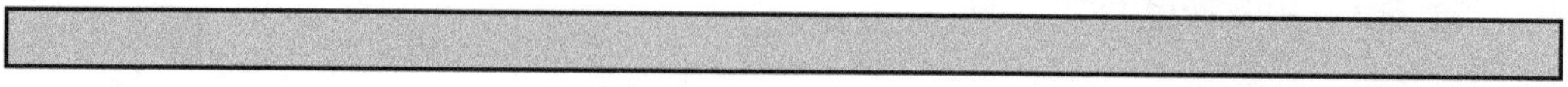

Time for action - Moving the background

The scene will create a graphics item for each part of the background and store pointers to them in the `m_sky`, `m_grass`, and `m_trees` private fields. Now the question is how to move them at different speeds. The solution is quite simple—the slowest one, the sky, is the smallest image. The fastest background, the ground and the grass, are the largest images. Now when we take a look at the end of the `movePlayer()` function's slot, we see this:

```
qreal ratio = qreal(m_worldShift) / maxWorldShift;
applyParallax(ratio, m_sky);
applyParallax(ratio, m_grass);
applyParallax(ratio, m_trees);
```

The `applyParallax()` helper method contains the following code:

```
void MyScene::applyParallax(qreal ratio, QGraphicsItem* item) {
    item->setX(-ratio * (item->boundingRect().width() - width()));
}
```

What just happened?

What are we doing here? At the beginning, the sky's left border is the same as the view's left border, both at point (0, 0). At the end, when Benjamin has walked to the maximum right, the sky's right border should be the same as the view's right border. So, at this position, the shift of the sky will be equal to the sky's width (`m_sky->boundingRect().width()`) minus the width of the view (`width()`). The shift of the sky depends on the position of the camera and, consequently, the value of the `m_worldShift` variable; if it is far to the left, the sky isn't shifted, and if the camera is far to the right, the sky is maximally shifted. Thus, we have to multiply the sky's maximum shift value with a factor based on the current position of the camera. The relation to the camera's position is the reason this is handled in the `movePlayer()` function. The factor we have to calculate has to be between 0 and 1. So we get the minimum shift (`0 * shift`, which equals 0) and the maximum shift (`1 * shift`, which equals `shift`). We name this factor as `ratio`.

How far the world was shifted is saved in `m_worldShift`, so by dividing `m_worldShift` by `maxWorldShift`, we get the needed factor. It is 0 when the player is to the far left and 1 if they are to the far right. Then, we have to simply multiply `ratio` with the maximum shift of the sky.

The same calculation is used for the other background items, so it is moved to a separate function. The calculation also explains why a smaller image is moving slower. It's because the overlap of the smaller image is less than that of the larger one, and since the backgrounds are moved in the same time period, the larger one has to move faster.

Have a go hero - Adding new background layers

Try to add additional background layers to the game, following the preceding example. As an idea, you can add a barn behind the trees or let an airplane fly through the sky.

The Animation framework

For now, we have calculated and applied new positions for our graphics items manually. However, Qt provides a way to do it automatically, called the Animation framework.

The framework is an abstract implementation of animations, so it can be applied to any `QObject`, such as widgets, or even plain variables. Graphics, items can be animated too, and we will get to this topic soon. Animations are not restricted to the object's coordinates. You can animate color, opacity, or a completely invisible property.

To create an animation, you typically need to perform the following steps:

1. Create an animation object (such as `QPropertyAnimation`)
2. Set the object that should be animated
3. Set the name of the property to be animated
4. Define how exactly the value should change (for example, set starting and ending values)
5. Start the animation

As you probably know, calling an arbitrary method by name is not possible in C++, and yet, the animation objects are able to change arbitrary properties at will. This is possible because "property" is not only a fancy name, but also another powerful feature of the `QObject` class and Qt meta-object compiler.

Properties

In `Chapter 3`, *Qt GUI Programming*, we edited predefined properties of widgets in the form editor and used their getter and setter methods in the code. However, until now, there wasn't a real reason for us to declare a new property. It'll be useful with the Animation framework, so let's pay more attention to properties.

Only classes that inherit `QObject` can declare properties. To create a property, we first need to declare it in a private section of the class (usually right after the `Q_OBJECT` mandatory macro) using a special `Q_PROPERTY` macro. That macro allows you to specify the following information about the new property:

- The property name—a string that identifies the property in the Qt meta system.
- The property type—any valid C++ type can be used for a property, but animations will only work with a limited set of types.
- Names of the getter and setter method for this property. If declared in `Q_PROPERTY`, you must add them to your class and implement them properly.
- Name of the signal that is emitted when the property changes. If declared in `Q_PROPERTY`, you must add the signal and ensure that it's properly emitted.

There are more configuration options, but they are less frequently needed. You can learn more about them from the **The Property System** documentation page.

> The Animation framework supports the following property types: `int`, `unsigned int`, `double`, `float`, `QLine`, `QLineF`, `QPoint`, `QPointF`, `QSize`, `QSizeF`, `QRect`, `QRectF`, and `QColor`. Other types are not supported, because Qt doesn't know how to interpolate them, that is, how to calculate intermediate values based on the start and end values. However, it's possible to add support for custom types if you really need to animate them.

Similar to signals and slots, properties are powered by **moc**, which reads the header file of your class and generates extra code that enables Qt (and you) to access the property at runtime. For example, you can use the `QObject::property()` and `QObject::setProperty()` methods to get and set properties by name.

Time for action - Adding a jump animation

Go to the `myscene.h` file and add a private `qreal m_jumpFactor` field. Next, declare a getter, a setter, and a change signal for this field:

```
public:
    //...
    qreal jumpFactor() const;
    void setJumpFactor(const qreal &jumpFactor);
signals:
    void jumpFactorChanged(qreal);
```

In the header file, we declare the `jumpFactor` property by adding the following code just after the `Q_OBJECT` macro:

```
Q_PROPERTY(qreal jumpFactor
           READ jumpFactor
           WRITE setjumpFactor
           NOTIFY jumpFactorChanged)
```

Here, `qreal` is the type of the property, `jumpFactor` is the registered name, and the following three lines register the corresponding member functions of the `MyScene` class in the property system. We'll need this property to make Benjamin jump, as we will see later on.

The `jumpFactor()` getter function simply returns the `m_jumpFactor` private member, which is used to store the actual position. The implementation of the setter looks like this:

```
void MyScene::setjumpFactor(const qreal &pos) {
    if (pos == m_jumpFactor) {
        return;
    }
    m_jumpFactor = pos;
    emit jumpFactorChanged(m_jumpFactor);
}
```

It is important to check whether `pos` will change the current value of `m_jumpFactor`. If this is not the case, exit the function, because we don't want the change signal to be emitted even if nothing has changed. Otherwise, we set `m_jumpFactor` to `pos` and emit the signal that informs about the change.

Property animations

We implemented the horizontal movement using a `QTimer`. Now, let's try a second way to animate items—the Animation framework.

Time for action - Using animations to move items smoothly

Let's add a new private member called `m_jumpAnimation` of the `QPropertyAnimation *` type, and initialize it in the constructor of `MyScene`:

```
m_jumpAnimation = new QPropertyAnimation(this);
m_jumpAnimation->setTargetObject(this);
m_jumpAnimation->setPropertyName("jumpFactor");
m_jumpAnimation->setStartValue(0);
m_jumpAnimation->setKeyValueAt(0.5, 1);
m_jumpAnimation->setEndValue(0);
m_jumpAnimation->setDuration(800);
m_jumpAnimation->setEasingCurve(QEasingCurve::OutInQuad);
```

What just happened?

For the instance of `QPropertyAnimation` created here, we define the item as a parent; thus, the animation will get deleted when the scene deletes the item, and we don't have to worry about freeing the used memory. Then, we define the target of the animation—our `MyScene` class—and the property that should be animated, `jumpFactor`, in this case. Then, we define the start and the end value of that property; in addition to that, we also define a value in between, by setting `setKeyValueAt()`. The first argument of the `qreal` type defines time inside the animation, where 0 is the beginning and 1 the end, and the second argument defines the value that the animation should have at that time. So your `jumpFactor` element will get animated from 0 to 1 and back to 0 in 800 milliseconds. This was defined by `setDuration()`. Finally, we define how the interpolation between the start and end value should be done and call `setEasingCurve()`, with `QEasingCurve::OutInQuad` as an argument.

> Qt defines up to 41 different easing curves for linear, quadratic, cubic, quartic, quintic, sinusoidal, exponential, circular, elastic, back easing, and bounce functions. These are too many to describe here. Instead, take a look at the documentation; simply search for `QEasingCurve::Type`.

In our case, `QEasingCurve::OutInQuad` ensures that the jump speed of Benjamin looks like an actual jump: fast in the beginning, slow at the top, and fast at the end again. We start this animation with the `jump` function:

```
void MyScene::jump()
{
    if (QAbstractAnimation::Stopped == m_jumpAnimation->state()) {
        m_jumpAnimation->start();
    }
}
```

We only start the animation by calling `start()` when the animation isn't running. Therefore, we check the animation's state to see whether it has been stopped. Other states could be `Paused` or `Running`. We want this jump action to be activated whenever the player presses the Space key on their keyboard. Therefore, we expand the `switch` statement inside the key press event handler using this code:

```
case Qt::Key_Space:
    jump();
    break;
```

Now the property gets animated, but Benjamin will still not jump. Therefore, we handle the changes of the `jumpFactor` value at the end of the `setJumpFactor` function:

```
void MyScene::setJumpFactor(const qreal &jumpFactor)
{
    //...
    qreal groundY = (m_groundLevel - m_player->boundingRect().height()
                                                                  / 2);
    qreal y = groundY - m_jumpAnimation->currentValue().toReal() *
                                                     m_jumpHeight;
    m_player->setY(y);
    //...
}
```

When our `QPropertyAnimation` is running, it will call our `setJumpFactor()` function to update the property's value. Inside that function, we calculate the *y* coordinate of the player item to respect the ground level defined by `m_groundLevel`. This is done by subtracting half of the item's height from the ground level's value since the item's origin point is in its center. Then, we subtract the maximum jump height, defined by `m_jumpHeight`, which is multiplied by the actual jump factor. Since the factor is in the range of 0 and 1, the new *y* coordinate stays inside the allowed jump height. Then, we alter the player item's *y* position by calling `setY()`, leaving the *x* coordinate as the same. Et voilà, Benjamin is jumping!

Have a go hero - Letting the item handle Benjamin's jump

Since the scene is already a `QObject`, adding a property to it was easy. However, imagine that you want to create a game for two players, each controlling a separate `Player` item. In this case, the jump factors of two elephants need to be animated independently, so you want to make an animated property in the `Player` class, instead of putting it to the scene.

The `QGraphicsItem` item and all standard items introduced so far don't inherit `QObject` and thus can't have slots or emit signals; they don't benefit from the `QObject` property system either. However, we can make them use `QObject`! All you have to do is add `QObject` as a base class and add the `Q_OBJECT` macro:

```
class Player : public QObject, public QGraphicsPixmapItem {
    Q_OBJECT
//...
};
```

Now you can use properties, signals, and slots with items too. Be aware that `QObject` must be the first base class of an item.

> **A word of warning**
> Only use `QObject` with items if you really need its capabilities. `QObject`
> adds a lot of overhead to the item, which will have a noticeable impact on performance when you have many items, so use it wisely and not only because you can.

If you make this change, you can move the jumpFactor property from MyScene to Player, along with a lot of related code. You can make the code even more consistent by handling the horizontal movement in Player as well. Let MyScene handle the input events and forward the movement commands to Player.

Time for action - Keeping multiple animations in sync

Now we'll start implementing the coin class. We can use a simple QGraphicsEllipseItem object, but we'll need to animate its properties, so let's create a new Coin class and derive it from QObject and QGraphicsEllipseItem. Define two properties: opacity of the qreal type and rect of the QRect type. This is done only by the following code:

```
class Coin : public QObject, public QGraphicsEllipseItem
{
    Q_OBJECT
    Q_PROPERTY(qreal opacity READ opacity WRITE setOpacity)
    Q_PROPERTY(QRectF rect READ rect WRITE setRect)
//...
};
```

No function or slot was added, because we simply used built-in functions of QGraphicsItem and associated them with the properties.

> **TIP:** If you want an item that inherits from QObject and QGraphicsItem, you can directly inherit QGraphicsObject. Moreover, it already registers all general QGraphicsItem properties in the metasystem, including pos, scale, rotation, and opacity. All properties come with corresponding notification signals, such as opacityChanged(). However, when you inherit QGraphicsObject, you cannot, at the same time, inherit QGraphicsEllipseItem or any other item class. So in this case, we will need to either implement painting of the ellipse manually or add a child QGraphicsEllipseItem that can perform the painting for us.

Next, we'll create the explode() function that will start some animations when the player collects the coin. Create a Boolean private field in the class and use it to ensure that each coin can only explode once:

```
void Coin::explode()
{
    if (m_explosion) {
        return;
    }
    m_explosion = true;
    //...
}
```

We want to animate our two properties by two `QPropertyAnimation` objects. One fades the coin out, while the other scales the coin in. To ensure that both animations get started at the same time, we use `QParallelAnimationGroup`, as follows:

```
QPropertyAnimation *fadeAnimation =
    new QPropertyAnimation(this, "opacity");
//...
QPropertyAnimation *scaleAnimation = new QPropertyAnimation(this,
"rect");
//...
QParallelAnimationGroup *group = new QParallelAnimationGroup(this);
group->addAnimation(scaleAnimation);
group->addAnimation(fadeAnimation);
connect(group, &QParallelAnimationGroup::finished,
        this,  &Coin::deleteLater);
group->start();
```

What just happened?

You already know how to set up a single property animation, so we omitted the code for it. After setting up both animations, we add them to the group animation by calling `addAnimation()` on the group, while passing a pointer to the animation we would like to add. Then, when we start the group; `QParallelAnimationGroup` ensures that all assigned animations start at the same time.

When both animations have finished, `group` will emit the `finished()` signal. We connected that signal to the `deleteLater()` slot of our class so that the coin object gets deleted when it's no longer visible. This handy slot is declared in the `QObject` class and is useful in many cases.

> **TIP**
> In some cases, you may want to stop an animation. You can do that by calling the `stop()` method. It's also possible to pause and resume an animation using `pause()` and `resume()`. Using these methods on a `QParallelAnimationGroup` will affect all transformations added to that group.

Chaining multiple animations

What if we wanted to perform an animation at the end of another animation? We could connect the `finished()` signal of the first animation to the `start()` slot of the second one. However, a much more convenient solution is to use `QSequentialAnimationGroup`. For example, if we want coins to scale and *then* to fade, the following code will do the trick:

```
QSequentialAnimationGroup *group = new
QSequentialAnimationGroup(this);
group->addAnimation(scaleAnimation);
group->addAnimation(fadeAnimation);
group->start();
```

Adding gamepad support

The player can use the keyboard to play our game, but it would be nice to also allow playing it using a gamepad. Fortunately, Qt provides the Qt Gamepad add-on that allows us to do this easily. As opposed to Qt Essentials (for example, Qt Widgets), add-ons may be supported on a limited number of platforms. As of Qt 5.9, Qt Gamepad supports Windows, Linux, Android, macOS, iOS, and tvOS (including the tvOS remote).

Working with gamepads in Qt

The starting point of the gamepad API is the `QGamepadManager` class. The singleton object of this class can be obtained using the `QGamepadManager::instance()` function. It allows you to request the list of identifiers of the available gamepads using the `connectedGamepads()` function. The `gamepadConnected()` signal can be used to detect new gamepads on the fly. `QGamepadManager` also provides API for configuring buttons and axes on the gamepad and is able to save the configuration to the specified settings file.

After you detected that one or multiple gamepads are available in the system, you should create a new `QGamepad` object and pass the obtained device identifier as a constructor's argument. You can use the first available gamepad or allow the user to select which gamepad to use. In this case, you can utilize the gamepad's `name` property that returns a readable name of the device.

The `Gamepad` object contains a dedicated property for each axis and button. This gives you two ways to receive the information about the state of the controls. First, you can use the getter of the property to check the current state of a button or an axis. For example, the `buttonL1()` function will return `true` if the L1 button is currently pressed, and the `axisLeftX()` will return the current horizontal position of the left stick as a `double` value that is in the range of -1 to 1. For trigger buttons (for example, `buttonL2()`), the property contains a `double` value that ranges from 0 (not pressed) to 1 (fully pressed).

The second way is to use the signals corresponding to each property. For example, you can connect to the gamepad's `buttonL1Changed(bool value)` and `axisLeftXChanged(double value)` signals to monitor the changes of the corresponding properties.

Finally, the `QGamepadKeyNavigation` class can be used to quickly add gamepad support to a keyboard-oriented application. When you create an object of this class, your application will begin receiving key events caused by gamepads. By default, `GamepadKeyNavigation` will emulate up, down, left, right, back, forward, and return keys when the corresponding gamepad buttons are pressed. However, you can override the default mapping or add your own mapping for other gamepad buttons.

Time for action - Handling gamepad events

Let's start with adding the Qt Gamepad add-on to our project by editing the `jrgame.pro` file:

```
QT += core gui widgets gamepad
```

This will make the headers of the library available to our project and tell `qmake` to link the project against this library. Now add the following code to the constructor of the `MyScene` class:

```
QList<int> gamepadIds =
QGamepadManager::instance()->connectedGamepads();
if (!gamepadIds.isEmpty()) {
    QGamepad *gamepad = new QGamepad(gamepadIds[0], this);
    connect(gamepad, &QGamepad::axisLeftXChanged,
            this, &MyScene::axisLeftXChanged);
    connect(gamepad, &QGamepad::axisLeftYChanged,
            this, &MyScene::axisLeftYChanged);
}
```

The code is pretty straightforward. First, we use `QGamepadManager::connectedGamepads` to get the list of IDs of the available gamepads. If some gamepads were found, we create a `QGamepad` object for the first found gamepad. We pass `this` to its constructor, so it becomes a child of our `MyScene` object, and we don't need to worry about deleting it. Finally, we connect the gamepad's `axisLeftXChanged()` and `axisLeftYChanged()` signals to new slots in the `MyScene` class. Now, let's implement these slots:

```
void MyScene::axisLeftXChanged(double value)
{
    int direction;
    if (value > 0) {
        direction = 1;
    } else if (value < 0) {
        direction = -1;
    } else {
        direction = 0;
    }
    m_player->setDirection(direction);
    checkTimer();
}

void MyScene::axisLeftYChanged(double value)
{
    if (value < -0.25) {
        jump();
    }
}
```

The `value` argument of the signals contains a number from -1 to 1. It allows us not only to detect whether a thumbstick was pressed, but also to get more precise information
about its position. However, in our simple game, we don't need this precision.
In the `axisLeftXChanged()` slot, we calculate and set the
elephant's `direction` based on the sign of the received value.
In the `axisLeftYChanged()` slot, if we receive a large enough negative value, we interpret it as a `jump` command. This will help us avoid accidental jumps. That's all! Our game now supports both keyboards and gamepads.

> **TIP:** If you need to react to other buttons and thumbsticks of the gamepad, use the other signals of the `QGamepad` class. It's also possible to read multiple gamepads at the same time by creating multiple `QGamepad` objects with different IDs.

Item collision detection

Whether the player item collides with a coin is checked by the scene's `checkColliding()` function, which is called after the player item has moved horizontally or vertically.

Time for action - Making the coins explode

The implementation of `checkColliding()` looks like this:

```
void MyScene::checkColliding()
{
    for(QGraphicsItem* item: collidingItems(m_player)) {
        if (Coin *c = qgraphicsitem_cast<Coin*>(item)) {
            c->explode();
        }
    }
}
```

What just happened?

First, we call the scene's `QGraphicsScene::collidingItems()` function, which takes the item for which colliding items should be detected as a first argument. With the second, optional argument, you can define how the collision should be detected. The type of that argument is `Qt::ItemSelectionMode`, which was explained earlier. By default, an item will be considered colliding with `m_player` if the shapes of the two items intersect.

Next, we loop through the list of found items and check whether the current item is a `Coin` object. This is done by trying to cast the pointer to `Coin`. If it is successful, we explode the coin by calling `explode()`. Calling the `explode()` function multiple times is no problem, since it will not allow more than one explosion. This is important since `checkColliding()` will be called after each movement of the player. So the first time the player hits a coin, the coin will explode, but this takes time. During this explosion, the player will most likely be moved again and thus collides with the coin once more. In such a case, `explode()` may be called multiple times.

The `qgraphicsitem_cast<>()` is a faster alternative to `dynamic_cast<>()`. However, it will properly work for custom types only if they implement `type()` properly. This virtual function must return a different value for each custom item class in the application.

The `collidingItems()` function will always return the background items as well, since the player item is above all of them most of the time. To avoid the continuous check if they actually are coins, we use a trick. Instead of using `QGraphicsPixmapItem` directly, we subclass it and reimplement its virtual `shape()` function, as follows:

```
QPainterPath BackgroundItem::shape() const {
  return QPainterPath();
}
```

We already used the `QPainterPath` class in the previous chapter. This function just returns an empty `QPainterPath`. Since the collision detection is done with the item's shape, the background items can't collide with any other item since their shape is permanently empty. Don't try this trick with `boundingRect()` though, because it must always be valid.

Had we done the jumping logic inside `Player`, we could have implemented the item collision detection from within the item itself. `QGraphicsItem` also offers a `collidingItems()` function that checks against colliding items with itself. So `scene->collidingItems(item)` is equivalent to `item->collidingItems()`.

TIP: If you are only interested in whether an item collides with another item, you can call `collidesWithItem()` on the item, passing the other item as an argument.

Finishing the game

The last part we have to discuss is the scene's initialization. Set the initial values for all fields and the constructor, create the `initPlayField()` function that will set up all the items, and call that function in the constructor. First, we initialize the sky, trees, ground, and player item:

```
void MyScene::initPlayField()
{
    setSceneRect(0, 0, 500, 340);
```

```
    m_sky = new BackgroundItem(QPixmap(":/sky"));
    addItem(m_sky);
    BackgroundItem *ground = new BackgroundItem(QPixmap(":/ground"));
    addItem(ground);
    ground->setPos(0, m_groundLevel);
    m_trees = new BackgroundItem(QPixmap(":/trees"));
    m_trees->setPos(0, m_groundLevel -
m_trees->boundingRect().height());
    addItem(m_trees);
    m_grass = new BackgroundItem(QPixmap(":/grass"));
    m_grass->setPos(0,m_groundLevel -
m_grass->boundingRect().height());
    addItem(m_grass);
    m_player = new Player();
    m_minX = m_player->boundingRect().width() * 0.5;
    m_maxX = m_fieldWidth - m_player->boundingRect().width() * 0.5;
    m_player->setPos(m_minX, m_groundLevel -
m_player->boundingRect().height() / 2);
    m_currentX = m_minX;
    addItem(m_player);
    //...
}
```

Next, we create coin objects:

```
m_coins = new QGraphicsRectItem(0, 0, m_fieldWidth, m_jumpHeight);
m_coins->setPen(Qt::NoPen);
m_coins->setPos(0, m_groundLevel - m_jumpHeight);
const int xRange = (m_maxX - m_minX) * 0.94;
for (int i = 0; i < 25; ++i) {
    Coin *c = new Coin(m_coins);
    c->setPos(m_minX + qrand() % xRange, qrand() % m_jumpHeight);
}
addItem(m_coins);
```

In total, we are adding 25 coins. First, we set up an invisible item with the size of the virtual world, called `m_coins`. This item should be the parent to all coins. Then, we calculate the width between `m_minX` and `m_maxX`. That is the space where Benjamin can move. To make it a little bit smaller, we only take 94 percent of that width. Then, in the `for` loop, we create a coin and randomly set its *x* and *y* position, ensuring that Benjamin can reach them by calculating the modulo of the available width and of the maximal jump height. After all 25 coins are added, we place the parent item holding all the coins on the scene. Since most coins are outside the actual view's rectangle, we also need to move the coins while Benjamin is moving.

Therefore, `m_coins` must behave like any other background. For this, we simply add the following code to the `movePlayer()` function, where we also move the background by the same pattern:

```
applyParallax(ratio, m_coins);
```

Have a go hero - Extending the game

That's it. This is our little game. Of course, there is much room to improve and extend it. For example, you can add some barricades Benjamin has to jump over. Then, you would have to check whether the player item collides with such a barricade item when moving forward, and if so, refuse movement. You have learned all the necessary techniques you need for that task, so try to implement some additional features to deepen your knowledge.

A third way of animation

Besides `QTimer` and `QPropertyAnimation`, there is a third way to animate the scene. The scene provides a slot called `advance()`. If you call that slot, the scene will forward that call to all items it holds by calling `advance()` on each one. The scene does that twice. First, all item `advance()` functions are called with `0` as an argument. This means that the items are about to advance. Then, in the second round, all items are called passing 1 to the item's `advance()` function. In that phase, each item should advance, whatever that means—maybe moving, maybe a color change, and so on. The scene's slot advance is typically called by a `QTimeLine` element; with this, you can define how many times during a specific period of time the timeline should be triggered.

```
QTimeLine *timeLine = new QTimeLine(5000, this);
timeLine->setFrameRange(0, 10);
```

This timeline will emit the `frameChanged()` signal every 5 seconds for 10 times. All you have to do is connect that signal to the scene's `advance()` slot, and the scene will advance 10 times in 50 seconds. However, since all items receive two calls for each advance, this may not be the best animation solution for scenes with a lot of items where only a few should advance.

Pop quiz

Q1. Which of the following is a requirement for animating a property?

1. The name of the property must start with "`m_`".
2. Getter and setter of the property must be slots.
3. The property must be declared using the `Q_PROPERTY` macro.

Q2. Which class sends a signal when a gamepad button is pressed or released?

1. `QGamepad`
2. `QWidget`
3. `QGraphicsScene`

Q3. What is the difference between the `shape()` and `boundingRect()` functions of `QGraphicsItem`?

1. `shape()` returns the bounding rectangle as a `QPainterPath` instead of a `QRectF`
2. `shape()` causes the item to be repainted.
3. `share()` can return a more precise description of the item's boundaries than `boundingRect()`

Summary

In this chapter, you deepened your knowledge about items, about the scene, and about the view. While developing the game, you became familiar with different approaches of how to animate items, and you were taught how to detect collisions. As an advanced topic, you were introduced to parallax scrolling.

After having completed the two chapters describing Graphics View, you should now know almost everything about it. You are able to create complete custom items, you can alter or extend standard items, and with the information about the level of detail, you even have the power to alter an item's appearance, depending on its zoom level. You can transform items and the scene, and you can animate items and thus the entire scene.

Furthermore, as you saw while developing the game, your skills are good enough to develop a jump-and-run game with parallax scrolling, as it is used in highly professional games. We also learned how to add gamepad support to our game. To keep it fluid and highly responsive, finally we saw some tricks on how to get the most out of Graphics View.

When we worked with widgets and the Graphics View framework, we had to use some general purpose Qt types, such as `QString` or `QVector`. In simple cases, their API is pretty obvious. However, these and many other classes provided by Qt Core module are very powerful, and you will greatly benefit from deeper knowledge of them. When you develop a serious project, it's very important to understand how these basic types work and what dangers they may pose when used incorrectly. In the next chapter, we will turn our attention to this topic. You will learn how you can work with text in Qt, which containers you should use in different cases, and how to manipulate various kind of data and implement a persistent storage. This is essential for any game that is more complicated than our simple examples.

6
Qt Core Essentials

This chapter will help you master Qt ways of basic data processing and storage. First of all, you will learn how to handle textual data and how to match text against regular expressions. Next, we will provide an overview of Qt containers and describe common pitfalls related to them. Then, you will see how to store and fetch data from files and how to use different storage formats for text and binary data. By the end of this chapter, you will be able to implement non-trivial logic and data processing in your games efficiently. You will also know how to load external data in your games and how to save your own data in permanent storage for future use.

Main topics covered in this chapter:

- Text handling
- Qt containers
- Serialization to INI, JSON, XML, and binary data
- Saving the application's settings

Text handling

Applications with a graphical user interface (and games surely fall into this category) are able to interact with users by displaying text and by expecting textual input from the user. We have already scratched the surface of this topic in the previous chapters using the `QString` class. Now, we will go into further detail.

String encodings

The C++ language does not specify encoding of strings. Thus, any `char*` array and any `std::string` object can use an arbitrary encoding. When using these types for interaction with native APIs and third-party libraries, you have to refer to their documentation to find out which encoding they use. The encoding used by native APIs of the operating system usually depends on the current locale. Third-party libraries often use the same encoding as native APIs, but some libraries may expect another encoding, for example, UTF-8.

A string literal (that is, each bare text you wrap in quotation marks) will use an implementation defined encoding. Since C++11, you have an option to specify the encoding your text will have:

- `u8"text"` will produce a UTF-8 encoded `const char[]` array
- `u"text"` will produce a UTF-16 encoded `const char16_t[]` array
- `U"text"` will produce a UTF-32 encoded `const char32_t[]` array

Unfortunately, the encoding used for interpreting the source files is still implementation defined, so it's not safe to put non-ASCII symbols in string literals. You should use escape sequences (such as `\unnnn`) to write such literals.

Text in Qt is stored using the `QString` class that uses Unicode internally. Unicode allows us to represent characters in almost all languages spoken in the world and is the de facto standard for native encoding of text in most modern operating systems. There are multiple Unicode-based encodings. Memory representation of the content of `QString` resembles UTF-16 encoding. Basically, it consists of an array of 16-bit values where each Unicode character is represented by either 1 or 2 values.

When constructing a `QString` from a `char` array or an `std::string` object, it's important to use a proper conversion method that depends on the initial encoding of the text. By default, `QString` assumes UTF-8 encoding of the input text. UTF-8 is compatible with ASCII, so passing UTF-8 or ASCII-only text to `QString(const char *str)` is correct. `QString` provides a number of static methods to convert from other encodings such as `QString::fromLatin1()` or `QString::fromUtf16()`. `QString::fromLocal8Bit()` method assumes the encoding corresponding to the system locale.

If you have to combine both `QString` and `std::string` in one program, `QString` offers you the `toStdString()` and `fromStdString()` methods to perform a conversion. These methods also assume UTF-8 encoding of `std::string`, so you can't use them if your strings are in another encoding.

Default representation of string literals (for example, `"text"`) is not UTF-16, so each time you convert it to a `QString`, an allocation and conversion happens. This overhead can be avoided using the `QStringLiteral` macro:

```
QString str = QStringLiteral("I'm writing my games using Qt");
```

`QStringLiteral` does two things:

- It adds a `u` prefix to your string literal to ensure that it will be encoded in UTF-16 at compile time
- It cheaply creates a `QString` and instructs it to use the literal without performing any allocation or encoding conversion

It's a good habit to wrap all your string literals (except the ones that need to be translated) into `QStringLiteral` but it is not required, so don't worry if you forget to do that.

QByteArray and QString

`QString` always contains UTF-16 encoded strings, but what if you have data in an unknown (yet) encoding? Also, what if the data is not even text? In these cases, Qt uses the `QByteArray` class. When you read data directly from a file or receive it from a network socket, Qt will return the data as a `QByteArray`, indicating that this is an arbitrary array of bytes without any information about the encoding:

```
QFile file("/path/to/file");
file.open(QFile::ReadOnly);
QByteArray array = file.readAll();
```

The closest equivalent of `QByteArray` in the standard library would be `std::vector<char>`. As the name implies, this is just an array of bytes with some helpful methods. In the preceding example, if you know that the file you read is in UTF-8, you can convert the data to a string, as follows:

```
QString text = QString::fromUtf8(array);
```

If you have no idea what encoding the file uses, it may be best to use the system encoding, so `QString::fromLocal8Bit` would be better. Similarly, when writing to a file, you need to convert the string to a byte array before passing it to the `write()` function:

```
QString text = "new file content\n";
QFile file("/path/to/file");
file.open(QFile::WriteOnly);
QByteArray array = text.toUtf8();
file.write(array);
```

You can use `file.close()` to close the file. `QFile` will also automatically close the file when deleted, so if your `QFile` object goes out of scope immediately after you've finished working with the file, there is no need for an explicit `close()` call.

Using other encodings

As we've already mentioned, `QString` has convenient methods for decoding and encoding data in the most popular encodings, such as UTF-8, UTF-16, and Latin1. However, Qt knows how to handle many other encodings as well. You can access them using the `QTextCodec` class. For example, if you have a file in Big-5 encoding, you can ask Qt for a codec object by its name and make use of the `fromUnicode()` and `toUnicode()` methods:

```
QByteArray big5Encoded = big5EncodedFile.readAll();
QTextCodec *big5Codec = QTextCodec::codecForName("Big5");
QString text = big5Codec->toUnicode(big5Encoded);
QByteArray big5EncodedBack = big5Codec->fromUnicode(text);
```

TIP

You can list the codecs supported on your installation using the `QTextCodec::availableCodecs()` static method. In most installations, Qt can handle almost 1,000 different text codecs.

Basic string operations

The most basic tasks that involve text strings are the ones where you add or remove characters from the string, concatenate strings, and access the string's content. In this regard, `QString` offers an interface that is compatible with `std::string`, but it also goes beyond that, exposing many more useful methods.

Adding data at the beginning or at the end of the string can be done using the `prepend()` and `append()` methods. Inserting data in the middle of a string can be done with the `insert()` method that takes the position of the character where we need to start inserting as its first argument and the actual text as its second argument. All these methods have a couple of overloads that accept different objects that can hold textual data, including the classic `const char*` array.

Removing characters from a string is similar. The basic way to do this is to use the `remove()` method that accepts the position at which we need to delete characters, and the number of characters to delete is as shown:

```
QString str = QStringLiteral("abcdefghij");
str.remove(2, 4); // str = "abghij"
```

There is also a `remove()` overload that accepts another string. When called, all its occurrences are removed from the original string. This overload has an optional argument that states whether comparison should be done in the default case-sensitive (`Qt::CaseSensitive`) or case-insensitive (`Qt::CaseInsensitive`) way:

```
QString str = QStringLiteral("Abracadabra");
str.remove(QStringLiteral("ab"), Qt::CaseInsensitive);
// str = "racadra"
```

To concatenate strings, you can either simply add two strings together, or you can append one string to the other:

```
QString str1 = QStringLiteral("abc");
QString str2 = QStringLiteral("def");
QString str1_2 = str1 + str2;
QString str2_1 = str2;
str2_1.append(str1);
```

Accessing strings can be divided into two use cases. The first is when you wish to extract a part of the string. For this, you can use one of these three methods—`left()`, `right()`, and `mid()`—that return the given number of characters from the beginning or end of the string or extract a substring of a specified length, starting from a given position in the string:

```
QString original = QStringLiteral("abcdefghij");
QString l = original.left(3); // "abc"
QString r = original.right(2); // "ij"
QString m = original.mid(2, 5); // "cdefg"
```

The second use case is when you wish to access a single character of the string. The use of the index operator works with `QString` in a similar fashion as with `std::string`, returning a copy or non-const reference to a given character that is represented by the `QChar` class, as shown in the following code:

```
QString str = "foo";
QChar f = str[0]; // const
str[0] = 'g'; // non-const
```

In addition to this, Qt offers a dedicated method—`at()`—that returns a copy of the character:

```
QChar f = str.at(0);
```

TIP: You should prefer to use `at()` instead of the index operator for operations that do not modify the character, as this explicitly uses a constant method.

The string search and lookup

The second group of functionalities is related to searching for the string. You can use methods such as `startsWith()`, `endsWith()`, and `contains()` to search for substrings in the beginning or end or in an arbitrary place in the string. The number of occurrences of a substring in the string can be retrieved using the `count()` method.

TIP: Be careful, there is also a `count()` method that doesn't take any parameters and returns the number of characters in the string.

If you need to know the exact position of the match, you can use `indexOf()` or `lastIndexOf()` to receive the position in the string where the match occurs. The first call works by searching forward, and the other one searches backwards. Each of these calls takes two optional parameters—the second one determines whether the search is case-sensitive (similar to how `remove` works). The first one is the position in the string where the search begins. It lets you find all the occurrences of a given substring:

```
int pos = -1;
QString str = QStringLiteral("Orangutans like bananas.");
do {
```

```
    pos = str.indexOf("an", pos + 1);
    qDebug() << "'an' found starts at position" << pos;
} while(pos != -1);
```

Dissecting strings

There is one more group of useful string functionalities that makes `QString` different from `std::string`, that is, cutting strings into smaller parts and building larger strings from smaller pieces.

Very often, a string contains substrings that are glued together by a repeating separator (for example, `"1,4,8,15"`). While you can extract each field from the record using functions that you already know (for example, `indexOf`), an easier way exists. `QString` contains a `split()` method that takes the separator string as its parameter and returns a list of strings that are represented in Qt by the `QStringList` class. Then, dissecting the record into separate fields is as easy as calling the following code:

```
QString record = "1,4,8,15,16,24,42";
QStringList items = record.split(",");
for(const QString& item: items) {
    qDebug() << item;
}
```

The inverse of this method is the `join()` method present in the `QStringList` class, which returns all the items in the list as a single string merged with a given separator:

```
QStringList fields = { "1", "4", "8", "15", "16", "24", "42" };
QString record = fields.join(",");
```

Converting between numbers and strings

`QString` also provides some methods for convenient conversion between textual and numerical values. Methods such as `toInt()`, `toDouble()`, or `toLongLong()` make it easy to extract numerical values from strings. All such methods take an optional `bool *ok` parameter. If you pass a pointer to a `bool` variable as this parameter, the variable will be set to `true` or `false`, depending on whether the conversion was successful or not. Methods returning integers also take the second optional parameter that specifies the numerical base (for example, binary, octal, decimal, or hexadecimal) of the value:

```
bool ok;
int v1 = QString("42").toInt(&ok, 10);
```

```
// v1 = 42, ok = true
long long v2 = QString("0xFFFFFF").toInt(&ok, 16);
// v2 = 16777215, ok = true
double v3 = QString("not really a number").toDouble(&ok);
//v3 = 0.0, ok = false
```

A static method called `number()` performs the conversion in the other direction—it takes a numerical value and number base and returns the textual representation of the value:

```
QString txt = QString::number(42); // txt = "42"
```

This function has some optional arguments that allow you to control the string representation of the number. For integers, you can specify the numerical base. For doubles, you can choose the scientific format `'e'` or the conventional format `'f'` and specify the number of digits after the decimal delimiter:

```
QString s1 = QString::number(42, 16); // "2a"
QString s2 = QString::number(42.0, 'f', 6); // "42.000000"
QString s3 = QString::number(42.0, 'e', 6); // "4.200000e+1"
```

TIP

Some of the other classes that represent values also provide conversions to and from `QString`. An example of such a class is `QDate`, which represents a date and provides the `fromString()` and `toString()` methods.

These methods are nice and easy to use for technical purposes, for example, for reading and writing numbers to configuration files. However, they are not suitable when you need to display a number to the user or parse a user input because numbers are written differently in different countries. This brings us to the topic of *internationalization*.

Internationalization

Most real projects have a target audience in multiple countries. The most notable difference between them is the spoken language, but there are other aspects some developers may not think of. For example, dot `"."` and comma `","` are both fairly common as the decimal separator throughout the world. Date formats are also very different and incompatible, and using a wrong format (for example, `mm/dd/yyyy` instead of `dd/mm/yyyy`) will result in a completely different date.

Qt provides the `QLocale` class for dealing with locale-dependent operations, including conversions between numbers in strings. In the following code, `text` and `number` may have different values, depending on the system locale:

```
QLocale locale = QLocale::system();
QString text = locale.toString(1.2);
double number = locale.toDouble(QStringLiteral("1,2"));
```

`QLocale` also provides methods for formatting dates and prices, and allows us to request additional information about local conventions.

As for translations, we've already mentioned that any text visible to users should be wrapped in a `tr()` function. Now we will explain this requirement.

Qt's translation system makes it possible for developing and translation teams to work independently. The project goes through the following steps:

1. Developers create an application and wrap all text that should be translated in special translation functions (such as `tr()`). Visible text in forms is automatically wrapped in translation functions.
2. A special Qt tool (**lupdate**) searches for all strings wrapped in translation functions and generates a translation file (`.ts`).
3. Translators open this file in a special application called **Qt Linguist**. In that application, they are able to see all strings grouped by *context*, which is usually the class this text belongs to. They can add translations and save them in the translation file.
4. When this new translation file is copied back to the project and applied using the `QCoreApplication::installTranslator` function, the translation functions start returning translated text instead of simply returning the argument.
5. As the application evolves and a new untranslated text appears, it's shown untranslated by default. However, it can be automatically added to translation files, and translators can add new translations for new content, without losing the existing translations.

We will not go into the details of this process. As a developer, you only need to ensure that all visible strings are wrapped in a translation function and a proper context is provided. The context is necessary because a short text (for example, one word on a button) may not be enough to understand the meaning and provide a proper translation, but how do we specify the context?

The main translation function is `QCoreApplication::translate()`. It accepts three arguments: the context, the text to translate, and an optional disambiguation text. The disambiguation argument is rarely needed. It can be used to distinguish between multiple instances of the same text in the same context and when they should have different translations.

Instead of `QCoreApplication::translate()`, you should usually use the `tr()` function, which is declared in each class that inherits `QObject`. `MyClass::tr(text, disambiguation)` is a shortcut for `QCoreApplication::translate("MyClass", text, disambiguation)`. Due to this, all translatable texts located in one class will share the same `context` string, so they will be grouped in Qt Linguist to make the translator's job easier.

If you have a translatable text outside of a subclass of `QObject`, the `tr()` function will not be available by default. In this case, you have the following options:

- Use the `QCoreApplication::translate()` function and write the `context` argument explicitly
- Reuse the `tr()` function of a relevant class (for example, `MyClass::tr()`)
- Declare the `tr()` function in your (non-`QObject`-based) class by adding the `Q_DECLARE_TR_FUNCTIONS(context)` macro at the top of the class declaration

Note that the translation functions should receive the string literals directly. Otherwise, **lupdate** will not be able to understand which text is being translated. The following code is incorrect, because the two strings will not be seen by translators:

```
const char* text;
if (condition) {
    text = "translatable1";
} else {
    text = "translatable2";
}
QString result = tr(text); // not recognized!
```

The simplest way to fix this issue is to apply the `tr()` function directly to each string literal:

```
QString result;
if (condition) {
    result = tr("translatable1");
} else {
    result = tr("translatable2");
}
```

Another solution is to mark translatable text with the `QT_TR_NOOP` macro:

```
if (condition) {
    text = QT_TR_NOOP("translatable1");
} else {
    text = QT_TR_NOOP("translatable2");
}
QString result = tr(text);
```

The `QT_TR_NOOP` macro returns its argument as is, but **lupdate** will recognize that these strings must be translated.

It's also possible to add a comment for the translator using a special form of C++ comments: `//: ...` or `/*: ... */`. Consider this example:

```
//: The button for sending attachment files
QPushButton *button = new QPushButton(tr("Send"));
```

> In this section, we only described the absolute minimum you need to know before starting work on a multilanguage game. This knowledge can save you a lot of time, because it's much easier to mark some text for translation as you write it than to go through a large code base and do it later. However, you will need to learn more to actually implement internationalization in your project. We will cover this topic in depth later (*Online chapter*, `https://www.packtpub.com/sites/default/files/downloads/MiscellaneousandAdvancedConcepts.pdf`).

Using arguments in strings

A common task is to have a string that needs to be dynamic in such a way that its content depends on the value of some external variable—for instance, you would like to inform the user about the number of files being copied, showing "copying file 1 of 2" or "copying file 2 of 5" depending on the value of counters that denote the current file and the total number of files. It might be tempting to do this by assembling all the pieces together using one of the available approaches:

```
QString str = "Copying file " + QString::number(current)
            + " of " + QString::number(total);
```

There are a number of drawbacks to such an approach; the biggest one is the problem of translating the string into other languages, wherein different languages their grammar might require the two arguments to be positioned differently than in English.

Instead, Qt allows us to specify positional parameters in strings and then replace them with real values. This approach is called **string interpolation**. Positions in the string are marked with the `%` sign (for example, `%1`, `%2`, and so on) and they are replaced by making a call to `arg()` and passing it the value that is used to replace the next lowest marker in the string. Our file copy message construction code then becomes this:

```
QString str = tr("Copying file %1 of %2").arg(current).arg(total);
```

Contrary to the behavior of the `printf()` built-in function, you don't need to specify the types of values in the placeholders (like `%d` or `%s`). Instead, the `arg()` method has a number of overloads that accept single characters, strings, integers, and real numbers. The `arg()` method has the same optional arguments that `QString::number()` has, allowing you to configure how numbers are formatted. Additionally, the `arg()` method has the `fieldWidth` argument that forces it to always output the string of a specified length, which is convenient for formatting tables:

```
const int fieldWidth = 4;
qDebug() << QStringLiteral("%1 | %2").arg(5, fieldWidth).arg(6,
fieldWidth);
qDebug() << QStringLiteral("%1 | %2").arg(15, fieldWidth).arg(16,
fieldWidth);
// output:
// "   5 |    6"
// "  15 |   16"
```

If you want to use a character other than space to fill empty spaces, use the `fillChar` optional argument of `arg()`.

Regular expressions

Let's briefly talk about **regular expressions**—usually shortened as "regex" or "regexp". You will need these regular expressions whenever you have to check whether a string or part of it matches a given pattern or when you want to find specific parts inside the text and possibly want to extract them.

Both the validity check and the finding/extraction are based on the so-called pattern of the regular expression, which describes the format a string must have to be valid, to be found, or to be extracted. Since this book is focused on Qt, there is unfortunately no time to cover regular expressions in depth. This is not a huge problem, however, since you can find plenty of good websites that provide introductions to regular expressions on the internet.

Even though there are many flavors of the regular expression's syntax, the one that Perl uses has become the *de facto* standard. In Qt, the `QRegularExpression` class provides Perl-compatible regular expressions.

> `QRegularExpression` was first introduced with Qt 5.0. In the previous versions, the only regular exception class was `QRegExp`, and it's still available for compatibility. Since `QRegularExpression` is closer to the Perl standard and since its execution speed is much faster as compared to `QRegExp`, we advise you to use `QRegularExpression` whenever possible. Nevertheless, you can read the `QRegExp` documentation, which contains a nice general introduction of regular expressions.

Time for action – A simple quiz game

To introduce you to the main usage of `QRegularExpression`, let's imagine this game: a photo, showing an object, is shown to multiple players, and each of them has to estimate the object's weight. The player whose estimate is closest to the actual weight wins. The estimates will be submitted via `QLineEdit`. Since you can write anything in a line edit, we have to ensure that the content is valid.

So what does valid mean? In this example, we define that a value between 1g and 999kg is valid. Knowing this specification, we can construct a regular expression that will verify the format. The first part of the text is a number, which can be between 1 and 999. Thus, the corresponding pattern looks like `[1-9]\d{0,2}`, where `[1-9]` allows—and demands—exactly one digit, except zero. It's optionally followed by up to two digits, including zero. This is expressed through `\d{0,2}`, where `\d` means "any digit", 0 is the minimal allowed count, and 2 is the maximal allowed count. The last part of the input is the weight's unit. With a pattern such as `(mg|g|kg)`, we allow the weight to be input in milligrams (`mg`), grams (`g`), or kilograms (`kg`). With `\s*`, we finally allow an arbitrary number of whitespace characters between the number and unit.

Let's combine it all together and test our regular expression right away:

```
QRegularExpression regex("[1-9]\\d{0,2}\\s*(mg|g|kg)");
regex.setPatternOptions(QRegularExpression::CaseInsensitiveOption);
qDebug() << regex.match("100 kg").hasMatch();       // true
qDebug() << regex.match("I don't know").hasMatch(); // false
```

What just happened?

In the first line, we constructed the aforementioned `QRegularExpression` object, while passing the regular expression's pattern as a parameter to the constructor. Note that we have to escape the `\` character, because it has special meaning in C++ syntax.

Regular expressions are case-sensitive by default. However, we want to allow the input to be in uppercase or mixed case. To achieve this, we can, of course, write `(mg|mG|Mg|MG|g|G|kg|kG|Kg|KG)` or convert the string to lowercase before matching, but there is a much cleaner and more readable solution. On the second line of the code example, you see the answer—a pattern option. We used `setPatternOptions()` to set the `QRegularExpression::CaseInsensitiveOption` option, which does not respect the case of the characters used. Of course, there are a few more options that you can read about in Qt's documentation on `QRegularExpression::PatternOption`. Instead of calling `setPatternOptions()`, we could also have passed the option as a second parameter to the constructor of `QRegularExpression`:

```
QRegularExpression regex("[1-9]\\d{0,2}\\s*(mg|g|kg)",
      QRegularExpression::CaseInsensitiveOption);
```

When we need to test an input, all we have to do is call `match()`, passing the string we would like to check against it. In return, we get an object of the `QRegularExpressionMatch` type that contains all the information that is further needed—and not only to check the validity. With `QRegularExpressionMatch::hasMatch()`, we then can determine whether the input matches our criteria, as it returns `true` if the pattern could be found. Otherwise, of course, `false` is returned.

Our pattern is not quite finished. The `hasMatch()` method would also return `true` if we matched it against "foo 142g bar". So, we have to define that the pattern is checked from the beginning to the end of the matched string. This is done by the `\A` and `\z` anchors. The former marks the start of a string and the latter the end of a string. Don't forget to escape the slashes when you use such anchors. The correct pattern will then look like this:

```
QRegularExpression regex("\\A[1-9]\\d{0,2}\\s*(mg|g|kg)\\z",
    QRegularExpression::CaseInsensitiveOption);
```

Extracting information out of a string

After we have checked that the sent guess is well formed, we have to extract the actual weight from the string. In order to be able to easily compare the different guesses, we further need to transform all values to a common reference unit. In this case, it should be a milligram, the lowest unit. So, let's see what `QRegularExpressionMatch` can offer us for this task.

With `capturedTexts()`, we get a string list of the pattern's captured groups. In our example, this list will contain "23kg" and "kg". The first element is always the string that was fully matched by the pattern. The next elements are all the substrings captured by the used brackets. Since we are missing the actual number, we have to alter the pattern's beginning to `([1-9]\d{0,2})`. Now, the list's second element is the number, and the third element is the unit. Thus, we can write the following:

```
int getWeight(const QString &input) {
    QRegularExpression regex("\\A([1-9]\\d{0,2})\\s*(mg|g|kg)\\z");
regex.setPatternOptions(QRegularExpression::CaseInsensitiveOption);
    QRegularExpressionMatch match = regex.match(input);
    if(match.hasMatch()) {
        const QString number = match.captured(1);
        int weight = number.toInt();
        const QString unit = match.captured(2).toLower();
        if (unit == "g") {
            weight *= 1000;
        } else if (unit == "kg") {
            weight *= 1000000 ;
        }
        return weight;
    } else {
        return -1;
    }
}
```

In the function's first two lines, we set up the pattern and its option. Then, we match it against the passed argument. If `QRegularExpressionMatch::hasMatch()` returns `true`, the input is valid and we extract the number and unit. Instead of fetching the entire list of captured text with `capturedTexts()`, we query specific elements directly by calling `QRegularExpressionMatch::captured()`. The passed integer argument signifies the element's position inside the list. So, calling `captured(1)` returns the matched digits as a `QString`.

> Be aware that adding a group at a later time will shift the indices of all the following groups by 1, and you will have to adjust your code! If you have long patterns or if there is a high probability that further brackets will be added in future, you can use **named groups** to make your code more maintainable. There is a `QRegularExpressionMatch::captured()` overload that allows you to specify the group name instead of index. For example, if you have written `(?<number>[1-9][0-9]{0,2})`, then you can get the digits by calling `match.captured("number")`.

To be able to calculate using the extracted number, we need to convert `QString` into an integer. This is done by calling `QString::toInt()`. The result of this conversion is then stored in the `weight` variable. Next, we fetch the unit and transform it to lowercase characters on the fly. This way, we can, for example, easily determine whether the user's guess is expressed in grams by checking the unit against the lowercase "g". We do not need to take care of the capital "G" or the variants "KG", "Kg", and the unusual "kG" for kilogram.

To get the standardized weight in milligrams, we multiply `weight` by 1,000 or 1,000,000, depending on whether this was expressed in g or kg. Lastly, we return this standardized weight. If the string wasn't well formed, we return `-1` to indicate that the given guess was invalid. It is then the caller's duty to determinate which player's guess was the best.

> Pay attention to whether your chosen integer type can handle the weight's value. For our example, 999 million is the biggest possible result, and, fortunately, it's smaller than the maximum possible value of a signed 32-bit integer (2,147,483,647). If you're unsure whether the type you use is big enough on all target systems, use a fixed width integer type (for example, `int64_t`).

As an exercise, try to extend the example by allowing decimal numbers so that "23.5g" is a valid guess. To achieve this, you have to alter the pattern in order to enter decimal numbers, and you also have to deal with `double` instead of `int` for the standardized weight.

Finding all pattern occurrences

Lastly, let's take a final look at how to find, for example, all numbers inside a string, even those leading with zeros:

```
QString input = QStringLiteral("123 foo 09 1a 3");
```

```
QRegularExpression regex("\\b\\d+\\b");
QRegularExpressionMatchIterator i = regex.globalMatch(input);
while (i.hasNext()) {
    QRegularExpressionMatch match = i.next();
    qDebug() << match.captured();
}
```

The `input` string contains an exemplary text in which we would like to find all numbers. The "foo" as well as "1a" variables should not be found by the pattern, since these are not valid numbers. Therefore, we set up the pattern, defining that we require at least one digit, `\d+`, and that this digit—or these digits—should be wrapped by word boundaries, `\b`. Note that you have to escape the slashes. With this pattern, we initiate the `QRegularExpression` object and call `globalMatch()` on it. Inside the passed argument, the pattern will be searched. This time, we do not get `QRegularExpressionMatch` back; instead, we get an iterator of the `QRegularExpressionMatchIterator` type. Since `QRegularExpressionMatchIterator` has a convenient `hasNext()` method, we check whether there is a further match and if so, we bring up the next match by calling `next()`. The type of the returned match is then `QRegularExpressionMatch`, which you already know.

> TIP: If you need to know about the next match inside the `while` loop, you can use `QRegularExpressionMatchIterator::peekNext()` to receive it. The benefit of this function is that it does not move the iterator.

This way, you can iterate all pattern occurrences in the string. This is helpful if you, for example, want to highlight a search string in text.

Our example will give the output of `"123"`, `"09"`, and `"3"`.

Taking into account that this was just a brief introduction to regular expressions, we would like to encourage you to read the **Detailed Description** section in the documentation to `QRegularExpression`, `QRegularExpressionMatch`, and `QRegularExpressionMatchIterator`. Regular expressions are very powerful and useful, so, in your daily programming life, you can benefit from the profound knowledge of regular expressions!

Containers

When you need to store a collection of objects, you need a container to hold them. The C++ standard library provides many powerful containers, such as `std::vector`, `std::list`, or `std::map`. However, Qt doesn't use these containers (actually, it hardly uses any standard library classes at all) and provides its own alternative implementation of containers instead. When Qt containers were introduced, they provided significantly more consistent performance on different platforms compared to standard library implementations, so they were required to create reliable cross-platform applications. This is not really the case now, as STL implementations and compilers have since evolved and gained new optimizations and features. However, there are still reasons to use Qt containers, especially in an application that heavily uses other Qt classes:

- Qt API always uses Qt containers. When you receive a `QList`, it will almost never be more efficient or convenient to convert it to a standard library container. Before calling a method that accepts `QList`, you should populate the input data in a `QList` instead of converting it from an STL container.
- Qt containers provide unique features, like implicit sharing (we will discuss it later in this chapter) or Java-style iterators, and some convenience methods STL containers lack.
- Qt containers follow Qt's naming scheme and its API conventions, so they look more natural in an application that is centered around Qt. For example, `QVector::isEmpty()` is more Qt-like than `std::vector::empty()`.

In addition, Qt containers provide STL-compatible API (for example, the `append()` method has the `push_back()` alias) that allows us to replace Qt containers with STL ones without changing much of the code. Range based `for` loop and some of the standard library algorithms are also compatible with Qt containers. That being said, if you need some features that are not available in Qt containers, using STL containers is a good idea.

Main container types

When you interact with a Qt API method, you don't have much choice on the container type, because you need to use the container the method uses. However, generally, you are free to choose containers to store your data. Let's go through the main Qt containers and learn when to use them.

We will only give a brief overview of Qt containers and won't go into details such as the algorithmic complexity of different operations. For most Qt containers, there is a similar STL container that we will name. The topic of choosing the right container is widely discussed, and it's not hard to find more information on it, especially for STL containers. You can also find more information on the **Container Classes** Qt documentation page.

`QVector` stores items in a continuous region of memory. The items are densely packed, meaning that this type is the most memory efficient and cache friendly. Its STL equivalent is `std::vector`. `QVector` should be the container of default choice, meaning that you should only use a different container if you have a reason to do it. `QVector` provides fast lookup by item number, fast on average appending items to the end and removing items from the end. Inserting and removing items from the beginning or middle of the vector is slow, because it causes all items to the right to shift in memory. Using `QVector` is straightforward:

```
QVector<int> numbers;
numbers.append(1);
numbers.append(5);
numbers.append(7);
qDebug() << numbers.count(); // 3
qDebug() << numbers[1];      // 5
```

The `QLinkedList` container, as the name implies, implements a linked list. Its STL equivalent is `std::list`. As opposed to `QVector`, it provides fast inserting and removing items at any location (the beginning, middle, or the end), but slow lookup by index, because it needs to iterate over items from the beginning to find the item by its index. `QLinkedList` is suitable when you need to insert or remove items at the middle of a huge list multiple times. However, note that in practice, `QVector` still may sometimes be more performant in this case, because `QLinkedList` is not densely packed in memory, which adds some overhead.

`QSet`, a Qt equivalent of `std::unordered_set`, is an unordered collection of unique items. Its advantage is the ability to efficiently add items, remove items, and check whether a particular item is present in a collection. The other list classes are not able to do the last operation quickly, because they need to iterate over all items and compare each item with the argument. Like with any other collection, you can iterate over the set's items, but the iteration order is not specified, that is, any item may appear on the first iteration, and so on. An example of the `QSet` API is shown in the following code:

```
QSet<QString> names;
```

```
names.insert("Alice");
names.insert("Bob");
qDebug() << names.contains("Alice"); // true
qDebug() << names.contains("John"); // false
for(const QString &name: names) {
    qDebug() << "Hello," << name;
}
```

The last flat collection is `QList`. Using it is currently not recommended, except when interacting with methods that accept or produce `QList` objects. Its performance and memory efficiency depends on the item type, and the rules that define "good" item types are complicated. For a "bad" type, `QList` is represented as a vector of `void *`, with each item stored as a separately allocated object on the heap. It's possible that `QList` implementation will change in Qt 6, but there is no official information about this yet.

There are some specialized list containers that provide extra functionality for a particular item type:

- The already familiar `QString` class is essentially a vector of `QChar` (16-bit Unicode characters)
- The familiar `QByteArray` is a vector of `char`
- `QStringList` is a `QList<QString>` with additional convenient operations
- `QBitArray` provides a memory-efficient array of bits with some useful APIs

Next, there are two main key-value collections: `QMap<K, T>` and `QHash<K, T>`. They allow you to associate a value (or multiple values) of type `T` with a key of type `K`. They both provide relatively fast lookup by key. When iterating over a `QMap` (similar to `std::map`), the items are sorted by keys, regardless of the insertion order:

```
QMap<int, QString> map;
map[3] = "three";
map[1] = "one";
map[2] = "two";
for(auto i = map.begin(); i != map.end(); ++i) {
    qDebug() << i.key() << i.value();
}
// output:
// 1 "one"
// 2 "two"
// 3 "three"
```

QHash (similar to std::unordered_map) has very similar APIs to QMap, but will iterate over items in unspecified order, like QSet. You can replace QMap with QHash in the previous example and see that the iteration order will change even when running the same program repeatedly. In exchange, QHash provides faster on-average insertions and lookups by key than QMap. You should use QHash instead of QMap if the iteration order doesn't matter to you.

An attentive reader may wonder how the code that looks very deterministic can produce random results. This randomness was intentionally introduced to protect against *algorithmic complexity attacks* on QHash and QSet. You can read the corresponding section of the QHash documentation page for more details about the attack and ways to configure the randomization.

Finally, QPair<T1, T2> is a simple class that can hold two values of different types, just like std::pair. You can use the qMakePair() function to make a pair out of two values.

Convenience containers

In addition to the containers described earlier, there are a few containers built on top of them that provide APIs and behavior that are more convenient in some special cases:

Container	Description
QStack	A QVector implementing the **last in, first out** (**LIFO**) structure. It contains the push() function for adding items to the stack, the pop() function for removing the top element, and the top() function for reading the top element without removing it.
QQueue	A QList implementing the **first in, first out** (**FIFO**) structure. Use enqueue() to append an item to the queue, dequeue() to take the head item from the queue, and head() to read the head item without removing it.
QMultiMap	A QMap with an API tailored for having multiple values for one key. QMap already allows us to do it; for example, you can add multiple items with one key using the QMap::insertMulti() method. However, QMultiMap renames it to insert() and hides the original QMap::insert() method that doesn't allow multiple values per key.
QMultiHash	Similar to QMultiMap, it's a QHash with a more convenient API for storing multiple values per key.

`QCache`	A key-value storage similar to `QHash` that allows you to implement a cache. `QCache` will delete its elements when they weren't recently used to keep the size of cache under the maximum allowed size. Since there is no way to know how much space an arbitrary item actually consumes, you can manually specify a *cost* for each item and the maximum total cost for a particular `QCache` object.
`QContiguousCache`	A flat container that allows you to cache a sublist of a large list. This is useful, for example, when implementing a viewer for a large table, where reads and writes are likely to happen near the current scroll location.

It's a good idea to use one of these classes when your task matches their use case.

Allowed item types

Not all types can be put in containers. All containers can only hold types that provide a default constructor, a copy constructor, and an assignment operator. All primitive types and most Qt data types (such as `QString` or `QPointF`) satisfy these requirements. Simple structs also can be stored in a container because the required constructors and operators are generated for them automatically, as per C++ standard.

A particular type usually cannot be put in a container because it doesn't have a constructor without arguments or copying this type was deliberately disabled. This is actually the case for `QObject` and all its descendants. The usage patterns of `QObject` suggest that you usually want to store pointers to a `QObject` to refer to it later. If that object was moved to a container or moved within a container, the pointer would be invalidated, so there is no copy constructor for these types. However, you can put pointers to `QObject` in containers (for example, `QVector<QObject *>`) because a pointer is a primitive type that satisfies all requirements. In this case, you have to manually ensure that your container will not contain any dangling pointers after the objects are deleted.

The preceding restrictions apply to items of lists and *values* of key-value collections, but what about their keys? It turns out that the key types have more restrictions that depend on the collection type.

`QMap<K, T>` additionally requires that the key type `K` has the comparison operator `operator<` that provides a *total order* (that is, satisfies a particular set of axioms). As an exception, pointer types are also allowed as a key type.

`QHash<K, T>` and `QSet<K>` require that the `K` type has `operator==`, and a `qHash(K key)` function overload exists. Qt provides these overloads for a large number of types for which it's possible, and you can create an overload for your custom type if needed.

Implicit sharing

One of the most significant differences between standard library containers and Qt's is the implicit sharing feature. In STL, creating a copy of a container immediately results in a memory allocation and copying the data buffer:

```
std::vector<int> x { 1, 2, 3};
std::vector<int> y = x; // full copy
```

If you don't intend to edit the copy, this is essentially a waste of resources, and you want to avoid it. This can be easily done in some cases by providing a reference (`const std::vector<int> &`) instead of making a copy. However, sometimes it becomes hard to ensure that the reference will be valid long enough, for example, if you want to store it in a class field. An alternative way to solve this task is to wrap a vector in a `shared_ptr` to explicitly share it between multiple objects. This becomes unnecessary when you work with Qt containers and some other Qt types.

In Qt, all main container types implement **implicit sharing** or **copy-on-write** semantics. Copying a `QVector` will not result in a new memory allocation until either of the two vectors is changed:

```
QVector<int> x { 1, 2, 3};
QVector<int> y = x;
// x and y share one buffer now
y[0] = 5; // new allocation happens here
// x and y have different buffers now
```

As long as no edits are made to the copy or the original object, the copying is very cheap. This allows you to cheaply and easily share constant data between objects without cluttering the code with manual management of shared objects. This feature is also implemented for `QString`, `QPen`, and many other Qt value types. Any copy operation still has some runtime overhead caused by reference counting, so you are encouraged to pass references instead of making copies when it's easy. However, this overhead is insignificant in most cases, except places with heavy computations.

If you like implicit sharing, you can implement it in your own data types using `QSharedDataPointer`. Refer to its documentation for the in-depth instructions.

In most cases, you can just use the containers as if they didn't implement implicit sharing, but there are a few cases where you have to be aware of it.

Pointer invalidation

First, implicit sharing means that holding any references or pointers to the container's content is disallowed when there is a possibility of changing this object or any object that shares the same buffer. The following small example illustrates the problem:

```
// don't do this!
QVector<int> x { 1, 2, 3 };
int *x0 = x.begin();
QVector<int> y = x;
x[0] = 42;
qDebug() << *x0; // output: 1
```

We initialized the `x0` variable with the pointer to the first element of the `x` vector. However, when we set a new value for that element and then tried to read it using the pointer, we got the old value again.

What just happened?

As we copied the `x` vector to `y`, the state of two vectors became shared and the original buffer was available to both of them. However, when we modified `x` using `operator[]`, it became **detached**, that is, a new buffer was allocated for it, and `y` retained the original buffer. The `x0` pointer continues to point at the original buffer, which is now only available to `y`. If you remove the `QVector<int> y = x;` line, the output will change to the expected 42. The general rule is that you should avoid storing pointers or references to the object's content while it's changed or shared with another object.

Unnecessary allocation

The next question is what actions on the object trigger the actual allocation of a new buffer? Obviously, `x[0] = 42` will trigger an allocation because the vector needs a buffer to write the new data to. However, `int i = x[0]` will also trigger an allocation if `x` is not declared as a `const` value or reference. That happens because in C++ this code triggers the non-const overload of `operator[]` if it's available, even though it's not necessary in this case. The vector doesn't know whether the requested item will or will not be changed, so it has to assume that it will be, and it triggers an allocation before returning a reference to the item in the new buffer.

The same issue takes effect when using other methods that have const and non-const overloads, for example, `begin()` or `data()`. The range-based `for` loop also calls `begin()`, so it will also detach if you iterate over a non-const value.

If you explicitly declare the container variable as const (for example, `const QVector<int> y` or `const QVector<int> &y`), the non-const methods will not be available, and it will not be possible to trigger an allocation using this variable. An alternative solution is to use special method aliases that are only available for const versions, such as `at()` for `operator=`, `constBegin()` for `begin()`, and `constData()` for `data()`. This solution is not usable with range-based `for` loop, though.

Range-based for and Qt foreach macro

Qt provides the `foreach` macro for iterating over Qt containers:

```
QVector<int> x { 1, 2, 3 };
foreach(const int i, x) {
    qDebug() << i;
}
```

This macro was available long before the range-based `for` loop made it into the C++ standard, so it's still very common in Qt code, and you should be familiar with it. The `foreach` loop always creates a temporary constant copy of the iterated object. Since it uses implicit sharing, this is very cheap. If you edit `x` while iterating over it, the changes will not affect the values of `i` because the iteration uses a copy, but this also means that such an operation is safe. Note that when using range-based `for` loop, STL-style iterators, or Java-style iterators, editing the same container you're iterating over is generally not safe. For example, changing item values may be permitted, but deleting an item may result in undefined behavior.

We discussed how range-based `for` loop can cause a deep copy of the containers. The `foreach` macro by itself will never cause a deep copy. However, if you edit the container while iterating over it, this will result in a deep copy, because two versions of data have to be stored somewhere.

When using the range-based `for` loop, you should be careful not to pass a reference to a temporary object. For example, this code looks legitimate, but it results in undefined behavior:

```
// don't do this!
for(QChar c: QString("abc").replace('a', 'z')) {
    qDebug() << c;
}
```

What just happened?

We created a temporary `QString` object and called its `replace()` method. This method' s return type is `QString &`, so it doesn't own the string's data. If we immediately assigned this value to an owning variable, it would be correct because the life of the original temporary `QString` lasts until the end of the full expression (in this case, the assignment):

```
QString string = QString("abc").replace('a', 'z');
for(QChar c: string) { // correct
    qDebug() << c;
}
```

However, the temporary object in the original example doesn't live until the end of the `for` loop, so this will result in a use-after-free bug. The `foreach` version of this code would contain an implicit assignment to a variable, so it would be correct.

On the other hand, the macro nature of `foreach` is its disadvantage. For example, the following code does not compile because the item type contains a comma:

```
QVector<QPair<int, int>> x;
foreach(const QPair<int, int>& i, x) {
    //...
}
```

The error is "macro `Q_FOREACH` passed 3 arguments, but takes just 2". To fix this issue, you have to create a `typedef` for the item type.

Since C++11, range-based `for` loop is a native, clean alternative to `foreach`, so we suggest that you prefer the native construct over the macro, but keep in mind the pitfalls we described.

Data storage

When implementing games, you will often have to work with persistent data; you will need to store the saved game data, load maps, and so on. For that, you have to learn about the mechanisms that let you use the data stored on digital media.

Files and devices

The most basic and low-level mechanism that is used to access data is to save and load it from the files. While you can use the classic file access approaches provided by C and C++, such as `stdio` or `iostream`, Qt provides its own file abstraction that hides platform-dependent details and provides a clean API that works across all platforms in a uniform manner.

The two basic classes that you will work with when using files are `QDir` and `QFile`. The former represents the contents of a directory, lets you traverse filesystems, creates and remove directories, and finally, accesses all files in a particular directory.

Traversing directories

Traversing directories with `QDir` is really easy. The first thing to do is to have an instance of `QDir` in the first place. The easiest way to do this is to pass the directory path to the `QDir` constructor.

Qt handles file paths in a platform-independent way. Even though the regular directory separator on Windows is a backward slash character (\) and on other platforms it is the forward slash (/), Qt internally always uses the forward slash, and paths returned by most Qt methods never contain backward slashes. You can always use forward slashes when passing paths to Qt methods, even on Windows. If you need to convert the Qt's path representation to the native form (for example, for passing it to the standard library or a third-party library), you can use `QDir::toNativeSeparators()`. `QDir::fromNativeSeparators()` to perform the inverse operation.

Qt provides a number of static methods to access some special directories. The following table lists these special directories and functions that access them:

Access function	Directory
`QDir::current()`	The current working directory
`QDir::home()`	The home directory of the current user
`QDir::root()`	The root directory—usually / for Unix and `C:\` for Windows
`QDir::temp()`	The system temporary directory

The `QStandardPaths` class provides information about other standard locations present in the system. For example, `QStandardPaths::writableLocation(QStandardPaths::MusicLocation)` returns path to the user's music folder.

Refer to the `QStandardPaths::StandardLocation` enum documentation for the list of available locations.

When you already have a valid `QDir` object, you can start moving between directories. To do that, you can use the `cd()` and `cdUp()` methods. The former moves to the named subdirectory, while the latter moves to the parent directory. You should always check that these commands were successful. If they return `false`, your `QDir` object will remain in the same directory!

To list files and subdirectories in a particular directory, you can use the `entryList()` method, which returns a list of entries in the directory that match the criteria passed to `entryList()`. The `filters` argument takes a list of flags that correspond to the different attributes that an entry needs to have to be included in the result. The most useful flags are listed in the following table:

Filter	**Meaning**
`QDir::Dirs`, `QDir::Files`, `QDir::Drives`	List directories, files, or Windows drives. You should specify at least one of these filters to get any results.
`QDir::AllEntries`	List directories, files, and drives. This is a shortcut for `Dirs | Files | Drives`.
`QDir::AllDirs`	List directories even if they don't match the name filters.
`QDir::NoDotAndDotDot`	Don't list `.` (current directory) and `..` (parent directory) entries. If `Dirs` flag is present and `NoDotAndDotDot` is not, these entries will always be listed.
`QDir::Readable`, `QDir::Writable`, `QDir::Executable`	List only entries that can be read, written to, or executed.
`QDir::Hidden`, `QDir::System`	List hidden files and system files. If these flags are not specified, hidden and system flags will not be listed.

The `sort` argument of `entryList()` allows you to choose the ordering of the results:

Flag	**Meaning**
`QDir::Unsorted`	The order of entries is undefined. It's a good idea to use it if the order doesn't matter to you, since it may be faster.
`QDir::Name`, `QDir::Time`, `QDir::Size`, `QDir::Type`	Sort by appropriate entry attributes.
`QDir::DirsFirst`, `QDir::DirsLast`	Determines whether directories should be listed before or after files. If neither flag is specified, directories will be mixed with files in the output.
`QDir::Reversed`	Reverses the order.

Additionally, there is an overload of `entryList()` that accepts a list of file name patterns in the form of `QStringList` as its first parameter. Here's an example call that returns all JPEG files in the directory sorted by size:

```
QStringList nameFilters = { QStringLiteral("*.jpg"),
QStringLiteral("*.jpeg") };
QStringList entries = dir.entryList(nameFilters,
    QDir::Files | QDir::Readable, QDir::Size);
```

Besides `entryList()`, there is the `entryInfoList()` method that wraps each returned file name in a `QFileInfo` object that has many convenient functions. For example, `QFileInfo::absoluteFilePath()` returns the absolute path to the file, and `QFileInfo::suffix()` returns the extension of the file.

> TIP: If you need to traverse directories recursively (for example, for finding all files in all subdirectories), you can use the `QDirIterator` class.

Reading and writing files

Once you know the path to a file (for example, using `QDir::entryList()`, `QFileDialog::getOpenFileName()`, or some external source), you can pass it to `QFile` to receive an object that acts as a handle to the file. Before the file contents can be accessed, the file needs to be opened using the `open()` method. The basic variant of this method takes a mode in which we need to open the file. The following table explains the modes that are available:

Mode	Description
`ReadOnly`	This file can be read from.
`WriteOnly`	This file can be written to.
`ReadWrite`	This file can be read from and written to.
`Append`	All data writes will be written at the end of the file.
`Truncate`	If the file is present, its content is deleted before we open it.
`Text`	When reading, all line endings are transformed to `\n`. When writing, all `\n` symbols are transformed to the native format (for example, `\r\n` on Windows or `\n` on Linux).
`Unbuffered`	The flag prevents the file from being buffered.

The `open()` method returns `true` or `false`, depending on whether the file was opened or not. The current status of the file can be checked by calling `isOpen()` on the file object. Once the file is open, it can be read from or written to, depending on the options that are passed when the file is opened. Reading and writing is done using the `read()` and `write()` methods. These methods have a number of overloads, but we suggest that you focus on using those variants that accept or return the already familiar `QByteArray` objects, because they manage the memory automatically. If you are working with plain text, then a useful overload for `write` is the one that accepts the text directly as input. Just remember that the text has to be null terminated. When reading from a file, Qt offers a number of other methods that might come in handy in some situations. One of these methods is `readLine()`, which tries to read from the file until it encounters a new line character. If you use it along with the `atEnd()` method that tells you whether you have reached the end of the file, you can realize the line-by-line reading of a text file:

```
QStringList lines;
while(!file.atEnd()) {
    QByteArray line = file.readLine();
    lines.append(QString::fromUtf8(line));
}
```

Another useful method is `readAll()`, which simply returns the file content, starting from the current position of the file pointer until the end of the file.

You have to remember, though, that when using these helper methods, you should be really careful if you don't know how much data the file contains. It might happen that when reading line by line or trying to read the whole file into memory in one step, you exhaust the amount of memory that is available for your process. If you only intend to work with small files that fit into memory, you can check the size of the file by calling `size()` on the `QFile` instance and abort if the file is too large. If you need to handle arbitrary files, however, you should process the file's data in steps, reading only a small portion of bytes at a time. This makes the code more complex but allows us to manage the available resources better.

If you require constant access to the file, you can use the `map()` and `unmap()` calls that add and remove mappings of the parts of a file to a memory address that you can then use like a regular array of bytes:

```
QFile f("myfile");
if(!f.open(QFile::ReadWrite)) {
    return;
}
uchar *addr = f.map(0, f.size());
if(!addr) {
```

```
        return;
    }
    f.close();
    doSomeComplexOperationOn(addr);
```

The mapping will automatically be removed when the `QFile` object is destroyed.

Devices

`QFile` is really a descendant class of `QIODevice` ("input/output device"), which is a Qt interface used to abstract entities related to reading and writing of blocks of data. There are two types of devices: sequential and random access devices. `QFile` belongs to the latter group; it has the concepts of start, end, size, and current position that can be changed by the user with the `seek()` method. Sequential devices, such as sockets and pipes, represent streams of data—there is no way to rewind the stream or check its size; you can only keep reading the data sequentially—piece by piece, and you can check how far away you currently are from the end of data. We will work with such devices in `Chapter 7`, *Networking*.

All I/O devices can be opened and closed. They all implement the `open()`, `read()`, and `write()` interfaces. Writing to the device queues the data for writing; when the data is actually written, the `bytesWritten()` signal is emitted that carries the amount of data that was written to the device. If more data becomes available in the sequential device, it emits the `readyRead()` signal, which informs you that if you call `read` now, you can expect to receive some data from the device.

Time for action – Implementing a device to encrypt data

Let's implement a really simple device that encrypts or decrypts the data that is streamed through it using a very simple algorithm—the Caesar cipher. When encrypting, it shifts each character in the plaintext by a number of characters defined by the key. It does the reverse when decrypting. Thus, if the key is `2` and the plaintext character is `a`, the ciphertext becomes `c`. Decrypting `z` with the key `4` will yield the value `v`.

First, create a new empty project by selecting the **Empty qmake Project** template from the **Other Project** category. Next, add a `main.cpp` file and a new `CaesarCipherDevice` class derived from `QIODevice`. The basic interface of the class will accept an integer key and set an underlying device that serves as the source or destination of data. This is all simple coding that you should already understand, so it shouldn't need any extra explanation, as shown:

```
class CaesarCipherDevice : public QIODevice
{
    Q_OBJECT
    Q_PROPERTY(int key READ key WRITE setKey)
public:
    explicit CaesarCipherDevice(QObject *parent = 0)
        : QIODevice(parent) {
        m_key = 0;
        m_baseDevice = 0;
    }
    void setBaseDevice(QIODevice *dev) {
        m_baseDevice = dev;
    }
    QIODevice *baseDevice() const {
        return m_baseDevice;
    }
    void setKey(int k) {
        m_key = k;
    }
    inline int key() const {
        return m_key;
    }
private:
    int m_key;
    QIODevice *m_baseDevice;
};
```

The next thing is to ensure that the device cannot be used if there is no device to operate on (that is, when `m_baseDevice == nullptr`). For this, we have to reimplement the `QIODevice::open()` method and return `false` when we want to prevent operating on our device:

```
bool CaesarCipherDevice::open(OpenMode mode) {
    if(!m_baseDevice) {
        return false;
    }
    if(!m_baseDevice->isOpen()) {
        return false;
    }
    if(m_baseDevice->openMode() != mode) {
```

```
        return false;
    }
    return QIODevice::open(mode);
}
```

The method accepts the mode that the user wants to open the device with. We perform an additional check to verify that the base device was opened in the same mode before calling the base class implementation that will mark the device as open.

TIP

It's a good idea to call `QIODevice::setErrorString` to let the user know about an error. Additionally, you can use `qWarning("message")` to print a warning to the console when an error occurs.

To have a fully functional device, we still need to implement the two protected pure virtual methods, which do the actual reading and writing. These methods are called by Qt from other methods of the class when needed. Let's start with `writeData()`, which accepts a pointer to a buffer containing the data and size equal to that of a buffer:

```
qint64 CaesarCipherDevice::writeData(const char *data, qint64 len) {
    QByteArray byteArray;
    byteArray.resize(len);
    for(int i = 0; i < len; ++i) {
        byteArray[i] = data[i] + m_key;
    }
    int written = m_baseDevice->write(byteArray);
    emit bytesWritten(written);
    return written;
}
```

First, we create a local byte array and resize it to the length of the input. Then, we iterate bytes of the input, add the value of the key to each byte (which effectively performs the encryption) and put it in the byte array. Finally, we try to write the byte array to the underlying device. Before informing the caller about the amount of data that was really written, we emit a signal that carries the same information.

The last method we need to implement is the one that performs decryption by reading from the base device and adding the key to each cell of the data. This is done by implementing `readData()`, which accepts a pointer to the buffer that the method needs to write to and the size of the buffer.

The code is quite similar to that of `writeData()`, except that we are subtracting the key value instead of adding it:

```
qint64 CaesarCipherDevice::readData(char *data, qint64 maxlen) {
    QByteArray baseData = m_baseDevice->read(maxlen);
    const int size = baseData.size();
    for(int i = 0; i < size; ++i) {
        data[i] = baseData[i] - m_key;
    }
    return size;
}
```

First, we try to read `maxlen` bytes from the underlying device and store the data in a byte array. Note that the byte array can contain fewer bytes than `maxlen` (for example, if we reached the end of the file) but it can't contain more. Then, we iterate the array and set subsequent bytes of data buffer to the decrypted value. Finally, we return the amount of data that was really read.

A simple `main()` function that can test the class looks as follows:

```
int main(int argc, char **argv) {
    QByteArray ba = "plaintext";
    QBuffer buf;
    buf.open(QIODevice::WriteOnly);
    CaesarCipherDevice encrypt;
    encrypt.setKey(3);
    encrypt.setBaseDevice(&buf);
    encrypt.open(buf.openMode());
    encrypt.write(ba);
    qDebug() << buf.data();

    CaesarCipherDevice decrypt;
    decrypt.setKey(3);
    decrypt.setBaseDevice(&buf);
    buf.open(QIODevice::ReadOnly);
    decrypt.open(buf.openMode());
    qDebug() << decrypt.readAll();
    return 0;
}
```

We use the `QBuffer` class that implements the `QIODevice` API and acts as an adapter for `QByteArray` or `QString`.

What just happened?

We created an encryption object and set its key to `3`. We also told it to use a `QBuffer` instance to store the processed content. After opening it for writing, we sent some data to it that gets encrypted and written to the base device. Then, we created a similar device, passing the same buffer again as the base device, but now, we open the device for reading. This means that the base device contains ciphertext. After this, we read all data from the device, which results in reading data from the buffer, decrypting it, and returning the data so that it can be written to the debug console.

Have a go hero – A GUI for the Caesar cipher

You can combine what you already know by implementing a full-blown GUI application that is able to encrypt or decrypt files using the Caesar cipher `QIODevice` class that we just implemented. Remember that `QFile` is also `QIODevice`, so you can pass its pointer directly to `setBaseDevice()`.

This is just a starting point for you. The `QIODevice` API is quite rich and contains numerous methods that are virtual, so you can reimplement them in subclasses.

Text streams

Much of the data produced by computers nowadays is based on text. You can create such files using a mechanism that you already know—opening `QFile` to write, converting all data into strings using `QString::arg()`, optionally encoding strings using `QTextCodec`, and dumping the resulting bytes to the file by calling `write`. However, Qt provides a nice mechanism that does most of this automatically for you in a way similar to how the standard C++ `iostream` classes work. The `QTextStream` class operates on any `QIODevice` API in a stream-oriented way. You can send tokens to the stream using the << operator, where they get converted into strings, separated by spaces, encoded using a codec of your choice, and written to the underlying device. It also works the other way round; using the >> operator, you can stream data from a text file, transparently converting it from strings to appropriate variable types. If the conversion fails, you can discover it by inspecting the result of the `status()` method—if you get `ReadPastEnd` or `ReadCorruptData`, it means that the read has failed.

> **TIP:** While `QIODevice` is the main class that `QTextStream` operates on, it can also manipulate `QString` or `QByteArray`, which makes it useful for us to compose or parse strings.

Using `QTextStream` is simple—you just pass a device to its constructor, and you're good to go. The `QTextStream` object will read to or write from that device. By default, `QTextStream` uses the encoding specified by the current locale, but if it encounters a UTF-16 or UTF-32 BOM (byte order mark), it will switch to the encoding specified by the BOM. The stream accepts strings and numerical values:

```
QFile file("output.txt");
file.open(QFile::WriteOnly | QFile::Text);
QTextStream stream(&file);
stream << "Today is " << QDate::currentDate().toString() << endl;
QTime t = QTime::currentTime();
stream << "Current time is " << t.hour() << " h and "
       << t.minute() << "m." << endl;
```

Apart from directing content into the stream, the stream can accept a number of manipulators, such as `endl`, which have a direct or indirect influence on how the stream behaves. For instance, you can tell the stream to display a number as decimal and another as hexadecimal with uppercase digits using the following code (highlighted in the code are all manipulators):

```
for(int i = 0;i < 10; ++i) {
    int num = qrand() % 100000;  // random number between 0 and 99999
    stream << dec << num
           << showbase << hex << uppercasedigits << num << endl;
}
```

This is not the end of the capabilities of `QTextStream`. It also allows us to display data in a tabular manner by defining column widths and alignments. Consider a game player record defined by the following structure:

```
struct Player {
    QString name;
    qint64 experience;
    QPoint position;
    char direction;
};
```

Suppose you have a set of records for players stored in a `QVector<Player> players` variable. Let's dump such information into a file in a tabular manner:

```
QFile file("players.txt");
file.open(QFile::WriteOnly | QFile::Text);
QTextStream stream(&file);
stream << center;
stream << qSetFieldWidth(16) << "Player" << qSetFieldWidth(0) << " ";
stream << qSetFieldWidth(10) << "Experience" << qSetFieldWidth(0) << "
```

```
";
stream << qSetFieldWidth(13) << "Position" << qSetFieldWidth(0) << "
";
stream << "Direction" << endl;

for(const Player &player: players) {
    stream << left << qSetFieldWidth(16) << player.name
           << qSetFieldWidth(0) << " ";
    stream << right << qSetFieldWidth(10) << player.experience
           << qSetFieldWidth(0) << " ";
    stream << right << qSetFieldWidth(6) << player.position.x()
           << qSetFieldWidth(0) << " ";
    stream << qSetFieldWidth(6) << player.position.y()
           << qSetFieldWidth(0) << " ";
    stream << center << qSetFieldWidth(10);

    switch(player.direction) {
    case 'n' : stream << "north"; break;
    case 's' : stream << "south"; break;
    case 'e' : stream << "east"; break;
    case 'w' : stream << "west"; break;
    default: stream << "unknown"; break;
    }
    stream << qSetFieldWidth(0) << endl;
}
```

The program creates a file that should look like this:

```
     Player      Experience  Position     Direction
Gondael               46783     10      -5   north
Olrael               123648     -5     103    east
Nazaal             99372641     48     634   south
```

One last thing about `QTextStream` is that it can operate on standard C file structures, which makes it possible for us to use `QTextStream` to, for example, write to `stdout` or read from `stdin`, as shown in the following code:

```
QTextStream stdoutStream(stdout);
stdoutStream << "This text goes to standard output." << endl;
```

Binary streams

More than often, we have to store object data in a device-independent way so that it can be restored later, possibly on a different machine with a different data layout and so on. In computer science, this is called **serialization**. Qt provides several serialization mechanisms and now we will take a brief look at some of them.

If you look at `QTextStream` from a distance, you will note that what it really does is serialize and deserialize data to a text format. Its close cousin is the `QDataStream` class that handles serialization and deserialization of arbitrary data to a binary format. It uses a custom data format to store and retrieve data from `QIODevice` in a platform-independent way. It stores enough data so that a stream written on one platform can be successfully read on a different platform.

`QDataStream` is used in a similar fashion as `QTextStream`—the << and >> operators are used to redirect data into or out of the stream. The class supports most of the built-in Qt data types so that you can operate on classes such as `QColor`, `QPoint`, or `QStringList` directly:

```
QFile file("outfile.dat");
file.open(QFile::WriteOnly | QFile::Truncate);
QDataStream stream(&file);
double dbl = 3.14159265359;
QColor color = Qt::red;
QPoint point(10, -4);
QStringList stringList { "foo", "bar" };
stream << dbl << color << point << stringList;
```

If you want to serialize custom data types, you can teach `QDataStream` to do that by implementing proper redirection operators.

Time for action – Serialization of a custom structure

Let's perform another small exercise by implementing functions that are required to use `QDataStream` to serialize the same simple structure that contains the player information that we used for text streaming:

```
struct Player {
    QString name;
    qint64 experience;
    QPoint position;
    char direction;
};
```

For this, two functions need to be implemented, both returning a `QDataStream` reference that was taken earlier as an argument to the call. Apart from the stream itself, the serialization operator accepts a constant reference to the class that is being saved. The most simple implementation just streams each member into the stream and returns the stream afterward:

```
QDataStream& operator<<(QDataStream &stream, const Player &p) {
    stream << p.name;
    stream << p.experience;
    stream << p.position;
    stream << p.direction;
    return stream;
}
```

Complementary to this, deserializing is done by implementing a redirection operator that accepts a mutable reference to the structure that is filled by data that is read from the stream:

```
QDataStream& operator>>(QDataStream &stream, Player &p) {
     stream >> p.name;
     stream >> p.experience;
     stream >> p.position;
     stream >> p.direction;
     return stream;
}
```

Again, at the end, the stream itself is returned.

Now we can use `QDataStream` to write our object to any I/O device (for example, a file, a buffer, or a network socket):

```
Player player = /* ... */;
QDataStream stream(device);
stream << player;
```

Reading the object back is just as simple:

```
Player player;
QDataStream stream(device);
stream >> player;
```

What just happened?

We provided two standalone functions that define redirection operators for the `Player` class to and from a `QDataStream` instance. This lets your class be serialized and deserialized using mechanisms offered and used by Qt.

XML streams

XML has become one of the most popular standards that is used to store hierarchical data. Despite its verbosity and difficulty to read by human eye, it is used in virtually any domain where data persistency is required, as it is very easy to read by machines. Qt provides support for reading and writing XML documents in two modules:

- The Qt Xml module provides access using the **Document Object Model** (**DOM**) standard with classes such as `QDomDocument`, `QDomElement`, and others
- The Qt Core module contains `QXmlStreamReader` and `QXmlStreamWriter` classes that implement streaming API

One of the downsides of `QDomDocument` is that it requires us to load the whole XML tree into the memory before parsing it. Additionally, Qt Xml is not actively maintained. Therefore, we will focus on the streaming approach provided by Qt Core.

In some situations, downsides of the DOM approach are compensated for by its ease of use as compared to a streamed approach, so you can consider using it if you feel that you have found the right task for it. If you want to use the DOM access to XML in Qt, remember to enable the `QtXml` module in your applications by adding a `QT += xml` line in the project configuration file.

Time for action – Implementing an XML parser for player data

In this exercise, we will create a parser to fill data that represents players and their inventory in an RPG game. First, let's create the types that will hold the data:

```
class InventoryItem {
    Q_GADGET
public:
```

```
    enum class Type {
        Weapon,
        Armor,
        Gem,
        Book,
        Other
    };
    Q_ENUM(Type)

    Type type;
    QString subType;
    int durability;

    static Type typeByName(const QStringRef &r);
};

class Player {
public:
    QString name;
    QString password;
    int experience;
    int hitPoints;
    QVector<InventoryItem> inventory;
    QString location;
    QPoint position;
};

struct PlayerInfo {
    QVector<Player> players;
};
```

What just happened?

We want to use the `Q_ENUM` macro on our enum, because it will allow us to easily convert enum values to strings and back, which is very useful for serialization. Since `InventoryItem` is not a `QObject`, we need to add a `Q_GADGET` macro to the beginning of the class declaration to make the `Q_ENUM` macro work. Think of `Q_GADGET` as of a lightweight variation of `Q_OBJECT` that enables some of its features but not others.

The `typeByName()` method will receive a string and return the corresponding enum variant. We can implement this method as follows:

```
InventoryItem::Type InventoryItem::typeByName(const QStringRef &r) {
    QMetaEnum metaEnum = QMetaEnum::fromType<InventoryItem::Type>();
    QByteArray latin1 = r.toLatin1();
    int result = metaEnum.keyToValue(latin1.constData());
    return static_cast<InventoryItem::Type>(result);
}
```

The implementation may look complicated, but it's much less error-prone than manually writing a bunch of `if` statements to choose the correct return value manually. First, we use the `QMetaEnum::fromType<T>()` template method to get the `QMetaEnum` object corresponding to our `enum`. The `keyToValue()` method of this object performs the conversion that we need, but it needs to be accompanied with a few conversions.

You can note that we are using a class called `QStringRef`. It represents a string reference—a substring in an existing string—and is implemented in a way that avoids expensive string construction; therefore, it is very fast. The similar `std::string_view` type was added to the standard library in C++17. We use it as the argument type because `QXmlStreamReader` will provide strings in this format.

However, the `keyToValue()` method expects a `const char *` argument, so we use the `toLatin1()` method to convert our string to `QByteArray`, and then use `constData()` to get the `const char *` pointer to its buffer. Finally, we use `static_cast` to convert the result from `int` to our `enum` type.

Save the following XML document somewhere. We will use it to test whether the parser can read it:

```
<PlayerInfo>
    <Player hp="40" exp="23456">
        <Name>Gandalf</Name>
        <Password>mithrandir</Password>
        <Inventory>
            <InvItem type="Weapon" durability="3">
                <SubType>Long sword</SubType>
            </InvItem>
            <InvItem type="Armor" durability="10">
                <SubType>Chain mail</SubType>
            </InvItem>
        </Inventory>
        <Location name="room1">
            <Position x="1" y="0"/>
```

```
        </Location>
    </Player>
</PlayerInfo>
```

Let's create a class called `PlayerInfoReader` that will wrap `QXmlStreamReader` and expose a parser interface for the `PlayerInfo` instances:

```
class PlayerInfoReader {
public:
    PlayerInfoReader(QIODevice *device);
    PlayerInfo read();
private:
    QXmlStreamReader reader;
};
```

The class constructor accepts a `QIODevice` pointer that the reader will use to retrieve data as it needs it. The constructor is trivial, as it simply passes the device to the `reader` object:

```
PlayerInfoReader(QIODevice *device) {
    reader.setDevice(device);
}
```

Before we go into parsing, let's prepare some code to help us with the process. First, let's add an enumeration type to the class that will list all the possible tokens—tag names that we want to handle in the parser:

```
enum class Token {
    Invalid = -1,
    PlayerInfo, // root tag
    Player,     // in PlayerInfo
    Name, Password, Inventory, Location, // in Player
    Position,   // in Location
    InvItem     // in Inventory
};
```

Then, just like we did in the `InventoryItem` class, we use the `Q_GADGET` and `Q_ENUM` macros and implement the `PlayerInfoReader::tokenByName()` convenience method.

Now, let's implement the entry point of the parsing process:

```
PlayerInfo PlayerInfoReader::read() {
    if(!reader.readNextStartElement()) {
        return PlayerInfo();
    }
    if (tokenByName(reader.name()) != Token::PlayerInfo) {
```

```
            return PlayerInfo();
        }
        PlayerInfo info;
        while(reader.readNextStartElement()) {
            if(tokenByName(reader.name()) == Token::Player) {
                Player p = readPlayer();
                info.players.append(p);
            } else {
                reader.skipCurrentElement();
            }
        }
        return info;
    }
```

First, we call `readNextStartElement()` on the reader to make it find the starting tag of the first element, and if it is found, we check whether the root tag of the document is what we expect it to be. If not, we return a default-constructed `PlayerInfo`, indicating that no data is available.

Next, we create a `PlayerInfo` variable. We iterate all the starting sub-elements in the current tag (`PlayerInfo`). For each of them, we check whether it is a `Player` tag and call `readPlayer()` to descend into the level of parsing data for a single player. Otherwise, we call `skipCurrentElement()`, which fast-forwards the stream until a matching ending element is encountered.

The other methods in this class will usually follow the same pattern. Each parsing method iterates all the starting elements, handling those it knows and ignoring all others. Such an approach lets us maintain forward compatibility, since all tags introduced in the newer versions of the document are silently skipped by an older parser.

The structure of `readPlayer()` is similar; however, it is more complicated, as we also want to read data from the attributes of the `Player` tag itself. Let's take a look at the function piece by piece. First, we get the list of attributes associated with the opening tag and ask for values of the two attributes that we are interested in:

```
Player p;
const QXmlStreamAttributes& playerAttrs = reader.attributes();
p.hitPoints = playerAttrs.value("hp").toString().toInt();
p.experience = playerAttrs.value("exp").toString().toInt();
```

After this, we loop all child tags and fill the `Player` structure based on the tag names. By converting tag names to tokens, we can use a `switch` statement to neatly structure the code in order to extract information from different tag types, as in the following code:

```
while(reader.readNextStartElement()) {
    Token t = tokenByName(reader.name());
    switch(t) {
    case Token::Name:
        p.name = reader.readElementText();
        break;
    case Token::Password:
        p.password = reader.readElementText();
        break;
    case Token::Inventory:
        p.inventory = readInventory();
        break;
    //...
    }
}
```

If we are interested in the textual content of the tag, we can use `readElementText()` to extract it. This method reads until it encounters the closing tag and returns the text contained within it. For the `Inventory` tag, we call the dedicated `readInventory()` method.

For the `Location` tag, the code is more complex than earlier as we again descend into reading child tags, extracting the required information and skipping all unknown tags:

```
case Token::Location:
    p.location = reader.attributes().value("name").toString();
    while(reader.readNextStartElement()) {
        if(tokenByName(reader.name()) == Token::Position) {
            const QXmlStreamAttributes& attrs = reader.attributes();
            p.position.setX(attrs.value("x").toString().toInt());
            p.position.setY(attrs.value("y").toString().toInt());
            reader.skipCurrentElement();
        } else {
            reader.skipCurrentElement();
        }
    }
    break;
```

Next, we again skip the tags that didn't match any known tokens. At the end of `readPlayer()`, we simply return the populated `Player` value.

The last method is similar in structure to the previous one—iterate all the tags, skip everything that we don't want to handle (everything that is not an inventory item), fill the inventory item data structure, and append the item to the list of already parsed items, as follows:

```
QVector<InventoryItem> PlayerInfoReader::readInventory() {
    QVector<InventoryItem> inventory;
    while(reader.readNextStartElement()) {
        if(tokenByName(reader.name()) != Token::InvItem) {
            reader.skipCurrentElement();
            continue;
        }
        InventoryItem item;
        const QXmlStreamAttributes& attrs = reader.attributes();
        item.durability =
attrs.value("durability").toString().toInt();
        item.type = InventoryItem::typeByName(attrs.value("type"));
        while(reader.readNextStartElement()) {
            if(reader.name() == "SubType") {
                item.subType = reader.readElementText();
            }
            else {
                reader.skipCurrentElement();
            }
        }
        inventory << item;
    }
    return inventory;
}
```

In `main()` of your project, write some code that will check whether the parser works correctly. You can use the `qDebug()` statements to output the sizes of lists and contents of variables. Take a look at the following code for an example:

```
QFile file(filePath);
file.open(QFile::ReadOnly | QFile::Text);
PlayerInfoReader reader(&file);
PlayerInfo playerInfo = reader.read();
if (!playerInfo.players.isEmpty()) {
    qDebug() << "Count:" << playerInfo.players.count();
    qDebug() << "Size of inventory:" <<
                playerInfo.players.first().inventory.size();
    qDebug() << "Inventory item:"
             << playerInfo.players.first().inventory[0].type
             << playerInfo.players.first().inventory[0].subType;
    qDebug() << "Room:" << playerInfo.players.first().location
             << playerInfo.players.first().position;
}
```

What just happened?

The code you just wrote implements a full top-down parser of the XML data. First, the data goes through a tokenizer, which returns identifiers that are much easier to handle than strings. Then, each method can easily check whether the token it receives is an acceptable input for the current parsing stage. Based on the child token, the next parsing function is determined and the parser descends to a lower level until there is nowhere to descend to. Then, the flow goes back up one level and processes the next child. If, at any point, an unknown tag is found, it gets ignored. This approach supports a situation when a new version of software introduces new tags to the file format specification, but an old version of software can still read the file by skipping all the tags that it doesn't understand.

Have a go hero – An XML serializer for player data

Now that you know how to parse XML data, you can create the complementary part—a module that will serialize `PlayerInfo` structures into XML documents using `QXmlStreamWriter`. Use methods such as `writeStartDocument()`, `writeStartElement()`, `writeCharacters()`, and `writeEndElement()` for this. Verify that the documents saved with your code can be parsed with what we implemented together.

QVariant

`QVariant` is a class that can hold values of multiple types:

```
QVariant intValue = 1;
int x = intValue.toInt();
QVariant stringValue = "ok";
QString y = stringValue.toString();
```

When you assign a value to a `QVariant` object, that value is stored inside along with the type information. You can use its `type()` method to find out which type of value it holds. The default constructor of `QVariant` creates an invalid value that you can detect using the `isValid()` method.

`QVariant` supports a great amount of types, including Qt value types such as `QDateTime`, `QColor`, and `QPoint`. You can also register your own types to store them in `QVariant`. One of the most powerful features of `QVariant` is the ability to store a collection or a hierarchy of values. You can use the `QVariantList` type (which is a `typedef` for `QList<QVariant>`) to create a list of `QVariant` objects, and you can actually put the whole list into a single `QVariant` object! You'll be able to retrieve the list and examine individual values:

```
QVariant listValue = QVariantList { 1, "ok" };
for(QVariant item: listValue.toList()) {
  qDebug() << item.toInt() << item.toString();
}
```

Similarly, you can use `QVariantMap` or `QVariantHash` to create a key-value collection with `QString` keys and `QVariant` values. Needless to say, you can store such a collection in a single `QVariant` as well. This allows you to construct a hierarchy with unlimited depth and arbitrary structure.

As you can see, `QVariant` is a pretty powerful class, but how can we use it for serializing? For a start, `QVariant` is supported by `QDataStream`, so you can use the binary serialization described earlier to serialize and restore any `QVariant` value you can construct. For example, instead of putting each field of your structure into `QDataStream`, you can put them into a `QVariantMap` and then put it into the stream:

```
Player player;
QVariantMap map;
map["name"] = player.name;
map["experience"] = player.experience;
//...
stream << map;
```

Loading the data is also straightforward:

```
QVariantMap map;
stream >> map;
Player player;
player.name = map["name"].toString();
player.experience = map["experience"].toLongLong();
```

This approach allows you to store arbitrary data in an arbitrary location. However, you can also use `QVariant` along with `QSettings` to conveniently store the data in an appropriate location.

QSettings

While not strictly a serialization issue, the aspect of storing application settings is closely related to the described subject. A Qt solution for this is the `QSettings` class. By default, it uses different backends on different platforms, such as system registry on Windows or INI files on Linux. The basic use of `QSettings` is very easy—you just need to create the object and use `setValue()` and `value()` to store and load data from it:

```
QSettings settings;
settings.setValue("level", 4);
settings.setValue("playerName", "Player1");
// ...
int level = settings.value("level").toInt();
```

The only thing you need to remember is that it operates on `QVariant`, so the return value needs to be converted to the proper type if needed, like `toInt()` in the preceding code. A call to `value()` can take an additional argument that contains the value to be returned if the requested key is not present in the map. This allows you to handle default values, for example, in a situation when the application is first started and the settings are not saved yet:

```
int level = settings.value("level", 1).toInt();
```

If you don't specify the default value, an invalid `QVariant` will be returned when nothing is stored, and you can check for that using the `isValid()` method.

In order for the default settings location to be correct, you need to set the organization name and the application name. They determine where exactly `QSettings` store data by default and ensure that the stored data will not conflict with another application. This is typically done at the beginning of your `main()` function:

```
int main(int argc, char *argv[]) {
    QApplication app(argc, argv);
    QCoreApplication::setOrganizationName("Packt");
    QCoreApplication::setApplicationName("Game Programming using Qt");
    //...
}
```

Settings hierarchy

The simplest scenario assumes that settings are "flat", in that all keys are defined on the same level. However, this does not have to be the case—correlated settings can be put into named groups. To operate on a group, you can use the `beginGroup()` and `endGroup()` calls:

```
settings.beginGroup("server");
QString serverIP = settings.value("host").toString();
int port = settings.value("port").toInt();
settings.endGroup();
```

When using this syntax, you have to remember to end the group after you are done with it. An alternative way to do the same thing is to pass the group name directly to invocation of `value()`, using / to separate it from the value name:

```
QString serverIP = settings.value("server/host").toString();
int port = settings.value("server/port").toInt();
```

You can create multiple nested groups by calling `beginGroup()` multiple times (or, equivalently, writing multiple slashes in the value name).

There is another way to introduce a non-flat structure to `QSettings`. It can handle composite `QVariant` values—`QVariantMap` and `QVariantList`. You can simply convert your data to a `QVariant`, much like we converted it to a `QJsonValue` earlier:

```
QVariant inventoryItemToVariant(const InventoryItem &item) {
    QVariantMap map;
    map["type"]       = InventoryItem::typeToName(item.type);
    map["subtype"]    = item.subType;
    map["durability"] = item.durability;
    return map;
}
```

This `QVariant` value can be passed to `QSettings::setValue()`. Of course, you will need to implement the inverse operation as well. More than that, nothing stops you from converting your data to JSON and saving it to `QSettings` as a `QByteArray`. However, these approaches may be slower than proper serialization, and the resulting settings file will be hard to edit manually.

Various Qt classes have methods that are meant to be used with `QSettings` to easily save a set of properties. For example, `QWidget::saveGeometry()` and `QWidget::restoreGeometry()` helpers allow you to save the window's position and size to `QSettings`:

```
settings.setValue("myWidget/geometry", myWidget->saveGeometry());
//...
myWidget->restoreGeometry(
    settings.value("myWidget/geometry").toByteArray());
```

Similarly, multiple widget classes
have `saveState()` and `restoreState()` methods to save information about the widget's state:

- `QMainWindow` can save positions of toolbars and dock widgets
- `QSplitter` can save positions of its handles
- `QHeaderView` can save sizes of the table's rows or columns
- `QFileDialog` can save the dialog's layout, history, and current directory

These methods are a great way to preserve all changes the user has made in your application's interface.

Customizing the settings location and format

The constructor of the `QSettings` class has a number of overloads that allow you to change the location where the data will be stored by a particular `QSettings` object, instead of using the default location. First, you can override the organization name and the application name:

```
QSettings settings("Packt", "Game Programming using Qt");
```

Next, you can use the system-wide storage location by passing `QSettings::SystemScope` as the `scope` argument:

```
QSettings settings(QSettings::SystemScope,
    "Packt", "Game Programming using Qt");
```

In this case, `QSettings` will try to read the settings for all users and then fall back to the user-specific location. Note that a system-wide location may not be writable, so using `setValue()` on it won't have the desired effect.

You can also opt out of the preferred format detection using the `QSettings::setDefaultFormat()` function. For example, use the following code on Windows to disable using the registry:

```
QSettings::setDefaultFormat(QSettings::IniFormat);
```

Finally, there is one more option available for total control of where the settings data resides—tell the constructor directly where the data should be located:

```
QSettings settings(
    QStandardPaths::writableLocation(QStandardPaths::ConfigLocation) +
        "/myapp.ini",
    QSettings::IniFormat
);
```

If you pass `QSettings::NativeFormat` to this constructor, the meaning of the path will depend on the platform. For example, it will be interpreted as a registry path on Windows.

Since you can use `QSettings` to read and write to an arbitrary INI file, it's a convenient and easy way to implement serialization of an object to the INI format, which is suitable in simple cases.

`QSettings` also allows you to register your own formats so that you can control the way your settings are stored, for example, by storing them using XML or by adding on-the-fly encryption. This is done using `QSettings::registerFormat()`, where you need to pass the file extension and two pointers to functions that perform reading and writing of the settings, respectively, as follows:

```
bool readCCFile(QIODevice &device, QSettings::SettingsMap &map) {
    CeasarCipherDevice ccDevice;
    ccDevice.setBaseDevice(&device);
    // ...
    return true;
}
bool writeCCFile(QIODevice &device, const QSettings::SettingsMap &map)
{
    // ...
}
const QSettings::Format CCFormat = QSettings::registerFormat(
    "ccph", readCCFile, writeCCFile);
```

JSON files

JSON stands for "JavaScript Object Notation", which is a popular lightweight textual format that is used to store object-oriented data in a human-readable form. It comes from JavaScript where it is the native format used to store object information; however, it is commonly used across many programming languages and a popular format for web data exchange. Qt Core supports JSON format, as we'll see in the following code. A simple JSON-formatted definition looks as follows:

```
{
    "name": "Joe",
    "age": 14,
    "inventory": [
        { "type": "gold", "amount": "144000" },
        { "type": "short_sword", "material": "iron" }
    ]
}
```

JSON objects can contain values of the following types:

Type	Description
bool	A boolean value (`true` or `false`).
double	A number value (for example, `42.1`).
string	A quoted string (for example, `"Qt"`).
array	A collection of values of any type enclosed in square brackets (for example, `[42.1, "Qt"]`).
object	A set of key-value pairs enclosed in braces. Keys are strings, and values can be of any type (for example, `{ "key1": 42.1, "key2": [42.1, "Qt"] }`).
null	A special value (`null`) indicating lack of data.

A proper **JSON document** must have either an array or an object at the top level. In the preceding example, we had an object containing three properties: name, age, and inventory. The first two properties are simple values, and the last property is an array that contains two objects with two properties each.

Qt can create and read JSON descriptions using the `QJsonDocument` class. A document can be created from the UTF-8-encoded text using the `QJsonDocument::fromJson()` static method, and can later be stored in a textual form again using `toJson()`. Once a JSON document is created, you can check whether it represents an object or an array using one of the `isArray()` and `isObject()` calls. Then, the document can be transformed into `QJsonArray` or `QJsonObject` using the `array()` or `object()` methods.

> Since the structure of JSON closely resembles that of `QVariant` (which can also hold key-value pairs using `QVariantMap` and arrays using `QVariantList`), conversion methods `QJsonDocument::fromVariant()` and `QJsonDocument::toVariant()` also exist.

`QJsonObject` is an iterable type that can be queried for a list of keys (using `keys()`) or asked for a value of a specific key (with a `value()` method or `operator[]`). Values are represented using the `QJsonValue` class, which can store any of the value types listed earlier. New properties can be added to the object using the `insert()` method that takes a key as a string, and a value can be added as `QJsonValue`. The existing properties can be removed using `remove()`.

`QJsonArray` is also an iterable type that contains a classic list API; it contains methods such as `append()`, `insert()`, `removeAt()`, `at()`, and `size()` to manipulate entries in the array, again working on `QJsonValue` as the item type.

Time for action – The player data JSON serializer

Our next exercise is to create a serializer of the same `PlayerInfo` structure as we used for the XML exercise, but this time the destination data format will be JSON.

Start by creating a `PlayerInfoJson` class and give it an interface similar to the one shown in the following code:

```
class PlayerInfoJson {
public:
    PlayerInfoJson() {}
    QByteArray playerInfoToJson(const PlayerInfo &pinfo);
};
```

All that is really required is to implement the `playerInfoToJson` method. Generally, we need to convert our `PlayerInfo` data to a `QJsonArray` and then use `QJsonDocument` to encode it as JSON:

```
QByteArray PlayerInfoJson::playerInfoToJson(const PlayerInfo &pinfo)
{
    QJsonDocument doc(toJson(pinfo));
    return doc.toJson();
}
```

Now, let's start implementing the `toJson()` method:

```
QJsonArray PlayerInfoJson::toJson(const PlayerInfo &pinfo) {
    QJsonArray array;
    for(const Player &p: pinfo.players) {
        array << toJson(p);
    }
    return array;
}
```

Since the structure is really a list of players, we can iterate over it, convert each player to a `QJsonValue`, and append the result to `QJsonArray`. Having this function ready, we can descend a level and implement an overload for `toJson()` that takes a `Player` object:

```
QJsonValue PlayerInfoJson::toJson(const Player &player) {
    QJsonObject object;
    object["name"]       = player.name;
    object["password"]   = player.password;
    object["experience"] = player.experience;
    object["hitpoints"]  = player.hitPoints;
    object["location"]   = player.location;
    object["position"]   = QJsonObject({ { "x", player.position.x() },
                                         { "y", player.position.y() }
});
    object["inventory"]  = toJson(player.inventory);
    return object;
}
```

This time, we are using `QJsonObject` as our base type, since we want to associate values with keys. For each key, we use the index operator to add entries to the object. The position key holds a `QPoint` value, which is not a valid JSON value, so we convert the point to a `QJsonObject` with two keys (`x` and `y`) using the C++11 initializer list. The situation is different with the inventory—again, we have to write an overload for `toJson` that will perform the conversion:

```
QJsonValue PlayerInfoJson::toJson(const QVector<InventoryItem> &items)
{
    QJsonArray array;
    for(const InventoryItem &item: items) {
        array << toJson(item);
    }
    return array;
}
```

The code is almost identical to the one handling `PlayerInfo` objects, so let's focus on the last overload of `toVariant`—the one that accepts `Item` instances:

```
QJsonValue PlayerInfoJson::toJson(const InventoryItem &item) {
    QJsonObject object;
    object["type"] = InventoryItem::typeToName(item.type);
    object["subtype"] = item.subType;
    object["durability"] = item.durability;
    return object;
}
```

There is not much to comment here—we add all keys to the object, converting the item type to a string. For this, we have to add the static `InventoryItem::typeToName()` method that is the reverse of `typeByName()`, that is, it takes a enum variant and outputs its name as a string:

```
const char *InventoryItem::typeToName(InventoryItem::Type value)
{
    QMetaEnum metaEnum = QMetaEnum::fromType<InventoryItem::Type>();
    return metaEnum.valueToKey(static_cast<int>(value));
}
```

This is pretty much a wrapper over the `QMetaEnum::valueToKey()` method that does all the magic that wouldn't be possible without Qt.

The serializer is complete! Now you can use `PlayerInfoJson::playerInfoToJson()` to convert `PlayerInfo` into a `QByteArray` containing the JSON. It's suitable for writing it to a file or sending it over the network. However, to make it more useful, we need to implement the reverse operation (deserialization).

Time for action – Implementing a JSON parser

Let's extend the `PlayerInfoJSON` class and equip it with a `playerInfoFromJson()` method:

```
PlayerInfo PlayerInfoJson::playerInfoFromJson(const QByteArray &ba) {
    QJsonDocument doc = QJsonDocument::fromJson(ba);
    if(!doc.isArray()) {
        return PlayerInfo();
    }
    QJsonArray array = doc.array();
    PlayerInfo pinfo;
    for(const QJsonValue &value: array) {
        pinfo.players << playerFromJson(value.toObject());
    }
    return pinfo;
}
```

First, we read the document and check whether it is valid and holds the expected array. Upon failure, an empty structure is returned; otherwise, we iterate over the received array and convert each of its elements to an object. Similar to the serialization example, we create a helper function for each complex item of our data structure. Thus, we write a new `playerFromJson()` method that converts `QJsonObject` to a `Player`, that is, performs a reverse operation as compared to `toJson(Player)`:

```
Player PlayerInfoJson::playerFromJson(const QJsonObject &object) {
    Player player;
    player.name       = object["name"].toString();
    player.password   = object["password"].toString();
    player.experience = object["experience"].toDouble();
    player.hitPoints  = object["hitpoints"].toDouble();
    player.location   = object["location"].toString();
    QJsonObject positionObject = object["position"].toObject();
    player.position   = QPoint(positionObject["x"].toInt(),
                               positionObject["y"].toInt());
    player.inventory  =
inventoryFromJson(object["inventory"].toArray());
    return player;
}
```

In this function, we used `operator[]` to extract data from `QJsonObject`, and then we used different functions to convert the data to the desired type. Note that in order to convert to `QPoint`, we first converted it to `QJsonObject` and then extracted the values before using them to build `QPoint`. In each case, if the conversion fails, we get a default value for that type (for example, an empty string or a zero number). To read the inventory, we employ another custom method:

```
QVector<InventoryItem> PlayerInfoJson::inventoryFromJson(
    const QJsonArray &array)
{
    QVector<InventoryItem> inventory;
    for(const QJsonValue &value: array) {
      inventory << inventoryItemFromJson(value.toObject());
    }
    return inventory;
}
```

What remains is to implement `inventoryItemFromJson()`:

```
InventoryItem PlayerInfoJson::inventoryItemFromJson(
    const QJsonObject &object)
{
    InventoryItem item;
    item.type = InventoryItem::typeByName(object["type"].toString());
    item.subType = object["subtype"].toString();
    item.durability = object["durability"].toDouble();
    return item;
}
```

Unfortunately, our `typeByName()` function requires `QStringRef`, not `QString`. We can fix this by adding a couple of overloads and forwarding them to a single implementation:

```
InventoryItem::Type InventoryItem::typeByName(const QStringRef &r) {
    return typeByName(r.toLatin1());
}
InventoryItem::Type InventoryItem::typeByName(const QString &r) {
    return typeByName(r.toLatin1());
}
InventoryItem::Type InventoryItem::typeByName(const QByteArray
&latin1) {
    QMetaEnum metaEnum = QMetaEnum::fromType<InventoryItem::Type>();
    int result = metaEnum.keyToValue(latin1.constData());
    return static_cast<InventoryItem::Type>(result);
}
```

What just happened?

The class that was implemented can be used for bidirectional conversion between `Item` instances and a `QByteArray` object, which contains the object data in the JSON format. We didn't do any error checking here; instead, we relied on Qt's rule that an error results in a sensible default value.

> What if you want to perform error checking? The most straightforward solution in this case is to use exceptions, as they will automatically propagate from the multiple nested calls to the caller's location. Ensure that you catch any exceptions you throw, or the application will terminate. A more Qt-like solution is to create a `bool *ok` argument in all methods (including internal ones) and set the boolean value to `false` in case of any error.

Pop quiz

Q1. What is the closest equivalent of `std::string` in Qt?

1. `QString`
2. `QByteArray`
3. `QStringLiteral`

Q2. Which strings match the `\A\d\z` regular expression?

1. Strings consisting of digits
2. Strings consisting of a single digit
3. This is not a valid regular expression

Q3. Which of the following container types can you use to store a list of widgets?

1. `QVector<QWidget>`
2. `QList<QWidget>`
3. `QVector<QWidget*>`

Q4. Which class can you use to convert a text string containing JSON to a Qt JSON representation?

1. `QJsonValue`
2. `QJsonObject`
3. `QJsonDocument`

Summary

In this chapter, you learned a number of core Qt technologies, ranging from text manipulation and containers to accessing devices that can be used to transfer or store data, using a number of popular technologies such as XML or JSON. You should be aware that we have barely scratched the surface of what Qt offers and there are many other interesting classes you should familiarize yourself with, but this minimum amount of information should give you a head start and show you the direction to follow with your future research.

In the next chapter, we will go beyond the boundaries of your computer and explore ways to use the powerful world of the modern internet. You will learn how to interact with the existing network services, check the current network availability, and implement your own servers and clients. This knowledge will come in handy if you want to implement multiplayer networked games.

7
Networking

In this chapter, you will be taught how to communicate with internet servers and with sockets in general. First, we will take a look at `QNetworkAccessManager`, which makes sending network requests and receiving replies really easy. Building on this basic knowledge, we will then use Google's Distance API to get information about the distance between two locations and how long it would take to get from one to the other. This technique, and the respective knowledge, can also be used to include Facebook or Twitter in your application via their respective APIs. Then, we will take a look at Qt's Bearer API, which provides information about a device's connectivity state. In the last section, you will learn how to use sockets to create your own server and clients using TCP or UDP as the network protocol.

The main topics covered in this chapter are the following:

- Downloading files using `QNetworkAccessManager`
- Using Google's Distance Matrix API
- Implementing a TCP chat server and client
- Using UDP sockets

QNetworkAccessManager

All network-related functionality in Qt is implemented in the Qt Network module. The easiest way to access files on the internet is to use the `QNetworkAccessManager` class, which handles the complete communication between your game and the internet.

Setting up a local HTTP server

In our next example, we will be downloading a file over HTTP. If you don't have a local HTTP server, you can just use any publicly available HTTP or HTTPS resource to test your code. However, when you develop and test a network-enabled application, it is recommended that you use a private, local network if feasible. This way, it is possible to debug both ends of the connection, and errors will not expose sensitive data.

If you are not familiar with setting up a web server locally on your machine, there are, luckily, a number of all-in-one installers that are freely available. These will automatically configure Apache2, MySQL (or MariaDB), PHP, and many other servers on your system. On Windows, for example, you can use XAMPP (`https://www.apachefriends.org`), or the Uniform Server (`http://www.uniformserver.com`); on Apple computers, there is MAMP (`https://www.mamp.info`); and on Linux, you can open your preferred package manager, search for a package called `Apache2` or a similar one, and install it. Alternatively, take a look at your distribution's documentation.

Before you install Apache on your machine, think about using a virtual machine, such as VirtualBox (`http://www.virtualbox.org`) for this task. This way, you keep your machine clean, and you can easily try different settings for your test server. With multiple virtual machines, you can even test the interaction between different instances of your game. If you are on Unix, Docker (`http://www.docker.com`) might be worth taking a look at.

Preparing a URL for testing

If you've set up a local HTTP server, create a file called `version.txt` in the root directory of the installed server. This file should contain a small piece of text such as "I am a file on localhost" or something similar. As you might have guessed, a real-life scenario could be to check whether there is an updated version of your game or application on the server. To test whether the server and the file are correctly set up, start a web browser and open `http://localhost/version.txt`. You should then see the file's content:

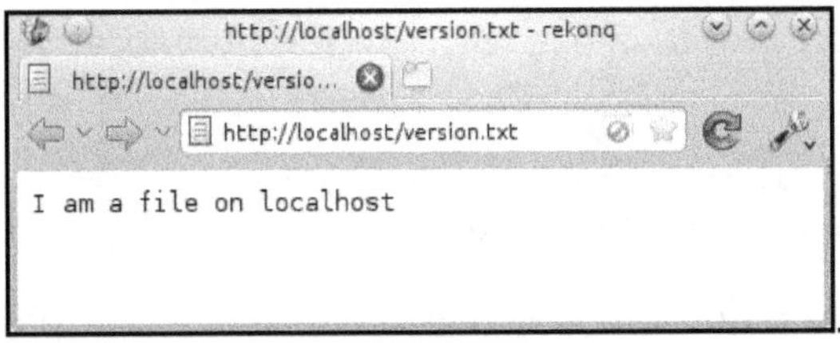

If this fails, it may be the case that your server does not allow you to display text files. Instead of getting lost in the server's configuration, just rename the file to `version.html`. This should do the trick!

If you don't have an HTTP server, you can use the URL of your favorite website, but be prepared to receive HTML code instead of plain text, as the majority of websites use HTML. You can also use the `https://www.google.com/robots.txt` URL, as it responds with plain text.

Time for action – Downloading a file

Create a Qt Widgets project and add a widget class named `FileDownload`. Add a button that will start the download and a plain text edit that will display the result. As always, you can look at the code files provided with the book if you need any help.

Next, enable the Qt Network module by adding `QT += network` to the project file. Then, create an instance of `QNetworkAccessManager` in the constructor and put it in a private field:

```
m_network_manager = new QNetworkAccessManager(this);
```

Since `QNetworkAccessManager` inherits `QObject`, it takes a pointer to `QObject`, which is used as a parent. Thus, you do not have delete the manager later on.

Secondly, we connect the manager's `finished()` signal to a slot of our choice; for example, in our class, we have a slot called `downloadFinished()`:

```
connect(m_network_manager, &QNetworkAccessManager::finished,
        this, &FileDownload::downloadFinished);
```

We have to do this because the API of `QNetworkAccessManager` is *asynchronous*. This means that none of the network requests, or the read or write operations, will block the current thread. Instead, when the data is available or another network event occurs, Qt will send a corresponding signal so that you can handle the data.

Thirdly, we actually request the `version.txt` file from localhost when the button is clicked:

```
QUrl url("http://localhost/version.txt");
m_network_manager->get(QNetworkRequest(url));
```

With `get()`, we send a request to get the contents of the file specified by the URL. The function expects a `QNetworkRequest` object, which defines all the information needed to send a request over the network. The main information for such a request is, naturally the URL of the file. This is the reason `QNetworkRequest` takes `QUrl` as an argument in its constructor. You can also set the URL with `setUrl()` to a request. If you wish to define a request header (for example, a custom user agent), you can use `setHeader()`:

```
QNetworkRequest request;
request.setUrl(QUrl("http://localhost/version.txt"));
request.setHeader(QNetworkRequest::UserAgentHeader, "MyGame");
m_network_manager->get(request);
```

The `setHeader()` function takes two arguments: the first is a value of the `QNetworkRequest::KnownHeaders` enumeration, which holds the most common (self-explanatory) headers, such as `LastModifiedHeader` or `ContentTypeHeader`, and the second is the actual value. You can also write the header using `setRawHeader()`:

```
request.setRawHeader("User-Agent", "MyGame");
```

When you use `setRawHeader()`, you have to write the header field names yourself. Besides this, it behaves like `setHeader()`. A list of all the available headers for the HTTP protocol Version 1.1 can be found in section 14 of RFC 2616 (`https://www.w3.org/Protocols/rfc2616/rfc2616-sec14.html#sec14`).

Getting back to our example, with the `get()` function, we requested the `version.txt` file from the localhost. All we have to do from now on is wait for the server to reply. As soon as the server's reply is finished, the `downloadFinished()` slot will be called that was defined by the preceding connection statement. A pointer to a `QNetworkReply` object will be passed as the argument to the slot, and we can read the reply's data and show it in `m_edit`, an instance of `QPlainTextEdit`, with the following:

```
void FileDownload::downloadFinished(QNetworkReply *reply) {
    const QByteArray content = reply->readAll();
    m_edit->setPlainText(QString::fromUtf8(content));
```

```
        reply->deleteLater();
    }
```

Since `QNetworkReply` inherits `QIODevice`, there are also other possibilities to read the content of the reply. For example, you can use `QDataStream` or `QTextStream` to read and interpret binary or textual data, respectively. Here, as the fourth command, `QIODevice::readAll()` is used to get the full content of the requested file in a `QByteArray` object. This is very similar to reading from files, which was shown in the previous chapter. The responsibility for the transferred pointer to the corresponding `QNetworkReply` lies with us, so we need to delete it at the end of the slot. However, be careful and do not call `delete` on the reply directly. Always use `deleteLater()`, as the documentation suggests!

> TIP: In the previous chapter, we warned you that you shouldn't use `readAll()` to read large files, as they can't fit in a single `QByteArray`. The same holds for `QNetworkReply`. If the server decides to send you a large response (for example, if you try to download a large file), the first portion of the response will be saved to a buffer inside the `QNetworkReply` object, and then the download will throttle down until you read some data from the buffer. However, you can't do that if you only use the `finished()` signal. Instead, you need to use the `QNetworkReply::readyRead()` signal and read each portion of the data in order to free the buffer and allow more data to be received. We will show how to do this later in this chapter.

The full source code can be found in the **FileDownload** example bundled with this book. If you start the small demo application and click on the **Load File** button, you should see the content of the loaded file:

FileDownload
User-agent: *
Disallow: /search
Allow: /search/about
Allow: /search/howsearchworks
Disallow: /sdch
Disallow: /groups
Disallow: /index.html?
Disallow: /?
Allow: /?hl=
Disallow: /?hl=*&
Allow: /?hl=*&gws_rd=ssl$
Disallow: /?hl=*&*&gws_rd=ssl
Load File

Have a go hero – Extending the basic file downloader

Of course, having to alter the source code in order to download another file is far from an ideal approach, so try to extend the dialog by adding a line edit in which you can specify the URL you want to download. Also, you can offer a file dialog to choose the location where the downloaded file will be saved. The simplest way of doing that is to use the `QFileDialog::getSaveFileName()` static function.

Single network manager per application

One single instance of `QNetworkAccessManager` is enough for an entire application. For example, you can create an instance of `QNetworkAccessManager` in your main window class and pass a pointer to it to all the other places where it's needed. For ease of use, you can also create a **singleton** and access the manager through that.

> TIP: A singleton pattern ensures that a class is instantiated only once. The pattern is useful for accessing application-wide configurations or—as in our case—an instance of `QNetworkAccessManager`.

A simple template-based approach to create a singleton will look like this (as a header file):

```
template <class T>
class Singleton
{
public:
    static T& instance()
    {
        static T static_instance;
        return static_instance;
    }
private:
    Singleton();
    ~Singleton();
    Singleton(const Singleton &);
    Singleton& operator=(const Singleton &);
};
```

In the source code, you will include that header file and acquire a singleton of a class called `MyClass` with this:

```
MyClass &singleton = Singleton<MyClass>::instance();
```

This singleton implementation is not *thread-safe*, meaning that attempting to access the instance from multiple threads simultaneously will result in undefined behavior. An example of thread-safe implementation of the singleton pattern can be found at `https://wiki.qt.io/Qt_thread-safe_singleton`.

If you are using Qt Quick—it will be explained in `Chapter 11`, *Introduction to Qt Quick*—with `QQmlApplicationEngine`, you can directly use the engine's instance of `QNetworkAccessManager`:

```
QQmlApplicationEngine engine;
QNetworkAccessManager *network_manager =
engine.networkAccessManager();
```

Time for action – Displaying a proper error message

If you do not see the content of the file, something went wrong. Just as in real life, this can often happen. So, we need to ensure that there is a good error handling mechanism in such cases to inform the user about what is going on. Fortunately, `QNetworkReply` offers several possibilities to do this.

In the slot called `downloadFinished()`, we first want to check whether an error occurred:

```
if (reply->error() != QNetworkReply::NoError) {
    // error occurred
}
```

The `QNetworkReply::error()` function returns the error that occurred while handling the request. The error is encoded as a value of the `QNetworkReply::NetworkError` type. The most common errors are probably these:

Error code	Meaning
`QNetworkReply::ConnectionRefusedError`	The program was not able to connect to the server at all (for example, if no server was running)
`QNetworkReply::ContentNotFoundError`	The server responded with HTTP error code 404, indicating that a page with the requested URL could not be found
`QNetworkReply::ContentAccessDenied`	The server responded with HTTP error code 403, indicating that you do not have the permission to access the requested file

There are more than 30 possible error types, and you can look them up in the documentation of the `QNetworkReply::NetworkError` enumeration. However, normally, you do not need to know exactly what went wrong. You only need to know whether everything worked out—`QNetworkReply::NoError` would be the return value in this case—or whether something went wrong. To provide the user with a meaningful error description, you can use `QIODevice::errorString()`. The text is already set up with the corresponding error message, and we only have to display it:

```
if (reply->error()) {
    const QString error = reply->errorString();
    m_edit->setPlainText(error);
    return;
}
```

In our example, assuming that we made an error in the URL and wrote `versions.txt` by mistake, the application will look like this:

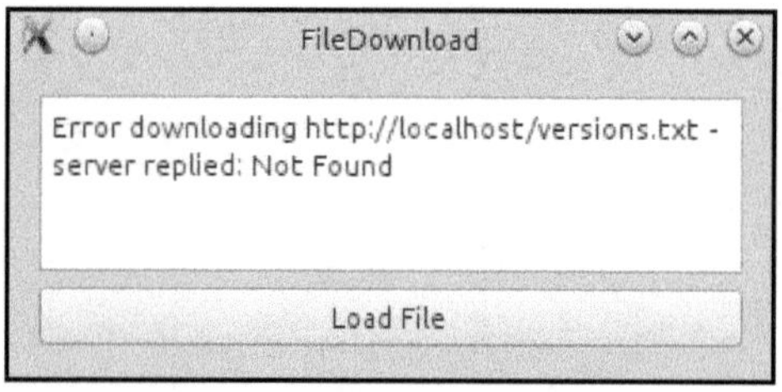

If the request was an HTTP request and the status code is of interest, it can be retrieved by `QNetworkReply::attribute()`:

```
int statusCode =
reply->attribute(QNetworkRequest::HttpStatusCodeAttribute).toInt();
```

Since it returns `QVariant`, you need to use `QVariant::toInt()` to get the code as an integer. Besides the HTTP status code, you can query a lot of other information through `attribute()`. Take a look at the description of the `QNetworkRequest::Attribute` enumeration in the documentation. There, you will also find `QNetworkRequest::HttpReasonPhraseAttribute`, which holds a human-readable reason phrase for the HTTP status code, for example, "Not Found" if an HTTP error 404 has occurred. The value of this attribute is used to set the error text for `QIODevice::errorString()`. So, you can either use the default error description provided by `errorString()` or compose your own by interpreting the reply's attributes.

> TIP: If a download failed and you want to resume it, or if you only want to download a specific part of a file, you can use the `Range` header. However, the server must support this.

In the following example, only the bytes from `300` to `500` will be downloaded:

```
QNetworkRequest request(url);
request.setRawHeader("Range", "bytes=300-500");
QNetworkReply *reply = m_network_manager->get(request);
```

> If you want to simulate sending a form on a website, you will usually need to send a POST request instead of GET. This is done by using the `QNetworkAccessManager::post()` function instead of the `get()` function we used. You will also need to specify the payload, for example, using the `QHttpMultiPart` class.

Downloading files over FTP

Downloading a file over FTP is as simple as downloading files over HTTP. If it is an anonymous FTP server for which you do not need an authentication, just use the URL as we did before. Assuming that there is again a file called `version.txt` on the FTP server on the localhost, type this:

```
m_network_manager->get(QNetworkRequest(
    QUrl("ftp://localhost/version.txt")));
```

That's all; everything else stays the same. If the FTP server requires an authentication, you'll get an error; consider this example:

Likewise, setting the username and password to access an FTP server is easy—either write it in the URL, or use the `setUserName()` and `setPassword()` functions of `QUrl`. If the server does not use a standard port, you can set the port explicitly with `QUrl::setPort()`.

TIP: To upload a file to an FTP server, use `QNetworkAccessManager::put()`, which takes `QNetworkRequest` as its first argument, calling a URL that defines the name of the new file on the server, and the actual data as its second argument, which should be uploaded. For small uploads, you can pass the content as `QByteArray`. For larger content, it's better to use a pointer to `QIODevice`. Ensure that the device is open and stays available until the upload is complete.

Downloading files in parallel

A very important note concerning `QNetworkAccessManager` is the fact that it works asynchronously. This means that you can post a network request without blocking the main event loop, and this is what keeps the GUI responsive. If you post more than one request, they are put in the manager's queue. Depending on the protocol used, they may be processed in parallel. If you are sending HTTP requests, normally up to six requests will be handled at a time. If more requests are queued, they will be automatically processed later. This will not block the application, as `QNetworkAccessManager` uses threads internally.

There is really no need to encapsulate `QNetworkAccessManager` in a thread; however, unfortunately, this unnecessary approach is frequently recommended all over the internet. Really, don't move `QNetworkAccessManager` to a thread unless you know exactly what you are doing.

If you send multiple requests, the slot connected to the manager's `finished()` signal is called in an arbitrary order, depending on how quickly a request gets a reply from the server. This is why you need to know to which request a reply belongs. This is one reason why every `QNetworkReply` carries its related `QNetworkRequest`. It can be accessed through `QNetworkReply::request()`.

Even if the determination of the replies and their purpose may work for a small application in a single slot, it will quickly get large and confusing if you send a lot of requests with different purposes. It would be better to connect requests to multiple slots that are specialized for a given task. Fortunately, this can be achieved very easily.

Any method that adds a request to `QNetworkAccessManager` (such as `get()`) returns a pointer to `QNetworkReply`. Using this pointer, you can then connect the reply's signals to your specific slots. For example, if you have several URLs, and you want to save all linked images from these sites to your hard drive, you request all web pages via `QNetworkAccessManager::get()` and connect their replies to a slot specialized for parsing the received HTML. If links to the images are found, this slot will request them again with `get()`. This time, however, the replies to these requests will be connected to a second slot, which is designed for saving the images to the disk. Thus, you can separate the two tasks: parsing HTML and saving data to a local drive.

The most important signals of `QNetworkReply` are discussed next.

The finished signal

The `finished()` signal is an equivalent of the `QNetworkAccessManager::finished()` signal that we used earlier. It is triggered as soon as a reply is returned—successfully or not. After this signal is emitted, neither the reply's data nor its metadata will be altered any more. With this signal, you are now able to connect a reply to a specific slot. This way, you can realize the scenario on saving images that was outlined in the previous section.

However, one problem remains: if you post simultaneous requests, you do not know which one has finished and thus called the connected slot. Unlike `QNetworkAccessManager::finished()`, `QNetworkReply::finished()` does not pass a pointer to `QNetworkReply`; this would actually be a pointer to itself in this case. We've already had a similar problem in `Chapter 3`, *Qt GUI Programming*, so let's remember how we can deal with it.

A quick solution to solve this problem is to use `sender()`. It returns a pointer to the `QObject` instance that has called the slot. Since we know that it was `QNetworkReply`, we can write the following:

```
QNetworkReply *reply = qobject_cast<QNetworkReply*>(sender());
if (!reply) {
    return;
}
```

In this code, we needed to cast the `QObject` pointer returned by `sender()` to a pointer of the `QNetworkReply` type.

> **TIP** Whenever you're casting classes that inherit `QObject`, use `qobject_cast`. Unlike `dynamic_cast`, it does not use RTTI and works across the dynamic library boundaries.

Although we can be pretty confident that the cast will work, do not forget to check whether the pointer is valid. If it is a null pointer, exit the slot.

Time for action – Writing the OOP conform code using QSignalMapper

A more elegant way that does not rely on `sender()` would be to use `QSignalMapper` to receive the reply object in the argument of the slot. First, you need to add the `QSignalMapper *m_imageFinishedMapper` private field to your class. When you call `QNetworkAccessManager::get()` to request each image, set up the mapper as follows:

```
for(const QString& url: urls) {
    QNetworkRequest request(url);
    QNetworkReply *reply = m_network_manager->get(request);
    connect(reply, SIGNAL(finished()),
            m_imageFinishedMapper, SLOT(map()));
    m_imageFinishedMapper->setMapping(reply, reply);
}
```

In a prominent place, most likely the constructor of the class, connect the mapper's `map()` signal to a custom slot. Take this example into consideration:

```
connect(m_imageFinishedMapper, SIGNAL(mapped(QObject*)),
        this, SLOT(imageFinished(QObject*)));
```

Now your slot receives the reply object as the argument:

```
void Object::imageFinished(QObject *replyObject)
{
    QNetworkReply *reply = qobject_cast<QNetworkReply *>(replyObject);
    //...
}
```

What just happened?

First, we posted the request and fetched the pointer to the `QNetworkReply` object. Then, we connected the reply's finished signal to the mapper's slot `map()`. Next, we called the `setMapping()` method of the mapper to indicate that the sender itself should be
sent as the slot's argument. The effect is very similar to the direct use of the `QNetworkAccessManager::finished(QNetworkReply *reply)` signal, but this way, we can use multiple slots dedicated to different purposes (with a separate mapper corresponding to each slot), all served by a single `QNetworkAccessManager` instance.

> TIP: `QSignalMapper` also allows you to map with `int` or `QString` as an identifier instead of `QObject *`, as used in the preceding code. So, you can rewrite the example and use the URL to identify the corresponding request.

The error signal

Instead of dealing with errors in the slot connected to the `finished()` signal, you can use the reply's `error()` signal, which passes the error of the `QNetworkReply::NetworkError` type to the slot. After the `error()` signal has been emitted, the `finished()` signal will, most likely, also be emitted shortly.

The readyRead signal

Until now, we have used the slot connected to the `finished()` signal to get the reply's content. This works perfectly if you are deal with small files. However, this approach is unsuitable when dealing with large files, as they will unnecessarily bind too many resources. For larger files, it is better to read and save the transferred data as soon as it is available. We are informed by `QIODevice::readyRead()` whenever new data is available to be read. So, for large files, you should use the following code:

```
QNetworkReply *reply = m_network_manager->get(request);
connect(reply, &QIODevice::readyRead,
        this, &SomeClass::readContent);
m_file.open(QIODevice::WriteOnly);
```

This will help you connect the reply's `readyRead()` signal to a slot, set up `QFile`, and open it. In the connected slot, type in the following snippet:

```
QNetworkReply *reply = /* ... */;
const QByteArray byteArray = reply->readAll();
m_file.write(byteArray);
m_file.flush();
```

Now, you can fetch the content, which has been transferred so far, and save it to the (already open) file. This way, the resources needed are minimized. Don't forget to close the file after the `finished()` signal is emitted.

In this context, it would be helpful if you knew upfront the size of the file you want to download. With this information, we can check upfront whether there is enough space left on the disk. We can use `QNetworkAccessManager::head()` for this purpose. It behaves like the `get()` function, but it does not request the content of the file. Only the headers are transferred, and if we are lucky, the server sends the `Content-Length` header, which holds the file size in bytes. To get that information, we type this:

```
int length =
reply->header(QNetworkRequest::ContentLengthHeader).toInt();
```

Time for action – Showing the download progress

Especially when a big file is downloaded, the user usually wants to know how much data has already been downloaded and approximately how long it will take for the download to finish.

In order to achieve this, we can use the reply's `downloadProgress()` signal. As the first argument, it passes the information on how many bytes have already been received and as the second argument, how many bytes there are in total. This gives us the possibility to indicate the progress of the download with `QProgressBar`. As the passed arguments are of the `qint64` type, we can't use them directly with `QProgressBar`, as it only accepts `int`. So, in the connected slot, we can do the following:

```
void SomeClass::downloadProgress(qint64 bytesReceived, qint64
bytesTotal) {
    qreal progress = (bytesTotal < 1) ? 1.0
                   : static_cast<qreal>(bytesReceived) / bytesTotal;
    progressBar->setValue(qRound(progress * progressBar->maximum()));
}
```

What just happened?

First, we calculate the percentage of the download progress. The calculated `progress` value will range from 0 (0%) to 1 (100%). Then, we set the new value for the progress bar where `progressBar` is the pointer to this bar. However, what value will `progressBar->maximum()` have and where do we set the range for the progress bar? What is nice is that you do not have to set it for every new download. It is only done once, for example, in the constructor of the class containing the bar. As range values, we would recommend this:

```
progressBar->setRange(0, 2048);
```

The reason is that if you take, for example, a range of 0 to 100 and the progress bar is 500 pixels wide, the bar would jump 5 pixels forward for every value change. This will look ugly. To get a smooth progression where the bar expands by 1 pixel at a time, a range of 0 to 99.999.999 would surely work, but it would be highly inefficient. This is because the current value of the bar would change a lot without any graphical depiction. So, the best value for the range would be 0 to the actual bar's width in pixels.

Unfortunately, the width of the bar can change depending on the actual widget width, and frequently querying the actual size of the bar every time the value changes is also not a good solution. Why 2048, then? It's just a nice round number that is bigger than any screen resolution we're likely to get. This ensures that the progress bar runs smoothly, even if it is fully expanded. If you are targeting smaller devices, choose a smaller, more appropriate number.

To be able to calculate the time remaining for the download to finish, you have to start a timer. In this case, use `QElapsedTimer`. After posting the request with `QNetworkAccessManager::get()`, start the timer by calling `QElapsedTimer::start()`. Assuming that the timer is called `m_timer`, the calculation will be as follows:

```
qreal remaining = m_timer.elapsed() *
                  (1.0 - progress) / progress;
int remainingSeconds = qRound(remaining / 1000);
```

`QElapsedTimer::elapsed()` returns the milliseconds that are counted from the moment the timer is started. Assuming that the download progress is linear, the ratio of the remaining time to the elapsed time equals `(1.0 - progress) / progress`. For example, if `progress` is 0.25 (25%), the expected remaining time will be three times bigger than the elapsed time: `(1.0 - 0.25) / 0.25) = 3`. If you divide the result by 1,000 and round it to the nearest integer, you'll get the remaining time in seconds.

`QElapsedTimer` is not to be confused with `QTimer`. `QTimer` is used to call a slot after a certain amount of time has passed. `QElapsedTimer` is merely a convenience class that is able to remember the start time and calculate the elapsed time by subtracting the start time from the current time.

Using a proxy

If you want to use a proxy, you first have to set up `QNetworkProxy`. You can define the type of proxy with `setType()`. As arguments, you will most likely want to pass `QNetworkProxy::Socks5Proxy` or `QNetworkProxy::HttpProxy`. Then, set up the hostname with `setHostName()`, the username with `setUserName()`, and the password with `setPassword()`. The last two properties are, of course, only needed if the proxy requires authentication. Once the proxy is set up, you can set it to the access manager via `QNetworkAccessManager::setProxy()`. Now, all new requests will use this proxy.

Connecting to Google, Facebook, Twitter, and co.

Since we discussed `QNetworkAccessManager`, you now have the knowledge you need to integrate Facebook, Twitter, or similar sites into your application. They all use the HTTPS protocol and simple requests in order to retrieve data from them. For Facebook, you have to use the so-called Graph API. It describes which interfaces are available and what options they offer. If you want to search for users who are called **Helena**, you have to request `https://graph.facebook.com/search?q=helena&type=user`. Of course, you can do this with `QNetworkManager`. You will find more information about the possible requests to Facebook at `https://developers.facebook.com/docs/graph-api`.

If you wish to display tweets in your game, you have to use Twitter's REST or Search API. Assuming that you know the ID of a tweet you would like to display, you can get it through `https://api.twitter.com/1.1/statuses/show.json?id=12345`, where `12345` is the actual ID for the tweet. If you would like to find tweets mentioning `#Helena`, you would write `https://api.twitter.com/1.1/search/tweets.json?q=%23Helena`. You can find more information about the parameters and the other possibilities of Twitter's API at `https://developer.twitter.com/en/docs`.

Since both Facebook and Twitter need an authentication to use their APIs, we will take a look at Google instead. Let's use Google's Distance Matrix API in order to get information about how long it would take for us to get from one city to another. The technical documentation for the API we will use can be found at `https://developers.google.com/maps/documentation/distancematrix`.

Time for action – Using Google's Distance Matrix API

The GUI for this example is kept simple—the source code is attached with the book. It consists of two line edits (`ui->from` and `ui->to`) that allow you to enter the origin and destination of the journey. It also provides you with a combobox (`ui->vehicle`) that allows you to choose a mode of transportation—whether you want to drive a car, ride a bicycle, or walk—a push button (`ui->search`) to start the request, and a text edit, or (`ui->result`) to show the results.

It looks like this:

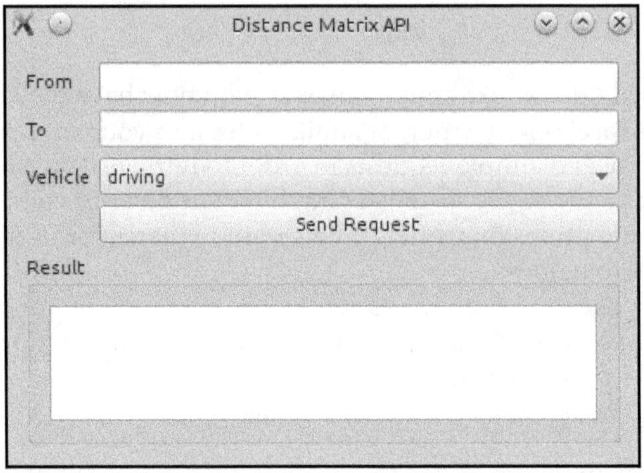

MainWindow—a subclass of QMainWindow—is the application's main class that holds two private members: m_network_manager, which is a pointer to QNetworkAccessManager, and m_reply, which is a pointer to QNetworkReply.

Time for action – Constructing the query

Whenever the button is pressed, the sendRequest() slot is called:

```
void MainWindow::sendRequest()
{
    if (m_reply != nullptr && m_reply->isRunning()) {
        m_reply->abort();
    }
    ui->result->clear();
    //...
}
```

In this slot, we first check whether there is an old request, which was stored in m_reply, and whether it is still running. If that is true, we abort the old request, as we are about to schedule a new one. Then, we also wipe out the result of the last request by calling QPlainTextEdit::clear() on the text edit.

Next, we will construct the URL for the request. We can do this by composing the string by hand where we add the query parameters to the base URL similar to the following:

```
// don't do this!
QString url = baseUrl + "?origin=" + ui->from->text() + "&...";
```

Besides the problem that this quickly becomes hard to read when we include multiple parameters, it is also rather error-prone. The values of the line edits have to be encoded to fit the criteria for a valid URL. For every user value, we, therefore, have to call `QUrl::toPercentEncoding()` explicitly. A much better approach, which is easier to read and less error-prone, is to use `QUrlQuery`. It circumvents the problem that may result when you forget to encode the data. So, we do this:

```
QUrlQuery query;
query.addQueryItem(QStringLiteral("sensor"),
QStringLiteral("false"));
query.addQueryItem(QStringLiteral("language"), QStringLiteral("en"));
query.addQueryItem(QStringLiteral("units"),
QStringLiteral("metric"));
query.addQueryItem(QStringLiteral("mode"),
ui->vehicle->currentText());
query.addQueryItem(QStringLiteral("origins"),  ui->from->text());
query.addQueryItem(QStringLiteral("destinations"), ui->to->text());
```

The usage is pretty clear: we create an instance and then add the query parameters with `addQueryItem()`. The first argument is taken as the key and the second as the value resulting in a string such as "key=value". The value will be automatically encoded when we use `QUrlQuery` in conjunction with `QUrl`. Other benefits of using `QUrlQuery` are that we can check whether we have already set a key with `hasQueryItem()`, taking the key as an argument, or removed a previously set key by calling `removeQueryItem()`.

Let's review which parameters we have set. The `sensor` key is set to `false` as we are not using a GPS device to locate our position. The `language` key is set to `English`, and for units, we favor metric over imperial. Then, the search-related parameters are set. The `origins` key holds the places we want to start from. As its value, the text of the `ui->from` line edit is chosen. If you want to query multiple starting positions, you just have to combine them using `|`. Equivalent to the origins, we set up the value for destinations. Last, we pass the value of the combo box to mode, which defines whether we want to go by a car, bicycle, or whether we want to walk. Next, we execute the request:

```
QUrl url(QStringLiteral(
```

```
    "https://maps.googleapis.com/maps/api/distancematrix/json"));
url.setQuery(query);
m_reply = m_network_manager->get(QNetworkRequest(url));
```

We create QUrl that contains the address to which the query should be posted. By including json at the end, we define that the server should transfer its reply using the JSON format. Google also provides the option for us to get the result as XML. To achieve this, simply replace json with xml. However, since the APIs of Facebook and Twitter return JSON, we will use this format.

Then, we set the previously constructed query to the URL by calling QUrl::setQuery(). This automatically encodes the values, so we do not have to worry about that. Last, we post the request by calling the get() function and store the returned QNetworkReply in m_reply.

Time for action – Parsing the server's reply

In the constructor, we have connected the manager's finished() signal to the finished() slot of the MainWindow class. It will thus be called after the request has been posted:

```
void MainWindow::finished(QNetworkReply *reply)
{
    if (m_reply != reply) {
        reply->deleteLater();
        return;
    }
    //...
}
```

First, we check whether the reply that was passed is the one that we have requested through m_network_manager. If this is not the case, we delete the reply and exit the function. This can happen if a reply was aborted by the sendRequest() slot. Since we are now sure that it is our request, we set m_reply to nullptr, because we have handled it and do not need this information any more:

```
m_reply = nullptr;
if (reply->error() != QNetworkReply::NoError) {
    ui->result->setPlainText(reply->errorString());
    reply->deleteLater();
    return;
}
```

Next, we check whether an error occurred, and if it did, we put the reply's error string in the text edit, delete the reply, and exit the function. After this, we can finally start decoding the server's response:

```
const QByteArray content = reply->readAll();
const QJsonDocument doc = QJsonDocument::fromJson(content);
if (!doc.isObject()) {
    ui->result->setPlainText(tr("Error while reading the JSON
file."));
    reply->deleteLater();
    return;
}
```

With `readAll()`, we get the content of the server's reply. Since the transferred data is not large, we do not need to use partial reading with `readyRead()`. The content is then converted to `QJsonDocument` using the `QJsonDocument::fromJson()` static function, which takes `QByteArray` as an argument and parses its data. If the document is not an object, the server's reply wasn't valid, as the API call should respond with a single object. In this case, we show an error message on the text edit, delete the reply, and exit the function. Let's look at the next part of the code:

```
const QJsonObject obj = doc.object();
const QJsonArray origins = obj.value("origin_addresses").toArray();
const QJsonArray destinations =
obj.value("destination_addresses").toArray();
```

Since we have now ensured that there is an object, we store it in `obj`. Furthermore, due to the API, we also know that the object holds the `origin_addresses` and `destination_addresses` keys. Both values are arrays that hold the requested origins and destinations. From this point on, we will skip any tests if the values exist and are valid since we trust the API. The object also holds a key called `status`, whose value can be used to check whether the query may have failed and if yes, why. The last two lines of the source code store the origins and destinations in two variables. With `obj.value("origin_addresses")`, we get `QJsonValue` that holds the value of the pair specified by the `origin_addresses` key, and `QJsonValue::toArray()` converts this value to `QJsonArray`. The returned JSON file for a search requesting the distance from Warsaw or Erlangen to Birmingham will look like this:

```
{
    "destination_addresses" : [ "Birmingham, West Midlands, UK" ],
    "origin_addresses" : [ "Warsaw, Poland", "Erlangen, Germany" ],
    "rows" : [ ... ],
    "status" : "OK"
}
```

The `rows` key holds the actual results as an array. The first object in this array belongs to the first origin, the second object to the second origin, and so on. Each object holds a key named `elements`, whose value is also an array of objects that belong to the corresponding destinations:

```
"rows" : [
    {
        "elements" : [{...}, {...}]
    },
    {
        "elements" : [{...}, {...}]
    }
  ],
```

Each JSON object (`{...}` in the preceding example) for an origin-destination pair consists of two pairs with the distance and duration keys. Both values of these keys are arrays that hold the `text` and `value` keys, where `text` is a human-readable phrase for `value`. The object for the Warsaw-Birmingham search looks as shown in the following snippet:

```
{
    "distance" : {
        "text" : "1,835 km",
        "value" : 1834751
    },
    "duration" : {
        "text" : "16 hours 37 mins",
        "value" : 59848
    },
    "status" : "OK"
}
```

As you can see, the value of `value` for distance is the distance expressed in meters—since we have used `units=metric` in the request—and the value of `text` is value transformed into kilometers with the "km" postfix. The same applies to duration. Here, value is expressed in seconds, and text is value converted into hours and minutes.

Now that we know how the returned JSON is structured, we display the value of each origin-destination pair in the text edit. Therefore, we loop through each possible pairing using the two `QJsonArray`. We need the indices as well as values, so we use the classic `for` loop instead of the range-based one:

```
QString output;
for (int i = 0; i < origins.count(); ++i) {
```

```
        const QString origin = origins.at(i).toString();
        const QJsonArray row =
    obj.value("rows").toArray().at(i).toObject()
                .value("elements").toArray();
        for (int j = 0; j < destinations.count(); ++j) {
```

First, we create an `output` string variable to cache the constructed text. Before starting the second loop, we calculate two variables that will be the same for all destinations. The `origin` variable holds the text representation of the current origin, and the `row` variable contains the corresponding row of the table. Whenever we try to get an item out of a `QJsonArray` or a `QJsonObject`, the returned value will have the `QJsonValue` type, so each time we do that, we need to convert it to an array, an object, or a string, depending on what we expect to get according to the API. When we calculate the `row` variable, starting at the reply's root object, we fetch the value of the `rows` key and convert it to an array (`obj.value("rows").toArray()`). Then, we fetch the value of the current row (`.at(i)`), convert it to an object, and fetch its `elements` key (`.toObject().value("elements")`). Since this value is also an array—the columns of the row—we convert it to an array.

The scope inside the two loops will be reached for each combination. Think of the transferred result as a table where the origins are rows and the destinations are columns:

```
output += tr("From: %1\n").arg(origin);
output += tr("To: %1\n").arg(destinations.at(j).toString());
```

First, we add the `"From:"` string and the current origin to output. The same is done for the destination, which results in the following as the value for output:

```
From: Warsaw, Poland
To: Birmingham, West Midlands, UK
```

Next, we will read the duration and distance from the corresponding `QJsonObject` from where we call `data`:

```
const QJsonObject data = row.at(j).toObject();
const QString status = data.value("status").toString();
```

In this code, we fetch the current column from the row (`at(j)`) and convert it to an object. This is the object that contains the distance and duration for an origin-destination pair in the `(i; j)` cell. Besides `distance` and `duration`, the object also holds a key called `status`. Its value indicates whether the search was successful (`OK`), whether the origin or destination could not be found (`NOT_FOUND`), or whether the search could not find a route between the origin and destination (`ZERO_RESULTS`). We store the value of `status` in a local variable that is also named `status`.

Next, we check the status and append the distance and the duration to the output:

```
if (status == "OK") {
    output += tr("Distance: %1\n").arg(
        data.value("distance").toObject().value("text").toString());
    output += tr("Duration: %1\n").arg(
        data.value("duration").toObject().value("text").toString());
} else { /*...*/ }
```

For distance, we want to show the phrased result. Therefore, we first get the JSON value of the distance key (`data.value("distance")`), convert it to an object, and request the value for the text key (`toObject().value("text")`). Lastly, we convert `QJsonValue` to `QString` using `toString()`. The same applies for duration. Finally, we need to handle the errors the API might return:

```
} else if (status == "NOT_FOUND") {
    output += tr("Origin and/or destination of this "
                 "pairing could not be geocoded.\n");
} else if (status == "ZERO_RESULTS") {
    output += tr("No route could be found.\n");
} else {
    output += tr("Unknown error.\n");
}
output += QStringLiteral("=").repeated(35) + QStringLiteral("\n");
```

At the end of the output for each cell, we add a line consisting of `35` equals signs (`QStringLiteral("=").repeated(35)`) to separate the result from the other cells. Finally, after all loops finish, we put the text into the text edit and delete the reply object:

```
ui->result->setPlainText(output);
reply->deleteLater();
```

The actual result then looks as follows:

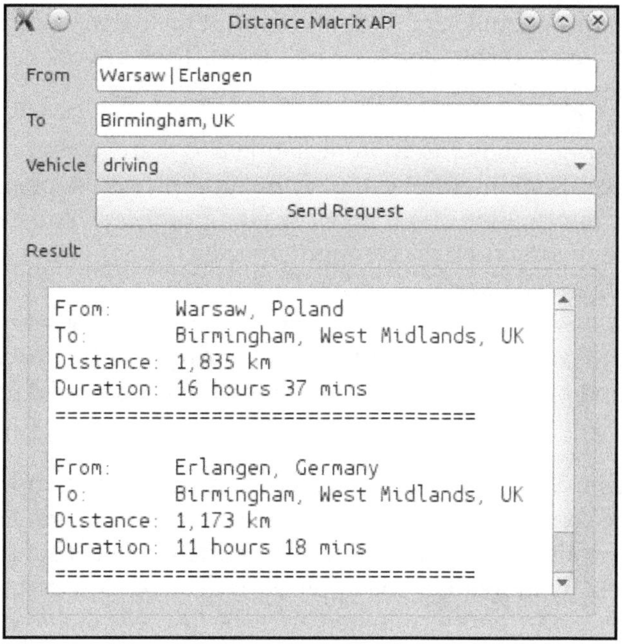

Have a go hero – Choosing XML as the reply's format

To hone your XML skills, you can use `https://maps.googleapis.com/maps/api/distancematrix/xml` as the URL to which you send the requests. Then, you can parse the XML file, as we did with JSON, and display the retrieved data likewise.

Controlling the connectivity state

Before trying to access a network resource, it's useful to check whether you have an active connection to the internet. Qt allows you to check whether the computer, mobile device, or tablet is online. You can even start a new connection if the operating system supports it.

The relevant API mainly consists of four classes. `QNetworkConfigurationManager` is the base and starting point. It holds all network configurations available on the system. Furthermore, it provides information about the network capabilities, for example, whether you can start and stop interfaces. The network configurations found by it are stored as `QNetworkConfiguration` classes.

`QNetworkConfiguration` holds all information about an access point but not about a network interface, as an interface can provide multiple access points. This class also provides only the information about network configurations. You can't configure an access point or a network interface through `QNetworkConfiguration`. The network configuration is up to the operating system and therefore `QNetworkConfiguration` is a read-only class. With `QNetworkConfiguration`, however, you can determine whether the type of connection is an Ethernet, WLAN, or 4G connection. This may influence what kind of data and, more importantly, what size of data you will download.

With `QNetworkSession`, you can then start or stop system network interfaces, which are defined by the configurations. This way, you gain control over an access point. `QNetworkSession` also provides session management that is useful when a system's access point is used by more than one application. The session ensures that the underlying interface only gets terminated after the last session has been closed. Lastly, `QNetworkInterface` provides classic information, such as the hardware address or interface name.

QNetworkConfigurationManager

`QNetworkConfigurationManager` manages all network configurations that are available on a system. You can access these configurations by calling `allConfigurations()`. Of course, you have to create an instance of the manager first:

```
QNetworkConfigurationManager manager;
QList<QNetworkConfiguration> cfgs = manager.allConfigurations();
```

The configurations are returned as a list. The default behavior of `allConfigurations()` is to return all possible configurations. However, you can also retrieve a filtered list. If you pass `QNetworkConfiguration::Active` as an argument, the list only contains configurations that have at least one active session. If you create a new session based on such a configuration, it will be active and connected. By passing `QNetworkConfiguration::Discovered` as an argument, you will get a list with configurations that can be used to immediately start a session. Note, however, that at this point, you cannot be sure whether the underlying interface can be started. The last important argument is `QNetworkConfiguration::Defined`. With this argument, `allConfigurations()` returns a list of configurations that are known to the system but are not usable right now. This may be a previously used WLAN hotspot, which is currently out of range.

You will be notified whenever the configurations change. If a new configuration becomes available, the manager emits the `configurationAdded()` signal. This may happen, for example, if mobile data transmission becomes available or if the user turns his/her device's WLAN adapter on. If a configuration is removed, for example, if the WLAN adapter is turned off, `configurationRemoved()` is emitted. Lastly, when a configuration is changed, you will be notified by the `configurationChanged()` signal. All three signals pass a constant reference to the configuration about what was added, removed, or changed. The configuration passed by the `configurationRemoved()` signal is, of course, invalid. It still contains the name and identifier of the removed configuration.

To find out whether any network interface of the system is active, call `isOnline()`. If you want to be notified about a mode change, track the `onlineStateChanged()` signal.

> TIP
>
> Since a WLAN scan takes a certain amount of time, `allConfigurations()` may not return all the available configurations. To ensure that configurations are completely populated, call `updateConfigurations()` first. Due to the long time it may take to gather all the information about the system's network configurations, this call is asynchronous. Wait for the `updateCompleted()` signal and only then, call `allConfigurations()`.

`QNetworkConfigurationManager` also informs you about the Bearer API's capabilities. The `capabilities()` function returns a flag of the `QNetworkConfigurationManager::Capabilities` type and describes the available possibilities that are platform-specific. The values you may be most interested in are as follows:

Value	**Meaning**
`CanStartAndStopInterfaces`	This means that you can start and stop access points.
`ApplicationLevelRoaming`	This indicates that the system will inform you if a more suitable access point is available, and that you can actively change the access point if you think there is a better one available.
`DataStatistics`	With this capability, `QNetworkSession` contains information about the transmitted and received data.

QNetworkConfiguration

`QNetworkConfiguration` holds, as mentioned earlier, information about an access point. With `name()`, you get the user-visible name for a configuration, and with `identifier()`, you get a unique, system-specific identifier. If you develop games for mobile devices, it may be of advantage to you to know which type of connection is being used. This might influence the data that you request; for example, the quality and thus, the size of a video. With `bearerType()`, the type of bearer used by a configuration is returned. The returned enumeration values are rather self-explanatory: `BearerEthernet`, `BearerWLAN`, `Bearer2G`, `BearerCDMA2000`, `BearerWCDMA`, `BearerHSPA`, `BearerBluetooth`, `BearerWiMAX`, and so on. You can look up the full-value list in the documentation for `QNetworkConfiguration::BearerType`.

With `purpose()`, you get the purpose of the configuration, for example, whether it is suitable to access a private network (`QNetworkConfiguration::PrivatePurpose`) or to access a public network (`QNetworkConfiguration::PublicPurpose`). The state of the configuration, if it is defined, discovered or active, as previously described, can be accessed through `state()`.

QNetworkSession

To start a network interface or to tell the system to keep an interface connected for as long as you need it, you have to start a session:

```
QNetworkConfigurationManager manager;
QNetworkConfiguration cfg = manager.defaultConfiguration();
QNetworkSession *session = new QNetworkSession(cfg, this);
session->open();
```

A session is based on a configuration. When there is more than one session and you are not sure which one to use, use `QNetworkConfigurationManager::defaultConfiguration()`. It returns the system's default configuration. Based on this, you can create an instance of `QNetworkSession`. The first argument, the configuration, is required. The second is optional but is recommended since it sets a parent, and we do not have to take care of the deletion. You may want to check whether the configuration is valid (`QNetworkConfiguration::isValid()`) first.

Calling `open()` will start the session and connect the interface if needed and supported. Since `open()` can take some time, the call is asynchronous. So, either listen to the `opened()` signal, which is emitted as soon as the session is open, or to the `error()` signal if an error happened. The error information is represented using the `QNetworkSession::SessionError` type. Alternatively, instead of checking the `opened()` signal, you can also watch the `stateChanged()` signal. The possible states for a session can be `Invalid`, `NotAvailable`, `Connecting`, `Connected`, `Closing`, `Disconnected`, and `Roaming`.

If you want to open the session in a synchronous way, call `waitForOpened()` right after calling `open()`. It will block the `event` loop until the session is open. This function will return `true` if successful and `false` otherwise. To limit the waiting time, you can define a time-out. Just pass the milliseconds that you are willing to wait as an argument to `waitForOpened()`. To check whether a session is open, use `isOpen()`.

To close the session, call `close()`. If no session is left on the interface, it will be shot down. To force an interface to disconnect, call `stop()`. This call will invalidate all the sessions that are based on that interface.

You may receive the `preferredConfigurationChanged()` signal, which indicates that the preferred configuration, that is, for example, the preferred access point, has changed. This may be the case if a WLAN network is now in range and you do not have to use 2G anymore. The new configuration is passed as the first argument, and the second one indicates whether changing the new access point will also alter the IP address. Besides checking for the signal, you can also inquire whether roaming is available for a configuration by calling `QNetworkConfiguration::isRoamingAvailable()`. If roaming is available, you have to decide to either reject the offer by calling `ignore()` or to accept it by calling `migrate()`. If you accept roaming, it will emit `newConfigurationActivated()` when the session is roamed. After you have checked the new connection, you can either accept the new access point or reject it. The latter means that you will return to the previous access point. If you accept the new access point, the previous one will be terminated.

QNetworkInterface

To get the interface that is used by a session, call `QNetworkSession::interface()`. It will return the `QNetworkInterface` object, which describes the interface. With `hardwareAddress()`, you get the low-level hardware address of the interface that is normally the MAC address. The name of the interface can be obtained by `name()`, which is a string such as "eth0" or "wlan0". A list of IP addresses as well as their netmasks and broadcast addresses registered with the interface is returned by `addressEntries()`. Furthermore, information about whether the interface is a loopback or whether it supports multicasting can be queried with `flags()`. The returned bitmask is a combination of these values: `IsUp`, `IsRunning`, `CanBroadcast`, `IsLoopBack`, `IsPointToPoint`, and `CanMulticast`.

Communicating between games

After having discussed Qt's high-level network classes such as `QNetworkAccessManager` and `QNetworkConfigurationManager`, we will now take a look at lower-level network classes and see how Qt supports you when it comes to implementing TCP or UDP servers and clients. This becomes relevant when you plan to extend your game by including a multiplayer mode. For such a task, Qt offers `QTcpSocket`, `QUdpSocket`, and `QTcpServer`.

Time for action – Realizing a simple chat program

To get familiar with `QTcpServer` and `QTcpSocket`, let's develop a simple chat program. This example will teach you the basic knowledge of network handling in Qt so that you can use this skill later to connect two or more copies of a game. At the end of this exercise, we want to see something like this:

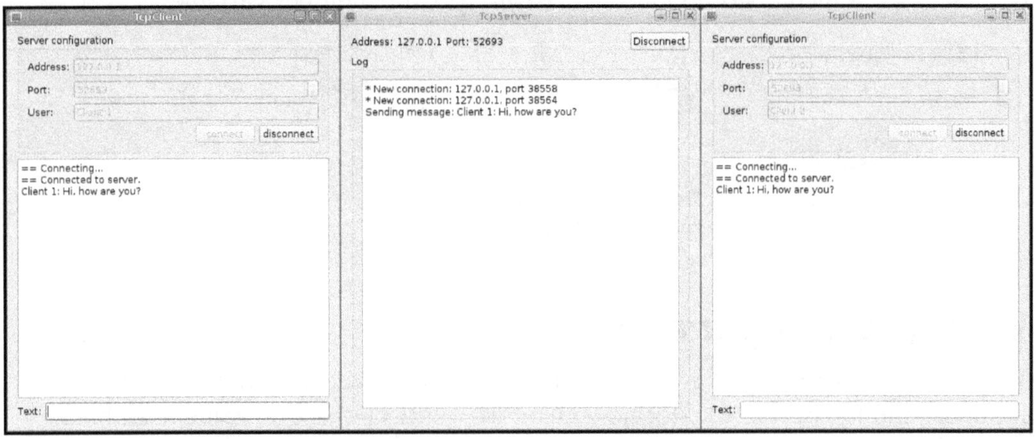

On both the left-hand side and the right-hand side of the preceding screenshot, you can see a client, whereas the server is in the middle. We'll start by taking a closer look at the server.

The server – QTcpServer

As a protocol for communication, we will use **Transmission Control Protocol** (**TCP**). You may know this network protocol from the two most popular internet protocols: HTTP and FTP. Both use TCP for their communication and so do the globally used protocols for email traffic: SMTP, POP3, and IMAP. The main advantage of TCP is its reliability and connection-based architecture. Data transferred by TCP is guaranteed to be complete, ordered, and without any duplicates. The protocol is furthermore stream oriented, which allows us to use `QDataStream` or `QTextStream`. A downside to TCP is its speed. This is because the missing data has to be retransmitted until the receiver fully receives it. By default, this causes a retransmission of all the data that was transmitted after the missing part. So, you should only choose TCP as a protocol if speed is not your top priority, but rather the completeness and correctness of the transmitted data. This applies if you send unique and nonrepetitive data.

Time for action – Setting up the server

A look at the server's GUI shows us that it principally consists of QPlainTextEdit (ui->log) that is used to display system messages and a button (ui->disconnectClients), which allows us to disconnect all the currently connected clients. On the top, next to the button, the server's address and port are displayed (ui->address and ui->port). After setting up the user interface in the constructor of the server's class TcpServer, we initiate the internally used QTcpServer, which is stored in the m_server private member variable:

```
if (!m_server->listen(QHostAddress::LocalHost, 52693)) {
    ui->log->setPlainText(tr("Failure while starting server: %1")
                          .arg(m_server->errorString()));
    return;
}
connect(m_server, &QTcpServer::newConnection,
        this, &TcpServer::newConnection);
```

What just happened?

With QTcpServer::listen(), we defined that the server should listen to the localhost and the port 52693 for new incoming connections. The value used here, QHostAddress::LocalHost of the QHostAddress::SpecialAddress enumeration, will resolve to 127.0.0.1. Instead, if you pass QHostAddress::Any, the server will listen to all IPv4 interfaces as well as to IPv6 interfaces. If you only want to listen to a specific address, just pass this address as QHostAddress:

```
m_server->listen(QHostAddress("127.0.0.1"), 0);
```

This will behave like the one in the preceding code, only in that the server will now listen to a port that will be chosen automatically. On success, listen() will return true. So, if something goes wrong in the example, it will show an error message on the text edit and exit the function. To compose the error message, we are using QTcpServer::errorString(), which holds a human-readable error phrase.

To handle the error in your game's code, the error string is not suitable. In any case where you need to know the exact error, use `QTcpServer::serverError()`, which returns the enumeration value of `QAbstractSocket::SocketError`. Based on this, you know exactly what went wrong, for example, `QAbstractSocket::HostNotFoundError`. If `listen()` was successful, we connect the server's `newConnection()` signal to the class's `newConnection()` slot. The signal will be emitted every time a new connection is available. Lastly, we show the server's address and port number that can be accessed through `serverAddress()` and `serverPort()`:

```
ui->address->setText(m_server->serverAddress().toString());
ui->port->setText(QString::number(m_server->serverPort()));
```

This information is required by the clients so that they are able to connect to the server.

Time for action – Reacting on a new pending connection

As soon as a client tries to connect to the server, the `newConnection()` slot will be called:

```
void TcpServer::newConnection()
{
    while (m_server->hasPendingConnections()) {
        QTcpSocket *socket = m_server->nextPendingConnection();
        m_clients << socket;
        ui->disconnectClients->setEnabled(true);
        connect(socket, &QTcpSocket::disconnected,
                this, &TcpServer::removeConnection);
        connect(socket, &QTcpSocket::readyRead,
                this, &TcpServer::readyRead);
        ui->log->appendPlainText(tr("* New connection: %1, port %2\n")
.arg(socket->peerAddress().toString())
                                .arg(socket->peerPort()));
    }
}
```

What just happened?

Since more than one connection may be pending, we use `hasPendingConnections()` to determine whether there is at least one more pending connection. Each one is then handled in the iteration of the `while` loop. To get a pending connection of the `QTcpSocket` type, we call `nextPendingConnection()` and add this connection to a private vector called `m_clients`, which holds all active connections. In the next line, as there is now at least one connection, we enable the button that allows all connections to be closed. The slot connected to the button's `click()` signal will call `QTcpSocket::close()` on each single connection. When a connection is closed, its socket emits a `disconnected()` signal. We connect this signal to our `removeConnection()` slot. With the last connection, we react to the socket's `readyRead()` signal, which indicates that new data is available. In such a situation, our `readyRead()` slot is called. Lastly, we print a system message that a new connection has been established. The address and port of the connecting client and peer can be retrieved by the socket's `peerAddress()` and `peerPort()` functions.

> TIP
>
> If a new connection can't be accepted, the `acceptError()` signal is emitted instead of `newConnection()`. It passes the reason for the failure of the `QAbstractSocket::SocketError` type as an argument. If you want to temporarily decline new connections, call `pauseAccepting()` on `QTcpServer`. To resume accepting new connections, call `resumeAccepting()`.

Time for action – Forwarding a new message

When a connected client sends a new chat message, the underlying socket—since it inherits `QIODevice`—emits `readyRead()`, and thus, our `readyRead()` slot will be called.

Before we take a look at this slot, there is something important that you need to keep in mind. Even though TCP is ordered and without any duplicates, this does not mean that all the data is delivered in one big chunk. So, before processing the received data, we need to ensure that we get the entire message. Unfortunately, there is neither an easy way to detect whether all data was transmitted nor a globally usable method for such a task. Therefore, it is up to you to solve this problem, as it depends on the use case. Two common solutions, however, are to either send magic tokens to indicate the start and end of a message, for example, single characters or XML tags, or you can send the size of the message upfront.

The second solution is shown in the Qt documentation where the length is put in a `quint16` in front of the message. We, on the other hand, will look at an approach that uses a simple magic token to handle the messages correctly. As a delimiter, we use the "End of Transmission Block" character—ASCII code 23—to indicate the end of a message. We also choose UTF-8 as the encoding of transmitted messages to ensure that clients with different locales can communicate with each other.

Since the processing of received data is quite complex, we will go through the code step by step this time:

```
void TcpServer::readyRead()
{
    QTcpSocket *socket = qobject_cast<QTcpSocket*>(sender());
    if (!socket) {
        return;
    }
    //...
}
```

To determine which socket called the slot, we use `sender()`. If the cast to `QTcpSocket` is unsuccessful, we exit the slot.

> Note that `sender()` is used for simplicity. If you write real-life code, it is better to use `QSignalMapper`.

Next, we read the transferred—potentially fragmentary—message with `readAll()`:

```
QByteArray &buffer = m_receivedData[socket];
buffer.append(socket->readAll());
```

Here, `QHash<QTcpSocket*, QByteArray> m_receivedData` is a private class member where we store the previously received data for each connection. When the first chunk of data is received from a client, `m_receivedData[socket]` will automatically insert an empty `QByteArray` into the hash and return a reference to it. On subsequent calls, it will return a reference to the same array. We use `append()` to append the newly received data to the end of the array. Finally, we need to identify the messages that were completely received by now, if there are any such messages:

```
while(true) {
    int endIndex = buffer.indexOf(23);
    if (endIndex < 0) {
        break;
    }
```

```
        QString message = QString::fromUtf8(buffer.left(endIndex));
        buffer.remove(0, endIndex + 1);
        newMessage(socket, message);
    }
```

On each iteration of the loop, we try to find the first separator character. If we didn't find one (`endIndex < 0`), we exit the loop, and leave the remaining partial message in `m_receivedData`. If we found a separator, we take the first message's data using the `left(endIndex)` function that returns the leftmost `endIndex` bytes from the array. To remove the first message from `buffer`, we use the `remove()` function that will remove the specified number of bytes, shifting the remaining bytes to the left. We want to remove `endIndex + 1` bytes (the message itself and the separator after it). Following our transmission protocol, we interpret the data as UTF-8 and call our `newMessage()` function that will handle the received message.

In the `newMessage()` function, we append the new message to the server log and send it to all clients:

```
void TcpServer::newMessage(QTcpSocket *sender, const QString &message)
{
    ui->log->appendPlainText(tr("Sending message:
%1\n").arg(message));
    QByteArray messageArray = message.toUtf8();
    messageArray.append(23);
    for(QTcpSocket *socket: m_clients) {
        if (socket->state() == QAbstractSocket::ConnectedState) {
            socket->write(messageArray);
        }
    }
    Q_UNUSED(sender)
}
```

In this function, we encode the message according to our transmission protocol. First, we use `toUtf8()` to convert `QString` to `QByteArray` in UTF-8 encoding. Next, we append the separator character. Finally, we iterate over the list of clients, check whether they are still connected, and send the encoded message to them. Since the socket inherits `QIODevice`, you can use most of the functions that you know from `QFile`. The current behavior of our server is very simple, so we have no use for the `sender` argument, so we add the `Q_UNUSED` macro to suppress the unused argument warning.

Have a go hero – Using QSignalMapper

As discussed earlier, using `sender()` is a convenient, but not an object-oriented, approach. Thus, try to use `QSignalMapper` instead to determine which socket called the slot. To achieve this, you have to connect the socket's `readyRead()` signal to a mapper and the slot directly. All the signal-mapper-related code will go into the `newConnection()` slot.

The same applies to the connection to the `removeConnection()` slot. Let's take a look at it next.

Time for action – Detecting a disconnect

When a client terminates the connection, we have to delete the socket from the local `m_clients` list. The socket's `disconnected()` signal is already connected to the `removeConnection()` slot, so we just need to implement it as follows:

```
void TcpServer::removeConnection()
{
    QTcpSocket *socket = qobject_cast<QTcpSocket*>(sender());
    if (!socket) {
        return;
    }
    ui->log->appendPlainText(tr("* Connection removed: %1, port %2\n")
                             .arg(socket->peerAddress().toString())
                             .arg(socket->peerPort()));
    m_clients.removeOne(socket);
    m_receivedData.remove(socket);
    socket->deleteLater();
    ui->disconnectClients->setEnabled(!m_clients.isEmpty());
}
```

What just happened?

After getting the socket that emitted the call through `sender()`, we post the information that a socket is being removed. Then, we remove the socket from `m_clients`, remove the associated buffer from `m_receivedData` and call `deleteLater()` on it. Do not use `delete`. Lastly, if no client is left, the disconnect button is disabled.

The server is ready. Now let's take a look at the client.

The client

The GUI of the client (TcpClient) is pretty simple. It has three input fields to define the server's address (ui->address), the server's port (ui->port), and a username (ui->user). Of course, there is also a button to connect to (ui->connect) and disconnect from (ui->disconnect) the server. Finally, the GUI has a text edit that holds the received messages (ui->chat) and a line edit (ui->text) to send messages.

Time for action – Setting up the client

After providing the server's address and port and choosing a username, the user can connect to the server:

```
void TcpClient::on_connect_clicked()
{
    //...
    if (m_socket->state() != QAbstractSocket::ConnectedState) {
        ui->chat->appendPlainText(tr("== Connecting..."));
        m_socket->connectToHost(ui->address->text(),
ui->port->value());
        //...
    }
}
```

What just happened?

The m_socket private member variable holds an instance of QTcpSocket. If this socket is already connected, nothing happens. Otherwise, the socket is connected to the given address and port by calling connectToHost(). Besides the obligatory server address and port number, you can pass a third argument to define the mode in which the socket will be opened. For possible values, you can use OpenMode just like we did for QIODevice.

Since this call is asynchronous, we print a notification to the chat so that the user is informed that the application is currently trying to connect to the server. When the connection is established, the socket sends the connected() signal that prints "Connected to server" on the chat to indicate that we have connected to a slot. Besides the messages in the chat, we also updated the GUI by, for example, disabling the connect button, but this is all basic stuff. You won't have any trouble understanding this if you have had a look at the sources. So, these details are left out here.

Of course, something could go wrong when trying to connect to a server, but luckily, we are informed about a failure as well through the `error()` signal, passing a description of error in the form of `QAbstractSocket::SocketError`. The most frequent errors will probably be `QAbstractSocket::ConnectionRefusedError` if the peer refused the connection or `QAbstractSocket::HostNotFoundError` if the host address could not be found. If the connection, however, was successfully established, it should be closed later on. You can either call `abort()` to immediately close the socket, whereas `disconnectFromHost()` will wait until all pending data has been written.

Time for action – Receiving text messages

In the constructor, we have connected the socket's `readyRead()` signal to a local slot. So, whenever the server sends a message through `QTcpSocket::write()`, we read the data and decode it:

```
m_receivedData.append(m_socket->readAll());
while(true) {
    int endIndex = m_receivedData.indexOf(23);
    if (endIndex < 0) {
        break;
    }
    QString message =
QString::fromUtf8(m_receivedData.left(endIndex));
    m_receivedData.remove(0, endIndex + 1);
    newMessage(message);
}
```

This code is very similar to the `readyRead()` slot of the server. It's even simpler because we only have one socket and one data buffer, so `m_receivedData` is a single `QByteArray`. The `newMessage()` implementation in the client is also much simpler than in the server:

```
void TcpClient::newMessage(const QString &message)
{
    ui->chat->appendPlainText(message);
}
```

Here, we just need to display the received message to the user.

Time for action – Sending text messages

What is left now is to describe how to send a chat message. On hitting return button inside the line edit, a local slot will be called that checks whether there is actual text to send and whether `m_socket` is still connected. If everything is ready, we construct a message that contains the self-given username, a colon, and the text of the line edit:

```
QString message = QStringLiteral("%1: %2")
                  .arg(m_user).arg(ui->text->text());
```

Then, we encode and send the message, just like we did on the server side:

```
QByteArray messageArray = message.toUtf8();
messageArray.append(23);
m_socket->write(messageArray);
```

That's all. It's like writing and reading from a file. For the complete example, take a look at the sources bundled with this book and run the server and several clients.

> You can see that the server and client share a significant amount of code. In a real project, you definitely want to avoid such duplication. You can move all repeating code to a common library used by both server or client. Alternatively, you can implement server and client in a single project and enable the needed functionality using command-line arguments or conditional compilation.

Have a go hero – Extending the chat server and client

This example has shown us how to send a simple text. If you now go on and define a schema for how the communication should work, you can use it as a base for more complex communication. For instance, if you want to enable the client to receive a list of all other clients (and their usernames), you need to define that the server will return such a list if it gets a special message from a client. You can use special text commands such as `/allClients`, or you can implement a more complex message structure using `QDataStream` or JSON serialization. Therefore, you have to parse all messages received by the server before forwarding them to all the connected clients. Go ahead and try to implement such a requirement yourself.

By now, it is possible that multiple users have chosen the same username. With the new functionality of getting a user list, you can prevent this from happening. Therefore, you have to send the username to the server that keeps track of them. In the current implementation, nothing stops the client from sending messages under a different username each time. You can make the server handle usernames instead of trusting the client's each message.

Synchronous network operations

The example we explained uses a nonblocking, asynchronous approach. For example, after asynchronous calls such as `connectToHost()`, we do not block the thread until we get a result, but instead, we connect to the socket's signals to proceed. On the Internet as well as Qt's documentation, on the other hand, you will find dozens of examples explaining the blocking and the synchronous approaches. You will easily spot them by their use of `waitFor...()` functions. These functions block the current thread until a function such as `connectToHost()` has a result—the time `connected()` or `error()` will be emitted. The corresponding blocking function to `connectToHost()` is `waitForConnected()`. The other blocking functions that can be used are `waitForReadyRead()`, which waits until new data is available on a socket for reading; `waitForBytesWritten()`, which waits until the data has been written to the socket; and `waitForDisconnected()`, which waits until the connection has been closed.

Look out! Even if Qt offers these `waitFor...()` functions, do not use them! The synchronous approach is not the smartest one, since it will freeze your game's GUI. A frozen GUI is the worst thing that can happen in your game, and it will annoy every user. So, when working inside the GUI thread, you are better to react to the `QIODevice::readyRead()`, `QIODevice::bytesWritten()`, `QAbstractSocket::connected()`, and `QAbstractSocket::disconnected()` signals.

`QAbstractSocket` is the base class of `QTcpSocket` as well as of `QUdpSocket`.

Following the asynchronous approach shown, the application will only become unresponsive while your own slots are being executed. If your slots contain more heavy computations, you will need to move them to an extra thread. Then, the GUI thread will only get signals, passing the new messages, and to send, it will simply pass the required data to the worker thread. This way, you will get a super fluent velvet GUI.

Using UDP

In contrast to TCP, UDP is unreliable and connectionless. Neither the order of packets nor their delivery is guaranteed. These limitations, however, allow UDP to be very fast. So, if you have frequent data, which does not necessarily need to be received by the peer, use UDP. This data could, for example, be real-time positions of a player that get updated frequently or live video/audio streaming. Since `QUdpSocket` is mostly the same as `QTcpSocket`—both inherit `QAbstractSocket`—there is not much to explain. The main difference between them is that TCP is stream-oriented, whereas UDP is datagram-oriented. This means that the data is sent in small packages, containing among the actual content, the sender's as well as the receiver's IP address and port number.

Unlike `QTcpSocket` and `QTcpServer`, UDP does not need a separate server class because it is connectionless. A single `QUdpSocket` can be used as a server. In this case, you have to use `QAbstractSocket::bind()` instead of `QTcpServer::listen()`. Like `listen()`, `bind()` takes the addresses and ports that are allowed to send datagrams as arguments. Note that TCP ports and UDP ports are completely unrelated to each other.

Whenever a new package arrives, the `QIODevice::readyRead()` signal is emitted. To read the data, use the `receiveDatagram()` or `readDatagram()` function. The `receiveDatagram()` function accepts an optional `maxSize` argument that allows you to limit the size of the received data. This function returns a `QNetworkDatagram` object that contains the datagram and has a number of methods to get the data. The most useful of them are `data()`, which returns the payload as a `QByteArray` as well as `senderAddress()` and `senderPort()` that allow you to identify the sender.

The `readDatagram()` function is a more low-level function that takes four parameters. The first one of the `char*` type is used to write the data in, the second specifies the amount of bytes to be written, and the last two parameters of the `QHostAddress*` and `quint16*` types are used to store the sender's IP address and port number. This function is less convenient, but you can use it more efficiently than `receiveDatagram()`, because it's possible to use the same data buffer for all datagrams instead of allocating a new one for each datagram.

`QUdpSocket` also provides the overloaded `writeDatagram()` function for sending the data. One of the overloads simply accepts a `QNetworkDatagram` object. You can also supply the data in the form of `QByteArray` or a `char*` buffer with a size, but in these cases, you also need to specify the recipient's address and port number as separate arguments.

Time for action – Sending a text via UDP

As an example, let's assume that we have two sockets of the QUdpSocket type. We will call the first one socketA and the other socketB. Both are bound to the localhost, socketA to the 52000 port and socketB to the 52001 port. So, if we want to send the string Hello! from socketA to socketB, we have to write in the application that is holding socketA:

```
socketA->writeDatagram(QByteArray("Hello!"),
                       QHostAddress("127.0.0.1"), 52001);
```

The class that holds socketB must have the socket's readyRead() signal connected to a slot. This slot will then be called because of our writeDatagram() call, assuming that the datagram is not lost! In the slot, we read the datagram and the sender's address and port number with:

```
while (socketB->hasPendingDatagrams()) {
    QNetworkDatagram datagram = socketB->receiveDatagram();
    qDebug() << "received data:" << datagram.data();
    qDebug() << "from:" << datagram.senderAddress()
             << datagram.senderPort();
}
```

As long as there are pending datagrams—this is checked by hasPendingDatagrams()—we read them using the high-level QNetworkDatagram API. After the datagram was received, we use the getter functions to read the data and identify the sender.

Have a go hero – Connecting players of the Benjamin game

With this introductory knowledge, you can go ahead and try some stuff by yourself. For example, you can take the game Benjamin the elephant and send Benjamin's current position from one client to another. This way, you can either clone the screen from one client to the other, or both clients can play the game and, additionally, can see where the elephant of the other player currently is. For such a task, you would use UDP, as it is important that the position is updated very fast while it isn't a disaster when one position gets lost.

Keep in mind that we only scratched the surface of networking due to its complexity. Covering it fully would have exceeded this beginner's guide. For a real game, which uses a network, you should learn more about Qt's possibilities for establishing a secure connection via SSL or some other mechanism.

Pop quiz

Q1. Which class can you use to read the data received over the network?

1. `QNetworkReply`
2. `QNetworkRequest`
3. `QNetworkAccessManager`

Q2. What should you usually do with the `QNetworkReply *reply` object in the `finished()` signal handler?

1. Delete it using `delete reply`
2. Delete it using `reply->deleteLater()`
3. Don't delete it

Q3. How to ensure that your application won't freeze because of processing an HTTP request?

1. Use `waitForConnected()` or `waitForReadyRead()` functions
2. Use `readyRead()` or `finished()` signals
3. Move `QNetworkAccessManager` to a separate thread

Q4. Which class can you use to create a UDP server?

1. `QTcpServer`
2. `QUdpServer`
3. `QUdpSocket`

Summary

In the first part of this chapter, you familiarized yourself with `QNetworkAccessManager`. This class is at the heart of your code whenever you want to download or upload files to the internet. After having gone through the different signals that you can use to fetch errors, to get notified about new data or to show the progress, you should now know everything you need on that topic.

The example about the Distance Matrix API depended on your knowledge of `QNetworkAccessManager`, and it shows you a real-life application case for it. Dealing with JSON as the server's reply format was a summary of `Chapter 4`, *Qt Core Essentials*, but it was highly needed since Facebook and Twitter only use JSON to format their network replies.

In the last section, you learned how to set up your own TCP server and clients. This enables you to connect different instances of a game to provide the multiplayer functionality. Alternatively, you were taught how to use UDP.

You are now familiar with Qt widgets, the Graphics View framework, the core Qt classes, and the networking API. This knowledge will already allow you to implement games with rich and advanced functionality. The only large and significant part of Qt we will explore is Qt Quick. However, before we get to that, let's consolidate our knowledge of what we already know and investigate some advanced topics.

Now we are returning to the world of widgets. In `Chapter 3`, *Qt GUI Programming*, we only used the widget classes provided by Qt. In the next chapter, you will learn to create your own widgets and integrate them into your forms.

8
Custom Widgets

We have so far been using only ready-made widgets for the user interface, which resulted in the crude approach of using buttons for a tic-tac-toe game. In this chapter, you will learn about much of what Qt has to offer with regard to custom widgets. This will let you implement your own painting and event handling, incorporating content that is entirely customized.

The main topics covered in this chapter are as follows:

- Working with `QPainter`
- Creating custom widgets
- Image handling
- Implementing a chess game

Raster and vector graphics

When it comes to graphics, Qt splits this domain into two separate parts. One of them is raster graphics (used by widgets and the Graphics View, for example). This part focuses on using high-level operations (such as drawing lines or filling rectangles) to manipulate colors of a grid of points that can be visualized on different devices, such as images, printers, or the display of your computer device. The other is vector graphics, which involves manipulating vertices, triangles, and textures. This is tailored for maximum speed of processing and display, using hardware acceleration provided by modern graphics cards.

t abstracts graphics using the concept of a surface (represented by the `QSurface` class) that it draws on. The type of the surface determines which drawing operations can be performed on the surface: surfaces that support software rendering and raster graphics have the `RasterSurface` type, and surfaces that support the OpenGL interface have the `OpenGLSurface` type.

In this chapter, you will deepen your knowledge of Qt's raster painting system. We will come back to the topic of OpenGL in the next chapter.

> `QSurface` objects can have other types, but they are needed less often. `RasterGLSurface` is intended for internal Qt use. `OpenVGSurface` supports OpenVG (a hardware accelerated 2D vector graphics API) and is useful on embedded devices that support OpenVG but lack OpenGL support. Qt 5.10 introduces `VulkanSurface`, which supports Vulkan graphics API.

Raster painting

When we talk about GUI frameworks, raster painting is usually associated with drawing on widgets. However, since Qt is something more than a GUI toolkit, the scope of raster painting that it offers is much broader.

In general, Qt's drawing architecture consists of three parts. The most important part is the device the drawing takes place on, represented by the `QPaintDevice` class. Qt provides a number of paint device subclasses, such as `QWidget` or `QImage` and `QPrinter` or `QPdfWriter`. You can see that the approach for drawing on a widget and printing on a printer is quite the same. The difference is in the second component of the architecture—the paint engine (`QPaintEngine`). The engine is responsible for performing the actual paint operations on a particular paint device. Different paint engines are used to draw on images and to print on printers. This is completely hidden from you, as a developer, so you really don't need to worry about it.

For you, the most important piece is the third component—`QPainter`—which is an adapter for the whole painting framework. It contains a set of high-level operations that can be invoked on the paint device. Behind the scenes, the whole work is delegated to an appropriate paint engine. While talking about painting, we will be focusing solely on the painter object, as any painting code can be invoked on any of the target devices only by using a painter initialized on a different paint device. This effectively makes painting in Qt device agnostic, as in the following example:

```
void doSomePainting(QPainter *painter) {
    painter->drawLine(QPoint(0,0), QPoint(100, 40));
}
```

The same code can be executed on a painter working on any possible `QPaintDevice` class, be it a widget, an image, or an OpenGL context (through the use of `QOpenGLPaintDevice`). We've already seen `QPainter` in action in `Chapter 4`, *Custom 2D Graphics with Graphics View*, when we created a custom graphics item. Now, let's learn more about this important class.

The `QPainter` class has a rich API. The most important methods in this class can be divided into three groups:

- Setters and getters for attributes of the painter
- Methods, with names starting with `draw` and `fill`, that perform drawing operations on the device
- Methods that allow manipulating the coordinate system of the painter

Painter attributes

Let's start with the attributes. The three most important ones are the pen, brush, and font. The pen holds properties of the outline drawn by the painter, and the brush determines how it will fill shapes. We've already described pens and brushes in `Chapter 4`, *Custom 2D Graphics with Graphics View*, so you should already understand how to work with them.

The `font` attribute is an instance of the `QFont` class. It contains a large number of methods for controlling font parameters such as font family, style (italic or oblique), font weight, and font size (either in points or device-dependent pixels). All the parameters are self-explanatory, so we will not discuss them here in detail. It is important to note that `QFont` can use any font installed on the system. In case more control over fonts is required or a font that is not installed in the system needs to be used, you can take advantage of the `QFontDatabase` class. It provides information about the available fonts (such as whether a particular font is scalable or bitmap or what writing systems it supports) and allows adding new fonts into the registry by loading their definitions directly from files.

An important class, when it comes to fonts, is the `QFontMetrics` class. It allows calculating how much space is needed to paint particular text using a font or calculates text eliding. The most common use case is to check how much space to allocate for a particular user-visible string; consider this example:

```
QFontMetrics fm = painter.fontMetrics();
QRect rect = fm.boundingRect("Game Programming using Qt");
```

This is especially useful when trying to determine `sizeHint` for a widget.

Coordinate systems

The next important aspect of the painter is its coordinate system. The painter in fact has two coordinate systems. One is its own logical coordinate system that operates on real numbers, and the other is the physical coordinate system of the device the painter operates on. Each operation on the logical coordinate system is mapped to physical coordinates in the device and applied there. Let's start with explaining the logical coordinate system first, and then we'll see how this relates to physical coordinates.

The painter represents an infinite cartesian canvas, with the horizontal axis pointing right and the vertical axis pointing down by default. The system can be modified by applying affine transformations to it—translating, rotating, scaling, and shearing. This way, you can draw an analog clock face that marks each hour with a line by executing a loop that rotates the coordinate system by 30 degrees for each hour and draws a line that is vertical in the newly-obtained coordinate system. Another example is when you wish to draw a simple plot with an x axis going right and a y axis going up. To obtain the proper coordinate system, you would scale the coordinate system by –1 in the vertical direction, effectively reversing the direction of the vertical axis.

What we described here modifies the world transformation matrix for the painter represented by an instance of the `QTransform` class. You can always query the current state of the matrix by calling `transform()` on the painter, and you can set a new matrix by calling `setTransform()`. `QTransform` has methods such as `scale()`, `rotate()`, and `translate()` that modify the matrix, but `QPainter` has equivalent methods for manipulating the world matrix directly. In most cases, using these would be preferable.

Each painting operation is expressed in logical coordinates, goes through the world transformation matrix, and reaches the second stage of coordinate manipulation, which is the view matrix. The painter has the concept of `viewport()` and `window()` rectangles. The `viewport` rectangle represents the physical coordinates of an arbitrary rectangle, while the `window` rectangle expresses the same rectangle but in logical coordinates. Mapping one to another gives a transformation that needs to be applied to each drawn primitive to calculate the area of the physical device that is to be painted.

By default, the two rectangles are identical to the rectangle of the underlying device (thus, no `window–viewport` mapping is done). Such transformation is useful if you wish to perform painting operations using measurement units other than the pixels of the target device. For example, if you want to express coordinates using percentages of the width and height of the target device, you would set both the window width and height to `100`. Then, to draw a line starting at 20% of the width and 10% of the height and ending at 70% of the width and 30% of the height, you would tell the painter to draw the line between `(20, 10)` and `(70, 30)`. If you wanted those percentages to apply not to the whole area of an image but to its left half, you would set the viewport rectangle only to the left half of the image.

> TIP: Setting the `window` and `viewport` rectangles only defines coordinate mapping; it does not prevent drawing operations from painting outside the `viewport` rectangle. If you want such behavior, you have to enable **clipping** in the painter and define the clipping region or path.

Drawing operations

Once you have the painter properly set, you can start issuing painting operations. `QPainter` has a rich set of operations for drawing different kinds of primitives. All of these operations have the `draw` prefix in their names, followed by the name of the primitive that is to be drawn. Thus, operations such as `drawLine`, `drawRoundedRect`, and `drawText` are available with a number of overloads that usually allow us to express coordinates using different data types. These may be pure values (either integer or real), Qt's classes, such as `QPoint` and `QRect`, or their floating point equivalents—`QPointF` and `QRectF`. Each operation is performed using current painter settings (font, pen, and brush).

> TIP: Refer to the documentation of the `QPainter` class for the list of all drawing operations.

Before you start drawing, you have to tell the painter which device you wish to draw on. This is done using the `begin()` and `end()` methods. The former accepts a pointer to a `QPaintDevice` instance and initializes the drawing infrastructure, and the latter marks the drawing as complete. Usually, we don't have to use these methods directly, as the constructor of `QPainter` calls `begin()` for us, and the destructor invokes `end()`.

Thus, the typical workflow is to instantiate a painter object, pass it to the device, then do the drawing by calling the `set` and `draw` methods, and finally let the painter be destroyed by going out of scope, as follows:

```
{
    QPainter painter(this); // paint on the current object
    QPen pen(Qt::red);
    pen.setWidth(2);
    painter.setPen(pen);
    painter.setBrush(Qt::yellow);
    painter.drawRect(0, 0, 100, 50);
}
```

We will cover more methods from the `draw` family in the following sections of this chapter.

Creating a custom widget

It is time to actually get something onto the screen by painting on a widget. A widget is repainted as a result of receiving a paint event, which is handled by reimplementing the `paintEvent()` virtual method. This method accepts a pointer to the event object of the `QPaintEvent` type that contains various bits of information about the repaint request. Remember that you can only paint on the widget from within that widget's `paintEvent()` call.

Time for action – Custom-painted widgets

Let's immediately put our new skills in to practice! Start by creating a new **Qt Widgets Application** in Qt Creator, choosing `QWidget` as the base class, and ensuring that the **Generate Form** box is unchecked. The name of our widget class will be `Widget`.

Switch to the header file for the newly created class, add a protected section to the class, and type `void paintEvent` in that section. Then, press *Ctrl* + *Space* on your keyboard and Creator will suggest the parameters for the method. You should end up with the following code:

```
protected:
    void paintEvent(QPaintEvent *);
```

Creator will leave the cursor positioned right before the semicolon. Pressing *Alt* + *Enter* will open the refactoring menu, letting you add the definition in the implementation file. The standard code for a paint event is one that instantiates a painter on the widget, as shown:

```
void Widget::paintEvent(QPaintEvent *)
{
    QPainter painter(this);
}
```

If you run this code, the widget will remain blank. Now we can start adding the actual painting code there:

```
void Widget::paintEvent(QPaintEvent *)
{
    QPainter painter(this);
    QPen pen(Qt::black);
    pen.setWidth(4);
    painter.setPen(pen);
    QRect r = rect().adjusted(10, 10, -10, -10);
    painter.drawRoundedRect(r, 20, 10);
}
```

Build and run the code, and you'll obtain the following output:

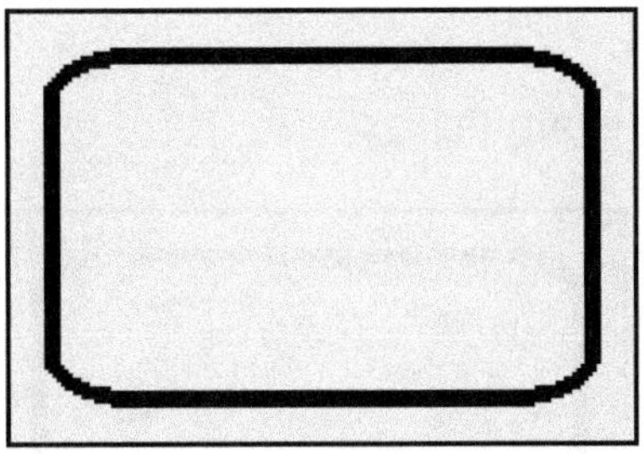

What just happened?

First, we set a four pixels wide black pen for the painter. Then, we called `rect()` to retrieve the geometry rectangle of the widget. By calling `adjusted()`, we receive a new rectangle with its coordinates (in the left, top, right, and bottom order) modified by the given arguments, effectively giving us a rectangle with a 10 pixel margin on each side.

> **TIP:** Qt usually offers two methods that allow us to work with modified data. Calling `adjusted()` returns a new object with its attributes modified, while if we had called `adjust()`, the modification would have been done in place. Pay special attention to which method you use to avoid unexpected results. It's best to always check the return value for a method—whether it returns a copy or void.

Finally, we call `drawRoundedRect()`, which paints a rectangle with its corners rounded by the number of pixels (in the *x*, *y* order) given as the second and third argument. If you look closely, you will note that the rectangle has nasty jagged rounded parts. This is caused by the effect of aliasing, where a logical line is approximated using the limited resolution of the screen; due to this, a pixel is either fully drawn or not drawn at all. As we learned in `Chapter 4`, *Custom 2D Graphics with Graphics View*, Qt offers a mechanism called anti-aliasing to counter this effect using intermediate pixel colors where appropriate. You can enable this mechanism by setting a proper render hint on the painter before you draw the rounded rectangle, as shown:

```
void Widget::paintEvent(QPaintEvent *)
{
    QPainter painter(this);
    painter.setRenderHint(QPainter::Antialiasing, true);
    // ...
}
```

Now you'll get the following output:

Of course, this has a negative impact on performance, so use anti-aliasing only where the aliasing effect is noticeable.

Time for action – Transforming the viewport

Let's extend our code so that all future operations focus only on drawing within the border boundaries after the border is drawn. Use the `window` and `viewport` transformation, as follows:

```
void Widget::paintEvent(QPaintEvent *) {
    QPainter painter(this);
    painter.setRenderHint(QPainter::Antialiasing, true);
    QPen pen(Qt::black);
    pen.setWidth(4);
    painter.setPen(pen);
    QRect r = rect().adjusted(10, 10, -10, -10);
    painter.drawRoundedRect(r, 20, 10);
    painter.save();
    r.adjust(2, 2, -2, -2);
    painter.setViewport(r);
    r.moveTo(0, -r.height() / 2);
    painter.setWindow(r);
    drawChart(&painter, r);
    painter.restore();
}
```

Also, create a protected method called `drawChart()`:

```
void Widget::drawChart(QPainter *painter, const QRect &rect) {
    painter->setPen(Qt::red);
    painter->drawLine(0, 0, rect.width(), 0);
}
```

Let's take a look at our output:

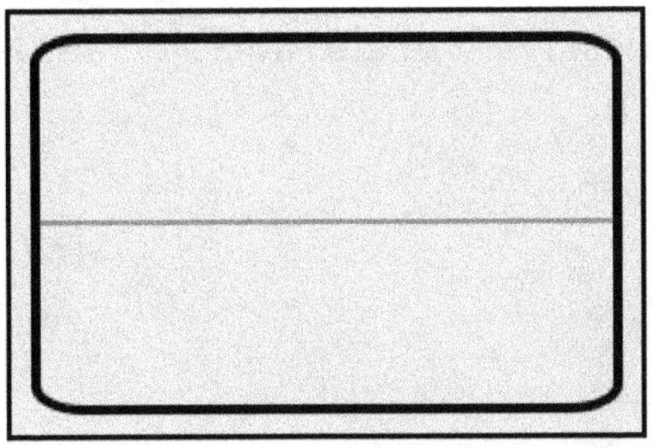

What just happened?

The first thing we did in the newly added code is call painter.save(). This call stores all parameters of the painter in an internal stack. We can then modify the painter state (by changing its attributes, applying transformations, and so on) and then, if at any point we want to go back to the saved state, it is enough to call painter.restore() to undo all the modifications in one go.

> **TIP**
> The save() and restore() methods can be called as many times as needed. States are stored in a stack, so you can save multiple times in a row and then restore to undo each change. Just remember to always pair a call to save() with a similar call to restore(), or the internal painter state will get corrupted. Each call to restore() will revert the painter to the last saved state.

After the state is saved, we modify the rectangle again by adjusting for the width of the border. Then, we set the new rectangle as the viewport, informing the painter about the physical range of coordinates to operate on. Then, we move the rectangle by half its height and set that as the painter window. This effectively puts the origin of the painter at half the height of the widget. Then, the drawChart() method is called, whereby a red line is drawn on the *x* axis of the new coordinate system.

Time for action – Drawing an oscillogram

Let's further extend our widget to become a simple oscillogram renderer. For that, we have to make the widget remember a set of values and draw them as a series of lines.

Let's start by adding a QVector<quint16> member variable that holds a list of unsigned 16-bit integer values. We will also add slots for adding values to the list and for clearing the list, as shown:

```
class Widget : public QWidget
{
    // ...
public slots:
    void addPoint(unsigned yVal) {
        m_points << qMax(0u, yVal);
        update();
    }
    void clear() {
        m_points.clear();
        update();
    }
```

```
protected:
    // ...
    QVector<quint16> m_points;
};
```

Note that each modification of the list invokes a method called `update()`. This schedules a paint event so that our widget can be redrawn with the new values.

Drawing code is also easy; we just iterate over the list and draw symmetric blue lines based on the values from the list. Since the lines are vertical, they don't suffer from aliasing and so we can disable this render hint, as shown:

```
void Widget::drawChart(QPainter *painter, const QRect &rect) {
    painter->setPen(Qt::red);
    painter->drawLine(0, 0, rect.width(), 0);
    painter->save();
    painter->setRenderHint(QPainter::Antialiasing, false);
    painter->setPen(Qt::blue);
    for(int i = 0; i < m_points.size(); ++i) {
        painter->drawLine(i, -m_points.at(i), i, m_points.at(i));
    }
    painter->restore();
}
```

To see the result, let's fill the widget with data in the `main()` function:

```
for(int i = 0; i < 450; ++i) {
    w.addPoint(qrand() % 120);
}
```

This loop takes a random number between `0` and `119` and adds it as a point to the widget. A sample result from running such code can be seen in the following screenshot:

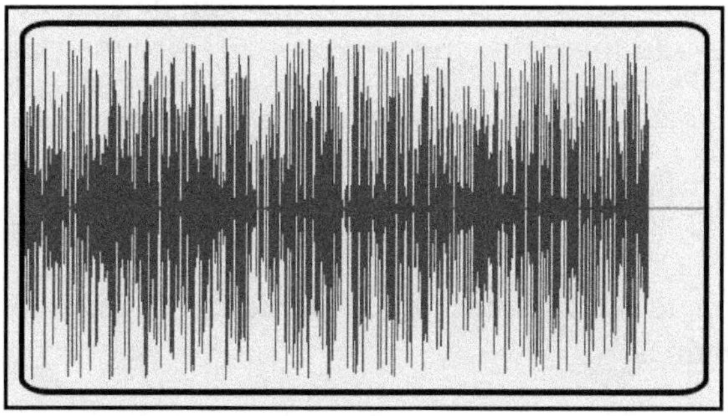

> **TIP:** If you scale down the window, you will note that the oscillogram extends past the boundaries of the rounded rectangle. Remember about clipping? You can use it now to constrain the drawing by adding a simple `painter.setClipRect(r)` call just before you call `drawChart()`.

So far, the custom widget was not interactive at all. Although the widget content could be manipulated from within the source code (say by adding new points to the plot), the widget was deaf to any user actions (apart from resizing the widget, which caused a repaint). In Qt, any interaction between the user and the widget is done by delivering events to the widget. Such a family of events is generally called input events and contains events such as keyboard events and different forms of pointing-device events—mouse, tablet, and touch events.

In a typical mouse event flow, a widget first receives a mouse press event, then a number of mouse move events (when the user moves the mouse around while the mouse button is kept pressed), and finally, a mouse release event. The widget can also receive an additional mouse double-click event in addition to these events. It is important to remember that by default, mouse move events are only delivered if a mouse button is pressed when the mouse is moved. To receive mouse move events when no button is pressed, a widget needs to activate a feature called **mouse tracking**.

Time for action – Making oscillograms selectable

It's time to make our oscillogram widget interactive. We will teach it to add a couple of lines of code to it that let the user select part of the plot. Let's start with storage for the selection. We'll need two integer variables that can be accessed via read-only properties; therefore, add the following two properties to the class:

```
Q_PROPERTY(int selectionStart READ selectionStart
                              NOTIFY selectionChanged)
Q_PROPERTY(int selectionEnd   READ selectionEnd
                              NOTIFY selectionChanged)
```

Next, you need to create corresponding private fields (you can initialize them both to –1), getters, and signals.

The user can change the selection by dragging the mouse cursor over the plot. When the user presses the mouse button over some place in the plot, we'll mark that place as the start of the selection. Dragging the mouse will determine the end of the selection. The scheme for naming events is similar to the paint event; therefore, we need to declare and implement the following two protected methods:

```
void Widget::mousePressEvent(QMouseEvent *mouseEvent) {
    m_selectionStart = m_selectionEnd = mouseEvent->pos().x() - 12;
    emit selectionChanged();
    update();
}
void Widget::mouseMoveEvent(QMouseEvent *mouseEvent) {
    m_selectionEnd = mouseEvent->pos().x() - 12;
    emit selectionChanged();
    update();
}
```

The structure of both event handlers is similar. We update the needed values, taking into consideration the left padding (12 pixels) of the plot, similar to what we do while drawing. Then, a signal is emitted and `update()` is called to schedule a repaint of the widget.

What remains is to introduce changes to the drawing code. We suggest that you add a `drawSelection()` method similar to `drawChart()`, but that it is called from the paint event handler immediately before `drawChart()`, as shown:

```
void Widget::drawSelection(QPainter *painter, const QRect &rect) {
    if(m_selectionStart < 0) {
        return;
    }
    painter->save();
    painter->setPen(Qt::NoPen);
    painter->setBrush(palette().highlight());
    QRect selectionRect = rect;
    selectionRect.setLeft(m_selectionStart);
    selectionRect.setRight(m_selectionEnd);
    painter->drawRect(selectionRect);
    painter->restore();
}
```

First, we check whether there is any selection to be drawn at all. Then, we save the painter state and adjust the pen and brush of the painter. The pen is set to `Qt::NoPen`, which means the painter should not draw any outline. To determine the brush, we use `palette()`; this returns an object of the `QPalette` type holding basic colors for a widget. One of the colors held in the object is the color of the highlight often used for marking selections. If you use an entry from the palette instead of manually specifying a color, you gain an advantage because when the user of the class modifies the palette, this modification is taken into account by our widget code.

> TIP: You can use other colors from the palette in the widget for other things we draw in the widget. You can even define your own `QPalette` object in the constructor of the widget to provide default colors for it.

Finally, we adjust the rectangle to be drawn and issue the drawing call.

When you run this program, you will note that the selection color doesn't contrast very well with the plot itself. To overcome this, a common approach is to draw the "selected" content with a different (often inverted) color. This can easily be applied in this situation by modifying the `drawChart()` code slightly:

```
for(int i = 0; i < m_points.size(); ++i) {
    if(m_selectionStart <= i && m_selectionEnd >=i) {
        painter->setPen(Qt::white);
    } else {
        painter->setPen(Qt::blue);
    }
    painter->drawLine(i, -m_points.at(i), i, m_points.at(i));
}
```

Now you see the following output:

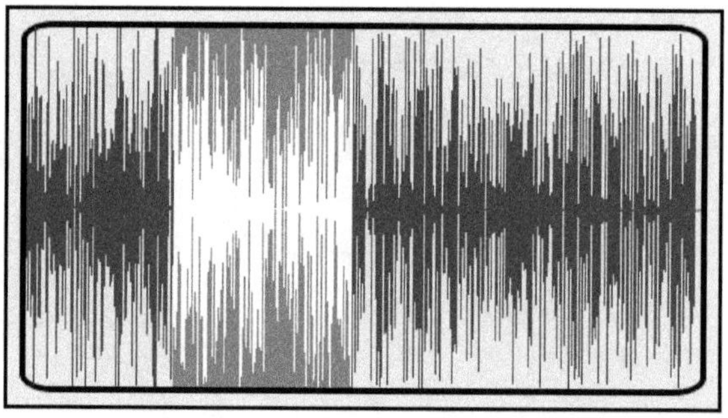

Have a go hero – Reacting only to the left mouse button

As an exercise, you can modify the event handling code so that it only changes the selection if the mouse event was triggered by the left mouse button. To see which button triggered the mouse press event, you can use the `QMouseEvent::button()` method, which returns `Qt::LeftButton` for the left button, `Qt::RightButton` for the right, and so on.

Touch events

Handling touch events is different. For any such event, you receive a call to the `touchEvent()` virtual method. The parameter of such a call is an object that can retrieve a list of points currently touched by the user with additional information regarding the history of user interaction (whether the touch was just initiated or the point was pressed earlier and moved) and what force is applied to the point by the user. Note that this is a low-level framework that allows you to precisely follow the history of touch interaction. If you are more interested in higher-level gesture recognition (pan, pinch, and swipe), there is a separate family of events available for it.

Handling gestures is a two-step procedure. First, you need to activate gesture recognition on your widget by calling `grabGesture()` and passing in the type of gesture you want to handle. A good place for such code is the widget constructor.

Then, your widget will start receiving gesture events. There are no dedicated handlers for gesture events but, fortunately, all events for an object flow through its `event()` method, which we can reimplement. Here's some example code that handles pan gestures:

```
bool Widget::event(QEvent *e) {
  if(e->type() == QEvent::Gesture) {
    QGestureEvent *gestureEvent = static_cast<QGestureEvent*>(e);
    QGesture *pan  = gestureEvent->gesture(Qt::PanGesture);
    if(pan) {
      handlePanGesture(static_cast<QPanGesture*>(pan));
    }
  }
  return QWidget::event(e);
}
```

First, a check for the event type is made; if it matches the expected value, the event object is cast to `QGestureEvent`. Then, the event is asked whether `Qt::PanGesture` was recognized. Finally, a `handlePanGesture` method is called. You can implement such a method to handle your pan gestures.

Working with images

Qt has two classes for handling images. The first one is `QImage`, more tailored toward direct pixel manipulation. You can check the size of the image or check and modify the color of each pixel. You can convert the image into a different internal representation (say from 8-bit color map to full 32-bit color with a premultiplied alpha channel). This type, however, is not that fit for rendering. For that, we have a different class called `QPixmap`. The difference between the two classes is that `QImage` is always kept in the application memory, while `QPixmap` can only be a handle to a resource that may reside in the graphics card memory or on a remote X server. Its main advantage over `QImage` is that it can be rendered very quickly at the cost of the inability to access pixel data. You can freely convert between the two types, but bear in mind that on some platforms, this might be an expensive operation. Always consider which class serves your particular situation better. If you intend to crop the image, tint it with some color, or paint over it, `QImage` is a better choice, but if you just want to render a bunch of icons, it's best to keep them as `QPixmap` instances.

Loading

Loading images is very easy. Both `QPixmap` and `QImage` have constructors that simply accept a path to a file containing the image. Qt accesses image data through plugins that implement reading and writing operations for different image formats. Without going into the details of plugins, it is enough to say that the default Qt installation supports reading the following image types:

Type	Description
BMP	Windows Bitmap
GIF	Graphics Interchange Format
JPG/JPEG	Joint Photography Experts Group
PNG	Portable Network Graphics
PPM/PBM/PGM	Portable anymap
XBM	X Bitmap

Type	Description
XPM	X Pixmap

As you can see, the most popular image formats are available. The list can be further extended by installing additional plugins.

> **TIP:** You can ask Qt for a list of supported image types by calling a static method, `QImageReader::supportedImageFormats()`, which returns a list of formats that can be read by Qt. For a list of writable formats, call `QImageWriter::supportedImageFormats()`.

An image can also be loaded directly from an existing memory buffer. This can be done in two ways. The first one is to use the `loadFromData()` method (it exists in both `QPixmap` and `QImage`), which behaves the same as when loading an image from a file—you pass it a data buffer and the size of the buffer and based on that, the loader determines the image type by inspecting the header data and loads the picture into `QImage` or `QPixmap`. The second situation is when you don't have images stored in a "filetype" such as JPEG or PNG; rather, you have raw pixel data itself. In such a situation, `QImage` offers a constructor that takes a pointer to a block of data together with the size of the image and format of the data. The format is not a file format such as the ones listed earlier but a memory layout for data representing a single pixel.

The most popular format is `QImage::Format_ARGB32`, which means that each pixel is represented by 32-bits (4 bytes) of data divided equally between alpha, red, green, and blue channels—8-bits per channel. Another popular format is `QImage::Format_ARGB32_Premultiplied`, where values for the red, green, and blue channels are stored after being multiplied by the value of the alpha channel, which often results in faster rendering. You can change the internal data representation using a call to `convertToFormat()`. For example, the following code converts a true-color image to 256 colors, where color for each pixel is represented by an index in a color table:

```
QImage trueColor("image.png");
QImage indexed = trueColor.convertToFormat(QImage::Format_Indexed8);
```

The color table itself is a vector of color definitions that can be fetched using `colorTable()` and replaced using `setColorTable()`. For example, you can convert an indexed image to grayscale by adjusting its color table, as follows:

```
QImage indexed = ...;
QVector<QRgb> colorTable = indexed.colorTable();
for(QRgb &item: colorTable) {
    int gray = qGray(item);
    item = qRgb(gray, gray, gray);
}
indexed.setColorTable(colorTable);
```

However, there is a much cleaner solution to this task. You can convert any image to the `Format_Grayscale8` format:

```
QImage grayImage =
coloredImage.convertToFormat(QImage::Format_Grayscale8);
```

This format uses 8 bits per pixel and doesn't have a color table, so it can only store grayscale images.

Modifying

There are two ways to modify image pixel data. The first one works only for `QImage` and involves direct manipulation of pixels using the `setPixel()` call, which takes the pixel coordinates and color to be set for that pixel. The second one works for both `QImage` and `QPixmap` and makes use of the fact that both these classes are subclasses of `QPaintDevice`. Therefore, you can open `QPainter` on such objects and use its drawing API. Here's an example of obtaining a pixmap with a blue rectangle and red circle painted over it:

```
QPixmap px(256, 256);
px.fill(Qt::transparent);
QPainter painter(&px);
painter.setPen(Qt::NoPen);
painter.setBrush(Qt::blue);
QRect r = px.rect().adjusted(10, 10, -10, -10);
painter.drawRect(r);
painter.setBrush(Qt::red);
painter.drawEllipse(r);
```

First, we create a 256 x 256 pixmap and fill it with transparent color. Then, we open a painter on it and invoke a series of calls that draws a blue rectangle and red circle.

`QImage` also offers a number of methods for transforming the image, including `scaled()`, `mirrored()`, `transformed()`, and `copy()`. Their API is intuitive, so we won't discuss it here.

Painting

Painting images in its basic form is as simple as calling `drawImage()` or `drawPixmap()` from the `QPainter` API. There are different variants of the two methods, but, basically, all of them allow one to specify which portion of a given image or pixmap is to be drawn and where. It is worth noting that painting pixmaps is preferred to painting images, as an image has to first be converted into a pixmap before it can be drawn.

If you have a lot of pixmaps to draw, a class called `QPixmapCache` may come in handy. It provides an application-wide cache for pixmaps. Using it, you can speed up pixmap loading while introducing a cap on memory usage.

Finally, if you just want to show a pixmap as a separate widget, you can use `QLabel`. This widget is usually used for displaying text, but you can configure it to show a pixmap instead with the `setPixmap()` function. By default, the pixmap is displayed without scaling. When the label is larger than the pixmap, it's position is determined by the label's alignment that you can change with the `setAlignment()` function. You can also call `setScaledContents(true)` to stretch the pixmap to the whole size of the label.

Painting text

Drawing text using `QPainter` deserves a separate explanation, not because it is complicated, but because Qt offers much flexibility in this regard. In general, painting text takes place by calling `QPainter::drawText()` or `QPainter::drawStaticText()`. Let's focus on the former first, which allows the drawing of generic text.

The most basic call to paint some text is a variant of this method, which takes *x* and *y* coordinates and the text to draw:

```
painter.drawText(10, 20, "Drawing some text at (10, 20)");
```

The preceding call draws the given text at position 10 horizontally and places the baseline of the text at position 20 vertically. The text is drawn using the painter's current font and pen. The coordinates can alternatively be passed as `QPoint` instances, instead of being given *x* and *y* values separately. The problem with this method is that it allows little control over how the text is drawn. A much more flexible variant is one that lets us give a set of flags and expresses the position of the text as a rectangle instead of a point. The flags can specify the alignment of the text within the given rectangle or instruct the rendering engine about wrapping and clipping the text. You can see the result of giving a different combination of flags to the call in the following diagram:

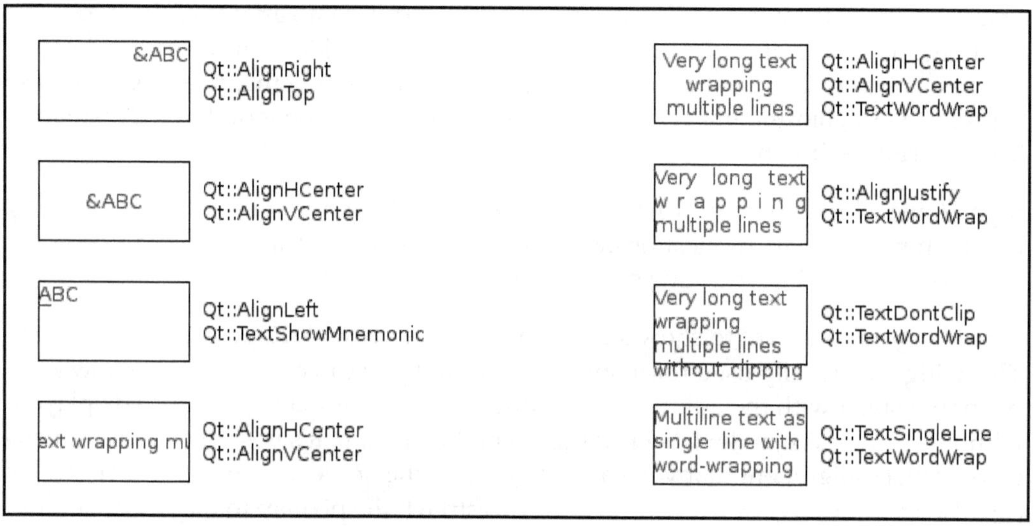

In order to obtain each of the preceding results, run code similar to the following:

```
painter.drawText(rect, Qt::AlignLeft | Qt::TextShowMnemonic, "&ABC");
```

You can see that unless you set the `Qt::TextDontClip` flag, the text is clipped to the given rectangle; setting `Qt::TextWordWrap` enables line wrapping, and `Qt::TextSingleLine` makes the engine ignore any newline characters encountered.

Static text

Qt has to perform a number of calculations when laying out the text, and this has to be done each time the text is rendered. This will be a waste of time if the text and its attributes have not changed since the last time. To avoid the need to recalculate the layout, the concept of static text was introduced.

To use it, instantiate `QStaticText` and initialize it with the text you want to render along with any options you might want it to have (kept as the `QTextOption` instance). Then, store the object somewhere, and whenever you want the text to be rendered, just call `QPainter::drawStaticText()`, passing the static text object to it. If the layout of the text has not changed since the previous time the text was drawn, it will not be recalculated, resulting in improved performance. Here's an example of a custom widget that simply draws text using the static text approach:

```
class TextWidget : public QWidget {
public:
    TextWidget(QWidget *parent = nullptr) : QWidget(parent) {}
    void setText(const QString &txt) {
        m_staticText.setText(txt);
        update();
    }
protected:
    void paintEvent(QPaintEvent *) {
        QPainter painter(this);
        painter.drawStaticText(0, 0, m_staticText);
    }
private:
    QStaticText m_staticText;
};
```

Optimizing widget painting

As an exercise, we will modify our oscillogram widget so that it only rerenders the part of its data that is required.

Time for action – Optimizing oscillogram drawing

The first step is to modify the paint event handling code to fetch information about the region that needs updating and pass it to the method drawing the chart. The changed parts of the code have been highlighted here:

```
void Widget::paintEvent(QPaintEvent *event)
{
    QRect exposedRect = event->rect();
    ...
    drawSelection(&painter, r, exposedRect);
    drawChart(&painter, r, exposedRect);
    painter.restore();
}
```

The next step is to modify `drawSelection()` to only draw the part of the selection that intersects with the exposed rectangle. Luckily, `QRect` offers a method to calculate the intersection for us:

```
void Widget::drawSelection(QPainter *painter, const QRect &rect,
                           const QRect &exposedRect)
{
    // ...
    QRect selectionRect = rect;
    selectionRect.setLeft(m_selectionStart);
    selectionRect.setRight(m_selectionEnd);
    painter->drawRect(selectionRect.intersected(exposedRect));
    painter->restore();
}
```

Finally, `drawChart` needs to be adjusted to omit the values outside the exposed rectangle:

```
void Widget::drawChart(QPainter *painter, const QRect &rect,
                       const QRect &exposedRect)
{
    painter->setPen(Qt::red);
    painter->drawLine(exposedRect.left(), 0, exposedRect.width(), 0);
    painter->save();
    painter->setRenderHint(QPainter::Antialiasing, false);
    const int lastPoint = qMin(m_points.size(),
                               exposedRect.right() + 1);
    for(int i = exposedRect.left(); i < lastPoint; ++i) {
      if(m_selectionStart <= i && m_selectionEnd >=i) {
        painter->setPen(Qt::white);
```

```
        } else
        painter->setPen(Qt::blue);
        painter->drawLine(i, -m_points.at(i), i, m_points.at(i));
    }
    painter->restore();
    Q_UNUSED(rect)
}
```

What just happened?

By implementing these changes, we have effectively reduced the painted area to the rectangle received with the event. In this particular situation, we will not save much time as drawing the plot is not that time-consuming; in many situations, however, you will be able to save a lot of time using this approach. For example, if we were to plot a very detailed aerial map of a game world, it would be very expensive to replot the whole map if only a small part of it were modified. We can easily reduce the number of calculations and drawing calls by taking advantage of the information about the exposed area.

Making use of the exposed rectangle is already a good step toward efficiency, but we can go a step further. The current approach requires that we redraw each and every line of the plot within the exposed rectangle, which still takes some time. Instead, we can paint those lines only once into a pixmap, and then whenever the widget needs repainting, tell Qt to render part of the pixmap to the widget.

Have a go hero – Caching the oscillogram in a pixmap

Now, it should be very easy for you to implement this approach for our example widget. The main difference is that each change to the plot contents should not result in a call to `update()` but in a call that will rerender the pixmap and then call `update()`. The `paintEvent` method then becomes simply this:

```
void Widget::paintEvent(QPaintEvent *event)
{
    QRect exposedRect = event->rect();
    QPainter painter(this);
    painter.drawPixmap(exposedRect, m_pixmap, exposedRect);
}
```

You'll also need to rerender the pixmap when the widget is resized. This can be done from within the `resizeEvent()` virtual function.

> While it is useful to master the available approaches to optimization, it's always important to check whether they actually make your application faster. There are often cases where the straightforward approach is more optimal than a clever optimization. In the preceding example, resizing the widget (and subsequently resizing the pixmap) can trigger a potentially expensive memory allocation. Use this optimization only if direct painting on the widget is even more expensive.

Implementing a chess game

At this point, you are ready to employ your newly gained skills in rendering graphics with Qt to create a game that uses widgets with custom graphics. The hero of today will be chess and other chess-like games.

Time for action – Developing the game architecture

Create a new **Qt Widgets Application** project. After the project infrastructure is ready, choose **New File or Project** from the **File** menu and choose to create a **C++ Class**. Call the new class `ChessBoard` and set `QObject` as its base class. Repeat the process to create a `ChessAlgorithm` class derived from `QObject` and another one called `ChessView`, but choose `QWidget` as the base class this time. You should end up with a file named `main.cpp` and four classes:

- `MainWindow` will be our main window class that contains a `ChessView`
- `ChessView` will be the widget that displays our chess board
- `ChessAlgorithm` will contain the game logic
- `ChessBoard` will hold the state of the chess board and provide it to `ChessView` and `ChessAlgorithm`

Now, navigate to the header file for `ChessAlgorithm` and add the following methods to the class:

```
public:
    ChessBoard* board() const;
public slots:
    virtual void newGame();
signals:
    void boardChanged(ChessBoard*);
protected:
    virtual void setupBoard();
    void setBoard(ChessBoard *board);
```

Also, add a private `m_board` field of the `ChessBoard*` type. Remember to either include `chessboard.h` or forward-declare the `ChessBoard` class. Implement `board()` as a simple getter method for `m_board`. The `setBoard()` method will be a protected setter for `m_board`:

```
void ChessAlgorithm::setBoard(ChessBoard *board)
{
    if(board == m_board) {
        return;
    }
    delete m_board;
    m_board = board;
    emit boardChanged(m_board);
}
```

Next, let's provide a base implementation for `setupBoard()` to create a default chess board with eight ranks and eight columns:

```
void ChessAlgorithm::setupBoard()
{
    setBoard(new ChessBoard(8, 8, this));
}
```

The natural place to prepare the board is in a function executed when a new game is started:

```
void ChessAlgorithm::newGame()
{
    setupBoard();
}
```

The last addition to this class for now is to extend the provided constructor to initialize `m_board` to a null pointer.

In the last method shown, we instantiated a `ChessBoard` object, so let's focus on that class now. First, extend the constructor to accept two additional integer parameters besides the regular parent argument. Store their values in private `m_ranks` and `m_columns` fields (remember to declare the fields themselves in the class header file).

In the header file, just under the `Q_OBJECT` macro, add the following two lines as property definitions:

```
Q_PROPERTY(int ranks READ ranks NOTIFY ranksChanged)
Q_PROPERTY(int columns READ columns NOTIFY columnsChanged)
```

Declare signals and implement getter methods to cooperate with those definitions. Also, add two protected methods:

```
protected:
    void setRanks(int newRanks);
    void setColumns(int newColumns);
```

These will be setters for the rank and column properties, but we don't want to expose them to the outside world, so we will give them `protected` access scope.

Put the following code into the `setRanks()` method body:

```
void ChessBoard::setRanks(int newRanks)
{
    if(ranks() == newRanks) {
        return;
    }
    m_ranks = newRanks;
    emit ranksChanged(m_ranks);
}
```

Next, in a similar way, you can implement `setColumns()`.

The last class we will deal with now is our custom widget, `ChessView`. For now, we will provide only a rudimentary implementation for one method, but we will expand it later as our implementation grows. Add a public `setBoard(ChessBoard *)` method with the following body:

```
void ChessView::setBoard(ChessBoard *board)
{
    if(m_board == board) {
        return;
    }
    if(m_board) {
        // disconnect all signal-slot connections between m_board and
```

```
this
        m_board->disconnect(this);
    }
    m_board = board;
    // connect signals (to be done later)
    updateGeometry();
}
```

Now, let's declare the `m_board` member. As we are not the owners of the board object (the algorithm class is responsible for managing it), we will use the `QPointer` class, which tracks the lifetime of `QObject` and sets itself to null once the object is destroyed:

```
private:
    QPointer<ChessBoard> m_board;
```

`QPointer` initializes its value to null, so we don't have to do it ourselves in the constructor. For completeness, let's provide a getter method for the board:

```
ChessBoard *ChessView::board() const {
    return m_board;
}
```

What just happened?

In the last exercise, we defined the base architecture for our solution. We can see that there are three classes involved: `ChessView` acting as the user interface, `ChessAlgorithm` for driving the actual game, and `ChessBoard` as a data structure shared between the view and the engine. The algorithm will be responsible for setting up the board (through `setupBoard()`), making moves, checking win conditions, and so on. The view will be rendering the current state of the board and will signal user interaction to the underlying logic.

Most of the code is self-explanatory. You can see in the `ChessView::setBoard()` method that we are disconnecting all signals from an old board object, attaching the new one (we will come back to connecting the signals later when we have already defined them), and finally telling the widget to update its size and redraw itself with the new board.

Time for action – Implementing the game board class

Now we will focus on our data structure. Add a new private member to `ChessBoard`, a vector of characters that will contain information about pieces on the board:

```
QVector<char> m_boardData;
```

Consider the following table that shows the piece type and the letters used for it:

Piece type		White	Black
	King	K	k
	Queen	Q	q
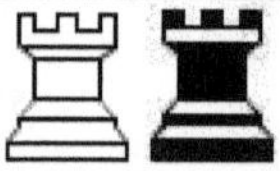	Rook	R	r
	Bishop	B	b
	Knight	N	n
	Pawn	P	P

You can see that white pieces use uppercase letters and black pieces use lowercase variants of the same letters. In addition to that, we will use a space character (0x20 ASCII value) to denote that a field is empty. We will add a protected method for setting up an empty board based on the number of ranks and columns on the board and a `boardReset()` signal to inform that the position on the board has changed:

```
void ChessBoard::initBoard()
{
    m_boardData.fill(' ', ranks() * columns());
    emit boardReset();
}
```

We can update our methods for setting rank and column counts to make use of that method:

```
void ChessBoard::setRanks(int newRanks)
{
    if(ranks() == newRanks) {
        return;
    }
    m_ranks = newRanks;
    initBoard();
    emit ranksChanged(m_ranks);
}

void ChessBoard::setColumns(int newColumns)
{
    if(columns() == newColumns) {
        return;
    }
    m_columns = newColumns;
    initBoard();
    emit columnsChanged(m_columns);
}
```

The `initBoard()` method should also be called from within the constructor, so place the call there as well.

Next, we need a method to read which piece is positioned in a particular field of the board:

```
char ChessBoard::data(int column, int rank) const
{
    return m_boardData.at((rank-1) * columns() + (column - 1));
}
```

Ranks and columns have indexes starting from 1, but the data structure is indexed starting from 0; therefore, we have to subtract 1 from both the rank and column index. It is also required to have a method to modify the data for the board. Implement the following public method:

```
void ChessBoard::setData(int column, int rank, char value)
{
    if(setDataInternal(column, rank, value)) {
        emit dataChanged(column, rank);
    }
}
```

The method makes use of another one that does the actual job. However, this method should be declared with `protected` access scope. Again, we adjust for index differences:

```
bool ChessBoard::setDataInternal(int column, int rank, char value)
{
    int index = (rank-1) * columns() + (column - 1);
    if(m_boardData.at(index) == value) {
        return false;
    }
    m_boardData[index] = value;
    return true;
}
```

Since `setData()` makes use of a signal, we have to declare it as well:

```
signals:
    void ranksChanged(int);
    void columnsChanged(int);
    void dataChanged(int c, int r);
    void boardReset();
```

The signal will be emitted every time there is a successful change to the situation on the board. We delegate the actual work to the protected method to be able to modify the board without emitting the signal.

Having defined `setData()`, we can add another method for our convenience:

```
void ChessBoard::movePiece(int fromColumn, int fromRank,
                           int toColumn, int toRank)
{
    setData(toColumn, toRank, data(fromColumn, fromRank));
    setData(fromColumn, fromRank, ' ');
}
```

Can you guess what it does? That's right! It moves a piece from one field to another one, leaving an empty space behind.

There is still one more method worth implementing. A regular chess game contains 32 pieces, and there are variants of the game where starting positions for the pieces might be different. Setting the position of each piece through a separate call to `setData()` would be very cumbersome. Fortunately, there is a neat chess notation called the **Forsyth-Edwards Notation** (**FEN**), with which the complete state of the game can be stored as a single line of text.

If you want the complete definition of the notation, you can look it up yourself. In short, we can say that the textual string lists piece placement rank by rank, starting from the last rank where each position is described by a single character interpreted as in our internal data structure (`K` for white king, `q` for black queen, and so on). Each rank description is separated by a `/` character. If there are empty fields on the board, they are not stored as spaces, but as a digit specifying the number of consecutive empty fields. Therefore, the starting position for a standard game can be written as follows:

```
"rnbqkbnr/pppppppp/8/8/8/8/PPPPPPPP/RNBQKBNR"
```

This can be interpreted visually, as follows:

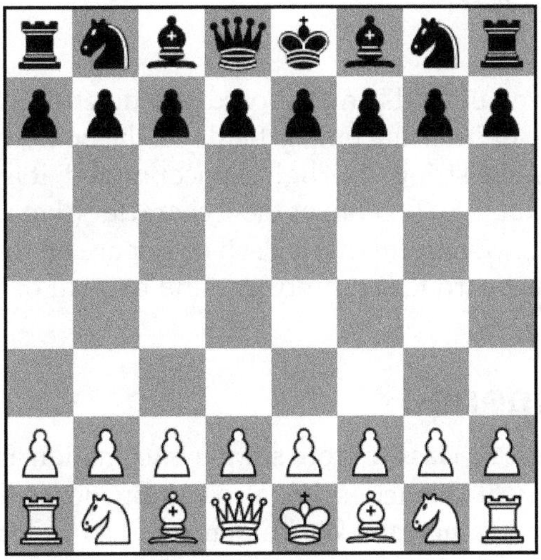

Let's write a method called `setFen()` to set up the board based on an FEN string:

```
void ChessBoard::setFen(const QString &fen)
{
    int index = 0;
    int skip = 0;
    const int columnCount = columns();
    QChar ch;
    for(int rank = ranks(); rank > 0; --rank) {
        for(int column = 1; column <= columnCount; ++column) {
            if(skip > 0) {
                ch = ' ';
                skip--;
            } else {
                ch = fen.at(index++);
```

```
                if(ch.isDigit()) {
                    skip = ch.toLatin1() - '0';
                    ch = ' ';
                    skip--;
                }
            }
            setDataInternal(column, rank, ch.toLatin1());
        }
        QChar next = fen.at(index++);
        if(next != '/' && next != ' ') {
            initBoard();
            return; // fail on error
        }
    }
    emit boardReset();
}
```

The method iterates over all fields on the board and determines whether it is currently in the middle of inserting empty fields on the board or should rather read the next character from the string. If a digit is encountered, it is converted into an integer by subtracting the ASCII value of the 0 character (that is, `'7' - '0'` = 7). After setting each rank, we require that a slash or a space be read from the string. Otherwise, we reset the board to an empty one and bail out of the method.

What just happened?

We taught the `ChessBoard` class to store simple information about chess pieces using a one-dimensional array of characters. We also equipped it with methods that allow querying and modifying game data. We implemented a fast way of setting the current state of the game by adopting the FEN standard. The game data itself is not tied to classic chess. Although we comply with a standard notation for describing pieces, it is possible to use other letters and characters outside the well-defined set for chess pieces. This creates a versatile solution for storing information about chess-like games, such as checkers, and possibly any other custom games played on a two-dimensional board of any size with ranks and columns. The data structure we came up with is not a stupid one—it communicates with its environment by emitting signals when the state of the game is modified.

Time for action – Understanding the ChessView class

This is a chapter about doing graphics, so it is high time we focus on displaying our chess game. Our widget currently displays nothing, and our first task will be to show a chess board with rank and column symbols and fields colored appropriately.

By default, the widget does not have any proper size defined, and we will have to fix that by implementing `sizeHint()`. However, to be able to calculate the size, we have to decide how big a single field on the board will be. Therefore, in `ChessView`, you should declare a property containing the size of the field, as shown:

```
Q_PROPERTY(QSize fieldSize
           READ fieldSize WRITE setFieldSize
           NOTIFY fieldSizeChanged)
```

To speed up coding, you can position the cursor over the property declaration, hit the *Alt* + *Enter* combination, and choose the **Generate missing Q_PROPERTY members** fix-up from the pop-up menu. Creator will provide minor implementations for the getter and setter for you. You can move the generated code to the implementation file by positioning the cursor over each method, hitting *Alt* + *Enter*, and choosing the **Move definition to chessview.cpp file** fixup. While the generated getter method is fine, the setter needs some adjusting. Modify it by adding the following highlighted code:

```
void ChessView::setFieldSize(QSize arg)
{
    if (m_fieldSize == arg) {
        return;
    }
    m_fieldSize = arg;
    emit fieldSizeChanged(arg);
    updateGeometry();
}
```

This tells our widget to recalculate its size whenever the size of the field is modified. Now we can implement `sizeHint()`:

```
QSize ChessView::sizeHint() const
{
    if(!m_board) {
        return QSize(100,100);
    }
    QSize boardSize = QSize(fieldSize().width()
        * m_board->columns() + 1,
```

```
        m_fieldSize.height() * m_board->ranks() + 1);
    // 'M' is the widest letter
    int rankSize = fontMetrics().width('M') + 4;
    int columnSize = fontMetrics().height() + 4;
    return boardSize + QSize(rankSize, columnSize);
}
```

First, we check whether we have a valid board definition and if not, return a sane size of 100 x 100 pixels. Otherwise, the method calculates the size of all the fields by multiplying the size of each of the fields by the number of columns or ranks. We add one pixel to each dimension to accommodate the right and bottom border. A chess board not only consists of fields themselves but also displays rank symbols on the left edge of the board and column numbers on the bottom edge of the board.

Since we use letters to enumerate ranks, we check the width of the widest letter using the `QFontMetrics` class. We use the same class to check how much space is required to render a line of text using the current font so that we have enough space to put column numbers. In both cases, we add 4 to the result to make a 2 pixel margin between the text and the edge of the board and another 2 pixel margin between the text and the edge of the widget.

Actually, the widest letter in the most common fonts is W, but it won't appear in our game.

It is very useful to define a helper method for returning a rectangle that contains a particular field, as shown:

```
QRect ChessView::fieldRect(int column, int rank) const
{
    if(!m_board) {
        return QRect();
    }
    const QSize fs = fieldSize();
    QPoint topLeft((column - 1) * fs.width(),
                   (m_board->ranks()-rank) * fs.height());
    QRect fRect = QRect(topLeft, fs);
    // offset rect by rank symbols
    int offset = fontMetrics().width('M');
    return fRect.translated(offset+4, 0);
}
```

Since rank numbers decrease from the top toward the bottom of the board, we subtract the desired rank from the maximum rank there is while calculating `fRect`. Then, we calculate the horizontal offset for rank symbols, just like we did in `sizeHint()`, and translate the rectangle by that offset before returning the result.

Finally, we can move on to implementing the event handler for the paint event. Declare the `paintEvent()` method (the fixup menu available under the *Alt* + *Enter* keyboard shortcut will let you generate a stub implementation of the method) and fill it with the following code:

```
void ChessView::paintEvent(QPaintEvent *)
{
    if(!m_board) {
        return;
    }
    QPainter painter(this);
    for(int r = m_board->ranks(); r > 0; --r) {
        painter.save();
        drawRank(&painter, r);
        painter.restore();
    }
    for(int c = 1; c <= m_board->columns(); ++c) {
        painter.save();
        drawColumn(&painter, c);
        painter.restore();
    }
    for(int r = 1; r <= m_board->ranks(); ++r) {
        for(int c = 1; c <= m_board->columns(); ++c) {
            painter.save();
            drawField(&painter, c, r);
            painter.restore();
        }
    }
}
```

The handler is quite simple. First, we instantiate the `QPainter` object that operates on the widget. Then, we have three loops: the first one iterates over ranks, the second over columns, and the third over all fields. The body of each loop is very similar; there is a call to a custom draw method that accepts a pointer to the painter and index of the rank, column, or both of them, respectively. Each of the calls is surrounded by executing `save()` and `restore()` on our `QPainter` instance. What are the calls for here? The three draw methods—`drawRank()`, `drawColumn()`, and `drawField()`—will be virtual methods responsible for rendering the rank symbol, the column number, and the field background.

It will be possible to subclass `ChessView` and provide custom implementations for those renderers so that it is possible to provide a different look of the chess board. Since each of these methods takes the painter instance as its parameter, overrides of these methods can alter attribute values of the painter behind our back. Calling `save()` before handing over the painter to such override stores its state on an internal stack, and calling `restore()` after returning from the override resets the painter to what was stored with `save()`. Note that the painter can still be left in an invalid state if the override calls `save()` and `restore()` a different number of times.

> TIP
>
> Calling `save()` and `restore()` very often introduces a performance hit, so you should avoid saving and restoring painter states too often in time-critical situations. As our painting is very simple, we don't have to worry about that when painting our chess board.

Having introduced our three methods, we can start implementing them. Let's start with `drawRank` and `drawColumn`. Remember to declare them as virtual and put them in protected access scope (that's usually where Qt classes put such methods), as follows:

```
void ChessView::drawRank(QPainter *painter, int rank)
{
    QRect r = fieldRect(1, rank);
    QRect rankRect = QRect(0, r.top(), r.left(), r.height())
        .adjusted(2, 0, -2, 0);
    QString rankText = QString::number(rank);
    painter->drawText(rankRect,
       Qt::AlignVCenter | Qt::AlignRight, rankText);
}

void ChessView::drawColumn(QPainter *painter, int column)
{
    QRect r = fieldRect(column, 1);
    QRect columnRect =
        QRect(r.left(), r.bottom(), r.width(), height() - r.bottom())
        .adjusted(0, 2, 0, -2);
    painter->drawText(columnRect,
        Qt::AlignHCenter | Qt::AlignTop, QChar('a' + column - 1));
}
```

Both methods are very similar. We use `fieldRect()` to query for the left-most column and bottom-most rank, and, based on that, we calculate where rank symbols and column numbers should be placed. The call to `QRect::adjusted()` is to accommodate the 2 pixel margin around the text to be drawn. Finally, we use `drawText()` to render appropriate text. For the rank, we ask the painter to align the text to the right edge of the rectangle and to center the text vertically. In a similar way, when drawing the column, we align to the top edge and center the text horizontally.

Now we can implement the third draw method. It should also be declared protected and virtual. Place the following code in the method body:

```
void ChessView::drawField(QPainter *painter, int column, int rank)
{
    QRect rect = fieldRect(column, rank);
    QColor fillColor = (column + rank) % 2 ?
        palette().color(QPalette::Light) :
        palette().color(QPalette::Mid);
    painter->setPen(palette().color(QPalette::Dark));
    painter->setBrush(fillColor);
    painter->drawRect(rect);
}
```

In this method, we use the `QPalette` object coupled with each widget to query for `Light` (usually white) and `Mid` (darkish) color, depending on whether the field we are drawing on the chess board is considered white or black. We do that instead of hardcoding the colors to make it possible to modify colors of the tiles without subclassing simply by adjusting the palette object. Then, we use the palette again to ask for the `Dark` color and use that as a pen for our painter. When we draw a rectangle with such settings, the pen will stroke the border of the rectangle to give it a more elegant look. Note how we modify attributes of the painter in this method and do not set them back afterward. We can get away with it because of the `save()` and `restore()` calls surrounding the `drawField()` execution.

We are now ready to see the results of our work. Let's switch to the `MainWindow` class and equip it with the following two private variables:

```
ChessView *m_view;
ChessAlgorithm *m_algorithm;
```

Then, modify the constructor by adding the following highlighted code to set up the view and the game engine:

```
MainWindow::MainWindow(QWidget *parent) :
  QMainWindow(parent),
  ui(new Ui::MainWindow)
{
    ui->setupUi(this);
    m_view = new ChessView;
    m_algorithm = new ChessAlgorithm(this);
    m_algorithm->newGame();
    m_view->setBoard(m_algorithm->board());
    setCentralWidget(m_view);
    m_view->setSizePolicy(QSizePolicy::Fixed, QSizePolicy::Fixed);
    m_view->setFieldSize(QSize(50,50));
    layout()->setSizeConstraint(QLayout::SetFixedSize);
}
```

Afterward, you should be able to build the project. When you run it, you should see a result similar to the one in the following screenshot:

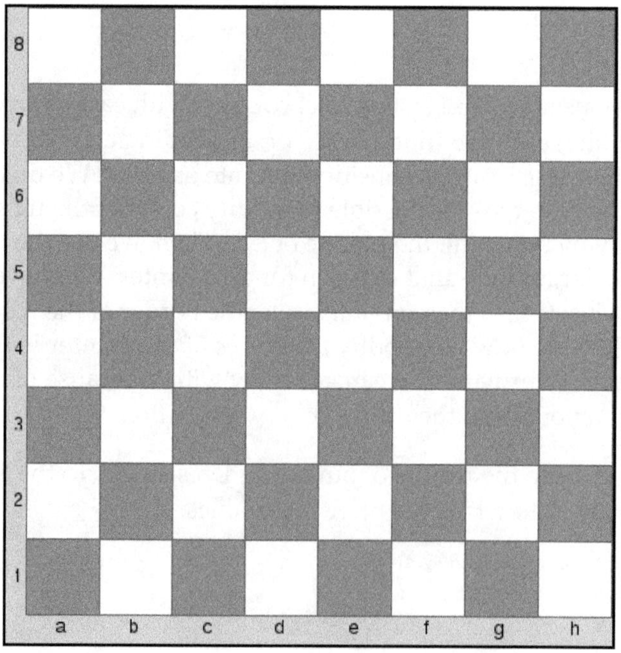

What just happened?

In this exercise, we did two things. First, we provided a number of methods for calculating the geometry of important parts of the chess board and the size of the widget. Second, we defined three virtual methods for rendering visual primitives of a chess board. By making the methods virtual, we provided an infrastructure to let the look be customized by subclassing and overriding base implementations. Furthermore, by reading color from `QPalette`, we allowed customizing the colors of the primitives even without subclassing.

The last line of the main window constructor tells the layout of the window to force a fixed size of the window equal to what the size hint of the widget inside it reports.

Time for action – Rendering the pieces

Now that we can see the board, it is time to put the pieces on it. We will use images for that purpose. In my case, we found a number of SVG files with chess pieces and decided to use them. SVG is a vector graphics format where all curves are defined not as a fixed set of points but as mathematic curves. Their main benefit is that they scale very well without causing an aliasing effect.

Let's equip our view with a registry of images to be used for "stamping" a particular piece type. Since each piece type is identified with char, we can use it to generate keys for a map of images. Let's put the following API into `ChessView`:

```
public:
    void setPiece(char type, const QIcon &icon);
    QIcon piece(char type) const;
private:
    QMap<char, QIcon> m_pieces;
```

For the image type, we do not use `QImage` or `QPixmap` but `QIcon`. This is because `QIcon` can store many pixmaps of different sizes and use the most appropriate one when we request an icon of a given size to be painted. It doesn't matter if we use vector images, but it does matter if you choose to use PNG or other types of image. In such cases, you can use `addFile()` to add many images to a single icon.

Going back to our registry, the implementation is very simple. We just store the icon in a map and ask the widget to repaint itself:

```
void ChessView::setPiece(char type, const QIcon &icon)
{
    m_pieces.insert(type, icon);
```

```
    update();
}

QIcon ChessView::piece(char type) const
{
    return m_pieces.value(type, QIcon());
}
```

Now we can fill the registry with actual images right after we create the view inside the `MainWindow` constructor. Note that we stored all the images in a resource file, as shown:

```
m_view->setPiece('P', QIcon(":/pieces/Chess_plt45.svg")); // pawn
m_view->setPiece('K', QIcon(":/pieces/Chess_klt45.svg")); // king
m_view->setPiece('Q', QIcon(":/pieces/Chess_qlt45.svg")); // queen
m_view->setPiece('R', QIcon(":/pieces/Chess_rlt45.svg")); // rook
m_view->setPiece('N', QIcon(":/pieces/Chess_nlt45.svg")); // knight
m_view->setPiece('B', QIcon(":/pieces/Chess_blt45.svg")); // bishop

m_view->setPiece('p', QIcon(":/pieces/Chess_pdt45.svg")); // pawn
m_view->setPiece('k', QIcon(":/pieces/Chess_kdt45.svg")); // king
m_view->setPiece('q', QIcon(":/pieces/Chess_qdt45.svg")); // queen
m_view->setPiece('r', QIcon(":/pieces/Chess_rdt45.svg")); // rook
m_view->setPiece('n', QIcon(":/pieces/Chess_ndt45.svg")); // knight
m_view->setPiece('b', QIcon(":/pieces/Chess_bdt45.svg")); // bishop
```

The next thing to do is to extend the `paintEvent()` method of the view to actually render our pieces. For that, we will introduce another protected virtual method called `drawPiece()`. We'll call it when iterating over all the ranks and columns of the board, as shown:

```
void ChessView::paintEvent(QPaintEvent *)
{
    // ...
    for(int r = m_board->ranks(); r > 0; --r) {
        for(int c = 1; c <= m_board->columns(); ++c) {
            drawPiece(&painter, c, r);
        }
    }
}
```

It is not a coincidence that we start drawing from the highest (top) rank to the lowest (bottom) one. By doing that, we allow a pseudo-3D effect; if a piece drawn extends past the area of the field, it will intersect the field from the next rank (which is possibly occupied by another piece). By drawing higher rank pieces first, we cause them to be partially covered by pieces from the lower rank, which imitates the effect of depth. By thinking ahead, we allow reimplementations of `drawPiece()` to have more freedom in what they can do.

The final step is to provide a base implementation for this method, as follows:

```
void ChessView::drawPiece(QPainter *painter, int column, int rank)
{
    QRect rect = fieldRect(column, rank);
    char value = m_board->data(column, rank);
    if(value != ' ') {
        QIcon icon = piece(value);
        if(!icon.isNull()) {
            icon.paint(painter, rect, Qt::AlignCenter);
        }
    }
}
```

The method is very simple; it queries for the rectangle of a given column and rank and then asks the `ChessBoard` instance about the piece occupying the given field. If there is a piece there, we ask the registry for the proper icon; if we get a valid one, we call its `paint()` routine to draw the piece centered in the field's rect. The image drawn will be scaled to the size of the rectangle. It is important that you only use images with a transparent background (such as PNG or SVG files and not JPEG files) so that the color of the field can be seen through the piece.

What just happened?

To test the implementation, you can modify the algorithm to fill the board with the default piece set up by introducing the following change to the `ChessAlgorithm` class:

```
void ChessAlgorithm::newGame()
{
  setupBoard();
  board()->setFen(
      "rnbqkbnr/pppppppp/8/8/8/8/PPPPPPPP/RNBQKBNR w KQkq - 0 1"
  );
}
```

Running the program should show the following result:

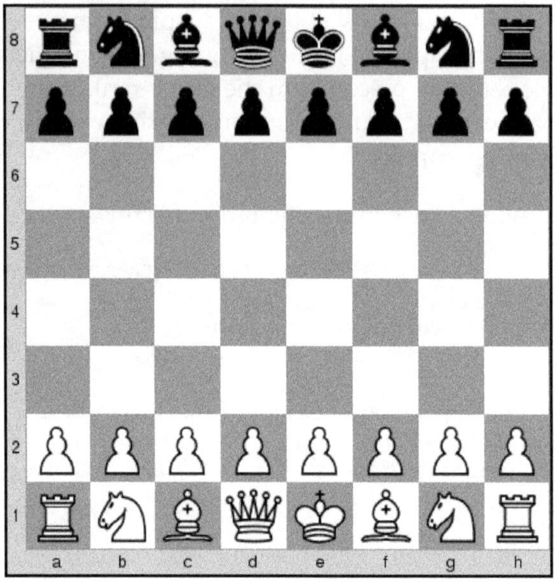

The modification we did in this step was very simple. First, we provided a way to tell the board what each piece type looks like. This includes not only standard chess pieces but anything that fits into char and can be set inside the `ChessBoard` class's internal data array. Second, we made an abstraction for drawing the pieces with the simplest possible base implementation: taking an icon from the registry and rendering it to the field. By making use of `QIcon`, we can add several pixmaps of different sizes to be used with different sizes of a single field. Alternatively, the icon can contain a single vector image that scales very well all by itself.

Time for action – Making the chess game interactive

We have managed to display the chess board, but to actually play a game, we have to tell the program what moves we want to play. We can do that by adding the `QLineEdit` widget where we will input the move in algebraic form (for example, `Nf3` to move a knight to `f3`), but a more natural way is to click on a piece with the mouse cursor (or tap it with a finger) and then click again on the destination field. To obtain such functionality, the first thing to do is to teach `ChessView` to detect mouse clicks.

Therefore, add the following method:

```
QPoint ChessView::fieldAt(const QPoint &pt) const
{
    if(!m_board) {
        return QPoint();
    }
    const QSize fs = fieldSize();
    int offset = fontMetrics().width('M') + 4;
    // 'M' is the widest letter
    if(pt.x() < offset) {
        return QPoint();
    }
    int c = (pt.x() - offset) / fs.width();
    int r = pt.y() / fs.height();
    if(c < 0 || c >= m_board->columns() ||
       r < 0 || r >= m_board->ranks()) {
        return QPoint();
    }
    return QPoint(c + 1, m_board->ranks() - r);
    // max rank - r
}
```

The code looks very similar to the implementation of `fieldRect()`. This is because `fieldAt()` implements its reverse operation—it transforms a point in the widget coordinate space to the column and rank index of a field the point is contained in. The index is calculated by dividing point coordinates by the size of the field. You surely remember that, in the case of columns, the fields are offset by the size of the widest letter and a margin of 4, and we have to consider that in our calculations here as well. We do two checks: first we check the horizontal point coordinate against the offset to detect whether the user clicked on the part of the widget where column symbols are displayed, and then we check whether the rank and column calculated fit the range represented in the board. Finally, we return the result as a `QPoint` value, since this is the easiest way in Qt to represent a two-dimensional value.

Now we need to find a way to make the widget notify its environment that a particular field was clicked on. We can do this through the signal-slot mechanism. Switch to the header file of `ChessView` (if you currently have `chessview.cpp` opened in Qt Creator, you can simply press the *F4* key to be transferred to the corresponding header file) and declare a `clicked(const QPoint &)` signal:

```
signals:
  void clicked(const QPoint &);
```

To detect mouse input, we have to override one of the mouse event handlers a widget has: either `mousePressEvent` or `mouseReleaseEvent`. It seems obvious that we should choose the former event; this would work, but it is not the best decision. Just think about the semantics of a mouse click: it is a complex event composed of pushing and releasing the mouse button. The actual "click" takes place after the mouse is released. Therefore, let's use `mouseReleaseEvent` as our event handler:

```
void ChessView::mouseReleaseEvent(QMouseEvent *event)
{
    QPoint pt = fieldAt(event->pos());
    if(pt.isNull()) {
        return;
    }
    emit clicked(pt);
}
```

The code is simple; we use the method we just implemented and pass it the position read from the `QMouseEvent` object. If the returned point is invalid, we quietly return from the method. Otherwise, `clicked()` is emitted with the obtained column and rank values.

We can make use of the signal now. Go to the constructor of `MainWindow` and add the following line to connect the widget's clicked signal to a custom slot:

```
connect(m_view, &ChessView::clicked,
        this,   &MainWindow::viewClicked);
```

Declare the slot and implement it, as follows:

```
void MainWindow::viewClicked(const QPoint &field)
{
    if(m_clickPoint.isNull()) {
        m_clickPoint = field;
    } else {
      if(field != m_clickPoint) {
        m_view->board()->movePiece(
          m_clickPoint.x(), m_clickPoint.y(),
          field.x(), field.y()
        );
      }
      m_clickPoint = QPoint();
    }
}
```

The function uses a class member variable—m_clickPoint—to store the clicked field. The variable value is made invalid after a move is made. Thus, we can detect whether the click we are currently handling has "select" or "move" semantics. In the first case, we store the selection in m_clickPoint; in the other case, we ask the board to make a move using the helper method we implemented some time ago. Remember to declare m_clickPoint as a private member variable of MainWindow.

All should be working now. However, if you build the application, run it, and start clicking around on the chess board, you will see that nothing happens. This is because we forgot to tell the view to refresh itself when the game position on the board is changed. We have to connect the signals that the board emits to the update() slot of the view. Open the setBoard() method of the widget class and fix it, as follows:

```
void ChessView::setBoard(ChessBoard *board)
{
    // ...
    m_board = board;
    // connect signals
    if(board) {
      connect(board, SIGNAL(dataChanged(int,int)),
              this,  SLOT(update()));
      connect(board, SIGNAL(boardReset()),
              this,  SLOT(update()));
    }
    updateGeometry();
}
```

If you run the program now, moves you make will be reflected in the widget, as shown:

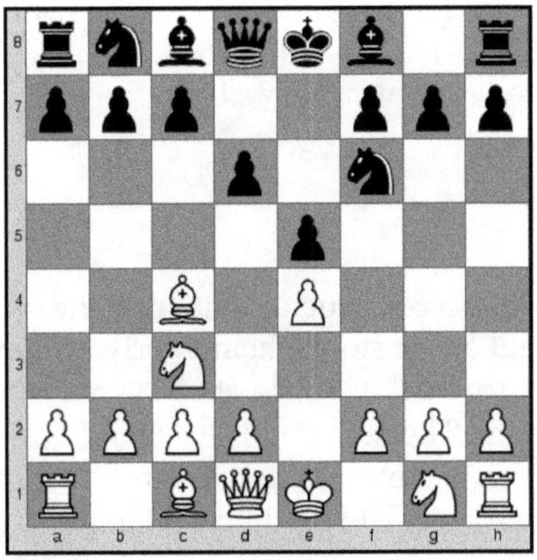

At this point, we might consider the visual part of the game as finished, but there is still one problem you might have spotted while testing our latest additions. When you click on the board, there is no visual hint that any piece was actually selected. Let's fix that now by introducing the ability to highlight any field on the board.

To do that, we will develop a generic system for different highlights. Begin by adding a `Highlight` class as an internal class to `ChessView`:

```
class ChessView : public QWidget
    // ...
public:
    class Highlight {
    public:
        Highlight() {}
        virtual ~Highlight() {}
        virtual int type() const { return 0; }
    };
    // ...
};
```

It is a minimalistic interface for highlights and only exposes a method returning the type of the highlight using a virtual method. In our exercise, we will focus on just a basic type that marks a single field with a given color. Such a situation will be represented by the `FieldHighlight` class:

```
class FieldHighlight : public Highlight {
public:
    enum { Type = 1 };
    FieldHighlight(int column, int rank, QColor color)
      : m_field(column, rank), m_color(color) {}
    inline int column() const { return m_field.x(); }
    inline int rank() const { return m_field.y(); }
    inline QColor color() const { return m_color; }
    int type() const { return Type; }
private:
    QPoint m_field;
    QColor m_color;
};
```

You can see that we provided a constructor that takes the column and rank indices and a color for the highlight and it stores them in private member variables. Also, `type()` is redefined to return `FieldHighlight::Type`, which we can use to easily identify the type of highlight. The next step is to extend `ChessView` with abilities to add and remove highlights. As the container declares a private `QList<Highlight*> m_highlights` member variable, add method declarations:

```
public:
    void addHighlight(Highlight *hl);
    void removeHighlight(Highlight *hl);
    inline Highlight *highlight(int index) const {
        return m_highlights.at(index);
    }
    inline int highlightCount() const {
        return m_highlights.size();
    }
```

Next, provide implementations for non-inline methods:

```
void ChessView::addHighlight(ChessView::Highlight *hl) {
    m_highlights.append(hl);
    update();
}

void ChessView::removeHighlight(ChessView::Highlight *hl) {
    m_highlights.removeOne(hl);
    update();
}
```

Drawing the highlights is really easy; we will use yet another virtual `draw` method. Place the following call in the `paintEvent()` implementation right before the loop that is responsible for rendering pieces:

```
drawHighlights(&painter);
```

The implementation simply iterates over all the highlights and renders those it understands:

```
void ChessView::drawHighlights(QPainter *painter)
{
    for(int idx = 0; idx < highlightCount(); ++idx) {
        Highlight *hl = highlight(idx);
        if(hl->type() == FieldHighlight::Type) {
            FieldHighlight *fhl = static_cast<FieldHighlight*>(hl);
            QRect rect = fieldRect(fhl->column(), fhl->rank());
            painter->fillRect(rect, fhl->color());
        }
    }
}
```

By checking the type of the highlight, we know which class to cast the generic pointer to. Then, we can query the object for the needed data. Finally, we use `QPainter::fillRect()` to fill the field with the given color. As `drawHighlights()` is called before the piece painting loop and after the field painting loop, the highlight will cover the background but not the piece.

That's the basic highlighting system. Let's make our `viewClicked()` slot use it:

```
void MainWindow::viewClicked(const QPoint &field)
{
    if(m_clickPoint.isNull()) {
        if(m_view->board()->data(field.x(), field.y()) != ' ') {
            m_clickPoint = field;
            m_selectedField = new ChessView::FieldHighlight(
              field.x(), field.y(), QColor(255, 0, 0, 50)
            );
            m_view->addHighlight(m_selectedField);
        }
    } else {
        if(field != m_clickPoint) {
            m_view->board()->movePiece(
                m_clickPoint.x(), m_clickPoint.y(), field.x(),
field.y()
            );
        };
        m_clickPoint = QPoint();
        m_view->removeHighlight(m_selectedField);
        delete m_selectedField;
        m_selectedField = nullptr;
    }
}
```

Note how we check that a field can only be selected if it is not empty (that is, there is an existing piece occupying that field).

You should also add a `ChessView::FieldHighlight *m_selectedField` private member variable and initialize it with a null pointer in the constructor. You can now build the game, execute it, and start moving pieces around:

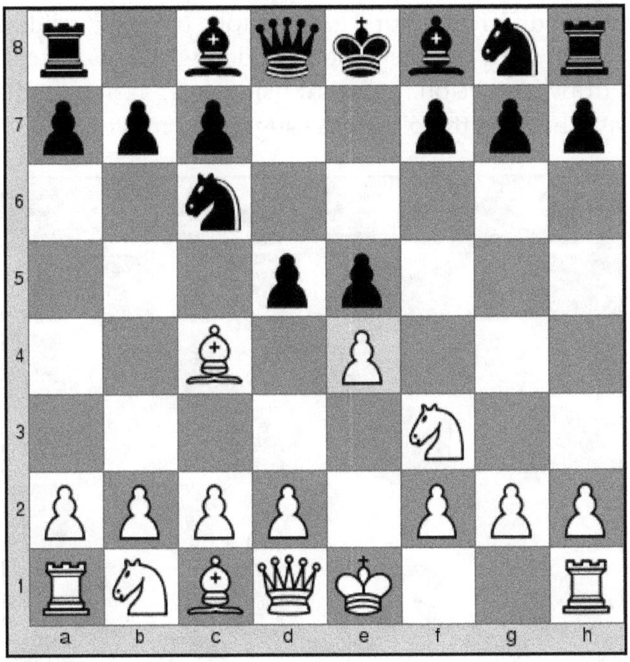

What just happened?

By adding a few lines of code, we managed to make the board clickable. We connected a custom slot that reads which field was clicked on and can highlight it with a semitransparent red color. Clicking on another field will move the highlighted piece there. The highlighting system we developed is very generic. We use it to highlight a single field with a solid color, but you can mark as many fields as you want with a number of different colors, for example, to show valid moves after selecting a piece. The system can easily be extended with new types of highlights; for example, you can draw arrows on the board using `QPainterPath` to have a complex hinting system (say, showing the player the suggested move).

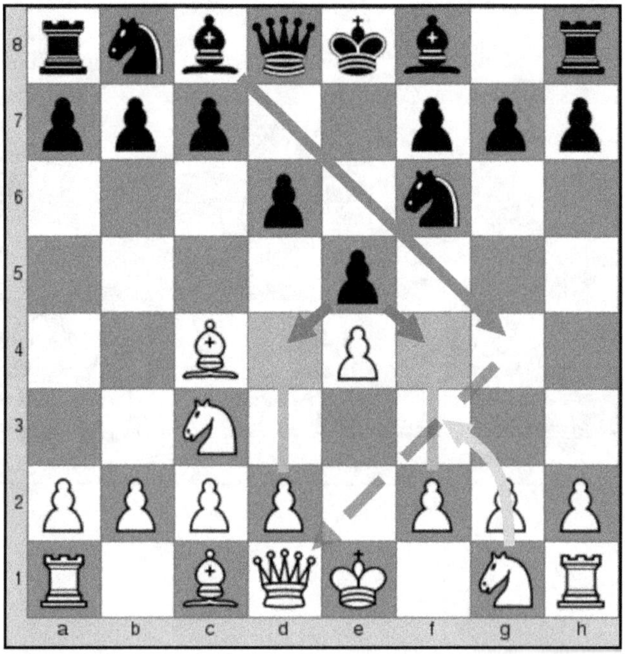

Time for action – Connecting the game algorithm

It would take us too long to implement a full chess game algorithm here, so instead, we will settle for a much simpler game called Fox and Hounds. One of the players has four pawns (hounds), which can only move over black fields and the pawn can only move in a forward fashion (toward higher ranks).

The other player has just a single pawn (fox), which starts from the opposite side of the board:

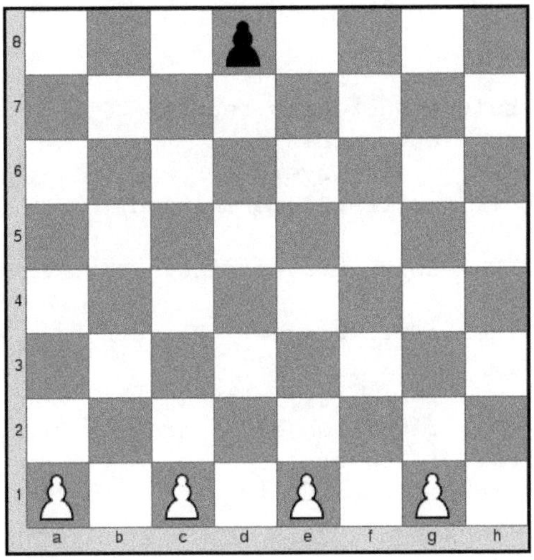

It can also move only over black fields; however it can move both forward (toward higher ranks) as well as backward (toward lower ranks). Players move their pawns in turn. The goal of the fox is to reach the opposite end of the board; the goal of the hounds is to trap the fox so that it can't make a move:

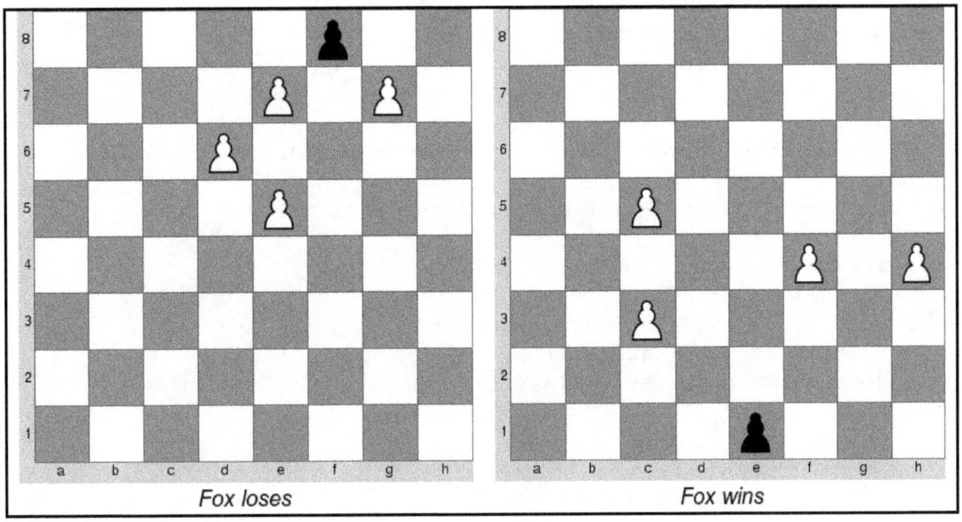

It's time to get to work! First, we will extend the `ChessAlgorithm` class with the required interface:

```
class ChessAlgorithm : public QObject
{
    Q_OBJECT
    Q_PROPERTY(Result result READ result)
    Q_PROPERTY(Player currentPlayer
               READ currentPlayer
               NOTIFY currentPlayerChanged)
public:
    enum Result { NoResult, Player1Wins, Draw, Player2Wins };
    Q_ENUM(Result)
    enum Player { NoPlayer, Player1, Player2 };
    Q_ENUM(Player)

    explicit ChessAlgorithm(QObject *parent = 0);
    ChessBoard* board() const;
    inline Result result() const {
        return m_result;
    }
    inline Player currentPlayer() const {
        return m_currentPlayer;
    }

signals:
    void boardChanged(ChessBoard*);
    void gameOver(Result);
    void currentPlayerChanged(Player);

public slots:
    virtual void newGame();
    virtual bool move(int colFrom, int rankFrom, int colTo, int
rankTo);
    bool move(const QPoint &from, const QPoint &to);

protected:
    virtual void setupBoard();
    void setBoard(ChessBoard *board);
    void setResult(Result);
    void setCurrentPlayer(Player);
private:
    ChessBoard *m_board;
    Result m_result;
    Player m_currentPlayer;
};
```

There are two sets of members here. First, we have a number of enums, variables, signals, and methods that are related to the state of the game: which player should make their move now and what is the result of the game currently. The `Q_ENUM` macro is used to register enumerations in Qt's metatype system so that they can be used as values for properties or arguments in signals. Property declarations and getters for them don't need any extra explanation. We have also declared protected methods for setting the variables from within subclasses. Here's their suggested implementation:

```
void ChessAlgorithm::setResult(Result value)
{
    if(result() == value) {
        return;
    }
    if(result() == NoResult) {
        m_result = value;
        emit gameOver(m_result);
    } else {
        m_result = value;
    }
}

void ChessAlgorithm::setCurrentPlayer(Player value)
{
    if(currentPlayer() == value) {
        return;
    }
    m_currentPlayer = value;
    emit currentPlayerChanged(m_currentPlayer);
}
```

Remember about initializing `m_currentPlayer` and `m_result` to `NoPlayer` and `NoResult` in the constructor of the `ChessAlgorithm` class.

The second group of functions is methods that modify the state of the game: the two variants of `move()`. The virtual variant is meant to be reimplemented by the real algorithm to check whether a given move is valid in the current game state and if that is the case, to perform the actual modification of the game board. In the base class, we can simply reject all possible moves:

```
bool ChessAlgorithm::move(int colFrom, int rankFrom,
   int colTo, int rankTo)
{
    Q_UNUSED(colFrom)
    Q_UNUSED(rankFrom)
    Q_UNUSED(colTo)
```

```
        Q_UNUSED(rankTo)
        return false;
    }
```

The overload is simply a convenience method that accepts two `QPoint` objects instead of four integers:

```
bool ChessAlgorithm::move(const QPoint &from, const QPoint &to)
{
    return move(from.x(), from.y(), to.x(), to.y());
}
```

The interface for the algorithm is ready now, and we can implement it for the Fox and Hounds game. Subclass `ChessAlgorithm` to create a `FoxAndHounds` class:

```
class FoxAndHounds : public ChessAlgorithm
{
public:
    FoxAndHounds(QObject *parent = 0);
    void newGame();
    bool move(int colFrom, int rankFrom, int colTo, int rankTo);
};
```

The implementation of `newGame()` is pretty simple: we set up the board, place pieces on it, and signal that it is time for the first player to make their move:

```
void FoxAndHounds::newGame()
{
    setupBoard();
    board()->setFen("3p4/8/8/8/8/8/8/P1P1P1P1 w");
     // 'w' - white to move
    m_fox = QPoint(5,8);
    setResult(NoResult);
    setCurrentPlayer(Player1);
}
```

The algorithm for the game is quite simple. Implement `move()` as follows:

```
bool FoxAndHounds::move(int colFrom, int rankFrom,
   int colTo, int rankTo)
{
    if(currentPlayer() == NoPlayer) {
        return false;
    }

    // is there a piece of the right color?
    char source = board()->data(colFrom, rankFrom);
    if(currentPlayer() == Player1 && source != 'P') return false;
```

```
    if(currentPlayer() == Player2 && source != 'p') return false;

    // both can only move one column right or left
    if(colTo != colFrom + 1 && colTo != colFrom - 1) return false;

    // do we move within the board?
    if(colTo < 1  || colTo  > board()->columns()) return false;
    if(rankTo < 1 || rankTo > board()->ranks())   return false;

    // is the destination field black?
    if((colTo + rankTo) % 2) return false;

    // is the destination field empty?
    char destination = board()->data(colTo, rankTo);
    if(destination != ' ') return false;

    // is white advancing?
    if(currentPlayer() == Player1 && rankTo <= rankFrom) return false;

    board()->movePiece(colFrom, rankFrom, colTo, rankTo);
    // make the move
    if(currentPlayer() == Player2) {
      m_fox = QPoint(colTo, rankTo); // cache fox position
    }
    // check win condition
    if(currentPlayer() == Player2 && rankTo == 1) {
        setResult(Player2Wins); // fox has escaped
    } else if(currentPlayer() == Player1 && !foxCanMove()) {
        setResult(Player1Wins); // fox can't move
    } else {
        // the other player makes the move now
        setCurrentPlayer(currentPlayer() == Player1 ? Player2 :
Player1);
    }
    return true;
}
```

Declare a protected `foxCanMove()` method and implement it using the following code:

```
bool FoxAndHounds::foxCanMove() const
{
    if(emptyByOffset(-1, -1) || emptyByOffset(-1, 1) ||
       emptyByOffset( 1, -1) || emptyByOffset( 1, 1)) {
        return true;
    }
    return false;
}
```

Then, do the same with `emptyByOffset()`:

```
bool FoxAndHounds::emptyByOffset(int x, int y) const
{
    const int destCol = m_fox.x() + x;
    const int destRank = m_fox.y() + y;
    if(destCol < 1 || destRank < 1 ||
       destCol >  board()->columns() ||
       destRank > board()->ranks()) {
        return false;
    }
    return (board()->data(destCol, destRank) == ' ');
}
```

Lastly, declare a private `QPoint m_fox` member variable.

The simplest way to test the game is to make two changes to the code. First, in the constructor of the main window class, replace `m_algorithm = new ChessAlgorithm(this)` with `m_algorithm = new FoxAndHounds(this)`. Second, modify the `viewClicked()` slot, as follows:

```
void MainWindow::viewClicked(const QPoint &field)
{
    if(m_clickPoint.isNull()) {
        // ...
    } else {
        if(field != m_clickPoint) {
            m_algorithm->move(m_clickPoint, field);
        }
        // ...
    }
}
```

You can also connect signals from the algorithm class to custom slots of the view or window to notify about the end of the game and provide a visual hint as to which player should make their move now.

What just happened?

We created a very simplistic API for implementing chess-like games by introducing the `newGame()` and `move()` virtual methods to the algorithm class. The former method simply sets up everything. The latter uses simple checks to determine whether a particular move is valid and whether the game has ended.

We use the `m_fox` member variable to track the current position of the fox to be able to quickly determine whether it has any valid moves. When the game ends, the `gameOver()` signal is emitted and the result of the game can be obtained from the algorithm. You can use the exact same framework for implementing all chess rules.

Have a go hero – Implementing the UI around the chess board

During the exercise, we focused on developing the game board view and necessary classes to make the game actually run. However, we completely neglected the regular user interface the game might possess, such as toolbars and menus. You can try designing a set of menus and toolbars for the game. Make it possible to start a new game, save a game in progress (say by implementing a FEN serializer), load a saved game (say by leveraging the existing FEN string parser), or choose different game types that will spawn different `ChessAlgorithm` subclasses. You can also provide a settings dialog for adjusting the look of the game board. If you feel like it, you can add chess clocks or implement a simple tutorial system that will guide the player through the basics of chess using text and visual hints via the highlight system we implemented.

Have a go hero – Connecting a UCI-compliant chess engine

If you really want to test your skills, you can implement a `ChessAlgorithm` subclass that will connect to a **Universal Chess Interface** (**UCI**) chess engine such as StockFish (`http://stockfishchess.org`) and provide a challenging artificial intelligence opponent for a human player. UCI is the de facto standard for communication between a chess engine and a chess frontend. Its specification is freely available, so you can study it on your own. To talk to a UCI-compliant engine, you can use `QProcess`, which will spawn the engine as an external process and attach itself to its standard input and standard output. Then, you can send commands to the engine by writing to its standard input and read messages from the engine by reading its standard output. To get you started, here's a short snippet of code that starts the engine and attaches to its communication channels:

```
class UciEngine : public QObject {
    Q_OBJECT
public:
```

```
    UciEngine(QObject *parent = 0) : QObject(parent) {
        m_uciEngine = new QProcess(this);
        m_uciEngine->setReadChannel(QProcess::StandardOutput);
        connect(m_uciEngine, SIGNAL(readyRead()),
SLOT(readFromEngine()));
    }
public slots:
    void startEngine(const QString &enginePath) {
        m_uciEngine->start(enginePath);
    }
    void sendCommand(const QString &command) {
        m_uciEngine->write(command.toLatin1());
    }
private slots:
    void readFromEngine() {
        while(m_uciEngine->canReadLine()) {
            QString line =
QString::fromLatin1(m_uciEngine->readLine());
            emit messageReceived(line);
        }
    }
signals:
    void messageReceived(QString);
private:
    QProcess *m_uciEngine;
};
```

Pop quiz

Q1. Which class should you use to load a JPEG image from a file and change a few pixels in it?

1. `QImage`
2. `QPixmap`
3. `QIcon`

Q2. Which function can be used to schedule a repaint of the widget?

1. `paintEvent()`
2. `update()`
3. `show()`

Q3. Which function can be used to change the color of the outline drawn by `QPainter`?

1. `setColor()`
2. `setBrush()`
3. `setPen()`

Summary

In this chapter, we learned about using raster graphics with Qt Widgets. What was presented in this chapter will let you implement custom widgets with painting and event handling. We also described how to handle image files and do some basic painting on images. This chapter concludes our overview of CPU rendering in Qt.

In the next chapter, we will switch from raster painting to accelerated vector graphics and explore Qt capabilities related to OpenGL and Vulkan.

9
OpenGL and Vulkan in Qt applications

Hardware acceleration is crucial for implementing modern games with advanced graphics effects. Qt Widgets module uses traditional approach optimized for CPU-based rendering. Even though you can make any widget use OpenGL, the performance will usually not be maximized. However, Qt allows you to use OpenGL or Vulkan directly to create high-performance graphics limited only by the graphics card's processing power. In this chapter, you will learn about employing your OpenGL and Vulkan skills to display fast 3D graphics. If you are not familiar with these technologies, this chapter should give you a kickstart for further research in this topic. We will also describe multiple Qt helper classes that simplify usage of OpenGL textures, shaders, and buffers. By the end of the chapter, you will be able to create 2D and 3D graphics for your games using OpenGL and Vulkan classes offered by Qt and integrate them with the rest of the user interface.

The main topics covered in this chapter are as listed:

- OpenGL in Qt applications
- Immediate mode
- Textures
- Shaders
- OpenGL buffers
- Vulkan in Qt applications

Introduction to OpenGL with Qt

We are not experts on OpenGL, so in this part of the chapter, we will not teach you to do any fancy stuff with OpenGL and Qt but will show you how to enable the use of your OpenGL skills in Qt applications. There are a lot of tutorials and courses on OpenGL out there, so if you're not that skilled with OpenGL, you can still benefit from what is described here by employing the knowledge gained here to more easily learn fancy stuff. You can use external materials and a high-level API offered by Qt, which will speed up many of the tasks described in the tutorials.

OpenGL windows and contexts

There are many ways you can perform OpenGL rendering in Qt. The most straightforward way that we will mainly use is to subclass `QOpenGLWindow`. It allows OpenGL to render your content directly to a whole window and is suitable if you draw everything in your application with OpenGL. You can make it a fullscreen window if you want. However, later we will also discuss other approaches that will allow you to integrate OpenGL content into a widget-based application.

The OpenGL context represents the overall state of the OpenGL pipeline, which guides the process of data processing and rendering to a particular device. In Qt, it is represented by the `QOpenGLContext` class. A related concept that needs explanation is the idea of an OpenGL context being "current" in a thread. The way OpenGL calls work is that they do not use any handle to any object containing information on where and how to execute the series of low-level OpenGL calls. Instead, it is assumed that they are executed in the context of the current machine state. The state may dictate whether to render a scene to a screen or to a frame buffer object, which mechanisms are enabled, or the properties of the surface OpenGL is rendering on. Making a context "current" means that all further OpenGL operations issued by a particular thread will be applied to this context. To add to that, a context can be "current" only in one thread at the same time; therefore, it is important to make the context current before making any OpenGL calls and then marking it as available after you are done accessing OpenGL resources.

`QOpenGLWindow` has a very simple API that hides most of the unnecessary details from the developer. Apart from constructors and a destructor, it provides a small number of very useful methods. First, there are auxiliary methods for managing the OpenGL context: `context()`, which returns the context, and `makeCurrent()` as well as `doneCurrent()` for acquiring and releasing the context. The class also provides a number of virtual methods we can re-implement to display OpenGL graphics.

We will be using the following three virtual methods:

- `initializeGL()` is invoked by the framework once, before any painting is actually done so that you can prepare any resources or initialize the context in any way you require.
- `paintGL()` is the equivalent of `paintEvent()` for the widget classes. It gets executed whenever the window needs to be repainted. This is the function where you should put your OpenGL rendering code.
- `resizeGL()` is invoked every time the window is resized. It accepts the width and height of the window as parameters. You can make use of that method by re-implementing it so that you can prepare yourself for the fact that the next call to `paintGL()` renders to a viewport of a different size.

Before calling any of these virtual functions, `QOpenGLWindow` ensures that the OpenGL context is current, so there is no need to manually call `makeCurrent()` in them.

Accessing OpenGL functions

Interaction with OpenGL is usually done through calling functions provided by the OpenGL library. For example, in a regular C++ OpenGL application, you can see calls to OpenGL functions such as `glClearColor()`. These functions are resolved when your binary is linked against the OpenGL library. However, when you write a cross-platform application, resolving all the required OpenGL functions is not trivial. Luckily, Qt provides a way to call OpenGL functions without having to worry about the platform-specific details.

In a Qt application, you should access OpenGL functions through a family of `QOpenGLFunctions` classes. The `QOpenGLFunctions` class itself only provides access to functions that are part of OpenGL ES 2.0 API. This subset is expected to work at most desktop and embedded platforms supported by Qt (where OpenGL is available at all). However, this is a really limited set of functions, and sometimes you may want to use a more recent OpenGL version at the cost of supporting less platforms. For each known OpenGL version and profile, Qt provides a separate class that contains the set of available functions. For example, the `QOpenGLFunctions_3_3_Core` class will contain all functions provided by the OpenGL 3.3 core profile.

The approach recommended by Qt is to select the OpenGL functions class corresponding to the version you want to use and add this class an the second base class of your window or widget. This will make all OpenGL functions from that version available within your class. This approach allows you to use code that was using the OpenGL library directly without changing it. When you put such code in your class, the compiler will, for example, use the `QOpenGLFunctions::glClearColor()` function instead of the global `glClearColor()` function provided by the OpenGL library.

However, when using this approach, you must be careful to only use functions provided by your base class. You can accidentally use a global function instead of a function provided by Qt classes if the Qt class you choose does not contain it. For example, if you use `QOpenGLFunctions` as the base class, you can't use the `glBegin()` function, as it is not provided by this Qt class. Such erroneous code may work on one operating system and then suddenly not compile on another because you don't link against the OpenGL library. As long as you only use OpenGL functions provided by Qt classes, you don't have to think about linking with the OpenGL library or resolving functions in a cross-platform way.

If you want to ensure that you only use Qt OpenGL function wrappers, you can use the Qt class as a private field instead of a base class. In that case, you have to access every OpenGL function through the private field, for example, `m_openGLFunctions->glClearColor()`. This will make your code more verbose, but at least you will be sure that you don't accidentally use a global function.

Before using Qt OpenGL functions, you have to call the `initializeOpenGLFunctions()` method of the functions class in the current OpenGL context. This is usually done in the `initializeGL()` function of the window. The `QOpenGLFunctions` class is expected to always initialize successfully, so its `initializeOpenGLFunctions()` method doesn't return anything. In all the other functions' classes, this function returns `bool`. If it returns `false`, it means that Qt was not able to resolve all the required functions successfully, and your application should exit with an error message.

In our examples, we will use the `QOpenGLFunctions_1_1` class that contains all OpenGL functions we'll use. When you're creating your own project, think about the OpenGL profile you want to target and select the appropriate functions class.

Using OpenGL in immediate mode

We will start with the most basic approach that's called **immediate mode**. In this mode, no additional setup of OpenGL buffers or shaders is required. You can just supply a bunch of geometric primitives and get the result right away. Immediate mode is now deprecated because it works much slower and is less flexible than more advanced techniques. However, it's so much easier than them that basically every OpenGL tutorial starts with describing the immediate mode calls. In this section, we'll show how to perform some simple OpenGL drawing with very little code. A more modern approach will be covered in the next section of this chapter.

Time for action – Drawing a triangle using Qt and OpenGL

For the first exercise, we will create a subclass of `QOpenGLWindow` that renders a triangle using simple OpenGL calls. Create a new project, starting with **Empty qmake Project** from the **Other Project** group as the template. In the project file, put the following content:

```
QT = core gui
TARGET = triangle
TEMPLATE = app
```

> Note that our project does not include Qt Widgets module. Using the `QOpenGLWindow` approach allows us to remove this unnecessary dependency and make our application more lightweight.

Note that Qt Core and Qt GUI modules are enabled by default, so you don't have to add them to the `QT` variable, but we prefer to explicitly show that we are using them in our project.

Having the basic project setup ready, let's define a `SimpleGLWindow` class as a subclass of `QOpenGLWindow` and `QOpenGLFunctions_1_1`. Since we don't want to allow external access to OpenGL functions, we use protected inheritance for the second base. Next, we override the
virtual `initializeGL()` method of `QOpenGLWindow`. In this method, we initialize our `QOpenGLFunctions_1_1` base class and use the `glClearColor()` function that it provides:

```
class SimpleGLWindow : public QOpenGLWindow,
```

```
                            protected QOpenGLFunctions_1_1
{
public:
    SimpleGLWindow(QWindow *parent = 0) :
        QOpenGLWindow(NoPartialUpdate, parent) {
    }
protected:
    void initializeGL() {
        if (!initializeOpenGLFunctions()) {
            qFatal("initializeOpenGLFunctions failed");
        }
        glClearColor(1, 1, 1, 0);
    }
};
```

In `initializeGL()`, we first call `initializeOpenGLFunctions()`, which is a method of the `QOpenGLFunctions_1_1` class, one of the base classes of our window class. The method takes care of setting up all the functions according to the parameters of the current OpenGL context (thus, it is important to first make the context current, which luckily is done for us behind the scenes before `initializeGL()` is invoked). If this function fails, we use the `qFatal()` macro to print an error message to `stderr` and abort the application. Then, we use the `QOpenGLFunctions_1_1::glClearColor()` function to set the clear color of the scene to white.

The next step is to re-implement `paintGL()` and put the actual drawing code there:

```
void SimpleGLWindow::paintGL() {
    glClear(GL_COLOR_BUFFER_BIT);
    glViewport(0, 0, width(), height());
    glBegin(GL_TRIANGLES);
    {
        glColor3f(1, 0, 0);
        glVertex3f( 0.0f, 1.0f, 0.0f);
        glColor3f(0, 1, 0);
        glVertex3f( 1.0f, -1.0f, 0.0f);
        glColor3f(0, 0, 1);
        glVertex3f(-1.0f, -1.0f, 0.0f);
    }
    glEnd();
}
```

This function first clears the color buffer and sets the OpenGL viewport of the context to be the size of the window. Then, we tell OpenGL to start drawing using triangles with the `glBegin()` call and passing `GL_TRIANGLES` as the drawing mode. Then, we pass three vertices along with their colors to form a triangle. Finally, we inform the pipeline, by invoking `glEnd()`, that we are done drawing using the current mode.

What is left is a trivial `main()` function that sets up the window and starts the event loop. Add a new **C++ Source File**, call it `main.cpp`, and implement `main()`, as follows:

```
int main(int argc, char **argv) {
    QGuiApplication app(argc, argv);
    SimpleGLWindow window;
    window.resize(600, 400);
    window.show();
    return app.exec();
}
```

This function is very similar to what we usually have in the `main()` function, but we use `QGuiApplication` instead of `QApplication`, because we only use the Qt GUI module. After running the project, you should see the following:

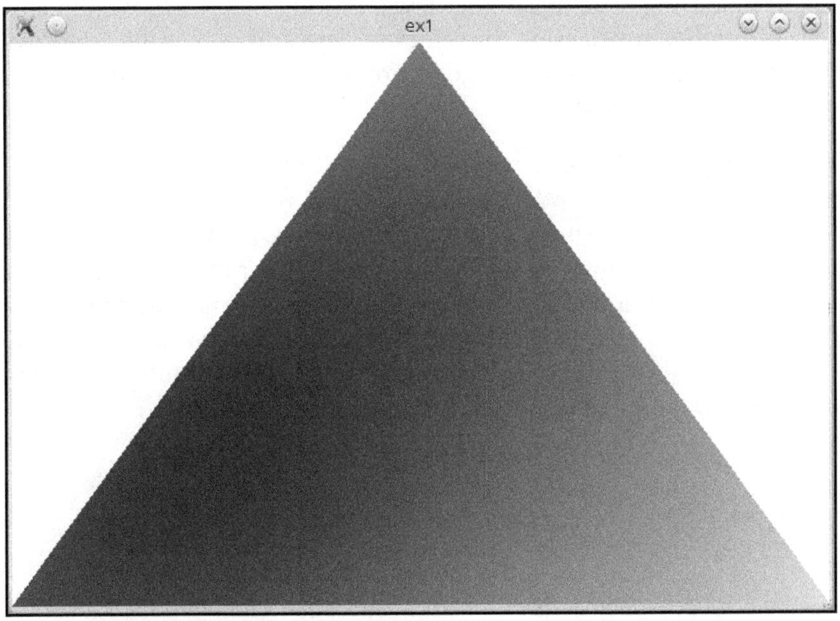

Multisampling

You can see that the triangle has jagged edges. That's because of the aliasing effect. You can counter it by enabling multisampling for the window, which will make OpenGL render the contents as if the screen had higher resolution and then average the result, which acts as anti-aliasing. To do that, add the following code to the constructor of the window:

```
QSurfaceFormat fmt = format();
fmt.setSamples(16); // multisampling set to 16
setFormat(fmt);
```

Note that multisampling is resource-demanding, so setting a high number of samples may cause your application to fail if your hardware or driver can't handle it. If the application doesn't work after enabling multisampling, try to lower the number of samples or just disable it.

Time for action – Scene-based rendering

Let's take our rendering code to a higher level. Putting OpenGL code directly into the window class requires subclassing the window class and makes the window class more and more complex. Let's follow good programming practice and separate rendering code from window code.

Create a new class and call it `AbstractGLScene`. It will be the base class for definitions of OpenGL scenes. We also derive the class (with protected scope) from `QOpenGLFunctions_1_1` to make accessing different OpenGL functions easier. Make the scene class accept a pointer to `QOpenGLWindow`, either in the constructor or through a dedicated setter method. Ensure that the pointer is stored in the class for easier access, as we will rely on that pointer for accessing physical properties of the window. Add methods for querying the window's OpenGL context. You should end up with code similar to the following:

```
class AbstractGLScene : protected QOpenGLFunctions_1_1 {
public:
    AbstractGLScene(QOpenGLWindow *window = nullptr) {
        m_window = window;
    }
    QOpenGLWindow* window() const { return m_window; }
    QOpenGLContext* context() {
       return m_window ? m_window->context() : nullptr;
    }
```

```
    const QOpenGLContext* context() const {
        return m_window ? m_window->context() : nullptr;
    }
private:
    QOpenGLWindow *m_window = nullptr;
};
```

Now the essential part begins. Add two pure virtual methods called `paint()` and `initialize()`. Also, remember to add a virtual destructor.

> **TIP:** Instead of making `initialize()` a pure virtual function, you can implement its body in such a way that it will call `initializeOpenGLFunctions()` to fulfill the requirements of the `QOpenGFunctions` class. Then, subclasses of `AbstractGLScene` can ensure that the functions are initialized properly by calling the base class implementation of `initialize()`.

Next, create a subclass of `QOpenGLWindow` and call it `SceneGLWindow`. Add an `AbstractGLScene *m_scene` private field and implement a getter and a setter for it. Create a constructor using the following code:

```
SceneGLWindow::SceneGLWindow(QWindow *parent) :
    QOpenGLWindow(NoPartialUpdate, parent)
{
}
```

This constructor forwards the parent argument to the base constructor and assigns `NoPartialUpdate` as the window's `UpdateBehavior`. This option means that the window will be fully painted on each `paintGL()` call and thus no framebuffer is needed. This is the default value of the first argument, but since we provide the second argument, we are obligated to provide the first argument explicitly.

Then, re-implement the `initializeGL()` and `paintGL()` methods and make them call appropriate equivalents in the scene:

```
void SceneGLWindow::initializeGL() {
    if(m_scene) {
        m_scene->initialize();
    }
}
void SceneGLWindow::paintGL() {
```

```
        if(m_scene) {
            m_scene->paint();
        }
    }
```

Finally, instantiate `SceneGLWindow` in the `main()` function.

What just happened?

We have just set up a class chain that separates the window code from the actual OpenGL scene. The window forwards all calls related to scene contents to the scene object so that when the window is requested to repaint itself, it delegates the task to the scene object. Note that prior to doing that, the window will make the OpenGL context current; therefore, all OpenGL calls that the scene makes will be related to that context. You can store the code created in this exercise for later reuse in further exercises and your own projects.

Time for action – Drawing a textured cube

Create a new class named `CubeGLScene` and derive it from `AbstractGLScene`. Implement the constructor to forward its argument to the base class constructor. Add a method to store a `QImage` object in the scene that will contain texture data for the cube. Add a `QOpenGLTexture` pointer member as well, which will contain the texture, initialize it to `nullptr` in the constructor, and delete it in the destructor. Let's call the `m_textureImage` image object and the `m_texture` texture. Now add a protected `initializeTexture()` method and fill it with the following code:

```
void CubeGLScene::initializeTexture() {
    m_texture = new QOpenGLTexture(m_textureImage.mirrored());
m_texture->setMinificationFilter(QOpenGLTexture::LinearMipMapLinear);
    m_texture->setMagnificationFilter(QOpenGLTexture::Linear);
}
```

The function first mirrors the image vertically. This is because the *y* axis in OpenGL points up by default, so a texture would be displayed "upside down". Then, we create a `QOpenGLTexture` object, passing it our image. After that, we set minification and magnification filters so that the texture looks better when it is scaled.

We are now ready to implement the `initialize()` method that will take care of setting up the texture and the scene itself:

```
void CubeGLScene::initialize() {
    AbstractGLScene::initialize();
    m_initialized = true;
    if(!m_textureImage.isNull()) {
        initializeTexture();
    }
    glClearColor(1, 1, 1, 0);
    glShadeModel(GL_SMOOTH);
}
```

We make use of a flag called `m_initialized`. This flag is needed to prevent the texture from being set up too early (when no OpenGL context is available yet). Then, we check whether the texture image is set (using the `QImage::isNull()` method); if so, we initialize the texture. Then, we set some additional properties of the OpenGL context.

> TIP
>
> In the setter for `m_textureImage`, add code that checks whether `m_initialized` is set to `true` and, if so, calls `initializeTexture()`. This is to make certain that the texture is properly set regardless of the order in which the setter and `initialize()` are called. Also remember to set `m_initialized` to `false` in the constructor.

The next step is to prepare the cube data. We will define a special data structure for the cube that groups vertex coordinates and texture data in a single object. To store coordinates, we will use classes tailored to that purpose—`QVector3D` and `QVector2D`:

```
struct TexturedPoint {
    QVector3D coord;
    QVector2D uv;
    TexturedPoint(const QVector3D& pcoord = QVector3D(),
                  const QVector2D& puv = QVector2D()) :
        coord(pcoord), uv(puv) {
    }
};
```

> `QVector2D`, `QVector3D`, and `QVector4D` are helper classes that represent a single point in space and provide some convenient methods. For instance, `QVector2D` stores two `float` variables (`x` and `y`), much like the `QPointF` class does. These classes are not to be confused with `QVector<T>`, a container template class that stores a collection of elements.

`QVector<TexturedPoint>` will hold information for the whole cube. The vector is initialized with data using the following code:

```
void CubeGLScene::initializeCubeData() {
    m_data = {
        // FRONT FACE
        {{-0.5, -0.5,  0.5}, {0, 0}}, {{ 0.5, -0.5,  0.5}, {1, 0}},
        {{ 0.5,  0.5,  0.5}, {1, 1}}, {{-0.5,  0.5,  0.5}, {0, 1}},

        // TOP FACE
        {{-0.5,  0.5,  0.5}, {0, 0}}, {{ 0.5,  0.5,  0.5}, {1, 0}},
        {{ 0.5,  0.5, -0.5}, {1, 1}}, {{-0.5,  0.5, -0.5}, {0, 1}},
        //...
    };
}
```

The code uses C++11 initializer list syntax to set the vector's data. The cube consists of six faces and is centered on the origin of the coordinate system. The following diagram presents the same data in graphical form:

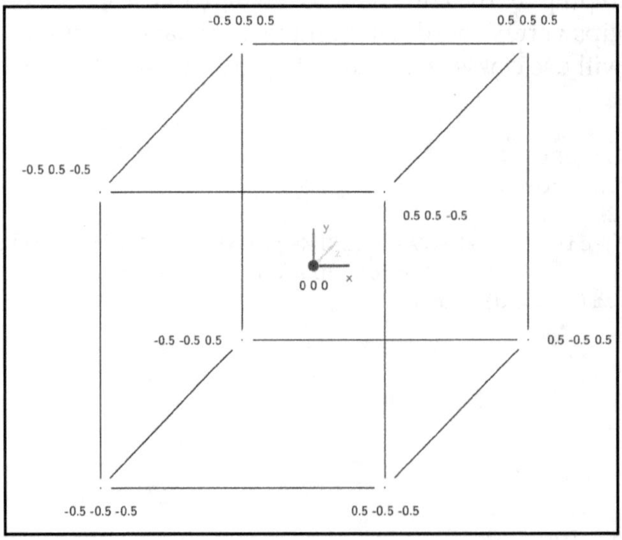

`initializeCubeData()` should be called from the scene constructor or from the `initialize()` method. What remains is the painting code:

```
  void CubeGLScene::paint() {
    glClear(GL_COLOR_BUFFER_BIT | GL_DEPTH_BUFFER_BIT);
    glViewport(0, 0, window()->width(), window()->height());
    glLoadIdentity();

    glRotatef(45, 1.0, 0.0, 0.0);
    glRotatef(45, 0.0, 1.0, 0.0);

    glEnable(GL_DEPTH_TEST);
    glEnable(GL_CULL_FACE);
    glCullFace(GL_BACK);
    paintCube();
}
```

First, we set up the viewport and then we rotate the view. Before calling `paintCube()`, which will render the cube itself, we enable depth testing and face culling so that only visible faces are drawn. The `paintCube()` routine looks as follows:

```
void CubeGLScene::paintCube() {
    if(m_texture) {
        m_texture->bind();
    }
    glEnable(GL_TEXTURE_2D);
    glBegin(GL_QUADS);
    for(const TexturedPoint &point: m_data) {
        glTexCoord2d(point.uv.x(), point.uv.y());
        glVertex3f(point.coord.x(), point.coord.y(), point.coord.z());
    }
    glEnd();
    glDisable(GL_TEXTURE_2D);
}
```

First, the texture is bound and texturing is enabled. Then, we enter the quad drawing mode and stream in data from our data structure. Finally, we disable texturing again.

For completeness, here's a `main()` function that executes the scene:

```
int main(int argc, char **argv) {
    QGuiApplication app(argc, argv);
    SceneGLWindow window;
    QSurfaceFormat fmt;
    fmt.setSamples(16);
    window.setFormat(fmt);
```

```
    CubeGLScene scene(&window);
    window.setScene(&scene);
    scene.setTexture(QImage(":/texture.jpg"));
    window.resize(600, 600);
    window.show();
    return app.exec();
}
```

Note the use of `QSurfaceFormat` to enable multisample antialiasing for the scene. We have also put the texture image into a resource file to avoid problems with the relative path to the file.

Have a go hero – Animating a cube

Try modifying the code to make the cube animated. To do that, have the scene inherit `QObject`, add an angle property of the `float` type to it (remember about the `Q_OBJECT` macro). Then, modify one of the `glRotatef()` lines to use the angle value instead of a constant value. Put the following code in `main()`, right before calling `app.exec()`:

```
QPropertyAnimation animation(&scene, "angle");
animation.setStartValue(0);
animation.setEndValue(359);
animation.setDuration(5000);
animation.setLoopCount(-1);
animation.start();
```

Remember to put a call to `window()->update()` in the setter for the angle property so that the scene is redrawn.

Modern OpenGL with Qt

The OpenGL code shown in the previous section uses a very old technique of streaming vertices one by one into a fixed OpenGL pipeline. Nowadays, modern hardware is much more feature-rich and not only does it allow faster processing of vertex data but also offers the ability to adjust different processing stages, with the use of reprogrammable units called **shaders**. In this section, we will take a look at what Qt has to offer in the domain of a "modern" approach to using OpenGL.

Shaders

Qt can make use of shaders through a set of classes based around `QOpenGLShaderProgram`. This class allows compiling, linking, and executing of shader programs written in GLSL. You can check whether your OpenGL implementation supports shaders by inspecting the result of a static `QOpenGLShaderProgram::hasOpenGLShaderPrograms()` call that accepts a pointer to an OpenGL context. All modern hardware and all decent graphics drivers should have some support for shaders.

Qt supports all kinds of shaders, with the most common being vertex and fragment shaders. These are both part of the classic OpenGL pipeline. You can see an illustration of the pipeline in the following diagram:

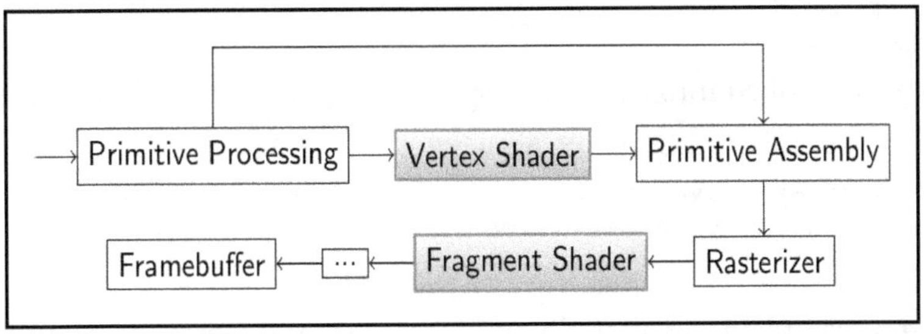

A single shader is represented by an instance of the `QOpenGLShader` class. You need to specify the type of the shader in the constructor of this class. Then, you can compile the shader's source code by calling `QOpenGLShader::compileSourceCode()`, which has a number of overloads for handling different input formats, or `QOpenGLShader::compileSourceFile()`. The `QOpenGLShader` object stores the ID of the compiled shader for future use.

When you have a set of shaders defined, you can assemble a complete program using `QOpenGLShaderProgram::addShader()`. After all shaders are added, you can `link()` the program and `bind()` it to the current OpenGL context. The program class has a number of methods for setting values of different input parameters—uniforms and attributes both in singular and array versions. Qt provides mappings between its own types (such as `QSize` or `QColor`) to GLSL counterparts (for example, `vec2` and `vec4`) to make the programmer's life even easier.

A typical code flow for using shaders for rendering is as follows (first a vertex shader is created and compiled):

```
QOpenGLShader vertexShader(QOpenGLShader::Vertex);
vertexShader.compileSourceCode(
    "uniform vec4 color;\n"
    "uniform highp mat4 matrix;\n"
    "void main(void) { gl_Position = gl_Vertex * matrix; }"
);
```

The process is repeated for a fragment shader:

```
QOpenGLShader fragmentShader(QOpenGLShader::Fragment);
fragmentShader.compileSourceCode(
    "uniform vec4 color;\n"
    "void main(void) { gl_FragColor = color; }"
);
```

Then, shaders are linked into a single program in a given OpenGL context:

```
QOpenGLShaderProgram program(context);
program.addShader(&vertexShader);
program.addShader(&fragmentShader);
program.link();
```

When shaders are linked together, OpenGL searches for common variables (such as uniforms or buffers) in them and maps them together. This allows you, for example, to pass a value from the vertex shader to the fragment shader. Behind the scenes, the `link()` function uses the `glLinkProgram()` OpenGL call.

Whenever the program is used, it should be bound to the current OpenGL context and filled with the required data:

```
program.bind();
QMatrix4x4 matrix = /* ... */;
QColor color = Qt::red;
program.setUniformValue("matrix", matrix);
program.setUniformValue("color", color);
```

After that, calls activating the render pipeline will use the bound program:

```
glBegin(GL_TRIANGLE_STRIP);
//...
glEnd();
```

Time for action – Shaded objects

Let's convert our last program so that it uses shaders. To make the cube better, we will implement a smooth lighting model using the Phong algorithm. At the same time, we will learn to use some helper classes that Qt offers for use with OpenGL.

The basic goals for this miniproject are as follows:

- Use vertex and fragment shaders for rendering a complex object
- Handle model, view, and projection matrices
- Use attribute arrays for faster drawing

Start by creating a new subclass of `AbstractGLScene`. Let's give it the following interface:

```
class ShaderGLScene : public QObject, public AbstractGLScene {
    Q_OBJECT
public:
    ShaderGLScene(SceneGLWindow *window);
    void initialize();
    void paint();
protected:
    void initializeObjectData();
private:
    struct ScenePoint {
        QVector3D coords;
        QVector3D normal;
        ScenePoint(const QVector3D &c = QVector3D(),
                   const QVector3D &n = QVector3D()) :
            coords(c), normal(n)
        {
        }
    };
    QOpenGLShaderProgram m_shader;
    QMatrix4x4 m_modelMatrix;
    QMatrix4x4 m_viewMatrix;
    QMatrix4x4 m_projectionMatrix;
    QVector<ScenePoint> m_data;
};
```

We're not using textures in this project, so `TexturedPoint` was simplified to `ScenePoint` with UV texture coordinates removed. Update the `main()` function to use the `ShaderGLScene` class.

We can start implementing the interface with the `initializeObjectData()` function that will be called in the constructor. This function must fill the `m_data` member with information about vertices and their normals. The implementation will depend on the source of your data.

TIP

In the sample code that comes with this book, you can find code that loads data from a file in the PLY format generated with the Blender 3D program. To export a model from Blender, ensure that it consists of just triangles (for that, select the model, go into the **Edit** mode by pressing *Tab*, open the **Faces** menu with *Ctrl* + *F*, and choose **Triangulate Faces**). Then, click on **File** and **Export**; choose **Stanford (.ply)**. You will end up with a text file containing vertex and normal data as well as face definitions for the vertices. We add the PLY file to the project's resources so that it is always available to our program. Then, we use the `PlyReader` C++ class that implements the parsing.

You can always reuse the cube object from the previous project. Just be aware that its normals are not calculated properly for smooth shading; thus, you will have to correct them.

Before we can set up the shader program, we have to be aware of what the actual shaders look like. Shader code will be loaded from external files, so the first step is to add a new file to the project. In Creator, right-click on the project in the project tree and choose **Add New...**; from the left pane, choose **GLSL**, and from the list of available templates, choose **Vertex Shader (Desktop OpenGL)**. Call the new file `phong.vert` and input the following code:

```
uniform highp mat4 modelViewMatrix;
uniform highp mat3 normalMatrix;
uniform highp mat4 projectionMatrix;
uniform highp mat4 mvpMatrix;

attribute highp vec4 Vertex;
attribute mediump vec3 Normal;

varying mediump vec3 N;
varying highp vec3 v;

void main(void) {
    N = normalize(normalMatrix * Normal);
    v = vec3(modelViewMatrix * Vertex);
    gl_Position = mvpMatrix * Vertex;
}
```

The code is very simple. We declare four matrices representing different stages of coordinate mapping for the scene. We also define two input attributes—`Vertex` and `Normal`—which contain the vertex data. The shader will output two pieces of data—a normalized vertex normal and a transformed vertex coordinate as seen by the camera. Of course, apart from that, we set `gl_Position` to be the final vertex coordinate. In each case, we want to be compliant with the OpenGL/ES specification, so we prefix each variable declaration with a precision specifier.

Next, add another file, call it `phong.frag`, and make it a fragment shader (Desktop OpenGL). The content of the file is a typical ambient, diffuse, and specular calculation:

```
struct Material {
    lowp vec3 ka;
    lowp vec3 kd;
    lowp vec3 ks;
    lowp float shininess;
};

struct Light {
    lowp vec4 position;
    lowp vec3 intensity;
};

uniform Material mat;

uniform Light light;

varying mediump vec3 N;
varying highp vec3 v;

void main(void) {
    vec3 n = normalize(N);
    vec3 L = normalize(light.position.xyz - v);
    vec3 E = normalize(-v);
    vec3 R = normalize(reflect(-L, n));

    float LdotN = dot(L, n);
    float diffuse = max(LdotN, 0.0);
    vec3 spec = vec3(0, 0, 0);

    if(LdotN > 0.0) {
        float RdotE = max(dot(R, E), 0.0);
        spec = light.intensity * pow(RdotE, mat.shininess);
    }
```

```
    vec3 color = light.intensity * (mat.ka + mat.kd * diffuse + mat.ks
* spec);
    gl_FragColor = vec4(color, 1.0);
}
```

Apart from using the two varying variables to obtain the interpolated normal (`N`) and fragment (`v`) position, the shader declares two structures for keeping light and material information. Without going into the details of how the shader itself works, it calculates three components—ambient light, diffused light, and specular reflection—adds them together, and sets that as the fragment color. Since all the per vertex input data is interpolated for each fragment, the final color is calculated individually for each pixel.

Once we know what the shaders expect, we can set up the shader program object. Let's go through the `initialize()` method. First, we call the base class implementation and set the background color of the scene to black, as shown in the following code:

```
void initialize() {
    AbstractGLScene::initialize();
    glClearColor(0, 0, 0, 0);
    //...
}
```

Add both shader files to the project's resources. Then, use the following code to read shaders from these files and link the shader program:

```
m_shader.addShaderFromSourceFile(QOpenGLShader::Vertex,
":/phong.vert");
m_shader.addShaderFromSourceFile(QOpenGLShader::Fragment,
":/phong.frag");
m_shader.link();
```

The `link()` function returns a Boolean value, but, we skip the error check here for simplicity. The next step is to prepare all the input data for the shader, as shown:

```
m_shader.bind();
m_shader.setAttributeArray("Vertex", GL_FLOAT,
                           &m_data[0].coords, 3, sizeof(ScenePoint));
m_shader.enableAttributeArray("Vertex");

m_shader.setAttributeArray("Normal", GL_FLOAT,
                           &m_data[0].normal, 3, sizeof(ScenePoint));
m_shader.enableAttributeArray("Normal");

m_shader.setUniformValue("mat.ka", QVector3D(0.1, 0, 0.0));
```

```
m_shader.setUniformValue("mat.kd", QVector3D(0.7, 0.0, 0.0));
m_shader.setUniformValue("mat.ks", QVector3D(1.0, 1.0, 1.0));
m_shader.setUniformValue("mat.shininess", 128.0f);

m_shader.setUniformValue("light.position", QVector3D(2, 1, 1));
m_shader.setUniformValue("light.intensity", QVector3D(1, 1, 1));
```

First, the shader program is bound to the current context so that we can operate on it. Then, we enable the setup of two attribute arrays—one for vertex coordinates and the other for their normals. In our program, the data is stored in a `QVector<ScenePoint>`, where each `ScenePoint` has `coords` and normal `fields`, so there are no separate C++ arrays for coordinates and normals. Fortunately, OpenGL is smart enough to use our memory layout as is. We just need to map our vector to two attribute arrays.

We inform the program that an attribute called `Vertex` is an array. Each item of that array consists of three values of the `GL_FLOAT` type. The first array item is located at `&m_data[0].coords`, and data for the next vertex is located at `sizeof(ScenePoint)` bytes later than the data for the current point. Then we have a similar declaration for the `Normal` attribute, with the only exception that the first piece of data is stored at `&m_data[0].normal`. By informing the program about layout of the data, we allow it to quickly read all the vertex information when needed.

After attribute arrays are set, we pass values for uniform variables to the shader program, which concludes the shader program setup. You will note that we didn't set values for uniforms representing the various matrices; we will do that separately for each repaint. The `paint()` method takes care of that:

```
void ShaderGLScene::paint() {
    m_projectionMatrix.setToIdentity();
    float aspectRatio = qreal(window()->width()) / window()->height();
    m_projectionMatrix.perspective(90, aspectRatio, 0.5, 40);

    m_viewMatrix.setToIdentity();
    QVector3D eye(0, 0, 2);
    QVector3D center(0, 0, 0);
    QVector3D up(0, 1, 0);
    m_viewMatrix.lookAt(eye, center, up);
    //...
}
```

In this method, we make heavy use of the `QMatrix4x4` class that represents a 4 × 4 matrix in a so-called row-major order, which is suited to use with OpenGL. At the beginning, we reset the projection matrix and use the `perspective()` method to give it a perspective transformation based on the current window size. Afterward, the view matrix is also reset and the `lookAt()` method is used to prepare the transformation for the camera; center value indicates the center of the view that the eye is looking at. The `up` vector dictates the vertical orientation of the camera (with respect to the eye position).

The next couple of lines are similar to what we had in the previous project:

```
glClear(GL_COLOR_BUFFER_BIT | GL_DEPTH_BUFFER_BIT);
glViewport(0, 0, window()->width(), window()->height());
glEnable(GL_DEPTH_TEST);
glEnable(GL_CULL_FACE);
glCullFace(GL_BACK);
```

After that, we do the actual painting of the object:

```
m_modelMatrix.setToIdentity();
m_modelMatrix.rotate(45, 0, 1, 0);
QMatrix4x4 modelViewMatrix = m_viewMatrix * m_modelMatrix;
paintObject(modelViewMatrix);
```

We start by setting the model matrix, which dictates where the rendered object is positioned relative to the center of the world (in this case, we say that it is rotated 45 degrees around the *y* axis). Then we assemble the model-view matrix (denoting the position of the object relative to the camera) and pass it to the `paintObject()` method:

```
void ShaderGLScene::paintObject(const QMatrix4x4& mvMatrix) {
    m_shader.bind();
    m_shader.setUniformValue("projectionMatrix", m_projectionMatrix);
    m_shader.setUniformValue("modelViewMatrix", mvMatrix);
    m_shader.setUniformValue("mvpMatrix",
m_projectionMatrix*mvMatrix);
    m_shader.setUniformValue("normalMatrix", mvMatrix.normalMatrix());
    glDrawArrays(GL_TRIANGLES, 0, m_data.size());
}
```

This method is very easy, since most of the work was done when setting up the shader program. First, the shader program is activated, and then all the required matrices are set as uniforms for the shader. Included is the normal matrix calculated from the model-view matrix.

Finally, a call to `glDrawArrays()` is issued, telling it to render with the `GL_TRIANGLES` mode using active arrays, starting from the beginning of the array (offset `0`) and reading in the `m_data.size()` entities from the array.

After you run the project, you should get a result similar to the following one, which happens to contain the Blender monkey, Suzanne:

GL buffers

Using attribute arrays can speed up programming, but for rendering all data still needs to be copied to the graphics card on each use. This can be avoided with OpenGL buffer objects. Qt provides a neat interface for such objects with its `QOpenGLBuffer` class. The currently supported buffer types are vertex buffers (where the buffer contains vertex information), index buffers (where the content of the buffer is a set of indexes to other buffers that can be used with `glDrawElements()`), and also less-commonly-used pixel pack buffers and pixel unpack buffers. The buffer is essentially a block of memory that can be uploaded to the graphics card and stored there for faster access. There are different usage patterns available that dictate how and when the buffer is transferred between the host memory and the GPU memory. The most common pattern is a one-time upload of vertex information to the GPU that can later be referred to during rendering as many times as needed. Changing an existing application that uses an attribute array to use vertex buffers is very easy. First, a buffer needs to be instantiated:

```
ShaderGLScene::ShaderGLScene(SceneGLWindow *window) :
    AbstractGLScene(window),
m_vertexBuffer(QOpenGLBuffer::VertexBuffer)
{ /* ... */ }
```

Then, its usage pattern needs to be set. In case of a one-time upload, the most appropriate type is `StaticDraw`:

```
m_vertexBuffer.setUsagePattern(QOpenGLBuffer::StaticDraw);
```

Then, the buffer itself has to be created and bound to the current context (for example, in the `initializeGL()` function):

```
m_vertexBuffer.create();
m_vertexBuffer.bind();
```

The next step is to actually allocate some memory for the buffer and initialize it:

```
m_vertexBuffer.allocate(m_data.constData(),
                        m_data.count() * sizeof(ScenePoint));
```

To change data in the buffer, there are two options. First, you can attach the buffer to the application's memory space, using a call to `map()` and then fill the data, using a returned pointer:

```
ScenePoint *buffer = static_cast<ScenePoint*>(
    vbo.map(QOpenGLBuffer::WriteOnly));
assert(buffer != nullptr);
for(int i = 0; i < vbo.size(); ++i) {
    buffer[i] = ...;
}
vbo.unmap();
```

An alternative approach is to write to the buffer directly, using `write()`:

```
vbo.write(0, m_data.constData(), m_data.size() * sizeof(ScenePoint));
```

Finally, the buffer can be used in the shader program in a way similar to an attribute array:

```
vbo.bind();
m_shader.setAttributeBuffer("Vertex", GL_FLOAT,
                            0, 3, sizeof(ScenePoint));
m_shader.enableAttributeArray("Vertex");
m_shader.setAttributeBuffer("Normal", GL_FLOAT,
                            sizeof(QVector3D), 3, sizeof(ScenePoint));
m_shader.enableAttributeArray("Normal");
```

The result is that all the data is uploaded to the GPU once and then used as needed by the current shader program or other OpenGL call-supporting buffer objects.

Using multiple OpenGL versions

Earlier in this chapter, we discussed a family of `QOpenGLFunctions` classes that provide access to OpenGL functions included in a specific OpenGL profile. If your whole application can use one profile, you can just select the appropriate Qt class and use it. However, sometimes you don't want the application to shut down completely if the requested profile is not supported on the current system. Instead, you can relax your requirements and use an older OpenGL version and provide simplified but still working rendering for systems that don't support the new profile. In Qt, you can implement such an approach using `QOpenGLContext::versionFunctions()`:

```
class MyWindow : public QOpenGLWindow {
protected:
    QOpenGLFunctions_4_5_Core *glFunctions45;
    QOpenGLFunctions_3_3_Core *glFunctions33;
    void initializeGL()
    {
        glFunctions33 =
context()->versionFunctions<QOpenGLFunctions_3_3_Core>();
        glFunctions45 =
context()->versionFunctions<QOpenGLFunctions_4_5_Core>();
    }
    void paintGL() {
        if (glFunctions45) {
            // OpenGL 4.5 rendering
            // glFunctions45->...
        } else if (glFunctions33) {
            // OpenGL 3.3 rendering
            // glFunctions33->...
        } else {
            qFatal("unsupported OpenGL version");
        }
    }
};
```

In the `initializeGL()` function, we try to request wrapper objects for multiple OpenGL versions. If the requested version is not currently available, `versionFunctions()` will return `nullptr`. In the `paintGL()` function, we use the best available version to perform the actual rendering.

Next, you can use the `QSurfaceFormat` class to specify the OpenGL version and profile you want to use:

```
MyWindow window;
QSurfaceFormat format = window.format();
format.setVersion(4, 0);
format.setProfile(QSurfaceFormat::CoreProfile);
window.setFormat(format);
window.show();
```

By requesting the core profile, you can ensure that old deprecated functionality will not be available in our application.

Offscreen rendering

Sometimes, it is useful to render an OpenGL scene not to the screen but to some image that can be later processed externally or used as a texture in some other part of rendering. For that, the concept of **Framebuffer Objects** (**FBO**) was created. An FBO is a rendering surface that behaves like the regular device frame buffer, with the only exception that the resulting pixels do not land on the screen. An FBO target can be bound as a texture in an existing scene or dumped as an image to regular computer memory. In Qt, such an entity is represented by a `QOpenGLFramebufferObject` class.

Once you have a current OpenGL context, you can create an instance of `QOpenGLFramebufferObject`, using one of the available constructors. A mandatory parameter to pass is the size of the canvas (either as a `QSize` object or as a pair of integers describing the width and height of the frame). Different constructors accept other parameters, such as the type of texture the FBO is to generate or a set of parameters encapsulated in `QOpenGLFramebufferObjectFormat`.

When the object is created, you can issue a `bind()` call on it, which switches the OpenGL pipeline to render to the FBO instead of the default target. A complementary method is `release()`, which restores the default rendering target. Afterward, the FBO can be queried to return the ID of the OpenGL texture (using the `texture()` method) or to convert the texture to `QImage` (by invoking `toImage()`).

Vulkan in Qt applications

OpenGL has undergone significant changes as graphics cards hardware has evolved. Many old parts of OpenGL API are now deprecated, and even up-to-date API is not ideal for utilizing the capabilities of modern hardware. Vulkan was designed as an attempt to create an API more suitable for this purpose.

Vulkan is a new API that can be used instead of OpenGL to perform hardware-accelerated rendering and computation. While Vulkan is more verbose and complex than OpenGL, it closely represents the actual interaction between CPU and GPU. This allows Vulkan users to achieve better control over utilizing GPU resources, which can lead to better performance. The first stable version of Vulkan API was released in 2016.

While Vulkan is a cross-platform solution, a Vulkan application still needs to contain a bit of platform-specific code, mainly related to window creation and event handling. Since Version 5.10, Qt provides a way to use Vulkan along with Qt's existing window and event infrastructure. You still retain full access to the original Vulkan API for rendering, but, at the same time, you can use the already familiar Qt API for everything else.

As with OpenGL, we will not give an in-depth guide of Vulkan here. We will only provide simple examples and cover the interaction between Qt and Vulkan. If you need more information about Vulkan, you can refer to its official page at `https://www.khronos.org/vulkan/`.

Preparing the developing environment

Before you can start developing games with Vulkan and Qt, you need to make a few preparations. First, you need to install the Vulkan SDK. To do that, head to `https://www.lunarg.com/vulkan-sdk/`, download a file for your operating system, and execute or unpack it. Examine the `index.html` file in the `doc` subdirectory in the installation folder to see whether you need to perform any additional actions.

Next, you need a Qt build with Vulkan support; it must be Qt 5.10 or later. If you have installed the most recent version available through the installer, it may already be suitable.

To check whether your Qt version has Vulkan support, create a new **Qt Console Application**, ensure that you select the kit corresponding to the most recently installed Qt version. The Vulkan SDK also requires you to set some environment variables, such as `VULKAN_SDK`, `PATH`, `LD_LIBRARY_PATH`, and `VK_LAYER_PATH` (exact names and values can depend on the operating system, so refer to the SDK documentation). You can edit environment variables for your project by switching to Qt Creator's **Projects** pane and expanding the **Build Environment** section.

Put the following code in `main.cpp`:

```
#include <QGuiApplication>
#include <vulkan/vulkan.h>
#include <QVulkanInstance>
int main(int argc, char *argv[]) {
    QGuiApplication app(argc, argv);
    QVulkanInstance vulkan;
    return app.exec();
}
```

Additionally, adjust the project file so that we actually have a Qt GUI application instead of a console application:

```
QT += gui
CONFIG += c++11
DEFINES += QT_DEPRECATED_WARNINGS
SOURCES += main.cpp
```

If the project builds successfully, your setup is complete.

If the compiler can't find the `vulkan/vulkan.h` header, then the Vulkan SDK was not installed properly or its headers are not located in the default include path. Check the Vulkan SDK documentation to see whether you have missed something. You can also switch to the Projects pane of Qt Creator and edit the build environment of the project to make the installed headers visible. Depending on the compiler, you may need to set the `INCLUDEPATH` or `CPATH` environment variable.

If you have a compile error corresponding to the `QVulkanInstance` header, you are using a Qt version prior to 5.10. Ensure that you install a recent version and select the correct kit on the **Projects** pane of Qt Creator.

However, if the `QVulkanInstance` includes directive works, but the `QVulkanInstance` class is still not defined, it means that your Qt build lacks Vulkan support. In this case, first try to install the most recent version using the official installer, if you haven't done so already:

1. Close Qt Creator
2. Launch the **Maintenance Tool** executable from the Qt installation directory
3. Select **Add or remove components**
4. Select the most recent Desktop Qt version
5. Confirm the changes

After the installation is done, re-open Qt Creator, switch to the **Projects** pane, and select the new kit for the project.

> Unfortunately, at the time of writing, the Qt builds available through the official installer do not have Vulkan support. It's possible (and likely) that it will be enabled in the future versions.

If the `QVulkanInstance` class is still not recognized, you have to build Qt from sources. This process varies depending on the operating system and the Qt version, so we will not cover the details in the book. Go to the `http://doc.qt.io/qt-5/build-sources.html` page and follow the instructions corresponding to your operating system. If the Vulkan SDK is properly installed, the output of the `configure` command should contain **Vulkan ... yes**, indicating that Vulkan support is enabled. After you build Qt, open Qt Creator's options dialog and set up a Qt version and a kit, as described in `Chapter 2`, *Installation*.

Finally, select the new kit for the project on the **Projects** pane:

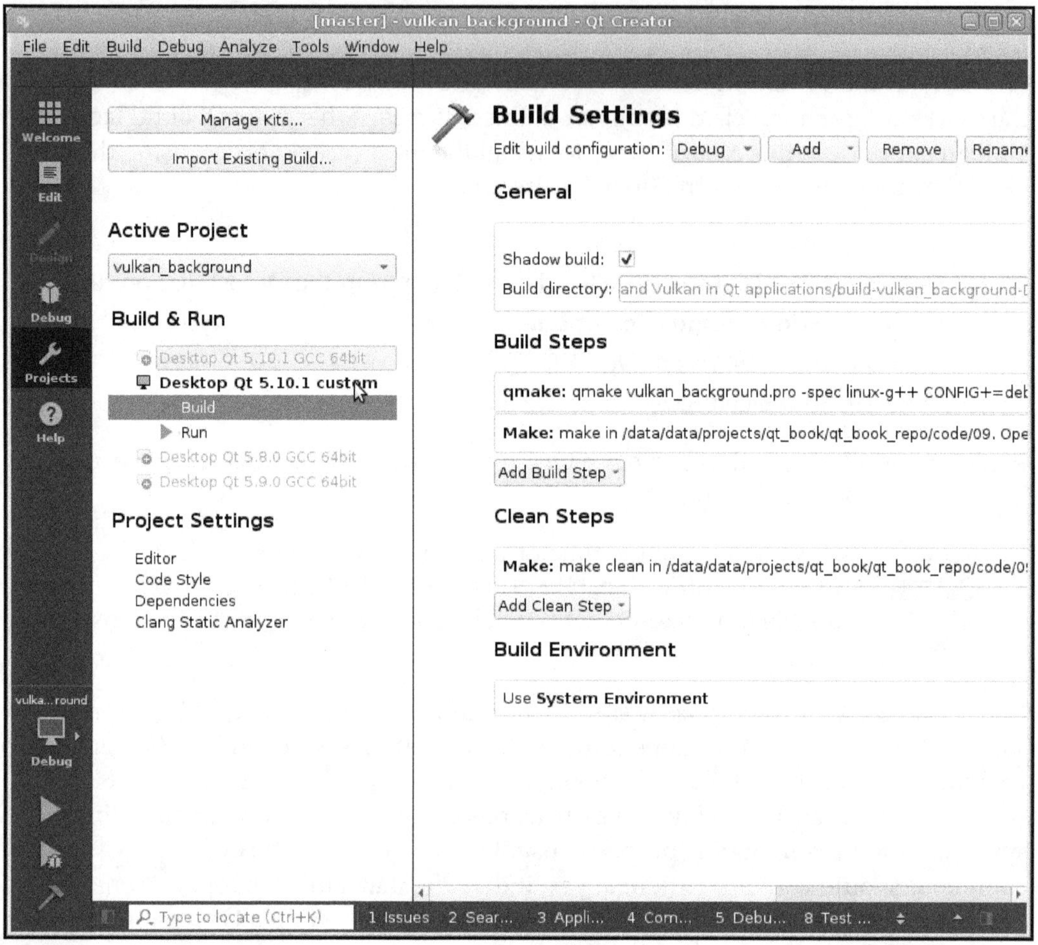

If you've done everything correctly, the project should now build and execute successfully.

Vulkan instance, window, and renderer

Before we start creating our first minimal Vulkan application, let's get familiar with the Qt classes we'll need for the task.

Unlike OpenGL, Vulkan doesn't have a global state. Interaction with Vulkan starts with the instance object represented by the `VkInstance` type. An application usually creates a single `VkInstance` object that contains the application-wide state. All other Vulkan objects can only be created from the instance object. In Qt, the corresponding class is `QVulkanInstance`. This class provides a convenient way to configure Vulkan and then initialize it with the given configuration. You can also use its `supportedExtensions()` and `supportedLayers()` functions to query supported features before using them. After the configuration is done, you should call the `create()` function that actually triggers loading Vulkan library and creating a `VkInstance` object. If this function returns `true`, the Vulkan instance object is ready to be used.

The next step is to create a window capable of Vulkan rendering. This is done by subclassing the `QVulkanWindow` class. Similar to `QOpenGLWindow`, `QVulkanWindow` extends `QWindow` and provides functionality required for utilizing Vulkan capabilities as well as some convenience functions. You can also use virtual functions inherited from `QWindow` to handle any events dispatched by Qt's event system. However, subclasses of `QVulkanWindow` should not perform any actual rendering. This task is delegated to the `QVulkanWindowRenderer` class. The `QVulkanWindow::createRenderer()` virtual function will be called once after the window is first shown, and you should reimplement this function to return your renderer object.

Now, about the renderer itself: `QVulkanWindowRenderer` is a simple class containing nothing more than a set of virtual functions. You can create your own renderer by subclassing `QVulkanWindowRenderer` and re-implementing the only pure virtual function called `startNextFrame()`. This function will be called when the drawing of the next frame is requested. You can perform all required drawing operations in this function and end it with a call to `QVulkanWindow::frameReady()` to indicate that the drawing is complete. You can also re-implement other virtual functions of the renderer. The most useful of them are `initResources()` and `releaseResources()`, which allow you to create required resources, store them in private members of your renderer class, and then destroy them when necessary.

These three classes define the basic structure of your Vulkan application. Let's see them in action.

Time for action – Creating the minimal Vulkan project

We've already created a project while testing the developing environment. Now let's add two new classes to the project. One class named `MyWindow` should be derived from `QVulkanWindow`, and the other class named `MyRenderer` should be derived from `QVulkanWindowRenderer`. Implement the window's `createRenderer()` virtual function:

```
QVulkanWindowRenderer *MyWindow::createRenderer() {
    return new MyRenderer(this);
}
```

Add the `QVulkanWindow *m_window` private field to the renderer class. Implement the constructor to initialize this field and override the `startNextFrame()` virtual function, as shown:

```
MyRenderer::MyRenderer(QVulkanWindow *window)
{
    m_window = window;
}
void MyRenderer::startNextFrame() {
    m_window->frameReady();
}
```

Finally, edit the `main()` function:

```
int main(int argc, char *argv[]) {
    QGuiApplication app(argc, argv);
    QVulkanInstance vulkan;
    if (!vulkan.create()) {
        qFatal("Failed to create Vulkan instance: %d",
vulkan.errorCode());
    }
    MyWindow window;
    window.resize(1024, 768);
    window.setVulkanInstance(&vulkan);
    window.show();
    return app.exec();
}
```

When you compile and run the project, a blank window with a black background should appear.

What just happened?

We've created a window that will be rendered using Vulkan. The `main()` function initializes Vulkan, creates a window, passes the instance object to the window, and shows it on the screen. As usual, the final call to `exec()` starts Qt's event loop. When the window is shown, Qt will call the `createRenderer()` function on the window and a new renderer object will be created in your implementation of this function. The renderer is attached to the window and will automatically be deleted along with it, so there is no need to delete it manually. Each time the window needs to be painted, Qt will call the renderer's `startNextFrame()` function. We don't perform any painting yet, so the window remains blank.

It's important that the drawing of every frame ends with a call to `frameReady()`. Until this function is called, processing of the frame cannot be completed. However, it's not required to call this function directly from the `startNextFrame()` function. You can delay this call if you need, for example, to wait for calculations to complete in a separate thread.

> TIP: Similar to how `paintEvent()` works, `startNextFrame()` will not be called continuously by default. It will only be called once after showing the window. It will also be called each time a part of the window is exposed (for example, as a result of moving a window or restoring a minimized window). If you need to render a dynamic scene continuously, call `m_window->requestUpdate()` after calling `m_window->frameReady()`.

Using Vulkan types and functions

We can let Qt handle loading the Vulkan library and resolving functions for us. It works similar to the `QOpenGLFunctions` set of classes. Qt provides two functions classes for Vulkan:

- The `QVulkanFunctions` class provides access to the Vulkan functions that are not device-specific
- The `QVulkanDeviceFunctions` class provides functions that work on a specific `VkDevice`

You can obtain these objects by calling the `functions()` and `deviceFunctions(VkDevice device)` methods of the `QVulkanInstance` class, respectively. You will usually use the device functions a lot in the renderer, so a common pattern is to add the `QVulkanDeviceFunctions *m_devFuncs` private field to your renderer class and initialize it in the `initResources()` virtual function:

```
void MyRenderer::initResources()
{
    VkDevice device = m_window->device();
    m_devFuncs = m_window->vulkanInstance()->deviceFunctions(device);
    //...
}
```

Now you can use `m_devFuncs` to access the Vulkan API functions. We won't use them directly, so we don't need to figure out how to link against the Vulkan library on each platform. Qt does this job for us.

As for structures, unions, and typedefs, we can use them directly without worrying about the platform details. It's enough to have the Vulkan SDK headers present in the system.

Time for action – Drawing with a dynamic background color

Let's see how we can use the Vulkan API in our Qt project to change the background color of the window. We'll cycle through all possible hues of the color while retaining constant saturation and lightness. This may sound complicated when you think about a color in RGB space, but it's actually very easy if you work with the HSL (Hue, Saturation, Lightness) color model. Luckily, `QColor` supports multiple color models, including HSL.

First, add and initialize the `m_devFuncs` private field, as just shown. Next, add the `float m_hue` private field that will hold the current hue of the background color. Set its initial value to zero. We can now start writing our `startNextFrame()` function that will do all the magic. Let's go through it piece by piece. First, we increment our `m_hue` variable and ensure that we don't go out of bounds; then, we use the `QColor::fromHslF()` function to construct a `QColor` value based on given hue, saturation, and lightness (each of them ranges from 0 to 1):

```
void MyRenderer::startNextFrame()
{
    m_hue += 0.005f;
```

```
        if (m_hue > 1.0f) {
            m_hue = 0.0f;
        }
        QColor color = QColor::fromHslF(m_hue, 1, 0.5);
        //...
    }
```

Next, we use this `color` variable to construct a `VkClearValue` array that we'll use for setting the background color:

```
VkClearValue clearValues[2];
memset(clearValues, 0, sizeof(clearValues));
clearValues[0].color = {
    static_cast<float>(color.redF()),
    static_cast<float>(color.greenF()),
    static_cast<float>(color.blueF()),
    1.0f
};
clearValues[1].depthStencil = { 1.0f, 0 };
```

To start a new render pass in Vulkan, we need to initialize a `VkRenderPassBeginInfo` structure. It requires a lot of data, but, luckily, `QVulkanWindow` provides most of the data for us. We just need to put it into the structure and use the `clearValues` array we set up earlier:

```
VkRenderPassBeginInfo info;
memset(&info, 0, sizeof(info));
info.sType = VK_STRUCTURE_TYPE_RENDER_PASS_BEGIN_INFO;
info.renderPass = m_window->defaultRenderPass();
info.framebuffer = m_window->currentFramebuffer();
const QSize imageSize = m_window->swapChainImageSize();
info.renderArea.extent.width = imageSize.width();
info.renderArea.extent.height = imageSize.height();
info.clearValueCount = 2;
info.pClearValues = clearValues;
```

Finally, it's time to perform the rendering:

```
VkCommandBuffer commandBuffer = m_window->currentCommandBuffer();
m_devFuncs->vkCmdBeginRenderPass(commandBuffer, &info,
                                 VK_SUBPASS_CONTENTS_INLINE);
m_devFuncs->vkCmdEndRenderPass(commandBuffer);
m_window->frameReady();
m_window->requestUpdate();
```

The `vkCmdBeginRenderPass()` Vulkan API function will begin the render pass, which will result in clearing the window with the color we've set. Since we don't have anything else to draw, we complete the render pass immediately using the `vkCmdEndRenderPass()` function. Then, we indicate that we've already done everything we want for this frame by calling the `frameReady()` function. This allows Qt to advance the rendering loop. As the final step, we request an update of the window to ensure that the new frame will be requested soon and the color animation will go on.

If you run the project now, you should see a window that constantly changes its background color:

We would love to show a more advanced example. However, even drawing a simple triangle in Vulkan usually requires a few hundred lines of code, because Vulkan requires you to explicitly set up a lot of things. While Qt provides a lot of helper classes for OpenGL rendering, it does not contain any similar classes that would help with Vulkan rendering or computation (as of Qt 5.10), so there is nothing specific to Qt in these tasks.

If you want to deepen your knowledge of Vulkan, you can study the documentation and tutorials present on its official website and the Vulkan SDK website. Qt also includes several good examples based on Vulkan, such as **Hello Vulkan Triangle**, **Hello Vulkan Texture**, and **Hello Vulkan Cubes**.

Logs and validation

Qt automatically receives messages from the Vulkan library and puts them into Qt's own logging system. The critical errors will be passed to `qWarning()`, so they will appear in the application output by default. However, Qt also logs additional information that can be useful when debugging. This information is hidden by default, but you can make it visible by adding the following line to the `main()` function just after the construction of `QGuiApplication`:

```
QLoggingCategory::setFilterRules(QStringLiteral("qt.vulkan=true"));
```

The Vulkan API does not perform any sanity checks by default. If you pass an invalid parameter to a Vulkan API function, the application may silently crash, or work inconsistently. However, you can enable **validation layers** for your Vulkan instance. They do not change the functionality of the API calls, but they enable additional checks when possible. It's a good idea to enable validation layers in a debug build. You can do that by calling `setLayers()` on the instance object before calling `create()`:

```
vulkan.setLayers({ "VK_LAYER_LUNARG_standard_validation" });
```

Keep in mind that an attempt to request a currently unsupported layer or extension will be ignored by Qt.

Let's test the validation layers by inserting an invalid parameter to our code:

```
info.renderArea.extent.width = -5; // invalid
```

When you run the application, Qt should print a warning to the application output:

```
vkDebug: CORE: 4: Cannot execute a render pass with renderArea not
within the bound of the framebuffer. RenderArea: x 0, y 0, width -5,
height 768. Framebuffer: width 1024, height 768.
```

If the warning does not appear, it means that the validation layers are not available or they failed to load. Check the application output for the presence of validation layers (they will be printed after the "Supported Vulkan instance layers" line) and any library loading errors. Ensure that you've set up the Vulkan SDK and the project's environment variables according to the documentation.

However, keep in mind that validation layers have a performance impact on your application. You should probably disable them in your final builds. You can also disable redirecting Vulkan's debug output to the Qt logging system, using the following code:

```
QVulkanInstance vulkan;
vulkan.setFlags(QVulkanInstance::NoDebugOutputRedirect);
```

Combining OpenGL or Vulkan with Qt Widgets

Sometimes you want to combine the powers of accelerated graphics and Qt Widgets. While OpenGL and Vulkan are great for rendering high-performance 2D and 3D scenes, the Qt Widgets module is far easier to use for creating user interfaces. Qt offers a few ways to combine them into a single powerful interface. This can be useful if your application depends heavily on widgets (for example, the 3D view is only one of the views in your application and is controlled using a bunch of other widgets surrounding the main view).

The first way is the `QWidget::createWindowContainer()` function. It takes an arbitrary `QWindow` and creates a `QWidget` that keeps the window within its bounds. That widget can be put into another widget and can be managed by a layout. While the window appears to be embedded into another window, it still remains a native window from the operating system's perspective, and any accelerated rendering will be performed directly on the window without a heavy performance impact. This approach has a few limitations, though. For example, the embedded window will always stack on top of other widgets. However, it's suitable in most cases.

Let's return to our OpenGL cube project and put it into a layout with an additional label:

```
QWidget widget;
QVBoxLayout* layout = new QVBoxLayout(&widget);
layout->addWidget(new QLabel("Scene"), 0);
QWidget* container = QWidget::createWindowContainer(&window, &widget);
layout->addWidget(container, 1);
widget.resize(600, 600);
widget.show();
```

Instead of showing the OpenGL window, we created a widget and put the window into the layout of that widget:

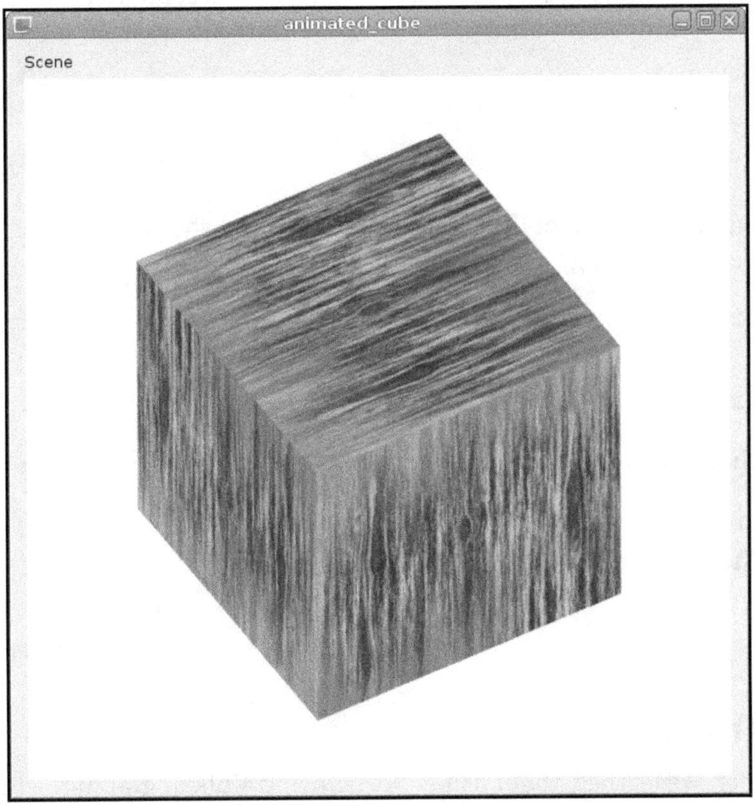

You can apply this approach to any `QWindow`, including Vulkan-based windows and Qt Quick windows, which we'll work with in subsequent chapters.

There is another way to solve the same task, but it only works with OpenGL. You can simply replace `QOpenGLWindow` with `QOpenGLWidget` to turn a window into a fully featured widget. The API of `QOpenGLWidget` (including virtual functions) is compatible with `QOpenGLWindow`, so it can act as a drop-in replacement. There are no limitations for the stacking order, focus, or opacity of `QOpenGLWidget`. You can even mix the OpenGL rendering with `QPainter` operations. However, this solution has a performance cost. `QOpenGLWindow` renders directly to the given window, while `QOpenGLWidget` first renders to an offscreen buffer that is then rendered to the widget, so it will be slower.

Pop quiz

Q1. Which of the following programming languages is accepted by the `QOpenGLShader::compileSourceCode()` function?

1. C
2. C++
3. GLSL

Q2. Which virtual function of the `QOpenGLWindow` class should you implement to perform OpenGL painting?

1. `paintGL()`
2. `paintEvent()`
3. `makeCurrent()`

Q3. When should you delete the object of your `QVulkanWindowRenderer` subclass?

1. In the destructor of the `QVulkanWindow` subclass
2. After deleting the `QVulkanInstance` object
3. Never

Summary

In this chapter, we learned about using OpenGL and Vulkan graphics with Qt. With this knowledge, you can create hardware accelerated 2D and 3D graphics. We also explored Qt classes that simplify usage of these technologies in Qt applications. If you want to sharpen your OpenGL and Vulkan skills, you can study numerous books and articles focused on these topics. Qt provides very transparent access to hardware accelerated graphics, so adapting any pure OpenGL or Vulkan approaches for Qt should be easy. If you prefer to have a higher-level API for accelerated graphics, you should turn your attention to Qt Quick and Qt 3D. We will cover it in the last part of this book.

In the next chapter, you will learn to implement scripting in your game. This will make it more extensible and easier to modify. Scripting can also be used to enable modding in your game, allowing players to customize the gameplay how they want.

10
Scripting

In this chapter, you will learn how to bring scripting facilities to your programs. You will gain knowledge of how to use JavaScript to implement the logic and details of your game, without having to rebuild the main game engine. These skills will also be useful in the last part of the book when we work with Qt Quick. Although the environment we will focus on blends best with Qt applications, there are other options if you don't like JavaScript. We will also show how you can use Python to make your games scriptable.

The main topics covered in this chapter are as listed:

- Executing JavaScript code
- Interaction between C++ and JavaScript
- Implementing a scripting game
- Integrating the Python interpreter

Why script?

You might ask yourself, "why should I use any scripting language if I can implement everything I need in C++"? There are a number of benefits to providing a scripting environment to your games. Most modern games really consist of two parts. One is the main game engine that implements the core of the game (data structures, processing algorithms, and the rendering layer) and exposes an API to the other component, which provides details, behavior patterns, and action flows for the game. This other component is sometimes written in a scripting language. The main benefit of this is that story designers can work independently from the engine developers, and they don't have to rebuild the whole game just to modify some of its parameters or check whether the new quest fits well into the existing story. This makes the development much quicker compared to the monolithic approach.

Another benefit is that this development opens the game to modding—skilled end users can extend or modify the game to provide some added value to the game. It's also a way to implement extensions of the game on top of the existing scripting API without having to redeploy the complete game binary to every player. Finally, you can reuse the same game driver for other games and just replace the scripts to obtain a totally different product.

In this chapter, we will use the Qt QML module to implement scripting. This module implements QML language used in Qt Quick. Since QML is JavaScript-based, Qt QML includes a JavaScript engine and provides API for running JavaScript code. It also allows you to expose C++ objects to JavaScript and vice versa.

We will not discuss the details of the JavaScript language itself, as there are many good books and websites available where you can learn JavaScript. Besides, the JavaScript syntax is very similar to that of C, and you shouldn't have any problems understanding the scripts that we use in this chapter even if you haven't seen any JavaScript code before.

Evaluating JavaScript expressions

To use Qt QML in your programs, you have to enable the script module for your projects by adding the `QT += qml` line to the project file.

C++ compilers do not understand JavaScript. Therefore, to execute any script, you need to have a running interpreter that will parse the script and evaluate it. In Qt, this is done with the `QJSEngine` class. This is a JavaScript runtime that handles the execution of script code and manages all the resources related to scripts. It provides the `evaluate()` method, which can be used to execute JavaScript expressions. Let's look at a "Hello World" program using `QJSEngine`:

```
#include <QCoreApplication>
#include <QJSEngine>

int main(int argc, char **argv) {
    QCoreApplication app(argc, argv);
    QJSEngine engine;
    engine.installExtensions(QJSEngine::ConsoleExtension);
    engine.evaluate("console.log('Hello World!');");
    return 0;
}
```

This program is very simple. First, it creates an application object that is required for the script environment to function properly and instantiates a `QJSEngine` object. Next, we ask `QJSEngine` to install the console extension—the global `console` object that can be used to print messages to the console. It's not part of the ECMAScript standard, so it's not available by default, but we can easily enable it using the `installExtensions()` function. Finally, we call the `evaluate()` function to execute the script source given to it as a parameter. After building and running the program, you will see a well-known `Hello World!` printed to the console with the `js:` prefix.

> By default, `QJSEngine` provides built-in objects defined by ECMA-262 standard, including `Math`, `Date`, and `String`. For example, a script can use `Math.abs(x)` to get the absolute value of a number.

If you don't get any output, it probably means that the script didn't get executed properly, possibly because of an error in the script's source code. To verify that, we can check the value returned from `evaluate()`:

```
QJSValue result = engine.evaluate("console.log('Hello World!')");
if (result.isError()) {
    qDebug() << "JS error:" << result.toString();
}
```

This code checks whether there is an exception or a syntax error and if yes, it displays the corresponding error message. For example, if you omit the closing single quote in the script source text and run the program, the following message will be displayed:

```
JS error: "SyntaxError: Expected token `)'"
```

You can see that `evaluate()` returns a `QJSValue`. This is a special type that is used to exchange data between the JavaScript engine and the C++ world. Like `QVariant`, it can hold a number of primitive types (`boolean`, `integer`, `string`, and so on). However, it is in fact much more powerful, because it can hold a reference to a JavaScript object or function that lives in the JavaScript engine. Copying a `QJSValue` will produce another object that references the same JavaScript object. You can use the member functions of `QJSValue` to interact with the objects from C++. For example, you can use `property()` and `setProperty()` to manipulate the object's properties and `call()` to call the function and get the returned value as another `QJSValue`.

In the previous example, `QJSEngine::evaluate()` returned an `Error` object. When the JavaScript code runs successfully, you can use the returned value later in your C++ code. For example, the script can calculate the amount of damage done to a creature when it is hit with a particular weapon. Modifying our code to use the result of the script is very simple. All that is required is to store the value returned by `evaluate()` and then it can be used elsewhere in the code:

```
QJSValue result = engine.evaluate("(7 + 8) / 2");
if (result.isError()) {
    //...
} else {
    qDebug() << result.toNumber();
}
```

Time for action – Creating a JavaScript editor

Let's do a simple exercise and create a graphical editor to write and execute scripts. Start by creating a new Qt Widgets project and implement a main window composed of two plain text edit widgets (`ui->codeEditor` and `ui->logWindow`) that are separated using a vertical splitter. One of the edit boxes will be used as an editor to input code and the other will be used as a console to display script results. Then, add a menu and toolbar to the window and create actions to open (`ui->actionOpenDocument`) and save (`ui->actionSaveDocument` and `ui->actionSaveDocumentAs`) the document, create a new document (`ui->actionNewDocument`), execute the script (`ui->actionExecuteScript`), and to quit the application (`ui->actionQuit`). Remember to add them to the menu and toolbar.

As a result, you should receive a window similar to the one shown in the following screenshot:

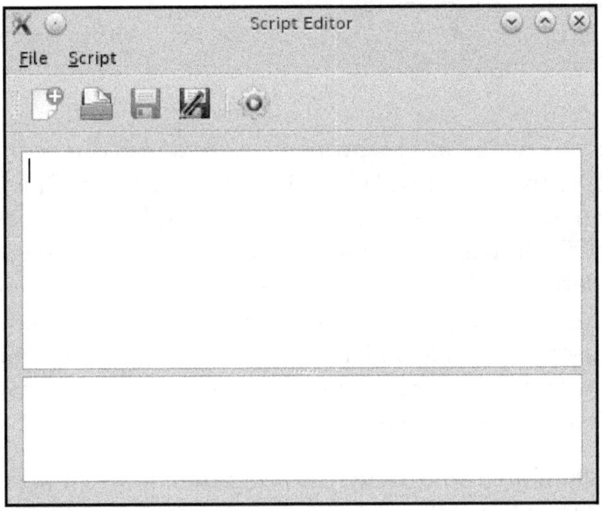

Connect the quit action to the `QApplication::quit()` slot. Then, create an `openDocument()` slot and connect it to the `triggered` signal of the appropriate action. In the slot, use `QFileDialog::getOpenFileName()` to ask the user for a document path, as follows:

```
void MainWindow::openDocument()
{
    QString filePath = QFileDialog::getOpenFileName(
        this, tr("Open Document"),
        QDir::homePath(), tr("JavaScript Documents (*.js)"));
    if(filePath.isEmpty()) {
        return;
    }
    open(filePath);
}
```

In a similar fashion, implement the **New**, **Save**, and **Save As** action handlers. Lastly, create the `open(const QString &filePath)` slot that should read the document and put its contents into the code editor:

```
void MainWindow::open(const QString &filePath)
{
    QFile file(filePath);
    if(!file.open(QFile::ReadOnly | QFile::Text)) {
        QMessageBox::critical(this, tr("Error"), tr("Can't open
```

```
file."));
        return;
    }
    setWindowFilePath(filePath);
    ui->codeEditor->setPlainText(QString::fromUtf8(file.readAll()));
    ui->logWindow->clear();
}
```

The `windowFilePath` property of `QWidget` can be used to associate a file with a window. When this property is set, Qt will automatically adjust the window title and even add a proxy icon on macOS, allowing convenient access to the file. You can then use this property in actions related to using the file—when saving a document, you can check whether this property is empty and ask the user to provide a filename. Then, you can reset this property when creating a new document or when the user provides a new path for the document.

At this point, you should be able to run the program and use it to create scripts and save and reload them in the editor.

Now, to execute the scripts, add a `QJSEngine m_engine` member variable to the window class. Create a new slot, call it `run`, and connect it to the execute action. Put the following code in the body of the slot:

```
void MainWindow::run()
{
    ui->logWindow->clear();
    QTextCursor logCursor = ui->logWindow->textCursor();
    QString scriptSourceCode = ui->codeEditor->toPlainText();
    QJSValue result = m_engine.evaluate(scriptSourceCode,
                                        windowFilePath());
    if(result.isError()) {
        QTextCharFormat errFormat;
        errFormat.setForeground(Qt::red);
        logCursor.insertText(tr("Exception at line %1:\n")
            .arg(result.property("lineNumber").toInt()), errFormat);
        logCursor.insertText(result.toString(), errFormat);
        logCursor.insertBlock();
        logCursor.insertText(result.property("stack").toString(),
                             errFormat);
    } else {
        QTextCharFormat resultFormat;
        resultFormat.setForeground(Qt::blue);
        logCursor.insertText(result.toString(), resultFormat);
    }
```

```
}
```

Build and run the program. To do so, enter the following script in the editor:

```
function factorial(n) {
    if(n < 0) {
        return;
    }
    if(n == 0) {
        return 1;
    }
    return n * factorial(n - 1);
}

factorial(7)
```

Save the script in a file called `factorial.js` and then run it. You should get an output as shown:

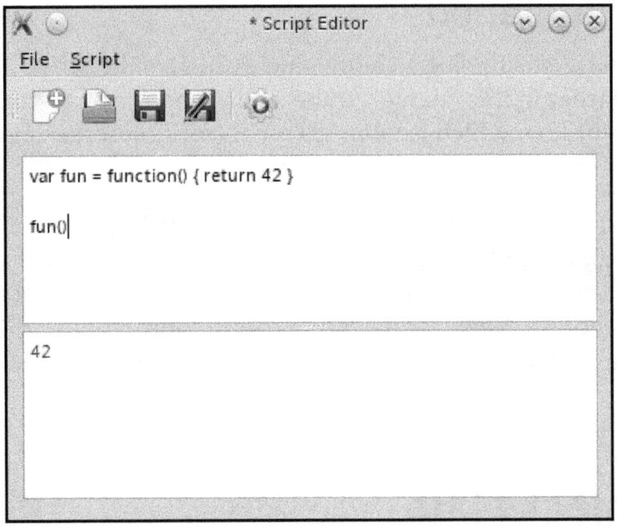

Next, replace the script with the following one:

```
function factorial(n) {
    return N;
}

factorial(7)
```

Running the script should yield the following result:

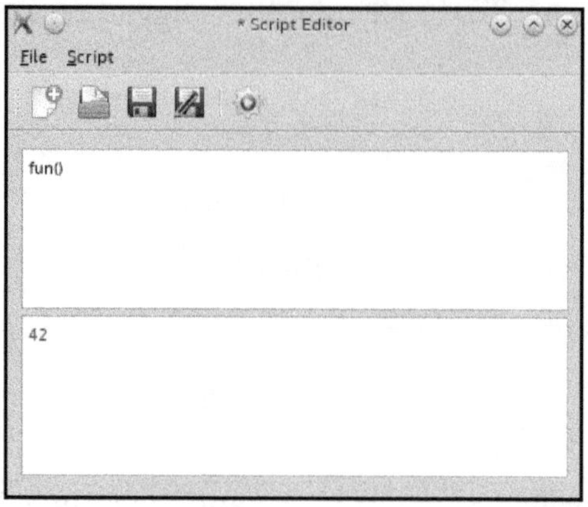

What just happened?

The `run()` method clears the log window and evaluates the script using the method that we learned earlier in this chapter. If the evaluation is successful, it prints the result in the log window, which is what we see in the first screenshot shown in the previous section.

In the second attempt, we made an error in the script using a nonexistent variable. Evaluating such code results in an exception. In addition to reporting the actual error, we also use the `lineNumber` property of the returned `Error` object to report the line that caused the problem. Next, we display the `stack` property of the error object, which returns the backtrace (a stack of function calls) of the problem, which we also print on the log.

Global object state

Let's try another script. The following code defines the `fun` local variable, which is assigned an anonymous function that returns a number:

```
var fun = function() {
    return 42;
}
```

You can then call `fun()` like a regular function, as follows:

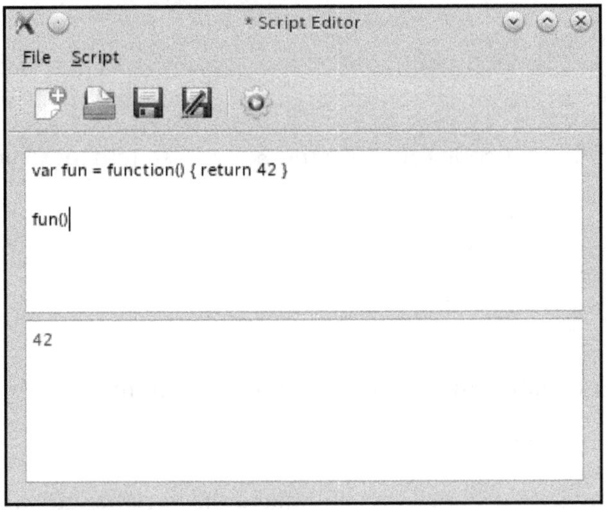

Now, let's look at what happens if we delete the definition of `fun` from the script, but still keep the invocation:

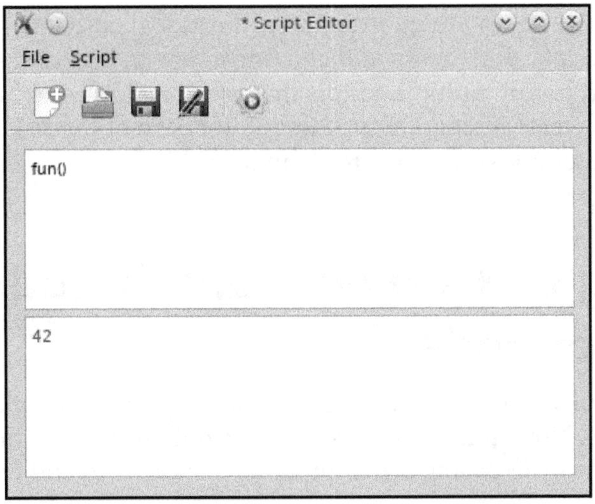

We still get the same result even though we didn't define what `fun` means! This is because any variables at the top scope become properties of the global object. The state of the global object is preserved during the existence of `QJSEngine`, so the `fun` variable will remain available until it's overwritten or the engine is destroyed.

To prevent users from accidentally changing the global object with local variables, we can wrap the provided code in an anonymous function:

```
QString wrappedCode =
    QStringLiteral("(function() { %1\n})()").arg(scriptSourceCode);
QJSValue result = m_engine.evaluate(wrappedCode, windowFilePath());
```

In this case, the JavaScript code must use the `return` statement to actually return a value to the editor:

```
var fun = function() {
    return 42;
}
return fun();
```

Removing the `fun` variable initialization will now result in an error:

```
ReferenceError: fun is not defined
```

However, removing the `var` keyword will make the variable global and preserved. A malicious user can also break the existing global object's properties. For example, evaluating `Math.floor = null;` will make the built-in `Math.floor` function unavailable in all subsequent calls.

There isn't really a good way to guard or reset the global object. If you are concerned about malicious scripts, destroying and creating a new `QJSEngine` object is the best option. If you need to run multiple scripts that are not allowed to interfere with each other, you have to create a separate `QJSEngine` for each of them. However, in most applications, such sandboxing seems to be an overkill.

Exposing C++ objects and functions to JavaScript code

So far, we were only evaluating some standalone scripts that can make use of built-in JavaScript features. Now, it is time to learn to use data from your programs in the scripts. This is done by exposing different kinds of entities to and from scripts.

Accessing C++ object's properties and methods

The simplest way to expose a C++ object to JavaScript code is to take advantage of Qt's meta-object system. QJSEngine is able to inspect QObject instances and detect their properties and methods. To use them in scripts, the object has to be visible to the script. The easiest way to make this happen is to add it to the engine's global object. As you remember, all data between the script engine and C++ is exchanged using the QJSValue class, so first we have to obtain a JS value handle for the C++ object:

```
QJSEngine engine;
QPushButton *button = new QPushButton("Button");
// ...
QJSValue scriptButton = engine.newQObject(button);
engine.globalObject().setProperty("pushButton", scriptButton);
```

QJSEngine::newQObject() creates a JavaScript object wrapping an existing QObject instance. We then set the wrapper as a property of the global object called pushButton. This makes the button available in the global context of the engine as a JavaScript object. All the properties defined with Q_PROPERTY are available as properties of the object, and every slot is accessible as a method of that object. In JavaScript, you will be able to use the pushButton object like this:

```
pushButton.text = 'My Scripted Button';
pushButton.checkable = true;
pushButton.setChecked(true);
pushButton.show();
```

Qt slots conventionally return void. They technically can have any return type, but Qt won't use the return value, so in most cases, there is no sense in returning any value. On the contrary, when you expose a C++ method to the JavaScript engine, you often want to return a value and receive it in JavaScript. In these cases, you should not create slots, as that will break the convention. You should make the method invokable instead. To do this, place the method declaration in a regular public scope and add Q_INVOKABLE before it:

```
public:
    Q_INVOKABLE int myMethod();
```

This macro instructs **moc** to make this method invokable in the meta-object system so that Qt will be able to call it at runtime. All invokable methods are automatically exposed to scripts.

Data type conversions between C++ and JavaScript

Qt will automatically convert arguments and return types of methods to its JavaScript counterparts. The supported conversions include the following:

- Basic types (bool, int, double, and such) are exposed without changes
- Qt data types (QString, QUrl, QColor, QFont, QDate, QPoint, QSize, QRect, QMatrix4x4, QQuaternion, QVector2D, and such) are converted to objects with the available properties
- QDateTime and QTime values are automatically converted to JavaScript Date objects
- Enums declared with Q_ENUM macro can be used in JavaScript
- Flags declared with Q_FLAG macro can be used as flags in JavaScript
- QObject* pointers will be automatically converted to JavaScript wrapper objects
- QVariant objects containing any supported types are recognized
- QVariantList is an equivalent of a JavaScript array with arbitrary items
- QVariantMap is an equivalent of a JavaScript object with arbitrary properties
- Some C++ list types (QList<int>, QList<qreal>, QList<bool>, QList<QString>, QStringList, QList<QUrl>, QVector<int>, QVector<qreal>, and QVector<bool>) are exposed to JavaScript without performing additional data conversions

If you want more fine-grained control over data type conversions, you can simply use QJSValue as an argument type or a return type. For example, this will allow you to return a reference to an existing JavaScript object instead of creating a new one each time. This approach is also useful for creating or accessing multidimensional arrays or other objects with complex structure. While you can use nested QVariantList or QVariantMap objects, creating QJSValue objects directly may be more efficient.

Qt will not be able to recognize and automatically convert a custom type. Attempting to access such method or property from JavaScript will result in an error. You can use the Q_GADGET macro to make a C++ data type available to JavaScript and use Q_PROPERTY to declare properties that should be exposed.

For more information on this topic, refer to the **Data Type Conversion Between QML and C++** documentation page.

Accessing signals and slots in scripts

`QJSEngine` also offers the capability to use signals and slots. The slot can be either a C++ method or a JavaScript function. The connection can be made either in C++ or in the script.

First, let's see how to establish a connection within a script. When a `QObject` instance is exposed to a script, the object's signals become the properties of the wrapping object. These properties have a `connect` method that accepts a function object that is to be called when the signal is emitted. The receiver can be a regular slot or a JavaScript function. The most common case is when you connect the signal to an anonymous function:

```
pushButton.toggled.connect(function() {
    console.log('button toggled!');
});
```

If you need to undo the connection, you will need to store the function in a variable:

```
function buttonToggled() {
    //...
}
pushButton.toggled.connect(buttonToggled);
//...
pushButton.toggled.disconnect(buttonToggled);
```

You can define the `this` object for the function by providing an extra argument to `connect()`:

```
var obj = { 'name': 'FooBar' };
pushButton.clicked.connect(obj, function() {
    console.log(this.name);
});
```

You can also connect the signal to a signal or slot of another exposed object. To connect the `clicked()` signal of an object called `pushButton` to a `clear()` slot of another object called `lineEdit`, you can use the following statement:

```
pushButton.clicked.connect(lineEdit.clear);
```

Emitting signals from within the script is also easy—just call the signal as a function and pass to it any necessary parameters:

```
pushButton.clicked();
spinBox.valueChanged(7);
```

To create a signal-slot connection on the C++ side where the receiver is a JavaScript function, you can utilize C++ lambda functions and the `QJSValue::call()` function:

```
QJSValue func = engine.evaluate(
    "function(checked) { console.log('func', checked); }");
QObject::connect(&button, &QPushButton::clicked, [func](bool checked)
{
    QJSValue(func).call({ checked });
});
```

Time for action – Using a button from JavaScript

Let's put all this together and build a complete example of a scriptable button:

```
int main(int argc, char *argv[]) {
    QApplication app(argc, argv);
    QJSEngine engine;
    engine.installExtensions(QJSEngine::ConsoleExtension);
    QPushButton button;
    engine.globalObject().setProperty("pushButton",
engine.newQObject(&button));
    QString script =
        "pushButton.text = 'My Scripted Button';\n"
        "pushButton.checkable = true;\n"
        "pushButton.setChecked(true);\n"
        "pushButton.toggled.connect(function(checked) {\n"
        "  console.log('button toggled!', checked);\n"
        "});\n"
        "pushButton.show();";
    engine.evaluate(script);

    QJSValue func = engine.evaluate(
```

```
            "function(checked) { console.log('button toggled 2!',
checked); }");
    QObject::connect(&button, &QPushButton::clicked, [func](bool
checked) {
        QJSValue(func).call({ checked });
    });
    return app.exec();
}
```

In this code, we expose the function to JavaScript and execute code that sets some properties of the button and accesses its `toggled` signal. Next, we create a JavaScript function, store a reference to it in the `func` variable, and connect the `toggled` signal of the button to this function from C++ side.

Restricting access to C++ classes from JavaScript

There are cases when you want to provide a rich interface for a class to manipulate it from within C++ easily, but to have strict control over what can be done using scripting, you want to prevent scripters from using some of the properties or methods of the class.

The safest approach is to create a wrapper class that only exposes the allowed methods and signals. This will allow you to design your original classes freely. For example, if you want to hide some methods, it's quite easy—just don't make them slots and don't declare them with `Q_INVOKABLE`. However, you may want them to be slots in the internal implementation. By creating a wrapper class, you can easily hide slots of the internal class from the JavaScript code. We'll show how to apply this approach later in this chapter.

Another issue may arise if the data types used by your internal object cannot be directly exposed to JavaScript. For example, if one of your methods returns a `QVector<QVector<int>>`, you will not be able to call such a method directly from JavaScript. The wrapper class is a good place to put the required data conversion operations.

You should also be aware that JavaScript code can emit any signals of exposed C++ objects. In some cases, this can break the logic of your application. If you're using a wrapper, you can just connect the signal of the internal class to the signal of the exposed wrapper. The script will be able to connect to the wrapper's signal, but it won't be able to emit the original signal. However, the script will be able to emit the wrapper's signal, and this can affect all the other JavaScript code in the engine.

If all or almost all APIs of the class are safe to expose to JavaScript, it's much easier to make the objects themselves available, instead of creating wrappers. If you want to restrict access to certain methods, keep in mind that JavaScript code can only access public and protected methods declared with `Q_INVOKABLE` and slots. Remember that you can still connect signals to non-slot methods if you use the `connect()` variant that takes a function pointer as an argument. JavaScript code also cannot access any private methods.

For properties, you can mark them inaccessible from scripts using the `SCRIPTABLE` keyword in the `Q_PROPERTY` declaration. By default, all properties are scriptable, but you can forbid their exposure to scripts by setting `SCRIPTABLE` to `false`, as shown in the following example:

```
Q_PROPERTY(QString internalName READ internalName SCRIPTABLE false)
```

Creating C++ objects from JavaScript

We've only exposed the existing C++ objects to JavaScript so far, but what if you want to create a new C++ object from JavaScript? You can do this using what you already know. A C++ method of an already exposed object can create a new object for you:

```
public:
    Q_INVOKABLE QObject* createMyObject(int argument) {
        return new MyObject(argument);
    }
```

> TIP
>
> We use `QObject*` instead of `MyObject*` in the function signature. This allows us to import the object into the JS engine automatically. The engine will take ownership of the object and delete it when there are no more references to it in JavaScript.

Using this method from JavaScript is also pretty straightforward:

```
var newObject = originalObject.createMyObject(42);
newObject.slot1();
```

This approach is fine if you have a good place for the `createMyObject` function. However, sometimes you want to create new objects independently of the existing ones, or you don't have any objects created yet. For these situations, there is a neat way to expose the constructor of the class to the JavaScript engine. First, you need to make your constructor invokable in the class declaration:

```
public:
    Q_INVOKABLE explicit MyObject(int argument, QObject *parent =
nullptr);
```

Then, you should use the `newQMetaObject()` function to import the *meta-object* of the class to the engine. You can immediately assign the imported meta-object to a property of the global object:

```
engine.globalObject().setProperty("MyObject",
     engine.newQMetaObject(&MyObject::staticMetaObject));
```

You can now invoke the constructor by calling the exposed object with the `new` keyword:

```
var newObject = new MyObject(42);
newObject.slot1();
```

Exposing C++ functions to JavaScript

Sometimes you just want to provide a single function instead of an object. Unfortunately, `QJSEngine` only supports functions that belong to `QObject`-derived classes. However, we can hide this implementation detail from the JavaScript side. First, create a subclass of `QObject` and add an invokable member function that proxies the original standalone function:

```
Q_INVOKABLE double factorial(int x) {
    return superFastFactorial(x);
}
```

Next, expose the wrapper object using the `newQObject()` function, as usual. However, instead of assigning this object to a property of the global object, extract the `factorial` property from the object:

```
QJSValue myObjectJS = engine.newQObject(new MyObject());
engine.globalObject().setProperty("factorial",
                                  myObjectJS.property("factorial"));
```

Now, the JavaScript code can access the method as if it were a global function, like `factorial(4)`.

Creating a JavaScript scripting game

Let's perfect our skills by implementing a game that allows players to use JavaScript. The rules are simple. Each player has a number of entities that move on the board. All entities move in turns; during each turn, the entity can stand still or move to an adjacent tile (cardinally or diagonally). If an entity moves to the tile occupied by another entity, that entity is killed and removed from the board.

At the beginning of the game, all entities are placed randomly on the board. An example of a starting position is displayed on the following image:

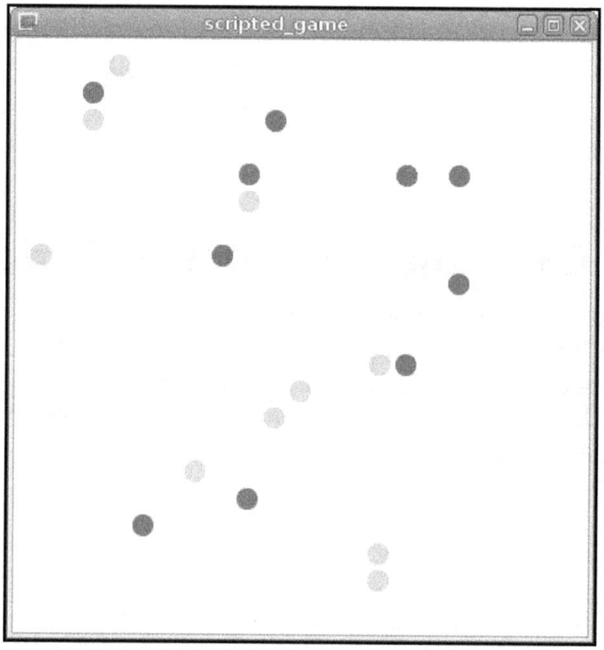

Each player must provide a JavaScript function that receives an entity object and returns its new position. This function will be called when one of the player's entities should move. Additionally, the player may provide an initialization function that will be called at the beginning of the game. The state of the board and entities on it will be exposed through a property of the global JavaScript object.

In our game, the players will compete to create the best survival strategy. Once the game is started, the players have no control over the entities, and the provided JavaScript functions must account for any possible game situation. When only entities of one player remain on the board, that player wins. The rules allow any number of players to participate, although we will only have two players in our example.

Time for action – Implementing the game engine

We will use the Graphics View framework to implement the board visualization. We will not provide too many details about the implementation, since we focus on scripting in this chapter. The basic skills you learned in `Chapter 4`, *Custom 2D Graphics with Graphics View*, should be enough for you to implement this game. The full code of this example is provided with the book. However, we will highlight the architecture of the project and briefly describe how it works.

The game engine implementation consists of two classes:

- The `Scene` class (derived from `QGraphicsScene`) manages the graphics scene, creates items, and implements the general game logic
- The `Entity` class (derived from `QGraphicsEllipseItem`) represents a single game entity on the board

Each `Entity` object is a circle with 0.4 radius and (0, 0) center. It is initialized in the constructor, using the following code:

```
setRect(-0.4, -0.4, 0.8, 0.8);
setPen(Qt::NoPen);
```

We will use the `pos` property (inherited from `QGraphicsItem`) to move the circle on the board. The tiles of the board will have a unit size, so we can just treat `pos` as integer `QPoint` instead of `QPointF` with `double` coordinates. We will zoom in to the graphics view to achieve the desired visible size of the entities.

The `Entity` class has two special properties with getters and setters. The `team` property is the number of the player this entity belongs to. This property also defines the color of the circle:

```
void Entity::setTeam(int team) {
    m_team = team;
    QColor color;
    switch(team) {
```

```
        case 0:
            color = Qt::green;
            break;
        case 1:
            color = Qt::red;
            break;
        }
        setBrush(color);
}
```

The `alive` flag indicates whether the entity is still in play. For simplicity, we will not immediately delete the killed entity objects. We will just hide them instead:

```
void Entity::setAlive(bool alive)
{
    m_alive = alive;
    setVisible(alive);
    //...
}
```

Let's turn our attention to the `Scene` class. First, it defines some game configuration options:

- The `fieldSize` property determines the two-dimensional size of the board
- The `teamSize` property determines how many entities each player has at the beginning of the game
- The `stepDuration` property determines the number of milliseconds passed between executing the next round of turns

The setter of the `fieldSize` property adjusts the scene rect so that the graphics view is correctly resized at the beginning of the game:

```
void Scene::setFieldSize(const QSize &fieldSize)
{
    m_fieldSize = fieldSize;
    setSceneRect(-1, -1,
                 m_fieldSize.width() + 2,
                 m_fieldSize.height() + 2);
}
```

The execution of each round of the game will be done in the `step()` function. In the constructor, we initialize a `QTimer` object responsible for calling this function:

```
m_stepTimer = new QTimer(this);
connect(m_stepTimer, &QTimer::timeout,
        this, &Scene::step);
m_stepTimer->setInterval(1000);
```

In the `setStepDuration()` function, we simply change the interval of this timer.

The `QVector<Entity*> m_entities` private field of the `Scene` class will contain all the entities in play. The game is started by calling the `start()` function. Let's take a look at it:

```
void Scene::start() {
    const int TEAM_COUNT = 2;
    for(int i = 0; i < m_teamSize; i++) {
        for(int team = 0; team < TEAM_COUNT; team++) {
            Entity* entity = new Entity(this);
            entity->setTeam(team);
            QPoint pos;
            do {
                pos.setX(qrand() % m_fieldSize.width());
                pos.setY(qrand() % m_fieldSize.height());
            } while(itemAt(pos, QTransform()));
            entity->setPos(pos);
            addItem(entity);
            m_entities << entity;
        }
    }
    //...
    m_stepTimer->start();
}
```

We create the requested number of entities for each team and place them at random locations on the board. If we happen to choose an already occupied place, we go on the next iteration of the `do-while` loop and choose another location. Next, we add the new item to the scene and to the `m_entities` vector. Finally, we start our timer so that the `step()` function will be called periodically.

In the `main()` function, we initialize the random number generator because we want to get new random numbers each time:

```
qsrand(QDateTime::currentMSecsSinceEpoch());
```

Then, we create and initialize the `Scene` object, and we create a `QGraphicsView` to display our scene.

The game engine is almost ready. We only need to implement the scripting.

Time for action – Exposing the game state to the JS engine

Before we move on to executing the players' scripts, we need to create a `QJSEngine` and insert some information into its global object. The scripts will use this information to decide the optimal move.

First, we add the `QJSEngine m_jsEngine` private field to the `Scene` class. Next, we create a new `SceneProxy` class and derive it from `QObject`. This class will expose the permitted API of `Scene` to the scripts. We pass a pointer to the `Scene` object to the constructor of the `SceneProxy` object and store it in a private variable:

```
SceneProxy::SceneProxy(Scene *scene) :
    QObject(scene), m_scene(scene)
{
}
```

Add two invokable methods to the class declaration:

```
Q_INVOKABLE QSize size() const;
Q_INVOKABLE QJSValue entities() const;
```

The implementation of the `size()` function is pretty straightforward:

```
QSize SceneProxy::size() const {
    return m_scene->fieldSize();
}
```

However, the `entities()` function is a bit trickier. We cannot add `Entity` objects to the JS engine because they are not based on `QObject`. Even if we could, we prefer to create a proxy class for entities as well.

Let's do this right now. Create the `EntityProxy` class, derive it from `QObject`, and pass a pointer to the underlying `Entity` object to the constructor, like we did in `SceneProxy`. Declare two invokable functions and a signal in the new class:

```
class EntityProxy : public QObject
{
```

```
    Q_OBJECT
public:
    explicit EntityProxy(Entity *entity, QObject *parent = nullptr);
    Q_INVOKABLE int team() const;
    Q_INVOKABLE QPoint pos() const;
    //...
signals:
    void killed();
private:
    Entity *m_entity;
};
```

Implementation of the methods just forward the calls to the underlying `Entity` object:

```
int EntityProxy::team() const
{
    return m_entity->team();
}

QPoint EntityProxy::pos() const
{
    return m_entity->pos().toPoint();
}
```

The `Entity` class will be responsible for creating its own proxy object. Add the following private fields to the `Entity` class:

```
EntityProxy *m_proxy;
QJSValue m_proxyValue;
```

The `m_proxy` field will hold the proxy object. The `m_proxyValue` field will contain the reference to the same object added to the JS engine. Initialize these fields in the constructor:

```
m_proxy = new EntityProxy(this, scene);
m_proxyValue = scene->jsEngine()->newQObject(m_proxy);
```

We modify the `Entity::setAlive()` function to emit the `killed()` signal when the entity is killed:

```
void Entity::setAlive(bool alive)
{
    m_alive = alive;
    setVisible(alive);
```

```
        if (!alive) {
            emit m_proxy->killed();
        }
    }
```

It's generally considered bad practice to emit signals from outside the class that owns the signal. If the source of the signal is another `QObject`-based class, you should create a separate signal in that class and connect it to the destination signal. In our case, we cannot do that, since `Entity` is not a `QObject`, so we choose to emit the signal directly to avoid further complication.

Create the `proxy()` and `proxyValue()` getters for these fields. We can now return to the `SceneProxy` implementation and use the entity proxy:

```
QJSValue SceneProxy::entities() const
{
    QJSValue list = m_scene->jsEngine()->newArray();
    int arrayIndex = 0;
    for(Entity *entity: m_scene->entities()) {
        if (entity->isAlive()) {
            list.setProperty(arrayIndex, entity->proxyValue());
            arrayIndex++;
        }
    }
    return list;
}
```

What just happened?

First, we ask the JS engine to create a new JavaScript array object. Then, we iterate over all entities and skip entities that were already killed. We use `QJSValue::setProperty` to add the proxy object of each entity to the array. We need to specify the index of the new array item, so we create the `arrayIndex` counter and increment it after each insertion. Finally, we return the array.

This function completes the `SceneProxy` class implementation. We just need to create a proxy object and add it to the JS engine in the constructor of the `Scene` class:

```
SceneProxy *sceneProxy = new SceneProxy(this);
m_sceneProxyValue = m_jsEngine.newQObject(sceneProxy);
```

Time for action – Loading scripts provided by users

Each player will provide their own strategy script, so the `Scene` class should have a field for storing all provided scripts:

```
QHash<int, QJSValue> m_teamScripts;
```

Let's provide the `setScript()` function that accepts the player's script and loads it into the JS engine:

```
void Scene::setScript(int team, const QString &script) {
    QJSValue value = m_jsEngine.evaluate(script);
    if (value.isError()) {
        qDebug() << "js error: " << value.toString();
        return;
    }
    if(!value.isObject()) {
        qDebug() << "script must return an object";
        return;
    }
    m_teamScripts[team] = value;
}
```

In this function, we try to evaluate the provided code. If the code returned a JavaScript object, we put it in the `m_teamScripts` hash table. We expect that the provided object has the `step` property containing the function that decides the entity's move. The object may also contain the `init` property that will be executed at the beginning of the game.

In the `main()` function, we load the scripts from the project's resources:

```
scene.setScript(0, loadFile(":/scripts/1.js"));
scene.setScript(1, loadFile(":/scripts/2.js"));
```

The `loadFile()` helper function simply loads the content of the file to a `QString`:

```
QString loadFile(const QString& path) {
    QFile file(path);
    if (!file.open(QFile::ReadOnly)) {
        qDebug() << "failed to open " << path;
        return QString();
    }
    return QString::fromUtf8(file.readAll());
}
```

If you want to allow users to provide their scripts without needing to recompile the project, you can accept the script files from the command-line arguments instead:

```
QStringList arguments = app.arguments();
if (arguments.count() < 3) {
    qDebug() << "usage: " << argv[0] << " path/to/script1.js
path/to/script2.js";
    return 1;
}
scene.setScript(0, loadFile(arguments[1]));
scene.setScript(1, loadFile(arguments[2]));
```

To set the command-line arguments for your project, switch to the **Projects** pane, select **Run** in the left column and locate the **Command line arguments** input box. The provided project contains two sample scripts in the `scripts` subdirectory.

Time for action – Executing the strategy scripts

First, we need to check whether the player provided an `init` function and execute it. We'll do it in the `Scene::start()` function:

```
for(int team = 0; team < TEAM_COUNT; team++) {
    QJSValue script = m_teamScripts.value(team);
    if (script.isUndefined()) {
        continue;
    }
    if (!script.hasProperty("init")) {
        continue;
    }
    m_jsEngine.globalObject().setProperty("field", m_sceneProxyValue);
    QJSValue scriptOutput = script.property("init").call();
    if (scriptOutput.isError()) {
        qDebug() << "script error: " << scriptOutput.toString();
        continue;
    }
}
```

In this code, we use `isUndefined()` to check whether the code was provided and parsed successfully. Next, we use `hasProperty()` to check whether the returned object contains the optional `init` function.

If we found it, we execute it using `QJSValue::call()`. We provide some information about the board by assigning our `SceneProxy` instance to the `field` property of the global object.

The most exciting part is the `step()` function that implements the actual game execution. Let's take a look at it:

```
void Scene::step() {
    for(Entity* entity: m_entities) {
        if (!entity->isAlive()) {
            continue;
        }
        QJSValue script = m_teamScripts.value(entity->team());
        if (script.isUndefined()) {
            continue;
        }
        m_jsEngine.globalObject().setProperty("field",
m_sceneProxyValue);

        QJSValue scriptOutput =
            script.property("step").call({ entity->proxyValue() });
        //...
    }
}
```

First, we iterate over all entities and skip the killed ones. Next, we use `Entity::team()` to determine which player this entity belongs to. We extract the corresponding strategy script from the `m_teamScripts` field and extract the `step` property from it. Then, we try to call it as a function and pass the current entity's proxy object as an argument. Let's see what we do with the script output:

```
if (scriptOutput.isError()) {
    qDebug() << "script error: " << scriptOutput.toString();
    continue;
}
QJSValue scriptOutputX = scriptOutput.property("x");
QJSValue scriptOutputY = scriptOutput.property("y");
if (!scriptOutputX.isNumber() || !scriptOutputY.isNumber()) {
    qDebug() << "invalid script output: " << scriptOutput.toVariant();
    continue;
}
QPoint pos(scriptOutputX.toInt(), scriptOutputY.toInt());
if (!moveEntity(entity, pos)) {
    qDebug() << "invalid move";
}
```

We try to interpret the function's return value as an object with `x` and `y` properties. If both properties contain numbers, we construct a `QPoint` from them and call our `moveEntity()` function that tries to execute the move chosen by the strategy.

We will not blindly trust the value returned by the user's script. Instead, we carefully check whether the move is valid:

```
bool Scene::moveEntity(Entity *entity, QPoint pos) {
    if (pos.x() < 0 || pos.y() < 0 ||
        pos.x() >= m_fieldSize.width() ||
        pos.y() >= m_fieldSize.height())
    {
        return false; // out of field bounds
    }
    QPoint posChange = entity->pos().toPoint() - pos;
    if (posChange.isNull()) {
        return true; // no change
    }
    if (qAbs(posChange.x()) > 1 || qAbs(posChange.y()) > 1) {
        return false; // invalid move
    }
    QGraphicsItem* item = itemAt(pos, QTransform());
    Entity* otherEntity = qgraphicsitem_cast<Entity*>(item);
    if (otherEntity) {
        otherEntity->setAlive(false);
    }
    entity->setPos(pos);
    return true;
}
```

We check that the new position is in bounds and is not too far from the entity's current position. If everything is correct, we execute the move. If another entity was on the destination tile, we mark it as killed. The function returns `true` if the move was successful.

That's it! Our game is ready to run. Let's create some strategy scripts to play with.

Time for action – Writing a strategy script

Our first script will simply select a random move:

```
{
    "step": function(current) {
        function getRandomInt(min, max) {
          return Math.floor(Math.random() * (max - min)) + min;
```

```
            }
            return {
                x: current.pos().x + getRandomInt(-1, 2),
                y: current.pos().y + getRandomInt(-1, 2),
            }
        }
    }
```

Of course, a more intelligent strategy can beat this script. You can find a more advanced script in the code bundle. First, when it sees an enemy entity nearby, it always goes for the kill. If there is no such enemy, it tries to move away from the closest ally, attempting to fill the whole board. This script will easily wipe out the randomly moving enemy:

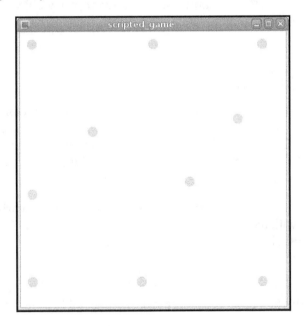

Of course, there is always room for improvement. Try to think of a better strategy and write a script that can win the game.

Have a go hero – Extending the game

There are a couple of ways for you to improve the game implementation. For example, you can detect when a player has won and display a pop-up message. You can also allow an arbitrary number of players.

You just need to replace the `TEAM_COUNT` constant with a new property in the `Scene` class and define more team colors. You can even create a GUI for users to provide their scripts instead of passing them as command-line arguments.

The scripting environment can also be improved. You can provide more helper functions (for example, a function to calculate the distance between two tiles) to make creating scripts easier. On the other hand, you can modify the rules and reduce the amount of available information so that, for example, each entity can only see other entities at a certain distance.

As discussed earlier, each script has ways to break the global object or emit the signals of the exposed C++ objects, affecting the other players. To prevent that, you can create a separate `QJSEngine` and a separate set of proxy objects for each player, effectively sandboxing them.

Python scripting

Qt QML is an environment that is designed to be part of the Qt world. Since not everyone knows or likes JavaScript, we will present another language that can easily be used to provide scripting environments for games that are created with Qt. Just be aware that this will not be an in-depth description of the environment—we will just show you the basics that can provide foundations for your own research.

A popular language used for scripting is Python. There are two variants of Qt bindings that are available for Python: PySide2 and PyQt. PySide2 is the official binding that is available under LGPL. PyQt is a third-party library that is available under GPL v3 and a commercial license.

PyQt is not available under LGPL, so for commercial closed-source products, you need to obtain a commercial license from Riverbank computing!

These bindings allow you to use the Qt API from within Python—you can write a complete Qt application using just Python. However, to call Python code from within C++, you will need a regular Python interpreter. Luckily, it is very easy to embed such an interpreter in a C++ application.

First, you will need Python installed, along with its development package. For example, for Debian-based systems, it is easiest to simply install the `libpythonX.Y-dev` package, where `X.Y` stands for the version of Python available in the repository:

```
sudo apt-get install libpython3.5-dev
```

We will use Python 3.5 in our example, but later minor versions should also be compatible with our code.

Then, you need to tell qmake to link your program against the library. For Linux, you can use `pkgconfig` to do this automatically:

```
CONFIG += link_pkgconfig no_keywords
# adjust the version number to suit your needs
PKGCONFIG += python-3.5m
```

> The `no_keywords` configuration option tells the build system to disable Qt-specific keywords (`signals`, `slots`, and `emit`). We have to do this because Python headers use the `slots` identifier that would conflict with the same Qt keyword. You can still access the Qt keywords if you write them as `Q_SIGNALS`, `Q_SLOTS`, and `Q_EMIT`.

For Windows, you need to manually pass information to the compiler:

```
CONFIG += no_keywords
INCLUDEPATH += C:\Python35\include
LIBS += -LC:\Python35\include -lpython35
```

To call Python code from within a Qt app, the simplest way is to use the following code:

```
#include <Python.h>
#include <QtCore>

int main(int argc, char **argv) {
    QCoreApplication app(argc, argv);
    Py_Initialize();
    const char *script = "print(\"Hello from Python\")";
    PyRun_SimpleString(script);
    Py_Finalize();
    return app.exec();
}
```

This code initializes a Python interpreter, then invokes a script by passing it directly as a string, and finally, it shuts down the interpreter before invoking Qt's event loop. Such code makes sense only for simple scripting. In real life, you'd want to pass some data to the script or fetch the result. For that, we have to write some more code. As the library exposes the C API only, let's write a nice Qt wrapper for it.

Time for action – Writing a Qt wrapper for embedding Python

As the first task, we will implement the last program using an object-oriented API. Create a new console project and add the following class to it:

```
class QtPython : public QObject {
    Q_OBJECT
public:
    QtPython(QObject *parent = 0);
    ~QtPython();
    void run(const QString &program);

private:
    QVector<wchar_t> programNameBuffer;
};
```

The implementation file should look like this:

```
#include <Python.h>
//...
QtPython::QtPython(QObject *parent) : QObject(parent) {
    QStringList args = qApp->arguments();
    if (args.count() > 0) {
        programNameBuffer.resize(args[0].count());
        args[0].toWCharArray(programNameBuffer.data());
        Py_SetProgramName(programNameBuffer.data());
    }
    Py_InitializeEx(0);
}

QtPython::~QtPython() {
    Py_Finalize();
}

void QtPython::run(const QString &program) {
    PyRun_SimpleString(qPrintable(program));
}
```

Then, add a `main()` function, as shown in the following snippet:

```
int main(int argc, char *argv[])
{
    QCoreApplication app(argc, argv);
    QtPython python;
    python.run("print('Hello from Python')");
    return 0;
}
```

Finally, open the `.pro` file and tell Qt to link with the Python library, as was shown earlier.

What just happened?

We created a class called `QtPython` that wraps the Python C API for us.

> **TIP:** Never use a `Q` prefix to call your custom classes, as this prefix is reserved for official Qt classes. This is to ensure that your code will never have a name clash with future code added to Qt. The Qt prefix, on the other hand, is meant to be used with classes that are extensions to Qt. You probably still shouldn't use it, but the probability of a name clash is much smaller and yields a lesser impact than clashes with an official class. It is best to come up with an application-specific prefix or use a namespace.

The class constructor creates a Python interpreter, and the class destructor destroys it. We use `Py_InitializeEx(0)`, which has the same functionality as `Py_Initialize()`, but it does not apply C signal handlers, as this is not something we would want when embedding Python. Prior to this, we use `Py_SetProgramName()` to inform the interpreter of our context. We also defined a `run()` method, taking `QString` and returning `void`. It uses `qPrintable()`, which is a convenience function that extracts a C string pointer from a `QString` object, which is then fed into `PyRun_SimpleString()`.

> **TIP:** Never store the output of `qPrintable()`, as it returns an internal pointer to a temporary byte array (this is equivalent to calling `toLocal8Bit().constData()` on a string). It is safe to use directly, but the byte array is destroyed immediately afterward; thus, if you store the pointer in a variable, the data may not be valid later when you try using that pointer.

The most difficult work when using embedded interpreters is to convert values between C++ and the types that the interpreter expects. With Qt Script, the `QScriptValue` type was used for this. We can implement something similar for our Python scripting environment.

Time for action – Converting data between C++ and Python

Create a new class and call it `QtPythonValue`:

```
class QtPythonValue {
public:
    QtPythonValue();
    QtPythonValue(const QtPythonValue &other);
    QtPythonValue& operator=(const QtPythonValue &other);

    QtPythonValue(int val);
    QtPythonValue(const QString &str);
    ~QtPythonValue();

    int toInt() const;
    QString toString() const;
    bool isNone() const;

private:
    QtPythonValue(PyObject *ptr);
    void incRef();
    void incRef(PyObject *val);
    void decRef();

    PyObject *m_value;
    friend class QtPython;
};
```

Next, implement the constructors, the assignment operator, and the destructor, as follows:

```
QtPythonValue::QtPythonValue() {
    incRef(Py_None);
}
QtPythonValue::QtPythonValue(const QtPythonValue &other) {
    incRef(other.m_value);
}
QtPythonValue::QtPythonValue(PyObject *ptr) {
    m_value = ptr;
```

```
}
QtPythonValue::QtPythonValue(const QString &str) {
    m_value = PyUnicode_FromString(qPrintable(str));
}
QtPythonValue::QtPythonValue(int val) {
    m_value = PyLong_FromLong(val);
}
QtPythonValue &QtPythonValue::operator=(const QtPythonValue &other) {
    if(m_value == other.m_value) {
        return *this;
    }
    decRef();
    incRef(other.m_value);
    return *this;
}
QtPythonValue::~QtPythonValue()
{
    decRef();
}
```

Then, implement the `incRef()` and `decRef()` functions:

```
void QtPythonValue::incRef(PyObject *val) {
    m_value = val;
    incRef();
}
void QtPythonValue::incRef() {
    if(m_value) {
        Py_INCREF(m_value);
    }
}
void QtPythonValue::decRef() {
    if(m_value) {
        Py_DECREF(m_value);
    }
}
```

Next, implement conversions from `QtPythonValue` to C++ types:

```
int QtPythonValue::toInt() const {
    return PyLong_Check(m_value) ? PyLong_AsLong(m_value) : 0;
}

QString QtPythonValue::toString() const {
    return PyUnicode_Check(m_value) ?
        QString::fromUtf8(PyUnicode_AsUTF8(m_value)) : QString();
```

```
}

bool QtPythonValue::isNone() const {
    return m_value == Py_None;
}
```

Finally, let's modify the `main()` function to test our new code:

```
int main(int argc, char *argv[]) {
    QCoreApplication app(argc, argv);
    QtPython python;
    QtPythonValue integer = 7, string = QStringLiteral("foobar"),
none;
    qDebug() << integer.toInt() << string.toString() << none.isNone();
    return 0;
}
```

When you run the program, you will see that the conversion between C++ and Python works correctly in both directions.

What just happened?

The `QtPythonValue` class wraps a `PyObject` pointer (through the `m_value` member), providing a nice interface to convert between what the interpreter expects and our Qt types. Let's see how this is done. First, take a look at the three private methods: two versions of `incRef()` and one `decRef()`. `PyObject` contains an internal reference counter that counts the number of handles on the contained value. When that counter drops to 0, the object can be destroyed. Our three methods use adequate Python C API calls to increase or decrease the counter in order to prevent memory leaks and keep Python's garbage collector happy.

The second important aspect is that the class defines a private constructor that takes a `PyObject` pointer, effectively creating a wrapper over the given value. The constructor is private; however, the `QtPython` class is declared as a friend of `QtPythonValue`, which means that only `QtPython` and `QtPythonValue` can instantiate values by passing `PyObject` pointers to it. Now, let's take a look at public constructors.

The default constructor creates an object pointing to a `None` value, which represents the absence of a value. The copy constructor and assignment operator are pretty standard, taking care of bookkeeping of the reference counter. Then, we have two constructors—one taking `int` and the other taking a `QString` value. They use appropriate Python C API calls to obtain a `PyObject` representation of the value.

Note that these calls already increase the reference count for us, so we don't have to do it ourselves.

The code ends with a destructor that decreases the reference counter and three methods that provide safe conversions from `QtPythonValue` to appropriate Qt/C++ types.

Have a go hero – Implementing the remaining conversions

Now, you should be able to implement other constructors and conversions for `QtPythonValue` that operates on the `float`, `bool`, or even on `QDate` and `QTime` types. Try implementing them yourself. If needed, take a look at the Python documentation to find appropriate calls that you should use.

> The documentation for Python 3.5 is available online at `https://docs.python.org/3.5/`. If you've installed a different Python version, you can find the documentation for your version on the same website.

We'll give you a head start by providing a skeleton implementation of how to convert `QVariant` to `QtPythonValue`. This is especially important, because Python makes use of two types whose equivalents are not available in C++, namely, tuples and dictionaries. We will need them later, so having a proper implementation is crucial. Here's the code:

```
QtPythonValue::QtPythonValue(const QVariant &variant)
{
    switch(variant.type()) {
    case QVariant::Invalid:
        incRef(Py_None);
        return;
    case QVariant::String:
        m_value =
PyUnicode_FromString(qPrintable(variant.toString()));
        return;
    case QVariant::Int:
        m_value = PyLong_FromLong(variant.toInt());
        return;
    case QVariant::LongLong:
        m_value = PyLong_FromLongLong(variant.toLongLong());
        return;
    case QVariant::List: {
```

```
        QVariantList list = variant.toList();
        const int listSize = list.size();
        PyObject *tuple = PyTuple_New(listSize);
        for(int i = 0; i < listSize; ++i) {
            PyTuple_SetItem(tuple, i,
QtPythonValue(list.at(i)).m_value);
        }
        m_value = tuple;
        return;
    }
    case QVariant::Map: {
        QVariantMap map = variant.toMap();
        PyObject *dict = PyDict_New();
        for(auto iter = map.begin(); iter != map.end(); ++iter) {
            PyDict_SetItemString(dict, qPrintable(iter.key()),
                                 QtPythonValue(iter.value()).m_value);
        }
        m_value = dict;
        return;
    }
    default:
        incRef(Py_None);
        return;
    }
}
```

The highlighted code shows how to create a tuple (which is a list of arbitrary elements) from `QVariantList` and how to create a dictionary (which is an associative array) from `QVariantMap`. You should also add a `QtPythonValue` constructor that takes `QStringList` and produces a tuple.

We have written quite a lot of code now, but there is no way of binding any data from our programs with Python scripting so far. Let's change that.

Time for action – Calling functions and returning values

The next task is to provide ways to invoke Python functions and return values from scripts. Let's start by providing a richer `run()` API. Implement the following method in the `QtPython` class:

```
QtPythonValue QtPython::run(const QString &program,
    const QtPythonValue &globals, const QtPythonValue &locals)
{
```

```
    PyObject *retVal = PyRun_String(qPrintable(program),
        Py_file_input, globals.m_value, locals.m_value);
    return QtPythonValue(retVal);
}
```

We'll also need a functionality to import Python modules. Add the following methods to the class:

```
QtPythonValue QtPython::import(const QString &name) const
{
    return QtPythonValue(PyImport_ImportModule(qPrintable(name)));
}

QtPythonValue QtPython::addModule(const QString &name) const
{
    PyObject *retVal = PyImport_AddModule(qPrintable(name));
    Py_INCREF(retVal);
    return QtPythonValue(retVal);
}

QtPythonValue QtPython::dictionary(const QtPythonValue &module) const
{
    PyObject *retVal = PyModule_GetDict(module.m_value);
    Py_INCREF(retVal);
    return QtPythonValue(retVal);
}
```

The last piece of the code is to extend `QtPythonValue` with this code:

```
bool QtPythonValue::isCallable() const {
    return PyCallable_Check(m_value);
}

QtPythonValue QtPythonValue::attribute(const QString &name) const {
    return QtPythonValue(PyObject_GetAttrString(m_value,
qPrintable(name)));
}

bool QtPythonValue::setAttribute(const QString &name, const
QtPythonValue &value) {
    int retVal = PyObject_SetAttrString(m_value, qPrintable(name),
value.m_value);
    return retVal != -1;
}

QtPythonValue QtPythonValue::call(const QVariantList &arguments) const
{
    return QtPythonValue(
```

```
        PyObject_CallObject(m_value,
QtPythonValue(arguments).m_value));
}

QtPythonValue QtPythonValue::call(const QStringList &arguments) const
{
    return QtPythonValue(
        PyObject_CallObject(m_value,
QtPythonValue(arguments).m_value));
}
```

Finally, you can modify `main()` to test the new functionality:

```
int main(int argc, char *argv[])
{
    QCoreApplication app(argc, argv);
    QtPython python;

    QtPythonValue mainModule = python.addModule("__main__");
    QtPythonValue dict = python.dictionary(mainModule);
    python.run("foo = (1, 2, 3)", dict, dict);
    python.run("print(foo)", dict, dict);

    QtPythonValue module = python.import("os");
    QtPythonValue chdir = module.attribute("chdir");
    chdir.call(QStringList() << "/home");
    QtPythonValue func = module.attribute("getcwd");
    qDebug() << func.call(QVariantList()).toString();

    return 0;
}
```

You can replace `/home` with a directory of your choice. Then, you can run the program.

What just happened?

We did two tests in the last program. First, we used the new `run()` method, passing to it the code that is to be executed and two dictionaries that define the current execution context—the first dictionary contains global symbols and the second contains local symbols. The dictionaries come from Python's `__main__` module (which, among other things, defines the `print` function). The `run()` method may modify the contents of the two dictionaries—the first call defines the tuple called `foo`, and the second call prints it to the standard output.

The second test calls a function from an imported module; in this case, we call two functions from the `os` module—the first function, `chdir`, changes the current working directory, and the other, called `getcwd`, returns the current working directory. The convention is that we should pass a tuple to `call()`, where we pass the needed parameters. The first function takes a string as a parameter; therefore, we pass a `QStringList` object, assuming that there is a `QtPythonValue` constructor that converts `QStringList` to a tuple (you need to implement it if you haven't done it already). Since the second function does not take any parameters, we pass an empty tuple to the call. In the same way, you can provide your own modules and call functions from them, query the results, inspect dictionaries, and so on. This is a pretty good start for an embedded Python interpreter. Remember that a proper component should have some error checking code to avoid crashing the whole application.

You can extend the functionality of the interpreter in many ways. You can even use PyQt5 to use Qt bindings in scripts, combining Qt/C++ code with Qt/Python code.

Have a go hero – Wrapping Qt objects into Python objects

At this point, you should be experienced enough to try and implement a wrapper for the `QObject` instances to expose signals and slots to Python scripting. If you decide to pursue the goal, `https://docs.python.org/3/` will be your best friend, especially the section about extending Python with C++. Remember that `QMetaObject` provides information about the properties and methods of Qt objects and `QMetaObject::invokeMethod()` allows you to execute a method by its name. This is not an easy task, so don't be hard on yourself if you are not able to complete it. You can always return to it once you gain more experience in using Qt and Python.

Before you head on to the next chapter, try testing your knowledge about scripting in Qt.

Pop quiz

Q1. Which is the method that you can use to execute JavaScript code?

1. `QJSValue::call()`
2. `QJSEngine::evaluate()`
3. `QJSEngine::fromScriptValue()`

Q2. What is the name of the class that serves as a bridge to exchange data between JS engine and C++?

1. `QObject`
2. `QJSValue`
3. `QVariant`

Q3. If you want to expose a C++ object to the script, which class must this object be derived from?

1. `QObject`
2. `QJSValue`
3. `QGraphicsItem`

Q4. Which of the following kinds of functions is not available to JavaScript code?

1. Signals
2. `Q_INVOKABLE` methods
3. Slots
4. Global functions

Q5. When is a `PyObject` instance destroyed?

1. When its value is set to `Py_None`
2. When its internal reference counter drops to 0
3. When the corresponding `QtPythonValue` is destroyed

Summary

In this chapter, you learned that providing a scripting environment to your games opens up new possibilities. Implementing a functionality using scripting languages is usually faster than doing the full write-compile-test cycle with C++, and you can even use the skills and creativity of your users who have no understanding of the internals of your game engine to make your games better and more feature-rich. You were shown how to use `QJSEngine`, which blends the C++ and JavaScript worlds together by exposing Qt objects to JavaScript and making cross-language signal-slot connections.

You also learned the basics of scripting with Python. There are other scripting languages available (for example, Lua), and many of them can be used along with Qt. Using the experience gained in this chapter, you should even be able to bring other scripting environments to your programs, as most embeddable interpreters offer similar approaches to that of Python.

In the next chapter, you will be introduced to Qt Quick—a library for creating fluid and dynamic user interfaces. It may not sound like it's related to this chapter, but Qt Quick is based on Qt QML. In fact, any Qt Quick application contains a `QJSEngine` object that executes JavaScript code of the application. Being familiar with this system will help you understand how such applications work. You will also be able to apply the skills you've learned here when you need to access C++ objects from Qt Quick and vice versa. Welcome to the world of Qt Quick.

You are treated [illegible] class of script [illegible] with [illegible] them [illegible] other scripts [illegible] [illegible] along with Qt. [illegible] this chapter you should [illegible] other [illegible] [illegible] debug interpreters [illegible] [illegible] Python.

In the [illegible] you [illegible] introduced [illegible] library [illegible] and dynamic [illegible] later. It may not [illegible] Qt [illegible] object that executes [illegible] will help you understand how [illegible] applications work [illegible] and [illegible] QtScript [illegible] Qt.

11
Introduction to Qt Quick

In this chapter, you will be introduced to a technology called **Qt Quick** that allows us to implement resolution-independent user interfaces with lots of eye-candy, animations, and effects that can be combined with regular Qt code that implements the logic of the application. You will learn the basics of the QML declarative language that forms the foundation of Qt Quick. You will create a simple Qt Quick application and see the advantages offered by the declarative approach.

The main topics covered in this chapter are these:

- QML basics
- Overview of Qt modules
- Using Qt Quick Designer
- Utilizing Qt Quick modules
- Property bindings and signal handling
- Qt Quick and C++
- States and transitions

Declarative UI programming

Although it is technically possible to use Qt Quick by writing C++ code, the module is accompanied by a dedicated programming language called **QML** (**Qt Modeling Language**). QML is an easy to read and understand declarative language that describes the world as a hierarchy of components that interact and relate to one another. It uses a JSON-like syntax and allows us to use imperative JavaScript expressions as well as dynamic property bindings. So, what is a declarative language, anyway?

Declarative programming is one of the programming paradigms that dictates that the program describes the logic of the computation without specifying how this result should be obtained. In contrast to imperative programming, where the logic is expressed as a list of explicit steps forming an algorithm that directly modifies the intermediate program state, a declarative approach focuses on what the ultimate result of the operation should be.

Time for action – Creating the first project

Let's create a project to better understand what QML is. In Qt Creator, select **File** and then **New File or Project** in the main menu. Choose **Application** in the left column and select the **Qt Quick Application - Empty** template. Name the project as `calculator` and go through the rest of the wizard.

Qt Creator created a sample application that displays an empty window. Let's examine the project files. The first file is the usual `main.cpp`:

```
#include <QGuiApplication>
#include <QQmlApplicationEngine>

int main(int argc, char *argv[])
{
    QGuiApplication app(argc, argv);
    QQmlApplicationEngine engine;
    engine.load(QUrl(QStringLiteral("qrc:/main.qml")));
    if (engine.rootObjects().isEmpty())
        return -1;
    return app.exec();
}
```

This code simply creates the application object, instantiates the QML engine, and asks it to load the `main.qml` file from the resources. If an error occurs, `rootObjects()` will return an empty list, and the application will terminate. If the QML file was loaded successfully, the application enters the main event loop.

The `*.qrc` file is a resource file. The concept of resource files should be familiar to you from `Chapter 3`, *Qt GUI Programming*. Basically, it contains the list of arbitrary project files that are required for project execution. During compilation, the contents of these files are embedded into the executable. You can then retrieve the content at runtime by specifying a virtual filename, such as `qrc:/main.qml` in the preceding code. You can expand the `Resources` section of the Project tree further to see all files added to the resource file.

In the sample project, `qml.qrc` references a QML file named `main.qml`. If you don't see it in the project tree, expand `Resources`, `qml.qrc`, and then `/` sections. The `main.qml` file is the top-level QML file that is loaded into the engine. Let's take a look at it:

```
import QtQuick 2.9
import QtQuick.Window 2.2

Window {
    visible: true
    width: 640
    height: 480
    title: qsTr("Hello World")
}
```

This file *declares* what objects should be created at the start of the application. As it uses some QML types provided by Qt, it contains two `import` directives at the top of the file. Each `import` directive contains the name and the version of the imported module. In this example, `import QtQuick.Window 2.2` enables us to use the `Window` QML type provided by this module.

The rest of the file is the declaration of the objects the engine should create. The `Window { ... }` construction tells QML to create a new object of the `Window` type. The code within this section assigns values to properties of this object. We explicitly assign a constant to the `visible`, `width`, and `height` properties of the window object. The `qsTr()` function is the translation function, just like `tr()` in C++ code. It returns the passed string without change by default. The `title` property will contain the result of evaluating the passed expression.

Time for action – Editing QML

Let's add some content to our window. Edit the `main.qml` file with the following code:

```
import QtQuick 2.9
import QtQuick.Window 2.2
import QtQuick.Controls 2.2
Window {
    visible: true
    width: 640
    height: 480
    title: qsTr("Hello World")
    TextField {
```

```
            text: "Edit me"
            anchors {
                top: parent.top
                left: parent.left
            }
        }
        Label {
            text: "Hello world"
            anchors {
                bottom: parent.bottom
                left: parent.left
            }
        }
    }
```

When you run the project, you will see a text field and a label in the window:

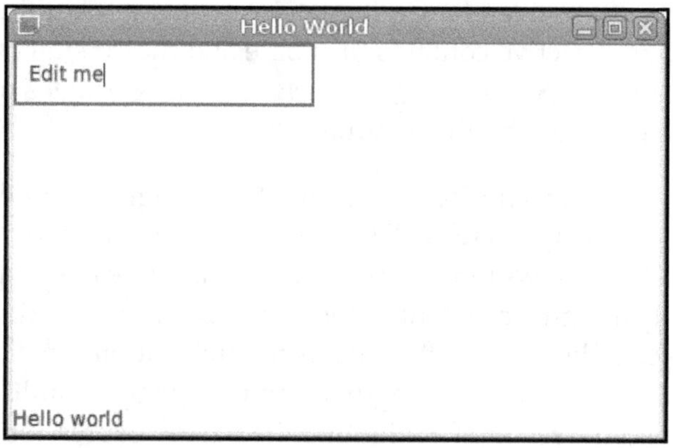

What just happened?

First, we added an import statement to make the `QtQuick.Controls` module available in the current scope. If you're not sure which version to use, invoke Qt Creator's code completion and use the most recent version. Due to the new import, we can now use the `TextField` and `Label` QML types in our QML file.

Next, we declared two **children** of the top-level `Window` object. QML objects form a parent-child relationship, much like `QObject` in C++. However, you don't need to explicitly assign parents to items. Instead, you declare the object within the declaration of its parent, and QML will automatically ensure that relationship. In our example, the `TextField { ... }` part tells QML to create a new QML object of the `TextField` type.

Since this declaration lies within the `Window { ... }` declaration, the `TextField` object will have the `Window` object as its parent. The same applies to the `Label` object. You can create multiple levels of nesting in a single file, if needed. You can use the `parent` property to access the parent item of the current item.

After declaring a new object, we assign values to its properties within its declaration. The `text` property is self-explanatory—it contains the text displayed in the UI. Note that the `TextField` object allows the user to edit the text. When the text is edited in the UI, the `text` property of the object will reflect the new value.

Finally, we assign value to the `anchors` **property group** to position the items as we like. We put the text field in the top-left corner of the window and put the label in the bottom-left corner. This step requires a more thorough explanation.

Property groups

Before we discuss anchors, let's talk about property groups in general. This is a new concept introduced in QML. Property groups are used when there are multiple properties with a similar purpose. For example, the `Label` type has a number of properties related to the font. They can be implemented as separate properties; consider the following example:

```
Label {
    // this code does not work
    fontFamily: "Helvetica"
    fontSize: 12
    fontItalic: true
}
```

However, such repetitive code is hard to read. Luckily, font properties are implemented as a property group, so you can set them using the **group notation** syntax:

```
Label {
    font {
        family: "Helvetica"
        pointSize: 12
        italic: true
    }
}
```

This code is much cleaner! Note that there is no colon character after `font`, so you can tell that this is a property group assignment.

In addition, if you only need to set one subproperty of the group, you can use the **dot notation** syntax:

```
Label {
    font.pointSize: 12
}
```

The dot notation is also used to refer to subproperties in the documentation. Note that you should prefer group notation if you need to set more than one subproperty.

That's all you need to know about property groups. Besides `font`, you can find many other property groups in some QML types, for example, `border`, `easing`, and `anchors`.

Anchors

Anchors allow you to manage item geometry by attaching certain points of some objects to points of another object. These points are called anchor lines. The following diagram shows the anchor lines that are available for each Qt Quick item:

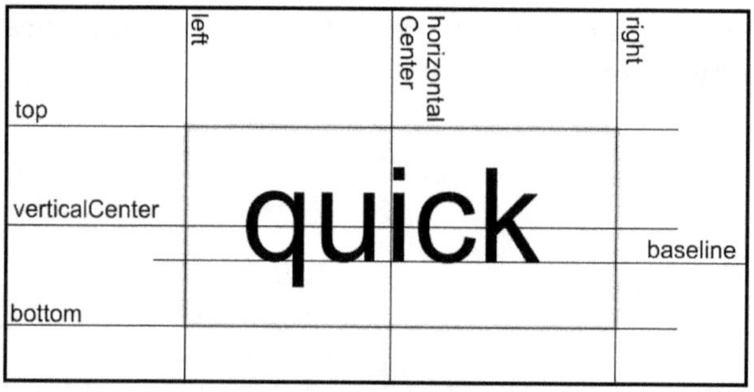

You can establish bindings between anchor lines to manage relative positioning of items. For each anchor line, there is a property that returns the current coordinate of that anchor line. For example, the `left` property returns the *x* coordinate of the left border of the item, and the `top` property returns the *y* coordinate of its top border. Next, each object contains the `anchors` property group that allows you to set coordinates of the anchor line for that item. For example, the `anchors.left` property can be used to request the position of the left border of the object. You can use these two kinds of properties together to specify relative positions of objects:

```
anchors.top: otherObject.bottom
```

This code declares that the top anchor line of the object must be bound to the bottom anchor line of the other object. It's also possible to specify a margin for such binding through properties, such as `anchors.topMargin`.

The `anchors.fill` property is the shortcut for binding the `top`, `bottom`, `left`, and `right` anchors to the specified object's respective anchor lines. As a result, the item will have the same geometry as the other object. The following code snippet is often used to expand the item to the whole area of its parent:

```
anchors.fill: parent
```

Time for action – Positioning items relative to each other

In our previous example, we used the following code to position the label:

```
anchors {
    bottom: parent.bottom
    left: parent.left
}
```

You should be able to understand this code by now. The `parent` property returns the reference to the parent QML object. In our case, it's the window. The `parent.bottom` expression returns the *y* coordinate of the parent's bottom anchor line. By assigning this expression to the `anchors.bottom` property, we ensure that the bottom anchor line of the label stays in the same position as the bottom anchor line of the window. The *x* coordinate is restricted in a similar way.

Now, let's see whether we can position the label just below the text field. In order to do that, we need to bind the `anchors.top` property of the label to the bottom anchor line of the text field. However, we have no way to access the text field from within the label yet. We can fix this by defining the `id` property of the text field:

```
TextField {
    id: textField
    text: "Edit me"
    anchors {
        top: parent.top
        left: parent.left
    }
}
Label {
    text: "Hello world"
```

```
        anchors {
            top: textField.bottom
            topMargin: 20
            left: parent.left
        }
    }
```

Setting an ID is similar to assigning the object to a variable. We can now use the `textField` variable to refer to our `TextField` object. The label is now positioned 20 pixels below the text field.

QML types, components, and documents

QML introduces some new concepts that you should be familiar with. A **QML type** is a concept similar to C++ class. Any value or object in QML should have some type and should be exposed to JavaScript code in a certain way. There are two major kinds of QML types:

- **Basic types** are types that hold a concrete value and do not refer to any other objects, for example, `string` or `point`
- **Object types** are types that can be used to create objects with certain functionality and consistent interface

Basic QML types are similar to C++ primitive types and data structures, such as `QPoint`. Object types are closer to widget classes, such as `QLineEdit`, but they are not necessarily tied to GUI.

There are numerous QML types provided by Qt. We've already used the `Window`, `TextField`, and `Label` types in our previous examples. You can also create your own custom QML types with unique functionality and behavior. The simplest way to create a QML type is to add a new `.qml` file with a capitalized name to the project. The base file name defines the name of the created QML type. For example, the `MyTextField.qml` file will declare a new `MyTextField` QML type.

Any complete and valid QML code is called a **document**. Any valid QML file contains a document. It's also possible to load documents from any source (for example, over the network). A **component** is a document loaded into the QML engine.

How does it work?

Qt Quick infrastructure hides most of the implementation details from the developer and allows you to keep your application code clean. Nevertheless, it's always important to understand what's going on.

The **QML engine** is a C++ class that understands QML code and executes the required actions to make it work. In particular, the QML engine is responsible for creating objects according to the requested hierarchy, assigning values to properties, and executing event handlers in response to events.

While QML language itself is quite far from JavaScript, it allows you to use any JavaScript expressions and code blocks for calculating values and handling events. This means that the QML engine must be capable of executing JavaScript. Under the hood, the implementation uses a very fast JavaScript engine, so you shouldn't usually worry about the performance of your JavaScript code.

The JavaScript code should be able to interact with QML objects, so every QML object is exposed as a JavaScript object with corresponding properties and methods. This integration uses the same mechanism that we learned in `Chapter 10`, *Scripting*. In C++ code, you have some control over the objects embedded into the QML engine and can even create new objects. We will get back to this topic later in the chapter.

While QML is a general purpose language, Qt Quick is a QML-based module that focuses on user interfaces. It provides a two-dimensional hardware accelerated canvas that contains a hierarchy of interconnected items. Unlike Qt Widgets, Qt Quick was designed to support visual effects and animations efficiently, so you can use its powers without significant performance degradation.

Qt Quick views are not based on a web browser engine. Browsers tend to be quite heavy, especially for mobile devices. However, you can use a web engine explicitly when you need it by adding the `WebView` or `WebEngine` object to your QML files.

Time for action – Property binding

QML is much more powerful than simple JSON. Instead of specifying an explicit value for a property, you can use an arbitrary JavaScript expression that will be automatically evaluated and assigned to the property. For example, the following code will display "ab" in the label:

```
Label {
    text: "a" + "b"
    //...
}
```

You can also refer to properties of the other objects in the file. As we saw earlier, you can use the `textEdit` variable to set relative position of the label. This is one example of a property binding. If the value of the `textField.bottom` expression changes for some reason, the `anchors.top` property of the label will be automatically updated with the new value. QML allows you to use the same mechanism for every property. To make the effect more obvious, let's assign an expression to the label's text property:

```
Label {
    text: "Your input: " + textField.text
    //...
}
```

Now the label's text will be changed according to this expression. When you change the text in the input field, the text of the label will be automatically updated!:

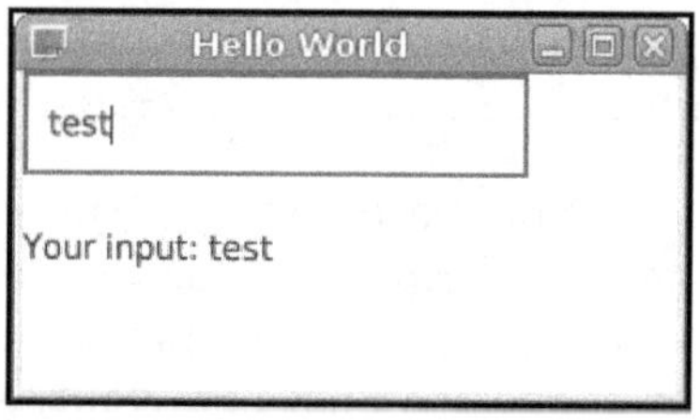

The property binding differs from a regular value assignment and binds the value of the property to the value of the supplied JavaScript expression. Whenever the expression's value changes, the property will reflect that change in its own value. Note that the order of statements in a QML document does not matter as you declare relations between properties.

This example shows one of the advantages of the declarative approach. We didn't have to connect signals or explicitly determine when the text should be changed. We just *declared* that the text should be influenced by the input field, and the QML engine will enforce that relation automatically.

If the expression is complex, you can replace it with a multiline block of text that works as a function:

```
text: {
    var x = textField.text;
    return "(" + x + ")";
}
```

You can also declare and use a named JavaScript function within any QML object declaration:

```
Label {
    function calculateText() {
        var x = textField.text;
        return "(" + x + ")";
    }
    text: calculateText()
    //...
}
```

A limitation of automatic property updates

QML does its best to determine when the function value may change, but it is not omnipotent. For our last function, it can easily determine that the function result depends on the value of the `textField.text` property, so it will re-evaluate the binding if that value changes. However, in some cases, it can't know that a function may return a different value the next time it is called, and in such situations, the statement will not be re-evaluated. Consider the following property binding:

```
Label {
    function colorByTime() {
        var d = new Date();
        var seconds = d.getSeconds();
        if(seconds < 15) return "red";
        if(seconds < 30) return "green";
        if(seconds < 45) return "blue";
        return "purple";
    }
    color: colorByTime()
    //...
```

```
}
```

The color will be set at the start of the application, but it will not work properly. QML will only call the `colorByTime()` function once when the object is initialized, and it will never call it again. This is because it has no way of knowing how often this function must be called. We will see how to overcome this in `Chapter 12`, *Customization in Qt Quick*.

Overview of QML types provided by Qt

Before we continue to work on our QML application, let's see what the built-in libraries are capable of. This will allow us to pick the right modules for the task. Qt provides a lot of useful QML types. In this section, we will provide an overview of the most useful modules available in Qt 5.9.

The following modules are important for building user interfaces:

- The `QtQuick` base module provides functionality related to drawing, event handling, positioning of elements, transformations, and many other useful types
- `QtQuick.Controls` provides basic controls for user interfaces, such as buttons and input fields
- `QtQuick.Dialogs` contains file dialogs, color dialogs, and message boxes
- `QtQuick.Extras` provides additional controls, such as dials, tumblers, and gauges
- `QtQuick.Window` enables window management
- `QtQuick.Layouts` provide layouts for automatic positioning of objects on screen
- `UIComponents` provides tab widget, progress bar, and switch types
- `QtWebView` allows you to add web content to the application
- `QtWebEngine` provides more sophisticated web browser functionality

If you want to implement rich graphics, the following modules may be of help:

- `QtCanvas3D` provides a canvas for 3D rendering
- `Qt3D` modules provide access to real-time simulation systems supporting 2D and 3D rendering
- `QtCharts` allows you to create sophisticated charts

- `QtDataVisualization` can be used to build 3D visualizations of datasets
- `QtQuick.Particles` allows you to add particle effects
- `QtGraphicalEffects` can apply graphical effects (such as blur or shadow) to other Qt Quick objects

Qt provides a lot of functionality commonly required on mobile devices:

- `QtBluetooth` supports basic communication with other devices over Bluetooth
- `QtLocation` allows you to display maps and find routes
- `QtPositioning` provides information about the current location
- `QtNfc` allows you to utilize NFC hardware
- `QtPurchasing` implements in-app purchases
- `QtSensors` provides access to on-board sensors, such as accelerometer or gyroscope
- `QtQuick.VirtualKeyboard` provides an implementation of an onscreen keyboard

Finally, there are two modules providing multimedia capabilities:

- `QtMultimedia` provides access to audio and video playback, audio recording, camera, and radio
- `QtAudioEngine` implements 3D positional audio playback

There are many more QML modules that we didn't mention here. You can find the full list on the **All QML Modules** documentation page. Note that some of the modules are not provided under LGPL license.

Qt Quick Designer

We can use QML to easily create a hierarchy of objects. If we need a few input boxes or buttons, we can just add some blocks to the code, just like we added the `TextField` and `Label` components in the previous example, and our changes will appear in the window. However, when dealing with complex forms, it's sometimes hard to position the objects properly. Instead of trying different `anchors` and relaunching the application, you can use the visual form editor to see the changes as you make them.

Time for action – Adding a form to the project

Locate the `qml.qrc` file in Qt Creator's project tree and invoke the **Add New...** option in its context menu. From **Qt** section, select the **QtQuick UI File** template. Input `Calculator` in the **Component name** field. The **Component form name** field will be automatically set to `CalculatorForm`. Finish the wizard.

Two new files will appear in our project. The `CalculatorForm.ui.qml` file is the form file that can be edited in the form editor. The `Calculator.qml` file is a regular QML file that can be edited manually to implement the behavior of the form. Each of these files introduces a new QML type. The `CalculatorForm` QML type is immediately used in the generated `Calculator.qml` file:

```
import QtQuick 2.4
CalculatorForm {
}
```

Next, we need to edit the `main.qml` file to add a `Calculator` object to the window:

```
import QtQuick 2.9
import QtQuick.Window 2.2
import QtQuick.Controls 2.2
Window {
    visible: true
    width: 640
    height: 480
    title: qsTr("Calculator")

    Calculator {
        anchors.fill: parent
    }
}
```

QML components are similar to C++ classes in some way. A QML component encapsulates an object tree so that you can use it without knowing about the exact content of the component. When the application is started, the `main.qml` file will be loaded into the engine, so the `Window` and `Calculator` objects will be created. The Calculator object, in turn, will contain a `CalculatorForm` object.
The `CalculatorForm` object will contain the items that we add later in the form editor.

Form editor files

When we worked with Qt Widgets form editor, you may have noted that a widget form is an XML file that is converted to a C++ class during compilation. This does not apply to Qt Quick Designer. In fact, the files produced by this form editor are completely valid QML files that are directly included in the project. However, the form editor files have a special extension (`.ui.qml`), and there are some artificial restrictions that protect you from doing bad things.

The `ui.qml` files should only contain content that is visible in the form editor. You do not need to edit these files by hand. It's not possible to call functions or execute JavaScript code from these files. Instead, you should implement any logic in a separate QML file that uses the form as a component.

> If you're curious about the content of a `ui.qml` file, you can click on the **Text Editor** tab that is positioned on the right border of the form editor's central area.

Form editor interface

When you open a `.ui.qml` file, Qt Creator goes to the **Design** mode and opens the Qt Quick Designer interface:

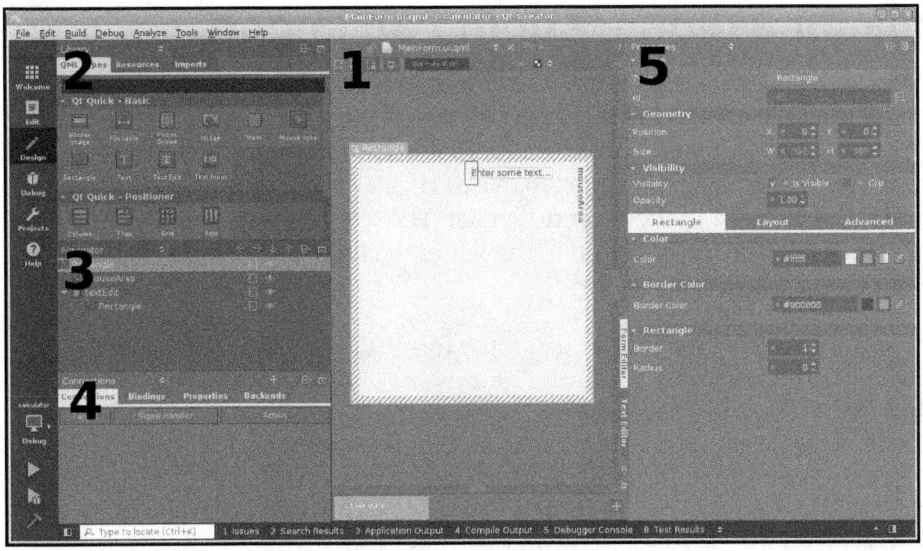

We've highlighted the following important parts of the interface:

- The main area (**1**) contains visualization of the document's content. You can click on the **Text Editor** tab at the right border of the main area to view and edit the QML code of the form without exiting the form editor. The bottom part of the main area displays list of states of the component.
- The **Library** pane (**2**) shows the available QML object types and allows you to create new objects by dragging them to the navigator or to the main area. The **Imports** tab contains a list of available QML modules and allows you to export a module and access more QML types.
- The **Navigator** pane (**3**) displays the hierarchy of the existing objects and their names. The buttons to the right of the names allow you to export an object as public property and toggle its visibility in the form editor.
- The **Connections** pane (**4**) provides ability to connect signals, change property bindings, and manage public properties of the form.
- The **Properties** pane (**5**) allows you to view and edit properties of the selected object.

We will now use the form editor to create a simple calculator application. Our form will contain two input boxes for operands, two radio buttons for selecting the operation, a label to display the result, and a button to reset everything to the original state.

Time for action – Adding an import

The default object palette contains a very minimal set of types provided by the `QtQuick` module. To access a richer set of controls, we need to add an `import` directive to our document. To do this, locate the **Library** pane in the top-left corner of the window and go to its **Imports** tab. Next, click on **Add Import** and select **QtQuick.Controls 2.2** in the drop-down list. The selected import will appear in the tab. You can click on the **×** button to the left of the import to remove it. Note that you cannot remove the default import.

> Adding the import using the form editor will result in adding the `import QtQuick.Controls 2.2` directive to the `.ui.qml` file. You can switch the main area to the **Text Editor** mode to see this change.

Now you can switch back to the **QML Types** tab of the **Library** pane. The palette will contain controls provided by the imported module.

Time for action – Adding items to the form

Locate the **Text Field** type in the **Qt Quick - Controls 2** section of the library pane and drag it to the main area. A new text field will be created. We will also need the **Radio Button**, **Label**, and **Button** types from the same section. Drag them to the form and arrange them as shown:

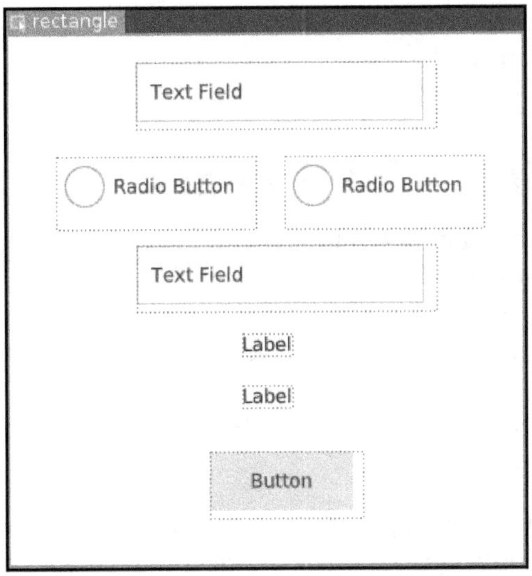

Next, you need to select each element and edit its properties. Click on the first text field in the main area or in the navigator. The blue frame around the object in the main area will indicate that it is selected. Now you can use the property editor to view and edit properties of the selected element. First, we want to set the `id` property that will be used to refer to the object in the code. Set the `id` property of the text edits to `argument1` and `argument2`. Locate the **Text** property under the **TextField** tab in the property editor. Set it to `0` for both text fields. The changed text will be immediately displayed in the main area.

Set `id` of the radio buttons to `operationAdd` and `operationMultiply`. Set their text to + and ×. Set the `checked` property of the `operationAdd` button to `true` by toggling the corresponding checkbox in the property editor.

The first label will be used to statically display the = sign. Set its `id` to `equalSign` and `text` to =. The second label will actually display the result. Set its `id` to `result`. We will take care of the `text` property later.

The button will reset the calculator to the original state. Set its `id` to `reset` and `text` to `Reset`.

You can run the application now. You will see that the controls are shown in the window, but they are not repositioned in respect to the window size. They always stay in the same positions. If you check out the text content of `CalculatorForm.ui.qml`, you will see that the form editor sets the `x` and `y` properties of each element. To make a more responsive form, we need to utilize the `anchors` property instead.

Time for action – Editing anchors

Let's see how we can edit anchors in the form editor and see the result on the fly. Select the `argument1` text field and switch to the **Layout** tab in the middle part of the **Properties** pane. The tab contains **Anchors** text, followed by a set of buttons for all anchor lines of this item. You can mouse over the buttons to see their tooltips. Click on the first button,
Anchor item to the top. A new set of controls will appear below the button, allowing you to configure this anchor.

First, you can select the target object, that is, the object containing the anchor line that will be used as the reference. Next, you can select the margin between the reference anchor line and the anchor line of the current object. To the right of the margin, there are buttons that allow you to choose which anchor line of the target to use as the reference. For example, if you choose the bottom line, our text field will retain its position relative to the bottom border of the form.

Anchor the top line of the text field to the top line of the **parent** and set **Margin** to **20**. Next, anchor the horizontal center line to **parent** with **Margin 0**. The property editor should look like this:

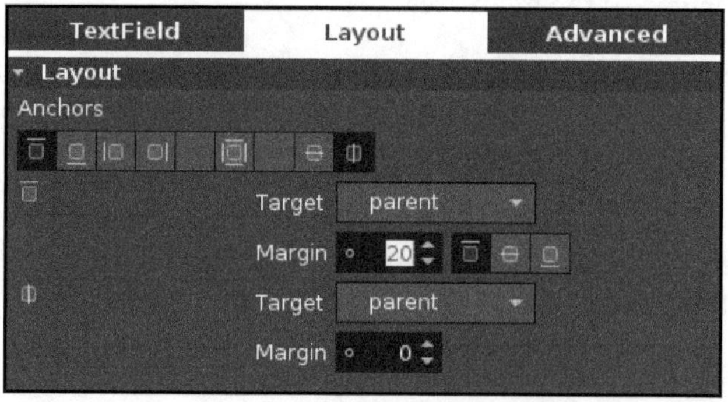

You can also verify the QML representation of these settings:

```
TextField {
    id: a
    text: qsTr("0")
    anchors.horizontalCenter: parent.horizontalCenter
    anchors.top: parent.top
    anchors.topMargin: 20
}
```

> If you drag the text field around using the mouse instead of setting the anchors, the form editor will set the `x` and `y` properties to position the element according to your actions. If you edit anchors of the item afterward, the `x` and `y` properties may remain set, but their effect will be overridden by the anchor effects.

Let's repeat this process for the `operationAdd` radio button. First, we need to adjust its horizontal position relative to the horizontal center of the form. Select the radio button, click on the **Anchor item to the right** button, leave `parent` as the target, and click on the **Anchor to the horizontal center of the target** button to the right of the margin input. Set margin to `10`. This will allow us to position the second radio button 10 points to the right of the horizontal center, and the space between the radio buttons will be 20.

Now, what about the top anchor? We can attach it to the parent and just set the margin that will look nice. However, ultimately, what we want is a specific vertical margin between the first text field and the first radio button. We can do this easily.

Enable the top anchor for the `operationAdd` radio button, select `argument1` in the **Target** drop-down list, click on the **Anchor to the bottom of the target** button to the right of the margin field, and input 20 in the margin field. Now the radio button is anchored to the text field above it. Even if we change the height of the text field, the vertical margin between the elements will stay intact. You can run the application and verify that the `argument1` and `operationAdd` elements now respond to window size changes.

Now, all we need is to repeat this process for the rest of the objects. However, this is quite a tedious task. It will get even more inconvenient in a larger form. Making changes to such forms will also be cumbersome. For example, to change the order of fields, you will need to carefully edit the anchors of involved objects. While anchors are good in simple cases, it's better to use a more automated approach for large forms. Luckily, Qt Quick provides layouts for this purpose.

Time for action – Applying layouts to the items

Before we apply layouts to objects, remove the anchors we had created. To do this, select each element and click on the buttons under **Anchors** text to uncheck them. The anchor properties below the buttons will disappear. The layout will now be able to position the objects.

First, import the `QtQuick.Layouts 1.3` module into the form, like we did earlier for `QtQuick.Controls`. Locate the **Qt Quick - Layouts** section in the palette and examine the available layouts:

- **Column Layout** will arrange its children vertically
- **Row Layout** will arrange its children horizontally
- **Grid Layout** will arrange its children vertically and horizontally in a grid
- **Stack Layout** will display only one of its children and hide the rest of them

Layouts are sensitive to the hierarchy of the objects. Let's use Navigator instead of the main area to manage our items. This will allow us to see the parent-child relationships between items more clearly. First, drag a **Row Layout** and drop it over the root item in the Navigator. A new `rowLayout` object will be added as a child of the root object. Next, drag the `operationAdd` and `operationMultiply` objects in the Navigator and drop them to the `rowLayout`. The radio buttons are now children of the row layout, and they are automatically positioned next to each other.

Now, drag a **Column Layout** to the root object. Select all other children of the root object, including `rowLayout`, in the Navigator, and drag them to the `columnLayout` object. If the items end up in wrong order, use the **Move up** and **Move down** buttons at the top part of the **Navigator** to arrange the items properly. You should get the following hierarchy:

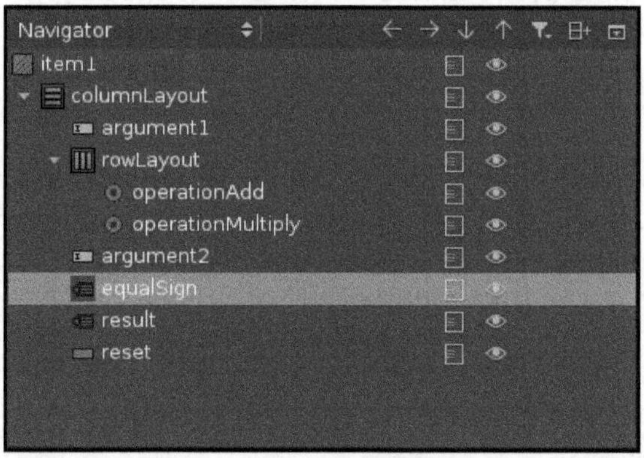

The `columnLayout` object will automatically position its children, but how to position the object itself? We should use anchors to do that. Select `columnLayout`, switch to the **Layout** tab in the property editor and click on the **Fill parent item** button. This will automatically create 4 anchor bindings and expand `columnLayout` to fill the form.

The items are now positioned automatically, but they are bound to the left border of the window. Let's align them to the middle. Select the first text field and switch to the **Layout** tab. As the object is now in a layout, the anchor settings are replaced with settings the layout understands. The **Alignment** property defines how the item is positioned within the available space. Select `AlignHCenter` in the first drop-down list. Repeat the process for each direct child of `columnLayout`.

You can now run the application and see how it reacts to changing window size:

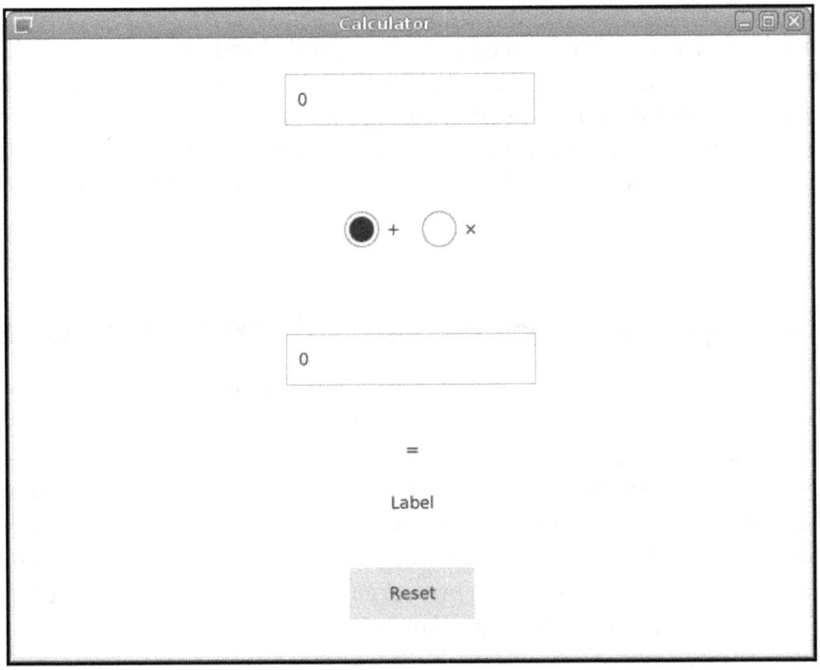

The form is ready. Let's implement the calculations now.

Time for action – Assigning an expression to the property

As you already saw, assigning constant text to a label is easy. However, you can also assign a dynamic expression to any property in the form editor. To do that, select the `result` label and mouse over the circle in the left part of **Text** property input field. When the circle turns into an arrow, click on it and select **Set Binding** in the menu. Input `argument1.text + argument2.text` in the binding editor and confirm the change.

If you run the application now, you will see that the `result` label will always display the concatenation of the strings the user inputs in the fields. That's because the `argument1.text` and `argument2.text` properties have the `string` type, so the + operation performs concatenation.

This feature is very useful if you need to apply simple bindings. However, it is not sufficient in our case, as we need to convert strings to numbers and select which arithmetic operation the user requested. Using functions in the form editor is not allowed, so we cannot implement this complex logic right here. We need to do it in the `Calculator.qml` file. This restriction will help us separate the view from the logic behind it.

Time for action – Exposing items as properties

Children of a component are not available from outside of it by default. This means that `Calculator.qml` cannot access input fields or radio buttons of our form. To implement the logic of the calculator, we need to access these objects, so let's expose them as public properties. Select the `argument1` text field in the Navigator and click on the **Toggles whether this item is exported as an alias property of the root item** button to the right of the object ID. After you click on the button, its icon will change to indicate that the item is exported. Now we can use the `argument1` public property in `Calculator.qml` to access the input field object.

Enable public properties for the `argument1`, `argument2`, `operationAdd`, `operationMultiply`, and `result` objects. The rest of the objects will remain hidden as implementation details of the form.

Now go to the `Calculator.qml` file and use the exposed properties to implement the calculator logic:

```
CalculatorForm {
    result.text: {
        var value1 = parseFloat(argument1.text);
        var value2 = parseFloat(argument2.text);
        if(operationMultiply.checked) {
            return value1 * value2;
        } else {
            return value1 + value2;
        }
    }
}
```

What just happened?

Since we exported objects as properties, we can access them by ID from outside of the form. In this code, we bind the `text` property of the `result` object to the return value of the code block that is enclosed in braces. We use `argument1.text` and `argument2.text` to access the current text of the input fields. We also use `operationMultiply.checked` to see whether the user checked the `operationMultiply` radio button. The rest is just straightforward JavaScript code.

Run the application and see how the result label automatically displays the result when the user interacts with the form.

Time for action – Creating an event handler

Let's implement the last bit of functionality. When the user clicks on the **Reset** button, we should change the form's values. Go back to the form editor and right-click on the `reset` button in the Navigator or in the main area. Select **Add New Signal Handler**. Qt Creator will navigate to the corresponding implementation file (`Calculator.qml`) and display the **Implement Signal Handler** dialog. Select the `clicked` signal in the drop-down list and click on the **OK** button to confirm the operation. This operation will do two things:

- The `reset` button will be automatically exported as a public property, just like we did it manually for the other controls
- Qt Creator will create a boilerplate for the new signal handler in the `Calculator.qml` file

Let's add our implementation to the automatically generated block:

```
reset.onClicked: {
    argument1.text = "0";
    argument2.text = "0";
    operationAdd.checked = true;
}
```

When the button is clicked on, this code will be executed. The text fields will be set to 0, and the `operationAdd` radio button will be checked. The `operationMultiply` radio button will be unchecked automatically.

Our calculator fully works now! We used declarative approach to implement a nicely looking and responsive application.

Qt Quick and C++

While QML has a lot of built-in functionality available, it will almost never be enough. When you're developing a real application, it always needs some unique functionality that is not available in QML modules provided by Qt. The C++ Qt classes are much more powerful, and third-party C++ libraries are also always an option. However, the C++ world is separated from our QML application by the restrictions of QML engine. Let's break that boundary right away.

Accessing C++ objects from QML

Let's say that we want to perform a heavy calculation in C++ and access it from our QML calculator. We will choose factorial for this project.

> The QML engine is really fast, so you can most likely calculate factorials directly in JavaScript without performance problems. We just use it here as a simple example.

Our goal is to inject our C++ class into the QML engine as a JavaScript object that will be available in our QML files. We will do that exactly like we did it in `Chapter 10`, *Scripting*. The `main` function creates a `QQmlApplicationEngine` object that inherits `QJSEngine`, so we have access to the API that is already familiar to us from that chapter. Here, we'll just show how we can apply this knowledge to our application without going into detail.

Go to the **Edit** mode, right-click on the project in the project tree and select **Add New**. Select the **C++ Class** template, input `AdvancedCalculator` as the class name and select **QObject** in the **Base Class** drop-down list.

Declare the invokable `factorial` function in the generated `advancedcalculator.h` file:

```
Q_INVOKABLE double factorial(int argument);
```

We can implement this function using the following code:

```
double AdvancedCalculator::factorial(int argument) {
    if (argument < 0) {
        return std::numeric_limits<double>::quiet_NaN();
    }
    if (argument > 180) {
      return std::numeric_limits<double>::infinity();
    }
    double r = 1.0;
    for(int i = 2; i <= argument; ++i) {
        r *= i;
    }
    return r;
}
```

We guard the implementation against too large inputs because `double` wouldn't be able to fit the resulting values anyway. We also return `NaN` on invalid inputs.

Next, we need to create an instance of this class and import it into the QML engine. We do this in the `main()`:

```
engine.globalObject().setProperty("advancedCalculator",
    engine.newQObject(new AdvancedCalculator));
return app.exec();
```

Our object is now available as the `advancedCalculator` global variable. Now we need to use this variable in the QML file. Open the form editor and add the third radio button to the `rowLayout` item. Set `id` of the radio button to `operationFactorial` and text to `!`. Export this radio button as a public property so that we can access it from the outside. Next, let's adjust the `result.text` property binding in the `Calculator.qml` file:

```
result.text: {
    var value1 = parseFloat(argument1.text);
    var value2 = parseFloat(argument2.text);
    if(operationMultiply.checked) {
```

```
        return value1 * value2;
    } else if (operationFactorial.checked) {
        return advancedCalculator.factorial(value1);
    } else {
        return value1 + value2;
    }
}
```

If the `operationFactorial` radio button is checked, this code will call the `factorial()` method of the `advancedCalculator` variable and return it as the result. The user will see it as text of the `result` label. When factorial operation is selected, the second text field is unused. We'll do something about that later in this chapter.

> For more information about exposing C++ API to JavaScript, refer to `Chapter 10`, *Scripting*. Most of the techniques described there apply to the QML engine as well.

We exposed a C++ object as a JavaScript object that is accessible from the QML engine. However, it is not a QML object, so you can't include it in the QML objects hierarchy or apply property bindings to properties of the object that was created this way. It's possible to create a C++ class that will work as a fully functional QML type, leading to a more powerful integration of C++ and QML. We will show that approach in `Chapter 12`, *Customization in Qt Quick*.

There is another way to expose our `AdvancedCalculator` class to JavaScript. Instead of adding it to the global object, we can register it as a singleton object in the QML module system using the `qmlRegisterSingletonType()` function:

```
qmlRegisterSingletonType("CalculatorApp", 1, 0, "AdvancedCalculator",
        [](QQmlEngine *engine, QJSEngine *scriptEngine) -> QJSValue {
    Q_UNUSED(scriptEngine);
    return engine->newQObject(new AdvancedCalculator);
});
QQmlApplicationEngine engine;
```

We pass the QML module name, major and minor versions, and the singleton name to this function. You can choose these values arbitrarily. The last argument is a callback function that will be called when this singleton object is accessed in the JS engine for the first time.

The QML code also needs to be slightly adjusted. First, import our new QML module into scope:

```
import CalculatorApp 1.0
```

Now you can just access the singleton by name:

```
return AdvancedCalculator.factorial(value1);
```

When this line is executed for the first time, Qt will call our C++ callback and create the singleton object. For subsequent calls, the same object will be used.

Accessing QML objects from C++

It is also possible to create QML objects from C++ and access the existing objects living in the QML engine (for example, those declared in some QML file). However, in general, doing this thing is bad practice. If we assume the most common case, which is that the QML part of our application deals with a user interface in Qt Quick for the logic written in C++, then accessing Qt Quick objects from C++ breaks the separation between logic and the presentation layer, which is one of the major principles in GUI programming. The user interface is prone to dynamic changes, relayouting up to a complete revamp. Heavy modifications of QML documents, such as adding or removing items from the design, will then have to be followed by adjusting the application logic to cope with those changes. In addition, if we allow a single application to have multiple user interfaces (skins), it might happen that because they are so different, it is impossible to decide upon a single set of common entities with hard-coded names that can be fetched from C++ and manipulated. Even if you managed to do that, such an application could crash easily if the rules were not strictly followed in the QML part.

That said, we have to admit that there are cases when it does make sense to access QML objects from C++, and that is why we decided to familiarize you with the way to do it. One of the situations where such an approach is desired is when QML serves us as a way to quickly define a hierarchy of objects with properties of different objects linked through more or fewer complex expressions, allowing them to answer to changes taking place in the hierarchy.

The `QQmlApplicationEngine` class provides access to its top-level QML objects through the `rootObjects()` function. All nested QML objects form a parent-child hierarchy visible from C++, so you can use `QObject::findChild` or `QObject::findChildren` to access the nested objects.

The most convenient way to find a specific object is to set its `objectName` property. For example, if we want to access the reset button from C++, we need to set its object name.

The form editor does not provide a way to set `objectName` for its items, so we need to use the text editor to make this change:

```
Button {
    id: reset
    objectName: "buttonReset"
    //...
}
```

We can now access this button from the `main` function:

```
if (engine.rootObjects().count() == 1) {
    QObject *window = engine.rootObjects()[0];
    QObject *resetButton = window->findChild<QObject*>("buttonReset");
    if (resetButton) {
        resetButton->setProperty("highlighted", true);
    }
}
```

In this code, we first access the top-level `Window` QML object. Then, we use the `findChild` method to find the object corresponding to our reset button. The `findChild()` method requires us to pass a class pointer as the template argument. Without knowing what class actually implements a given type, it is safest to simply pass `QObject*` as, once again, we know all QML objects inherit it. It is more important what gets passed as the function argument value—it is the name of the object we want returned. Note that it is not the `id` of the object but the value of the `objectName` property. When the result gets assigned to the variables, we verify whether the item has been successfully found and if that is the case, the generic `QObject` API is used to set its `highlighted` property to `true`. This property will change the appearance of the button.

> **TIP**
> The `QObject::findChild` and `QObject::findChildren` functions perform recursive search with unlimited depth. While they're easy to use, these functions may be slow if the object has many children. To improve performance, you can turn off recursive search by passing the `Qt::FindDirectChildrenOnly` flag to these functions. If the target object is not a direct child, consider calling `QObject::findChild` repeatedly to find each intermediate parent.

If you need to create a new QML object, you can use the `QQmlComponent` class for that. It accepts a QML document and allows you to create a QML object from it. The document is usually loaded from a file, but you can even provide it directly in C++ code:

```
QQmlComponent component(&engine);
component.setData(
    "import QtQuick 2.6\n"
    "import QtQuick.Controls 2.2\n"
    "import QtQuick.Window 2.2\n"
    "Window { Button { text: \"C++ button\" } }", QUrl());
QObject* object = component.create();
object->setProperty("visible", true);
```

The `component.create()` function instantiates our new component and returns a pointer to it as `QObject`. In fact, any QML object derives from `QObject`. You can use Qt meta-system to manipulate the object without needing to cast it to a concrete type. The object's properties can be accessed using the `property()` and `setProperty()` functions. In this example, we set the `visible` property of the `Window` QML object to `true`. When our code is executed, a new window with a button will appear on screen.

You can also call the object's methods using the `QMetaObject::invokeMethod()` function:

```
QMetaObject::invokeMethod(object, "showMaximized");
```

If you want to embed a new object into the existing QML form, you need to set *visual parent* of the new object. Let's say that we want to add a button to the calculator's form. First, you need to assign `objectName` to it in `main.qml`:

```
Calculator {
    anchors.fill: parent
    objectName: "calculator"
}
```

You can now add a button to this form from C++:

```
QQmlComponent component(&engine);
component.setData(
    "import QtQuick 2.6\n"
    "import QtQuick.Controls 2.2\n"
    "Button { text: \"C++ button2\" }", QUrl());
QObject *object = component.create();
QObject *calculator = window->findChild<QObject*>("calculator");
object->setProperty("parent", QVariant::fromValue(calculator));
```

In this code, we create a component and assign the main form as its `parent` property. This will make the object appear in the top-left corner of the form. Like with any other QML object, you can use the `anchors` property group to change position of the object.

When creating complex objects, it takes time for them to instantiate and at times, it is desired to not block the control flow for too long by waiting for the operation to complete. In such cases, you can create an object in the QML engine asynchronously using the `QQmlIncubator` object. This object can be used to schedule instantiation and continue the flow of the program. We can query the state of the incubator and when the object is constructed, we will be able to access it. The following code demonstrates how to use the incubator to instantiate an object and keep the application responding while waiting for the operation to complete:

```
QQmlComponent component(&engine,
    QUrl::fromLocalFile("ComplexObject.qml"));
QQmlIncubator incubator;
component.create(incubator);
while(!incubator.isError() && !incubator.isReady()) {
    QCoreApplication::processEvents();
}
QObject *object = incubator.isReady() ? incubator.object() : 0;
```

Bringing life into static user interfaces

Our user interface has been quite static until now. In this section, we will add a simple animation to our calculator. When the user selects the factorial operation, the second (unused) text field will fade out. It will fade in when another operation is selected. Let's see how QML allows us to implement that.

Fluid user interfaces

So far, we have been looking at graphical user interfaces as a set of panels embedded one into another. This is well reflected in the world of desktop utility programs composed of windows and subwindows containing mostly static content scattered throughout a large desktop area where the user can use a mouse pointer to move around windows or adjust their size.

However, this design doesn't correspond well with modern user interfaces that often try to minimize the area they occupy (because of either a small display size like with embedded and mobile devices or to avoid obscuring the main display panel like in games), at the same time providing rich content with a lot of moving or dynamically resizing items. Such user interfaces are often called "fluid", to signify that they are not formed as a number of separate different screens but contain dynamic content and layout where one screen fluently transforms into another. The `QtQuick` module provides a runtime to create rich applications with fluid user interfaces.

States and transitions

Qt Quick introduces a concept of **states**. Any Qt Quick object can have a predefined set of states. Each state corresponds to a certain situation in the application logic. For example, we can say that our calculator application has two states:

- When add or multiply operations are selected, the user has to input two operands
- When factorial operation is selected, the user has to input only one operand

States are identified by `string` names. Implicitly, any object has the base state with an empty name. To declare a new state, you need to specify the state name and a set of property values that are different in that state, compared to the base state.

Each Qt Quick object also has the `state` property. When you assign a state name to this property, the object goes to the specified state. This happens immediately by default, but it's possible to define **transitions** for the object and perform some visual effects when changing states.

Let's see how we can utilize states and transitions in our project.

Time for action – Adding states to the form

Open the `CalculatorForm.ui.qml` file in the form editor. The bottom part of the main area contains the states editor. The **base state** item is always present on the left. Click on the **Add a new state** button on the right of the states editor. A new state will appear in the editor. It contains a text field that you can use to set the state's name. Set the name to `single_argument`.

Only one of the states can be selected at a time. When a custom state is selected, any changes in the form editor will only affect the selected state. When the base state is selected, you can edit the base state and all the changes will affect all other states unless the changed property is overridden in some state.

Select the `single_argument` state by clicking on it in the state editor. It will also be automatically selected upon creation. Next, select the `argument2` text field and set its `opacity` property to 0. The field will become completely transparent, except for the blue outline provided by the form editor. However, this change only affects the `single_argument` state. When you switch to the base state, the text field will become visible. When you switch back to the second state, the text field will become invisible again.

You can switch to the text editor to see how this state is represented in the code:

```
states: [
    State {
        name: "single_argument"
        PropertyChanges {
            target: b
            opacity: 0
        }
    }
]
```

As you can see, the state does not contain a full copy of the form. Instead, it only records the difference between this state and the base state.

Now we need to ensure that the form's state is properly updated. You just need to bind the `state` property of the form to a function that returns the current state. Switch to the `Calculator.qml` file and add the following code:

```
CalculatorForm {
    state: {
        if (operationFactorial.checked) {
            return "single_argument";
        } else {
            return "";
        }
    }
    //...
}
```

As with any other property binding, the QML engine will automatically update the value of the `state` property when needed. When the user selects the factorial operation, the code block will return `"single_argument"`, and the second text field will be hidden. In other cases, the function will return an empty string that corresponds to the base state. When you run the application, you should be able to see this behavior.

Time for action – Adding smooth transition effect

Qt Quick allows us to easily implement smooth transition between states. It will automatically detect when some property needs to be changed, and if there is a matching animation attached to the object, that animation will take over the process of applying the change. You don't even need to specify the starting and ending values of the animated property; it's all done automatically.

To add a smooth transition to our form, add the following code to the `Calculator.qml` file:

```
CalculatorForm {
    //...
    transitions: Transition {
        PropertyAnimation {
            property: "opacity"
            duration: 300
        }
    }
}
```

Run the application and you will see that the text field's opacity changes gradually when the form transitions to another state.

What just happened?

The `transitions` property holds the list of `Transition` objects for this object. It's possible to specify a different `Transition` object for each pair of states if you want to perform different animations in different cases. However, you can also use a single `Transition` object that will affect all transitions. For convenience, QML allows us to assign a single object to a property that expects a list.

A `Transition` object must contain one or multiple animations that will be applied during this transition. In this example, we added `PropertyAnimation` that allows us to animate any property of any child object of the main form. The `PropertyAnimation` QML type has properties that allow you to configure what exactly it will do. We instructed it to animate the `opacity` property and take 300 ms to perform the animation. The opacity change will be linear by default, but you can use the `easing` property to select another easing function.

> As always, the Qt documentation is a great source of detailed information about available types and properties. Refer to **Transition QML Type** and **Animation QML Type** documentation pages for more information. We will also talk more about states and transitions in `Chapter 13`, *Animations in Qt Quick Games*.

Have a go hero – Adding an animation of the item's position

You can make the calculator's transition even more appealing if you make the text field fly away off screen while fading out. Just use the form editor to change the text field's position in the `single_argument` state, and then attach another `PropertyAnimation` to the `Transition` object. You can play with different easing types to see which looks better for this purpose.

Pop quiz

Q1. Which property allows you to position a QML object relative to another object?

1. `border`
2. `anchors`
3. `id`

Q2. Which file name extension indicates that the file cannot be loaded into a QML engine?

1. `.qml`
2. `.ui`
3. `.ui.qml`
4. All of the above are valid QML files

Q3. What is a Qt Quick transition?

1. A change of parent-child relationships among the existing Qt Quick objects
2. A set of properties that change when an event occurs
3. A set of animations that play when the object's state changes

Summary

In this chapter, you were introduced to with a declarative language called QML. The language is used to drive Qt Quick—a framework for highly dynamic and interactive content. You learned the basics of Qt Quick—how to create documents with a number of element types and how to create your own in QML, or in C++. You also learned how to bind expressions to properties to automatically reevaluate them. You saw how to expose the C++ core of your application to QML-based user interfaces. You learned to use the visual form editor and how to create animated transitions in the interface.

You also learned which QML modules are available. You were shown how to use the `QtQuick.Controls` and `QtQuick.Layouts` modules to build the application's user interface out of standard components. In the next chapter, we will see how you can make your own fully customized QML components with a unique look and feel. We will show how to implement custom graphics and event handling in QML applications.

12
Customization in Qt Quick

In the previous chapter, you learned how to use controls and layouts provided by Qt Quick to build the user interface of your application. Qt contains numerous QML types that can serve as building blocks for your game, providing rich functionality and a nice appearance. However, sometimes you need to create a custom component that satisfies the needs of your game. In this chapter, we will show a couple of convenient ways to extend your QML project with custom components. By the end of this chapter, you will know how to perform custom painting on a canvas, handle various input events, and implement lazy loading for your components. We will also see how to integrate a C++ object into QML's object tree.

The main topics covered in this chapter are as listed:

- Creating a custom component
- Handling mouse, touch, keyboard, and gamepad events
- Dynamic and lazy loading
- Painting on Canvas using JavaScript

Creating a custom QML component

We already touched the topic of custom components when we worked with the form editor in the previous chapter. Our QML files implemented reusable components with a clean interface that can be used in the rest of the application. We will now take a more low-level approach and create a new QML component directly from QML code using the basic Qt Quick building blocks. Our component will be a button with a rounded shape and a nice background. The button will hold definable text and an icon. Our component should look good for different texts and icons.

Time for action – Creating a button component

Start by creating a new project in Qt Creator. Choose **Qt Quick Application - Empty** as the project template. Name the project `custom_button` and leave the rest of the options unchanged.

At this point, you should end up with a QML document containing an empty window. Let's start by creating the button frame. Edit the `main.qml` file to add a new `Rectangle` item to the window:

```
import QtQuick 2.9
import QtQuick.Window 2.2

Window {
    visible: true
    width: 640
    height: 480
    title: qsTr("Hello World")

    Rectangle {
        id: button
        anchors.centerIn: parent
        border { width: 1; color: "black" }
        radius: 5
        width: 100; height: 30
        gradient: Gradient {
            GradientStop { position: 0; color: "#eeeeee" }
            GradientStop { position: 1; color: "#777777" }
        }
    }
}
```

After running the project, you should see a result similar to the following:

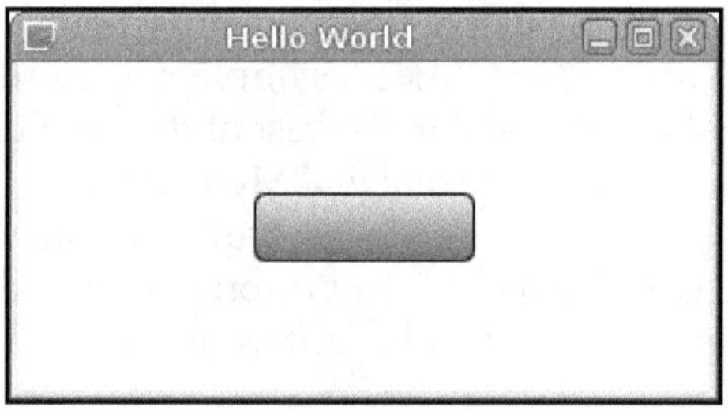

What just happened?

You can see that the rectangle is centered in the window using a `centerIn` anchor binding that we didn't mention before. This is one of the two special anchors that are provided for convenience, to avoid having to write too much code.
Using `centerIn` is equivalent to setting both `horizontalCenter` and `verticalCenter`. The other convenience binding is `fill`, which makes one item occupy the whole area of another item (similar to setting the left, right, top, and bottom anchors to their respective anchor lines in the destination item).

Instead of setting a solid color for the button, we declared the background to be a linear gradient. We bound a `Gradient` element to the `gradient` property and defined two `GradientStop` elements as its children, where we specified two colors to blend between. `Gradient` does not inherit from `Item` and thus is not a visual Qt Quick element. Instead, it is just a QML object that serves as a data holder for the gradient definition.

The `Item` type has a property called `children` that contains a list of the visual children (`Item` instances) of an item and another property called `resources`, which contains a list of non-visual objects (such as `Gradient` or `GradientStop`) for an item. Normally, you don't need to use these properties when adding visual or non-visual objects to an item, as the item will automatically assign child objects to appropriate properties. Note that in our code, the `Gradient` object is not a child object of the `Rectangle`; it is just assigned to its `gradient` property.

Time for action – Adding button content

The next step is to add text and an icon to the button. First, copy the icon file to the project directory. In Qt Creator, locate the `qml.qrc` resource file in the project tree. In the context menu of the resource file, select **Add Existing Files** and select your icon file. The file will be added to the resources and will appear in the project tree. Our example file is called `edit-undo.png`, and the corresponding resource URL is `qrc:/edit-undo.png`.

TIP

You can get the resource path or URL of a file by locating that file in the project tree and using the **Copy Path** or **Copy URL** option in its context menu.

Next, we will add the icon and the text to our button using another item type called `Row`, as shown:

```
Rectangle {
    id: button
    anchors.centerIn: parent
    border { width: 1; color: "black" }
    radius: 5
    gradient: Gradient {
        GradientStop { position: 0; color: "#eeeeee" }
        GradientStop { position: 1; color: "#777777" }
    }
    width: buttonContent.width + 8
    height: buttonContent.height + 8

    Row {
        id: buttonContent
        anchors.centerIn: parent
        spacing: 4

        Image {
            id: buttonIcon
            source: "qrc:/edit-undo.png"
        }
        Text {
            id: buttonText
            text: "ButtonText"
        }
    }
}
```

You'll get the following output:

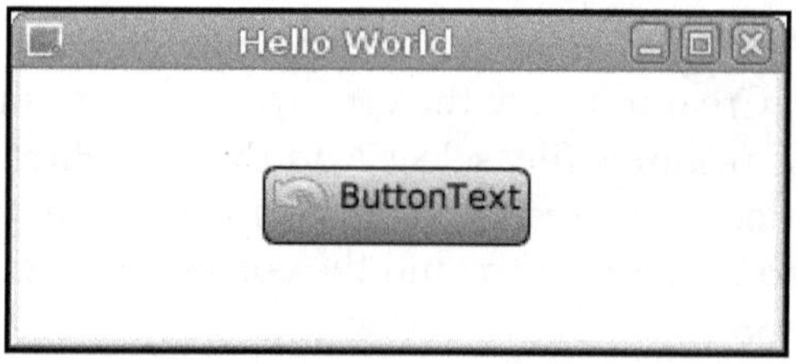

What just happened?

`Row` is a **positioner** QML type provided by the `QtQuick` module. Its purpose is similar to the `RowLayout` type from the `QtQuick.Layouts` module. The `Row` item spreads its children in a horizontal row. It makes it possible to position a series of items without using anchors. `Row` has the `spacing` property that dictates how much space to leave between items.

> The `QtQuick` module also contains the `Column` type that arranges children in a column, the `Grid` type that creates a grid of items, and the `Flow` type that positions its children side by side, wrapping as necessary.

Time for action – Sizing the button properly

Our current panel definition still doesn't behave well when it comes to sizing the button. If the button content is very small (for example, the icon doesn't exist or the text is very short), the button will not look good. Typically, push buttons enforce a minimum size—if the content is smaller than a specified size, the button will be expanded to the minimum size allowed. Another problem is that the user might want to override the width or height of the item. In such cases, the content of the button should not overflow past the border of the button. Let's fix these two issues by replacing the `width` and `height` property bindings with the following code:

```
clip: true
implicitWidth: Math.max(buttonContent.implicitWidth + 8, 80)
implicitHeight: buttonContent.implicitHeight + 8
```

What just happened?

The `implicitWidth` and `implicitHeight` properties can contain the desired size the item wants to have. It's a direct equivalent of `sizeHint()` from Qt Widgets. By using these two properties instead of `width` and `height` (which are bound to `implicitWidth` and `implicitHeight` by default), we allow the user of our component to override those implicit values. When this happens and the user does not set the width or height big enough to contain the icon and text of the button, we prevent the content from crossing the boundaries of the parent item by setting the `clip` property to `true`.

TIP Clipping can reduce performance of your game, so use it only when necessary.

Time for action – Making the button a reusable component

So far, we have been working on a single button. Adding another button by copying the code, changing the identifiers of all components, and setting different bindings to properties is a very tedious task. Instead, we can make our button item a real component, that is, a new QML type that can be instantiated on demand as many times as required.

First, position the text cursor in the beginning of our `Rectangle` item and press *Alt* + *Enter* on the keyboard to open the refactoring menu, like in the following screenshot:

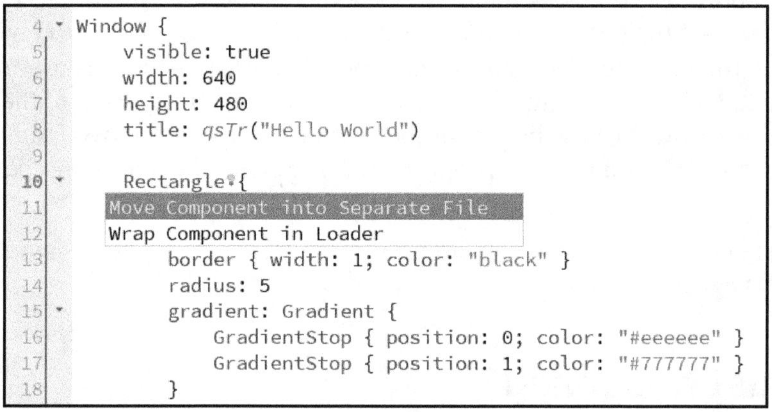
Window {
visible: true
width: 640
height: 480
title: qsTr("Hello World")
Rectangle {
Move Component into Separate File
Wrap Component in Loader
border { width: 1; color: "black" }
radius: 5
gradient: Gradient {
GradientStop { position: 0; color: "#eeeeee" }
GradientStop { position: 1; color: "#777777" }
}

From the menu, choose **Move Component into Separate File**. In the popup, type in a name for the new type (for example, `Button`) and check `anchors.centerIn` in the **Property assignments for main.qml** list:

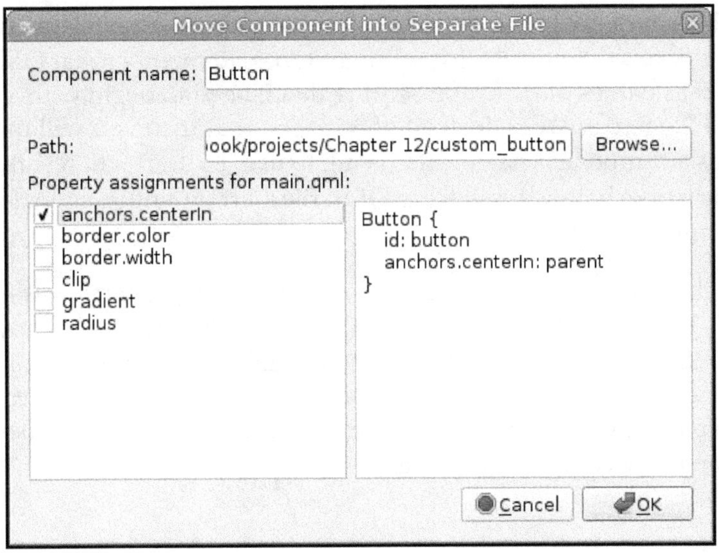

Accept the dialog by clicking on the **OK** button.

What just happened?

You can see that we have a new file called `Button.qml` in the project, which contains everything the button item used to have, with the exception of the `id` and `anchors.centerIn` properties. The main file was simplified to the following:

```
Window {
    visible: true
    width: 640
    height: 480
    title: qsTr("Hello World")

    Button {
        id: button
        anchors.centerIn: parent
    }
}
```

`Button` has become a component—a definition of a new type of element that can be used the same way as standard QML element types. Remember that QML component names, as well as names of files representing them, need to begin with a capital letter! If you name a file `button.qml` instead of `Button.qml`, then you will not be able to use `Button` as a component name, and trying to use "button" will result in an error message. This works both ways—every QML file starting with a capital letter can be treated as a component definition.

Since we checked `anchors.centerIn` in the dialog, this property was not moved to `Button.qml`. The reason for that choice is that our button can be put anywhere, so it can't possibly know how it should be positioned. Instead, positioning of the button should be done at the location where we use the component. Now we can edit `main.qml` to put the button into a layout or use other positioning properties without having to change the component's code.

Importing components

A component definition can be used directly by other QML files residing in the same directory as the component definition. In our example, the `main.qml` and `Button.qml` files are located in the same directory, so you can use the `Button` QML type inside `main.qml` without having to import anything.

If you need to access a component definition from a file residing elsewhere, you will have to first import the module containing the component in the file where you want to use it. The definition of a module is very simple—it is just a relative path to the *directory* containing QML files. This means that if you have a file named `Baz.qml` in a directory called `Base/Foo/Bar` and you want to use the `Baz` component from within the `Base/Foo/Ham.qml` file, you will have to put the following import statement in `Ham.qml`:

```
import "Bar"
```

If you want to use the same component from within the `Base/Spam.qml` file, you will have to replace the import statement with this:

```
import "Foo/Bar"
```

Importing a module makes all its components available for use. You can then declare objects of types imported from a certain module.

QML and virtual resource paths

Our project uses a Qt resource file to make our QML files embedded into the binary and ensure that they are always available to the application, even if the source directory is not present at the computer. During startup, we refer to the main QML file using the `qrc:/main.qml` URL. This means that the runtime only sees the file hierarchy in the resource file, and the actual source directory of the project is not taken into account.

The other QML file has the `qrc:/Button.qml` URL, so Qt considers them to be in the same virtual directory and everything still works. However, if you create a QML file but forget to add it to the project's resources, Qt will be unable to load that file. Even if the file is present in the same real directory as `main.qml`, Qt will only look for it in the virtual `qrc:/` directory.

> It's possible to add a file to the resources with a prefix, in which case it can have an URL like `qrc:/some/prefix/Button.qml`, and the runtime will consider it to be in another virtual directory. That being said, unless you explicitly create a new prefix, you should be fine. If your QML files are arranged in subdirectories, their hierarchy will be preserved when you add them to the resource file.

Event handlers

Qt Quick is meant to be used for creating user interfaces that are highly interactive. It offers a number of elements for taking input events from the user. In this section, we will go through them and see how you can use them effectively.

Time for action – Making the button clickable

So far, our component only looks like a button. The next task is to make it respond to mouse input.

The `MouseArea` QML type defines a transparent rectangle that exposes a number of properties and signals related to mouse input. Commonly used signals include `clicked`, `pressed`, and `released`. Let's do a couple of exercises to see how the element can be used.

Open the `Button.qml` file and add a `MouseArea` child item to the button and use anchors to make it fill the whole area of the button. Call the element `buttonMouseArea`. Put the following code in the body of the item:

```
Rectangle {
    id: button
    // ...
    Row { ... }
    MouseArea {
        id: buttonMouseArea
        anchors.fill: parent
        onClicked: button.clicked()
    }
}
```

In addition to this, set the following declaration in the button object just after its ID is declared:

```
Rectangle {
    id: button
    signal clicked()
    // ...
}
```

To test the modification, go to the `main.qml` file and add a signal handler to the button:

```
Button {
    id: button
    anchors.centerIn: parent
    onClicked: console.log("Clicked!")
}
```

Then, run the program and click on the button. You'll see your message printed to the Qt Creator's console.

What just happened?

With the `signal clicked()` statement, we declared that the button object can emit a signal called `clicked`. With the `MouseArea` item, we defined a rectangular area (covering the whole button) that reacts to mouse events. Then, we defined `onClicked`, which is a signal handler. For every signal an object has, a script can be bound to a handler named like the signal and prefixed with "on"; hence, for the `clicked` signal, the handler is called `onClicked`, and, for `valueChanged`, it is called `onValueChanged`.

In this particular case, we have two handlers defined—one for the button where we write a simple statement to the console, and the other for the `MouseArea` element where we call the button's signal function, effectively emitting that signal.

`MouseArea` has even more features, so now let's try putting them to the right use to make our button more feature-rich.

Time for action – Visualizing button states

Currently, there is no visual reaction to clicking on the button. In the real world, the button has some depth and when you push it and look at it from above, its contents seems to shift a little toward the right and downward. Let's mimic this behavior by making use of the pressed property `MouseArea` has, which denotes whether the mouse button is currently being pressed (note that the pressed property is different from the pressed signal that was mentioned earlier). The content of the button is represented by the `Row` element, so add the following statements inside its definition:

```
Row {
    id: buttonContent
    // ...
    anchors.verticalCenterOffset: buttonMouseArea.pressed ? 1 : 0
    anchors.horizontalCenterOffset: buttonMouseArea.pressed ? 1 : 0
    // ...
}
```

We can also make the text change color when the mouse cursor hovers over the button. For this, we have to do two things. First, let's enable receiving hover events on the `MouseArea` by setting its `hoverEnabled` property:

```
hoverEnabled: true
```

When this property is set, `MouseArea` will be setting its `containsMouse` property to `true` whenever it detects the mouse cursor over its own area. We can use this value to set the text color:

```
Text {
  id: buttonText
  text: "ButtonText"
  color: buttonMouseArea.containsMouse ? "white" : "black"
}
```

What just happened?

In the last exercise, we learned to use some properties and signals from `MouseArea` to make the button component more interactive. However, the element is much richer in features. In particular, if hover events are enabled, you can get the current mouse position in the item's local coordinate system through the `mouseX` and `mouseY` properties that return values. The cursor position can also be reported by handling the `positionChanged` signal. Speaking of signals, most `MouseArea` signals carry a `MouseEvent` object as their argument. This argument is called `mouse` and contains useful information about the current state of the mouse, including its position and buttons currently pressed. By default, `MouseArea` only reacts to the left mouse button, but you can use the `acceptedButtons` property to select which buttons it should handle. These features are shown in the following example:

```
MouseArea {
    id: buttonMouseArea
    anchors.fill: parent
    hoverEnabled: true
    acceptedButtons: Qt.LeftButton | Qt.MiddleButton | Qt.RightButton
    onClicked: {
        switch(mouse.button) {
            case Qt.LeftButton:
                console.log("Left button clicked"); break;
            case Qt.MiddleButton:
                console.log("Middle button clicked"); break;
            case Qt.RightButton:
                console.log("Right button clicked"); break;
        }
    }
    onPositionChanged: {
        console.log("Position: [" + mouse.x + "; " + mouse.y + "]");
    }
}
```

Time for action – Notifying the environment about button states

We have added some code to make the button look more natural by changing its visual aspects. Now, let's extend the button programming interface so that developers can use more features of the button.

The first thing we can do is make button colors definable by introducing some new properties for the button. Let's put the highlighted code at the beginning of the button component definition:

```
Rectangle {
    id: button
    property color topColor: "#eeeeee"
    property color bottomColor: "#777777"
    property color textColor: "black"
    property color textPressedColor: "white"
    signal clicked()
```

Then, we'll use the new definitions for the background gradient:

```
gradient: Gradient {
    GradientStop { position: 0; color: button.topColor }
    GradientStop { position: 1; color: button.bottomColor }
}
```

Now for the text color:

```
Text {
    id: buttonText
    text: "ButtonText"
    color: buttonMouseArea.pressed ?
        button.textPressedColor : button.textColor
}
```

As you can note, we used the `pressed` property of `MouseArea` to detect whether a mouse button is currently being pressed on the area. We can equip our button with a similar property. Add the following code to the top level `Rectangle` of the `Button` component:

```
property alias pressed: buttonMouseArea.pressed
```

What just happened?

The first set of changes introduced four new properties defining four colors that we later used in statements defining gradient and text colors for the button. In QML, you can define new properties for objects with the `property` keyword. The keyword should be followed by the property type and property name. QML understands many property types, the most common being `int`, `real`, `string`, `font`, and `color`. Property definitions can contain an optional default value for the property, preceded with a colon. The situation is different with the pressed property definition.

You can see that for the property type, the definition contains the word `alias`. It is not a property type but an indicator that the property is really an alias to another property—each time the `pressed` property of the button is accessed, the value of the `buttonMouseArea.pressed` property is returned, and every time the property is changed, it is the mouse area's property that really gets changed. With a regular property declaration, you can provide any valid expression as the default value because the expression is bound to the property. With a property alias, it is different—the value is mandatory and has to be pointing to an existing property of the same or another object.

Consider the following two definitions:

```
property int foo: someobject.prop
property alias bar: someobject.prop
```

At first glance, they are similar as they point to the same property and therefore the values returned for the properties are the same. However, the properties are really very different, which becomes apparent if you try to modify their values:

```
foo = 7
bar = 7
```

The first property actually has an expression bound to it, so assigning `7` to `foo` simply releases the binding and assigns the value `7` to the `foo` property, leaving `someobject.prop` with its original value. The second statement, however, is an alias; therefore, assigning a new value applies the modification to the `someobject.prop` property the alias is really pointing to.

Speaking of properties, there is an easy way to react when a property value is modified. For each existing property, there is a handler available that is executed whenever the property value is modified. The handler name is `on` followed by the property name, then followed by the word `Changed`, all in camel case—thus, for a `foo` property, it becomes `onFooChanged` and for `topColor`, it becomes `onTopColorChanged`. To log the current press state of the button to the console, all we need to do is implement the property change handler for this property:

```
Button {
    // ...

    onPressedChanged: {
        console.log("The button is currently " +
                    (pressed ? "" : "not ") + "pressed")
    }
```

```
}
```

In this example, we created a fully functional custom QML component. Our button reacts to mouse input and exposes some useful properties and signals to the user. This makes it a reusable and customizable object. In a real project, always think of the repeating parts of your UI and consider moving them into a single component to reduce code duplication.

Touch input

`MouseArea` is the simplest of input event elements. Nowadays, more and more devices have touch capabilities and Qt Quick can handle them as well. Currently, we have three ways of handling touch input.

First of all, simple touch events are also reported as mouse events. Tapping and sliding a finger on the screen can be handled using `MouseArea`, just like mouse input.

Time for action – Dragging an item around

Create a new **Qt Quick Application - Empty** project. Edit the `main.qml` file to add a circle to the window:

```
Rectangle {
    id: circle
    width: 60; height: width
    radius: width / 2
    color: "red"
}
```

Next, add a `MouseArea` to the circle and use its `drag` property to enable moving the circle by touch (or mouse):

```
Rectangle {
    //...
    MouseArea {
        anchors.fill: parent
        drag.target: circle
    }
}
```

Then, you can start the application and begin moving the circle around.

What just happened?

A circle was created by defining a rectangle with its height equal to width, making it a square and rounding the borders to half the side length. The `drag` property can be used to tell `MouseArea` to manage a given item's position using input events flowing into this `MouseArea` element. We denote the item to be dragged using the `target` subproperty. You can use other subproperties to control the axis the item is allowed to move along or constrain the move to a given area. An important thing to remember is that the item being dragged cannot be anchored for the axis on which the drag is requested; otherwise, the item will respect the anchor and not the drag. We didn't anchor our circle item at all since we want it to be draggable along both axes.

The second approach to handling touch input in Qt Quick applications is to use `PinchArea`, which is an item similar to `MouseArea`, but rather than dragging an item around, it allows you to rotate or scale it using two fingers (with a so called "pinch" gesture), as shown:

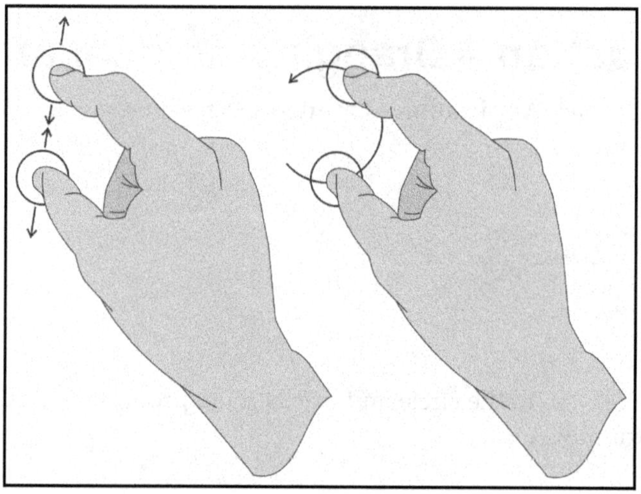

Be aware that `PinchArea` reacts only to touch input, so to test the example, you will need a real multitouch capable device.

Time for action – Rotating and scaling a picture by pinching

Start a new **Qt Quick Application - Empty** project. Add an image file to the resources, just like we previously did in the button project. In the `main.qml` file, add an image to the window and make it centered in its parent:

```
Image {
    id: image
    anchors.centerIn: parent
    source: "qrc:/wilanow.jpg"
}
```

Now, we will add a `PinchArea` element. This kind of item can be used in two ways—either by manually implementing signal handlers `onPinchStarted`, `onPinchUpdated`, and `onPinchFinished` to have total control over the functionality of the gesture, or using a simplified interface similar to the `drag` property of `MouseArea`. Since the simplified interface does exactly what we want, there is no need to handle pinch events manually. Let's add the following declaration to the file:

```
PinchArea {
    anchors.fill: parent
    pinch {
        target: image
        minimumScale: 0.2
        maximumScale: 2.0
        minimumRotation: -90
        maximumRotation: 90
    }
}
```

You'll get an output similar to the following screenshot:

What just happened?

Our simple application loads an image and centers it in the view. Then, there is a `PinchArea` item filling the view area that is told to operate on the image object. We define the range of the scaling and rotating of the item. The rest is left to the `PinchArea` item itself. If you start interacting with the application, you will see the item rotate and scale. What really happens behind the scenes is that `PinchArea` modifies the values of the two properties each Qt Quick item has—`rotation` and `scale`.

> `PinchArea` can also control the dragging of the item with `pinch.dragAxis`, just like `MouseArea` does with drag, but for simplicity, we didn't use this part of the API. Feel free to experiment with it in your own code.

Have a go hero – Rotating and scaling with a mouse

Of course, you don't have to use `PinchArea` to rotate or scale an item. Properties controlling those aspects are regular properties that you can read and write at any time. Try replacing `PinchArea` with `MouseArea` to obtain a result similar to what we just did by modifying the scale and rotation properties as a result of receiving mouse events—when the user drags the mouse while pressing the left button, the image is scaled and when the user does the same while pressing the right button, the image is rotated.

If you manage to do the task, try replacing `MouseArea` with `PinchArea` again, but then, instead of using the `pinch` property, handle events manually to obtain the same effect (the event object is called `pinch` and has a number of properties you can play with).

A third approach to handling touch input is using the `MultiPointTouchArea` item. It provides a low-level interface to gestures by reporting each touch point separately. It can be used to create custom high-level gesture handlers similar to `PinchArea`.

Keyboard input

So far, we've been dealing with pointer input, but user input is not just that—we can also handle keyboard input. This is quite simple and basically boils down to two easy steps.

First, you have to enable receiving keyboard events by stating that a particular item has keyboard focus:

```
focus: true
```

Then, you can start handling events by writing handlers in a similar fashion as for mouse events. However, `Item` doesn't provide its own handler for manipulating keys that is a counterpart for `keyPressEvent` and `keyReleaseEvent` of `QWidget`. Instead, adequate handlers are provided by the `Keys` attached property.

Attached properties are provided by elements that are not used as standalone elements but provide properties to other objects by getting attached to them as well. This is a way of adding support for new properties without modifying the API of the original element (it doesn't add new properties through an **is-a** relation, but rather through a **has-a** one). Each object that references an attached property gets its own copy of the attaching object that then handles the extra properties. We will come back to attached properties later in the chapter. For now, you just need to remember that in certain situations, an element can obtain additional properties that are not part of its API.

Let's go back to implementing event handlers for keyboard input. As we said earlier, each Item has a `Keys` attached property that allows us to install our own keyboard handlers. The basic two signals `Keys` adds to `Item` are `pressed` and `released`; therefore, we can implement the `onPressed` and `onReleased` handlers that have a `KeyEvent` argument providing similar information as `QKeyEvent` in the widget world. As an example, we can see an item that detects when the spacebar was pressed:

```
Rectangle {
    focus: true
    color: "black"
    width: 100
    height: 100
    Keys.onPressed: {
        if(event.key === Qt.Key_Space) {
             color = "red";
        }
    }
    Keys.onReleased: {
        if(event.key === Qt.Key_Space) {
            color = "blue";
        }
    }
}
```

It might become problematic if you want to handle many different keys in the same item, as the `onPressed` handler would likely contain a giant switch section with branches for every possible key. Fortunately, `Keys` offers more properties. Most of the commonly used keys (but not letters) have their own handlers that are called when the particular key is pressed. Thus, we can easily implement an item that takes a different color depending on which key was pressed last:

```
Rectangle {
    //...
    focus: true
```

```
        Keys.onSpacePressed:      color = "purple"
        Keys.onReturnPressed:     color = "navy"
        Keys.onVolumeUpPressed:   color = "blue"
        Keys.onRightPressed:      color = "green"
        Keys.onEscapePressed:     color = "yellow"
        Keys.onTabPressed:        color = "orange"
        Keys.onDigit0Pressed:     color = "red"
    }
```

Note that the `released` signal will still be emitted for every released key even if the key has its own pressed signal.

Now, consider another example:

```
Item {
    id: item
    property int number: 0
    width: 200; height: width
    focus: true
    Keys.onSpacePressed: {
        number++;
    }
    Text {
        text: item.number
        anchors.centerIn: parent
    }
}
```

We would expect that when we press and hold the spacebar, we will see the text change from `0` to `1` and stay on that value until we release the key. If you run the example, you will see that instead, the number keeps incrementing as long as you hold down the key. This is because by default, the keys autorepeat—when you hold the key, the operating system keeps sending a sequence of press-release events for the key (you can verify that by adding the `console.log()` statements to the `Keys.onPressed` and `Keys.onReleased` handlers). To counter this effect, you can differentiate between autorepeat and regular events. In Qt Quick, you can do this easily, as each key event carries the appropriate information. Simply replace the handler from the last example with the following one:

```
Keys.onSpacePressed: {
    if(!event.isAutoRepeat) {
        number++;
    }
}
```

The event variable we use here is the name of the parameter of the spacePressed signal. As we cannot declare our own names for the parameters like we can do in C++, for each signal handler, you will have to look up the name of the argument in the documentation. You can search for Keys in the documentation index to open the **Keys QML Type** page. The signal list will contain type and name of the signal's parameter, for example, spacePressed(KeyEvent event).

Whenever you process an event, you should mark it as accepted to prevent it from being propagated to other elements and handled by them:

```
Keys.onPressed: {
    if(event.key === Qt.Key_Space) {
        color = "blue";
        event.accepted = true;
    }
}
```

However, if you use a handler dedicated to an individual button (like onSpacePressed), you don't need to accept the event, as Qt will do that for you automatically.

In standard C++ applications, we usually use the *Tab* key to navigate through focusable items. With games (and fluid user interfaces in general), it is more common to use arrow keys for item navigation. Of course, we can handle this situation using the Keys attached property and adding Keys.onRightPressed, Keys.onTabPressed, and other signal handlers to each of our items where we want to modify the focus property of the desired item, but it would quickly clutter our code. Qt Quick comes to our help once again by providing a KeyNavigation attached property, which is meant to handle this specific situation and allows us to greatly simplify the needed code. Now, we can just specify which item should get into focus when a specific key is triggered:

```
Row {
    spacing: 5
    Rectangle {
        id: first
        width: 50; height: width
        color: focus ? "blue" : "lightgray"
        focus: true
        KeyNavigation.right: second
    }
    Rectangle {
        id: second
        width: 50; height: width
        color: focus ? "blue" : "lightgray"
```

```
                KeyNavigation.right: third
            }
            Rectangle {
                id: third
                width: 50; height: width
                color: focus ? "blue" : "lightgray"
            }
        }
```

Note that we made the first item get into focus in the beginning by explicitly setting the `focus` property. By setting the `KeyNavigation.right` property, we instruct Qt to focus on the specified item when this item receives a right key press event. The reverse transition is added automatically—when the left key is pressed on the second item, the first item will receive focus. Besides `right`, `KeyNavigation` contains the `left`, `down`, `up`, `tab`, and `backtab` (*Shift* + *Tab*) properties.

Both the `Keys` and `KeyNavigation` attached properties have a way to define the order in which each of the mechanisms receive the events. This is handled by the `priority` property, which can be set to either `BeforeItem` or `AfterItem`. By default, `Keys` will get the event first (`BeforeItem`), then the internal event handling can take place and finally, `KeyNavigation` will have a chance of handling the event (`AfterItem`). Note that if the key is handled by one of the mechanisms, the event is accepted and the remaining mechanisms will not receive that event.

Have a go hero – Practicing key-event propagation

As an exercise, you can expand our last example by building a larger array of items (you can use the `Grid` element to position them) and defining a navigation system that makes use of the `KeyNavigation` attached property. Have some of the items handle events themselves using the `Keys` attached property. See what happens when the same key is handled by both mechanisms. Try influencing the behavior using the `priority` property.

When you set the `focus` property of an item to `true`, any previously used item loses focus. This becomes a problem when you try to write a reusable component that needs to set focus to its children. If you add multiple instances of such a component to a single window, their focus requests will conflict with each other. Only the last item will have focus because it was created last. To overcome this problem, Qt Quick introduces a concept of **focus scopes**. By wrapping your component into a `FocusScope` item, you gain ability to set focus to an item inside the component without influencing the global focus directly.

When an instance of your component receives focus, the internal focused item will also receive focus and will be able to handle keyboard events. A good explanation of this feature is given on the **Keyboard Focus in Qt Quick** documentation page.

Text input fields

Apart from the attached properties we described, Qt Quick provides built-in elements for handling keyboard input. The two most basic types are `TextInput` and `TextEdit`, which are QML equivalents of `QLineEdit` and `QTextEdit`. The former are used for single-line text input, while the latter serves as its multiline counterpart. They both offer cursor handling, undo-redo functionality, and text selections. You can validate text typed into `TextInput` by assigning a validator to the `validator` property. For example, to obtain an item where the user can input a dot-separated IP address, we can use the following declaration:

```
TextInput {
    id: ipAddress
    width: 100
    validator: RegExpValidator {
        // four numbers separated by dots
        regExp: /\d+\.\d+\.\d+\.\d+/
    }
    focus: true
}
```

The regular expression only verifies the format of the address. The user can still insert bogus numbers. You should either do a proper check before using the address or provide a more complex regular expression that will constrain the range of numbers the user can enter.

One thing to remember is that neither `TextInput` nor `TextEdit` has any visual appearance (apart from the text and cursor they contain), so if you want to give the user some visual hint as to where the item is positioned, the easiest solution is to wrap it in a styled rectangle:

```
Rectangle {
  id: textInputFrame
  width: 200
  height: 40
  border { color: "black"; width: 2 }
  radius: 10
  antialiasing: true
  color: "darkGray"
```

```
    }
    TextInput {
      id: textInput
      anchors.fill: textInputFrame
      anchors.margins: 5
      font.pixelSize: height-2
      verticalAlignment: TextInput.AlignVCenter
      clip: true
    }
```

Note that the highlighted code—the `clip` property of `textInput`—is enabled such that by default, if the text entered in the box doesn't fit in the item, it will overflow it and remain visible outside the actual item. By enabling clipping, we explicitly say that anything that doesn't fit the item should not be drawn.

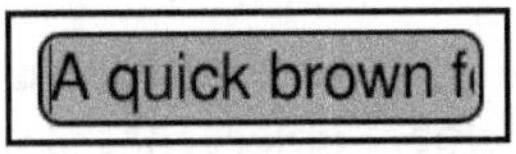

The `QtQuick.Controls` module provides more advanced text input controls, such as `TextField` and `TextArea`. We've already used them in our project in `Chapter 11`, *Introduction to Qt Quick*.

Gamepad input

Handling gamepad events is a very common task when developing a game. Fortunately, Qt provides Qt Gamepad module for this purpose. We already learned how to use it in C++. Now let's see how to do this in QML applications.

To enable Qt Gamepad module, add `QT += gamepad` to the project file. Next, import the QML module by adding the following line at the beginning of your QML file:

```
import QtGamepad 1.0
```

This import allows you to declare objects of the `Gamepad` type. Add the following object inside your top-level QML object:

```
Gamepad {
    id: gamepad
    deviceId: GamepadManager.connectedGamepads.length > 0 ?
        GamepadManager.connectedGamepads[0] : -1
}
```

The GamepadManager object allows us to list identifiers of gamepads available in the system. We use the first available gamepad if any are present in the system. If you want the game to pick up a connected gamepad on the fly, use the following code snippet:

```
Connections {
    target: GamepadManager
    onGamepadConnected: gamepad.deviceId = deviceId
}
```

What just happened?

The preceding code simply adds a signal handler for the gamepadConnected signal of the GamepadManager object. The usual way to add a signal handler is to declare it directly in the section of the sender. However, we can't do that in this case, since GamepadManager is an existing global object that is not part of our QML object tree. Thus, we use the Connections QML type that allows us to specify an arbitrary sender (using the target property) and attach a signal handler to it. You can think of Connections as a declarative version of QObject::connect calls.

The initialization is done, so we can now use the gamepad object to request information about the gamepad input. There are two ways to do that.

First, we can use property bindings to set properties of other objects depending on the buttons pressed on the gamepad:

```
Text {
    text: gamepad.buttonStart ? "Start!" : ""
}
```

Whenever the start button is pressed or released on the gamepad, the value of the gamepad.buttonStart property will be set to true or false, and the QML engine will automatically update the displayed text.

The second way is to add a signal handler to detect when a property changes:

```
Gamepad {
    //...
    onButtonStartChanged: {
        if (value) {
            console.log("start pressed");
        } else {
            console.log("start released");
        }
```

```
        }
    }
```

The `Gamepad` QML type has a separate property and signal for each gamepad button, just like the `QGamepad` C++ class.

You can also use the `GamepadKeyNavigation` QML type to introduce gamepad support to a game that supports keyboard input:

```
    GamepadKeyNavigation {
        gamepad: gamepad
        active: true
        buttonStartKey: Qt.Key_S
    }
```

When this object is declared in your QML file, gamepad events provided by the `gamepad` object will be automatically converted to key events. By default, `GamepadKeyNavigation` is able to emulate up, down, left, right, back, forward, and return keys when the corresponding gamepad buttons are pressed. However, you can override the default mapping or add your own mapping for other gamepad buttons. In the preceding example, we tell `GamepadKeyNavigation` that the start key on the gamepad should act as if the *S* key was pressed on the keyboard. You can now handle these events just as any regular keyboard event.

Sensor input

Qt is reaching out to more and more platforms that are used nowadays. This includes a number of popular mobile platforms. Mobile devices are usually equipped with additional hardware, less often seen on desktop systems. Let's see how to handle sensor input in Qt so that you can use it in your games.

Most of the features discussed in this section are not usually available on desktops. If you want to play with them, you need to set up running Qt applications on a mobile device. This requires a few configuration steps that depend on your target platform. Please refer to Qt documentation for exact instructions, as they will offer complete and up-to-date information that wouldn't be possible to provide in a book. Good starting points are **Getting Started with Qt for Android** and **Qt for iOS** documentation pages.

Access to sensors present on mobile devices is provided by the Qt Sensors module and must be imported before it can be used:

```
import QtSensors 5.0
```

There are a lot of QML types you can use to interact with sensors. Have a look at this impressive list:

QML type	Description
`Accelerometer`	Reports the device's linear acceleration along the *x*, *y*, and *z* axes.
`Altimeter`	Reports the altitude in meters relative to mean sea level.
`AmbientLightSensor`	Reports the intensity of the ambient light.
`AmbientTemperatureSensor`	Reports the temperature in degree Celsius of the current device's ambient.
`Compass`	Reports the azimuth of the device's top as degrees from magnetic north.
`DistanceSensor`	Reports distance in cm from an object to the device.
`Gyroscope`	Reports the device's movement around its axes in degrees per second.
`HolsterSensor`	Reports if the device is holstered in a specific pocket.
`HumiditySensor`	Reports on humidity.
`IRProximitySensor`	Reports the reflectance of the outgoing infrared light. The range is from 0 (zero reflection) to 1 (total reflection).
`LidSensor`	Reports on whether a device is closed.
`LightSensor`	Reports the intensity of light in lux.
`Magnetometer`	Reports the device's magnetic flux density along its axes.
`OrientationSensor`	Reports the orientation of the device.
`PressureSensor`	Reports the atmospheric pressure in Pascals.
`ProximitySensor`	Reports if an object is close to the device. Which distance is considered "close" depends on the device.
`RotationSensor`	Reports the three angles that define the orientation of the device in a three-dimensional space.
`TapSensor`	Reports if a device was tapped.

QML type	Description
`TiltSensor`	Reports the angle of tilt in degrees along the device's axes.

> Unfortunately, not all sensors are supported on all platforms. Check out the **Compatibility Map** documentation page to see which sensors are supported on your target platforms before trying to use them.

All these types inherit the `Sensor` type and provide similar API. First, create a sensor object and activate it by setting its `active` property to `true`. When the hardware reports new values, they are assigned to the sensor's `reading` property. As with any property in QML, you can choose between using the property directly, using it in a property binding, or using the `onReadingChanged` handler to react to each new value of the property.

The type of the `reading` object corresponds to the type of the sensor. For example, if you use a tilt sensor, you'll receive a `TiltReading` object that provides suitable properties to access the angle of tilt around the *x* (`xRotation`) and *y* (`yRotation`) axes. For each sensor type, Qt provides a corresponding reading type that contains the sensor data.

All readings also have the `timestamp` property that contains the number of microseconds since some fixed point. That point can be different for different sensor objects, so you can only use it to calculate time intervals between two readings of the same sensor.

The following QML code contains a complete example of using a tilt sensor:

```
import QtQuick 2.9
import QtQuick.Window 2.2
import QtSensors 5.0
Window {
    visible: true
    width: 640
    height: 480
    title: qsTr("Hello World")
    Text {
        anchors.centerIn: parent
        text: {
            if (!tiltSensor.reading) {
                return "No data";
            }
            var x = tiltSensor.reading.xRotation;
```

```
            var y = tiltSensor.reading.yRotation;
            return "X: " + Math.round(x) +
                   " Y: " + Math.round(y)
        }
    }
    TiltSensor {
        id: tiltSensor
        active: true
        onReadingChanged: {
            // process new reading
        }
    }
}
```

When this application receives a new reading, the text on screen will be automatically updated. You can also use the `onReadingChanged` handler to process new data in another way.

Detecting device location

Some modern games require information about the player's geographic location and other related data, such as movement speed. The Qt Positioning module allows you to access this information. Let's see a basic QML example of determining the location:

```
import QtQuick 2.9
import QtQuick.Window 2.2
import QtPositioning 5.0
Window {
    visible: true
    width: 640
    height: 480
    title: qsTr("Hello World")
    Text {
        anchors.centerIn: parent
        text: {
            var pos = positionSource.position;
            var coordinate = pos.coordinate;
            return "latitude: " + coordinate.latitude +
              "\nlongitude: " + coordinate.longitude;
        }
    }
    PositionSource {
        id: positionSource
        active: true
        onPositionChanged: {
            console.log("pos changed",
```

```
                                   position.coordinate.latitude,
                                   position.coordinate.longitude);
            }
        }
    }
```

First, we import the `QtPositioning` module into scope. Next, we create a `PositionSource` object and set its `active` property to true. The `position` property of the `PositionSource` object will be automatically updated as new information is available. In addition to latitude and longitude, this property also contains information about altitude, direction and speed of travel, and accuracy of location. Since some of values may not be available, each value is accompanied with a Boolean property that indicates if the data is present. For example, if `directionValid` is true, then `direction` value was set.

There are multiple ways to determine the player's location. The `PositionSource` type has a few properties that allow you to specify the source of the data. First, the `preferredPositioningMethods` property allows you to choose between satellite data, non-satellite data, or using both of them. The `supportedPositioningMethods` property holds information about currently available methods. You can also use the `nmeaSource` property to provide an NMEA position-specification data file which overrides any other data sources and can be used to simulate the device's location and movement which is very useful during development and testing of the game.

Creating advanced QML components

By now, you should be familiar with the very basics of QML and Qt Quick. Now, we can start combining what you know and fill the gaps with more information to build more advanced QML components. Our target will be to display an analog clock.

Time for action – A simple analog clock application

Create a new **Qt Quick Application - Empty** project. To create a clock, we will implement a component representing the clock needle, and we will use instances of that component in the actual clock element. In addition to this, we will make the clock a reusable component; therefore, we will create it in a separate file and instantiate it from within `main.qml`:

```
Window {
    visible: true
    width: 640
    height: 480
    title: qsTr("Hello World")

    Clock {
        id: clock
        anchors {
            fill: parent
            margins: 20
        }
    }
}
```

We use the `anchors` property group to expand the item to fit the whole window except for the 20-pixel margin for all four sides.

Before this code works, however, we need to add a new QML file for the `Clock` component. Locate the `qml.qrc` resource file in the project tree and select **Add New...** in its context menu. From the **Qt** category, select **QML File (Qt Quick 2)**, input `Clock` as the name and confirm the operation. A new file called `Clock.qml` will be created and added to the resources list.

Let's start by declaring a circular clock plate:

```
import QtQuick 2.9

Item {
    id: clock

    property color color: "lightgray"

    Rectangle {
        id: plate

        anchors.centerIn: parent
        width: Math.min(clock.width, clock.height)
        height: width
        radius: width / 2
        color: clock.color
        border.color: Qt.darker(color)
        border.width: 2
    }
}
```

If you run the program now, you'll see a plain gray circle hardly resembling a clock plate:

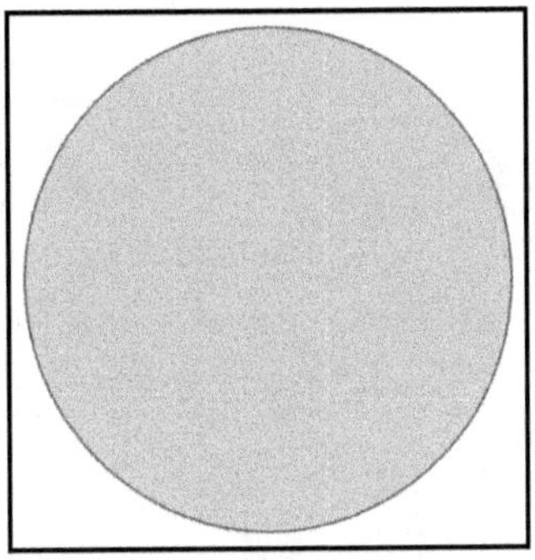

The next step is to add marks dividing the plate into 12 sections. We can do this by putting the following declaration inside the `plate` object:

```
Repeater {
    model: 12

    Item {
        id: hourContainer

        property int hour: index
        height: plate.height / 2
        transformOrigin: Item.Bottom
        rotation: index * 30
        x: plate.width/2
        y: 0

        Rectangle {
            width: 2
            height: (hour % 3 == 0) ? plate.height * 0.1
                                    : plate.height * 0.05
            color: plate.border.color
            antialiasing: true
            anchors.horizontalCenter: parent.horizontalCenter
            anchors.top: parent.top
            anchors.topMargin: 4
        }
    }
}
```

Running the program should now give the following result, looking much more like a clock plate:

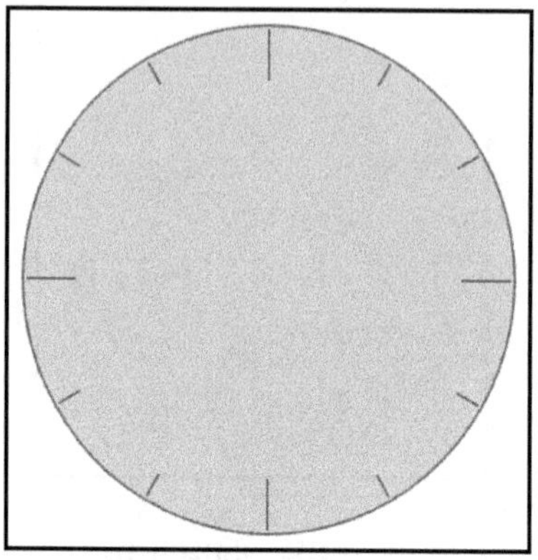

What just happened?

The code we just created introduces a couple of new features. Let's go through them one by one.

First of all, we used a new element called `Repeater`. It does exactly what its name says—it repeats items declared within it using a given model. For each entry in the model, it creates an instance of a component assigned to a property called `delegate` (the property name means that it contains an entity to which the caller delegates some responsibility, such as describing a component to be used as a stencil by the caller). `Item` declared in `Repeater` describes the delegate even though we cannot see it explicitly assigned to a property. This is because `delegate` is a default property of the `Repeater` type, which means anything unassigned to any property explicitly gets implicitly assigned to the default property of the type.

> The `Item` type also has a default property called `data`. It holds a list of elements that gets automatically split into two "sublists"—the list of the item's children (which creates the hierarchy of `Item` instances in Qt Quick) and another list called resources, which contains all "child" elements that do not inherit from `Item`. You have direct access to all three lists, which means calling `children[2]` will return the third `Item` element declared in the item, and `data[5]` will return the sixth element declared in the `Item`, regardless of whether the given element is a visual item (that inherits `Item`) or not.

The model can be a number of things, but in our case, it is simply a number denoting how many times the delegate should be repeated. The component to be repeated is a transparent item containing a rectangle. The item has a property declared called `hour` that has the `index` variable bound to it. The latter is a property assigned by `Repeater` to each instance of the delegate component. The value it contains is the index of the instance in the `Repeater` object—since we have a model containing twelve elements, `index` will hold values within a range of `0` to `11`. The item can make use of the `index` property to customize instances created by `Repeater`. In this particular case, we use `index` to provide values for a `rotation` property and by multiplying the index by `30`, we get values starting from `0` for the first instance and ending at `330` for the last one.

The `rotation` property brings us to the second most important subject—item transformations. Each item can be transformed in a number of ways, including rotating the item and scaling it in two-dimensional space, as we already mentioned earlier. Another property called `transformOrigin` denotes the origin point around which scale and rotation are applied. By default, it points to `Item.Center`, which makes the item scale and rotate around its center, but we can change it to eight other values, such as `Item.TopLeft` for the top-left corner or `Item.Right` for the middle of the right edge of the item. In the code we crafted, we rotate each item clockwise around its bottom edge. Each item is positioned horizontally in the middle of the plate using the `plate.width / 2` expression and vertically at the top of the plate with the default width of `0` and the height of half the plate's height; thus, each item is a thin vertical line spanning from within the top to the center of the plate. Then, each item is rotated around the center of the plate (each item's bottom edge) by 30 degrees more than a previous item effectively laying items evenly on the plate.

Finally, each item has a gray `Rectangle` attached to the top edge (offset by `4`) and horizontally centered in the transparent parent. Transformations applied to an item influence the item's children similar to what we have seen in Graphics View; thus, the effective rotation of the rectangle follows that of its parent. The height of the rectangle depends on the value of `hour`, which maps to the index of the item in `Repeater`. Here, you cannot use `index` directly as it is only visible within the topmost item of the delegate. That's why we create a real property called `hour` that can be referenced from within the whole delegate item hierarchy.

If you want more control over item transformations, then we are happy to inform you that apart from rotation and scale properties, each item can be assigned an array of elements such as `Rotation`, `Scale`, and `Translate` to a property called `transform`, which are applied in order, one at a time. These types have properties for fine-grained control over the transformation. For instance, using `Rotation`, you can implement rotation over any of the three axes and around a custom origin point (instead of being limited to nine predefined origin points as when using the `rotation` property of `Item`).

Time for action – Adding needles to the clock

The next step is to add the hour, minute, and second needles to the clock. Let's start by creating a new component called `Needle` in a file called `Needle.qml` (remember that component names and files representing them need to start with a capital letter):

```
import QtQuick 2.9

Rectangle {
    id: root

    property int value: 0
    property int granularity: 60
    property alias length: root.height

    width: 2
    height: parent.height / 2
    radius: width / 2
    antialiasing: true
    anchors.bottom: parent.verticalCenter
    anchors.horizontalCenter: parent.horizontalCenter
    transformOrigin: Item.Bottom
    rotation: 360 / granularity * (value % granularity)
}
```

`Needle` is basically a rectangle anchored to the center of its parent by its bottom edge, which is also the item's pivot. It also has the `value` and `granularity` properties driving the rotation of the item, where `value` is the current value the needle shows and `granularity` is the number of different values it can display. Also, anti-aliasing for the needle is enabled as we want the tip of the needle nicely rounded. Having such a definition, we can use the component to declare the three needles inside the clock plate object:

```
Needle {
    length: plate.height * 0.3
    color: "blue"
    value: clock.hours
    granularity: 12
}
Needle {
    length: plate.height * 0.4
    color: "darkgreen"
    value: clock.minutes
    granularity: 60
}
Needle {
    width: 1
    length: plate.height * 0.45
    color: "red"
    value: clock.seconds
    granularity: 60
}
```

The three needles make use of the `hours`, `minutes`, and `seconds` properties of clock, so these need to be declared as well:

```
property int hours: 0
property int minutes: 0
property int seconds: 0
```

By assigning different values to the properties of `Clock` in `main.qml`, you can make the clock show a different time:

```
import QtQuick 2.9

Clock {
    //...
    hours: 7
    minutes: 42
    seconds: 17
}
```

You'll get an output as shown:

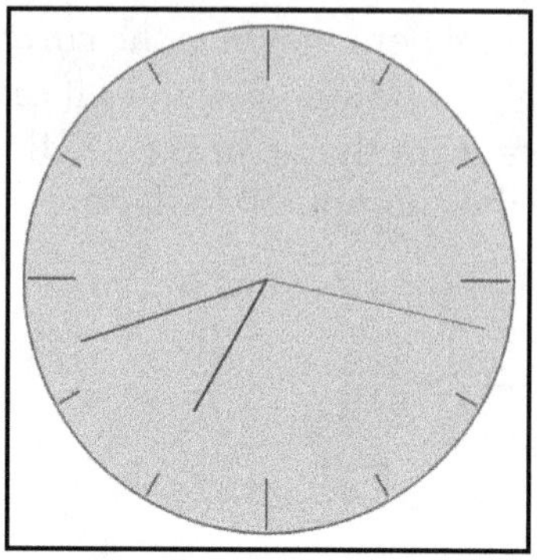

What just happened?

Most `Needle` functionality is declared in the component itself, including geometry and transformations. Then, whenever we want to use the component, we declare an instance of `Needle` and optionally customize the `length` and `color` properties as well as set its `value` and `granularity` to obtain the exact functionality we need.

Time for action – Making the clock functional

The final step in creating a clock is to make it actually show the current time. In JavaScript, we can query the current time using the `Date` object:

```
var currentDate = new Date();
var hours   = currentDate.getHours();
var minutes = currentDate.getMinutes();
var seconds = currentDate.getSeconds();
```

Therefore, the first thing that comes to mind is to use the preceding code to show the current time on the clock:

```
Item {
    id: clock
    property int hours:   currentDate.getHours()
    property int minutes: currentDate.getMinutes()
    property int seconds: currentDate.getSeconds()
    property date currentDate: new Date()
    // ...
}
```

This will indeed show the current time once you start the application, but the clock will not be updating itself as the time passes. This is because `new Date()` returns an object representing one particular moment in time (the date and time at the moment when the object was instantiated). While QML usually is capable of automatically updating a property when the value of the bound expression changes, it's unable to do so in this case. Even if QML was smart enough to see that the `new Date()` property always returns a different date, it doesn't know how often we want to update the value, and updating it as frequently as possible is generally a bad idea. Thus, we need a way to manually schedule periodic execution of an action.

To obtain this effect in QML, we can use a `Timer` element that is an equivalent of `QTimer` in C++ and lets us periodically execute some code. Let's modify the code to use a timer:

```
Item {
    id: clock
    //...
    property alias running: timer.running
    Timer {
        id: timer
        repeat: true
        interval: 500
        running: true
        onTriggered: clock.currentDate = new Date()
    }
    //...
}
```

What just happened?

By setting the `interval` property, we ask the timer to emit the `triggered` signal every 500 ms, causing our `currentDate` property to be updated with a new `Date` object representing the current time. The clock is also given the `running` property (pointing to its equivalent in the timer) that can control whether updates should be enabled. The timer's `repeat` property is set to `true`; otherwise, it will trigger just once.

To briefly sum up what you have learned so far, we can say that you know how to create hierarchies of objects by declaring their instances, and you also know how to program new types in separate files, making definitions available as components to be instantiated in other QML files. You can even use the `Repeater` element to declare a series of objects based on a common stencil.

Dynamic and lazy loading of QML objects

All our previous QML projects contain an explicit declaration of the object tree. We usually create a window and place multiple specific elements into it in specific order. The QML engine creates these objects on startup and keeps them alive until the application terminates. This is a very convenient approach that allows you to save a lot of time, as you could see in our previous examples. However, sometimes you need the object tree to be more flexible—for example, if you don't know upfront which elements should be created. QML offers a few ways to create objects dynamically and to delay creating an object until you really need it. Utilizing these features can make your QML application more performant and flexible.

Creating objects on request

The problem with predeclaring objects directly in a QML file is that you need to know upfront how many objects you will need. More often than not, you will want to dynamically add and remove objects to your scene, for example, in an alien invasion game, where, as the player progresses, new alien saucers will be entering the game screen and other saucers will be getting shot down and destroyed. Also, the player's ship will be "producing" new bullets streaking in front of the ship, eventually running out of fuel or otherwise disappearing from the game scene. By putting a good amount of effort into the problem, you will be able to use `Repeater` to obtain this effect, but there is a better tool at hand.

QML offers us another element type called `Component`, which is another way to teach the engine about a new element type by declaring its contents in QML. There are basically two approaches to doing this.

The first approach is to declare a `Component` element instance in the QML file and inline the definition of the new type directly inside the element:

```
Component {
    id: circleComponent
    Item {
        //...
    }
}
```

The other approach is to load the component definition from an existing QML file. Let's say that we have a `Circle.qml` file with the following content:

```
import QtQuick 2.9
Item {
    property int diameter: 20
    property alias color: rect.color
    property alias border: rect.border

    implicitWidth: diameter
    implicitHeight: diameter

    Rectangle {
        id: rect
        width: radius
        height: radius
        radius: diameter / 2
        anchors.centerIn: parent
    }
}
```

Such code declares a component that defines a circle and exposes its `diameter`, `color`, and `border` properties. Let's see how we can create instances of this component dynamically.

QML exposes a special global object called `Qt`, which provides a set of interesting methods. One of the methods allows the caller to create a component passing the URL of an existing QML document:

```
var circleComponent = Qt.createComponent("Circle.qml");
```

An interesting note is that `createComponent` can not only accept a local file path but also a remote URL, and if it understands the network scheme (for example, `http`), it will download the document automatically. In this case, you have to remember that it takes time to do that, so the component may not be ready immediately after calling `createComponent`. Since the current loading status is kept in the `status` property, you can connect to the `statusChanged` signal to be notified when this happens. A typical code path looks similar to the following:

```
Window {
    //...
    Component.onCompleted: {
        var circleComponent = Qt.createComponent("Circle.qml");
        if(circleComponent.status === Component.Ready) {
            addCircles(circleComponent);
        } else {
```

```
                circleComponent.statusChanged.connect(function() {
                    if(circleComponent.status === Component.Ready) {
                        addCircles(circleComponent);
                    }
                });
            }
        }
    }
```

In this example, we use the `Component.onCompleted` handler to run the code as soon as the window object is created. This handler is available in all Qt Quick items and is often used to perform initialization. You can also use any other signal handler here. For example, you can start loading the component when a button is pressed or a timer has expired.

> The counterpart of the `completed()` signal of `Component` is `destruction()`. You can use the `Component.onDestruction` handler to perform actions such as saving the state of the object to persistent storage or otherwise cleaning the object up.

If the component definition is incorrect or the document cannot be retrieved, the status of the object will change to `Error`. In that case, you can make use of the `errorString()` method to see what the actual problem is:

```
if(circleComponent.status === Component.Error) {
    console.warn(circleComponent.errorString());
}
```

Once you are sure that the component is ready, you can finally start creating objects from it. For this, the component exposes a method called `createObject`. In its simplest form, it accepts an object that is to become the parent of the newly born instance (similar to widget constructors accepting a pointer to a parent widget) and returns the new object itself so that you can assign it to some variable. Then, you can start setting the object's properties:

```
Window {
    //...
    ColumnLayout {
        id: layout
        anchors.fill: parent
    }
    function addCircles(circleComponent) {
        ["red", "yellow", "green"].forEach(function(color) {
            var circle = circleComponent.createObject(layout);
```

```
                circle.color = color;
                circle.Layout.alignment = Qt.AlignCenter;
            });
        }
        //...
    }
```

A more complex invocation lets us do both these operations (create the object and set its properties) in a single call by passing a second parameter to `createObject`:

```
var circle = circleComponent.createObject(layout,
    { diameter: 20, color: 'red' });
```

The second parameter is a JavaScript object whose properties are to be applied to the object being created. The advantage of the latter syntax is that all property values are applied to the object as one atomic operation and they won't trigger property change handlers (just like when the item is declared in a QML document) instead of a series of separate operations, each of which sets the value for a single property, possibly causing an avalanche of change handler invocations in the object.

After creation, the object becomes a first-class citizen of the scene, acting in the same way as items declared directly in the QML document. The only difference is that a dynamically created object can also be dynamically destructed by calling its `destroy()` method, which is similar to calling `delete` on C++ objects. When speaking of destroying dynamic items, we have to point out that when you assign a result of `createObject` to a variable (like `circle`, in our example) and that variable goes out of scope, the item will not be released and garbage collected as its parent still holds a reference to it, preventing it from being recycled.

We didn't mention this explicitly before, but we have already used inline component definitions earlier in this chapter when we introduced the `Repeater` element. The repeated item defined within the repeater is in fact not a real item, but a component definition that is instantiated as many times as needed by the repeater.

Delaying item creation

Another recurring scenario is that you do know how many elements you will need, but the problem is that you cannot determine upfront what type of elements they will be. At some point during the lifetime of your application, you will learn that information and will be able to instantiate an object. Until you gain the knowledge about the given component, you will need some kind of item placeholder where you will later put the real item. You can, of course, write some code to use the `createObject()` functionality of the component, but this is cumbersome.

Fortunately, Qt Quick offers a nicer solution in the form of a `Loader` item. This item type is exactly what we described it to be—a temporary placeholder for a real item that will be loaded on demand from an existing component. You can put `Loader` in place of another item and when you need to create this item, one way is to set the URL of a component to the `source` property:

```
Loader {
    id: loader
}
//...
onSomeSignal: loader.source = "Circle.qml"
```

You can also directly attach a real component to the `sourceComponent` of a `Loader`:

```
Loader {
    id: loader
    sourceComponent: shouldBeLoaded ? circleComponent : undefined
}
```

Immediately afterward, the magic begins and an instance of the component appears in the loader. If the `Loader` object has its size set explicitly (for example, by anchoring or setting the width and height), then the item will be resized to the size of the loader. If an explicit size is not set, then `Loader` will instead be resized to the size of the loaded element once the component is instantiated. In the following code, the loader has its size set explicitly, so when its item is created, it will respect the anchors and sizes declared here:

```
Loader {
    anchors {
        left: parent.left
        leftMargin: 0.2 * parent.width
        right: parent.right
        verticalCenter: parent.verticalCenter
    }
    height: 250
    source: "Circle.qml"
}
```

Imperative painting on Canvas using JavaScript

Declaring graphical items is nice and easy, but as programmers, we're more used to writing imperative code, and some things are easier expressed as an algorithm rather than as a description of the final result to be achieved. It is easy to use QML to encode a definition of a primitive shape such as a rectangle in a compact way—all we need is to mark the origin point of the rectangle, its width, height, and optionally, a color. Writing down a declarative definition of a complex shape consisting of many control points positioned in given absolute coordinates, possibly with an outline in some parts of it, maybe accompanied by an image or two, is still possible in a language such as QML; however, this will result in a much more verbose and much less readable definition. This is a case where using an imperative approach might prove more effective. HTML (being a declarative language) already exposes a proven imperative interface for drawing different primitives called a `Canvas` that is widely used in web applications. Fortunately, Qt Quick provides us with its own implementation of a `Canvas` interface similar to the one from the web by letting us instantiate `Canvas` items. Such items can be used to draw straight and curved lines, simple and complex shapes, and graphs and graphic images. It can also add text, colors, shadows, gradients, and patterns. It can even perform low-level pixel operations. Finally, the output may be saved as an image file or serialized to a URL usable as source for an `Image` item. There are many tutorials and papers available out there on using an HTML canvas, and they can usually be easily applied to a Qt Quick canvas as well (the reference manual even includes a list of aspects you need to pay attention to when porting HTML canvas applications to a Qt Quick Canvas), so here we will just give you the very basics of imperative drawing in Qt Quick.

Consider a game where the player's health is measured by the condition of his heart—the slower the beat, the healthier the player is. We will use this kind of visualization as our exercise in practicing painting using the `Canvas` element.

Time for action – Preparing Canvas for heartbeat visualization

Let's start with simple things by creating an empty Qt Quick project. Add the following code to the main.qml file:

```
Window {
    //...
    Canvas {
        id: canvas

        implicitWidth: 600
        implicitHeight: 300

        onPaint: {
            var ctx = canvas.getContext("2d");
            ctx.clearRect(0, 0, canvas.width, canvas.height);
            ctx.strokeRect(50, 50, 100, 100);
        }
    }
}
```

When you run the project, you will see a window containing a rectangle:

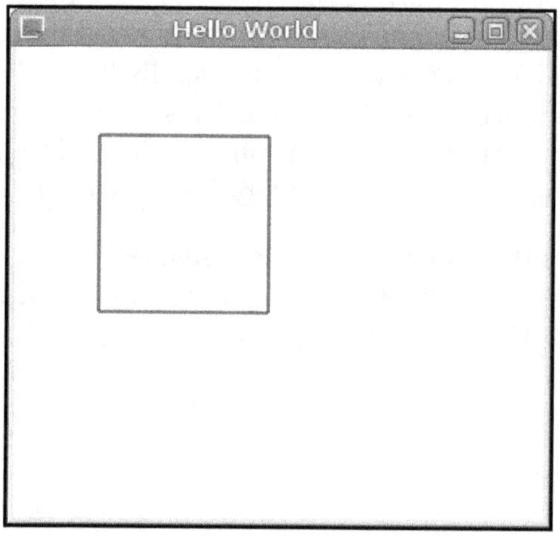

What just happened?

In the preceding code, we created a basic boilerplate code for using a canvas. First, we created a `Canvas` instance with an implicit width and height set. There, we created a handler for the `paint` signal that is emitted whenever the canvas needs to be redrawn. The code placed there retrieves a context for the canvas, which can be thought of as an equivalent to the `QPainter` instance we used when drawing on Qt widgets. We inform the canvas that we want its 2D context, which gives us a way to draw in two dimensions. A 2D context is the only context currently present for the `Canvas` element, but you still have to identify it explicitly—similar to HTML. Having the context ready, we tell it to clear the whole area of the canvas. This is different from the widget world in which when the `paintEvent` handler was called, the widget was already cleared for us and everything had to be redrawn from scratch. With `Canvas`, it is different; the previous content is kept by default so that you can draw over it if you want. Since we want to start with a clean sheet, we call `clearRect()` on the context. Finally, we use the `strokeRect()` convenience method that draws a rectangle on the canvas.

Time for action - drawing a heartbeat

We will extend our component now and implement its main functionality—drawing a heartbeat-like diagram.

Add the following property declarations to the `canvas` object:

```
property int lineWidth: 2
property var points: []
property real arg: -Math.PI
```

Inside the `Canvas` section, add a declaration for a timer that will trigger updates of the picture:

```
Timer {
    interval: 10
    repeat: true
    running: true
    onTriggered: {
        canvas.arg += Math.PI / 180;
        while(canvas.arg >= Math.PI) {
            canvas.arg -= 2 * Math.PI;
        }
    }
}
```

Then again, inside the `Canvas` section, define the handler for when the value of `arg` is modified:

```
onArgChanged: {
    points.push(func(arg));
    points = points.slice(-canvas.width);
    canvas.requestPaint();
}
```

This handler uses a custom JavaScript function—`func()`. Place the implementation of the function just above the handler:

```
function func(argument) {
    var a = (2 * Math.PI / 10);
    var b = 4 * Math.PI / 5;
    return Math.sin(20 * argument) * (
        Math.exp(-Math.pow(argument / a, 2)) +
        Math.exp(-Math.pow((argument - b) / a, 2)) +
        Math.exp(-Math.pow((argument + b) / a, 2))
    );
}
```

Finally, modify the `onPaint` signal handler:

```
onPaint: {
    var ctx = canvas.getContext("2d");
    ctx.reset();
    ctx.clearRect(0, 0, canvas.width, canvas.height);
    var pointsToDraw = points.slice(-canvas.width);
    ctx.translate(0, canvas.height / 2);
    ctx.beginPath();
    ctx.moveTo(0, -pointsToDraw[0] * canvas.height / 2);
    for(var i = 1; i < pointsToDraw.length; i++) {
        ctx.lineTo(i, -pointsToDraw[i] * canvas.height / 2);
    }
    ctx.lineWidth = canvas.lineWidth;
    ctx.stroke();
}
```

Then, you can run the code and see a heartbeat-like diagram appear on the canvas:

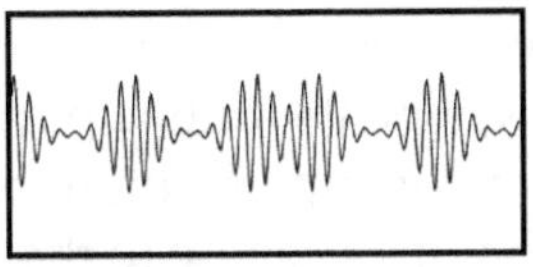

What just happened?

We added two kinds of properties to the element. By introducing `lineWidth`, we can manipulate the width of the line that visualizes the heartbeat. The `points` variable stores an array of already calculated function values. We initialize it to an empty array. The `arg` variable stores the function argument that was last evaluated. The argument of the function should be in the range from $-\pi$ to $+\pi$; thus, we initialize `arg` to `-Math.PI`. Then, we add a timer that ticks in regular intervals, incrementing `arg` by 1° until it reaches $+\pi$, in which case it is reset to the initial value.

Changes to `arg` are intercepted in the handler we implement next. In there, we push a new item to the array of points. The value is calculated by the `func` function, which is quite complicated, but it is sufficient to say that it returns a value from within a range of –1 to +1. The oldest records are removed from the array of points using `Array.slice()` so that at most, the last `canvas.width` items remain in the array. This is so that we can plot one point for each pixel of the width of the canvas, and we don't have to store any more data than required. At the end of the function, we invoke `requestPaint()`, which is an equivalent of `QWidget::update()` and schedules a repaint of the canvas.

That, in turn, calls our `onPaint` signal handler. There, after retrieving the context, we reset the canvas to its initial state and then calculate an array of points that is to be drawn again using `slice()`. Then, we prepare the canvas by translating and scaling it in the vertical axis so that the origin is moved to half of the height of the canvas (that's the reason for calling `reset()` at the beginning of the procedure—to revert this transformation). After that, `beginPath()` is called to inform the context that we are starting to build a new path. Then, the path is built segment by segment by appending lines. Each value is multiplied by `canvas.height / 2` so that values from the point array are scaled to the size of the item. The value is negated as the vertical axis of the canvas grows to the bottom, and we want positive values to be above the origin line. After that, we set the width of the pen and draw the path by calling `stroke()`.

Time for action – Hiding properties

If we convert our heartbeat canvas to a QML component, the `points` and `arg` properties will be the public properties visible to the user of the component. However, they are really implementation details we want to hide. We should only expose properties that make sense to the user of the component, such as `lineWidth` or `color`.

Since the `Timer` object inside the `Canvas` is not exported as public property, that timer object will be unavailable from the outside, so we can attach properties to the timer instead of attaching them to the top-level `Canvas` object. However, the properties do not belong to the timer logically, so this solution will be confusing. For such cases, there is a convention that you should create an empty `QtObject` child in the top-level object and move properties into it:

```
Canvas {
    id: canvas
    property int lineWidth: 2
    //...
    QtObject {
        id: d
        property var points: []
        property real arg: -Math.PI

        function func(argument) { /* ... */ }
        onArgChanged: { /* ... */ }
    }
    //...
}
```

`QtObject` is the QML representation of the `QObject` class. It is a QML type that doesn't have any particular functionality, but can hold properties. As part of the convention, we set `id` of this object to `d`. The `onArgChanged` handler is moved to the private object as well. In the `onTriggered` and `onPaint` handlers, we should now refer to the internal properties as `d.points` and `d.arg`. Consider this example:

```
onTriggered: {
    d.arg += Math.PI / 180;
    while(d.arg >= Math.PI) {
        d.arg -= 2 * Math.PI;
    }
}
```

The `points` and `arg` properties are now unavailable from the outside, leading to clean public interface of our heartbeat object.

Time for action – Making the diagram more colorful

The diagram serves its purpose, but it looks a bit dull. Add some shine to it by defining three new color properties in the canvas object—`color`, `topColor`, `bottomColor`—and setting their default values to `black`, `red`, and `blue`, respectively:

```
property color color: "black"
property color topColor: "red"
property color bottomColor: "blue"
```

Then, let's make use of these properties by extending `onPaint` implementation:

```
onPaint: {
    //...
    // fill:
    ctx.beginPath();
    ctx.moveTo(0, 0);
    var i;
    for(i = 0; i < pointsToDraw.length; i++) {
        ctx.lineTo(i, -pointsToDraw[i] * canvas.height/2);
    }
    ctx.lineTo(i, 0);
    var gradient = ctx.createLinearGradient(
            0, -canvas.height / 2, 0, canvas.height / 2);
    gradient.addColorStop(0.1, canvas.topColor);
    gradient.addColorStop(0.5, Qt.rgba(1, 1, 1, 0));
    gradient.addColorStop(0.9, canvas.bottomColor);
    ctx.fillStyle = gradient;
    ctx.fill();

    // stroke:
    ctx.beginPath();
    ctx.moveTo(0, -pointsToDraw[0] * canvas.height / 2);
    for(i = 1; i < pointsToDraw.length; i++) {
        ctx.lineTo(i, -pointsToDraw[i] * canvas.height / 2);
    }
    ctx.lineWidth = canvas.lineWidth;
    ctx.strokeStyle = canvas.color;
    ctx.stroke();
}
```

Upon running the preceding code snippet, you get the following output:

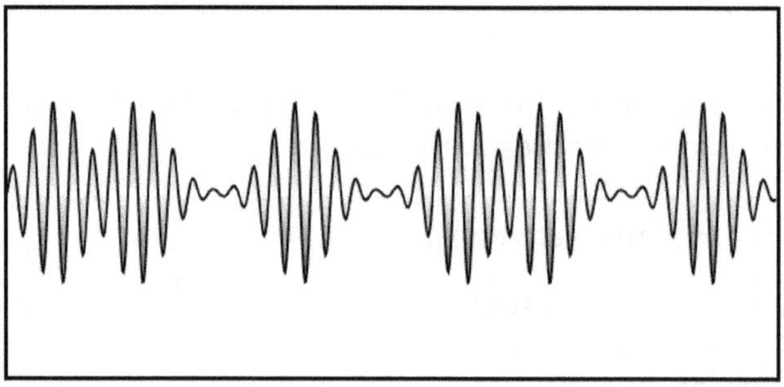

What just happened?

The modifications to `onPaint` that we implemented are creating another path and using that path to fill an area using a gradient. The path is very similar to the original one, but it contains two additional points that are the first and last points drawn projected onto the horizontal axis. This ensures that the gradient fills the area properly. Note that the canvas uses imperative code for drawing; therefore, the order of drawing the fill and the stroke matters—the fill has to be drawn first so that it doesn't obscure the stroke.

Using C++ classes as QML components

In the next exercise, we will implement a car dashboard that can be used in a racing game and will show a number of parameters such as current speed and motor revolutions per minute. The input data will be provided by a C++ object. We'll see how to include this object into the QML object tree and use property bindings to implement the dashboard.

The final result will look similar to the following:

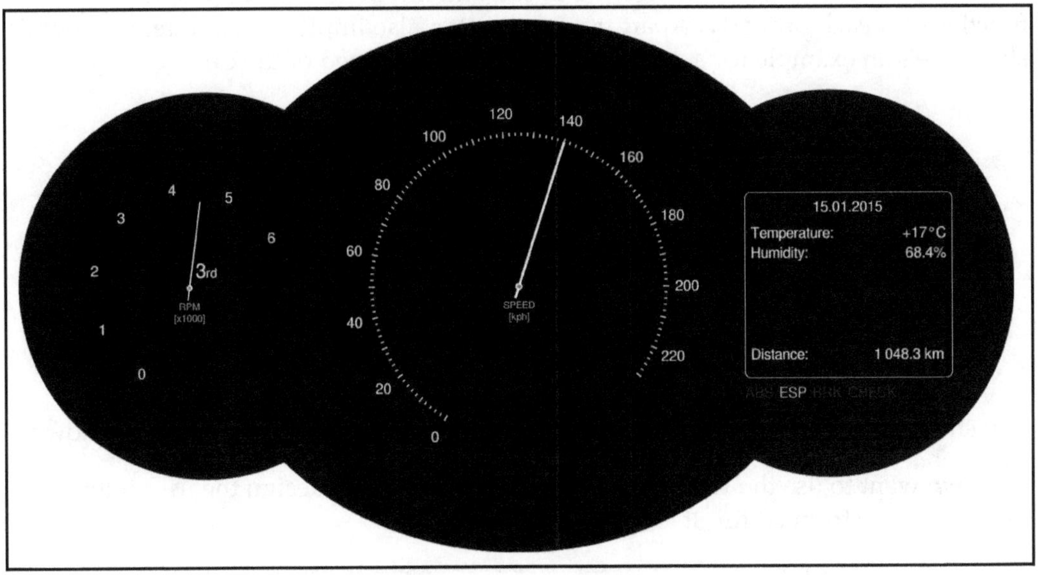

Time for action – Self-updating car dashboard

We will start with the C++ part. Set up a new Qt Quick application. This will generate the main function for you that instantiates `QGuiApplication` and `QQmlApplicationEngine` and sets them up to load a QML document.

Use the **File** menu to create **New file or Project** and create a new Qt Designer form class. Call it `CarInfo` and choose the `Widget` template. We will use this class for modifying values of different parameters so that we may observe how they influence what the Qt Quick scene displays. In the class declaration, add the following properties:

```
class CarInfo : public QWidget {
    Q_OBJECT
    Q_PROPERTY(int rpm READ rpm NOTIFY rpmChanged)
    Q_PROPERTY(int gear READ gear NOTIFY gearChanged)
    Q_PROPERTY(int speed READ speed NOTIFY speedChanged)
    Q_PROPERTY(double distance READ distance NOTIFY distanceChanged)
    //...
};
```

The properties are read-only, and the `NOTIFY` clause defines signals emitted when the respective property values change. Go ahead and implement the appropriate functions for each property. Apart from the getter, also implement a setter as a public slot. Here's an example for a property controlling the speed of the car:

```
int CarInfo::speed() const {
    return m_speed;
}
void CarInfo::setSpeed(int newSpeed) {
    if(m_speed == newSpeed) {
        return;
    }
    m_speed = newSpeed;
    emit speedChanged(m_speed);
}
```

You should be able to follow the example for the remaining properties on your own.

Since we want to use the widget to tweak property values, design the user interface for it using the form editor. It can look like this:

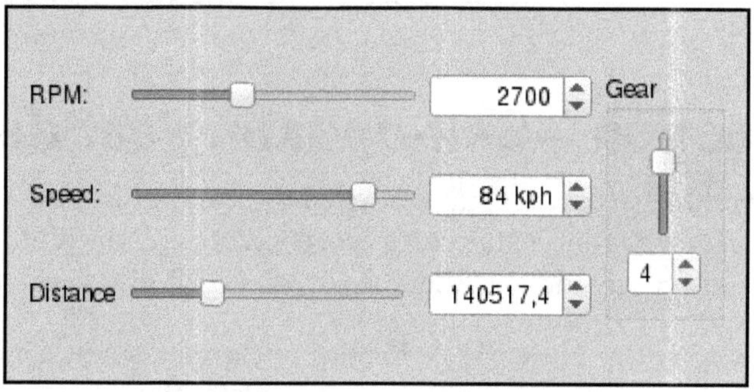

Make appropriate signal-slot connections in the widget so that modifying any of the widgets for a given parameter or using the setter slot directly updates all the widgets for that parameter.

TIP: Instead of adding member variables to the `CarInfo` class for properties such as `speed`, `rpm`, `distance`, or `gear`, you can operate directly on the widgets placed on the `ui` form, as shown further.

For example, a getter for the `distance` property will look like this:

```
qreal CarInfo::distance() const
{
    return ui->distanceBox->value();
}
```

The setter would then be modified to the following:

```
void CarInfo::setDistance(qreal newDistance)
{
    ui->distanceBox->setValue(newDistance);
}
```

You will then need to add `connect()` statements to the constructor to ensure that signals are propagated from the ui form:

```
connect(ui->distanceBox, SIGNAL(valueChanged(double)),
        this,            SIGNAL(distanceChanged(double)));
```

Next, you can test your work by running the widget. To do this, you have to alter the main function to look as follows:

```
int main(int argc, char **argv) {
    QApplication app(argc, argv);
    CarInfo cinfo;
    cinfo.show();
    return app.exec();
};
```

Since we are using widgets, we have to replace `QGuiApplication` with `QApplication` and enable the widgets module by placing `QT += widgets` in the project file (remember to run `qmake` from the project's context menu afterward). Ensure that everything works as expected (that is, that moving sliders and changing spinbox values reflect the changes to widget properties) before moving on to the next step.

We will now add Qt Quick to the equation, so let's start by updating our main function to display our scene. Introduce the highlighted changes to the code:

```
int main(int argc, char **argv) {
    QApplication app(argc, argv);
    CarInfo cinfo;
    QQmlApplicationEngine engine;
    engine.rootContext()->setContextProperty("carData", &cinfo);
    engine.load(QUrl(QStringLiteral("qrc:/main.qml")));
    if (engine.rootObjects().isEmpty())
```

```
        return -1;
    cinfo.show();
    return app.exec();
}
```

The modifications create a QML engine for our scene, export the `CarInfo` instance to the global context of the QML engine, and load and display the scene from a file located in a resource.

It is important to first export all the objects and only then load the scene. This is because we want all the names to be already resolvable when the scene is being initialized so that they can be used right away. If we reversed the order of calls, we would get a number of warnings on the console about the identities being undefined.

Finally, we can focus on the QML part. Look at the picture of the result we want to be shown at the beginning of the exercise. For the black background, we used a bitmap image created in a graphical editor (you can find the file in the materials for this book), but you can obtain a similar effect by composing three black rounded rectangles directly in Qt Quick—the two outer parts are perfect circles, and the inner module is a horizontally stretched ellipse.

If you decide to use our background file (or make your own prettier image), you should add it to the project's resources and put the following code into `main.qml`:

```
import QtQuick 2.9
import QtQuick.Window 2.3

Window {
    visible: true
    width: backgroundImage.width
    height: backgroundImage.height

    Image {
        id: backgroundImage
        source: "qrc:/dashboard.png"
        Item {
            id: leftContainer
            anchors.centerIn: parent
            anchors.horizontalCenterOffset: -550
            width: 400; height: width
        }
        Item {
            id: middleContainer
            anchors.centerIn: parent
            width: 700; height: width
        }
```

```
        Item {
            id: rightContainer
            anchors.centerIn: parent
            anchors.horizontalCenterOffset: 525
            width: 400; height: width
        }
    }
}
```

What we do here is add the image to the window and create three items to serve as containers for different elements of the dashboard. The containers are all centered in the parent, and we use a `horizontalCenterOffset` property to move the two outer items sideways. The values of the offset as well as the widths are based on the background image's geometry (note that all three containers are perfect squares). If instead of using our file, you settle for creating the three parts yourself using Qt Quick items, the containers will simply be anchored to the centers of the three black items.

The dials look complicated, but in reality, they are very easy to implement, and you have already learned everything you need to design them.

Let's start with the needle. Use the context menu of the resource file to create a new QML file and call it `Needle.qml`. Open the file and place the following content:

```
import QtQuick 2.9

Item {
    id: root
    property int length: parent.width * 0.4
    property color color: "white"
    property color middleColor: "red"
    property int size: 2

    Rectangle { //needle
        width: root.size
        height: length + 20
        color: root.color
        anchors.horizontalCenter: parent.horizontalCenter
        anchors.bottom: parent.bottom
        anchors.bottomMargin: -20
        antialiasing: true
    }

    Rectangle { //fixing
        anchors.centerIn: parent
        width: 8 + root.size
        height: width
```

```
            radius: width / 2
            color: root.color
            Rectangle { //middle dot
                anchors {
                    fill: parent
                    margins: parent.width * 0.25
                }
                color: root.middleColor
            }
        }
    }
```

The document defines an item with four attributes—the length of the needle (defaults to 80% of the dial's radius), the color of the needle, `middleColor`, which stands for the color of the needle's fixing, and the size, which defines how wide the needle is. The code is self-explanatory. The item itself does not have any dimensions and only acts as an anchor for visual elements—the needle itself is a thin rectangle oriented vertically with a fixing 20 units from the end. The fixing is a circle of the same color as the needle with a smaller circle in the middle that uses a different fill color. The smaller radius of the inner circle is obtained by filling the outer circle with a 25% margin from each side.

As for the dials, we will put their code inline in the main file since we just have two of them and they differ a bit, so the overhead of creating a separate component with a well-designed set of properties will outweigh the benefits of having nicely encapsulated objects.

If you think about what needs to be done to have the dial displayed and working, it seems that the hardest thing is to lay out the numbers nicely on the circle, so let's start with that. Here's an implementation of a function for calculating the position along a circle circumference, based on the radius of the circle and angle (in degrees) where an item should be positioned:

```
function calculatePosition(angle, radius) {
    if(radius === undefined) {
        radius = width / 2 * 0.8;
    }
    var a = angle * Math.PI / 180;
    var px = width / 2 + radius * Math.cos(a);
    var py = width / 2 + radius * Math.sin(a);
    return Qt.point(px, py);
}
```

The function converts degrees to radians and returns the desired point. The function expects the `width` property to be available that helps calculate the center of the circle and in case a radius was not given, serves as a means to calculate a feasible value for it.

With such a function available, we can use the already familiar `Repeater` element to position items where we want them. Let's put the function in `middleContainer` and declare the dial for car speed:

```
Item {
    id: middleContainer
    // ...
    function calculatePosition(angle, radius) { /* ... */ }
    Repeater {
        model: 24 / 2
        Item {
            property point pt:
            middleContainer.calculatePosition(120 + index * 12 * 2)
            x: pt.x
            y: pt.y
            Label {
                anchors.centerIn: parent
                text: index * 20
            }
        }
    }
    Needle {
        anchors.centerIn: parent
        length: parent.width * 0.35
        size: 4
        rotation: 210 + (carData.speed * 12 / 10)
        color: "yellow"
    }
}
```

You might have noted that we used an element called `Label`. We created it to avoid having to set the same property values for all the texts we use in the user interface:

```
import QtQuick 2.9

Text {
    color: "white"
    font.pixelSize: 24
}
```

The dial consists of a repeater that will create 12 elements. Each element is an item positioned using the earlier described function. The item has a label anchored to it that displays the given speed. We use `120 + index * 12 * 2` as the angle expression as we want "0" to be positioned at 120 degrees and each following item positioned 24 degrees further.

The needle is given rotation based on the value read from the `carData` object. Since the angular distance between consecutive 20 kph labels is 24 degrees, the distance for one kph is 1.2 and thus we multiply `carData.speed` by that factor. Item rotation is calculated with 0 degrees "pointing right"; therefore, we add 90 to the initial 120 degree offset of the first label to obtain starting coordinates matching those of the label system.

As you can see in the image of the final result at the beginning of this section, the speed dial contains small lines every 2 kph, with those divisible by 10 kph longer than others. We can use another `Repeater` to declare such ticks:

```
Repeater {
    model: 120 - 4

    Item {
        property point pt: middleContainer.calculatePosition(
            120 + index * 1.2 * 2, middleContainer.width * 0.35
        )
        x: pt.x
        y: pt.y
        Rectangle {
            width: 2
            height: index % 5 ? 5 : 10
            color: "white"
            rotation: 210 + index * 1.2 * 2
            anchors.centerIn: parent
            antialiasing: true
        }
    }
}
```

Finally, we can put a label for the dial:

```
Text {
    anchors.centerIn: parent
    anchors.verticalCenterOffset: 40
    text: "SPEED\n[kph]"
    horizontalAlignment: Text.AlignHCenter
    color: "#aaa"
    font.pixelSize: 16
```

```
}
```

Ensure that the label is declared before the dial needle, or give the needle a higher *z* value so that the label doesn't overpaint the needle.

Next, repeat the process on your own for the left container by creating an RPM dial reading values from the `carData.rpm` property. The dial also displays the current gear of the car's engine. Place the following code inside the `leftContainer` object definition:

```
Item {
    id: gearContainer
    anchors.centerIn: parent
    anchors.horizontalCenterOffset: 10
    anchors.verticalCenterOffset: -10

    Text {
        id: gear
        property int value: carData.gear
        property var gears: [
            "R", "N",
            "1<sup>st</sup>", "2<sup>nd</sup>", "3<sup>rd</sup>",
            "4<sup>th</sup>", "5<sup>th</sup>"
        ]
        text: gears[value + 1]
        anchors.left: parent.left
        anchors.bottom: parent.bottom
        color: "yellow"
        font.pixelSize: 32
        textFormat: Text.RichText
    }
}
```

The only part needing explanation is highlighted. It defines an array of gear labels starting with reverse, going through neutral, and then through five forward gears. The array is then indexed with the current gear and the text for that value is applied to the label. Note that the value is incremented by 1, which means the 0th index of the array will be used when `carData.gear` is set to `1`.

We will not show how to implement the right container. You can do that easily yourself now with the use of the `Grid` positioner to lay out the labels and their values. To display the series of controls on the bottom of the right container (with texts `ABS`, `ESP`, `BRK`, and `CHECK`), you can use `Row` of `Label` instances.

Now, start the program and begin moving the sliders on the widget. See how the Qt Quick scene follows the changes.

What just happened?

We have created a very simple QObject instance and exposed it as our "data model" to QML. The object has a number of properties that can receive different values. Changing a value results in emitting a signal, which in turn notifies the QML engine and causes bindings containing those properties to be reevaluated. As a result, our user interface gets updated.

Time for action – Grouping engine properties

The data interface between the QML and C++ worlds that we created is very simple and has a small number of properties. However, as the amount of data we want to expose grows, the object can become cluttered. Of course, we can counter that effect by dividing it into multiple smaller objects, each having separate responsibilities and then exporting all those objects to QML, but that is not always desirable. In our case, we can see that rpm and gear are properties of the engine subsystem, so we can move them to a separate object; however, in reality, their values are tightly coupled with the speed of the car and to calculate the speed, we will need to know the values of those two parameters. However, the speed also depends on other factors such as the slope of the road, so putting the speed into the engine subsystem object just doesn't seem right. Fortunately, there is a nice solution to that problem.

QML has a concept called grouped properties. You already know a number of them—the border property of the Rectangle element or the anchors property of the Item element, for example. Let's see how to define such properties for our exposed object.

Create a new QObject-derived class and call it CarInfoEngine. Move the property definitions of rpm and gear to that new class along with their getters, setters, and change signals. Add the following property declaration to CarInfo:

```
Q_PROPERTY(QObject* engine READ engine NOTIFY engineChanged)
```

Implement the getter and the private field:

```
    QObject* engine() const { return m_engine; }
private:
    CarInfoEngine *m_engine;
```

We will not use the signal right now. However, we had to declare it; otherwise, QML would complain we were binding expressions that depend on properties that are non-notifiable:

```
signals:
    void engineChanged();
```

Initialize `m_engine` in the constructor of `CarInfo`:

```
m_engine = new CarInfoEngine(this);
```

Next, update the code of `CarInfo` to modify properties of `m_engine` whenever respective sliders on the widget are moved. Provide a link the other way as well—if the property value is changed, update the user interface accordingly.

Update the QML document and replace `carData.gear` with `carData.engine.gear`. Do the same for `carData.rpm` and `carData.engine.rpm`. You should end up with something along the lines of the following:

```
Item {
    id: leftContainer
    // ...

    Item {
        id: gearContainer
        Text {
            id: gear
            property int value: carData.engine.gear
            // ...
        }
    }
    Needle {
        anchors.centerIn: parent
        length: parent.width * 0.35
        rotation: 210 + (carData.engine.rpm * 35)
    }
}
```

What just happened?

Essentially, what we did is expose a property in `CarInfo` that is itself an object that exposes a set of properties. This object of the `CarInfoEngine` type is bound to the `CarInfo` instance it refers to.

Time for action – Registering C++ class as QML type

So far, what we did was expose ourselves to QML single objects created and initialized in C++. However, we can do much more—the framework allows us to define new QML types. These can either be generic `QObject`-derived QML elements or items specialized for Qt Quick.

We will start with something simple—exposing the `CarInfo` type to QML so that instead of instantiating it in C++ and then exposing it in QML, we can directly declare the element in QML and still allow the changes made to the widget to be reflected in the scene.

To make a certain class (derived from `QObject`) instantiable in QML, all that is required is to register that class with the declarative engine using the `qmlRegisterType` template function. This function takes the class as its template parameter along a number of function arguments: the module `uri`, the major and minor version numbers, and the name of the QML type we are registering. The following call will register the `FooClass` class as the QML type `Foo`, available after importing `foo.bar.baz` in Version 1.0:

```
qmlRegisterType<FooClass>("foo.bar.baz", 1, 0, "Foo");
```

You can place this invocation anywhere in your C++ code; just ensure that this is before you try to load a QML document that might contain declarations of `Foo` objects. A typical place to put the function call is in the program's main function. Afterward, you can start declaring objects of the `Foo` type in your documents. Just remember that you have to import the respective module first:

```
import QtQuick 2.9
import foo.bar.baz 1.0

Item {
    Foo {
        id: foo
    }
}
```

Time for action – Making CarInfo instantiable from QML

First, we will update the QML document to create an instance of `CarInfo` present in the `CarInfo 1.0` module:

```
import QtQuick 2.9
import CarInfo 1.0

Image {
    source: "dashboard.png"

    CarInfo {
        id: carData
        visible: true // make the widget visible
    }
  // ...
}
```

As for registering `CarInfo`, it might be tempting to simply call `qmlRegisterType` on `CarInfo` and congratulate ourselves for a job well done:

```
int main(int argc, char **argv) {
    QGuiApplication app(argc, argv);
    QQmlApplicationEngine engine;
    // this code does not work
    qmlRegisterType<CarInfo>("CarInfo", 1, 0, "CarInfo");
    //...
}
```

In general, this would work (yes, it is as simple as that). However, it will not work with widgets. It's not possible to include `QWidget`-based objects into a QML object tree because a `QWidget` object can only have another `QWidget` object as its parent, and QML needs to set the outer QML object as the parent. To resolve this conflict, we need to ensure that what we instantiate is not a widget. For that, we will use a proxy object that will forward our calls to the actual widget. Therefore, create a new class called `CarInfoProxy` derived from `QObject` and make it have the same properties as `CarInfo`. Consider this example:

```
class CarInfoProxy : public QObject {
    Q_OBJECT
    Q_PROPERTY(QObject *engine READ engine NOTIFY engineChanged)
    Q_PROPERTY(int speed READ speed WRITE setSpeed NOTIFY
speedChanged)
    // ...
```

Declare one more property that will let us show and hide the widget on demand:

```
Q_PROPERTY(bool visible READ visible WRITE setVisible
                        NOTIFY visibleChanged)
```

Then, we can place the widget as a member variable of the proxy so that it is created and destroyed alongside its proxy:

```
private:
    CarInfo m_car;
```

This way, the `CarInfo` widget will have `nullptr` parent, so it will be displayed as a top-level window. The QML engine will create an object of the `CarInfoProxy` class and set its parent to be another QML object, but this will not affect the parent of the widget.

Next, implement the missing interface. For simplicity, we are showing you code for some of the properties. The others are similar, so you can fill in the gaps on your own:

```
public:
    CarInfoProxy(QObject *parent = nullptr) : QObject(parent) {
        connect(&m_car, &CarInfo::engineChanged,
                this, &CarInfoProxy::engineChanged);
        connect(&m_car, &CarInfo::speedChanged,
                this, &CarInfoProxy::speedChanged);
    }
    QObject *engine() const {
        return m_car.engine();
    }
    bool visible() const {
        return m_car.isVisible();
    }
    void setVisible(bool v) {
        if(v == visible()) return;
        m_car.setVisible(v);
        emit visibleChanged(v);
    }
    int speed() const {
        return m_car.speed();
    }
    void setSpeed(int v) {
        m_car.setSpeed(v);
    }
signals:
    void engineChanged();
    void visibleChanged(bool);
    void speedChanged(int);
```

```
};
```

You can see that we reuse the `CarInfoEngine` instance from the widget instead of duplicating it in the proxy class. Finally, we can register `CarInfoProxy` as `CarInfo`:

```
qmlRegisterType<CarInfoProxy>("CarInfo", 1, 0, "CarInfo");
```

If you run the code now, you will see that it works—`CarInfo` has become a regular QML element. Due to this, its properties can be set and modified directly in the document, right? If you try setting the speed or the distance, it will work just fine. However, try to set a property grouped in the `engine` property:

```
CarInfo {
    id: carData
    visible: true
    engine.gear: 3
}
```

QML runtime will complain with a message similar to the following one:

```
Cannot assign to non-existent property "gear"
             engine.gear: 3
                    ^
```

This is because the runtime does not understand the `engine` property—we declared it as `QObject` and yet we are using a property this class doesn't have. To avoid this issue, we have to teach the runtime about `CarInfoEngine`.

First, let's update the property declaration macro to use `CarInfoEngine` instead of `QObject`:

```
Q_PROPERTY(CarInfoEngine* engine READ engine NOTIFY engineChanged)
```

Also, the getter function itself:

```
CarInfoEngine* engine() const {
    return m_engine;
}
```

You should make these changes in both the `CarInfo` and `CarInfoProxy` classes. Then, we should teach the runtime about the type:

```
QString msg = QStringLiteral("Objects of type CarInfoEngine cannot be
created");
qmlRegisterUncreatableType<CarInfoEngine>("CarInfo", 1, 0,
"CarInfoEngine", msg);
```

What just happened?

In this exercise, we let the QML runtime know about two new elements. One of them is `CarInfo`, which is a proxy to our widget class. We told the engine that this is a full-featured class that is instantiable from QML. The other class, `CarInfoEngine`, also became known to QML; however, the difference is that every attempt to declare an object of this type in QML fails with a given warning message. There are other functions available for registering types in QML, but they are rarely used, so we will not be describing them here. If you are curious about them, type in `qmlRegister` in the **Index** tab of Creator's **Help** pane.

Pop quiz

Q1. Which QML type allows you to create a placeholder for an object that will be instantiated later?

1. `Repeater`
2. `Loader`
3. `Component`

Q2. Which QML type provides low-level access to individual touch events?

1. `PinchArea`
2. `MouseArea`
3. `MultiPointTouchArea`

Q3. When can you access a component defined in another QML file without an import statement?

1. You can do that if the component is registered using the `qmlRegisterType` function
2. You can do that if the component file is added to the project resources
3. You can do that if the component file is in the same directory as the current file

Summary

You are now familiar with multiple methods that can be used to extend Qt Quick with your own item types. You learned to use JavaScript to create custom visual items. You also know how to use C++ classes as non-visual QML elements fully integrated with your UI. We also discussed how to handle mouse, touch, keyboard, and gamepad events in Qt Quick applications. However, so far, despite us talking about "fluid" and "dynamic" interfaces, you haven't seen much of them. Do not worry; in the next chapter, we will focus on animations in Qt Quick as well as fancy graphics and applying what you learned in this chapter for creating nice-looking and interesting games. So, read on!

13
Animations in Qt Quick Games

In the previous two chapters, we introduced you to the basics of Qt Quick and QML. By now, you should be fluent enough with the syntax and understand the basic concepts of how Qt Quick works. In this chapter, we will show you how to make your games stand out from the crowd by introducing different kinds of animations that make your applications feel more like the real world. You will also learn to treat Qt Quick objects as separate entities programmable using state machines. A significant part of this chapter will introduce how to implement a number of important gaming concepts using Qt Quick. All this will be shown while we build a simple 2D action game using the presented concepts.

The main topics covered in this chapter are as follows:

- Animation framework in Qt Quick
- States and transitions in depth
- Implementing games in Qt Quick
- Sprite animations
- Using state machines for animation
- Parallax scrolling
- Collision detection

Animation framework in Qt Quick

In `Chapter 11`, *Introduction to Qt Quick,* we implemented a simple animation using Qt Quick states and transitions. We will now deepen our knowledge on this topic and learn how to add some dynamics into the user interfaces we create. Thus far, books cannot contain moving pictures, so you will have to test most things we describe here yourself by running the provided Qt Quick code.

Qt Quick provides a very extensive framework for creating animations. By that, we don't mean only moving items around. We define an animation as *changing an arbitrary value over time*. So, what can we animate? Of course, we can animate item geometry. However, we can also animate rotation, scale, other numeric values, and even colors, but let's not stop here. Qt Quick also lets you animate the parent-child hierarchy of items or anchor assignments. Almost anything that can be represented by an item property can be animated.

Moreover, the changes are rarely linear—if you kick a ball in the air, it first gains height quickly because its initial speed was large. However, the ball is a physical object being pulled down by the earth's gravity, which slows the climb down until the ball stops and then starts falling down, accelerating until it hits the ground. Depending on the properties of both the ground and the ball, the object can bounce off the surface into the air again with less momentum, repeating the spring-like motion until eventually it fades away, leaving the ball on the ground. Qt Quick lets you model all that using easing curves that can be assigned to animations.

Generic animations

Qt Quick provides a number of animation types derived from a generic `Animation` element that you will never use directly. The type exists only to provide an API common to different animation types.

Let's take a closer look at the animation framework by looking at a family of animation types derived from the most common animation type—`PropertyAnimation`. As the name implies, they provide the means to animate values of object properties. Despite the fact that you can use the `PropertyAnimation` element directly, it is usually more convenient to use one of its subclasses that specialises in dealing with the peculiarities of different data types.

The most basic property animation type is `NumberAnimation`, which lets you animate all kinds of numeric values of both integral and real numbers. The simplest way of using it is to declare an animation, tell it to animate a specific property in a specific object, and then set the length of the animation and the starting and ending value for the property:

```
import QtQuick 2.9

Item {
    id: root
    width: 600; height: width
    Rectangle {
```

```
        id: rect
        color: "red"
        width: 50; height: width
    }
    NumberAnimation {
        target: rect
        property: "x"
        from: 0; to: 550
        duration: 3000
        running: true
    }
}
```

Time for action – Scene for an action game

Let's try something new for our new project. Select **New File or Project** from the **File** menu of Qt Creator, switch to the **Other Project** category and choose the **Qt Quick UI Prototype** template. Qt Creator will create a main QML file and a project file with the `.qmlproject` extension. This kind of project file is different than regular project files with the `.pro` extension. This is a pure QML project that does not contain any C++ code and thus does not require compilation. However, you need a QML runtime environment to run this project. Your Qt installation provides such an environment, so you can run the project from the terminal using the `qmlscene main.qml` command or just let Qt Creator handle that. Note that the Qt resources system is not used with these projects, and the QML files are loaded directly from the filesystem.

TIP

If you need to add C++ code to your project or you intend to distribute compiled binaries of the project, use the **Qt Quick Application** templates instead. The **Qt Quick UI Prototype** template, as the name implies, is only good for prototypes.

In the project directory, make a subdirectory called `images` and from the game project that we have created using Graphics View, copy `grass.png`, `sky.png`, and `trees.png`. Then, put the following code into the QML document:

```
import QtQuick 2.9

Image {
    id: root
    property int dayLength: 60000 // 1 minute
    source: "images/sky.png"
```

```
        Item {
            id: sun
            x: 140
            y: root.height - 170
            Rectangle {
                id: sunVisual
                width: 40
                height: width
                radius: width / 2
                color: "yellow"
                anchors.centerIn: parent
            }
        }
        Image {
            source: "images/trees.png"
            x: -200
            anchors.bottom: parent.bottom
        }
        Image {
            source: "images/grass.png"
            anchors.bottom: parent.bottom
        }
    }
```

> **TIP**
> If you don't declare the top-level `Window` object, `qmlscene` will display the top-level Qt Quick item in a window automatically. Note that when writing a Qt Quick application driven by the `QQmlApplicationEngine` class, you need to declare the `Window` object explicitly.

When you run the project now, you will see a screen similar to this one:

What just happened?

We set up a very simple scene consisting of three images stacked up to form a landscape. Between the background layer (the sky) and the foreground (trees), we placed a yellow circle representing the sun. Since we will be moving the sun around in a moment, we anchored the center of the object to an empty item without physical dimensions so that we can set the sun's position relative to its center. We also equipped the scene with a `dayLength` property, which will hold information about the length of one day of game time. By default, we set it to 60 seconds so that things happen really quickly and we can see the animation's progress without waiting. After all things are set correctly, the length of the day can be balanced to fit our needs.

The graphical design lets us easily manipulate the sun while keeping it behind the tree line. Note how the stacking order is implicitly determined by the order of elements in the document.

Time for action – Animating the sun's horizontal movement

The everyday cruise of the sun in the sky starts in the east and continues west to hide beneath the horizon in the evening. Let's try to replicate this horizontal movement by adding animation to our `sun` object.

Open the QML document of our last project. Inside the `root` item, add the following declaration:

```
NumberAnimation {
    target: sun
    property: "x"
    from: 0
    to: root.width
    duration: dayLength
    running: true
}
```

Running the program with such modifications will produce a run with a horizontal movement of the sun. The following image is a composition of a number of frames of the run:

What just happened?

We introduced a `NumberAnimation` element that is set to animate the `x` property of the `sun` object. The animation starts at `0` and lasts until `x` reaches the `root` item's width (which is the right edge of the scene). The movement lasts for `dayLength` milliseconds. The `running` property of the animation is set to `true` to enable the animation. Since we didn't specify otherwise, the motion is linear.

You may be thinking that the animation runs in the wrong direction—"west" is on the left and "east" is on the right, yes? That's true, however, only if the observer faces north. If that were the case for our scene, we wouldn't be seeing the sun at all—at noon, it crosses the south direction.

Composing animations

The animation we made in the last section looks OK but is not very realistic. The sun should rise in the morning, reach its peak sometime before noon, and then, sometime later, start setting toward the evening, when it should cross the horizon and hide beneath the landscape.

To achieve such an effect, we can add two more animations for the `y` property of the sun. The first animation would start right at the beginning and decrease the vertical position of the sun (remember that the vertical geometry axis points down, so decreasing the vertical position means the object goes up). The animation would be complete at one-third of the day length. We would then need a way to wait for some time and then start a second animation that would pull the object down toward the ground. Starting and stopping the animation is easy—we can either call the `start()` and `stop()` functions on the animation item or directly alter the value of the `running` property. Each `Animation` object emits `started()` and `stopped()` signals. The delay can be implemented using a timer. We can provide a signal handler for the stopped signal of the first animation to trigger a timer to start the other one like this:

```
NumberAnimation {
    id: sunGoesUpAnim
    // ...
    onStopped: sunGoesDownAnimTimer.start()
}
Timer {
    id: sunGoesDownAnimTimer
    interval: dayLength / 3
    onTriggered: sunGoesDownAnim.start()
}
```

Even ignoring any side problems this would bring (for example, how to stop the animation without starting the second one), such an approach couldn't be called "declarative", could it?

Fortunately, similar to what we had in C++, Qt Quick lets us form animation groups that run either parallel to each other or in sequence. There are the `SequentialAnimation` and `ParallelAnimation` types where you can declare any number of child animation elements forming the group. To run two animations in parallel, we can declare the following hierarchy of elements:

```
ParallelAnimation {
    id: parallelAnimationGroup
    running: true
    NumberAnimation {
        target: obj1; property: "prop1"
        from: 0; to: 100
        duration: 1500
    }
    NumberAnimation {
        target: obj2; property: "prop2"
        from: 150; to: 0
```

```
        duration: 1500
    }
}
```

The same technique can be used to synchronize a larger group of animations, even if each component has a different duration:

```
SequentialAnimation {
    id: sequentialAnimationGroup
    running: true
    ParallelAnimation {
        id: parallelAnimationGroup
        NumberAnimation {
            id: animation1
            target: obj2; property: "prop2"
            from: 150; to: 0
            duration: 1000
        }
        NumberAnimation {
            id: animation2
            target: obj1; property: "prop1"
            from: 0; to: 100
            duration: 2000
        }
    }
    PropertyAnimation {
        id: animation3
        target: obj1; property: "prop1"
        from: 100; to: 300
        duration: 1500
    }
}
```

The group presented in the snippet consists of three animations. The first two animations are executed together as they form a parallel subgroup. One member of the group runs twice as long as the other. Only after the whole subgroup completes is the third animation started. This can be visualized using a **Unified Modeling Language** (**UML**) activity diagram where the size of each activity is proportional to the duration of that activity:

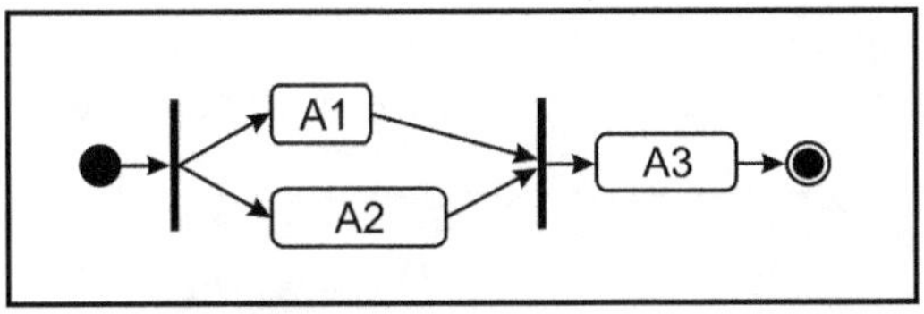

Time for action – Making the sun rise and set

Let's add vertical movement (animation of the `y` property) to our sun by adding a sequence of animations to the QML document. As our new animations will be running in parallel to the horizontal animation, we can enclose animations for both directions within a single `ParallelAnimation` group. It would work, but in our opinion, this will unnecessarily clutter the document. Another way of specifying parallel animations is to declare them as separate hierarchies of elements, making each animation independent of the other, and that is what we will do here.

Open our document from the last exercise, and right under the previous animation, place the following code:

```
SequentialAnimation {
    running: true
    NumberAnimation {
        target: sun
        property: "y"
        from: root.height + sunVisual.height
        to: root.height - 270
        duration: dayLength / 3
    }
    PauseAnimation { duration: dayLength / 3 }
    NumberAnimation {
        target: sun
        property: "y"
        from: root.height - 270
        to: root.height + sunVisual.height
        duration: dayLength / 3
    }
}
```

Running the program will result in the light source rising in the morning and setting in the evening. However, the trajectory of the move seems somewhat awkward:

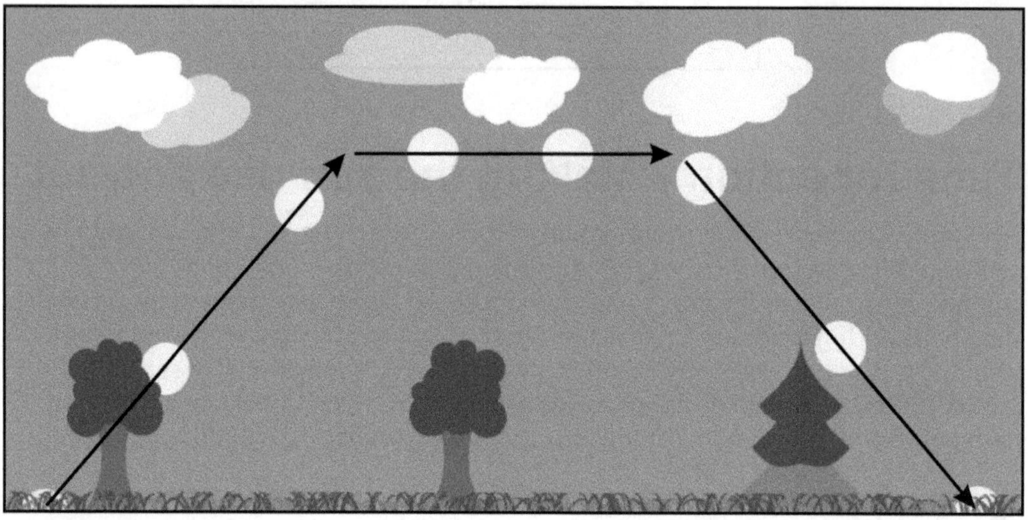

What just happened?

We declared a sequential animation group consisting of three animations, each taking one-third of the day length. The first member of the group makes the sun go up. The second member, which is an instance of a new element type—`PauseAnimation`—introduces a delay equal to its duration. This, in turn, lets the third component start its work in the afternoon to pull the sun down toward the horizon.

The problem with such a declaration is that the sun moves in a horribly angular way, as can be seen in the image.

Non-linear animations

The reason for the described problem is that our animations are linear. As we noted at the beginning of this chapter, linear animations rarely occur in nature, which usually makes their use yield a very unrealistic result.

We also said earlier that Qt Quick allows us to use easing curves to perform animations along non-linear paths. There are a large number of curves offered. Here's a diagram listing the available non-linear easing curves:

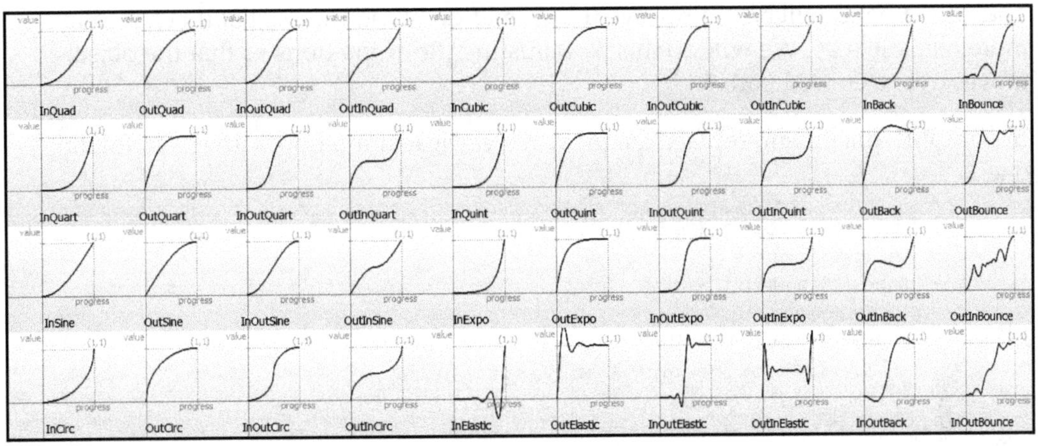

You can use any of the curves on an element of the `PropertyAnimation` type or one derived from it (for example, `NumberAnimation`). This is done using the `easing` property group, where you can set the `type` of the curve. Different curve types may further be tweaked by setting a number of properties in the `easing` property group, such as `amplitude` (for bounce and elastic curves), `overshoot` (for back curves), or `period` (for elastic curves).

Declaring an animation along an `InOutBounce` path is very easy:

```
NumberAnimation {
    target: obj
    property: prop
    from: startValue
    to: endValue
    easing.type: Easing.InOutBounce
    running: true
}
```

Time for action – Improving the path of the sun

The task at hand will be to improve the animation of the sun so that it behaves in a more realistic way. We will do this by adjusting the animations so that the object moves over a curved path.

In our QML document, replace the previous vertical animation with the following one:

```
SequentialAnimation {
    running: true
    NumberAnimation {
        target: sun
        property: "y"
        from: root.height + sunVisual.height
        to: root.height - 270
        duration: dayLength / 2
        easing.type: Easing.OutCubic
    }
    NumberAnimation {
        target: sun
        property: "y"
        to: root.height + sunVisual.height
        duration: dayLength / 2
        easing.type: Easing.InCubic
    }
}
```

The following picture shows how the sun will now move:

What just happened?

The sequence of three animations (two linear ones and a pause) was replaced by another sequence of two animations that follow a path determined by a cubic function. This makes our sun rise pretty fast and then slow down to an amount almost unnoticeable near the moment when the sun approaches noon. When the first animation is finished, the second one reverses the motion, making the sun descend very slowly and then increase its velocity as dusk approaches. As a result, the farther the sun is from the ground, the slower it seems to move. At the same time, the horizontal animation remains linear, as the speed of earth in its motion around the sun is practically constant. When we combine the horizontal and vertical animations, we get a path that looks very similar to what we can observe in the real world.

Property value sources

From the QML perspective, `Animation` and element types derived from it are called **property value sources**. This means they can be attached to a property and generate values for it. What is important is that it allows us to use animations using a much simpler syntax. Instead of explicitly declaring the target and property of an animation, you can attach the animation to a named property of the parent object.

To do this, instead of specifying `target` and `property` for `Animation`, use the `on` keyword, followed by the name of a property name for which the animation is to be a value source. For example, to animate the `rotation` property of an object with a `NumberAnimation` object, the following code can be used:

```
NumberAnimation on rotation {
    from: 0
    to: 360
    duration: 500
}
```

It is valid to specify more than one property value source for the same property of an object.

Time for action – Adjusting the sun's color

If you look at the sun at dusk or dawn, you will see that it is not yellow but becomes red the closer it is to the horizon. Let's teach our object representing the sun to do the same by providing a property value source for it.

Open the QML document, find the declaration for the `sunVisual` object, and extend it with the highlighted part:

```
Rectangle {
    id: sunVisual
    // ...
    SequentialAnimation on color {
        ColorAnimation {
            from: "red"
            to: "yellow"
            duration: 0.2 * dayLength / 2
        }
        PauseAnimation {
            duration: 2 * 0.8 * dayLength / 2
        }
        ColorAnimation {
            to: "red"
            duration: 0.2 * dayLength / 2
        }
        running: true
    }
}
```

What just happened?

An animation was attached to the `color` property of our rectangle modeling the visual aspects of the sun. The animation consists of three parts. First, we perform a transition from red to yellow using the `ColorAnimation` object. This is an `Animation` subtype dedicated to modifying colors. Since the rectangle color is not a number, using the `NumberAnimation` object will not work, as the type cannot interpolate color values. Therefore, we either have to use the `PropertyAnimation` or the `ColorAnimation` object. The duration for the animation is set to 20 percent of half the day length so that the yellow color is obtained very quickly. The second component is a `PauseAnimation` object to provide a delay before the third component is executed, which gradually changes the color back to red. For the last component, we do not provide a value for the `from` property. This causes the animation to be initiated with the value of the property current to the time when the animation is executed (in this case, the sun should be yellow).

Note that we only had to specify the property name for the top-level animation. This particular element is what serves as the property value source, and all descendant animation objects "inherit" the target property from that property value source.

Time for action – Furnishing sun animation

The animation of the sun looks almost perfect right now. We can still improve it, though. If you look into the sky in the early morning and then again at noon, you will note that the sun appears much bigger during sunrise or sunset compared to its size when it is at its zenith. We can simulate that effect by scaling the object.

In our scene document, add another sequential animation that operates on the `scale` property of the sun:

```
SequentialAnimation on scale {
    NumberAnimation {
      from: 1.6; to: 0.8
      duration: dayLength / 2
      easing.type: Easing.OutCubic
    }
    NumberAnimation {
      from: 0.8; to: 1.6
      duration: dayLength / 2
      easing.type: Easing.InCubic
    }
}
```

Let's examine the result again:

What just happened?

In this section, we just followed the path set for an earlier declaration—the vertical movement of the stellar body influences its perceived size; therefore, it seems like a good decision to bind the two animations together. Note that instead of specifying a new property value source for the scale, we might have modified the original animation and made the scale animation parallel to the animation that operates on the `y` property:

```
SequentialAnimation {
    ParallelAnimation {
        NumberAnimation {
            target: sun
            property: "y"
            from: root.height + sunVisual.height
            to: root.height - 270
            duration: dayLength / 2
            easing.type: Easing.OutCubic
        }
        NumberAnimation {
            target: sun
            property: "scale"
            from: 1.6; to: 0.8
            duration: dayLength / 2
            easing.type: Easing.OutCubic
        }
        // ...
    }
}
```

Have a go hero – Animating the sun's rays

By now, you should be an animation expert. If you want to try your skills, here's a task for you. The following code can be applied to the `sun` object and will display very simple red rays emitted from the sun:

```
Item {
    id: sunRays
    property int count: 10
    width: sunVisual.width
    height: width
    anchors.centerIn: parent
    z: -1
    Repeater {
        model: sunRays.count
```

```
        Rectangle {
            color: "red"
            rotation: index * 360 / sunRays.count
            anchors.fill: parent
        }
    }
}
```

The result is shown on the following picture:

The goal is to animate the rays so that the overall effect looks good and fits the tune like style of the scene. Try different animations—rotations, size changes, and colors. Apply them to different elements—all rays at once (for example, using the `sunRays` identifier) or only particular rectangles generated by the repeater.

Behaviors

In the previous chapter, we implemented a dashboard for a racing game where we had a number of clocks with needles. We could set values for each clock (for example, car speed) and a respective needle would immediately set itself to the given value. However, such an approach is unrealistic—in the real world, changes of a value happen over time. In our example, the car accelerates from 10 mph to 50 mph by going through 11 mph, 12 mph, and so on, until after some time it reaches the desired value. We call this the **behavior** of a value—it is essentially a model that tells how the parameter reaches its destined value. Defining such models is a perfect use case for declarative programming. Fortunately, QML exposes a `Behavior` element that lets us model behaviors of property changes in Qt Quick.

The `Behavior` elements let us associate an animation with a given property so that every time the property value is to be changed, it is done by running the given animation instead of by making an immediate change to the property value.

Consider a simple scene defined by the following code:

```
import QtQuick 2.9

Item {
    width: 600; height: width
    Item {
        id: empty
        x: parent.width / 2; y: parent.height / 2
        Rectangle {
            id: rect
            width: 100; height: width
            color: "red"
            anchors.centerIn: parent
        }
    }
    MouseArea {
        anchors.fill: parent
        onClicked: {
            empty.x = mouse.x;
            empty.y = mouse.y;
        }
    }
}
```

This scene contains a red rectangle anchored to an empty item. Whenever the user clicks somewhere within the scene, the empty item is moved there, dragging along the rectangle. Let's see how to use the `Behavior` element to smoothly change the position of the empty item. Similar to `Animation` and other property value sources, the `Behavior` element can be used with the on-property syntax:

```
Item {
    id: empty
    x: parent.width / 2; y: parent.height / 2
    Rectangle {
        id: rect
        width: 100; height: width
        color: "red"
        anchors.centerIn: parent
    }
    Behavior on x {
        NumberAnimation { }
    }
```

```
        Behavior on y {
            NumberAnimation { }
        }
    }
```

By adding the two marked declarations, we define behaviors for the `x` and `y` properties that follow animations defined by `NumberAnimation`. We do not include start or end values for the animation as these will depend on the initial and final value for the property. We also don't set the property name in the animation because by default, the property for which the behavior is defined will be used. As a result, we get a linear animation of a numerical property from the original value to the destined value over the default duration.

> TIP: Using linear animations for real-world objects rarely looks good. Usually, you will get much better results if you set an easing curve for the animation so that it starts slowly and then gains speed and decelerates just before it is finished.

Animations that you set on behaviors can be as complex as you want:

```
Behavior on x {
    SequentialAnimation {
        PropertyAction {
            target: rect
            property: "color"
            value: "yellow"
        }
        ParallelAnimation {
            NumberAnimation {
                easing.type: Easing.InOutQuad
                duration: 1000
            }
            SequentialAnimation {
                NumberAnimation {
                    target: rect
                    property: "scale"
                    from: 1.0; to: 1.5
                    duration: 500
                }
                NumberAnimation {
                    target: rect
                    property: "scale"
                    from: 1.5; to: 1.0
                    duration: 500
                }
            }
        }
```

```
            PropertyAction {
                target: rect
                property: "color"
                value: "red"
            }
        }
    }
```

The behavioral model declared in the last piece of code performs a sequential animation. It first changes the color of the rectangle to yellow using the `PropertyAction` element, which performs an immediate update of a property value (we will talk about this more a bit later). The color will be set back to red after the last step of the model. In the meantime, a parallel animation is performed. One of its components is a `NumberAnimation` class that executes the actual animation of the `x` property of `empty` (since the target and property of the animation are not explicitly set). The second component is a sequential animation of the `scale` property of the rectangle, which first scales the item up by 50 percent during the first half of the animation and then scales it back down in the second half of the animation.

Time for action – Animating the car dashboard

Let's employ the knowledge we just learned to improve the car dashboard we created in the previous chapter. We will use animations to show some realism in the way the clocks update their values.

Open the dashboard project and navigate to the `main.qml` file. Find the declaration of the `Needle` object, which is responsible for visualizing the speed of the vehicle. Add the following declaration to the object:

```
Behavior on rotation {
    SmoothedAnimation {
        velocity: 50
    }
}
```

Repeat the process for the left clock. Set the velocity of the animation to `100`. Build and run the project. See how the needles behave when you modify the parameter values in spin boxes. Adjust the `velocity` of each animation until you get a realistic result.

What just happened?

We have set the property value sources on needle rotations that are triggered whenever a new value for the property is requested. Instead of immediately accepting the new value, the `Behavior` element intercepts the request and starts the `SmoothedAnimation` class to gradually reach the requested value. The `SmoothedAnimation` class is an animation type that animates numeric properties. The speed of the animation is not determined by its duration; instead, a `velocity` property is set. This property dictates how fast a value is to be changed. However, the animation is using a non-linear path—it starts slowly, then accelerates to the given velocity, and, near the end of the animation, decelerates in a smooth fashion. This yields an animation that is attractive and realistic and, at the same time, is of shorter or longer duration, depending on the distance between the starting and ending values.

> You can implement custom property value sources by subclassing `QQmlPropertyValueSource` and registering the class in the QML engine.

States

When you look at real-world objects, it is often very easy to define their behavior by extracting a number of states the object may take and describing each of the states separately. A lamp can be turned either on or off. When it is "on", it is emitting light of a given color, but it is not doing that when in the "off" state. Dynamics of the object can be defined by describing what happens if the object leaves one of the states and enters another one. Considering our lamp example, if you turn the lamp on, it doesn't momentarily start emitting light with its full power, but the brightness of the light gradually increases to reach its final power after a very short period.

Qt Quick supports *state-driven* development by letting us declare states and transitions between them for items. The model fits the declarative nature of Qt Quick very well.

By default, each item has a single anonymous state, and all properties you define take values of the expressions you bind or assign to them imperatively based on different conditions. Instead of this, a set of states can be defined for the object and for each of the state properties of the object itself; in addition, the objects defined within it can be programmed with different values or expressions. Our example lamp definition could be similar to this:

```
Item {
    id: lamp
    property bool lampOn: false
    width: 200
    height: 200
    Rectangle {
        id: lightsource
        anchors.fill: parent
        color: "transparent"
    }
}
```

We could, of course, bind the `color` property of `lightsource` to `lamp.lampOn ? "yellow" : "transparent"`; instead, we can define an "on" state for the lamp and use a `PropertyChanges` element to modify the rectangle color:

```
Item {
    id: lamp
    property bool lampOn: false
    // ...
    states: State {
        name: "on"
        PropertyChanges {
            target: lightsource
            color: "yellow"
        }
    }
}
```

Each item has a `state` property that you can read to get the current state, but you can also write to it to trigger transition to a given state. By default, the `state` property is set to an empty string that represents the anonymous state. Note that with the preceding definition, the item has two states—the "on" state and the anonymous state (which is used when the lamp is off in this case). Remember that state names have to be unique as the `name` parameter is what identifies a state in Qt Quick.

To enter a state, we can, of course, use an event handler fired when the value of the `lampOn` parameter is modified:

```
onLampOnChanged: state = lampOn ? "on" : ""
```

Such imperative code works, but it can be replaced with a declarative definition in the state itself:

```
State {
    name: "on"
    when: lamp.lampOn
    PropertyChanges {
        target: lightsource
        color: "yellow"
    }
}
```

Whenever the expression bound to the `when` property evaluates to `true`, the state becomes active. If the expression becomes `false`, the object will return to the default state or will enter a state for which its own `when` property evaluates to `true`.

To define more than one custom state, it is enough to assign a list of state definitions to the `states` property:

```
states: [
    State {
        name: "on"
        when: lamp.lampOn
        PropertyChanges { /*...*/ }

    },
    State {
        name: "off"
        when: !lamp.lampOn
    }
]
```

The `PropertyChanges` element is the most often used change in a state definition, but it is not the only one. In exactly the same way that the `ParentChange` element can assign a different parent to an item and the `AnchorChange` element can update anchor definitions, it is also possible to run a script when a state is entered using the `StateChangeScript`
element. All these element types are used by declaring their instances as children in a `State` object.

Transitions

The second part of the state machine framework is defining how an object transits from one state to another. Similar to the `states` property, all items have a `transitions` property, which takes a list of definitions represented by the `Transition` objects and provides information about animations that should be played when a particular transition takes place.

A transition is identified by three attributes—the source state, the destination state, and a set of animations. Both the source state name (set to the `from` property) and the target state name (set to the `to` property) can be empty, in which case they should be interpreted as "any". If a `Transition` exists that matches the current state change, its animations will be executed. A more concrete transition definition (which is one where `from` and/or `to` are explicitly set) has precedence over a more generic one.

Suppose that we want to animate the opacity of the lamp rectangle from `0` to `1` when the lamp is switched on. We can do it as an alternative to manipulating the color. Let's update the lamp definition:

```
Item {
    id: lamp
    property bool lampOn: false
    Rectangle {
        id: lightsource
        anchors.fill: parent
        color: "yellow"
        opacity: 0
    }
    MouseArea {
        anchors.fill: parent
        onPressed: {
            lamp.lampOn = !lamp.lampOn;
        }
    }
    states: State {
        name: "on"
        when: lamp.lampOn
        PropertyChanges {
            target: lightsource
            opacity: 1
        }
    }
    transitions: Transition {
        NumberAnimation {
            duration: 500
```

```
                property: "opacity"
            }
        }
    }
```

The transition is triggered for any source and any target state—it will be active when the lamp goes from the anonymous to the "on" state as well as in the opposite direction. It defines a single `NumberAnimation` element that works on `opacity` property and lasts for 500 miliseconds. The animation does not define the target object; thus, it will be executed for any object that needs updating as part of the transition—in the case of the lamp, it will only be the `lightsource` object.

If more than one animation is defined in a transition, all animations will run in parallel. If you need a sequential animation, you need to explicitly use a `SequentialAnimation` element:

```
Transition {
    SequentialAnimation {
        NumberAnimation {
            target: lightsource
            property: "opacity"
            duration: 500
        }
        ScriptAction {
            script: {
                console.log("Transition has ended");
            }
        }
    }
}
```

TIP: States are a feature of all `Item` types as well as its descendent types. It is, however, possible to use states with elements not derived from the `Item` object using a `StateGroup` element, which is a self-contained functionality of states and transitions with exactly the same interface as what is described here regarding `Item` objects.

More animation types

The animation types we discussed earlier are used for modifying values of types that can be described using physical metrics (position, sizes, colors, angles). However, there are more types available.

The first group of special animations consists of the `AnchorAnimation` and `ParentAnimation` elements.

The `AnchorAnimation` element is useful if a state change should cause a change to defined anchors for an item. Without it, the item would immediately snap into its place. By using the `AnchorAnimation` element, we trigger all anchor changes to be gradually animated.

The `ParentAnimation` element, on the other hand, makes it possible to define animations that should be present when an item receives a new parent. This usually causes an item to be moved to a different position in the scene. By using the `ParentAnimation` element in a state transition, we can define how the item gets into its target position. The element can contain any number of child animation elements that will be run in parallel during a `ParentChange` element.

The second special group of animations is action animations—`PropertyAction` and `ScriptAction`. These animation types are not stretched in time but perform a given one-time action.

The `PropertyAction` element is a special kind of animation that performs an immediate update of a property to a given value. It is usually used as part of a more complex animation to modify a property that is not animated. It makes sense to use it if a property needs to have a certain value during an animation.

`ScriptAction` is an element that allows the execution of an imperative piece of code during an animation (usually at its beginning or end).

Quick game programming

Here, we will go through the process of creating a platform game using Qt Quick. It will be a game similar to Benjamin the Elephant from `Chapter 6`, *Qt Core Essentials*. The player will control a character that will be walking through the landscape and collecting coins. The coins will be randomly appearing in the world. The character can access highly placed coins by jumping.

Throughout this chapter as well as the previous one, we prepared a number of pieces that we will be reusing for this game. The layered scene that was arranged when you learned about animations will serve as our game scene. The animated sun will represent the passing of time.

We will guide you through implementing the main features of the game. At the end of the chapter, you will have a chance to test your skills by adding more game mechanics to our project.

Game loops

Most games revolve around some kind of game loop. It is usually some kind of function that is called repeatedly, and its task is to progress the game—process input events, move objects around, calculate and execute actions, check win conditions, and so on. Such an approach is very imperative and usually results in a very complex function that needs to know everything about everybody (this kind of anti-pattern is sometimes called a **god object** pattern). In QML (which powers the Qt Quick framework), we aim to separate responsibilities and declare well-defined behaviors for particular objects. Therefore, although it is possible to set up a timer that will periodically call a game loop function, this is not the best possible approach in a declarative world.

Instead, we suggest using a natural time-flow mechanism already present in Qt Quick—one that controls the consistency of animations. Remember how we defined the sun's travel across the sky at the beginning of this chapter? Instead of setting up a timer and moving the object by a calculated number of pixels, we created an animation, defined a total running time for it, and let Qt take care of updating the object. This has the great benefit of neglecting delays in function execution. If you used a timer and some external event introduced a significant delay before the timeout function was run, the animation would start lagging behind. When Qt Quick animations are used, the framework compensates for such delays, skipping some of the frame updates to ensure that the requested animation duration is respected. Thanks to that, you will not have to take care of it all by yourself.

To overcome the second difficult aspect of a game loop—the god object anti-pattern—we suggest encapsulating the logic of each item directly in the item itself using the states and transitions framework we introduced earlier. If you define an object using a natural time flow describing all states it can enter during its lifetime and actions causing transitions between states, you will be able to just plop the object with its included behavior wherever it is needed and thus easily reuse such definitions in different games, reducing the amount of work necessary to make the object fit into the game.

Input processing

A usual approach in games is to read input events and call functions responsible for actions associated with particular events:

```
void Scene::keyEvent(QKeyEvent *event) {
    switch(event->key()) {
    case Qt::Key_Right:
        player->goRight(); break;
    case Qt::Key_Left:
        player->goLeft();  break;
    case Qt::Key_Space:
        player->jump();    break;
    // ...
    }
}
```

This, however, has its drawbacks, one of which is the need to check events at even periods of time. This might be hard and is certainly not a declarative approach.

We already know that Qt Quick handles keyboard input via the `Keys` attached property. It is possible to craft QML code similar to the one just presented, but the problem with such an approach is that the faster the player taps keys on the keyboard, the more frequently the character will move, jump, or shoot. However, it's possible to overcome this problem, as we'll see as we move on.

Time for action – Character navigation

Create a new QML document and call it `Player.qml`. In the document, place the following declarations:

```
Item {
    id: player
```

```
        y: parent.height
        focus: true
        Keys.onRightPressed: x = Math.min(x + 20, parent.width)
        Keys.onLeftPressed: x = Math.max(0, x - 20)
        Keys.onUpPressed: jump()
        function jump() {
            jumpAnim.start();
        }
        Image {
            source: "images/elephant.png"
            anchors.bottom: parent.bottom
            anchors.horizontalCenter: parent.horizontalCenter
        }
        Behavior on x {
            NumberAnimation { duration: 100 }
        }
        SequentialAnimation on y {
            id: jumpAnim
            running: false
            NumberAnimation {
                to: player.parent.height - 50
                easing.type: Easing.OutQuad
            }
            NumberAnimation {
                to: player.parent.height
                easing.type: Easing.InQuad
            }
        }
    }
```

Next, open the document containing the main scene definition and declare the player character near the end of the document after all the background layers have been declared:

```
    Player {
        id: player
        x: 40
    }
```

What just happened?

The player itself is an empty item with a keyboard focus that handles presses of the right, left, and up arrow keys, causing them to manipulate the `x` and `y` coordinates of the player. The `x` property has a `Behavior` element set so that the player moves smoothly within the scene. Finally, anchored to the player item is the actual visualization of the player—our elephant friend.

When the right or left arrow keys are pressed, a new position for the character will be calculated and applied. Thanks to the `Behavior` element, the item will travel gradually (during one second) to the new position. Keeping the key pressed will trigger autorepeat and the handler will be called again. In a similar fashion, when the up arrow key is pressed, it will activate a prepared sequential animation that will lift the character up by 50 pixels and then move it down again to the initial position.

This approach works, but we can do better. Let's try something different.

Time for action – Another approach to character navigation

Replace the previous key handlers with the following code:

```
Item {
    id: player
    //...
    QtObject {
        id: flags
        readonly property int speed: 100
        property int horizontal: 0
    }
    Keys.onRightPressed: {
        recalculateDurations();
        flags.horizontal = 1;
    }
    Keys.onLeftPressed: {
        if(flags.horizontal != 0) {
            return;
        }
        recalculateDurations();
        flags.horizontal = -1;
    }
    Keys.onUpPressed: jump()
    Keys.onReleased: {
        if(event.isAutoRepeat) return;
        if(event.key === Qt.Key_Right) {
            flags.horizontal = 0;
        }
        if(event.key === Qt.Key_Left && flags.horizontal < 0) {
            flags.horizontal = 0;
        }
    }
```

```
    function recalculateDurations() {
        xAnimRight.duration = (xAnimRight.to - x) * 1000 /
flags.speed;
        xAnimLeft.duration = (x - xAnimLeft.to) * 1000 / flags.speed;
    }
    NumberAnimation on x {
        id: xAnimRight
        running: flags.horizontal > 0
        to: parent.width
    }
    NumberAnimation on x {
        id: xAnimLeft
        running: flags.horizontal < 0
        to: 0
    }
}
```

What just happened?

Instead of performing actions immediately, upon pressing a key, we are now setting flags (in a private object) for which direction the character should be moving in. In our situation, the right direction has priority over the left direction. Setting a flag triggers an animation that tries to move the character toward an edge of the scene. Releasing the button will clear the flag and stop the animation. Before the animation is started, we are calling the `recalculateDurations()` function, which checks how long the animation should last for the character to move at the desired speed.

> **TIP** If you want to replace keyboard-based input with something else, for example, accelerometer or custom buttons, the same principle can be applied. When using an accelerometer, you can even control the speed of the player by measuring how much the device is tilted. You can additionally store the tilt in the `flags.horizontal` parameter and make use of that variable in the `recalculateDurations()` function.

Have a go hero – Polishing the animation

What we have done is sufficient for many applications. However, you can try controlling the movement even more. As a challenge, try modifying the system in such a way that during a jump, inertia keeps the current horizontal direction and speed of movement of the character until the end of the jump. If the player releases the right or left keys during a jump, the character will stop only after the jump is complete.

Despite trying to do everything in a declarative fashion, some actions will still require imperative code. If some action is to be executed periodically, you can use the `Timer` item to execute a function on demand. Let's go through the process of implementing such patterns together.

Time for action – Generating coins

The goal of the game we are trying to implement is to collect coins. We will spawn coins now and then in random locations of the scene.

Create a new QML Document and call it `Coin.qml`. In the editor, enter the following code:

```
Item {
    id: coin
    Rectangle {
        id: coinVisual
        color: "yellow"
        border.color: Qt.darker(color)
        border.width: 2
        width: 30; height: width
        radius: width / 2
        anchors.centerIn: parent
        transform: Rotation {
            origin.x: coinVisual.width / 2
            origin.y: coinVisual.height / 2
            axis { x: 0; y: 1; z: 0 }
            NumberAnimation on angle {
                from: 0; to: 360
                loops: Animation.Infinite
                running: true
                duration: 1000
            }
        }
        Text {
```

```
                color: coinVisual.border.color
                anchors.centerIn: parent
                text: "1"
            }
        }
    }
```

Next, open the document where the scene is defined and enter the following code somewhere in the scene definition:

```
    Component {
        id: coinGenerator
        Coin {}
    }

    Timer {
        id: coinTimer
        interval: 1000
        repeat: true
        running: true
        onTriggered: {
            var cx = Math.floor(Math.random() * root.width);
            var cy = Math.floor(Math.random() * root.height / 3)
                    + root.height / 2;
            coinGenerator.createObject(root, { x: cx, y: cy });
        }
    }
```

What just happened?

First, we defined a new element type, `Coin`, consisting of a yellow circle with a number centered over an empty item. The rectangle has an animation applied that rotates the item around a vertical axis, resulting in a pseudo three-dimensional effect.

Next, a component able to create instances of a `Coin` element is placed in the scene. Then, a `Timer` element is declared that fires every second and spawns a new coin at a random location of the scene.

Sprite animation

The player character as well as any other component of the game should be animated. If the component is implemented using simple Qt Quick shapes, it is quite easy to do by changing the item's properties fluently, using property animations (as we did with the `Coin` object). Things get more difficult if a component is complex enough that it is easier to draw it in a graphics program and use an image in the game instead of trying to recreate the object using Qt Quick items. Then, you need a number of images—one for every frame of animation. Images would have to keep replacing one another to make a convincing animation.

Time for action – Implementing simple character animation

Let's try to make the player character animated in a simple way. In the materials that come with this book, you will find a number of images with different walking phases for Benjamin the Elephant. You can use them, or you can draw or download some other images to be used in place of those provided by us.

Put all images in one directory (for example, `images`) and rename them so that they follow a pattern that contains the base animation name followed by a frame number, for example, `walking_01`, `walking_02`, `walking_03`, and so on.

Next, open the `Player.qml` document and replace the image element showing `elephant.png` with the following code:

```
Image {
    id: elephantImage
    property int currentFrame: 1
    property int frameCount: 7
    source: "images/walking_" + currentFrame + ".png"
    mirror: player.facingLeft
    anchors.bottom: parent.bottom
    anchors.horizontalCenter: parent.horizontalCenter
    NumberAnimation on currentFrame {
        from: 1
        to: frameCount
        loops: Animation.Infinite
        duration: elephantImage.frameCount * 40
        running: player.walking
    }
}
```

In the root element of `Player.qml`, add the following properties:

```
property bool walking: flags.horizontal !== 0
property bool facingLeft: flags.horizontal < 0
```

Start the program and use the arrow keys to see Benjamin move.

What just happened?

A number of images were prepared following a common naming pattern containing a number. All the images have the same size. This allows us to replace one image with another just by changing the value of the `source` property to point to a different image. To make it easier, we introduced a property called the `currentFrame` element that contains the index of the image to be displayed. We used the `currentFrame` element in a string, forming an expression bound to the `source` element of the image. To make substituting frames easy, a `NumberAnimation` element was declared to modify the values of the `currentFrame` element in a loop from `1` to the number of animation frames available (represented by the `frameCount` property) so that each frame is shown for 40 milliseconds.

The animation is playing if the `walking` property evaluates to `true` (based on the value of the `flags.horizontal` element in the player object). Finally, we use the `mirror` property of the `Image` parameter to flip the image if the character is walking left.

The preceding approach works, but it's not perfect. The complexity of the declaration following this pattern grows much faster than required when we want to make movement animation more complex (for example, if we want to introduce jumping). This is not the only problem, though. Loading images does not happen instantly. The first time a particular image is to be used, the animation can stall for a moment while the graphics get loaded, which may ruin the user experience. Lastly, it is simply messy to have a bunch of pictures here and there for every image animation.

A solution to this is to use a **sprite sheet**—a set of small images combined into a single larger image for better performance. Qt Quick supports sprite sheets through its sprite engine that handles loading sequences of sprites from a single image, animating them, and transitioning between different sprites.

In Qt Quick, a sprite sheet can be an image of any type supported by Qt that contains an image strip with all frames of the animation. Subsequent frames should form a continuous line flowing from left to right and from the top to the bottom of the image. However, they do not have to start in the top-left corner of the containing image, nor do they have to end in its bottom-right corner—a single file can contain many sprites. A sprite is defined by providing the size of a single frame in pixels and a frame count. Optionally, you can specify an offset from the top-left corner where the first frame of the sprite is to be read from. The following diagram can be helpful in visualizing the scheme:

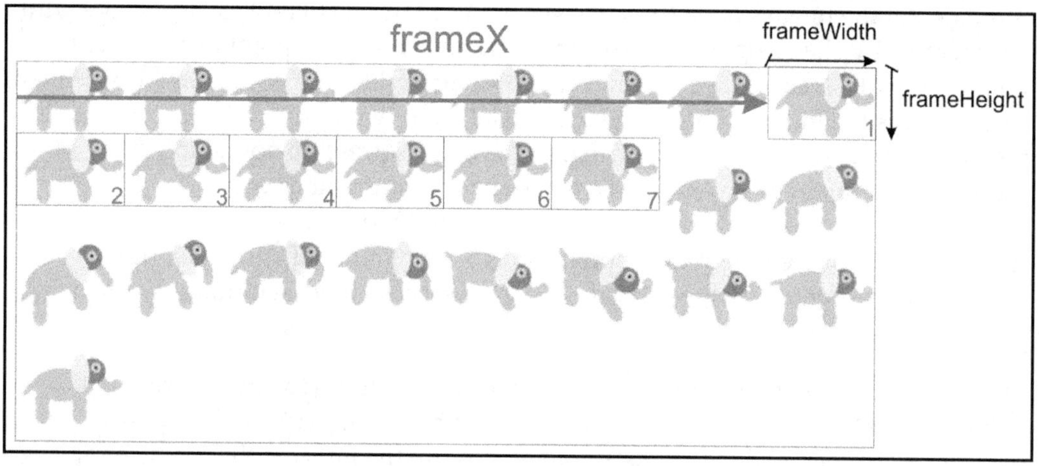

QML offers a `Sprite` element type with a `source` property pointing to the URL of the container image, the `frameWidth` and `frameHeight` properties determining the size of each frame, and a `frameCount` property defining the number of frames in the sprite. Offsetting the image can be achieved by setting values of the `frameX` and `frameY` properties. In addition to this, some additional properties are present; the most important three are `frameRate`, `frameDuration`, and `duration`. All these serve to determine the pace of the animation. If the `frameRate` element is defined, it is interpreted as a number of frames to cycle through per second. If this property is not defined, then the `frameDuration` element kicks in and is treated as a period of time in which to display a single frame (thus, it is directly an inverse of the `frameRate` element). If this property is not defined as well, the `duration` element is used, which carries the duration of the whole animation. You can set any of these three properties, but you don't need to set more than one of them.

Time for action – Animating characters using sprites

Let's wait no further. The task at hand is to replace the manual animation from the previous exercise with a sprite sheet animation.

Open the `Player.qml` document, remove the whole image element responsible for displaying the player character, and add the following code:

```
AnimatedSprite {
    id: sprite
    source: "images/sprite.png"
    frameX: 560
    frameY: 0
    frameWidth: 80
    frameHeight: 52
    frameCount: 7
    frameRate: 10
    interpolate: true
    width: frameWidth
    height: frameHeight

    running: player.walking
    anchors.bottom: parent.bottom
    anchors.horizontalCenter: parent.horizontalCenter

    transform: Scale {
        origin.x: sprite.width / 2
        xScale: player.facingLeft ? -1 : 1
    }
}
```

What just happened?

We replaced the previous static image with an ever-changing source with a different item. As the `Sprite` parameter is not an `Item` element but a data definition of a sprite, we cannot use it in place of the `Image` element. Instead, we will use the `AnimatedSprite` element, which is an item that can display a single animated sprite defined inline. It even has the same set of properties as the `Sprite` parameter. We defined a sprite embedded in `images/sprite.png` with a width of `80` and a height of `52` pixels. The sprite consists of seven frames that should be displayed at a rate of 10 frames per second. The `running` property is set up similar to the original `Animation` element. As the `AnimatedSprite` element does not have a `mirror` property, we emulate it by applying a scale transformation that flips the item horizontally if the `player.facingLeft` expression evaluates to `true`. Additionally, we set the `interpolate` property to `true`, which makes the sprite engine calculate smoother transitions between frames.

The result we are left with is similar to an earlier attempt, so if these two are similar, why bother using sprites? In many situations, you want more complex animation than just a single-frame sequence. What if we want to animate the way Benjamin jumps in addition to walking? Embedding more manual animations, although possible, would explode the number of internal variables required to keep the state of the object. Fortunately, the Qt Quick sprite engine can deal with that. The `AnimatedSprite` element we used provides a subset of features of the whole framework. By substituting the item with the `SpriteSequence` element, we gain access to the full power of sprites. Whilst we're on the subject of `Sprite`, we need to tell you about one additional property of the object, a property called `to` that contains a map of probabilities of transitioning from the current sprite to another one. By stating which sprites the current one migrates to, we create a state machine with weighted transitions to other sprites as well as cycling back to the current state.

Transitioning to another sprite is triggered by setting the `goalSprite` property on the `SpriteSequence` object. This will cause the sprite engine to traverse the graph until it reaches the requested state. It is a great way to fluently switch from one animation to another by going through a number of intermediate states.

Instead of asking the sprite machine to gracefully transit to a given state, you can ask it to force an immediate change by calling the `SpriteSequence` class's `jumpTo()` method and feeding it the name of the sprite that should start playing.

The last thing that needs to be clarified is how to actually attach the sprite state machine to the `SpriteSequence` class. It is very easy—just assign an array of the `Sprite` objects to the `sprites` property.

Time for action – Adding jumping with sprite transitions

Let's replace the `AnimatedSprite` class with the `SpriteSequence` class in the Bejamin the Elephant animation, adding a sprite to be played during the jumping phase.

Open the `Player.qml` file and replace the `AnimatedSprite` object with the following code:

```
SpriteSequence {
    id: sprite
    width: 80
    height: 52
    interpolate: false
    anchors.bottom: parent.bottom
    anchors.horizontalCenter: parent.horizontalCenter
    running: true

    Sprite {
        name: "still"
        source: "images/sprite.png"
        frameCount: 1
        frameWidth: 80; frameHeight: 52
        frameDuration: 100
        to: { "still": 1, "walking": 0, "jumping": 0 }
    }
    Sprite {
        name: "walking"
        source: "images/sprite.png"
        frameX: 560; frameY: 0
        frameCount: 7
        frameWidth: 80; frameHeight: 52
        frameRate: 20
        to: { "walking": 1, "still": 0, "jumping": 0 }
```

```
        }
        Sprite {
            name: "jumping"
            source: "images/sprite.png"
            frameX: 480; frameY: 52
            frameCount: 11
            frameWidth: 80; frameHeight: 70
            frameDuration: 50
            to: { "still" : 0, "walking": 0, "jumping": 1 }
        }

        transform: Scale {
            origin.x: sprite.width / 2
            xScale: player.facingLeft ? -1 : 1
        }
    }
```

Next, extend the `jumpAnim` object by adding the highlighted changes:

```
SequentialAnimation {
    id: jumpAnim
    running: false
    ScriptAction {
        script: {
            sprite.goalSprite = "jumping";
        }
    }
    NumberAnimation {
        target: player; property: "y"
        to: player.parent.height - 50
        easing.type: Easing.OutQuad
    }
    NumberAnimation {
        target: player; property: "y"
        to: player.parent.height
        easing.type: Easing.InQuad
    }
    ScriptAction {
        script: {
            sprite.goalSprite = "";
            sprite.jumpTo("still");
        }
    }
}
```

What just happened?

The `SpriteSequence` element we have introduced has its `Item` elements-related properties set up in the same way as the `AnimatedSprite` element. Apart from that, a sprite called "still" was explicitly set as the current one. We defined a number of `Sprite` objects as children of the `SpriteSequence` element. This is equivalent to assigning those sprites to the `sprites` property of the object. The complete state machine that was declared is presented in the following diagram:

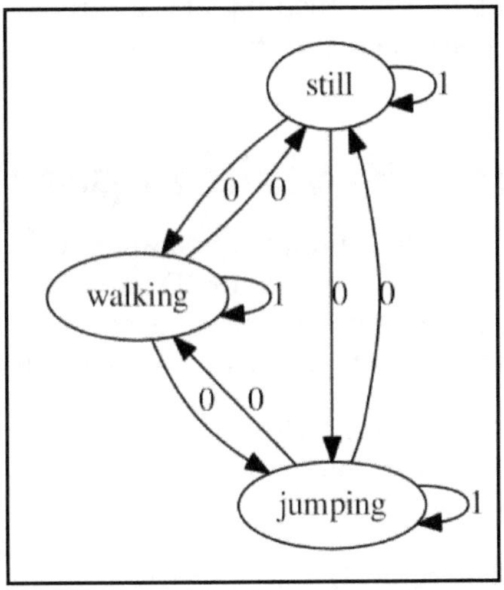

A sprite called "still" has just a single frame representing a situation when Benjamin doesn't move. The sprite keeps spinning in the same state due to the weighted transition back to the "still" state. The two remaining transitions from that state have their weights set to `0`, which means they will never trigger spontaneously, but they can be invoked by setting the `goalSprite` property to a sprite that can be reached by activating one of those transitions.

The sequential animation was extended to trigger sprite changes when the elephant lifts into the air.

Have a go hero – Making Benjamin wiggle his tail in anticipation

To practice sprite transitions, your goal is to extend the state machine of Benjamin's `SpriteSequence` element to make him wiggle his tail when the elephant is standing still. You can find the appropriate sprite in the materials that come included with this book. The sprite field is called `wiggling.png`. Implement the functionality by making it probable that Benjamin spontaneously goes from the "still" state to "wiggling". Pay attention to ensure that the animal stops wiggling and starts walking the moment the player activates the right or left arrow keys.

Time for action – Revisiting parallax scrolling

We already discussed the useful technique of parallax scrolling in `Chapter 6`, *Qt Core Essentials*. It gives the impression of depth for 2D games by moving multiple layers of background at a different speed depending on the assumed distance of the layer from the viewer. Let's see how easy it is to apply the same technique in Qt Quick.

We will implement parallax scrolling with a set of layers that move in the direction opposite to the one the player is moving in. Therefore, we will need a definition of the scene and a moving layer.

Create a new **QML File (Qt Quick 2)**. Call it `ParallaxScene.qml`. The scene will encompass the whole game "level" and will expose the position of the player to the moving layers. Put the following code in the file:

```
import QtQuick 2.9

Item {
    id: root
    property int currentPos
    x: -currentPos * (root.width - root.parent.width) / width
}
```

Then, create another QML file and call it `ParallaxLayer.qml`. Make it contain the following definition:

```
import QtQuick 2.9

Item {
    property real factor: 0
    x: factor > 0 ? -parent.currentPos / factor - parent.x : 0
}
```

Now, let's use the two new element types in the main QML document. We'll take elements from the earlier scene definition and make them into different parallax layers—the sky, the trees, and the grass:

```
Rectangle {
    id: view
    width: 600
    height: 380
    ParallaxScene {
        id: scene
        width: 1500; height: 380
        anchors.bottom: parent.bottom
        currentPos: player.x
        ParallaxLayer {
            factor: 7.5
            width: sky.width; height: sky.height
            anchors.bottom: parent.bottom
            Image { id: sky; source: "images/sky.png" }
            Item {
                 id: sun
                 //...
            }
        }
        ParallaxLayer {
            factor: 2.5
            width: trees.width; height: trees.height
            anchors.bottom: parent.bottom
            Image { id: trees; source: "images/trees.png" }
        }
        ParallaxLayer {
            factor: 0
            width: grass.width; height: grass.height
            anchors.bottom: parent.bottom
            Image { id: grass; source: "images/grass.png" }
        }
        Item {
            id: player
            // ...
```

```
        }
        Component {
            id: coinGenerator
            Coin {}
        }
        Timer {
            id: coinTimer
            //...
            onTriggered: {
                var cx = Math.floor(Math.random() * scene.width);
                var cy = Math.floor(Math.random() * scene.height / 3)
+
                    scene.height / 2;
                coinGenerator.createObject(scene, { x: cx, y: cy});
            }
        }
    }
}
```

You can now run the game and observe the movement of background layers when the player moves around:

What just happened?

The `ParallaxScene` element we implemented is a moving plane. Its horizontal offset depends on the character's current position and the size of the view. The range of scroll of the scene is determined by the difference between the scene size and the view size—it says how much scrolling we have to do when the character moves from the left edge to the right edge of the scene so that it is in view all the time. If we multiply that by the distance of the character from the left edge of the scene expressed as a fraction of the scene width, we will get the needed scene offset in the view (or otherwise speaking, a projection offset of the scene).

The second type—`ParallaxLayer`—is also a moving plane. It defines a distance factor that represents the relative distance (depth) of the layer behind the foreground, which influences how fast the plane should be scrolled compared to the foreground (scene). The value of `0` means that the layer should be moving with exactly the same speed as the foreground layer. The larger the value, the slower the layer moves as compared to the character. The offset value is calculated by dividing the character's position in the scene by the factor. Since the foreground layer is also moving, we have to take it into consideration when calculating the offset for each parallax layer. Thus, we subtract the horizontal position of the scene to get the actual layer offset.

Having the layers logically defined, we can add them to the scene. Each layer has a physical representation in our case, static images containing textures of the sky, trees, and grass. Each layer is defined separately and can live its own life, containing static and animated elements that have no influence on remaining layers. For example, we put the sun object into the sky layer, so it will move along with the sky layer in addition to playing its own animations.

Finally, since we no longer have the `root` element, we modified the `coinTimer` handler to use the `scene` element instead.

Have a go hero – Vertical parallax sliding

As an additional exercise, you may want to implement a vertical parallax sliding in addition to a horizontal one. Just make your scene bigger and have it expose the vertical scroll position in addition to the horizontal one reported by the `currentPos` element. Then, just repeat all the calculations for the `y` property of each layer and you should be done in no time. Remember that distance factors for `x` and `y` may be different.

Collision detection

There is no built-in support for collision detection in Qt Quick, but there are three ways of providing such support. First, you can use a ready collision system available in a number of 2D physics engines such as Box2D. Secondly, you can implement a simple collision system yourself in C++. Lastly, you can do collision checking directly in JavaScript by comparing object coordinates and bounding boxes.

Our game is very simple; therefore, we will use the last approach. If we had a larger number of moving objects involved in our game, we would probably choose the second approach. The first approach is best if you have an object of non-rectangular shapes that can rotate and bounce off other objects. In this case, having a physics engine at hand becomes really useful.

Time for action – Collecting coins

From Qt Creator's menu, access **File** — **New File or Project**. From **Qt** category, choose the **JS File** template. Call the `collisions.js` file. Put the following content into the document:

```
.pragma library

function boundingBox(object1) {
    var cR = object1.childrenRect;
    var mapped = object1.mapToItem(
         object1.parent, cR.x, cR.y, cR.width, cR.height);
    return Qt.rect(mapped.x, mapped.y, mapped.width, mapped.height);
}

function intersect(object1, object2) {
    var r1 = boundingBox(object1);
    var r2 = boundingBox(object2);
    return (r1.x <= r2.x+r2.width && // r1.left <= r2.right
            r2.x <= r1.x+r1.width && // r2.left <= r1.right
            r1.y <= r2.y+r2.height && // r1.top <= r2.bottom
            r2.y <= r1.y+r1.height); // r2.top <= r1.bottom
}
```

Create another JS File and call it `coins.js`. Enter the following:

```
.import "collisions.js" as Collisions

var coins = []
```

```
coins.collisionsWith = function(player) {
    var collisions = [];
    for(var index = 0; index < coins.length; ++index) {
        var obj = this[index];
        if(Collisions.intersect(player, obj)) {
            collisions.push(obj);
        }
    }
    return collisions;
};
coins.remove = function(obj) {
    var arr = Array.isArray(obj) ? obj : [ obj ];
    var L = arr.length;
    var idx, needle;
    while(L && this.length) {
        needle = arr[--L];
        idx = this.indexOf(needle);
        if(idx !== -1) {
            this.splice(idx, 1);
        }
    }
    return this;
};
```

Finally, open the `main.qml` file and add the following `import` statement:

```
import "coins.js" as Coins
```

In the player object, define the `checkCollisions()` function:

```
function checkCollisions() {
    var result = Coins.coins.collisionsWith(player);
    if(result.length === 0) return;
    result.forEach(function(coin) { coin.hit() });
    Coins.coins.remove(result) // prevent the coin from being hit
again
}
```

Next, modify the `coinTimer` handler to push new coins to the list:

```
Timer {
    id: coinTimer
    //...
    onTriggered: {
        var cx = Math.floor(Math.random() * scene.width);
        var cy = scene.height - 60 - Math.floor(Math.random() * 60);
        var coin = coinGenerator.createObject(scene, { x: cx, y: cy});
        Coins.coins.push(coin);
```

```
        }
    }
```

Lastly, in the same player object, trigger collision detection by handling the position changes of the player:

```
onXChanged: {
    checkCollisions();
}
onYChanged: {
    checkCollisions();
}
```

In the `Coin.qml` file, define an animation and a `hit()` function:

```
SequentialAnimation {
    id: hitAnim
    running: false
    NumberAnimation {
        target: coin
        property: "opacity"
        from: 1; to: 0
        duration: 250
    }
    ScriptAction {
        script: coin.destroy()
    }
}

function hit() {
    hitAnim.start();
}
```

What just happened?

The `collisions.js` file contains functions used to do collision checking. The first line of the file is a `.pragma library` statement, noting that this document only contains functions and does not contain any mutable object. This statement marks the document as a library that can be shared between documents that import it. This aids in reduced memory consumption and improved speed, as the engine doesn't have to reparse and execute the document each time it is imported.

The functions defined in the library are really simple. The first one returns a bounding rectangle of an object based on its coordinates and the size of its children. It assumes that the top-level item is empty and contains children that represent the visual aspect of the object. Children coordinates are mapped using the `mapToItem` function so that the rectangle returned is expressed in the parent item coordinates. The second function does a trivial checking of intersection between two bounding rectangles and returns `true` if they intersect and `false` otherwise.

The second document keeps a definition of an array of coins. It adds two methods to the array object. The first one—`collisionsWith`—performs a collision check between any of the items in the array and the given object using functions defined in `collisions.js`. That's why we import the library at the start of the document. The method returns another array that contains objects intersecting the `player` argument. The other method, called `remove`, takes an object or an array of objects and removes them from `coins`.

The document is not a library; therefore, each document that imports `coins.js` would get its own separate copy of the object. Thus, we need to ensure that `coins.js` is imported only once in the game so that all references to the objects defined in that document relate to the same instance of the object in our program memory.

Our main document imports `coins.js`, which creates the array for storing coin objects and makes its auxiliary functions available. This allows the defined `checkCollisions()` function to retrieve the list of coins colliding with the player. For each coin that collides with the player, we execute a `hit()` method; as a last step, all colliding coins are removed from the array. Since coins are stationary; collision can only occur when the player character enters an area occupied by a coin. Therefore, it is enough to trigger collision detection when the position of the player character changes—we use the `onXChanged` and `onYChanged` handlers.

As hitting a coin results in removing it from the array, we lose a reference to the object. The `hit()` method has to initiate removal of the object from the scene. A minimalistic implementation of this function would be to just call the `destroy()` function on the object, but we do more—the removal can be made smoother by running a fade-out animation on the coin. As a last step, the animation can destroy the object.

The number of objects we track on the scene is really small, and we simplify the shape of each object to a rectangle. This lets us get away with checking collisions in JavaScript. For a larger amount of moving objects, custom shapes, and handling rotations, it is much better to have a collision system based on C++. The level of complexity of such a system depends on your needs.

Have a go hero – Extending the game

You can polish your game development skills by implementing new game mechanics in our jumping elephant game. For example, you can introduce a concept of fatigue. The more the character jumps, the more tired they get and the slower they begin to move and have to rest to regain speed. To make the game more difficult, at times moving obstacles can be generated. When the character bumps into any of them, they get more and more tired. When the fatigue exceeds a certain level, the character dies and the game ends. The heartbeat diagram we previously created can be used to represent the character's level of fatigue—the more tired the character gets, the faster their heart beats.

There are many ways these changes can be implemented, and we want to give you a level of freedom, so we will not provide a step-by-step guide on how to implement a complete game. You already know a lot about Qt Quick, and this is a good opportunity to test your skills!

Pop quiz

Q1. Which of the following types cannot be used with the special on-property syntax?

1. `Animation`
2. `Transition`
3. `Behavior`

Q2. Which QML type allows you to configure a sprite animation with transitions between multiple states?

1. `SpriteSequence`
2. `Image`
3. `AnimatedSprite`

Q3. Which QML type is able to prevent any instant change of the property's value and perform a gradual change of value instead?

1. `Timer`
2. `Behavior`
3. `PropertyAction`

Summary

In this chapter, we showed you how to extend your Qt Quick skills to make your applications dynamic and attractive. We went through the process of recreating and improving a game created earlier in C++ to familiarize you with concepts such as collision detection, state-driven objects, and time-based game loops. You are now familiar with all the most important concepts required to make games using Qt Quick.

In the next chapter, we will turn our attention to techniques that will make your games even more visually appealing. We'll explore the built-in graphical effects Qt Quick provides. You will also learn to extend Qt Quick with custom painted items implemented in C++. This will give you the freedom to create any visual effects you have in mind.

14
Advanced Visual Effects in Qt Quick

Sprite animations and smooth transitions are not always enough to make the game visually appealing. In this chapter, we will explore many ways to add some eye candy to your games. Qt Quick provides a decent amount of built-in visual effects that will come in handy. However, from time to time, you will want to do something that is not possible to do with standard components—something unique and specific to your game. In these cases, you don't need to limit your imagination. We will teach you to dive deep into the C++ API of Qt Quick to implement truly unique graphics effects.

The main topics covered in this chapter are these:

- Auto-scaling user interfaces
- Applying graphical effects to the existing items
- Particle systems
- OpenGL painting in Qt Quick
- Using `QPainter` in Qt Quick

Making the game more attractive

A game should not just be based upon an interesting idea, and it should not only work fluently on a range of devices and give entertainment to those people playing it. It should also look nice and behave nicely. Whether people are choosing from a number of similar implementations of the same game or want to spend money on another similarly priced and entertaining game, there is a good chance that they'll choose the game that looks the best—having a lot of animations, graphics, and flashy content. We already learned a number of techniques to make a game more pleasing to the eye, such as using animations or implementing parallax effect. Here, we will show you a number of other techniques that can make your Qt Quick applications more attractive.

Auto-scaling user interfaces

The first extension you may implement is making your game auto-adjust to the device resolution it is running on. There are basically two ways to accomplish this. The first is to center the user interface in the window (or screen) and if it doesn't fit, enable scrolling. The other approach is to scale the interface to always fit the window (or screen). Which one to choose depends on a number of factors, the most important of which is whether your UI is good enough when upscaled. If the interface consists of text and non-image primitives (basically rectangles), or if it includes images but only vector ones or those with very high resolution, then it is probably fine to try and scale the user interface. Otherwise, if you use a lot of low-resolution bitmap images, you will have to choose one particular size for the UI (optionally allowing it to downscale, since the quality degradation should be less significant in this direction if you enable anti-aliasing).

Whether you choose to scale or to center and scroll, the basic approach is the same—you put your UI item in another item so that you have fine control over the UI geometry, regardless of what happens to the top-level window. Taking the centered approach is quite easy—just anchor the UI to the center of the parent. To enable scrolling, wrap the UI in the `Flickable` item and constrain its size if the size of the window is not big enough to fit the whole user interface:

```
Window {
    //...
    Flickable {
        id: uiFlickable
        anchors.centerIn: parent
        contentWidth: ui.width
```

```
        contentHeight: ui.height

        width: parent.width >= contentWidth ?
               contentWidth : parent.width
        height: parent.height >= contentHeight ?
                contentHeight : parent.height

        UI {
            id: ui
        }
    }
}
```

You can put the following simple code into the `UI.qml` file to see how `Flickable` positions the UI item:

```
import QtQuick 2.0
Rectangle {
    width: 300
    height: 300
    gradient: Gradient {
        GradientStop { position: 0.0; color: "lightsteelblue" }
        GradientStop { position: 1.0; color: "blue" }
    }
}
```

You should probably decorate the top-level item with a nice background if the UI item does not occupy the full area of its parent.

Scaling seems more complicated, but it is really easy with Qt Quick. Again, you have two choices—either stretch or scale. Stretching is as easy as executing the `anchors.fill: parent` command, which effectively forces the UI to recalculate the geometry of all its items, but it possibly allows us to use the space more efficiently. It is, in general, very time-consuming for the developer to provide expressions for calculating the geometry of each and every element in the user interface as the size of the view changes. This is usually not worth the effort. A simpler approach is to just scale the UI item to fit the window, which will implicitly scale the contained items. In such an event, their size can be calculated relative to the base size of the main view of the user interface. For this to work, you need to calculate the scale that is to be applied to the user interface to make it fill the whole space available. The item has a scale of 1 when its effective width equals its implicit width and its effective height equals its implicit height. If the window is larger, we want to scale up the item until it reaches the size of the window.

Therefore, the window's width divided by the item's implicit width will be the item's scale in the horizontal direction. This is shown in the following diagram:

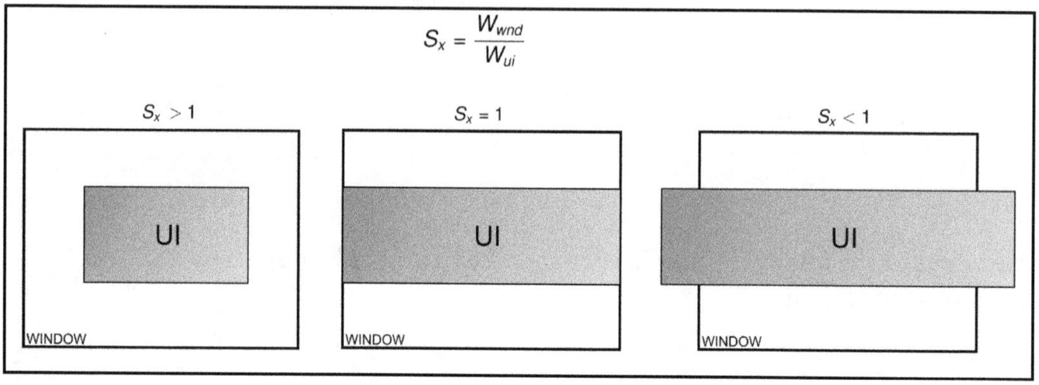

The same can be applied to the vertical direction, but if the UI has a different aspect ratio than the window, its horizontal and vertical scale factors will be different. For the UI to look nice, we have to take the lower of the two values—to only scale up as much as the direction with less space allows, leaving a gap in the other direction:

```
Window {
    //...
    UI {
        id: ui
        anchors.centerIn: parent
        scale: Math.min(parent.width / width,
                        parent.height / height)
    }
}
```

Again, it may be a good idea to put some background on the window item to fill in the gaps.

What if you want to save some margin between the user interface and the window? You can, of course, take that into consideration when calculating the scale (`(window.width - 2 * margin) / width`, and so on) but there is an easier way—simply put an additional item inside the window, leaving an appropriate margin, and put the user interface item in that additional item and scale it up to the additional item's size:

```
Window {
    //...
    Item {
```

```
            anchors {
                fill: parent
                margins: 10
            }
            UI {
                id: ui
                anchors.centerIn: parent
                scale: Math.min(parent.width / width,
                                parent.height / height)
            }
        }
    }
```

When you scale elements a lot, you should consider enabling anti-aliasing for items that can lose quality when rendered in a size different than their native size (for example, images). This is done very easily in Qt Quick, as each `Item` instance has a property called `antialiasing` which, when enabled, will cause the rendering backend to try to reduce distortions caused by the aliasing effect. Remember that this comes at the cost of increased rendering complexity, so try to find a balance between quality and efficiency, especially on low-end hardware. You may provide an option to the user to globally enable or disable anti-aliasing for all game objects or to gradually adjust quality settings for different object types.

Graphical effects

The basic two predefined items in Qt Quick are rectangle and image. You can use them in a variety of creative ways and make them more pleasant-looking by applying GLSL shaders. However, implementing a shader program from scratch is cumbersome and requires in-depth knowledge of the shader language. Luckily, a number of common effects are already implemented and ready to use in the form of the `QtGraphicalEffects` module.

To add a subtle black shadow to our canvas-based heartbeat element defined in the `HeartBeat.qml` file, use a code similar to the following that makes use of the `DropShadow` effect:

```
import QtQuick 2.9
import QtQuick.Window 2.2
import QtGraphicalEffects 1.0

Window {
    //...
    HeartBeat {
        id: heartBeat
```

```
            anchors.centerIn: parent
            visible: false
        }
        DropShadow {
            source: heartBeat
            anchors.fill: heartBeat
            horizontalOffset: 3
            verticalOffset: 3
            radius: 8
            samples: 16
            color: "black"
        }
    }
```

To apply a shadow effect, you need an existing item as the source of the effect. In our case, we are using an instance of the `HeartBeat` class centered in a top-level item. Then, the shadow effect is defined and its geometry follows that of its source using the `anchors.fill` element. Just as the `DropShadow` class renders the original item as well as the shadow, the original item can be hidden by setting its `visible` property to `false`:

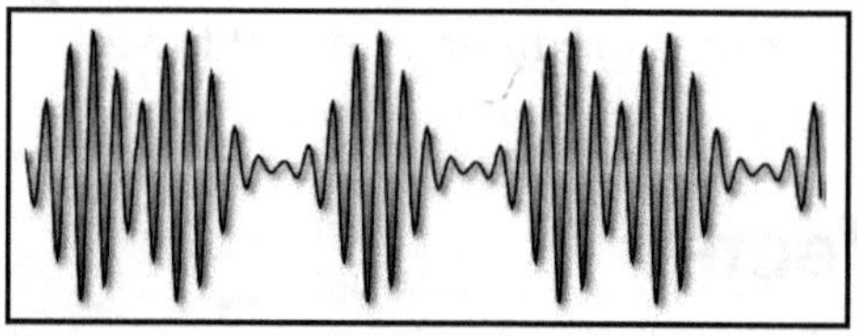

Most of the `DropShadow` class's properties are self-explanatory, but two properties—`radius` and `samples`—require some additional explanation. The shadow is drawn as a blurred monochromatic copy of the original item offset by a given position. The two mentioned properties control the amount of blur and its quality—the more samples used for blurring, the better the effect, but also the more demanding the computation that needs to be performed.

Speaking of blur, the plain blurring effect is also available in the graphics effects module through the `GaussianBlur` element type. To apply a blur instead of a shadow to the last example, simply replace the occurrence of the `DropShadow` class with the following code:

```
GaussianBlur {
    source: heartBeat
    anchors.fill: heartBeat
    radius: 12
    samples: 20
```

```
        transparentBorder: true
    }
```

This change will produce the following result:

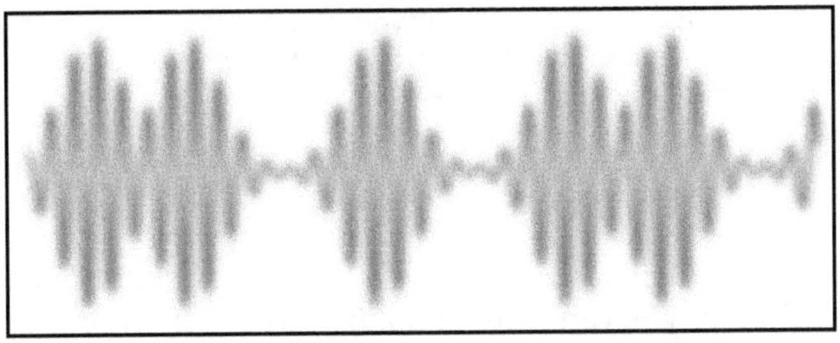

Here, you can see two earlier mentioned properties as well as a vaguely named `transparentBorder` one. Enabling this property fixes some artifacts on the edges of the blur and in general, you'll want to keep it that way.

Have a go hero – The blur parallax scrolled game view

The `blur` property is a very nice effect that can be used in many situations. For example, you can try to implement a feature within our elephant game whereby when the user pauses the game (for example, by pressing the *P* key on the keyboard), the view gets blurred. Make the effect smooth by applying an animation to the effect's `radius` property.

Another interesting effect is `Glow`. It renders a colored and blurred copy of the source element. An example use case for games is highlighting some parts of the user interface—you can direct the user's attention to the element (for example, button or badge) by making the element flash periodically:

```
Window {
    //...
    Badge {
        id: importantBadge
        anchors.centerIn: parent
    }
    Glow {
        source: importantBadge
        anchors.fill: source
        samples: 64
        color: "red"
```

```
            SequentialAnimation on radius {
                loops: Animation.Infinite
                running: true

                NumberAnimation { from: 0; to: 30; duration: 500 }
                PauseAnimation { duration: 100 }
                NumberAnimation { from: 30; to: 0; duration: 500 }
                PauseAnimation { duration: 1000 }
            }
        }
    }
```

The complete module contains 20 different effects. We cannot describe each effect in detail here. Nevertheless, you can learn about it yourself. If you clone the module's source git repository (found under `https://code.qt.io/cgit/qt/qtgraphicaleffects.git/`), in the `tests/manual/testbed` subdirectory of the cloned repository, you will find a nice application for testing the existing effects. To run the tool, open the `testBed.qml` file with `qmlscene`:

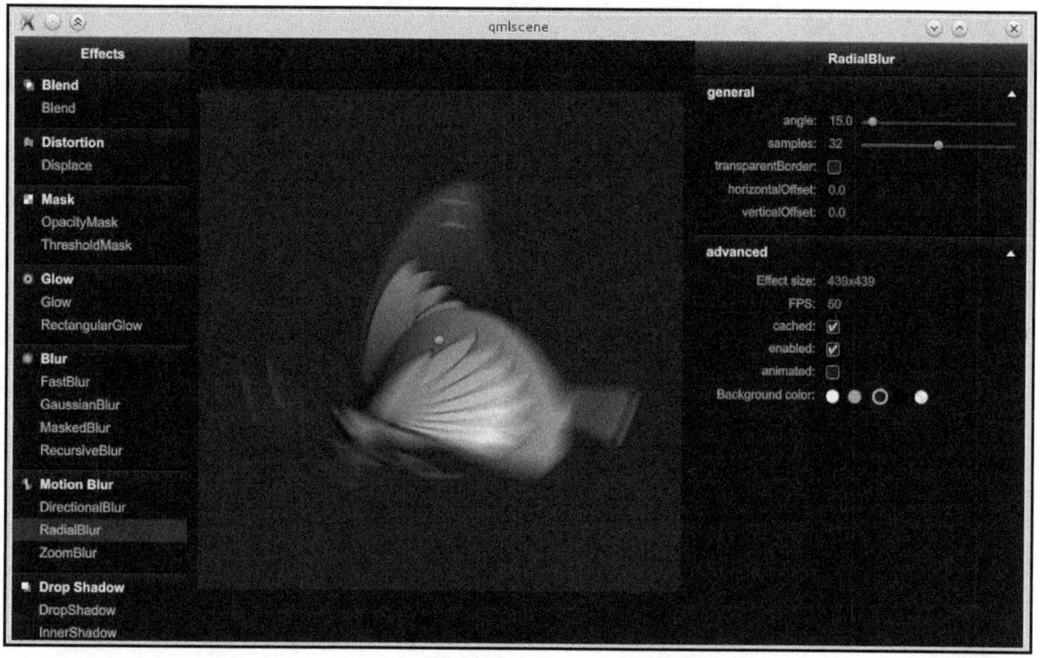

> **TIP**
> You can also access a complete list of effects and their short descriptions by searching for **QtGraphicalEffects** in the documentation index.

Particle systems

A commonly used visual effect in games is generating a large number of small, usually short-lived, often fast-moving, fuzzy objects such as stars, sparks, fumes, dust, snow, splinters, falling leaves, or the like. Placing these as regular items within a scene would greatly degrade performance. Instead, a special engine is used, which keeps a registry of such objects and tracks (simulates) their logical attributes without having physical entities in the scene. Such objects, called **particles**, are rendered upon request in the scene using very efficient algorithms. This allows us to use a large number of particles without having a negative impact on the rest of the scene.

Qt Quick provides a particle system in the `QtQuick.Particles` import. The `ParticleSystem` element provides the core for the simulation, which uses the `Emitter` elements to spawn particles. They are then rendered according to definitions in a `ParticlePainter` element. Simulated entities can be manipulated using the `Affector` objects, which can modify the trajectory or life span of particles.

Let's start with a simple example. The following code snippet declares the simplest possible particle system:

```
import QtQuick 2.0
import QtQuick.Window 2.2
import QtQuick.Particles 2.0

Window {
    visible: true
    width: 360
    height: 360
    title: qsTr("Particle system")

    ParticleSystem {
        id: particleSystem
        anchors.fill: parent

        Emitter { anchors.fill: parent }
        ImageParticle { source: "star.png" }
    }
}
```

The result can be observed in the following image:

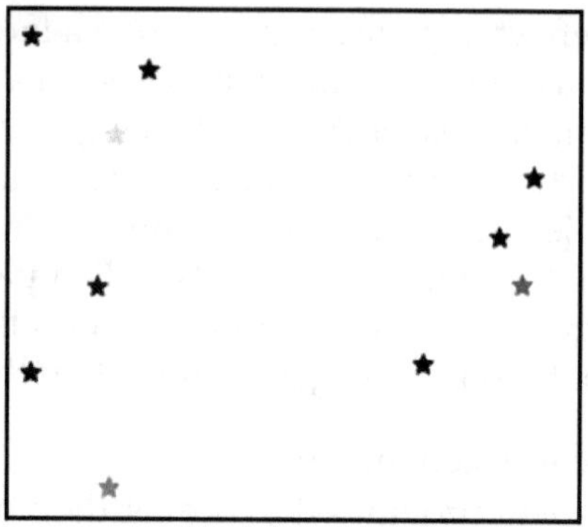

Let's analyze the code. After importing `QtQuick.Particles 2.0`, a `ParticleSystem` item is instantiated that defines the domain of the particle system. We define two objects within that system. The first object is the `Emitter` and defines an area where particles will be spawned. The area is set to encompass the whole domain. The second object is an object of the `ImageParticle` type, which is a `ParticlePainter` subclass. It determines that particles should be rendered as instances of a given image. By default, the `Emitter` object spawns 10 particles per second, each of which lives for one second and then dies and is removed from the scene. In the code presented, the `Emitter` and `ImageParticle` objects are direct children of the `ParticleSystem` class; however, this doesn't have to be the case. The particle system can be explicitly specified by setting the `system` property.

Tuning the emitter

You can control the amount of particles being emitted by setting the `emitRate` property of the emitter. Another property, called the `lifeSpan`, determines how many milliseconds it takes before a particle dies. To introduce some random behavior, you can use the `lifeSpanVariation` property to set a maximum amount of time (in milliseconds) the life span can be altered by the system (in both directions):

```
Emitter {
    anchors.fill: parent
    emitRate: 350
    lifeSpan: 1500
    lifeSpanVariation: 400 // effective: 1100-1900 ms
}
```

A possible result of this change is shown in the following picture:

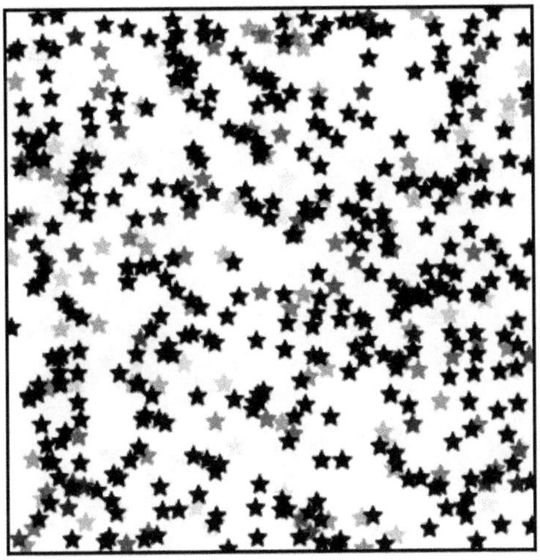

Increasing the emission rate and life span of particles can lead to a situation in which a very large number of particles have to be managed (and possibly rendered). This can degrade performance; thus, an upper limit of particles that can concurrently be alive can be set through the `maximumEmitted` property.

Tweaking the life span of particles makes the system more diverse. To strengthen the effect, you can also manipulate the size of each particle through the `size` and `sizeVariation` properties:

```
Emitter {
    anchors.fill: parent
    emitRate: 50
    size: 12
    sizeVariation: 6
    endSize: 2
}
```

This will give you particles of different sizes:

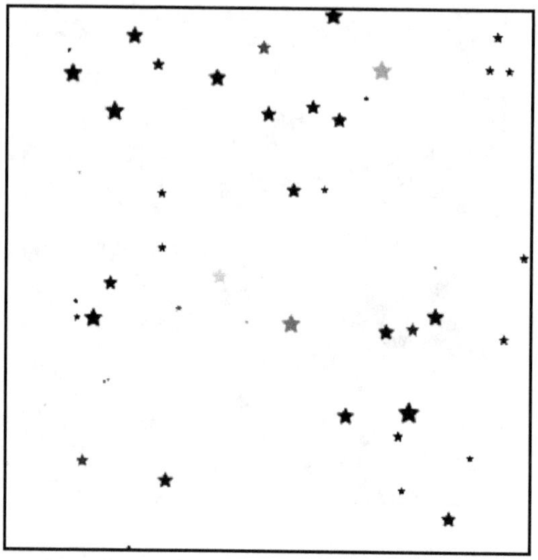

The range of functionality presented thus far should be enough to create many nice-looking and useful particle systems. However, particles are emitted from the whole area of the emitter, which is a regular `QQuickItem` and thus is rectangular. This doesn't have to be the case, though. The `Emitter` element contains a `shape` property, which is a way to declare the area that is to be giving birth to particles.
The `QtQuick.Particles` module defines three types of custom shape that can be used—`EllipseShape`, `LineShape`, and `MaskShape`. The first two are very simple, defining either an empty or filled ellipse inscribed in the item or a line crossing one of the two diagonals of the item. The `MaskShape` element is more interesting, as it makes it possible to use an image as a shape for the `Emitter` element:

```
Emitter {
    anchors.fill: parent
    emitRate: 1600
    shape: MaskShape { source: "star.png" }
}
```

Particles can now only spawn within the specified area:

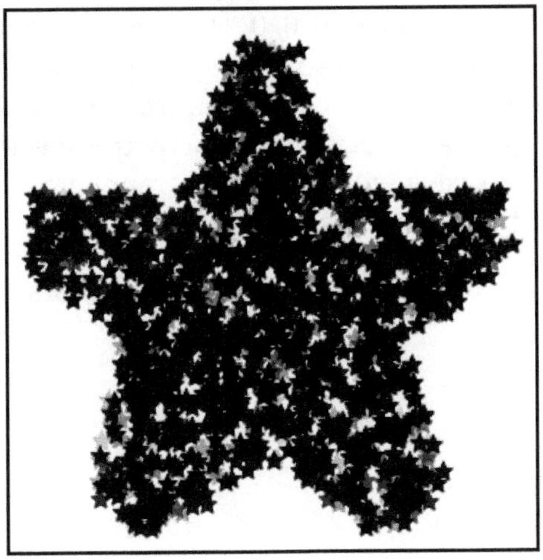

Rendering particles

So far, we have used a bare `ImageParticle` element to render particles. It is only one of the three `ParticlePainters` available, with the others being `ItemParticle` and `CustomParticle`. However, before we move on to other renderers, let's focus on tweaking the `ImageParticle` element to obtain some interesting effects.

The `ImageParticle` element renders each logical particle as an image. The image can be manipulated separately for each particle by changing its color and rotation, deforming its shape, or using it as a sprite animation.

To influence the color of particles, you can use any of the large number of dedicated properties—`alpha`, `color`, `alphaVariation`, `colorVariation`, `redVariation`, `greenVariation`, and `blueVariation`. The first two properties define the base value for the respective attributes, and the remaining properties set the maximum deviation of a respective parameter from the base value. In the case of opacity, there is only one type of variation you can use, but when defining the color, you can either set different values for each of the red, green, and blue channels, or you can use the global `colorVariation` property, which is similar to setting the same value for all three channels. Allowed values are any between the range of 0 (no deviation allowed) and 1.0 (100% in either direction).

TIP

Note that when a color is applied to an image, the respective components of the colors (red, green, blue, and alpha) are multiplied. Black color (0, 0, 0, 1) has all components set to 0 except for alpha, so applying a solid color to a black image will not have any effect. On the contrary, if your image contains white pixels (1, 1, 1, 1), they will be displayed in exactly the specified color. Transparent pixels will stay transparent because their alpha component will remain set to 0.

In our example, we can create particles with different colors using the following code:

```
ImageParticle {
    source: "star_white.png"
    colorVariation: 1
}
```

The result should look like this:

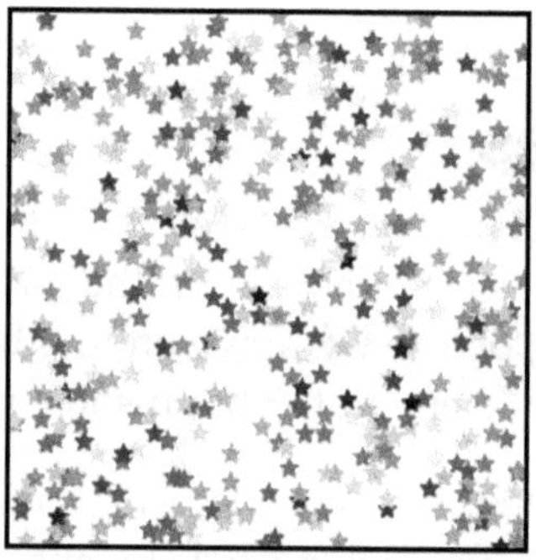

The properties mentioned are stationary—the particle obeys the constant value during its whole life. The `ImageParticle` element also exposes two properties, letting you control the color of particles relative to their age. First of all, there is a property called `entryEffect` that defines what happens with the particle at its birth and death. The default value is `Fade`, which makes particles fade in from 0 opacity at the start of their life and fades them back to 0 just before they die. You have already experienced this effect in all the earlier particle animations we demonstrated. Other values for the property are `None` and `Scale`. The first one is obvious—there is no entry effect associated with particles. The second one scales particles from 0 at their birth and scales them back to 0 at the end of their life.

The other time-related property is `colorTable`. You can feed it with a URL of an image to be used as a one-dimensional texture determining the color of each particle over its life. At the beginning, the particle gets color-defined by the left edge of the image and then progresses right in a linear fashion. It is most common to set an image here containing a color gradient to achieve smooth transitions between colors.

The second parameter that can be altered is the rotation of a particle. Here, we can also either use properties that define constant values for rotation (`rotation` and `rotationVariation`) specified in degrees or modify the rotation of particles in time with `rotationVelocity` and `rotationVelocityVariation`. The velocity defines the pace or rotation in degrees per second.

Particles can also be deformed. The `xVector` and `yVector` properties allow binding vectors, which define distortions in horizontal and vertical axes. We will describe how to set the vectors in the next section. Last but not least, using the `sprites` property, you can define a list of sprites that will be used to render particles. This works in a fashion similar to the `SpriteSequence` type described in the previous chapter.

Making particles move

Apart from fading and rotating, the particle systems we have seen so far were very static. While this is useful for making star fields, it is not at all useful for explosions, sparks, or even falling snow. This is because particles are mostly about movement. Here, we will show you two aspects of making your particles fly.

The first aspect is modeling how the particles are born. By that, we mean the physical conditions of the object creating the particles. During an explosion, matter is pushed away from the epicenter with a very large force that causes air and small objects to rush outward at an extremely high speed. Fumes from a rocket engine are ejected with high velocities in the direction opposite to that of the propelled craft. A moving comet draws along a braid of dust and gases put into motion by the inertia.

All these conditions can be modeled by setting the velocity or acceleration of the particles. These two metrics are described by vectors determining the direction and amount (magnitude or length) of the given quantity. In Qt Quick, such vectors are represented by an element type called `Direction`, where the tail of the vector is attached to the object and the position of the head is calculated by the `Direction` instance. Since we have no means of setting attributes on particles because we have no objects representing them, those two attributes—`velocity` and `acceleration`—are applied to emitters spawning the particles. As you can have many emitters in a single particle system, you can set different velocities and accelerations for particles of different origins.

There are four types of direction elements representing different sources of information about the direction. First, there is `CumulativeDirection`, which acts as a container for other direction types and works like a sum of directions contained within.

Then, there is `PointDirection`, where you can specify the *x* and *y* coordinates of a point where the head of the vector should be attached. To avoid the unrealistic effect of all particles heading in the same direction, you can specify `xVariation` and `yVariation` to introduce allowed deviation from a given point:

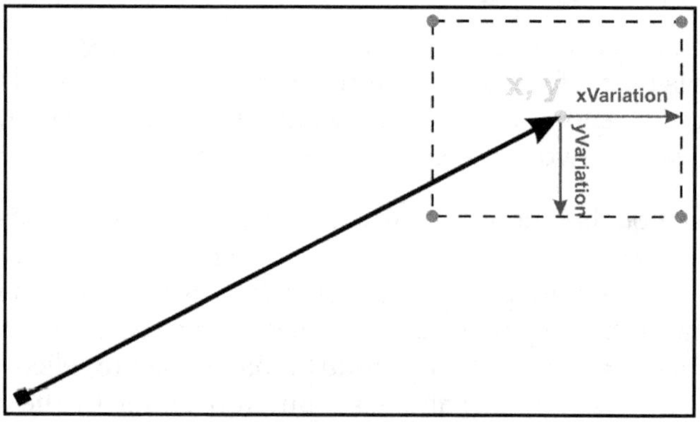

The third type is the most popular direction type—`AngleDirection`, which directly specifies the angle (in degrees clockwise from straight right) and magnitude (in pixels per second) of the vector. The angle can vary from the base by `angleVariation`, and similarly, `magnitudeVariation` can be used to introduce variation to the length of the vector:

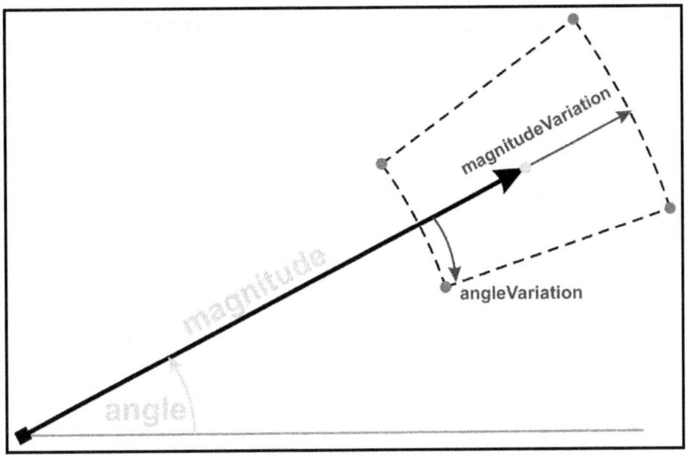

The last type is similar to the previous one. The `TargetDirection` vector can be used to point the vector toward the center of a given Qt Quick item (set with the `targetItem` property). The length of the vector is calculated by giving the `magnitude` and `magnitudeVariation`, and both can be interpreted as pixels per second or multiples of distance between the source and target points (depending on the value of the `proportionalMagnitude` property):

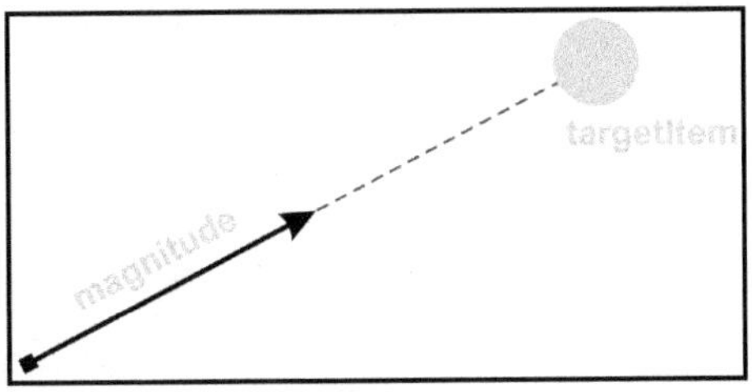

Let's get back to setting particle velocity. We can use the `AngleDirection` vector to specify that particles should be moving left, spreading at a maximum of 45 degrees:

```
Emitter {
    anchors.centerIn: parent
    width: 50; height: 50
    emitRate: 50
    velocity: AngleDirection {
        angleVariation: 45
        angle: 180
        magnitude: 200
    }
}
```

This code will produce the effect shown on the following picture:

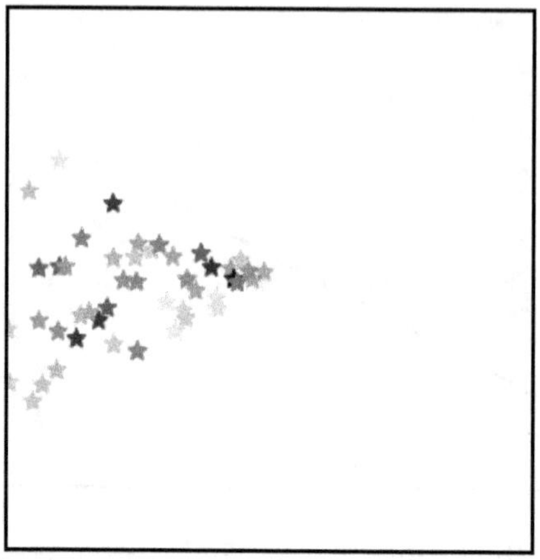

Setting acceleration works the same way. You can even set both the initial velocity and the acceleration each particle should have. It is very easy to shoot the particles in the left direction and start pulling them down:

```
Emitter {
    anchors.right: parent.right
    anchors.verticalCenter: parent.verticalCenter
    emitRate: 15
    lifeSpan: 5000
    velocity: AngleDirection {
        angle: 180
        magnitude: 200
    }
    acceleration: AngleDirection {
        angle: 90 // local left = global down
        magnitude: 100
    }
}
```

This code will produce particles moving along a single curve:

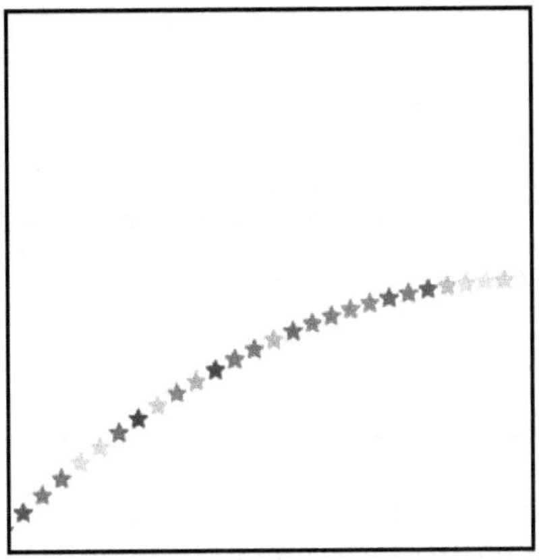

The `Emitter` element has one more nice property that is useful in the context of moving particles. Setting the `velocityFromMovement` parameter to a value different from `0` makes any movement of the `Emitter` element apply to the velocity of the particles. The direction of the additional vector matches the direction of the emitter's movement, and the magnitude is set to the speed of the emitter multiplied by the value set to `velocityFromMovement`. It is a great way to generate fumes ejected from a rocket engine:

```
Item {
    Image {
        id: image
        source: "rocket.png"
    }
    Emitter {
        anchors.right: image.right
        anchors.verticalCenter: image.verticalCenter
        emitRate: 500
        lifeSpan: 3000
        lifeSpanVariation: 1000
        velocityFromMovement: -20
        velocity: AngleDirection {
            magnitude: 100
            angleVariation: 40
        }
    }
    NumberAnimation on x {
        ...
    }
}
```

This is how the result could look like:

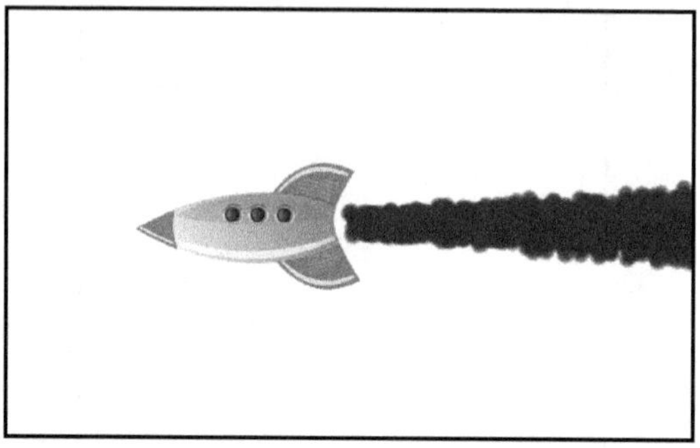

The second way of addressing the behavior of particles is to influence their attributes after they are born—in any particular moment of their life. This can be done using affectors. These are items inheriting affector, which can modify some attributes of particles currently traveling though the area of the affector. One of the simplest affectors is `Age`. It can advance particles to a point in their lifetime where they only have `lifeLeft` milliseconds of their life left:

```
Age {
    once: true
    lifeLeft: 500
    shape: EllipseShape { fill: true }
    anchors.fill: parent
}
```

Setting `once` to `true` makes each affector influence a given particle only once. Otherwise, each particle can have its attributes modified many times.

Another affector type is `Gravity`, which can accelerate particles in a given angle. `Friction` can slow particles down, and `Attractor` will affect the particle's position, velocity, or acceleration so that it starts traveling toward a given point. `Wander` is great for simulating snowflakes or butterflies flying in pseudo-random directions.

There are also other affector types available, but we will not go into their details here. We would like to warn you, however, against using affectors too often—they can severely degrade performance.

Time for action – Vanishing coins spawning particles

It is now time to practice our freshly acquired skills. The task is to add a particle effect to the game we created in the previous chapter. When the player collects a coin, it will explode into a sprinkle of colorful stars.

Start by declaring a particle system as filling the game scene, along with the particle painter definition:

```
ParticleSystem {
    id: coinParticles
    anchors.fill: parent // scene is the parent
    ImageParticle {
        source: "images/particle.png"
        colorVariation: 1
        rotationVariation: 180
        rotationVelocityVariation: 10
    }
}
```

Next, modify the definition of `Coin` to include an emitter:

```
Emitter {
    id: emitter
    system: coinParticles
    emitRate: 0
    lifeSpan: 1500
    lifeSpanVariation: 100
    velocity: AngleDirection {
        angleVariation: 180
        magnitude: 10
    }
    acceleration: AngleDirection {
        angle: 270
        magnitude: 30
    }
}
```

Finally, the `hit()` function has to be updated:

```
function hit() {
    emitter.burst(50);
    hitAnim.start();
}
```

Run the game and see what happens when Benjamin collects coins:

What just happened?

In this exercise, we defined a simple particle system that fills the whole scene. We defined a simple image painter for the particles where we allow particles to take on all the colors and start in all possible rotations. We used a star pixmap as our particle template.

Then, an `Emitter` object is attached to every coin. Its `emitRate` is set to `0`, which means it does not emit any particles on its own. We set a varying life span on particles and let them fly in all directions by setting their initial velocity with an angle variation of 180 degrees in both directions (giving a total of 360 degrees). By setting an acceleration, we give the particles a tendency to travel toward the top edge of the scene.

In the hit function, we call a `burst()` function on the emitter, which makes it give instant birth to a given number of particles.

Custom OpenGL-based Qt Quick items

In `Chapter 12`, *Customization in Qt Quick*, we learned to create new QML element types that can be used to provide dynamic data engines or some other type of non-visual objects. Now we will see how to provide new types of visual items to Qt Quick.

The first question you should ask yourself is whether you really need a new type of item. Maybe you can achieve the same goal with the already existing elements? Very often, you can use vector or bitmap images to add custom shapes to your applications, or you can use Canvas to quickly draw the graphics you need directly in QML.

If you decide that you do require custom items, you will be doing that by implementing subclasses of the `QQuickItem` C++ class, which is the base class for all items in Qt Quick. After creating the new type, you will always have to register it with QML using `qmlRegisterType`.

The scene graph

To provide very fast rendering of its scene, Qt Quick uses a mechanism called **scene graph**. The graph consists of a number of nodes of well-known types, each describing a primitive shape to be drawn. The framework makes use of knowledge of each of the primitives allowed and their parameters to find the most performance-wise optimal order in which items can be rendered. Rendering itself is done using OpenGL, and all the shapes are defined in terms of OpenGL calls.

Providing new items for Qt Quick boils down to delivering a set of nodes that define the shape using terminology the graph understands. This is done by subclassing `QQuickItem` and implementing the pure virtual `updatePaintNode()` method, which is supposed to return a node that will tell the scene graph how to render the item. The node will most likely be describing a geometry (shape) with a material (color, texture) applied.

Time for action – Creating a regular polygon item

Let's learn about the scene-graph by delivering an item class for rendering convex regular polygons. We will draw the polygon using the OpenGL drawing mode called "triangle fan". It draws a set of triangles that all have a common vertex. Subsequent triangles are defined by the shared vertex, the vertex from the previous triangle, and the next vertex specified. Take a look at the diagram to see how to draw a hexagon as a triangle fan using eight vertices as control points:

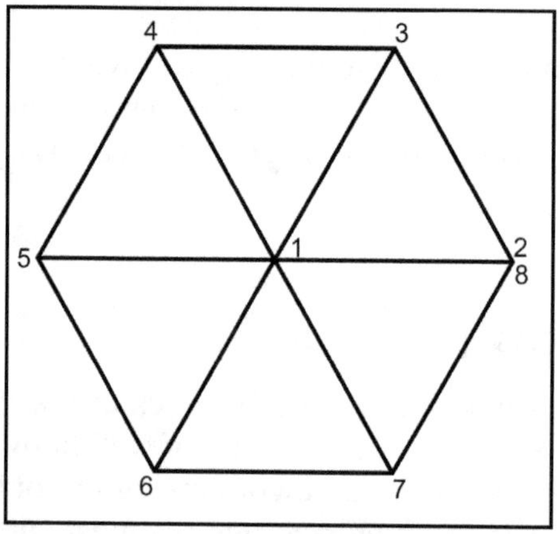

The same method applies for any regular polygon. The first vertex defined is always the shared vertex occupying the center of the shape. The remaining points are positioned on the circumference of a bounding circle of the shape at equal angular distances. The angle is easily calculated by dividing the full angle by the number of sides. For a hexagon, this yields 60 degrees.

Let's get down to business and the `QQuickItem` subclass. We will give it a very simple interface:

```
class RegularPolygon : public QQuickItem
{
    Q_OBJECT
    Q_PROPERTY(int vertices READ vertices WRITE setVertices
               NOTIFY verticesChanged)
    Q_PROPERTY(QColor color READ color WRITE setColor NOTIFY
colorChanged)
public:
    RegularPolygon();
    ~RegularPolygon();
```

```
    int vertices() const;
    void setVertices(int v);

    QColor color() const;
    void setColor(const QColor &c);

    QSGNode *updatePaintNode(QSGNode *, UpdatePaintNodeData *);

signals:
    void verticesChanged(int);
    void colorChanged(QColor);

private:
     int m_vertexCount;
     QColor m_color;
};
```

Our polygon is defined by the number of vertices and the fill color. We also get everything we inherited from `QQuickItem`, including the width and height of the item. Besides adding the obvious getters and setters for the properties, we override the virtual `updatePaintNode()` method, which is responsible for building the scene-graph.

Before we deal with updating graph nodes, let's deal with the easy parts first. Implement the constructor as follows:

```
RegularPolygon::RegularPolygon()
{
    setFlag(ItemHasContents, true);
    m_vertexCount = 6;
}
```

We make our polygon a hexagon by default. We also set a flag, `ItemHasContents`, which tells the scene-graph that the item is not fully transparent and should ask us how the item should be painted by calling `updatePaintNode()`. Existence of this flag allows Qt to avoid preparing the whole infrastructure if the item would not be painting anything anyway.

The setters are also quite easy to grasp:

```
void RegularPolygon::setVertices(int v) {
    v = qMax(3, v);
    if(v == vertices()) return;
    m_vertexCount = v;
    emit verticesChanged(v);
    update();
}
```

```
void RegularPolygon::setColor(const QColor &c) {
    if(color() == c) return;
    m_color = c;
    emit colorChanged(c);
    update();
}
```

A polygon has to have at least three sides; thus, we enforce this as a minimum, sanitizing the input value with `qMax`. After we change any of the properties that could influence the look of the item, we call `update()` to let Qt Quick know that the item needs to be rerendered. Let's tackle `updatePaintNode()` now. We'll disassemble it into smaller pieces so that it is easier for you to understand how the function works:

```
QSGNode *RegularPolygon::updatePaintNode(
    QSGNode *oldNode, QQuickItem::UpdatePaintNodeData *) {
```

When the function is called, it may receive a node it returned during a previous call. Be aware that the graph is free to delete all the nodes when it feels like it, so you should never rely on the node being there even if you returned a valid node during the previous run of the function. Let's move on to the next part of the function:

```
    QSGGeometryNode *node = nullptr;
    QSGGeometry *geometry = nullptr;
```

The node we will return is a geometry node that contains information about the geometry and the material of the shape being drawn. We will be filling those variables as we go through the method. Next, we check whether `oldNode` was provided:

```
        if (!oldNode) {
            node = new QSGGeometryNode;
            geometry = new QSGGeometry(
                QSGGeometry::defaultAttributes_Point2D(), m_vertexCount +
2);
            geometry->setDrawingMode(GL_TRIANGLE_FAN);
            node->setGeometry(geometry);
            node->setFlag(QSGNode::OwnsGeometry);
```

As we already mentioned, the function is called with the previously returned node as the argument, but we should be prepared for the node not being there and we should create it. Thus, if that is the case, we create a new `QSGGeometryNode` and a new `QSGGeometry` for it. The geometry constructor takes a so-called attribute set as its parameter, which defines a layout for data in the geometry.

Most common layouts have been predefined:

Attribute set	**Usage**	**First attribute**	**Second attribute**
`Point2D`	Solid colored shape	`float x, y`	-
`ColoredPoint2D`	Per-vertex color	`float x, y`	`uchar red, green, blue, alpha`
`TexturedPoint2D`	Per-vertex texture coordinate	`float x, y`	`float tx, float ty`

We will be defining the geometry in terms of 2D points without any additional information attached to each point; therefore, we pass `QSGGeometry::defaultAttributes_Point2D()` to construct the layout we need. As you can see in the preceding table for that layout, each attribute consists of two floating point values denoting the *x* and *y* coordinates of a point.

The second argument of the `QSGGeometry` constructor informs us about the number of vertices we will be using. The constructor will allocate as much memory as is needed to store the required number of vertices using the given attribute layout. After the geometry container is ready, we pass its ownership to the geometry node so that when the geometry node is destroyed, the memory for the geometry is freed as well. At this moment, we also mark that we will be rendering in the `GL_TRIANGLE_FAN` mode. The process is repeated for the material:

```
QSGFlatColorMaterial *material = new QSGFlatColorMaterial;
material->setColor(m_color);
node->setMaterial(material);
node->setFlag(QSGNode::OwnsMaterial);
```

We use `QSGFlatColorMaterial` as the whole shape will have one color that is set from `m_color`. Qt provides a number of predefined material types. For example, if we wanted to give each vertex a separate color, we would have used `QSGVertexColorMaterial` along with the `ColoredPoint2D` attribute layout.

The next piece of code deals with a situation in which `oldNode` did contain a valid pointer to a node that was already initialized:

```
} else {
    node = static_cast<QSGGeometryNode *>(oldNode);
    geometry = node->geometry();
    geometry->allocate(m_vertexCount + 2);
}
```

In this case, we only need to ensure that the geometry can hold as many vertices as we need in case the number of sides changed since the last time the function was executed. Next, we check the material:

```
QSGMaterial *material = node->material();
QSGFlatColorMaterial *flatMaterial =
        static_cast<QSGFlatColorMaterial*>(material);
if(flatMaterial->color() != m_color) {
    flatMaterial->setColor(m_color);
    node->markDirty(QSGNode::DirtyMaterial);
}
```

If the color differs, we reset it and tell the geometry node that the material needs to be updated by marking the `DirtyMaterial` flag.

Finally, we can set vertex data:

```
QRectF bounds = boundingRect();
QSGGeometry::Point2D *vertices = geometry->vertexDataAsPoint2D();

// first vertex is the shared one (middle)
QPointF center = bounds.center();

vertices[0].set(center.x(), center.y());

// vertices are distributed along circumference of a circle

qreal angleStep = 360.0 / m_vertexCount;

qreal radius = qMin(width(), height()) / 2;

for (int i = 0; i < m_vertexCount; ++i) {
    qreal rads = angleStep * i * M_PI / 180;
    qreal x = center.x() + radius * std::cos(rads);
    qreal y = center.y() + radius * std::sin(rads);
    vertices[1 + i].set(x, y);
}
vertices[1 + m_vertexCount] = vertices[1];
```

First, we ask the geometry object to prepare a mapping for us from the allocated memory to a `QSGGeometry::Point2D` structure, which can be used to conveniently set data for each vertex. Then, actual calculations are performed using the equation for calculating points on a circle. The radius of the circle is taken as the smaller part of the width and height of the item so that the shape is centered in the item. As you can see in the diagram at the beginning of the exercise, the last point in the array has the same coordinates as the second point in the array to close the fan into a regular polygon.

At the very end, we mark the geometry as changed and return the node to the caller:

```
    node->markDirty(QSGNode::DirtyGeometry);
    return node;
}
```

What just happened?

Rendering in Qt Quick can happen in a thread different that is than the main thread. Before calling the `updatePaintNode()` function, Qt performs synchronization between the GUI thread and the rendering thread to allow us safely access our item's data and other objects living in the main thread. The function executing the main thread is blocked while this function executes, so it is crucial that it executes as quickly as possible and doesn't do any unnecessary calculations as this directly influences performance. This is also the only place in your code where at the same time you can safely call functions from your item (such as reading properties) and interact with the scene-graph (creating and updating the nodes). Try not emitting any signals nor creating any objects from within this method as they will have affinity to the rendering thread rather than the GUI thread.

Having said that, you can now register your class with QML using `qmlRegisterType` and test it with the following QML document:

```
Window {
    width: 600
    height: 600
    visible: true
    RegularPolygon {
        id: poly
        anchors {
            fill: parent
            bottomMargin: 20
        }
        vertices: 5
        color: "blue"
```

```
    }
}
```

This should give you a nice blue pentagon. If the shape looks aliased, you can enforce anti-aliasing by setting the surface format for the application:

```
int main(int argc, char **argv) {
    QGuiApplication app(argc, argv);
    QSurfaceFormat format = QSurfaceFormat::defaultFormat();
    format.setSamples(16); // enable multisampling
    QSurfaceFormat::setDefaultFormat(format);

    qmlRegisterType<RegularPolygon>("RegularPolygon", 1, 0,
"RegularPolygon");

    QQmlApplicationEngine engine;
    engine.load(QUrl(QStringLiteral("qrc:/main.qml")));
    if (engine.rootObjects().isEmpty())
      return -1;
    return app.exec();
}
```

If the application produces a black screen after enabling anti-aliasing, try to lower the number of samples or disable it.

Have a go hero – Creating a supporting border for RegularPolygon

What is returned by `updatePaintNode()` may not just be a single `QSGGeometryNode` but also a larger tree of `QSGNode` items. Each node can have any number of child nodes. By returning a node that has two geometry nodes as children, you can draw two separate shapes in the item:

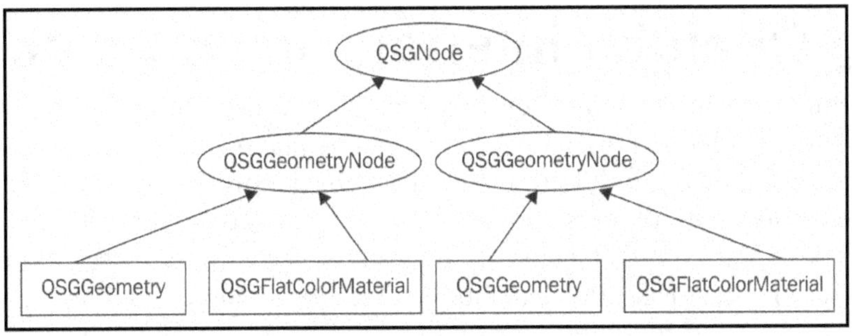

As a challenge, extend `RegularPolygon` to draw not only the internal filled part of the polygon but also an edge that can be of a different color. You can draw the edge using the `GL_QUAD_STRIP` drawing mode. Coordinates of the points are easy to calculate—the points closer to the middle of the shape are the same points that form the shape itself. The remaining points also lie on a circumference of a circle that is slightly larger (by the width of the border). Therefore, you can use the same equations to calculate them.

The `GL_QUAD_STRIP` mode renders quadrilaterals with every two vertices specified after the first four, composing a connected quadrilateral. The following diagram should give you a clear idea of what we are after:

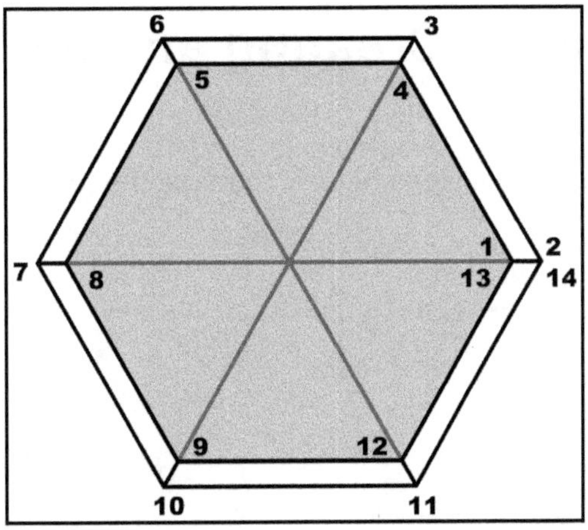

Using QPainter interface in Qt Quick

Implementing items in OpenGL is quite difficult—you need to come up with an algorithm of using OpenGL primitives to draw the shape you want, and then you also need to be skilled enough with OpenGL to build a proper scene graph node tree for your item. However, there is another way—you can create items by painting them with `QPainter`. This comes at a cost of performance as behind the scenes, the painter draws on an indirect surface (a frame buffer object or an image) that is then converted to OpenGL texture and rendered on a quad by the scene-graph. Even considering that performance hit, it is often much simpler to draw the item using a rich and convenient drawing API than to spend hours doing the equivalent in OpenGL or using Canvas.

To use that approach, we will not be subclassing `QQuickItem` directly but `QQuickPaintedItem`, which gives us the infrastructure needed to use the painter for drawing items.

Basically, all we have to do, then, is implement the pure virtual `paint()` method that renders the item using the received painter. Let's see this put into practice and combine it with the skills we gained earlier.

Time for action – Creating an item for drawing outlined text

The goal of the current exercise is to be able to make the following QML code work:

```
import QtQuick 2.9
import QtQuick.Window 2.3
import OutlineTextItem 1.0

Window {
    visible: true
    width: 800
    height: 400
    title: qsTr("Hello World")

    Rectangle {
        anchors.fill: parent
        OutlineTextItem {
            anchors.centerIn: parent
            text: "This is outlined text"
            fontFamily: "Arial"
```

```
            fontPixelSize: 64
            color: "#33ff0000"
            antialiasing: true
            border {
                color: "blue"
                width: 2
                style: Qt.DotLine
            }
        }
    }
}
```

Then, it produces the following result:

Start with an empty Qt Quick application project. Create a new C++ class and call it `OutlineTextItemBorder`. Place the following code into the class definition:

```
class OutlineTextItemBorder : public QObject {
    Q_OBJECT
    Q_PROPERTY(int width MEMBER m_width NOTIFY widthChanged)
    Q_PROPERTY(QColor color MEMBER m_color NOTIFY colorChanged)
    Q_PROPERTY(Qt::PenStyle style MEMBER m_style NOTIFY styleChanged)
public:
    OutlineTextItemBorder(QObject *parent = 0);

    int width() const;
    QColor color() const;
    Qt::PenStyle style() const;
    QPen pen() const;
signals:
    void widthChanged(int);
    void colorChanged(QColor);
    void styleChanged(int);
private:
    int m_width;
    QColor m_color;
    Qt::PenStyle m_style;
};
```

This is a simple `QObject`-based class holding a number of properties. You can see that `Q_PROPERTY` macros don't have the `READ` and `WRITE` keywords we've been using thus far. This is because we are taking a shortcut right now, and we let **moc** produce code that will operate on the property by directly accessing the given class member. Normally, we would recommend against such an approach as without getters; the only way to access the properties is through the generic `property()` and `setProperty()` calls. However, in this case, we will not be exposing this class to the public in C++ so we won't need the setters, and we implement the getters ourselves, anyway. The nice thing about the `MEMBER` keyword is that if we also provide the `NOTIFY` signal, the generated code will emit that signal when the value of the property changes, which will make property bindings in QML work as expected. We also need to implement the method that returns the actual pen based on values of the properties:

```
QPen OutlineTextItemBorder::pen() const {
    QPen p;
    p.setColor(m_color);
    p.setWidth(m_width);
    p.setStyle(m_style);
    return p;
}
```

The class will provide a grouped property for our main item class. Create a class called `OutlineTextItem` and derive it from `QQuickPaintedItem`, as follows:

```
class OutlineTextItem : public QQuickPaintedItem
{
    Q_OBJECT
    Q_PROPERTY(QString text MEMBER m_text
                            NOTIFY textChanged)
    Q_PROPERTY(QColor color MEMBER m_color
                            NOTIFY colorChanged)
    Q_PROPERTY(OutlineTextItemBorder* border READ border
                            NOTIFY borderChanged)
    Q_PROPERTY(QString fontFamily MEMBER m_fontFamily
                            NOTIFY fontFamilyChanged)
    Q_PROPERTY(int fontPixelSize MEMBER m_fontPixelSize
                            NOTIFY fontPixelSizeChanged)
public:
    OutlineTextItem(QQuickItem *parent = 0);
    void paint(QPainter *painter);
    OutlineTextItemBorder* border() const;
    QPainterPath shape(const QPainterPath &path) const;
private slots:
    void updateItem();
signals:
```

```
    void textChanged(QString);
    void colorChanged(QColor);
    void borderChanged();
    void fontFamilyChanged(QString);
    void fontPixelSizeChanged(int);
private:
    OutlineTextItemBorder* m_border;
    QPainterPath m_path;
    QRectF m_boundingRect;
    QString m_text;
    QColor m_color;
    QString m_fontFamily;
    int m_fontPixelSize;
};
```

The interface defines properties for the text to be drawn, in addition to its color, font, and the grouped property for the outline data. Again, we use `MEMBER` to avoid having to manually implement getters and setters. Unfortunately, this makes our constructor code more complicated, as we still need a way to run some code when any of the properties are modified. Implement the constructor using the following code:

```
OutlineTextItem::OutlineTextItem(QQuickItem *parent) :
    QQuickPaintedItem(parent)
{
    m_border = new OutlineTextItemBorder(this);
    connect(this, &OutlineTextItem::textChanged,
            this, &OutlineTextItem::updateItem);
    connect(this, &OutlineTextItem::colorChanged,
            this, &OutlineTextItem::updateItem);
    connect(this, &OutlineTextItem::fontFamilyChanged,
            this, &OutlineTextItem::updateItem);
    connect(this, &OutlineTextItem::fontPixelSizeChanged,
            this, &OutlineTextItem::updateItem);
    connect(m_border, &OutlineTextItemBorder::widthChanged,
            this, &OutlineTextItem::updateItem);
    connect(m_border, &OutlineTextItemBorder::colorChanged,
            this, &OutlineTextItem::updateItem);
    connect(m_border, &OutlineTextItemBorder::styleChanged,
            this, &OutlineTextItem::updateItem);
    updateItem();
}
```

We basically connect all the property change signals from both the object and its grouped property object to the same slot that will update the data for the item if any of its components are modified. We also call the same slot directly to prepare the initial state of the item. The slot can be implemented like this:

```
void OutlineTextItem::updateItem() {
    QFont font(m_fontFamily, m_fontPixelSize);
    m_path = QPainterPath();
    m_path.addText(0, 0, font, m_text);
    m_boundingRect = borderShape(m_path).controlPointRect();
    setImplicitWidth(m_boundingRect.width());
    setImplicitHeight(m_boundingRect.height());
    update();
}
```

At the beginning, the function resets a painter path object that serves as a backend for drawing outlined text and initializes it with the text drawn using the font set. Then, the slot calculates the bounding rect for the path using the `borderShape()` function that we will shortly see. We use `controlPointRect()` to calculate the bounding rectangle as it is much faster than `boundingRect()` and returns an area greater than or equal to the one `boundingRect()`, which is OK for us. Finally, it sets the calculated size as the size hint for the item and asks the item to repaint itself with the `update()` call. Implement the `borderShape()` function using the following code:

```
QPainterPath OutlineTextItem::borderShape(const QPainterPath &path)
const
{
    QPainterPathStroker pathStroker;
    pathStroker.setWidth(m_border->width());
    QPainterPath p = pathStroker.createStroke(path);
    p.addPath(path);
    return p;
}
```

The `borderShape()` function returns a new painter path that includes both the original path and its outline created with the `QPainterPathStroker` object. This is so that the width of the stroke is correctly taken into account when calculating the bounding rectangle.

What remains is to implement the `paint()` routine itself:

```
void OutlineTextItem::paint(QPainter *painter) {
    if(m_text.isEmpty()) return;
    painter->setPen(m_border->pen());
    painter->setBrush(m_color);
    painter->setRenderHint(QPainter::Antialiasing, true);
    painter->translate(-m_boundingRect.topLeft());
    painter->drawPath(m_path);
}
```

The code is really simple—we bail out early if there is nothing to draw. Otherwise, we set up the painter using the pen and color obtained from the item's properties. We enable anti-aliasing and calibrate the painter coordinates with that of the bounding rectangle of the item. Finally, we draw the path on the painter.

What just happened?

During this exercise, we made use of the powerful API of Qt's raster graphics engine to complement an existing set of Qt Quick items with a simple functionality. This is otherwise very hard to achieve using predefined Qt Quick elements and even harder to implement using OpenGL. We agreed to take a small performance hit in exchange for having to write just about a hundred lines of code to have a fully working solution. Remember to register the class with QML if you want to use it in your code:

```
qmlRegisterUncreatableType<OutlineTextItemBorder>(
     "OutlineTextItem", 1, 0, "OutlineTextItemBorder", "");
qmlRegisterType<OutlineTextItem>(
     "OutlineTextItem", 1, 0, "OutlineTextItem");
```

Pop quiz

Q1. Which QML type can be used to enable scrolling of a large item inside a smaller viewport?

1. `Rectangle`
2. `Flickable`
3. `Window`

Q2. What is the purpose of the `Affector` QML type?

1. `Affector` allows you to change properties of QML items during an animation
2. `Affector` influences properties of particles spawned by a particle system
3. `Affector` allows you to control initial properties of particles spawned by a particle system

Q3. What happens when you use `QPainter` to draw on a Qt Quick item?

1. Every call to the `QPainter` API is translated to an equivalent OpenGL call
2. `QPainter` paints on an invisible buffer that is then loaded as an OpenGL texture
3. The item painted by `QPainter` is displayed without hardware acceleration

Summary

You are now familiar with Qt Quick's capabilities that allow you to add astonishing graphical effects to your games. You can configure particle systems and implement OpenGL painting in the Qt Quick's scene graph. You are also able to utilize the skills acquired in the first parts of the book to implement painted Qt Quick items.

Of course, Qt Quick is much richer than all this, but we had to stop somewhere. The set of skills we have hopefully passed on to you should be enough to develop many great games. However, many of the elements have more properties than we have described here. Whenever you want to extend your skills, you can check the reference manual to see whether the element type has more interesting attributes. Qt Quick is still in active development, so it's a good idea to go through the changelogs of the recent Qt versions to see the new features that could not be covered in this book.

In the next chapter, we'll turn our attention to the Qt 3D module, which is a relatively recent addition to the Qt framework. Qt 3D provides a rich QML API that will allow us to use many of the skills we learned while working with Qt Quick. However, instead of user interface and 2D graphics, you will now create games that display hardware accelerated 3D graphics. When you learn to use Qt 3D, you will be able to take your games to a completely new level!

15
3D Graphics with Qt

Many modern games take place in 3D worlds. Graphics processing units are constantly evolving, allowing developers to create more and more visually appealing and detailed worlds. While you can use OpenGL or Vulkan directly to render 3D objects, this can prove to be quite challenging. Luckily, the Qt 3D module provides an implementation of 3D rendering with a high-level API. In this chapter, we'll learn to use its capabilities and see how we can create a 3D game with Qt.

Qt 3D is not limited to rendering. You'll also learn to handle user input and implement game logic in a 3D game. Qt 3D was designed to be highly efficient and fully extensible, so it allows you to implement your own additions to all Qt 3D systems.

Qt 3D offers both C++ and QML API with mostly equivalent functionality. While the C++ API allows you to modify and extend the implementation, we will use the QML approach, that will allow us to write clean and declarative code and use the techniques we've learned in the previous chapters. By combining Qt 3D with the powers of QML, you will be able to make amazing games in no time!

The main topics covered in this chapter are:

- Rendering 3D objects
- Handling user input
- Performing animations
- Integration with 3D editors
- Working with Qt 3D using C++
- Integration with Qt Widgets and Qt Quick

Qt 3D overview

Before we see Qt 3D in action, let's go through the important parts of its architecture.

Entities and components

Qt 3D is not just a 3D rendering tool. When sufficiently evolved, it can become a full-featured game engine. This is supported by its original architecture. Qt 3D introduces a new set of abstractions that are particularly useful for its task.

You may have noticed that most of the Qt API heavily uses inheritance. For example, each widget type is derived from `QWidget`, which in turn is derived from `QObject`. Qt forms large family trees of classes to provide common and specialized behavior. In contrast, elements of a Qt 3D scene are constructed using **composition** instead of inheritance. A single part of a Qt 3D scene is called an **entity** and represented by the `Entity` type. However, an `Entity` object by itself doesn't have any particular effect or behavior. You can add pieces of behavior to an entity in the form of **components**.

Each component controls some part of the entity's behavior. For example, the `Transform` component controls the entity's position within the scene, the `Mesh` component defines its shape, and the `Material` component controls the properties of the surface. This approach allows you to assemble entities from only the components that you need. For example, if you need to add a light source to the scene, you can create an entity with the `PointLight` component. You still want to choose a location of the light source, so you'll need the `Transform` component as well. However, `Mesh` and `Material` components do not make sense for a light source, so you don't need to use them.

Entities are arranged in a classic parent–child relationship, like any other QML objects or QObjects. A tree of entities form a Qt 3D scene. The topmost entity is usually responsible for defining scene-wide configuration. These settings are specified by attaching special components (such as `RenderSettings` and `InputSettings`) to the top level `Entity`.

Qt 3D modules

Qt 3D is split into a number of modules that you can choose to use in your project. It may be hard to see which of them you need, so let's see what each module is made for.

Stable modules

The `Qt3DCore` module implements the base structure of Qt 3D. It provides `Entity` and `Component` types, as well as base classes for other Qt 3D systems. `Qt3DCore` itself does not implement any behavior, providing only the framework that's used by other modules.

The `Qt3DRender` module implements 3D rendering, so it's one of the most feature-rich modules. Let's list some important pieces of its functionality:

- `GeometryRenderer` is the base component type that defines the visible shape of an entity
- The `Mesh` component allows you to import the entity's geometry from a file
- The `Material` component is the base component type that defines visible properties of the entity's surface
- The `SceneLoader` component allows you to import a hierarchy of entities with meshes and materials from a file
- Light components (`DirectionalLight`, `EnvironmentLight`, `PointLight`, and `SpotLight`) allow you to control the scene's lighting
- The `FrameGraph` API provides a way of defining how exactly your scene should be rendered. It allows you to set up the camera, implement multiple viewports, shadow mapping, custom shaders, and much more
- The `ObjectPicker` component allows you to find out which entities are positioned at a particular window point.

Next, `Qt3DLogic` is a very small module that provides the `FrameAction` component. This component allows you to execute an arbitrary action for each frame of your entity.

Finally, the `Qt3DInput` module is focused on user input. It provides a few components that allow you to handle keyboard and mouse events in your game. `Qt3DInput` also contains types that can be used to configure the input devices.

Experimental modules

At the time of writing, all the other Qt 3D modules are still in **tech preview**, so their API may be incomplete. Future Qt versions may introduce incompatible changes in these modules, so don't be surprised if you need to make a few changes in the provided code to make it work (our code was tested on Qt 5.10). These modules should eventually be stabilized in the future, so you should check the Qt documentation to find out their current status.

The `Qt3DAnimation` module, as the name implies, is responsible for animations in the Qt 3D scene. It's able to handle keyframe animations on the entity's `Transform` component, as well as blend-shape and vertex-blend animations. However, we won't be using this module in this chapter, as the already familiar animation framework of Qt Quick is more than enough for us.

The `Qt3DExtras` module provides components that are not strictly necessary for working with Qt 3D, but are very useful for building first simple projects. They are:

- Mesh generators for basic geometric shapes (cubes, spheres, and so on)
- The `ExtrudedTextMesh` component that allows you to show 3D text in the scene
- Many standard material components, such as `DiffuseSpecularMaterial` and `GoochMaterial`

Additionally, `Qt3DExtras` provides two convenience classes that allow the user to control the position of the camera using mouse and keyboard:

- `OrbitCameraController` moves the camera along an orbital path
- `FirstPersonCameraController` moves the camera as in a first-person game

The `Qt3DQuickExtras` module provides the `Qt3DExtras::Quick::Qt3DQuickWindow` C++ class. This is a window that displays a QML-based Qt 3D scene.

Finally, the `Qt3DQuickScene2D` module provides the ability to embed Qt Quick items into the Qt 3D scene, and the `QtQuick.Scene3D` QML module allows you to embed a Qt 3D scene into a Qt Quick application.

As you can see, the capabilities of Qt 3D are not limited by rendering. You can also use it to handle user input and implement the game logic for your entities. Qt 3D is fully extensible, so you can use its C++ API to implement your own components, or modify existing ones. However, we will mainly use the QML-based API in this chapter.

> Note that Qt 3D objects are not Qt Quick items, so not all Qt Quick capabilities are open for you when you work with Qt 3D. For example, you can't use `Repeater` to instantiate multiple Qt 3D entities. However, you can still use Qt Quick animations because they can handle any QML objects. It's also possible to embed a Qt 3D scene into a Qt Quick interface using the `Scene3D` QML type.

Using modules

Before using each of the Qt 3D modules, you have to enable the module separately in the project file. For example, the following line will enable all currently documented modules:

```
QT += 3dcore 3drender 3dinput 3dlogic 3danimation \
      qml quick 3dquick 3dquickextras 3dquickscene2d
```

When using QML, each module must also be separately imported:

```
import Qt3D.Core 2.10
import Qt3D.Render 2.10
import Qt3D.Extras 2.10
import Qt3D.Input 2.0
import Qt3D.Logic 2.0
import QtQuick.Scene2D 2.9
import QtQuick.Scene3D 2.0
```

> You can see that different Qt 3D modules have different QML module versions. Some modules were updated in Qt 5.10 and have new features that we'd like to use in our code, so you have to specify the last version (2.10) to make new QML types available. On the other hand, some modules weren't updated, so 2.0 is the only available version. The up-to-date versions will change in the future as new Qt releases come out. The Qt documentation should hopefully contain the correct import statements.

All C++ types of a Qt 3D module are placed in a namespace. In other regards, Qt naming conventions apply. For example, the `Entity` QML type corresponds to the `QEntity` C++ class in the `Qt3DCore` namespace. The corresponding include directive is `#include <QEntity>`.

Qt 3D also introduces a concept of **aspects**. An aspect is simply a piece of behavior that can be added to the Qt 3D engine. The `Qt3DQuickWindow` class contains a built-in aspect engine that automatically enables `QRenderAspect`, `QInputAspect`, and `QLogicAspect` aspects, allowing Qt 3D to render the scene, process user input, and execute frame actions. If you decide to use the `Qt3DAnimation` module, you should also enable `QAnimationAspect`. You can do that using the `Qt3DWindow::registerAspect()` method. Other Qt 3D modules don't require a separate aspect. It's also possible to create a new aspect, but it's usually not necessary.

Rendering 3D objects

Each item of the Qt 3D scene is represented by the `Entity` type. However, not all entities are visible 3D objects. In order for an entity to be visible, it has to have a **mesh** component and a **material** component.

Mesh, material, and transform

The mesh defines the geometrical shape of the entity. It contains information about vertices, edges, and faces required to render the object. The base type of all mesh components is `GeometryRenderer`. However, you'll usually use one of its descendants:

- `Mesh` imports geometry data from a file
- `ConeMesh`, `CuboidMesh`, `CylinderMesh`, `PlaneMesh`, `SphereMesh`, and `TorusMesh` provide access to primitive geometric shapes
- `ExtrudedTextMesh` defines the entity's shape based on a specified text and font

While the mesh defines where the object's surface will be drawn, the material defines how exactly it will be drawn. The most obvious property of a surface is its color, but depending on the reflection model, there can be all sorts of properties, such as coefficients of diffuse and specular reflection. Qt 3D provides a lot of different material types:

- `PerVertexColorMaterial` allows you to set color properties for each vertex and renders ambient and diffuse reflections
- `TextureMaterial` renders a texture and ignores lighting
- `DiffuseSpecularMaterial` implements the Phong reflection model and allows you to set ambient, diffuse, and specular components of the reflection
- `GoochMaterial` implements the Gooch shading model
- `MetalRoughMaterial` renders a metal-like surface using PBR (physically based rendering)
- `MorphPhongMaterial` also follows the Phong reflection model but also supports morph animations of the `Qt3DAnimation` module

The third common component of a visible 3D object is `Transform`. While not strictly required, it's usually necessary for setting the position of the object in the scene. You can set the position using the `translation` property. It's also possible to scale the object using the `scale3D` property that allows you to set different scale coefficients for each `axis`, or the `scale` property that accepts a single coefficient that applies to all axes. Similarly, you can either set the rotation quaternion using the `rotation` property or set individual Euler angles using `rotationX`, `rotationY`, and `rotationZ` properties. Finally, you can set the `matrix` property to apply an arbitrary transformation matrix.

TIP

Note that transformations apply not only to the current entity, but to all its children as well.

Lighting

Some of the available materials will take the lighting into account. Qt 3D allows you to add different types of lights to the scene and configure them. You can do that by adding a new `Entity` to the scene and attaching a `DirectionalLight`, `PointLight`, or `SpotLight` component to it. Each of these components has the `color` property that allows you to configure the color of the light and the `intensity` property that allows you to choose how bright the light is. The rest of the properties are specific to the light type.

Directional light (also called "distant light" or "sunlight") casts parallel rays in the direction defined by the `worldDirection` property of the `DirectionalLight` type. Position and rotation of the entity have no influence on the lighting effect of a directional light, so there is no need for a `Transform` component.

Point light emits light from its position in all directions. The position of the light can be changed via the `Transform` component attached to the same entity.
The `PointLight` component allows you to configure how bright the light will be at a distance by setting the `constantAttenuation`, `linearAttenuation`, and `quadraticAttenuation` properties.

While point light can be interpreted as a sphere of light, **spotlight** is a cone of light. It emits light from its position, but the directions are limited by the `localDirection` property that defines where the spotlight is facing and the `cutOffAngle` property that configures how wide the light cone is. The position and direction of the spotlight can be influenced by the translation and rotation of the `Transform` component attached to the same entity. `SpotLight` also has the same attenuation properties as `PointLight`.

TIP

If no lights are present in the scene, Qt will automatically add an implicit point light so that the scene is somewhat visible.

The fourth type of light is different from the others. It's called **environment light** and can be configured by adding the `EnvironmentLight` component to an entity. It defines the surrounding lighting of the scene using two textures assigned to its `irradiance` and `specular` properties. Unlike other light types, this component does not have `color` or `intensity` properties. There can only be one environment light in a scene.

Note that light sources themselves are invisible. Their only purpose is to influence the appearance of 3D objects that use certain material types.

Time for action – creating a 3D scene

In this chapter, we will create an implementation of the famous Tower of Hanoi game. This puzzle game contains three rods and multiple disks of different sizes. The disks can slide onto the rods, but a disk cannot be placed on top of a smaller disk. At the starting position, all the rods are placed on one of the disks. The goal is to move them all to another rod. The player can only move one disk at a time.

> As usual, you will find the complete project in the resources that come with the book.

Create a new **Qt Quick Application - Empty** project and call it `hanoi`. While we will use some Qt Quick utilities, our project will not really be based on Qt Quick. Qt 3D will do most of the work. Nevertheless, the **Qt Quick Application - Empty** is the most suitable of currently present templates, so we choose to use it. Edit the `hanoi.pro` file to enable the Qt modules that we'll need:

```
QT += 3dcore 3drender 3dinput quick 3dquickextras
```

We will use the `Qt3DQuickWindow` class to instantiate our QML objects instead of the `QQmlApplicationEngine` class we usually use with Qt Quick. To do that, replace the `main.cpp` file with the following code:

```
#include <QGuiApplication>
#include <Qt3DQuickWindow>

int main(int argc, char* argv[])
{
    QGuiApplication app(argc, argv);
    Qt3DExtras::Quick::Qt3DQuickWindow window;
    window.setSource(QUrl("qrc:/main.qml"));
    window.show();
    return app.exec();
}
```

Next, replace the `main.qml` file with the following code:

```
import Qt3D.Core 2.10
import Qt3D.Render 2.10
import Qt3D.Input 2.0
import Qt3D.Extras 2.10

Entity {
    components: [
        RenderSettings {
            activeFrameGraph: ForwardRenderer {
                clearColor: "black"
                camera: Camera {
                    id: camera
                    projectionType: CameraLens.PerspectiveProjection
                    fieldOfView: 45
                    nearPlane : 0.1
                    farPlane : 1000.0
                    position: Qt.vector3d(0.0, 40.0, -40.0)
                    upVector: Qt.vector3d(0.0, 1.0, 0.0)
                    viewCenter: Qt.vector3d(0.0, 0.0, 0.0)
                }
            }
        },
        InputSettings {}
    ]
}
```

This code declares a single `Entity` object that contains two components. The `RenderSettings` component defines how Qt 3D should render the scene. The `activeFrameGraph` property of `RenderSettings` can hold a tree of render operations, but the simplest possible frame graph is a single `ForwardRenderer` object that takes care of all the rendering. `ForwardRenderer` renders objects one by one directly to the OpenGL framebuffer. We use the `clearColor` property to set the background color of our scene to black. The `camera` property of the `ForwardRenderer` holds the `Camera` object it will use for calculating the transformation matrix.

Let's go through the properties of the `Camera` object we've used in our code:

- The `projectionType` property defines the type of the projection. Besides the `PerspectiveProjection`, you can use `OrthographicProjection`, `FrustumProjection`, or `CustomProjection`.
- The `fieldOfView` property contains the field of view parameter of the perspective projection. You can change it to achieve a zoom in/out effect.
- The `nearPlane` and `farPlane` properties define the positions of the nearest and the furthest planes that will be visible in the camera (they correspond to the visible *z* axis values in the viewport coordinates).
- The `position` vector defines the position of the camera in the world coordinates.
- The `upVector` vector in the world coordinates is the vector that would appear pointing up when viewing it through the camera.
- The `viewCenter` vector in the world coordinates is the point that will appear in the center of the viewport.

When using the perspective projection, you usually need to set the aspect ratio according to the window size. The `Camera` object has the `aspectRatio` property for that, but we don't need to set it, since the `Qt3DQuickWindow` object will update this property automatically.

You can disable this feature by adding `window.setCameraAspectRatioMode(Qt3DExtras::Quick::Qt3DQuickWindow::UserAspectRatio)` to the `main.cpp` file.

If you want to use an orthographic projection instead of a perspective one, you can use the `top`, `left`, `bottom`, and `right` properties of the `Camera` object to set the visible area.

Finally, the second component of our `Entity` is the `InputSettings` component. Its `eventSource` property should point to the object that provides the input events. As with `aspectRatio`, we don't need to set this property manually. The `Qt3DQuickWindow` will find the `InputSettings` object and set itself as the `eventSource`.

You can run the project to verify that it compiles successfully and doesn't produce any runtime errors. You should receive an empty black window as a result.

Now let's add something visible to our scene. Edit the `main.qml` file to add a few child objects to the root `Entity`, as shown:

```
Entity {
    components: [
        RenderSettings { /* ... */ },
        InputSettings {}
    ]
    FirstPersonCameraController {
        camera: camera
    }
    Entity {
        components: [
            DirectionalLight {
                color: Qt.rgba(1, 1, 1)
                intensity: 0.5
                worldDirection: Qt.vector3d(0, -1, 0)
            }
        ]
    }
    Entity {
        components: [
            CuboidMesh {},
            DiffuseSpecularMaterial { ambient: "#aaa"; shininess: 100;
},
            Transform { scale: 10 }
        ]
    }
}
```

As a result, you should see a cube at the center of the window:

More than that, you can use the arrow keys, the **Page Up** and **Page Down** keys, and the left mouse button to move the camera around.

What just happened?

We added a few objects to our scene graph. First, the `FirstPersonCameraController` object allows the user to freely control the camera. This is quite useful for testing the game while you don't have your own camera controlling code yet. Next, an entity with a single `DirectionalLight` component works as a light source in the scene. We use the properties of this component to set the color, intensity, and direction of the light.

Finally, we added an entity that represents a regular 3D object. Its shape is provided by the `CuboidMesh` component that generates a unit cube. The appearance of its surface is defined by the `DiffuseSpecularMaterial` component that conforms to the widely used Phong reflection model. You can use `ambient`, `diffuse`, and `specular` color properties to control different components of the reflected light. The `shininess` property defines how smooth the surface is. We use the `Transform` component to scale the cube to a larger size.

Time for action – constructing the Tower of Hanoi scene

Our next task will be to create a foundation and three rods for our puzzle. We will take advantage of QML's modular system and split our code into multiple components. First, let's leave camera and lighting settings in the `main.qml` and put our actual scene content to a new `Scene` component. In order to do that, put the text cursor onto the Entity declaration of the cube, press *Alt* + *Enter* and select **Move Component into Separate File**. Input `Scene` as the component name and confirm the operation. Qt Creator will create a new `Scene.qml` file and add it to the project's resources. The `main.qml` now contains just an instantiation of our scene component:

```
Entity {
    //...
    Scene { }
}
```

The actual properties of the entity are moved to the `Scene.qml` file. Let's adjust it to the following form:

```
Entity {
    id: sceneRoot
    Entity {
        components: [
            DiffuseSpecularMaterial {
                ambient: "#444"
            },
            CuboidMesh {},
            Transform {
                scale3D: Qt.vector3d(40, 1, 40)
            }
        ]
    }
}
```

Our scene will contain multiple items, so we introduced a new `Entity` object and called it `sceneRoot`. This entity doesn't have any components, so it will not have any visible effect on the scene. This is similar to how an object of `Item` type usually serves as a container for Qt Quick items without providing any visual content.

The cube entity is now a child of `sceneRoot`. We use the `scale3D` property of the `Transform` component to change the dimensions of our cube. Now it looks like a tabletop that will serve as a foundation for the rest of the objects.

Now let's work on the rods. Naturally, we want to have a `Rod` component because it is a repeating part of our scene. Invoke the context menu of `qml.qrc` in the project tree and choose **Add New**. From the **Qt** category, choose **QML File (Qt Quick 2)** and input `Rod` as the filename. Let's see how we can implement this component:

```
import Qt3D.Core 2.10
import Qt3D.Render 2.10
import Qt3D.Extras 2.10
Entity {
    property int index
    components: [
        CylinderMesh {
            id: mesh
            radius: 0.5
            length: 9
            slices: 30
        },
        DiffuseSpecularMaterial {
            ambient: "#111"
```

```
            },
            Transform {
                id: transform
                translation: {
                    var radius = 8;
                    var step = 2 * Math.PI / 3;
                    return Qt.vector3d(radius * Math.cos(index * step),
                                       mesh.length / 2 + 0.5,
                                       radius * Math.sin(index * step));

                }
            }
        ]
    }
```

Similar to the cube entity, our rod consists of a mesh, a material, and a `Transform` component. Instead of the `CubeMesh`, we use the `CylinderMesh` component that will create a cylinder for us. The `radius` and `length` properties define the dimensions of the object, and the `slices` property impacts the number of generated triangles. We chose to increase the number of slices to make the cylinders look better, but be aware that it has a performance impact that may become noticeable if you have many objects.

Our `Rod` component has the index property that contains the positional number of the rod. We use this property to calculate the *x* and *z* coordinates of the rod so that all three rods are placed on a circle with an eight radius. The *y* coordinate is set to ensure that the rod is positioned on top of the foundation. We assign the calculated position vector to the `translation` property of the `Transform` component. Finally, add three `Rod` objects to the `Scene.qml` file:

```
Entity {
    id: sceneRoot
    //...
    Rod { index: 0 }
    Rod { index: 1 }
    Rod { index: 2 }
}
```

When you run the project, you should see the foundation and the rods:

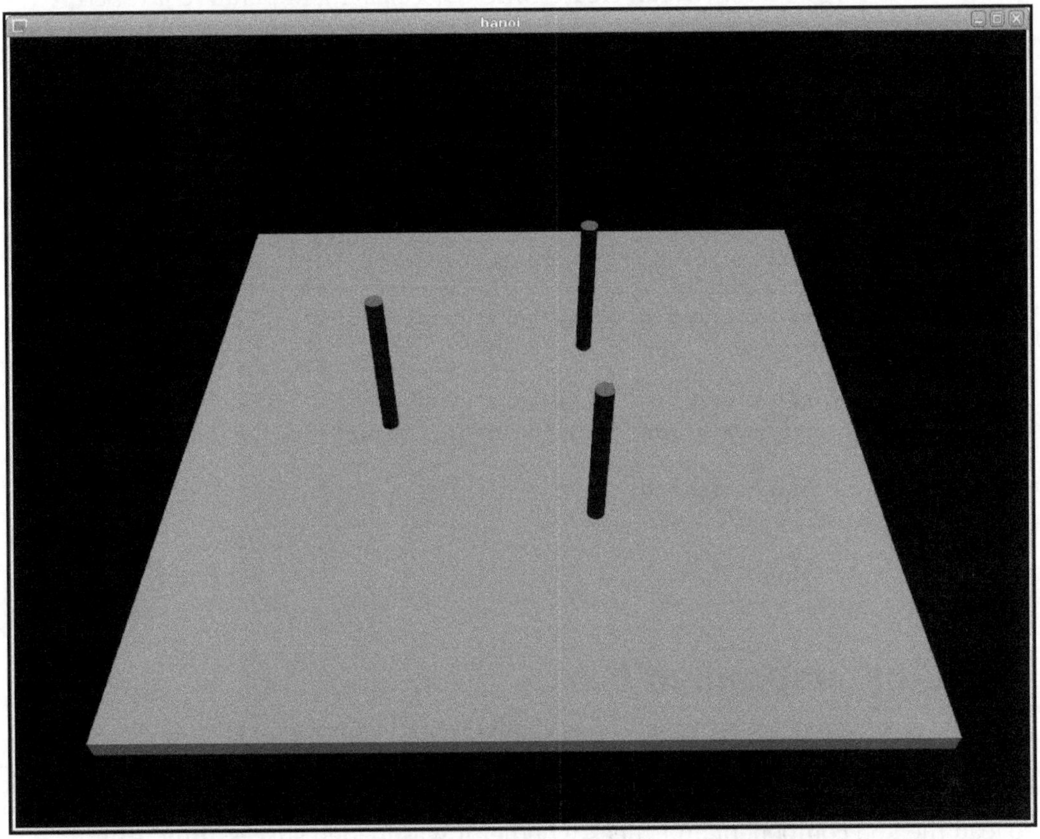

Time for action – repeating 3D objects

Our code works, but the way we create the rods is not ideal. First, enumerating rods and their indices in `Scene.qml` is inconvenient and error-prone. Second, we'll need to have a way to access a `Rod` object by its index, and the current approach doesn't allow that. In the previous chapters, we dealt with repeating Qt Quick objects using the `Repeater` QML type. However, `Repeater` doesn't work for `Entity` objects. It's only able to handle types that inherit from Qt Quick `Item`.

The solution to our problem is already familiar to you since Chapter 12, *Customization in Qt Quick*. We can create QML objects using imperative JavaScript code. Remove Rod objects from the Scene.qml file and make the following additions instead:

```
Entity {
    id: sceneRoot
    property variant rods: []
    Entity { /* ... */}
    Component.onCompleted: {
        var rodComponent = Qt.createComponent("Rod.qml");
        if(rodComponent.status !== Component.Ready) {
            console.log(rodComponent.errorString());
            return;
        }
        for(var i = 0; i < 3; i++) {
            var rod = rodComponent.createObject(sceneRoot, { index: i
});
            rods.push(rod);
        }
    }
}
```

What just happened?

First, we created a property called rods that will hold an array of created Rod objects. Next, we used the Component.onCompleted attached property to run some JavaScript code after the QML engine instantiates our root object. Our first action was to load the Rod component and check whether it was loaded successfully. After obtaining a functioning component object, we used its createObject() method to create three new rods. We used the arguments of this function to pass the root object and value of the index property. Finally, we pushed the Rod object into the array.

Time for action – creating disks

Our next task is to create eight disks that will slide onto rods. We'll do it in a similar way to how we handled rods. First, create a new file called Disk.qml for our new component. Put the following content into the file:

```
import Qt3D.Core 2.10
import Qt3D.Render 2.10
import Qt3D.Extras 2.10
```

```
Entity {
    property int index
    property alias pos: transform.translation
    components: [
        DiffuseSpecularMaterial {
            ambient: Qt.hsla(index / 8, 1, 0.5)
        },
        TorusMesh {
            minorRadius: 1.1
            radius: 2.5 + 1 * index
            rings: 80
        },
        Transform {
            id: transform
            rotationX: 90
            scale: 0.45
        }
    ]
}
```

Like rods, disks are identified by their index. In this case, index influences the color and size of the disk. We calculate the disk's color using the `Qt.hsla()` function that takes hue, saturation, and lightness values and returns a `color` value that can be assigned to the `ambient` property of the material. This formula will give us eight colorful disks of different hues.

The position of the disk is defined by the `translation` property of the `Transform` component. We want to be able to read and change the position of the disk from the outside, so we set up a property alias called `pos` that exposes the `transform.translation` property value.

Next, we use the `TorusMesh` component to define the shape of our disks. A torus shape is not really suitable for playing the Tower of Hanoi game in reality, but it will have to do for now. Later in this chapter, we'll replace it with a more suitable shape. The properties of the `TorusMesh` component allow us to adjust some of its measurements, but we also have to apply rotation and scale to the object to achieve the desired size and position.

Instead of putting all the disk objects into a single array, let's create an array for each rod. When we move a disk from one rod to another one, we'll remove the disk from the first rod's array and add it to the second rod's array. We can do that by adding a property to the `Rod` component. While we're at it, we should also expose the rod's position to the outside. We'll need it to position the disks on the rods. Declare the following properties in the top level `Entity` in `Rod.qml`:

```
readonly property alias pos: transform.translation
property var disks: []
```

The `pos` property will follow the value of the `translation` property of the `Transform` component. Since this value is calculated based on the `index` property, we declare the `pos` property as `readonly`.

Next, we need to adjust the `Component.onCompleted` handler of the `Scene` component. Initialize the `diskComponent` variable, just like we did with `rodComponent`. Then you can create disks using the following code:

```
var startingRod = rods[0];
for(i = 0; i < 8; i++) {
    var disk = diskComponent.createObject(sceneRoot, { index: i });
    disk.pos = Qt.vector3d(startingRod.pos.x, 8 - i,
startingRod.pos.z);
    startingRod.disks.unshift(disk);
}
```

After creating each disk, we set its position based on its index and the position of the chosen rod. We accumulate all disks in the `disks` property of the rod. We choose the order of disks in the array so that the bottom disk is at the beginning and the top disk is at the end. The `unshift()` function adds the item to the array at the beginning, giving the desired order.

If you run the project, you should see all eight tori on one of the rods:

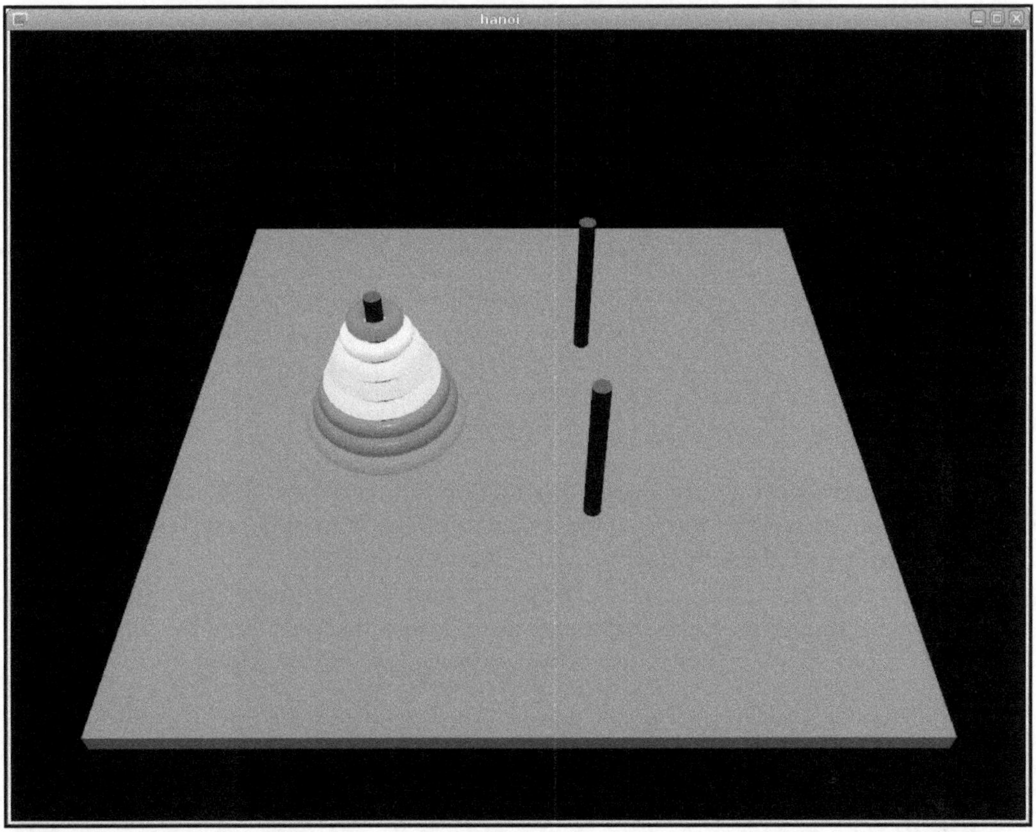

The next piece of functionality we'll need is the ability to move disks from one rod to another. However, it's the player who makes the decision, so we'll also need some way to receive input from the user. Let's see what options we have for handling user input.

Handling user input

The first way of receiving events in Qt 3D is to use Qt GUI capabilities. The `Qt3DQuickWindow` class we use inherits from `QWindow`. That allows you to subclass `Qt3DQuickWindow` and reimplement some of its virtual functions, such as `keyPressEvent()` or `mouseMoveEvent()`. You are already familiar with this part of Qt API because it's roughly the same as provided by Qt Widgets and Graphics View. Qt 3D doesn't introduce anything special here, so we won't give this approach much attention.

Similar to Qt Quick, Qt 3D introduces a higher-level API for receiving input events. Let's see how we can use it.

Devices

Qt 3D is focused on providing a good abstraction for every aspect it handles. This applies to input as well. In terms of Qt 3D, an application may have access to an arbitrary number of **physical devices**. They are represented by the `AbstractPhysicalDevice` type. At the time of writing, there are two built-in types of physical devices: keyboard and mouse. You can access them by declaring an object of `KeyboardDevice` or `MouseDevice` type in your QML file.

You can use properties of the device object to configure its behavior. There is currently only one such property: the `MouseDevice` type has a `sensitivity` property that affects how mouse movement is converted to axis inputs.

It's allowed to create multiple objects of the same device type in a single application. All devices will handle all received inputs, but you can set different values of properties for different device objects.

You typically don't want to handle events directly from the physical devices. Instead, you should set up a **logical device** that receives events from the physical devices and converts them to actions and inputs that make sense for your application. You can specify a set of **actions** and **axes** for your device using the `actions` and `axes` properties of the `LogicalDevice` type, and Qt 3D will recognize the described inputs and notify your objects about them.

We will provide a few code examples to demonstrate how to handle various kinds of input in Qt 3D. You can test the code by putting it into the `main.qml` file of the `hanoi` project or create a separate project for that.

Keyboard and mouse buttons

An action is represented by the `Action` type. An action can be triggered by pressing a single key, a key combination, or a key sequence. This is defined by the `inputs` property of the `Action` type. The most simple kind of input is `ActionInput` which reacts to a single key.

When the action is triggered, its `active` property will change from `false` to `true`. When the corresponding key or key combination is released, `active` changes back to `false`. You can use the usual QML features to track changes of the property:

```
Entity {
    //...
    KeyboardDevice { id: keyboardDevice }
    MouseDevice { id: mouseDevice }
    LogicalDevice {
        actions: [
            Action {
                inputs: ActionInput {
                    sourceDevice: keyboardDevice
                    buttons: [Qt.Key_A]
                }
                onActiveChanged: {
                    console.log("A changed: ", active);
                }
            },
            Action {
                inputs: ActionInput {
                    sourceDevice: keyboardDevice
                    buttons: [Qt.Key_B]
                }
                onActiveChanged: {
                    console.log("B changed: ", active);
                }
            },
            Action {
                inputs: ActionInput {
                    sourceDevice: mouseDevice
                    buttons: [MouseEvent.RightButton]
                }
```

```
                    onActiveChanged: {
                        console.log("RMB changed: ", active);
                    }
                }
            ]
        }
    }
```

As you can see, keyboard and mouse button events are handled in the same way. However, they come from different physical devices, so make sure you specify the correct device in the `sourceDevice` property of `ActionInput`.

You can specify multiple buttons for `ActionInput`. In this case, the action will trigger if any of the specified buttons are pressed. For example, use the following code to handle both the main *Enter* key and the *Enter* key on the keypad:

```
Action {
    inputs: ActionInput {
        sourceDevice: keyboardDevice
        buttons: [Qt.Key_Return, Qt.Key_Enter]
    }
    onActiveChanged: {
        if (active) {
            console.log("enter was pressed");
        } else {
            console.log("enter was released");
        }
    }
}
```

TIP: Note that it's not required to put the input handling code into the root object of the scene. You can put it into any `Entity`. It's also possible to have multiple entities handling input events at the same time.

Input chords

The `InputChord` type allows you to trigger an action when multiple keys are pressed at the same time:

```
Action {
    inputs: InputChord {
        timeout: 500
        chords: [
            ActionInput {
```

```
                sourceDevice: keyboardDevice
                buttons: [Qt.Key_Q]
            },
            ActionInput {
                sourceDevice: keyboardDevice
                buttons: [Qt.Key_W]
            },
            ActionInput {
                sourceDevice: keyboardDevice
                buttons: [Qt.Key_E]
            }
        ]
    }
    onActiveChanged: {
        console.log("changed: ", active);
    }
}
```

The `onActiveChanged` handler will be called when *Q*, *W*, and *E* keys are pressed within 500 milliseconds and held together.

Analog (axis) input

Axis in Qt 3D is an abstraction of analog one-dimensional input. A typical source of axis input is an analog stick of a gamepad. As the name implies, `Axis` only represents movement along a single axis, so a stick can be represented by two axes—one for vertical movement and one for horizontal movement. A pressure-sensitive button can be represented by a single axis. An axis input produces a `float` value ranging from –1 to 1, with zero corresponding to the neutral position.

That being said, there is no gamepad support in Qt 3D at the time of writing. It's possible that it will be added in future versions. You can also use the extensible C++ API of Qt 3D to implement the gamepad device using Qt Gamepad. However, the simplest solution is to use Qt Gamepad directly. Nothing prevents you from using QML or C++ API of Qt Gamepad in an application that uses Qt 3D.

The `inputs` property of the `Axis` type allows you to specify which input events should be redirected to this axis. You can use the `AnalogAxisInput` type to access the axis data provided by a physical device. The `MouseDevice` provides four virtual axes that are emulated based on the mouse input. Two of them are based on the vertical and horizontal scroll. Two others are based on vertical and horizontal pointer movement, but they only work while any mouse button is pressed.

The `ButtonAxisInput` type allows you to emulate an axis based on the button pressed. You can use the `scale` property to set the axis value corresponding to each button. When multiple buttons are pressed together, the mean of their axis values is used.

Both mouse-based and button-based axes are demonstrated in the following example:

```
LogicalDevice {
    axes: [
        Axis {
            inputs: [
                AnalogAxisInput {
                    sourceDevice: mouseDevice
                    axis: MouseDevice.X
                }
            ]
            onValueChanged: {
                console.log("mouse axis value", value);
            }
        },
        Axis {
            inputs: [
                ButtonAxisInput {
                    sourceDevice: keyboardDevice
                    buttons: [Qt.Key_Left]
                    scale: -1.0
                },
                ButtonAxisInput {
                    sourceDevice: keyboardDevice
                    buttons: [Qt.Key_Right]
                    scale: 1
                }
            ]
            onValueChanged: {
                console.log("keyboard axis value", value);
            }
        }
    ]
}
```

Object picker

Object picker is a component that allows an entity to interact with the mouse pointer. This component does not interact with the previously described input API directly. For example, you don't need to provide a mouse device for it. All you need to do is to attach the `ObjectPicker` component to an entity that also contains a mesh. The signals from `ObjectPicker` will notify you about input events related to this entity:

Signal	Explanation
`clicked(pick)`	The object was clicked.
`pressed(pick)`	The mouse button was pressed over the object.
`released(pick)`	The mouse button was released after `pressed(pick)` was triggered.
`moved(pick)`	The mouse pointer was moved.
`entered()`	The mouse pointer entered the object's area.
`exited()`	The mouse pointer exited the object's area.

Additionally, the `pressed` property will be set to `true` while a mouse button is pressed over the object, and the `containsMouse` property will be set to `true` while the mouse pointer is over the object's area. You can attach change handlers to these properties or use them in a property binding, as with any other property in QML:

```
Entity {
    components: [
        DiffuseSpecularMaterial { /* ... */ },
        TorusMesh { /* ... */ },
        ObjectPicker {
            hoverEnabled: true
            onClicked: {
                console.log("clicked");
            }
            onContainsMouseChanged: {
                console.log("contains mouse?", containsMouse);
            }
        }
    ]
}
```

Depending on your scene, picking can be a heavy computational task. By default, the most simple and efficient options are used. The default object picker will only handle mouse press and release events. You can set its `dragEnabled` property to `true` to handle mouse movements after `pressed(pick)` was triggered. You can also set the `hoverEnabled` property to `true` to handle all mouse movements, even when mouse buttons aren't pressed. There properties belong to the `ObjectPicker` component, so you can set them separately for each entity.

There are also global picking settings that affect the whole window. They are stored in the `pickingSettings` property of the `RenderSettings` component that is normally attached to the root entity. The settings can be changed like this:

```
Entity {
    components: [
        RenderSettings {
            activeFrameGraph: ForwardRenderer { /*...*/ }
            pickingSettings.pickMethod:
PickingSettings.TrianglePicking
        },
        InputSettings {}
    ]
    //...
}
```

Let's go through the possible settings. The `pickResultMode` property defines the behavior of overlapping pickers. If it's set to `PickingSettings.NearestPick`, only the object nearest to the camera will receive the event. If `PickingSettings.AllPicks` is specified, all objects will receive the event.

The `pickMethod` property allows you to choose how pickers decide whether the mouse pointer overlaps with the object. The default value is `PickingSettings.BoundingVolumePicking`, meaning that only the bounding box of the object is taken into account. This is a fast but inaccurate method. To achieve higher accuracy, you can set the `PickingSettings.TrianglePicking` method, which takes all mesh triangles into account.

Finally, the `faceOrientationPickingMode` property allows you to choose if the front face, back face, or both faces will be used for the triangle picking.

Frame-based input handling

In all the previous examples, we used property change signal handlers to execute code when the state of the logical device or object picker changes. This allows you, for example, to execute a function at the moment a button is pressed or released. However, sometimes you want to execute a continuous action (for example, accelerate an object) while a button is pressed. This is easy to do with just a few changes to the code.

First, you need to attach an `id` to the object with interesting properties (for example `Action`, `Axis`, or `ObjectPicker`):

```
LogicalDevice {
    actions: [
        Action {
            id: myAction
            inputs: ActionInput {
                sourceDevice: keyboardDevice
                buttons: [Qt.Key_A]
            }
        }
    ]
}
```

This will allow you to refer to its properties. Next, you need to use the `FrameAction` component provided by the `Qt3DLogic` module. This component will simply emit the `triggered()` signal each frame. You can attach it to any entity and use the input data as you want:

```
Entity {
    components: [
        //...
        FrameAction {
            onTriggered: {
                console.log("A state: ", myAction.active);
            }
        }
    ]
```

You can use the `FrameAction` component to run any code that should be executed once per frame. However, don't forget that QML allows you to use property bindings, so you can set property values based on user input without having to write imperative code at all.

Time for action – receiving mouse input

Our game is pretty simple, so the only action the player has to do is pick two rods for a move. Let's use `ObjectPicker` to detect when the player clicks on a rod.

First, set the `pickingSettings.pickMethod` property of the `RenderSettings` object to `PickingSettings.TrianglePicking` in the `main.qml` file (you can use the code example from the previous section). Our scene is very simple, and triangle picking shouldn't be too slow. This setting will greatly increase the picker's accuracy.

The next set of changes will go to the `Rod.qml` file. First, add an ID to the root entity and declare a signal that will notify the outside world that the rod was clicked:

```
Entity {
    id: rod
    property int index
    readonly property alias pos: transform.translation
    property var disks: []
    signal clicked()
    //...
}
```

Next, add an `ObjectPicker` to the `components` array and emit the public `clicked()` signal when the picker reports that it was clicked:

```
Entity {
    //...
    components: [
        //...
        ObjectPicker {
            id: picker
            hoverEnabled: true
            onClicked: rod.clicked()
        }
    ]
}
```

Finally, let's give the player a hint that the rod is clickable by highlighting it when it intersects with the mouse pointer:

```
DiffuseSpecularMaterial {
    ambient: {
        return picker.containsMouse? "#484" : "#111";
    }
},
```

When the player puts the mouse pointer over a rod, the `picker.containsMouse` property will become `true`, and QML will update the material's color automatically. You should see this behavior when running the project. The next task is to access the rod's `clicked()` signal from the `Scene` component. To do that, you'll need to make the following changes to the code:

```
Component.onCompleted: {
    //...
    var setupRod = function(i) {
        var rod = rodComponent.createObject(sceneRoot, { index: i });
        rod.clicked.connect(function() {
            rodClicked(rod);
        });
        return rod;
    }

    for(var i = 0; i < 3; i++) {
        rods.push(setupRod(i));
    }
    //...

}
function rodClicked(rod) {
    console.log("rod clicked: ", rods.indexOf(rod));
}
```

As a result of these changes, the game should print a message to the application output, whenever a rod is clicked.

What just happened?

First, we added a `setupRod()` helper function that creates a new rod and connects its signal to the new `rodClicked()` function. Then we simply called `setupRod()` for each index and accumulated the rod object into the `rods` array. The `rodClicked()` function will contain the rest of our game logic, but for now it only prints the index of the clicked rod to the application output.

Note that the content of the `setupRod()` function cannot be placed directly into the body of the `for` loop over `i`. The `clicked()` signal is connected to a closure that captures the `rod` variable. Within the function, each rod will connect to a closure that captures the corresponding `Rod` object. Within the `for` loop, all closures would capture the common `rod` variable that will hold the last `Rod` object for all the closures.

Performing animations

Animations are essential for making a good game. Qt 3D provides a separate module for performing animations, but at the time of writing it's still experimental. Luckily, Qt already provides multiple ways to play animations. When using C++ API, you can use the Animation Framework (we learned about it in `Chapter 5`, *Animations in Graphics View*). When using QML, you can use the powerful and convenient animation system provided by Qt Quick. We already worked with it a lot in previous chapters, so here we'll see how we can apply our knowledge to Qt 3D.

Qt Quick animations can be applied to almost any property of any QML object (strictly speaking, there are property types it can't handle, but we won't deal with those types here). If you look at the QML files of our project, you'll see that basically everything in our scene is defined by properties. That means that you can animate positions, colors, dimensions of objects and almost everything else.

Our current task will be to create an animation of the disk sliding up from the rod, moving across the table to the other rod, and sliding down that rod. The property we'll animate is `pos` which is the property alias for `transform.translation`.

Time for action – animating disk movements

Our animation will consist of three parts, so it will require a fair amount of code. Instead of putting all that code directly into the `Scene` component, let's put the animation into a separate component. Create a new file called `DiskAnimation.qml` and fill it with the following code:

```
import QtQuick 2.10

SequentialAnimation {
    id: rootAnimation
    property variant target: null
```

```
    property vector3d rod1Pos
    property vector3d rod2Pos
    property int startY
    property int finalY

    property int maxY: 12

    Vector3dAnimation {
        target: rootAnimation.target
        property: "pos"
        to: Qt.vector3d(rod1Pos.x, maxY, rod1Pos.z)
        duration: 30 * (maxY - startY)

    }
    Vector3dAnimation {
        target: rootAnimation.target
        property: "pos"
        to: Qt.vector3d(rod2Pos.x, maxY, rod2Pos.z)
        duration: 400
    }
    Vector3dAnimation {
        target: rootAnimation.target
        property: "pos"
        to: Qt.vector3d(rod2Pos.x, finalY, rod2Pos.z)
        duration: 30 * (maxY - finalY)
    }
}
```

What just happened?

Our animation has a lot of properties because it should be flexible enough to handle all the cases we need. First, it should be able to animate any disk, so we added the `target` property that will contain the disk we currently move. Next, the rods that participate in the movement influence the intermediate and final coordinates of the disk (more specifically, its *x* and *z* coordinates). The `rod1Pos` and `rod2Pos` properties will hold the coordinates of the rods in play. The `startY` and `finalY` properties define the starting and final coordinates of the disk. These coordinates will depend on the current number of disks stored on each rod. Finally, the `maxY` property simply defines the maximum height the disk will raise at while moving.

The property we animated is of the `vector3d` type, so we needed to use the `Vector3dAnimation` type that is able to correctly interpolate all three components of the vector. We set the same `target` and `property` for all three parts of the animation. Then, we carefully calculated the final position of the disk after each stage and assigned it to the `to` property. There is no need to set the `from` property, as the animation will automatically use the current position of the disk as the starting point. Finally, we calculated the `duration` of each step to ensure steady movement of the disk.

Of course, we want to test the new animation right away. Add a `DiskAnimation` object to the `Scene` component and initialize the animation at the end of the `Component.onCompleted` handler:

```
DiskAnimation { id: diskAnimation }
Component.onCompleted: {
    //...
    var disk1 = rods[0].disks.pop();
    diskAnimation.rod1Pos = rods[0].pos;
    diskAnimation.rod2Pos = rods[1].pos;
    diskAnimation.startY = disk1.pos.y;
    diskAnimation.finalY = 1;
    diskAnimation.target = disk1;
    diskAnimation.start();

}
```

When you run the application, you should see the top disk moving from one rod to another.

Time for action – implementing game logic

Most of the required preparations are done, and now it's time to make our game functional. The player should be able to make a move by clicking on a rod and then clicking on another rod. After the first rod is selected, the game should remember it and show it in a different color.

First, let's prepare the `Rod` component. We need it to have a new property that indicates that this rod was selected as the first rod for the next move:

```
property bool isSourceRod: false
```

It's easy to make the rod change color depending on the `isSourceRod` value using a property binding:

```
DiffuseSpecularMaterial {
    ambient: {
        if (isSourceRod) {
            return picker.containsMouse? "#f44" : "#f11";
        } else {
            return picker.containsMouse? "#484" : "#111";
        }
    }
},
```

Now let's turn our attention to the `Scene` component. We'll need a property that contains the currently selected first rod:

```
Entity {
    id: sceneRoot
    property variant rods: []
    property variant sourceRod
    //...
}
```

All that remains is the implementation of the `rodClicked()` function. Let's go through it in two steps:

```
function rodClicked(rod) {
    if (diskAnimation.running) { return; }
    if (rod.isSourceRod) {
        rod.isSourceRod = false;
        sourceRod = null;
    } else if (!sourceRod) {
        if (rod.disks.length > 0) {
            rod.isSourceRod = true;
            sourceRod = rod;
        } else {
            console.log("no disks on this rod");
        }
    } else {
        //...
    }
}
```

First, we check whether the move animation is already running, and ignore the event if it is. Next, we check whether the clicked rod was already selected. In this case, we simply deselect the rod. This allows the player to cancel the move if they accidentally selected an incorrect rod.

If `sourceRod` is unset, that means that we're in the first phase of the move. We check that the clicked rod has some disks on it, otherwise a move would not be possible. If everything is all right, we set the `sourceRod` property and the rod's `isSourceRod` property.

The rest of the function handles the second phase of the move:

```
var targetRod = rod;
if (targetRod.disks.length > 0 &&
    targetRod.disks[targetRod.disks.length - 1].index <
    sourceRod.disks[sourceRod.disks.length - 1].index)
{
    console.log("invalid move");
} else {
    var disk = sourceRod.disks.pop();
    targetRod.disks.push(disk);
    diskAnimation.rod1Pos = sourceRod.pos;
    diskAnimation.rod2Pos = targetRod.pos;
    diskAnimation.startY = disk.pos.y;
    diskAnimation.finalY = targetRod.disks.length;
    diskAnimation.target = disk;
    diskAnimation.start();
}
sourceRod.isSourceRod = false;
sourceRod = null;
```

In this branch, we already know that we have the first rod object stored in the `sourceRod` property. We store the clicked rod object in the `targetRod` variable. Next, we check whether the player tries to put a larger disk on top of the smaller one. If that's the case, we refuse to make the invalid move.

If everything is correct, we finally perform the move. We use the `pop()` function to remove the disk from the end of the `sourceRod.disks` array. This is the disk that will be moved to the other rod. We immediately push the disk object to the `disks` array of the other rod. Next, we carefully set up all properties of the animation and start it. At the end of the function, we clear the rod's `isSourceRod` property and the scene's `sourceRod` property to allow the player to make the next move.

Have a go hero – improving the game

Try to make your own modifications to the game. For example, you can notify the player about an invalid move by flashing the background color or the color of the foundation object. You can even add a 3D text to the scene using the `ExtrudedTextMesh` component. Try to play with different easing modes to make the animations look better.

The properties and functions of the `Scene` object are visible to the outside world, but they really are implementation details. You can fix that by putting them into an internal `QtObject`, as we described in `Chapter 12`, *Customization in Qt Quick*.

> Qt 3D is very flexible when it comes to rendering. While it's straightforward to use with the simple `ForwardRenderer`, you can create a much more complex render graph if you want. It's possible to render to multiple viewports, use off-screen textures, apply custom shaders, and create your own graphics effects and materials. We can't discuss all these possibilities in this book, but you can look at Qt examples to see how this can be done. Some of the relevant examples are Qt3D: Multi Viewport QML, Qt3D: Shadow Map QML, and Qt3D: Advanced custom material QML.

Integration with 3D modeling software

Geometric shapes provided by the `Qt3DExtras` module are great for prototyping. As we saw, these mesh generators come in handy when you want to create and test a new game quickly. However, a real game usually contains more complex figures than spheres and cubes. The meshes are usually prepared using specialized 3D modelling software. Qt 3D provides wide capabilities for importing 3D data from external files.

The first way of importing such data is the `Mesh` component. You only need to attach this component to an entity and specify the path to the file using the `source` property. As of Qt 5.10, `Mesh` supports OBJ, PLY, STL, and Autodesk FBX file formats.

As always, you can use a real filename or a Qt resource path. However, note that the source property expects an URL, not a path. A correct absolute resource path should start with `qrc:/`, and an absolute file path should start with `file://`. You can also use relative paths that will be resolved relatively to the current QML file.

If you're using OBJ files, `Mesh` provides you with an additional option to only load a sub-mesh from the `source` file. You can do it by specifying the name of the sub-mesh in the `meshName` property of the `Mesh` component. Instead of the exact name, you can also specify a regular expression to load all sub-meshes matching that expression.

Time for action – using OBJ files for the disks

Qt 3D doesn't provide a suitable mesh for the disks, but we can use a 3D modelling software to make any shape we want and then use it in our project. You will find the required OBJ files in the resources that come with the book. The files are named from `disk0.obj` to `disk7.obj`. If you want to practice with a 3D modelling software, you can prepare the files yourself.

Create a subdirectory named `obj` in your project directory and put the OBJ files there. Invoke the context menu of `qml.qrc` in the Qt Creator's project tree and select **Add Existing Files**. Add all OBJ files to the project. To put these files to work, we need to edit the `Disk.qml` file. Remove scale and rotation from the `Transform` component. Replace `TorusMesh` with `Mesh` and specify the resource path to the OBJ file as the `source` property:

```
components: [
    DiffuseSpecularMaterial { /*...*/ },
    Mesh {
        source: "qrc:/obj/disk" + index + ".obj"
    },
    Transform {
        id: transform
    }
]
```

Qt 3D will now use our new models for the disks:

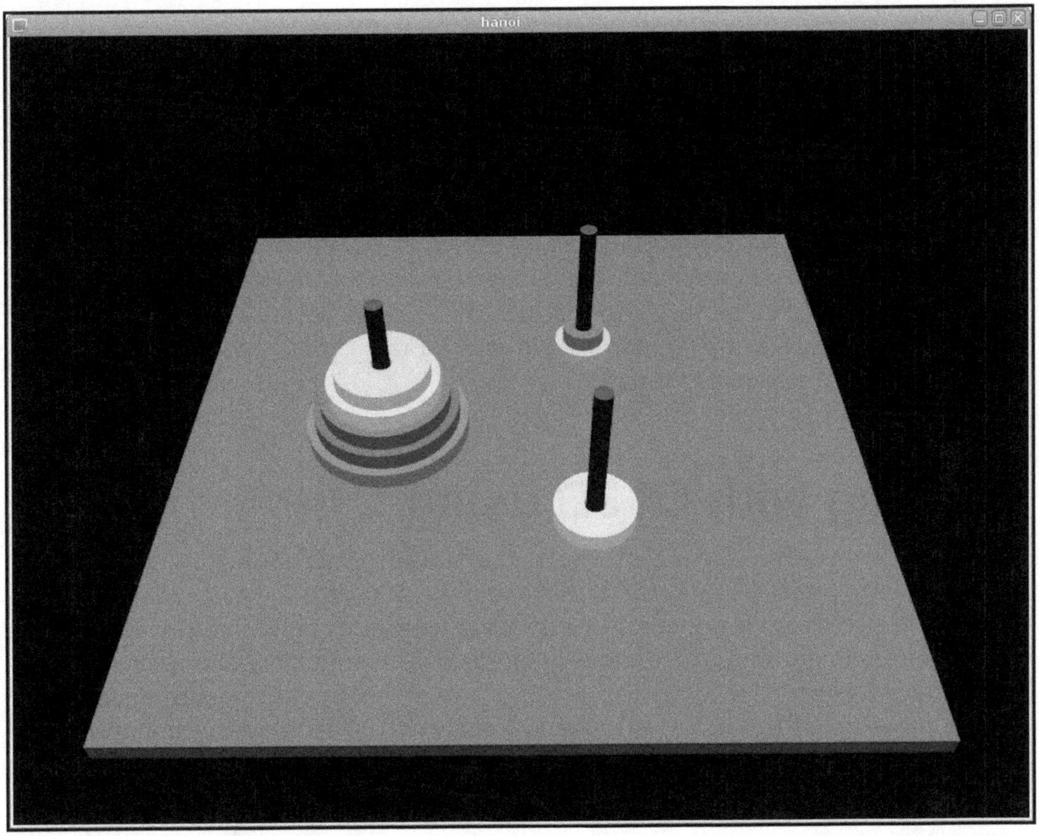

Loading a 3D scene

The `Mesh` component is useful when you want to import a single object's shape from an external file. However, sometimes you want to import multiple objects from a single file. For example, you could prepare some decorations surrounding your game action and then import them all at once. This is where the `SceneLoader` component becomes useful.

It can be used similar to the `Mesh` component:

```
Entity {
    components: [
        SceneLoader {
            source: "path/to/scene/file"
        }
    ]
}
```

However, instead of providing shape for its entity, `SceneLoader` creates a whole tree of `Entity` objects that become children of the `SceneLoader`'s entity. Each new entity will be provided with a mesh, a material, and a transform according to the file data. `SceneLoader` uses Assimp (Open Asset Import Library) to parse the source files, so it supports many common 3D formats.

Working with Qt 3D using C++

While QML is a powerful and convenient way of using Qt 3D, sometimes you may have reasons to prefer C++ over QML. For example, if your project has a large C++ codebase or your team is not familiar with JavaScript, sticking with C++ might be the right solution. If you want to extend a Qt 3D class with your custom implementation, you'll have to use the C++ approach. Additionally, if you deal with large amounts of objects, processing them in C++ may be noticeably faster than doing that in QML. Qt allows you to choose between C++ and QML freely.

The QML API of Qt 3D for the most part consists of C++ classes exposed without many changes. That means that most of the code you've seen in this chapter so far can be transparently translated to the equivalent C++ code with minimal effort. When you elect not to use QML, you lose its property bindings, syntax sugar, and the ability to declare trees of objects that are automatically instantiated. However, as long as you're familiar with the core of Qt C++ API, you shouldn't have any issues. You'll have to create objects manually and assign parents to them. In place of property bindings, you'll have to connect to property change signals and perform the required updates manually. If you studied the earlier chapters of this book, you should have no problems with doing that.

Time for action – creating a 3D scene using C++

Let's see how we can recreate our first Qt 3D scene using only C++ code. Our scene will contain a light source, a cube, and a first person camera controller. You can use the **Qt Console Application** template to create the project. Don't forget to enable the Qt 3D modules you want to use in the project file:

```
QT += 3dextras
CONFIG += c++11
```

The first change compared to the QML approach is that you need to use the `Qt3DWindow` class instead of `Qt3DQuickWindow`. The `Qt3DWindow` class performs a few actions that are typically needed in a Qt 3D application. It sets up a `QForwardRenderer`, a camera, and initializes the `QInputSettings` object needed for processing events. You can access the default frame graph using the `defaultFrameGraph()` method. The default camera is available using the `camera()` method. The aspect ratio of the default camera is updated automatically according to the window size. If you want to set up a custom frame graph, use the `setActiveFrameGraph()` method.

All the code from our small example will be put into the `main()` function. Let's go through it piece by piece. First, we initialize the usual `QGuiApplication` object, create a `Qt3DWindow` object, and apply our preferred settings to its frame graph and camera:

```
int main(int argc, char *argv[]) {
    QGuiApplication app(argc, argv);

    Qt3DExtras::Qt3DWindow window;
    window.defaultFrameGraph()->setClearColor(Qt::black);

    Qt3DRender::QCamera *camera = window.camera();
    camera->lens()->setPerspectiveProjection(45.0f, 16.0f / 9.0f,
0.1f, 1000.0f);
    camera->setPosition(QVector3D(0, 40.0f, -40.0f));
    camera->setViewCenter(QVector3D(0, 0, 0));
    //...
}
```

Next, we create a root entity object that will hold all our other entities and create a camera controller attached to the camera:

```
Qt3DCore::QEntity *rootEntity = new Qt3DCore::QEntity();
Qt3DExtras::QFirstPersonCameraController *cameraController =
    new Qt3DExtras::QFirstPersonCameraController(rootEntity);
cameraController->setCamera(camera);
```

Next, we set up a light entity:

```
Qt3DCore::QEntity *lightEntity = new Qt3DCore::QEntity(rootEntity);
Qt3DRender::QDirectionalLight *lightComponent = new
Qt3DRender::QDirectionalLight();
lightComponent->setColor(Qt::white);
lightComponent->setIntensity(0.5);
lightComponent->setWorldDirection(QVector3D(0, -1, 0));
lightEntity->addComponent(lightComponent);
```

It's important that we pass the root entity to the `QEntity` constructor to ensure that the new entity will be a part of our scene. To add a component to the entity, we use the `addComponent()` function. The next step is to set up the cube 3D object:

```
Qt3DCore::QEntity *cubeEntity = new Qt3DCore::QEntity(rootEntity);
Qt3DExtras::QCuboidMesh *cubeMesh = new Qt3DExtras::QCuboidMesh();
Qt3DExtras::QDiffuseSpecularMaterial *cubeMaterial =
    new Qt3DExtras::QDiffuseSpecularMaterial();
cubeMaterial->setAmbient(Qt::white);
Qt3DCore::QTransform *cubeTransform = new Qt3DCore::QTransform();
cubeTransform->setScale(10);
cubeEntity->addComponent(cubeMesh);
cubeEntity->addComponent(cubeMaterial);
cubeEntity->addComponent(cubeTransform);
```

As you can see, this code simply creates a few objects and sets their properties to the same values we used in our QML example. The final lines of code complete our setup:

```
window.setRootEntity(rootEntity);
window.show();
return app.exec();
```

We pass the root entity to the window and show it on screen. That's all! Qt 3D will render the constructed scene in the same way it worked in our QML project.

All properties of Qt 3D classes are equipped with change notification signals, so you can use connect statements to react to external changes properties. For example, if you use the `Qt3DInput::QAction` component to receive keyboard or mouse events, you can use its `activeChanged(bool isActive)` signal to get notifications about the event. You can also perform animations in the 3D scene using C++ animation classes such as `QPropertyAnimation`.

Integration with Qt Widgets and Qt Quick

While Qt 3D is a very powerful module, sometimes it's not enough to make a complete game or application. Other Qt modules such as Qt Quick or Qt Widgets can be very helpful, for example, when working on the user interface of your game. Luckily, Qt provides a few ways to use different modules together.

When it comes to Qt Widgets, your best bet is the `QWidget::createWindowContainer()` function. It allows you to surround your 3D view with widgets and display them all in a single window. This approach was already discussed in `Chapter 9`, *OpenGL and Vulkan in Qt Applications*, and can be applied to Qt 3D without any changes.

However, the capabilities of Qt Widgets are still limited in the world of hardware-accelerated graphics. Qt Quick is much more promising in this area, and the synergy between QML APIs of Qt Quick and Qt 3D can prove to be very strong. Qt provides two ways to combine Qt Quick and Qt 3D in a single application without significant performance costs. Let's take a closer look at them.

Embedding Qt Quick UI into a 3D scene

Qt 3D allows you to embed an arbitrary Qt Quick item into your 3D scene using the `Scene2D` type. How does that work? First, you need to put your Qt Quick content into a new `Scene2D` object. Next, you need to declare a texture that will be used as a render target for the form. Whenever Qt Quick decides to update its virtual view, the `Scene2D` object will render it directly to the specified texture. You only need to display this texture as you want. The most simple way of doing that is to pass it to a `TextureMaterial` component attached to one of your 3D objects.

However, this is only one part of the job. It's nice to allow users to see your form, but they should also be able to interact with it. This is also supported by `Scene2D`! To make it work, you need to do the following:

1. Set `pickMethod` to `TrianglePicking` in the `RenderSettings`. This will allow object pickers to retrieve more accurate information about mouse events.
2. Attach an `ObjectPicker` component to all entities that use the texture created by `Scene2D`. It's a good idea to set the `hoverEnabled` and `dragEnabled` properties of the object picker to `true` to make mouse events work as expected.
3. Specify all these entities in the `entities` property of the `Scene2D` object.

This will allow `Scene2D` to forward mouse events to the Qt Quick content. Unfortunately, forwarding keyboard events is not available yet.

Let's see an example of this approach:

```
import Qt3D.Core 2.0
import Qt3D.Render 2.0
import Qt3D.Input 2.0
import Qt3D.Extras 2.10
import QtQuick 2.10
import QtQuick.Scene2D 2.9
import QtQuick.Controls 2.0
import QtQuick.Layouts 1.0
Entity {
    components: [
        RenderSettings {
            activeFrameGraph: ForwardRenderer { /*...*/ }
            pickingSettings.pickMethod:
PickingSettings.TrianglePicking
        },
        InputSettings {}
    ]
    Scene2D {
        output: RenderTargetOutput {
            attachmentPoint: RenderTargetOutput.Color0
            texture: Texture2D {
                id: texture
                width: 200
                height: 200
                format: Texture.RGBA8_UNorm
            }
        }
```

```
            entities: [cube, plane]
            Rectangle {
                color: checkBox1.checked? "#ffa0a0" : "#a0a0ff"
                width: texture.width
                height: texture.height
                ColumnLayout {
                    CheckBox {
                        id: checkBox1
                        text: "Toggle color"
                    }
                    CheckBox {
                        id: checkBox2
                        text: "Toggle cube"
                    }
                    CheckBox {
                        id: checkBox3
                        checked: true
                        text: "Toggle plane"
                    }
                }
            }
        }
        //...
    }
```

This code sets up a Qt 3D scene that contains a `Scene2D` object. `Scene2D` itself is not visible in the 3D scene. We declare a texture that will receive the rendered Qt Quick content. You can choose `width` and `height` of the texture depending on the size of the displayed content.

Next, we declare that we'll render this texture in two entities (we'll create them in the next piece of code). Finally, we place a Qt Quick item directly into the `Scene2D` object. Make sure you set this size for your Qt Quick item according to the size of the texture. In our example, we created a form containing three checkboxes in a layout.

The next part of code creates two items for displaying the Qt Quick-based texture:

```
Entity {
    id: cube
    components: [
        CuboidMesh {},
        TextureMaterial {
            texture: texture
        },
        Transform {
            scale: 10
            rotationY: checkBox2.checked ? 45 : 0
```

```
            },
            ObjectPicker {
                hoverEnabled: true
                dragEnabled: true
            }
        ]
    }
    Entity {
        id: plane
        components: [
            PlaneMesh {
                mirrored: true
            },
            TextureMaterial {
                texture: texture
            },
            Transform {
                translation: checkBox3.checked ? Qt.vector3d(-20, 0, 0) :
    Qt.vector3d(20, 0, 0)
                scale: 10
                rotationX: 90
                rotationY: 180
                rotationZ: 0
            },
            ObjectPicker {
                hoverEnabled: true
                dragEnabled: true
            }

        ]
    }
```

The first item is a cube, and the second item is a plane. Most of the properties are just arbitrary values that make the scene look good. The important part is that each item has a `TextureMaterial` component, and we passed the `texture` object into it. Each item also has an `ObjectPicker` component that allows the user to interact with the item. Note that we used the `mirrored` property of `PlaneMesh` to display the texture in its original (not mirrored) orientation.

One plane object is usually enough to display your form. We used two objects purely for demonstration purposes.

While Qt Quick items and Qt 3D entities live in different worlds and don't seem to interact with each other, they are still declared in a single QML file, so you can use property bindings and other QML techniques to make all these items work together. In our example, not only is the background color of the root Qt Quick item controlled by the checkbox, but the 3D objects are also influenced by checkboxes:

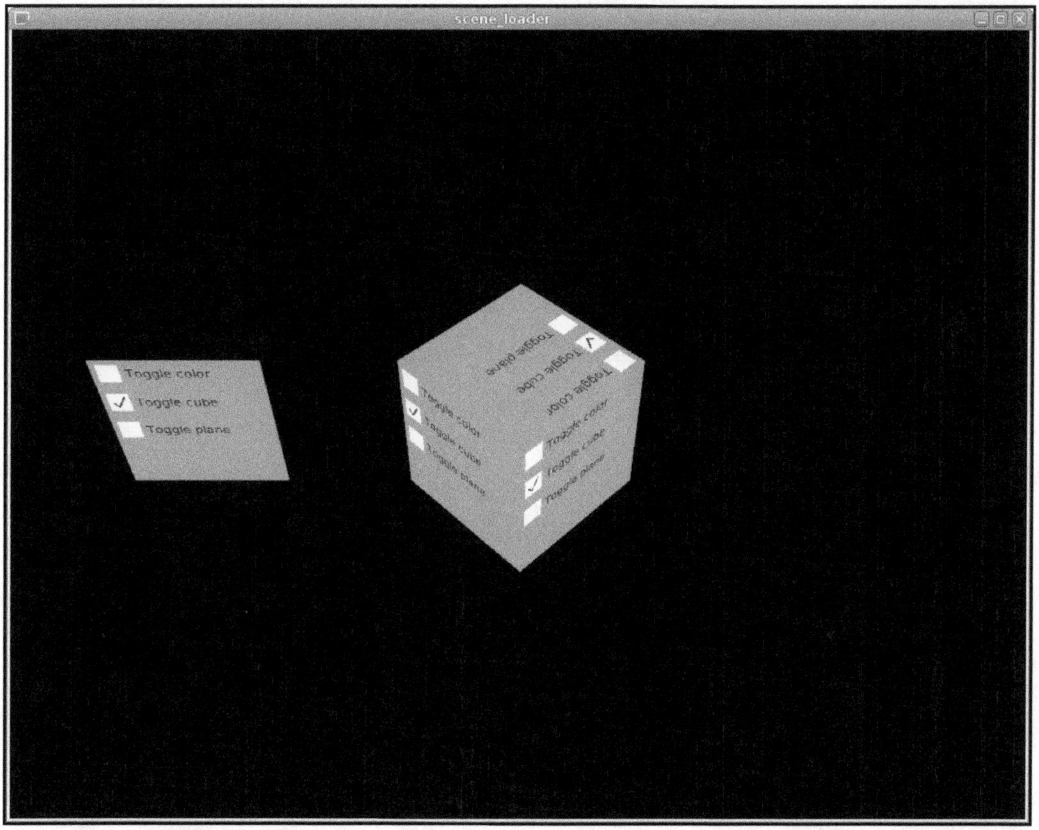

Embedding a Qt 3D scene into a Qt Quick form

Now let's see how we can perform the opposite task. This approach is useful if your application is built mainly around Qt Quick. This means that you use the `QQmlApplicationEngine` class in the `main()` function, and the root object of your `main.qml` file is usually the `Window` object. It's very easy to extend your Qt Quick application with a bit of 3D action.

We could place all the code into the `main.qml` file, but it's more convenient to split it because setting up a 3D scene requires quite a bit of code. Let's say you have a file named `My3DScene.qml` that contains the usual content of a 3D scene:

```
Entity {
    components: [
        RenderSettings {
            activeFrameGraph: ForwardRenderer { /*...*/ },
        InputSettings {}
    ]
    Entity { /*...*/ }
    Entity { /*...*/ }
    //...
}
```

To add this 3D scene into the `main.qml` file (or any other Qt Quick-based QML file), you should use the `Scene3D` QML type that can be imported from the `QtQuick.Scene3D` module. For example, this is how you can create a form with a button and a 3D view:

```
import QtQuick 2.10
import QtQuick.Layouts 1.0
import QtQuick.Controls 1.0
import QtQuick.Window 2.0
import QtQuick.Scene3D 2.0

Window {
    visible: true
    Button {
        id: button1
        text: "button1"
        anchors {
            top: parent.top
            left: parent.left
            right: parent.right
            margins: 10
```

```
        }
    }
    Scene3D {
        focus: true
        anchors {
            top: button1.bottom
            bottom: parent.bottom
            left: parent.left
            right: parent.right
            margins: 10
        }
        aspects: ["input", "logic"]
        My3DScene {}
    }
}
```

Most of the code is the usual content of a Qt Quick form. The `Scene3D` item does all the magic. The root 3D entity should be added to this item directly or, as in our case, in the form of a custom component. The `Scene3D` item sets up a Qt 3D engine and renders the passed scene:

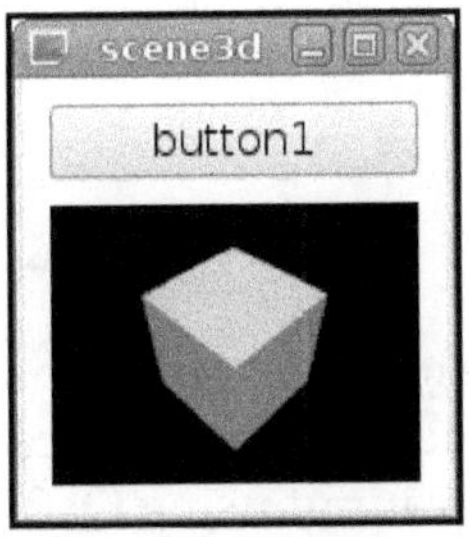

If you want to use `Qt3DInput` or `Qt3DLogic` modules, you need to enable the corresponding 3D aspects using the `aspects` property of `Scene3D`, as shown in the screenshot. Additionally, the `multisample` Boolean property can be used to enable multisampling. The `hoverEnabled` property can be used to enable handling of mouse events when mouse buttons are not pressed.

Similar to `Qt3DQuickWindow`, `Scene3D` sets the camera's aspect ratio automatically by default. You can disable it by setting its `cameraAspectRatioMode` property to `Scene3D.UserAspectRatio`.

This approach can also be used to display some UI controls on top of the 3D view. This will allow you to use the full power of Qt Quick to make the UI of your game amazing.

Pop quiz

Q1. Which component can be used to rotate a 3D object?

1. `CuboidMesh`
2. `RotationAnimation`
3. `Transform`

Q2. Which component is the most suitable for emulating the light of the sun?

1. `DirectionalLight`
2. `PointLight`
3. `SpotLight`

Q3. What is a Qt 3D material?

1. An object that allows you to load a texture from a file.
2. A component that defines the physical properties of the object.
3. A component that defines the visible properties of the object's surface.

Summary

In this chapter, we learned to create 3D games with Qt. We saw how to create and position 3D objects in the scene and configure the camera for rendering. Next, we examined how we can handle user input using Qt 3D. More than that, you learned to apply your existing animation skills to Qt 3D objects. Finally, we found out how to use Qt 3D together with other Qt modules.

Like Qt Quick, Qt 3D is rapidly evolving. At the time of writing, some of the modules are still experimental. You should expect the API of Qt 3D to be improved and extended, so make sure you check the Qt documentation for newer releases.

This concludes our book on game programming using Qt. We have taught you the general basics of Qt, described its widget realm to you, and introduced you to the fascinating world of Qt Quick and Qt 3D. Widgets (including Graphics View), Qt Quick, and Qt 3D are the main paths you can take when creating games using the Qt framework. We have also shown you ways of merging the two approaches by making use of any OpenGL or Vulkan skills you might have, going beyond what Qt already offers today. At this point, you should start playing around and experimenting, and if at any point you feel lost or simply lack the information on how to do something, the very helpful Qt reference manual should be the first resource you direct yourself to.

Good luck and have lots of fun!

Pop quiz answers

Chapter 3
Q1: 2
Q2: 2
Q3: 2
Q4: 1

Chapter 4
Q1: 1
Q2: 4
Q3: 2
Q4: 3

Chapter 5
Q1: 3
Q2: 1
Q3: 3

Chapter 6
Q1: 1
Q2: 2
Q3: 3
Q4: 3

Chapter 7
Q1: 1
Q2: 2
Q3: 2
Q4: 3

Chapter 8
Q1: 1
Q2: 2
Q3: 3

Chapter 9
Q1: 3
Q2: 1
Q3: 3

Chapter 10
Q1: 2
Q2: 2
Q3: 1
Q4: 4
Q5: 2

Chapter 11
Q1: 2
Q2: 2
Q3: 3

Chapter 12
Q1: 2
Q2: 3
Q3: 3

Chapter 13
Q1: 2
Q2: 1
Q3: 2

Chapter 14
Q1: 2
Q2: 2
Q3: 2

Chapter 15
Q1: 3
Q2: 1
Q3: 3

Chapter 16
Q1: 3
Q2: 2
Q3: 1
Q4: 3

Other Books You May Enjoy

If you enjoyed this book, you may be interested in these other books by Packt:

Learn QT 5
Nicholas Sherriff

ISBN: 978-1-78847-885-4

- Install and configure the Qt Framework and Qt Creator IDE
- Create a new multi-project solution from scratch and control every aspect of it with QMake
- Implement a rich user interface with QML
- Learn the fundamentals of QtTest and how to integrate unit testing
- Build self-aware data entities that can serialize themselves to and from JSON
- Manage data persistence with SQLite and CRUD operations
- Reach out to the internet and consume an RSS feed
- Produce application packages for distribution to other users

Qt 5 Projects
Marco Piccolino

ISBN: 978-1-78829-388-4

- Learn the basics of modern Qt application development
- Develop solid and maintainable applications with BDD, TDD, and Qt Test
- Master the latest UI technologies and know when to use them: Qt Quick, Controls 2, Qt 3D and Charts
- Build a desktop UI with Widgets and the Designer
- Translate your user interfaces with QTranslator and Linguist
- Get familiar with multimedia components to handle visual input and output
- Explore data manipulation and transfer: the model/view framework, JSON, Bluetooth, and network I/O
- Take advantage of existing web technologies and UI components with WebEngine

Leave a review - let other readers know what you think

Please share your thoughts on this book with others by leaving a review on the site that you bought it from. If you purchased the book from Amazon, please leave us an honest review on this book's Amazon page. This is vital so that other potential readers can see and use your unbiased opinion to make purchasing decisions, we can understand what our customers think about our products, and our authors can see your feedback on the title that they have worked with Packt to create. It will only take a few minutes of your time, but is valuable to other potential customers, our authors, and Packt. Thank you!

Index

C

D

E

P

Q

R

S

W

X